A Contemporary
ANABAPTIST
Theology

BIBLICAL, HISTORICAL, CONSTRUCTIVE

THOMAS N. FINGER

InterVarsity Press
Downers Grove, Illinois

InterVarsity Press
P.O. Box 1400, Downers Grove, IL 60515-1426
World Wide Web: www.ivpress.com
E-mail: mail@ivpress.com

InterVarsity Press® *is the book-publishing division of InterVarsity Christian Fellowship/USA*®, *a student movement active on campus at hundreds of universities, colleges and schools of nursing in the United States of America, and a member movement of the International Fellowship of Evangelical Students. For information about local and regional activities, write Public Relations Dept., InterVarsity Christian Fellowship/USA, 6400 Schroeder Rd., P.O. Box 7895, Madison, WI 53707-7895, or visit the IVCF website at* <*www.intervarsity.org*>.

Design: Cindy Kiple

ISBN 0-8308-2785-4

Printed in the United States of America ∞

Library of Congress Cataloging-in-Publication Data

Finger, Thomas N.
    A contemporary Anabaptist theology: biblical, historical,
    constructive/by Thomas N. Finger.
        p. cm.
    Includes bibliographical references and index.
    ISBN 0-8308-2785-4 (hardcover: alk. paper)
    1. Anabaptists—Doctrines. I. Title.
    BX4931.3.F45 2004
    230'.43,dc22

                                                                      2004017263

P	18	17	16	15	14	13	12	11	10	9	8	7	6	5	4	3	2	1
Y	18	17	16	15	14	13	12	11	10	09	08	07	06	05	04			

CONTENTS

PART I

CONTEMPORARY AND HISTORICAL CONTEXT

1

WHY THIS TASK?

As the twenty-first century dawns the role theology might play in Christian faith is quite uncertain. Current tendencies seem unfavorable to this discipline. While imagery bombards us almost everywhere, theology has relied on print. While sound bites reign in the media, extended exposition has been theology's métier. Even in religion, the experiential and practical aspects are deemed most relevant, but theology is intellectual.

Moreover, whereas pluralism is increasingly experienced and celebrated, theology seems concerned with universal truths. Theology usually has been pursued by ecclesiastical and intellectual leaders to formulate doctrines and behavioral norms valid for everyone. Is theology simply one of modernity's rationalistic, elitist, organizing and centralizing projects?[1] Amidst postmodernity's affective, popular, fragmenting and pluriform sensibilities is theology out of place?

Much of the theological interest that survives is attracted toward particularity—especially toward groups that have lacked recognizable voices and have struggled under oppression. What earlier written expressions they bequeathed were mostly unsystematic: song, sermon, letter, poem, tract. Theologians concerned with these movements retrieve hidden histories. And while it is often supposed that such groups had no theology, implicit theologies are being discovered and gradually taking explicit shape. These explications, however, frequently emphasize—sometimes radically—the distinctiveness of their respective traditions. Their significance for the broader church and society is often unclear.

Frequently, it is assumed that such marginalized groups, except gendered ones, originated beyond the West. Yet the West has its own hidden histories of repression.

---

[1]Since I will often mention modernity and postmodernity, an excursus at the end of this chapter briefly explains my fairly standard, somewhat loose usage of both terms. I find today's world significantly shaped by both these overall perspectives on reality.

Some Western peoples who are mostly white, middle class and male led today may appear to flow within society's mainstream. Yet some have descended from long-silenced minorities. In Western history, few groups suffered such severe persecution as the sixteenth-century Anabaptists. At least five thousand were cruelly racked, torn, burned and drowned. Most of the rest lost home, livelihood, possessions or civil status.

Eventually, survival often came to depend on cultural isolation, sometimes under overlords who offered protection in exchange for clearing swamps and forests and then farming. Gradually these descendants, mostly called Mennonites, won respect for their practical Christianity: their industry, thrift, honesty and increasingly their pacifism. Relatively few, though, attained more than practical literacy. Many of their writings—sermons, letters, devotional thoughts—were unsophisticated and occasional.

Anabaptism's ethics and its particular history have affected other Christians and even society somewhat. It is usually assumed, though, that Anabaptists have nothing to offer theology. And if Anabaptism's value lies in its distinct practices, does it matter? Should not Christian "families" simply appreciate each other's unique gifts and celebrate their diversity? Why be concerned about formulating theological generalizations? Why even ask whether marginalized groups might contribute to them?

My brief response is that while current culture often valorizes particularity, other, perhaps stronger, trends are rapidly drawing all peoples and nations together. It is increasingly recognized, for instance, that environmental degradation in some regions (e.g., rain forests) adversely affects many others. Former boundaries, moreover, are being swiftly erased by telecommunications. Billions of dollars, even entire companies, can change hands on several continents with a few clicks of the keyboard. The accelerating velocity of telecommunications parallels the growing dominance of a single economic system, capitalism, freeing it from many local political and social constraints. Many particular, historically oppressed peoples are being swept into and often under these advancing global waves.

To be sure, rapid communications can also enable marginalized groups to express their identities and organize to resist homogenizing tendencies. These and other globalizing forces can also facilitate the churches' worldwide mission. However, if today's diverse communities simply celebrate their diversities, they likely will underestimate the power and scope of these global processes and become increasingly vulnerable to them.

It appears that in our differentiating, postmodern world, modern homogenizing forces are nearing their apex of power. Their momentum often seems irresistible. They tend to impose their values—unbridled consumerism and desire for profit—on all activities and structures in all societies.[2] Christians treasure other values. Yet if churches are to communicate and incarnate these in the face of such totalizing trends, they must often act together. Common efforts, however, require clarity about common aims and values.

In Christian faith common aims and values are inseparable from shared convictions about human nature, life's meaning, ultimate reality; in other words they are inseparable from theology. Yet Christians have often differed over these—long before today's celebration of diversity. Diversities, of course, are valuable, particularly when they contribute insights from marginalized Christian families, and they help churches minister among vastly different cultures. But if theology simply revels in particularities, can churches form a vision strong, clear and unified enough to interact with today's globalizing forces? Not, I propose, unless theology's traditional quest for universal affirmations also plays a role.

If so, what traditions could best aid the broader church? At first glance, "mainline" theologies, whose outlook has often been global, seem obvious choices (Catholic, Orthodox, Reformed, Anglican, Lutheran, etc.). Marginalized groups, like Anabaptists, could help missions aid particular, oppressed peoples by sharing their historical experiences and ethics. But Anabaptists could hardly help articulate common theological themes. Or couldn't they?

Historical studies indicate that sixteenth-century Anabaptists shared many Protestant concerns, such as biblical authority and critique of ecclesiastical hierarchy. Yet their pursuit of holiness seemed so Catholic that Protestants could deride them as "new monks." In Anabaptism, that is, these and many other emphases that divided Catholics and Protestants were intertwined in practice. Now what if this harmony were supported by a theological rationale, even if it was often unarticulated? If it were more clearly articulated, might it aid understanding among Protestants and Catholics today?

Further, Mennonites have often stressed biblical authority and mission in ways that sound "evangelical." Yet their promotion of ethical living and social betterment seems strangely "liberal." In these days of evangelical-liberal ecumenical tensions around the world, might Anabaptist theology suggest ways of affirming elements of both?

In short, I am proposing that in today's culture, which prizes particularity yet where many tendencies press swiftly toward globality, an unlikely, very particular

---

[2]For ways in which companies and even national economies seem compelled to adopt certain procedures to survive, see Thomas Friedman, especially on the golden straitjacket and the electronic herd (*The Lexus and the Olive Tree* [New York: Anchor, 2000], pp. 101-42). I am implying that consumerism or profit motives are non-Christian in "unbridled" form, but not all forms.

Christian communion, the Anabaptists, can aid theology in addressing both dimensions. It can help bring voices from the underside to fuller expression and also help guide conflicts among majority traditions toward understanding. My main task will be to render explicit the largely implicit theology that has guided Anabaptists in order to address issues facing today's churches and societies.

SOME HISTORICAL CONSIDERATIONS

I am not alone in attempting such an explication. Self-conscious theologizing within the Anabaptist perspective is about two decades old. Several ways of undertaking such theologizing have crystallized somewhat by now. Nonetheless, it is not always clear what their proponents mean by "Anabaptist," and what their theological norms and methods really are. This engenders confusion among today's Anabaptists and others wanting to understand them. For this reason I believe I can best further Anabaptist theologizing not only by constructing a contemporary expression but also by elucidating my norms, sources and methods. This will require showing how I read historic Anabaptism. Many diverse interpretations of it also exist, and theologies can vary significantly if they follow one or another.

The complexities involved in retrieving historic Anabaptist theology resemble those affecting many submerged minority traditions. Anabaptism was largely a peasant-artisan movement, an illegal one at that. Most of its few educated leaders died within its first years. Anabaptist beliefs were usually passed on orally, and undercover, in the vernacular.[3] Arrests along with confiscations of the few circulating manuscripts often interrupted communication. Ironically, we know less about Anabaptists when they covered their tracks and considerably more about when they got caught! Much of what we know comes from court trials, descriptions and defamations by their enemies. Educated Anabaptists were banned from further formal study and most publishing and public speaking. No explicit theological tradition, like those undergirding the Lutheran and Reformed movements, could develop.

Anabaptism, further, sprang from not a single historical source but at least three (most commonly identified as Swiss, South German-Austrian and Dutch). Tensions, even sharp conflicts, sometimes arose among them. Each movement faced somewhat different challenges, and these often preoccupied their writings. Each source, further, drew upon differing theological traditions, vocabularies and motifs. Moreover, all this comes down to us through centuries of highly partisan interpretation.

Nevertheless, no historical movement coalesces from diverse origins, especially amidst savage persecution, unless its branches share important commonalities. For

---

[3]C. Arnold Snyder, *Anabaptist History and Theology* (Kitchener, Ont.: Pandora, 1995), pp. 101-4.

Anabaptists these included common theological convictions worth dying for. Anabaptists, moreover, did collect various writings of their leaders, some unsystematic but others not. Enough remain to detect unifying theological threads within and among authors.

To indicate what role historic Anabaptism plays in my theology, I must devote about half of each doctrinal chapter to showing how I handle the sources: how I weigh data from different streams and various spokespersons, episodes and subcurrents within them, not to mention how I sift the scholarly interpretations through which all this comes.

OVERVIEW

Before my answers can be very helpful, many readers will need some sketch of Anabaptist history. Chapter two outlines the period that I call historic Anabaptism (from about 1525-1575). Next I outline various scholarly interpretations, beginning roughly with Harold Bender's *The Anabaptist Vision* (1944) and then some major efforts at current Anabaptist theology, most of them post-1980 (chap. 3). With these in mind, I set forth my own procedures, assumptions and methodology as transparently as possible (chap. 4). These first four chapters constitute part one: "Contemporary and Historical Context."

Each chapter in parts two and three considers a specific theological locus (e.g., the church), sometimes by dividing it into sections (e.g., baptism, Lord's Supper). Each chapter or section thereof first presents historic Anabaptist views and my reading of them. The second half develops my constructive theology on these topics. There I dialogue with current theological movements, generally a different one for each locus. To indicate the broad potential relevance of Anabaptist insights, I engage contemporary Catholic, Lutheran, Reformed, Orthodox, liberation, feminist, neo-orthodox and evangelical as well as other Anabaptist theologies. My resulting affirmations are substantive. But due to diversities among my dialogue partners, they may be more nearly samples than comprehensive expositions of my theology.

Part two, "The Coming of the New Creation" (chaps. 5-7), proposes and explicates a center for a theology informed by Anabaptism. I present this not as an essence but simply one helpful vantage point for exploring the whole. Neither does it consist simply of "distinctives" that would constitute Anabaptism, even were other features eliminated or altered.[4] Historical movements and theologies attain

---

[4]For an impressive classification and analysis of numerous scholarly views on historic Anabaptism's essence and goals, see Calvin Redekop, "The Community of Scholars and the Essence of Anabaptism," *MQR* 67, no. 4 (1993): 429-50.

distinctive shape not only from features which distinguish them but also from how they incorporate those affirmed by others.

This center will be the coming of the new creation in three inseparable dimensions: personal, communal and missional. Anabaptism's salvific impetus can be characterized as intertwining these aspects, which other traditions often separate. Chapter five, "The Personal Dimension," shows how Anabaptists did and today can interconnect themes stressed by Protestants (justification), by Catholics (sanctification) and by Orthodoxy (divinization).

Chapter six indicates how the personal dimension is expressed through and shaped by "the communal dimension"—and how the latter must be energized and informed by the former. Its four sections cover ecclesial practices: baptism, the Lord's Supper, discipline and economic sharing. Chapter seven, "The Missional Dimension," shows how the first two dimensions give rise to and yet originate from the church's mission. Here I discuss evangelism, especially the universality of the Christian message, which is often challenged by postmodernism. I also ponder the church's interactions with the rest of the world.

Part three (chaps. 8-10), "The Convictional Framework," considers this salvific center. Here I ponder three loci sometimes regarded as more formally theological: Christology, anthropology and eschatology. Although the salvific center (chaps. 5-7) more often occupied historic Anabaptist awareness, this framework was no less essential. Had Anabaptists understood Jesus, humankind and the coming end other than they did, their soteriology would have been quite different.

Chapter eight, "Jesus and Divine Reality," discusses in three sections Jesus' work, his person and God's triune character. Chapter nine, "Human Nature," centers around the human will and body. Chapter ten, "The Last Things," portrays the intensity with which historic Anabaptists anticipated the new creation's coming, and how their expectation, despite some excesses, can function today. Space simply does not allow for other loci. Creation would perhaps be next most important; it appears at various points. So does revelation, most succinctly in my basic assumptions (chap. 4). A brief concluding chapter (11) sketches the contours of the theology developed.

EXCURSUS

Modernity. Modernity crystallized at the Enlightenment (c. A.D. 1680-1800). Among its main features, very broadly considered, is reason's primacy for knowing reality and guiding behavior. Humans are intrinsically valuable because they possess reason and free will. Reason can rise above the distortive, subjective influences of emotions, traditions and cultural particularities to attain impartial, objective knowledge. This it formulates in universal laws, for reason aims at comprehensiveness. Physical science is its supreme form, showing that matter's basic units are individual particles, and, applied to society, that its basic units are individual people.

Though these physical and personal individual units often repel each other, free interplay among them results in overarching harmony. To achieve this in society, individuals must be liberated from authority, superstition and tradition to follow their reason and free will. Then, through democracy, humans will create laws to balance their conflicting interests. Through capitalism, which allows free interplay among competing economic interests, humans can become wealthy and self-sufficient. Through technology, the practical application of science, wealth will greatly increase and fund unprecedented educational, medical and other social advances. Intellectual, industrial, social and moral progress is inevitable: this is a universal historical law. This metanarrative guides modernity.

Though competition among individuals (and other interests) creates losers, this is justified by collective progress and, after Darwin, elimination of the least fit to advance by the most fit. Nations and individuals which are less intellectual, democratic or economically successful have developed their human potential less and deserve happiness less. Modernity devalues traits and values other than those that advance it, and tends to homogenize differences. By dissolving or subordinating "inferior" cultures and most traditions, and by continually reshaping society to further progress, modernity alienates many competing groups and individuals from each other, and individuals from corporate contexts of identity and meaning. Religion is valued if it furthers moral and intellectual development and continuing transformation of reality by modernity's universal values, but not if it appeals to emotions, traditions, authority or a reality transcending the immanent, progressive, rationally knowable historical process.

Postmodernity. According to postmodernity, which has become increasingly widespread over the last thirty years, behavior, knowledge and reason itself are significantly shaped by cultural, traditional, physical and emotional particularities. Postmodernity challenges the possibility of objective knowledge and stresses variety among epistemological perspectives—so strongly that the term itself is perhaps indefinable. Postmodernity raises the question of epistemological relativism, though many postmodernists do not affirm it.

Among postmodernism's main features, very broadly considered, are valuing many ways of knowing (aesthetic, intuitive, bodily and so forth), of which science is only one, and many expressions of knowledge (symbols, gestures, rituals and so forth), of which mathematics and print are only two. Knowledge serves power and is shaped by powerful interests. Universal truths, values and metanarratives are suspect because they are often affirmed by the powerful to promote and mask their real interests. Human willing is neither guided by pure reason nor free from cultural and biological forces, but is largely determined by those forces.

Human and nonhuman reality consist not of individual units but interrelated structures and processes. Democracy and capitalism, which portray individuals as primary, overlook individuals' subordination to much larger, more powerful forces whose operations they mask. Technology, despite its benefits, tends to serve these forces. Humans, however, are intrinsically social, shaped by specific relationships, cultures and traditions. Therefore homogenizing trends, which subordinate and marginalize "the other," must be opposed along with competition, which disadvantages them and alienates individuals and groups from one another. Local cultures, governments and economies should be valued. Religion is valued if it strengthens individual and group identity. Postmodernity is open to mystery and reality that transcends the rationally knowable historical process, but postmodernity often is suspicious of universal claims about this.

2

A Tumultuous History

I am proposing that the largely implicit theology of the relatively little-known Anabaptist movement offers surprisingly significant resources for theology today. It can contribute, in particular, to issues that often distance Protestants from Catholics, evangelicals from ecumenicals and marginalized from mainstream communions. Any retrieval and explication of this theology, of course, requires some awareness of the movement as a whole. This is not easily gained, for Anabaptism began as an extraordinarily diverse, largely peasant-artisan phenomenon. It was rich in tales both heroic and horrific. It was less prolific, however, in theological expression. No summa comparable to Calvin's *Institutes* or Melanchthon's *Loci Communes* provides entrance to its thought world.

Anabaptism is best approached as a dynamic interweaving among social, economic, ecclesiastical and missional forces. Its largely implicit theology can be detected through repeating patterns in individual and group behavior as well as in written exhortations and expositions. Taking this approach, this chapter will provide glimpses of historic Anabaptism's dynamism. Though numerous theological issues are latent in what follows, I will not explicate many of them here but will do so more gradually in later chapters. I will sketch Anabaptism's origination from three relatively independent sources—Swiss, South German-Austrian and Dutch—and also a Polish stream with some Italian provenance. Readers familiar with these events (from about 1525 to 1575) may want to skim or skip this chapter.

SWITZERLAND

It is almost 1523. The frosty air of Zurich, Switzerland, tingles with tension and apprehension. Speculations and rumors swirl around the latest crusade of the controversial "people's priest," Ulrich Zwingli. Upon arriving in 1519 this serious, articulate scholar had initiated the unprecedented practice of preaching straight through books of the Bible. Launching out from this biblical base, he began vigorously denouncing many civic and church practices, even critiquing prominent citizens by name.

Just now Zwingli is attacking the collection of tithes and interest. Tithes provide the financial sustenance for all local ecclesiastical institutions, including Zwingli's own church, the Great Minster, with its twenty-four canons. Interest constitutes a pillar of the economic system.[1] But Zwingli claims that Scripture describes tithes, which the church has represented as divine obligations, simply as voluntary contributions. All Zurich tenses. Will the city councils and church hierarchy finally clamp down on Zwingli? Or will he muster enough support to continue his path toward reformation?

The broad controversy is largely resolved at the First Zurich Disputation on January 29, 1523, attended by about six hundred of Zurich's five thousand residents. Various charges are raised against the people's priest, but the city council rejects them. Zwingli, to the consternation of Catholic officials, treats this gathering as an official assembly of the Zurich church, and the city council, composed of the social and economic elite, as empowered to make binding decisions.

In the countryside, however, resentment against tithes and interest is escalating. Peasants contribute disproportionately to support Zurich's institutions and are more pressed than city dwellers by rising rents and interest. Rural priests Wilhelm Reublin and Simon Stumpf tell their congregations to cease paying tithes. Finally by June, six country churches beseech the Zurich city council for relief. Another showdown arrives! Will Zwingli's radical vision alter even these venerable economic structures? To the peasants' disappointment, Zwingli moderates his tone. He begins to explain that even though tithing and charging interest are human practices, most forms are valid. Some changes, of course, are desirable. But these should be gradual to avoid economic disruption.[2] The peasant petition is refused. Zurich keeps tithing power in its hands.

Nonetheless, Zwingli's reforming vision is still fervently advocated by several

---

[1] Interest included obligatory payment for cash loans and taxes assessed on real estate, which were collected regardless of revenue obtained from the property (Ulrich Gaebler, *Huldrych Zwingli* [Philadelphia: Fortress, 1986], p. 50).

[2] Zwingli advocated a step-by-step recovery of tithing's original purpose: supporting the poor and paying preachers (ibid., p. 94). As church institutions such as monasteries were dissolved, he wanted their wealth to go to the poor. Though this happened at first, these funds were soon diverted to secular purposes (ibid., p. 98). Zwingli continued to critique monopolies, money trading and currency devaluation (ibid., p. 94) and recommended regulating interest rates (ibid., p. 93). However, even in cases of clear abuse he advocated only gradual changes, stressing that existing agreements must be honored. By late 1525 the Zurich council "had not brought the peasants any decisive political or economic relief"(ibid., p. 96).

young scholars who study Scripture and Greek classics with him. One is Felix Mantz, highly educated son of one of Zwingli's fellow priests.[3] Another is Conrad Grebel, irresolute and dissolute sometime university student and son of a nobleman and Zurich council member.[4] All are inspired by the great Catholic humanist Erasmus, who promotes a simple, ethical faith based on Jesus' example while critiquing ecclesiastical hierarchy and theological complexity.

Within this circle, during 1522, Zwingli had praised pacifism and the early Christian community of goods (Acts 2:42-47; 4:32-37). He asserted that unbaptized children are not damned and that infant baptism lacks biblical foundation. His young disciples eagerly anticipated his reforming of Zurich solely on a scriptural basis.

The most explosive issues, images and the Catholic Mass, are debated at the Second Zurich Disputation on October 26-28, 1523. This time nine hundred crowd together, including many from surrounding areas. It is agreed that images will be removed from churches, but to avoid disturbances, only after several months' instruction in all congregations. Most participants find the Mass idolatrous. Zwingli, after some urging from Conrad Grebel to abolish it quickly, asks the town council to decide how to phase it out.

At just this juncture, however, Simon Stumpf, the rural priest opposed to tithes, protests to Zwingli, "You have no authority to place the decision in Milords' hands, for the decision is already made: the Spirit of God decides."[5] Zwingli rejoins that the council is not making the ultimate decision but only supervising its implementation. Yet a crucial disagreement between Zwingli and his radical followers has erupted. Grebel, Stumpf and others want such decisions made and implemented on the basis of Scripture alone by a body that is clearly a church. Zwingli wants government, or the government considered as a church, to promulgate and regulate such reforms.

Disheartened by Zwingli's apparent compromising of his earlier biblical vision, the radicals begin searching for an alternative. Soon after the Second Disputation (perhaps even before it) Grebel, Stumpf and Felix Mantz urge Zwingli to begin a new Protestant church composed only of the truly converted. They apparently expect most Zurichers to join it, for they assume that its members could elect a new, truly Christian town council. This church of the committed then would apparently be a state church, for it would comprise the majority of citizens, some of whom

---

[3]Though priests were supposed to be celibate, many lived and raised children with women with public knowledge and sometimes approval. Zwingli lived with Anna Reinhard from early 1522 until he married her on April 2, 1524.

[4]For Grebel's searching years and eventual conversion, see his many letters collected in *The Sources of Swiss Anabaptism*, ed. Leland Harder (Scottdale, Penn.: Herald, 1985).

[5]Ibid., p. 242.

would participate in government. Zwingli objects that no such church can be established in this fallen world because no congregation can avoid having some unregenerate members.

As the radicals seek a new course, they become convinced (following earlier hints from Zwingli) that baptism should be administered not to infants but only to those making a mature faith decision. If baptism, the gateway to church membership, were limited to such persons, the desired church of the committed could be assembled. But baptism's meaning would change. It might not symbolize the washing away of original sin but mark the entrance into a virtuous Christian life.

Refusals to baptize infants begin early in 1524 in rural Witikon, under Wilhelm Reublin, who had earlier opposed tithes, and in Zollikon, a village near Zurich, where tithing had been resisted too. Grebel and other Zurichers also refuse to baptize their infants, prompting a city council mandate in August for everyone to do so. Following inconclusive talks between the radicals and church leaders in December, and a public disputation in January 1525, the council reaffirms its mandate. It orders Grebel and Mantz to cease public opposition and expels all non-Zurichers, such as Reublin, associated with them.

Despairing of thoroughgoing church reform through Zwinglian channels, fifteen radicals gather at Felix Mantz's home on January 21, 1525. As the fear of God lies heavily upon them, one George Blaurock asks Grebel to baptize him. Grebel complies, and then he (or perhaps Blaurock) baptizes all the others. A new church has just originated. Its opponents, joining the Greek prefix *ana* (meaning "again") to *baptism*, will soon derisively call it Anabaptist.[6]

Immediately this new church launches into mission. During the next week some thirty-five persons, mostly small farmers and hired help, receive baptism in Zollikon. They soon remove locks from their doors and, though continuing to live in family households, make their possessions available to each other. Authorities from Zurich quickly arrest Mantz, Blaurock and twenty-five others, initiating a series of increasingly lengthy imprisonments. Many of the new Anabaptists, however, anticipate the imminent end of the age. In June 1525 women, men and children from Zollikon wind through Zurich, exhorting repentance and warning of coming judgment.

Anabaptist evangelists spread quickly into the countryside. Often they are well received by those who resent Zurich's political and economic domination, especially in neighboring territories that could be styled "peasant democracies."[7] In

---

[6]Since virtually every non-Jewish European had been baptized in infancy, baptism of mature believers was commonly regarded as a second baptism. "Anabaptists," however, insisted that this latter form alone was the true first, and not a second, baptism.

[7]Gaebler, *Huldrych Zwingli*, p. 3.

some locales veterans of the recent Peasants' War (see below) accept baptism. Armed peasants occasionally protect Anabaptist missionaries.[8] Though Grebel and others insist on following Jesus literally and thus renouncing all violence, no consensus on this among Anabaptists exists at this early date.

In St. Gall, about fifty miles east of Zurich, where Grebel's brother-in-law Vadian is mayor, Anabaptist preachers initially enjoy free reign. On Palm Sunday, 1525, Grebel baptizes multitudes at the river. Soon revivals flourish every evening in forests, mountains, fields and at the city gate.

Yet some people experience strange visions. Others speak in tongues while yet others seek signs of the End. With traditional restraints lifted, sexual promiscuity and antisocial behavior appear. By May's end Zwingli's *On Baptism*, composed to refute the Anabaptists, is publicly promoted in St. Gall.[9] By June the government forbids Anabaptist meetings. It imposes fines for rebaptism and convenes a militia to forestall any revolt. Mayor Vadian has at length opted for Zwingli's approach.

At this juncture, we will journey to the city of Waldshut, about thirty miles northeast of Zurich on the Rhine, under Austrian control. In 1520 Balthasar Hubmaier, a doctor in theology and former university rector, arrived as a priest and began gravitating toward Protestant convictions. He visited Erasmus, corresponded with Zwingli and spoke at the Second Zurich Disputation. By spring 1524 he had devised a plan for Protestant reform of Waldshut.

Hubmaier, however, had to deal with a movement that bypassed Zurich: the Peasants' War. Throughout the Germanic territories the fortunes of feudal lords were fading. As petty nobles sought to stem their decline and rising cities sought to increase their fortunes, burgeoning taxation and restrictive regulations descended on the peasants. Most peasants also felt that they were financially exploited by and had no voice in the Roman Church. But Protestantism, as they understood it, offered economic betterment and congregational participation.

By midsummer 1524 peasant armies were marching through northern Switzerland and the Black Forest presenting demands to their Austrian rulers. Waldshut's Protestant reform was also threatened by the Austrians. So the city allied with the peasants. Hubmaier found many of the peasants' demands "Christian and just" and helped them compose a declaration.[10] During that fall and winter, troops from Zurich reinforced Waldshut.

---

[8]C. Arnold Snyder, *Anabaptist History and Theology* (Kitchener, Ont.: Pandora, 1995), pp. 58-60; and James Stayer, *Anabaptism and the Sword*, 2nd ed. (Lawrence, Kans.: Coronado Press, 1976), pp. 109-13.
[9]In a letter to Vadian accompanying this booklet, Zwingli asserted that "The issue, is not baptism, but revolt, factions, heresy" (George Williams, *The Radical Reformation*, 3rd ed. [Kirksville, Mo.: 16th Century Journal, 1992], p. 224).
[10]Stayer, *Anabaptism and the Sword*, p. 107.

In March of 1525, however, Reublin and Grebel visit. On Easter, Reublin baptizes Hubmaier and about sixty others. Before long most citizens and city council members receive baptism, and Waldshut becomes an Anabaptist city—one of three to ever do so legally (with Nicholsburg in Moravia and Münster in North Germany, as we will see). Hubmaier expects these converts to participate in government and even armed defense. Waldshut continues to furnish the peasants with troops and supplies.

By July, Hubmaier authors *On the Christian Baptism of Believers*, a sophisticated reply to Zwingli's *On Baptism*. He insists, as nearly all Anabaptists would, that the biblical order of conversion places preaching first, repentance and belief second, and baptism third. In December of 1525, however, Waldshut finally falls to the Austrians. Hubmaier flees to Zurich, which is by now extremely hostile to Anabaptists.

Let us turn back to the peasant armies. In March 1525 they took over St. Peter's Benedictine monastery in the Black Forest. At about that time St. Peter's prior, Michael Sattler, left for good. Quite possibly he sympathized with the peasant's plight and/or their critique of the monastery's socioeconomic privilege. By summer 1526 Sattler, now baptized, will begin preaching in Swiss villages that had supported the peasants.

Later that year Sattler and his new wife, Margaretta, a former Beguine nun, will make their way to Strasbourg, a free city on the Rhine that is unusually hospitable to religious dissenters. Hans Denck, a mystical South German we will soon meet, is there. The Strasbourg reformers, especially Wolfgang Capito, will find Sattler's faith basically sound. Yet they will caution that he insists too legalistically on performing good works and separates the true church too sharply from society.

Returning to Zurich, Balthasar Hubmaier and his wife, Elsbeth, fleeing from fallen Waldshut, are arrested there in December 1525. A debate on baptism between Hubmaier and the city's church leaders follows. Both sides claim to have won. Gradually, however, Hubmaier, probably fearing extradition to the Austrians, is persuaded to renounce his views. Yet when led before a congregation to recant publicly, Hubmaier forcefully expounds the Anabaptist position. For this he is again imprisoned and repeatedly tortured. He recants once more (while being tried along with Mantz, Blaurock and Grebel, who stand firm). After reiterating his recantation in three churches, Balthasar, with Elsbeth, is allowed to flee eastward toward Moravia, where we will meet them again.

During 1525-1526, Anabaptist converts and leaders are jailed for extended periods, under increasingly harsh conditions.[11] Most often they are charged with

---

[11]Initially, Zurich church leaders sought to change the prisoners' minds through dialogue and won some back to the established church.

(1) denying that Christians can hold government office, (2) mandating sharing of goods, (3) insisting that sin after baptism is impossible and (4) fomenting revolution. They generally admit the first but emphasize their obedience to government's legitimate functions. They deny that they command sharing of goods, though it was often practiced in some form. And while they expect the baptized to lead transformed lives, they deny that sinlessness is attainable. Finally, while Anabaptism did appeal to some revolutionaries, its leaders absolutely deny encouraging any such thing.

Despite these defenses the Zurich city council, following the trial of Hubmaier, Blaurock, Grebel and Mantz in March 1526, decrees death by drowning for all "rebaptizers." In November this penalty expands to anyone hearing Anabaptist preaching. Though Grebel persists in baptizing, he escapes this fate by succumbing to the plague in August. Mantz, however, becomes Zurich's first Anabaptist martyr—he was drowned on January 5, 1527.

In two short years Anabaptism had spread through much of Switzerland. Yet its enthusiastic early communities were quickly scattered. Its adherents now lead a secretive, illegal existence. Despite this, its apostles and congregations are often in touch. Yet they differ on several important points.

First, Anabaptism involves deep experiences of spiritual renewal. For most these experiences energize a disciplined life. Yet some feel that such ecstasies free them from all rules. Second, the church's relationship to government, and especially the use of force, is unclear. On one hand, Anabaptism has often intermixed with peasant political aspirations. Moreover, the Zurich radicals and Hubmaier called for an Anabaptist government and state church early on. On the other hand, Grebel, Mantz and others denied that Christians should govern or use force.

To unify and coordinate the hardpressed Anabaptist movement, some theological agreement is necessary. A clandestine conference convenes at Schleitheim, northeast of Waldshut, in February 1527. It affirms a seven-point "brotherly union" drawn up by the ex-Benedictine, Michael Sattler.[12] This Schleitheim Confession insists that "there is nothing else in the world . . . than good or evil, believing and unbelieving . . . the world and those who are come out of the world . . . and none will have part with the other"(art. 4). Christian behavior, consequently, must be visibly distinct from "worldly" varieties. The church and its activities must be separate from the state and cultural life.

This means that "the sword," or violence, is "outside the perfection of Christ." No Christian should wield it (art. 6) or swear civic oaths (art. 7). The Schleitheim Confession also promulgates a distinctive understanding of church discipline (art.

---

[12] *The Legacy of Michael Sattler*, ed. John H. Yoder (Scottdale, Penn.: Herald, 1973), pp. 34-42.

2). Those who sin must be warned twice. If they pay no heed then, or at a subsequent meeting, they will be banned from the congregation. Schleitheim also outlines Anabaptist understandings of church practices: baptism (art. 1), the Lord's Supper (art. 3) and the role of a "shepherd" to lead congregations in exhorting, teaching, banning, and the Supper (art. 5). A "congregational order" probably circulated with the confession, directing that "none shall have anything of his own," but that a "common fund" should be established for the poor.

Schleitheim attendees also map out coordinated plans for far-flung mission. However, on their return to Horb, an Austrian-governed town on the Neckar River, Michael and Margaretta Sattler are apprehended. Largely due to widespread sympathy for them, considerable difficulties attend their incarceration and trial preparations. During his imprisonment Michael exhorts his congregation to steadfastness, for the escalating persecution surely heralds the End.[13]

The verdict at Michael's trial is sealed in advance. His tongue is severed and his flesh twice torn with red-hot tongs in the town square. Then he is torn five times more and burned at the place of execution.[14] Following this atrocity Margaretta is alternately threatened and offered mercy by a leading Austrian countess among others if she will recant. She repeatedly refuses and is drowned.

Michael's horrible death is broadcast widely. Wolfgang Capito, the tolerant Strasbourg reformer, excoriates the Austrian governors. Michael and his followers, Capito protests, were true, even if misguided, Christians. They should be corrected by persuasion, not coercion.[15]

Already by 1527 most Swiss Anabaptists are underground or on the run. Some, however, enjoy limited toleration in Bern, Switzerland's largest city. Several congregations in canton Bern survive today. Many other Anabaptists, however, flee to mountains, forests or Strasbourg. Still others form small communities scattered through other Germanic territories, sometimes crossbreeding Swiss Anabaptism with other varieties. By the 1550s some Swiss will spread down the Rhine and meet the Dutch. For many decades, even centuries, Swiss Anabaptists will maintain a distinctive ethos marked by fervent biblicism, ethical seriousness and a strict ban.

SOUTH GERMANY AND AUSTRIA

It is May 14, 1525. Today Waldshut is an Anabaptist city. Michael Sattler has left his monastery. In many Swiss regions Anabaptist evangelists are galvanizing large

---

[13]Ibid., pp. 55-63.

[14]Accounts of the punishment vary slightly in the descriptions of Michael's trial and martyrdom (see ibid., pp. 67-80).

[15]Ibid., pp. 86-93.

followings. But about two hundred miles to the north, in the forests and fields near Frankenhausen, two large armies square off. One appears smart and orderly. Its hosts of knights are garbed in the latest, least cumbersome, most protective armor. They sport the most advanced weapons. They muster in disciplined fashion.

The army opposite looks rag-tag and bedraggled. It sports every variety of make-shift, half-protective clothing and rusty, antiquated weapon. Yet above their uneven ranks flutter white flags crested with swords and great white banners emblazoned with rainbows, designed by their leader, the fiery priest, Thomas Müntzer.

The two forces have already skirmished. The ragtag, mostly German peasants have the edge. But now Philip of Hesse, leader of the opposing nobles, asks for a truce. He offers to let the peasants go if they hand over Müntzer. While the peasants debate this, the nobles steal toward more advantageous positions. Not surprisingly, Müntzer exhorts his side forward, ensuring it of God's favor in this climactic showdown of the Peasants' War. Suddenly a rainbow, the very symbol on the peasant banners, appears in the sky. The peasants rush forward.

Five to six thousand are butchered. Philip loses only six men.[16] The back of the pan-Germanic Peasant's War is broken (though it will continue to rage in the Austrian Tyrol into 1526).

Destructive as peasant depredations could be, their demands, which they normally presented well before fighting, were articulated in biblical fashion by educated advocates like Hubmaier. Their best-known declaration offered to revoke any demand inconsistent with Scripture.[17] It proposed that congregations choose and dismiss their own pastors. It refused to pay all tithes, and proposed that all collected tithes be distributed locally. The declaration insisted that since Christ redeemed everyone, no person can be another's property and serfdom must be abolished. The peasants requested that ancient privileges of equal access to local waters, forests and meadows be retained or restored. They rejected excessive demands for labor and rents and refused to pay the church's death tax.

As peasants began presenting such demands, they hoped that Martin Luther, himself from peasant stock, would champion them. Yet Luther denounced their demands as worldly and selfish. Christians, he said, rather than insisting on their own rights, should patiently suffer wrong.[18] Luther, however, also critiqued the nobles'

---

[16]Though Philip also backed the soldiers who slaughtered many Münsterites in 1534, he dealt leniently with Anabaptists in his own lands and resisted executing them (Williams, *Radical Reformation,* pp. 659-69).

[17]Martin Luther, "Admonition to Peace," in *Luther's Works* (Philadelphia, Fortress, 1967), 46:8-6.

[18]Ibid., pp. 23-40.

tyranny. He proposed that the current rebellion might be God's judgment and even called the peasant demands just.[19] Yet Luther's tract, "Against the Murdering Hordes of Peasants," exhorted "everyone who can, smite, slay, and stab, secretly or openly" any warring peasant, for "nothing can be more poisonous, hurtful, or devilish than a rebel."[20]

Most common people, however, thought that ideals like the peasants' were basic to the Reformation.[21] But by 1520 Luther had implored secular rulers to reform the church.[22] Like Zwingli, he granted the state an essential role in restructuring the church. Not surprisingly, then, Luther's backing of the nobility in the Peasants' War alienated enormous masses of common people. In many Germanic lands Anabaptism became their main Reformation option, appealing to victims of and even participants in the war.

But we return to Frankenfeld on May 14, 1525. Perhaps we can glimpse a stealthy figure slipping away from peasant lines. Though this wandering bookseller has not fought, he has promoted Thomas Müntzer's writings and even signed his "eternal covenant." Preaching a week later at his home town of Bibra, Hans Hut will still insist that "subjects should murder all the authorities, for the opportune time has arrived."[23]

Müntzer's revolutionary vision sprang from mystical medieval roots. Müntzer thought that Luther taught a "sweet Christ," who simply provided comfort when someone professed faith. For Müntzer, however, conversion involved God's purging of all attachments to created things. In this process the convert experiences the "bitter Christ": shares Christ's crucifixion, descends into hell, even loses faith in God. Eventually, however, the Spirit resurrects the person and illumines the Scripture. This involves not simply insight into its literal meaning, or letter, as Luther—and the Swiss Brethren—emphasized. The Spirit even surpasses the Bible, bestowing special revelations about the imminent end of the age.

On a social level, Müntzer taught, this inner purging of desires for created things will dethrone cravings for pleasure and wealth that dominate human activity and spawn social inequalities. This purging will take form as a common people's revolution, destroying the wealthy who control the economy. Commoners will then place

---

[19]Ibid., pp. 17-23.

[20]Martin Luther, "Against the Murdering Hordes of Peasants," *Luther's Works* (Philadelphia, Fortress, 1967), p. 50.

[21]James Stayer, *The German Peasants' War and the Anabaptist Community of Goods* (Montreal: McGill-Queen's University Press, 1991), pp. 45-60.

[22]Martin Luther, "The Address to the German Nobility," *Luther's Works* (Philadelphia: Fortress, 1966), 44:115-217.

[23]Williams, *Radical Reformation*, p. 167.

all creatures, which people now strive to own as property, back under God's sole dominion. They will live moderately, sharing things in common.[24] Why then did the peasants fail at Frankenhausen? Müntzer concludes that they were still too attached to material cravings. He is beheaded and his body is exhibited on a spear.

Not long after, Hans Hut, with wife and child, flees southward to Augsburg. There he encounters Anabaptists. In May 1526 he is baptized by Hans Denck. With extraordinary rapidity Hut plants Anabaptist congregations throughout south Germany and Austria. Many of his converts establish other congregations more widely.

Moving mostly among illiterates, and sometimes being illiterate themselves, these evangelists often memorize and preach from a list of Scriptures expressing Hut's major themes. Many evangelists are itinerant craftspeople; since craftspeople often work together in large rooms, the evangelists initiate clandestine discussions in these workrooms in town after town. Further, since suspected male leaders are closely watched, women are crucial in spreading this grassroots movement through ordinary encounters in daily tasks.[25]

While eschatological expectation was fairly strong among the Swiss, it is much more central for Hut. He understands baptism as the sealing of the final 144,000 (cf. Rev 7). It is also entrance into a Christian community that shares material goods. Hut calculates that Christ will return 3 1/2 years after the restoration of believers' baptism in Switzerland, on May 31, 1528. Until then Christians should not resist their enemies but suffer as Jesus did. At the very end, however, they can take up the sword against the godless. Hut, who heeds some dreams and special revelations, outlines the last days' course under "seven judgments," shared only with the mature.

Despite Hut's eschatological predilections, he understands salvation somewhat like Müntzer. Most people, he laments, want to be justified through a shallow, external faith profession. But true justification involves profound internal suffering and both spiritual and ethical purification. Hut can call this internal struggle the baptism of the Spirit. A valid outward baptism of water must witness to it. Thereafter, true Christians will experience a baptism of blood, consisting of daily mortification and perhaps literal martyrdom. Hut adds, however, that the Spirit eventually brings relief and joy.[26]

In May of 1527 Hut tangles with Balthasar Hubmaier, by now in Moravia, who

---

[24]Stayer, *German Peasants' War*, pp. 107-14.

[25]Snyder, *Anabaptist History and Theology*, pp. 101-4.

[26]Hans Hut, "On the Mystery of Baptism," in *Early Anabaptist Spirituality*, ed. Daniel Liechty (New York: Paulist Press, 1994), pp. 64-81.

sharply disagrees with him, especially over eschatology. In August, Hut attends a gathering of about sixty Anabaptist leaders in Augsburg, later dubbed the Martyr's Synod because by 1530 only two or three remained alive. Here again his eschatological preoccupations are challenged. Hut is captured in September, tortured, grilled regarding his teachings and finally asphyxiated by a fire in his cell.

South German-Austrian Anabaptism was also shaped by a quite different figure. Hans Denck was a young schoolteacher and translator trained in Hebrew, Greek and Latin. Reformation ideas reached him through the filter of humanist-mystical discussion groups in Nuremberg, about one hundred miles north of Augsburg. Müntzer visited him there in 1524, and Denck had some contact with his followers the next spring. When Protestantism triumphed in Nuremberg, its preachers complained that Denck downplayed the Bible, overstressed good works and rejected water baptism.[27] The city council banished him on January 21, 1525—Swiss Anabaptism's very birth day.

Denck met many Swiss Anabaptists in St. Gall that September and then exercised some leadership among their Augsburg counterparts. In May 1526 Balthasar Hubmaier, on the run from Zurich to Moravia, stopped by Augusburg and perhaps baptized Denck. When the Augsburg city council became suspicious, Denck feared a repeat of Nuremberg and fled to Strasbourg, that temporary haven for so many Anabaptist leaders.

Though Sattler and a Swiss group were active there, Denck chose an Anabaptist fellowship with spiritualist leanings. Soon, however, the authorities, finding him much less orthodox than Sattler, banished him. Denck then attended the Augsburg Martyr's Synod (August 1527). As debate swirled around Hut, Denck began wondering whether concern over fidelity to Scripture was really uniting Anabaptists or perhaps dividing them around diverging interpretations. He also began questioning the momentous significance ascribed to the "external" rite of water baptism.

Denck then departed for Basel, Switzerland. He increasingly felt that his Anabaptism had divided him from other Christians. He ceased to insist on external believers' baptism and affirmed an inner, nonphysical baptism and Lord's Supper. Therewith Denck exited Anabaptism and crossed over into Spiritualism. In November 1527, however, Denck succumbed to the plague. He was twenty-seven years old.

Denck was influenced by the medieval mystical themes that shaped Müntzer and Hut. Yet he shared little of their prophetic harshness or revolutionary fervor. For Denck, the divine Word, which most Christians identify uniquely with Jesus,

---

[27]Hans Denck, *The Spiritual Legacy of Hans Denck*, ed. Clarence Bauman (Leiden: E. J. Brill, 1991), pp. 51-71.

dwells in everyone—including Jews, Muslims and pagans—though most seldom notice it. Those who let this Word work within them experience inner crucifixion of their creaturely attachments, much as Müntzer and Hut said. The Word eventually fills them so fully that they become divinized.

Denck's theology raises problems. Does divinization mean actually becoming God? Is Denck's Jesus then simply a human who responded to the Word like others, though more fully? Denck often added that those being divinized would know how to act without Scripture and could fulfill God's law. They do not really need the biblical letter or "external" church ceremonies stressed by Anabaptists. True religion is inward, invisible and individual.

Due to Hut's and Denck's early deaths, their impact on South German-Austrian Anabaptism soon fades somewhat. Moreover, some who continue Hut's apocalypticism or Denck's mysticism extend them beyond Anabaptism.

After Hut's end-time prediction of May 31, 1528, fails, eschatological preoccupation declines markedly, except among a few who revise the final timetable. Some flee to Strasbourg. Others, like Augustin Bader, remain in south Germany. Bader, however, seeks to convince Anabaptists as far distant as Switzerland of his commission. When he fails, he organizes a commune from his last faithful followers (five men, three women, eight children). He announces that his infant son, born in late 1529, will be the new Messiah (a star was observed standing still over Bader's headquarters). Then 2 1/2 years later, after invading Turks destroy the godless authorities, Bader as regent for his son will announce a moneyless millennium of productive labor and social equality.

Soon thereafter a disciple beholds a gold crown and scepter descending toward Bader. Bader manufactures them as real objects, accompanied by a gilded sword, knife, chain, ring and golden canopy embroidered with stars. Unfortunately, Bader is executed over two years before they can be worn. Despite this, his wife, Sabrina, makes it to Strasbourg with her children. There the tolerant reformer Wolfgang Capito, recently widowed, is so smitten by her that he nearly becomes the Messiah's stepfather.[28]

Bader, like Denck, had migrated beyond Anabaptism. He announced that the time for teaching and baptizing was past, and he likely suspended the Lord's Supper. He excommunicated the Swiss who disbelieved his revelations—while they excommunicated him. Bader finally ceased worshiping Christ and prayed

---

[28]This is Werner Packull's phrase (*Mysticism and the Early South German-Austrian Anabaptists* [Scottdale, Penn.: Herald, 1977], p. 138). For Bader's activities, see ibid., pp. 131-38. On Sabrina Bader, see also C. Arnold Snyder and Lydia A. Huebert Hecht, *Profiles of Anabaptist Women* (Waterloo, Ont.: Wilfred Laurier University Press, 1996), pp. 106-10.

only to "God."

Denck's mystical proclivities are further extended by people like Hans Buenderlin and Christian Entfelder.[29] They escape in 1529 to Strasbourg, where both spiritualist and Anabaptist conventicles exist; they gravitate toward the former. Buenderlin eventually rejects all "external" ceremonies and opposes more literal readings of Scripture, such as the Swiss practiced. These, he feels, miss the deeper spiritual substance and produce divisive sectarianism. Similarly, Entfelder soon repudiates all organized churches and their ceremonies, and calls for inner spiritual unity among Christians.

Denck, Buenderlin and Entfelder show how close to Spiritualism Anabaptism could become. Like Anabaptists, Spiritualists stressed profound inner communion with God and exemplary ethical conduct. Both movements sharply critiqued domineering hierarchy, lavish ceremonialism and moral corruption among both Catholics and Protestants. Yet Anabaptists also emphasized ceremonies and structures that knit Christians into a visible, tangible body.

Another early South German-Austrian movement remained Anabaptist and survived. To tell its story, we will travel first to the Austrian Tyrol (western Austria and northern Italy today). This rugged, mountainous land was patchworked with local territories that prized their freedom. Gradually, however, the Austrians and foreign mining interests took over the government, church and economy. Yet most locals so deeply resented this that in May 1525, as peasant armies to the north are being crushed, crowds of petty burghers, peasants, miners and artisans in the Tyrol rise in revolt.

Their platform calls for lay leadership in the church, abolition of the Mass, and Scripture as sole authority. Their leader, Michael Gaismair, envisions the leveling of city walls to equalize burghers and peasants. He proposes relative autonomy of local communities, freedom from tariffs for artisans, nationalization of mines and commerce, cooperative community work projects and aid to the sick and poor. Throughout 1526, however, Austria relentlessly smothers this uprising. In mid-1527 George Blaurock, a Tyrolean native, brings Anabaptism back from Switzerland. Since Protestantism has made few inroads, Anabaptism offers the only serious alternative to Catholicism. It rapidly becomes a mass movement.

Several of Hut's converts swiftly perform multiple baptisms. Leonhard Schiemer had been a Franciscan monk and Hans Schlaffer, a parish priest. Both are well educated and write moving accounts of their faith—from prison. Both, echoing Hut and Denck, stress death to creaturely attachments through participation in Christ's suffering and divinization through participating in his resurrection.

---

[29]Packull, *Mysticism and the Early South German-Austrian Anabaptists*, pp. 155-75.

Yet they, like Hut, increasingly experience suffering, not only internally but also outwardly, through persecution. Both believe that the end is near, but they are more muted and less specific than Hut. After merely six months as an Anabaptist, and having evangelized in twenty-eight cities, Schiemer is martyred in January 1528. Seventy others will follow him on the same spot. In February the same fate overtakes Schlaffer.

Multiple executions later, Jacob Hutter emerges as Tyrolean Anabaptism's main leader. He visits Moravia, where local nobles are sheltering Anabaptist refugees. Persecution in the Tyrol is so severe that forming Anabaptist communities, which includes some sharing of goods, is next to impossible. Nevertheless Tyrolean Anabaptists still endeavor to gather the elect of the last days (but without highlighting dating schemes). Given local conditions, Hutter urges that this evangel include the literal call to Moravia, where alone true Christian life seems practicable.

To understand these migrations, we will backtrack a bit and journey to Moravia. In 1526 Balthasar Hubmaier, fleeing from Waldshut, Zurich and Augsburg, was invited to Moravia by Lord Leonard of Liechtenstein. Though officially under Austrian rule, the Moravian nobility cherished a fierce tradition of independence. They could usually flout most of their overlords' wishes.

As Anabaptist refugees began pouring in, Hubmaier assumed supremacy in Nicholburg's main congregation. He baptized about six thousand, including Lord Leonard. As he had done in Waldshut, Hubmaier was on the way to establishing an Anabaptist state church in Moravia. Its members included local governors who wielded the sword. Soon, however, a sizeable group began protesting his sanction of violence and also the mass baptisms, which to them seemed superficial.

In July 1527 the Austrians captured Balthasar and Elsbeth Hubmaier, despite Lord Leonard's attempted protection. From prison in January 1528, Balthasar composed a defense of his beliefs. Some he diluted, though not so far as he had in Zurich.[30] Under torture he confessed to treason at Waldshut, the most weighty charge against him. On March 10, 1528, this sensitive scholar, who had often wrestled with martyrdom's terror, was burned at the stake in Vienna. He had not abandoned his main Anabaptist convictions. Neither had Elsbeth, who was drowned in the Danube three days later.

---

[30]*Balthasar Hubmaier: Theologian of Anabaptism*, ed. Wayne Pipkin and John H. Yoder (Scottdale, Penn.: Herald, 1989), pp. 524-62. He offered, for example, to suspend his practice of baptism and the Lord's Supper until a churchwide council could be called to decide authoritatively about them (ibid., p. 557). He apparently meant that Catholics, Protestants, Anabaptists and all others claiming to be Christian would be involved. Hubmaier averred that Ferdinand of Austria, for whom he was composing this apology and perhaps the foremost persecutor of Anabaptists in Europe, would surely help call such a council.

That same month, back in Nicholsburg, the company that had opposed Hubmaier leaves Lord Leonard's realm, under Jacob Wiedemann. After a perilous journey they find refuge under the lords of Austerlitz, who exempt them from war taxes. En route they pool all their possessions. With this act the mystical teaching on detachment from creaturely things and the widespread Anabaptist practice of sharing goods join and culminate in total community of possessions.

Early on the Wiedemann group develops a distinctive authority structure. Its leaders receive a "double portion" of common goods (cf. I Tim 5:17). They are better fed and clothed than others. In 1530 Wilhelm Reublin, an original Zurich Anabaptist and baptizer of Hubmaier, visits. He complains that this inequality impoverishes many ordinary members; some infants have even died of malnutrition. He protests Wiedemann's authoritarian ways. Eventually Reublin is formally banned. With Joerg Zaunring he leads a dissident flock to nearby Auspitz. However, when Jacob Hutter next visits Moravia, he finds the Wiedemann group mostly to blame.

The next few years witness disheartening splits among groups seeking to devise biblical ways of communal living.[31] At Auspitz the wife of leader Zaunring is banned for adultery. Then Zaunring is banned for treating her sympathetically, even though he later serves as a missionary. One George Schuetzinger is installed. But Hutter finds him hoarding money. He is banned, although he publicly repents. Hutter then bans some other troublemakers. These take up with two nearby communities, the Philippites and Gabrielites, which challenge Hutter. After several stretches of fasting, however, Hutter's followers ban both of them in the Great Schism of 1533. These two groups issue counterbans but eventually disperse. Their opponents, soon called Hutterites, will persist to the present.

In 1536, though, Jacob Hutter is finally captured in the Tyrol. The magistrates, fearing great popular sympathy, want him beheaded in secret. But Ferdinand of Austria, who had publicly burned Hubmaier, demands the same for Hutter. Despite continuing persecution, Hutterite missionaries keep combing the Tyrol and adjacent lands, calling people to Moravia, that wilderness where God will protect the elect in the last days (cf. Rev 12:13-14). Of the missionaries commissioned, four-fifths eventually meet martyrdom!

Back in Moravia, the Hutterites do render the wilderness quite fruitful by 1542. Although Austrian depredations destroy much of this between 1545 and 1551, the Hutterites will regain stability and prosperity for the rest of the century. They will become skilled farmers, craftspeople, even doctors. The local populace will place

---

[31]Werner Packull, *Hutterite Beginnings* (Baltimore: Johns Hopkins, 1995), pp. 214-35.

their services in high demand. Yet Hutterites will consistently affirm as sharp a distinction between their true church and the state as the Swiss Schleitheim Confession does.

From 1542-1556 the Hutterites are co-led by Peter Riedemann, whose *Confession of Faith* provides historic Anabaptism's most systematic theological expression. Riedemann roots sin in "wrong taking": that lust for creaturely things which leads to private possessions.[32] Accordingly, surrender and sharing of possessions are integral to salvation.

Riedemann also understands salvation as divinization, or profound transformation through participation in the divine nature. Riedemann combines this South German-Austrian theme with obedience to tight communal structures enforced by the ban. The Hutterites, South Germany-Austria's surviving group, like Switzerland's survivors, the Swiss Brethren, place discipline and strict communal structures in the foreground.

Despite the flight of many South German-Austrian Anabaptists to Moravia, Strasbourg and elsewhere, scattered congregations remained in the homeland.[33] Their eschatological predictions evolved into calls to repentance, their emphasis on the inner cross into a theology of discipleship and martyrdom, their mysticism into practical moralism.[34]

One final major figure surfaced in this Anabaptist stream. Pilgram Marpeck hailed from a wealthy, influential Tyrolean family. His father had been mayor and city council member in Rattenberg. Pilgram also held these posts and often represented Rattenberg in dealings with the Austrian government. He was also mining magistrate for the district, directly responsible to the archduke. This meant that Marpeck not only ran the mines but also granted exploration rights, mediated all disputes and exercised almost complete civil jurisdiction.

But mining was mostly controlled by foreign interests. So in the spring of 1525 miners at nearby Schwaz take over their mines and join Michael Gaismair's rebellion. With help from Rattenberg, and perhaps even a loan from Pilgram, Ferdinand of Austria subdues them.[35] Soon thereafter Ferdinand, Hubmaier's

---

[32]Peter Rideman, *Confession of Faith* (Rifton, N.Y.: Plough, 1970), pp. 58-59. Instead of "wrong taking," John Friesen translates "embracing what is unrighteous." "Wrong taking," however, is more appropriate for the original "unrechten Annehmen," especially since he cites Genesis 3:6 in support (John Friesen, ed., *Peter Riedemann's Hutterite Confession of Faith* (Scottdale, Penn.: Herald, 1999).

[33]Packull, *Mysticism and the Early South German-Austrian Anabaptists*, pp. 118-29; Williams, *The Radical Reformation*, pp. 659-79.

[34]A few retained nostalgic memories of Müntzer's failed revolution, and violence occasionally flared on the margins (Stayer, *Anabaptism and the Sword*, pp. 189-201).

[35]Stephen Boyd, *Pilgram Marpeck* (Durham, N.C.: Duke University Press, 1992), p. 20.

and Hutter's executor, orders Marpeck to apprehend and punish Anabaptists. Pilgram requests release from this responsibility but is refused. Then Leonhard Schiemer is beheaded and burned in January 1528, about two hundred yards from Marpeck's home. Pilgram resigns his position almost immediately. Before questions can be asked, he and his wife Anna are en route to Strasbourg, likely via Moravia.

In Strasbourg an Anabaptist circle forms around them. Despite his aristocratic status, Pilgram joins the gardeners/wagoners guild, whose members feel strapped by usury, rents and tithes; he also joins a group collecting for the poor. At the same time he supervises massive logging and river transportation operations for the city. His superlative engineering skills will make him quite valuable to other cities where he will sojourn. These skills will win some toleration for him and his fellow Anabaptists. During Marpeck's stay in Strasbourg, Buenderlin and Entfelder are tilting toward Spiritualism. Pilgram's first publications, in contrast, underscore the importance of "outward" ceremonies and structures in forming any authentic, lasting church.[36]

Strasbourg's relatively tolerant rulers eventually request Marpeck to leave, as they did most Anabaptists. After various crisscrossing journeys we find him in Moravia in 1541. He is seeking to promote unity among the Swiss Brethren and Hutterites, even while critiquing the former's heavy discipline and the latter's mandating community of goods. The Hutterites, however, refuse to hear him. Pilgram, they report, responded that he would rather unite with the pope or the Turks. From 1544-1556 Marpeck works with water and lumber supply systems in Augsburg and leads an Anabaptist congregation.

Although Marpeck, as an Anabaptist, was never allowed to study theology formally, many historians consider this capable, educated man historic Anabaptism's most profound theologian. Above all, he sought balance among Anabaptist emphases. While nurturing a rich inner, mystical faith like spiritualists, he insisted that it be corporately mediated through outer sacraments and structures. Marpeck linked the latter with Christ's lowly, physical humanity. He also found this essential to both ethics and salvific mediation of Christ's divine reality. Though Marpeck stressed a disciplined life, he opposed overly strict banning, especially among the Swiss. He insisted that church and state be distinct, but not wholly disconnected, as did the Schleitheim Swiss and Hutterites. He served the state in civic—though not police or military—functions.

---

[36]Pilgram Marpeck, *The Writings of Pilgram Marpeck*, ed. and trans. William Klassen and Walter Klaassen (Scottdale, Penn.: Herald, 1978), pp. 44-67.

THE NETHERLANDS

It is June 1533. In Switzerland, Anabaptists have long since gone underground, except in several locales such as near Bern. In Moravia tensions are escalating among Philippites, Gabrielites and the group soon to be called Hutterites. In Strasbourg an earnest, voluble prophet is deliberately seeking incarceration. He is convinced that he is the Elijah of the last days, who in sixth months will be released. Then he will send forth 144,000 indestructible apostles for a final ingathering of God's elect. Melchior Hoffman attains his goal. He is imprisoned for a decade, until his demise.

Early Anabaptism in the Netherlands was propelled by eschatological expectation at least as strongly as in South Germany-Austria. Melchior Hoffman, a self-commissioned Lutheran lay evangelist, first appeared in Baltic regions in 1523. He preached justification by faith alone and that those who rely on works face God's imminent judgment. Hearers were fascinated—or repelled—by his prognostications and vivid portrayals of events to precede this judgment.

Hoffman bitterly criticized the dominant Catholic Church and won temporary endorsement from King Frederick of Denmark and Martin Luther himself. But as the Peasants' War raged to the south, Hoffman was chiefly attracting the lower classes and coincidentally appeared in the vicinity of civil disturbances fairly often. So he was banished from Stockholm, Kiel and many other places, and fled to Strasbourg in 1529. There he met Swiss Brethren, Denckites, Pilgramites (including Marpeck himself) and spiritualists. But he was especially intrigued by a circle of prophetic Anabaptists, some of them the late Hut's disciples, gathered around Barbara Rebstock and Leonard and Ursula Jost.[37]

Persuaded of believers' baptism, Hoffman then journeyed to the Netherlands and, as Hut had, commenced baptizing in droves. Like South German-Austrian Anabaptists, Hoffman taught converts to expect excruciating inner detachment from creaturely desires and subsequent divinization. Yet he promised them a nature more divinely spiritual and more rapidly acquired than Anabaptists in that region envisioned. In the Netherlands divinization began to sound more like actually becoming God, and it raised even higher behavioral expectations. Hoffman underlined this by teaching that Jesus did not receive his human "flesh" from Mary but brought it with him from heaven. Divinization came through participation in Jesus' flesh, so understood.

Numerous Netherlanders were ripe for conversion. For while still Catholic, many were Sacramentarians: people who denied that the eucharistic elements were

---

[37]Snyder and Hecht, eds., *Profiles of Anabaptist Women*, pp. 273-87.

Christ's literal body and blood. Once this central notion was questioned, critique of other Catholic teachings and structures followed.[38] Further, the Netherlands were ruled by Charles V, Most Catholic King of Spain and Holy Roman Emperor, with Austrian assistance. The natives resented this control and regarded the church hierarchy as Charles's instrument. In addition, economic hardship was shoving artisans, from whom most Anabaptists came, onto poverty's margins.

In March 1531, Sicke Snijder, one of Hoffman's most successful converts-turned-evangelist, became Dutch Anabaptism's first martyr. Ten more were executed in December. Rudely shocked, Hoffman, who had expected his divinized converts to be nearly invulnerable, suspended baptisms for two years. He also altered his eschatology. Hoffman began expecting less to occur by divine intervention and more by human agency. He even suggested that before Christ returned, the saints might in some way reign on earth and render judgment.

Following Hoffmann's imprisonment in 1533, even more dubious leadership surfaces in the Netherlands. The baker Jan Matthijs proclaims himself Enoch of the last days. (Hoffman is still Elijah.) He leaves his aging wife and takes up with a "pretty young slip of a girl" named Divara.[39] When Anabaptists in Amsterdam begin to doubt his claims, he threatens them with such dire damnation that they cave in. Matthijs reinstitutes baptism. Guided by visions and dreams, he commissions twelve apostles to announce that God will shortly rid the earth of tyrants, but that no Christian blood will be shed.

Two future Anabaptist leaders, Obbe and Dirk Philips, receive baptism from such emissaries. In March 1534 these emissaries and others stride through Amsterdam proclaiming woe. About sixteen are executed. Obbe Philips, who witnesses the gruesome proceedings, reports that when he saw the corpses, "we could not identify them, so frightfully were they changed by fire and smoke, and those on the wheels we could not recognize either, nor tell one from the other."[40]

Nevertheless, this hardly dissuades a dozen visionaries from running naked

---

[38]For Sacramentarianism's impact on Anabaptism, see Williams, *Radical Reformation*, pp. 95-108, 175-81.

[39]Ibid., p. 542.

[40]Obbe Philips, "A Confession," in *Spiritual and Anabaptist Writers*, ed. George Williams and Angel Mergal (Philadelphia: Westminster Press, 1957), p. 219. Obbe's vivid reminiscences are perhaps overstated, since he later left Anabaptism. Of Hoffman he says, "I know of no one who has so much calumniated and damned in his writings as this Melchior." Obbe and his colleagues considered it "a true, pure, and saintly thing to denounce [others] as heretics and godless and to damn those who were not receptive or disposed to our belief" (ibid., p. 209). Alluding to emphasis on rapid divinization, Obbe laments that "as soon as anyone was baptized, he was at once a pious Christian and slandered all people and admitted no one on earth to be good but himself and his fellow brethren" (ibid., p. 224).

through Amsterdam in February 1535. They are beheaded before it can be determined whether they caught pneumonia. Another forty to fifty seize the town hall briefly in May. Obbe and another leader are to reinforce the hall with Anabaptist troops, but both refuse. Obbe and Dirk feel almost alone in opposing violence.

These Amsterdam episodes are acts in a larger drama that Hoffman confusedly had begun to intimate: an inauguration of the saints' earthly reign preceding Christ's return. Attention eventually focuses on Münster, just east of today's Dutch-German border. There Anabaptists come to power through legal channels. At the same time, many eschatological predictions are placing a particular city at the center of God's final inbreaking. Hoffman had picked Strasbourg, but Matthijs and his apostles (expanded to twenty-seven) urge their converts toward Münster.

Thousands of Dutch Anabaptists, assaulted by poverty and severe persecution, flock to Münster. Houses, orchards and businesses are being abandoned by citizens opposed to the new government! All goods will henceforth be shared! In March 1534 authorities at Kampen halt twenty-seven ships. Aboard, they find three thousand armed Anabaptist men heading, with women and children, for Münster. Local authorities execute their leaders but refuse Austrian requests to sink all the boats.

In January 1534, Jan Matthijs and his apostles enter Münster and initiate believers' baptism. Those baptized expect never to suffer nor fight. But in February the local bishop assembles an army to retake the city. Hundreds of Münsterites now take up the defense. Thousands of reinforcements keep heading their way. Matthijs rules for six weeks. Possessions are equalized. All meals are taken together. Churches and monasteries are razed and plundered, their wealth transferred to the city council. Guilds are dissolved. Money is abolished. Though households are not broken up, all doors must remain open, day and night. On Easter, however, Matthijs feels divinely led to assault the besiegers almost alone, relying on miraculous intervention. He is hacked to pieces.

Immediately one Jan van Leyden takes charge and abolishes the city council. Stricter moral and social laws are imposed. Many infractions are punishable by death. When the Münsterites repulse a full-scale attack on May 25, van Leyden voids all existing marriages and commands everyone to marry. Polygamy is permitted (women outnumber men three to one); all women come under a husband's rule. Jan renounces his recently baptized wife and takes Matthijs's "pretty young slip" of a widow, Divara.[41] When forty-nine persons protest all this, he cruelly executes them.

After another victory on August 31, van Leyden promotes himself to king of

---

[41]Snyder and Hecht, eds., *Profiles of Anabaptist Women*, pp. 298-304; cf. Williams, *Radical Reformation*, p. 542.

righteousness, who will punish the unrighteous and reign over the saints world-wide. Three times daily, as he appears in the marketplace, his subjects prostrate themselves. Yet even though messengers rally many more toward Münster, few now arrive. On June 25, 1535, the city finally falls. Nearly all remaining inhabitants are slaughtered. Jan van Leyden and two other leaders go on exhibit throughout north Germany. They are publicly tortured with red-hot tongs and suspended from a Münster church tower in cages that still hang there today.

Needless to say, the remaining Dutch Anabaptists are in disarray. Most pacifists critical of Münster follow Dirk and Obbe Philips. Yet some, surprisingly, still thirst for vengeance and rally around a Jan van Battenburg. They decree that the time for baptizing is past, and they become bandits robbing churches, burning crops and occasionally dispatching the ungodly. A third Anabaptist faction, inclined toward spiritualism, follows one David Joris.

In 1536 Joris becomes the leading Dutch Anabaptist, uniting his group with most of the pacifists. But shortly thereafter Joris is suffused in an eight-day ecstasy. He envisions earthly rulers falling down and naked people all around. Joris begins interpreting sin chiefly as latent guilt about sexuality. He promotes a spiritual cleansing that will return persons to a childlike, Edenic state, free from sexual shame. Then, liberated from fleshly lusts, women and men will begin conceiving holy offspring. Polygamy will be allowed. As Jan van Leyden had, Joris now calls himself the Third David (following ancient Israel's king and Jesus) who will reign on earth during an imminent age of the Spirit.

Joris also seeks allegiance from the Melchiorite prophets at Strasbourg. But Barbara Rebstock thoroughly discredits his claims despite his effort to deny her, as a woman, the right to speak. Joris increasingly elevates the inner, revelatory Word over Scripture's outer words. Church ceremonies and structures become empty formalities, as they had for Denck, Buenderlin and Entfelder. In 1543, under an assumed name, Joris escapes with many followers to Basel. There they attend the state church, grow rich and enjoy a cultured life.

Dutch Anabaptism's future leadership now lies largely with a reluctant Catholic priest.[42] Early in his priesthood Menno Simons became convinced about justification by faith. Then, struck by Sicke Snijder's execution in 1531, he investigated and acknowledged believers' baptism. Menno even began preaching from Scripture in Protestant fashion and refuting Münsterites. Yet he remained in the priesthood out of fear.

Then in 1535, three hundred Anabaptists en route to Münster took over a nearby cloister. When the militia forcibly recovered the cloister, many Anabaptists

---

[42]Menno Simons, *The Complete Works of Menno Simons*, ed. J. C. Wenger (Scottdale, Penn.: Herald, 1956), pp. 668-73.

lost their lives. One was Menno's brother. Finally Menno could no longer bear it. He could not stand by while so many ignorant, impoverished, persecuted sheep were being so drastically misled!

In January 1536, Menno leaves the priesthood. About a year later several Anabaptists encourage him to begin preaching and teaching. After much agonized wrestling with fear of persecution, Menno is ordained bishop by Obbe Philips. He then embarks on repeated travel through the Netherlands and north Germany. Shortly after his ordination he marries Gertrude, perhaps from his home village, who travels with him. Always on the run, Menno often complains that he can seldom find even a shack safe for his sick wife, two daughters and one son. In 1542 Emperor Charles V decrees an enormous bounty on Menno's head and severe penalties for anyone sheltering him or even reading his books. Yet Menno will die in his bed in 1561.

Menno gradually assumes leadership of nearly all Dutch Anabaptists. In about 1541 Obbe Philips leaves the movement that will be called "Mennonite." His brother, Dirk, however, remains a bishop, assists Menno in many tasks and assumes Menno's mantle from 1561 until his own death in 1568. Dirk's *Enchiridion* becomes the second most systematic treatment of Anabaptist beliefs, after Riedemann's *Confession of Faith*.

Menno and Dirk retain the Dutch notion of divinization, or "new birth," that energizes very upright lives. Much like Hoffman but unlike Anabaptists elsewhere, they attribute this to participation in Jesus' flesh, which they concede came through Mary—but directly from God and not really from her. Menno and Dirk insist that this flesh is still fully human. Accordingly, they expect lofty behavior from those who partake of it. Indeed, this outlook is more sober than the still-present spiritualism, which sanctions aberrant behavior and disastrous extrabiblical revelations. To keep things sober, Menno and Dirk insist on following Scripture's letter, much as do the Swiss Brethren. Reacting against Münster they underscore Jesus' commands and example, with their pacifistic thrust, as do Anabaptists almost everywhere.

To keep the church pure later Dutch leaders, like the Swiss Brethren and Hutterites, advise frequent use of the ban. Turmoil erupts in 1555, however, when Dirk, Leenart Bouwens (1515-1582) and Menno (probably reluctantly) insist that a banned person's spouse must cease all normal relationships with—must shun— the one banned.

The first serious Mennonite split occurs in 1556. A group called Waterlanders rejects this strict shunning and eventually the strong bishops' role exemplified by Dirk, Menno and Leenart. By now Swiss Brethren and Mennonites are making contact, coming from opposite directions along the Rhine. The Swiss, though fairly keen on using the ban themselves, are disturbed by the Netherlanders' spousal shunning. A Swiss-Dutch conference in 1557 at Strasbourg fails to reconcile this difference, and the Dutch soon ban the Swiss.[43] Not until 1591 will this breach be healed.

Meanwhile to the northeast Anabaptism is flourishing in Flanders (in today's Belgium). Yet persecution is even more severe than in the Netherlands. During the 1560s thousands of Flemish Anabaptists flee north, many settling in the northern-most Netherlands, Friesland. Yet the Flemish and Frisians differ culturally and also in understanding the church. The former favor autonomy of local congregations. The latter prefer bishops. In 1560 four Frisian congregations unite in a fairly tight association, but the Flemish object. After seven years of convoluted recriminations and negotiations, Flemish-majority and Frisian-majority groups ban each other. (Dirk Philips and Leenart Bouwens themselves were banned by some groups!) By 1567 three major Mennonite groups exist: Waterlanders, Flemish and Frisians.

By Dirk's death (1568) three large, enduring Anabaptist bodies have emerged, one from each originating stream surveyed so far: Swiss Brethren, Hutterites (South Germany-Austria) and Mennonites (Netherlands).[44] Formal contacts are emerging among them. For all three groups faith is deeply transformative, and it energizes true Christians to live quite differently from others. Yet as life finally set-tles down, their distinctness becomes less the product of spiritual innovation and persecution, and more of adherence to strict communal ways.

POLAND (AND ITALY, LITHUANIA AND ROMANIA)

It is 1569, the year after Dirk Philip's death. In Rakow, a small, rural Polish village, artisans, scholars and peasants are assembling, along with nobles who have dis-persed all their wealth among the poor. Together they begin laboring manually: till-ing fields, erecting dwellings, establishing flourishing paper, pottery and cloth in-dustries. Clergy labor among them, no longer assuming leadership roles.

By this date Hutterites in Moravia have entered their golden years (1565-1578). Marpeck's Pilgramites, however, are becoming less visible. Some of the scat-tered Swiss Brethren have journeyed down the Rhine and encountered Dutch Men-nonites. These two have recently split over the ban, and the Dutch are struggling with several divisions among themselves. But back in Rakow, hopes for cooperative ventures run high. The fruits of the various labors are being shared. After day's work ends, religious discussions occupy the hours. Curious visitors drop by.

Eventually, however, the discussions turn into endless, often chaotic, debates. Lacking ministerial guidance, affairs become confused and disorganized. Some

---

[43] Anabaptists from many regions were beginning formal contacts. A 1555 conference on Christology in Strasbourg was attended by Swiss Brethren, Hutterites, Pilgramites and Mennonites. Another pan-Anabaptist conference gathered there in 1554, about which almost nothing is known.
[44] Marpeck's followers (Pilgramites) still exist in scattered locations, but will soon disappear.

groups and aspiring leaders exit, hoping to form more stable communities else-where. Will Rakow soon disintegrate or become more strictly structured, like Hut-terite colonies? Or does some different future await its residents, most of whom have received believers' baptism?

Although an enduring church body from each of Anabaptism's original branches has attained distinctive form by now, believers' baptism still spreads east-ward. Eventually, the groups who are now adopting this rite will cease practicing it or die out altogether. Yet various threads connect these groups to other strands of our story. The Polish Brethren, who will endure for about a century, constitute a branch of historic Anabaptism.

Several important impulses in this eastward drift originated, surprisingly, in It-aly. Until 1542, when a Roman Catholic inquisition began, Italian states were gen-erally more hospitable to radical groups than those to the north. Since many Ital-ians were irreligious and Mass was often poorly attended, groups that gathered elsewhere for religious activities often escaped notice. To the north, where state church attendance was high and sometimes mandatory, believers' baptism marked off its adherents sharply from society. But in Italy before 1542, where religiosity was more fluid and state control less pervasive, believers' baptism did not mark as decisively those who came to practice it.[45]

Italian Anabaptism emerged from two sources. To the south, many educated persons in Naples and Sicily were influenced by humanist arguments that some tra-ditional doctrines conflicted with biblical texts. Living in Rome's shadow, where church dogma and state power had linked hands for centuries, many Italian human-ists regarded creedal trinitarian formulations as vehicles of coercion. Failure to af-firm these could bring ecclesiastical *and* civil penalties.[46] Among those critical of the church, which included numerous aristocrats, circles formed for religious dis-cussion and aiding the poor.

Several south Italians who became Anabaptists imbibed the theory, taught es-pecially at the University of Padua (in the Venetian Republic), that Jesus was Joseph and Mary's natural son whom God later raised to deity. Like many of their north-ern counterparts, Italian Anabaptists generally expected Jesus to return soon and establish an earthly millennium. But unlike most northern Anabaptists, many Ital-ians emphasized predestination and bondage of the will. They regarded baptism more often as a sign of election than as incorporation into the church. Italians also were less inclined to ban.

Meanwhile, Anabaptism also flowed down from the north. As the Peasants' War

---

[45]Williams, *Radical Reformation*, pp. 945-46.
[46]Ibid., pp. 945-49.

and then Anabaptist evangelism spread southward through the Tyrol, Anabaptism eventually reach Italy. Thousands of peasant refugees from the war streamed into the Venetian Republic, which was ripe for the evangelism. Venice, a wealthy maritime state, enjoyed substantial immunity from pressures from Rome. It welcomed many religious dissenters, much like Strasbourg to the north. Anabaptist conventicles soon appeared.

Most north Italian Anabaptists were influenced by Austrian/Tyrolean Anabaptism, with its more traditional views on Jesus and the Trinity. To reach some resolution with southern teachings, a synod of about sixty Anabaptists convened in Venice in 1550. Through forty days of discussion, an affirmation on ten disputed issues crystallized. Jesus was declared Joseph and Mary's natural son, who benefits us solely through his ethical teaching and self-sacrificing testimony to God's love.[47] Though several delegates rejected these positions, a southern, more humanistic and unitarian Anabaptism had triumphed over the northern, Germanic type.

The synod also commissioned apostolic bishops to travel in pairs through much of Italy. In 1551, however, one of these, Peter Manelfi, unexpectedly defected to Rome. He provided information about numerous Anabaptist congregations and leaders. The well-organized inquisition soon captured or scattered most.

The few remaining leaders fled, as Tyrolean Anabaptists had, to Moravia. The Hutterites, however, turned away anyone affirming the Venice Synod. Consequently, many expatriate Italians formed their own communities there. Eventually, however, the masterminds of these migrations were intercepted, thoroughly examined and drowned. Still, in Italy, Anabaptists on the whole had been treated less gruesomely than in Germanic and Dutch lands.

Italian intellectual currents flowed toward Poland through Italian humanists who, fearing the inquisition, fled to Swiss and German university towns, where they attained wary toleration. Then in 1553 the Protestant city of Geneva, Switzerland, burns Michael Servetus for unorthodox trinitarian views and Anabaptism (though he was never a practicing Anabaptist). Italian humanists are enraged. Once again, they protest, trinitarian doctrine is functioning as a cudgel of civic and ecclesiastical conformity.[48] Many Polish students, sojourning in the same Swiss and German circles, take home this humanistic orientation in general and its trinitarian criti-

---

[47]Many who became Anabaptists also believed that the soul is not naturally immortal but "sleeps" between death and the final resurrection. Some affirmed, further, that only the righteous would be resurrected, while the unrighteous would simply remain dead. Many denied hell. The Venice Synod affirmed soul sleep and rejected hell (ibid., pp. 871-72).

[48]John Calvin, Geneva's leading reformer, supported this execution. The city council, however, refused his recommendations that Servetus be allowed to present his views publicly and be executed less painfully. On Italian radicals in Switzerland and Germany, see ibid., pp. 943-90.

cisms in particular. Various Italian radicals undertake similar journeys and disseminate the same outlook there.

In marked contrast to western Europe, Poland and neighboring Lithuania enjoy significant religious toleration. Nobles are at least as independent as their Moravian counterparts. Many promote religious reform on their own lands, which include numerous towns, though largely to oppose Catholic political power. With the support of these nobles, new church structures begin to form, and by 1550 much of Poland is, in effect, Protestant. Polish Anabaptists emerge from efforts to form an independent Reformed Church. Anabaptism, that is, arises not in opposition to legal processes but by means of them. Much of what we know comes from records of their synods. My account will be largely limited to the development of Polish Anabaptist Christology.

In 1556, at the Synod of Secemin, Peter Gonesius affirms that God the Father alone is truly God, that Christ therefore does not share in deity and that the Trinity is not a Christian teaching. The synod strongly rejects this. Gonesius had earned his doctorate at Padua, where Italian Anabaptists encountered the teaching that Jesus was Joseph's natural son. Gonesius was there during Servetus's execution and must have experienced an antitrinitarian reaction. En route back to Poland in 1555, he picked up some radical social teachings from the Hutterites.

Though Gonesius is rejected in 1556, he sparks a trinitarian debate among Polish Brethren, which occurs in roughly three phases.[49] From about 1562 to 1565, tritheism begins to prevail. Its proponents persuade the emerging Polish Brethren to use Scriptural terms alone to speak of God. They then add that words like *Trinity* and *person*, when applied to God, are misleading and postbiblical inventions. They affirm that Father, Son and Holy Spirit are each God but stress differences among them. They reject talk of one divine substance. Perhaps inconsistently, however, some tritheists regard the Father as God in the most fundamental sense, as Gonesius originally had, and as Source of the Son and Spirit.

Eventually, the Reformed Church condemns tritheism. This sparks the formation of a dissenting Minor Church in 1565, which becomes fully Anabaptist by about 1569. From 1566-1568 this Minor Church turns toward ditheism, which arises in reaction to Laelius Socinus, an Italian refugee via Switzerland. Socinus proposes that Jesus, though virgin-born (and thus not Joseph's son), was simply a man who did not exist before this birth but was later raised by God to deity. Ditheists, who soon include Gonesius, protest that this denial of Christ's preexistence contradicts Scripture. They affirm that the Son was divine from eternity, though

---

[49]Dariusz Jarmola, "The Origins and Development of Believers' Baptism among the Polish Brethren in the 16th Century" (Ph.D. diss., Louisville: Southern Baptist Seminary, 1990), pp. 63-72.

subordinate to the Father. However, they regard the Holy Spirit as a divine influence, not a divine person.

Unitarians, however, essentially concur with Socinus. Only the one called Father is God. Jesus was a man eventually adopted as God's Son. The Spirit, though, is an impersonal force, as ditheists claimed. Unitarians and ditheists debate vigorously at many synods, but by 1569 unitarianism prevails among the Minor Church, now often called Polish Brethren.

Controversy about God and Jesus undergoes one further phase, with origins in nearby Transylvania (northern Romania). Under a tolerant government like Poland's, unitarianism emerges from ecclesiastical discussions and becomes Transylvania's main reformed party in 1569. Many unitarians incline toward believers' baptism, which is strongly advocated by the influential leader, Francis David. However, Transylvanian unitarians officially adopt this rite only between 1578 and 1580, too briefly to really be considered Anabaptist.

David views Jesus as a human prophet who had ascended into heaven in confirmation of his messiahship. Yet he is not there now but will be resurrected as Judge at the end. Such a Christ, David concludes, should not be worshiped as divine. But Giorgio Biandrata, a unitarian, argues that since Jesus was raised to share the Father's glory, he can be called God and worshiped as such. Biandrata invites Faustus Socinus, nephew of Laelius (like him an Italian via Switzerland), to Transylvania to counteract David. By 1579 a unitarian synod definitively affirms adoration of Christ. Though nonadorationism makes little headway in Poland, it attracts followers in Lithuania for a while under Simon Budny. But it wanes considerably there after 1582, when Budny becomes one of the few leaders ever excommunicated by the nondogmatic Brethren.

Discussion of baptism also originates in the Reformed Synods. It begins in 1558 at Bresc Litewski with Gonesius's denial that infant baptism is scriptural. Debate ceases in 1569, after which believers' baptism increasingly, though not universally, prevails among the Polish Brethren. Meanwhile, a growing interest in communitarianism is sparked by increasing contacts with Hutterites. Many Poles hope to join forces with them but are rebuffed for several reasons. Hutterites are firmly trinitarian. They are uncomfortable with the higher social origins and education of many Poles. Finally, Hutterites regard themselves as the one true church and expect Poles to mostly adapt and submit to them.

As Hutterite contacts fail, Rakow becomes Polish Anabaptism's distinctive communal expression. But in its initial efforts at equality, Rakovians had rejected ministerial leadership and things disintegrated. Then unexpectedly in 1572, Rakow is reorganized under ministerial leadership. Many pastors are appointed in Poland and Lithuania.

Eventually, Rakow becomes Polish Anabaptism's center. Many synods convene there. A press in Rakow disseminates books throughout Europe. A library attracts scholars, some of whom teach in a local school stressing philosophy, theology and defense of Anabaptist faith. Yet adherents of other religious communions also attend. The student body often exceeds one thousand, about one-third of them nobility. Yet social distinctions remain leveled at Rakow as does sharing of labor and goods.

The Polish Brethren eventually organize their theology around the teachings of Faustus Socinus, Laelius's nephew.[50] Faustus, who never receives believers' baptism, is unitarian but emphasizes the resurrection and adoration of Jesus, and attainment of eternal life though him. In 1660 the Brethren, then called Socinians, will be driven from Poland. Before long they will disappear as an organized movement.

---

[50]Faustus Socinus died in 1604. In 1605 the Rakovian Cathechism appeared, the classic expression of Socinianism.

3

APPROACHING THE
THEOLOGICAL ENDEAVOR

The preceding chapter's convoluted, rapid-paced, sometimes admirable, sometimes appalling sagas can leave readers dizzy. We gasp at tales of heroic martyrdom and sordid vengeance. We watch some protagonists promote implausible spiritual revelations, and others, sober, literal legalism. Unbridled license breaks forth in some situations, zealous banning in others. We wonder: can any intelligible, underlying theology really be drawn from all this? Yet three stable communions emerged from the cacophony and continue today. They hardly could have, were they not guided by deep, interrelated convictions that formed at least implicit theologies.

Life today is shaped not only by postmodern trends toward diversity and particularity but also modern trends accelerating through globalization. To fulfill their mission, churches must understand and engage both (cf. chap. 1). Historic Anabaptism clearly resembles oppressed, minority churches and peoples whose distinct lifestyles and values are being submerged under globalization's homogenizing forces. Increased appreciation of historic Anabaptism can help today's churches better minister among such marginalized groups.

But does Anabaptism also display similarities with mainstream churches, with their global outlook? Can it also help churches formulate broader beliefs and strategies to address worldwide as well as local issues? To find out, I will now ask whether more general characteristics of historic Anabaptism, that is, common values and beliefs that emerged despite diversities of time, place and circumstance, can be identified and whether some of these can be retrieved today.

Such a theological retrieval, though fairly recent, is already underway. At this juncture it is highly creative but quite diverse, sometimes confusingly so. It can, I believe, be furthered through greater attention to the assumptions and methodologies operative in its various forms. In my own retrieval process, then, I will render my own assumptions and methods as transparent as possible. Since these will include my reading of historic Anabaptism, it will be helpful to first sketch some major interpretations of it over the last sixty years. Then I will review the development of contemporary theology in Anabaptist perspective, mainly over the last twenty years. These will raise the main issues, outline the field of inquiry and provide discussion partners for my own appropriation of Anabaptism's theology in chapters five to ten.

CONTEMPORARY APPROACHES TO HISTORIC ANABAPTISM

From the Reformation until at least the mid-nineteenth century, standard Catholic and Protestant readings prevailed. Anabaptists were presented as theological heretics and political traitors. Anabaptists, it was said, exalted conscience and "the Spirit" over the biblical letter, and individualism against the organized church and state. Thomas Müntzer was the obvious root, the failed Münster insurrection the inevitable fruit.

Several interpreters, however, came to view Anabaptism as the forerunner of a modern movement. In 1850, Friedrich Engels became the first of many Marxists to hail Anabaptism as communism's ancestor. This only solidified the mainline ecclesiastical interpretation. By century's end Ernst Troeltsch was praising Anabaptism for stressing conscience and inner personal freedom. Over time, Troeltsch said, this emphasis eroded theology's transcendent claims, destroyed authoritarian institutions and paved the way for technology's unchecked transformation of nature. Anabaptism heralded modern "progress" and liberal Christianity.[1]

By mid-twentieth century, however, another important reading had appeared. It presented Anabaptism as "the culmination of the Reformation, the fulfillment of the original vision of Luther and Zwingli"; as "consistent evangelical Protestantism seeking to recreate without compromise the original New Testament church,

---

[1]Along with Socinians, Arminians, mystics and spiritualists, "the sectarian Baptist groups" gave rise to literary criticism and the valuing of practical ethics over objective revelation, immediate experience over historical events and subjectivism over ritual and hierarchy. By Troeltsch's day all these had "irresistibly broken in upon the Protestant Churches, like a flood sweeping away old landmarks"(Ernst Troeltsch, *Protestantism and Progress* [Philadelphia: Fortress, 1986], pp. 37-38). As such ideals began spreading via the Enlightenment, "It was now at last the turn of the stepchildren of the Reformation to have their great hour in the history of the world"(p. 68). Troeltsch also elevated Anabaptism by identifying it as a sect, a valid organizational form different from the established church type, and also from the mystical type, in which people like Müntzer could be placed.

the vision of Christ and the apostles."[2] I must limit my account of this approach and its critics to North America.

The Anabaptist Vision

Harold Bender located himself in this line in his epochal 1944 address, "The Anabaptist Vision." Bender identified three themes as most basic to historic Anabaptism. First, the "essence of Christianity" for Anabaptists was discipleship. Second, the church was a voluntary brotherhood. Third, an "ethic of love and nonresistance as applied to all human relationships" was evident.[3] For Bender the Swiss (excluding Hubmaier) represented normative Anabaptism. Thus Bender marginalized mystics and revolutionaries or ruled them out.

It is significant that these three themes can be understood simply in social-ethical terms. This was not Bender's intention. Elsewhere he insisted that the church can be adequately called the "body of Christ" only in light of more "transcendent" phrases, such as "in Christ," which express "utter dependence and close intimacy between Christ and the Church."[4] In fact "'Lord' does not refer to the historical Jesus . . . but to the present living Lord, now at the right hand of the majesty . . . but present on earth in His body, the church, as His dwelling place through the Spirit."[5]

Nonetheless, a social-ethical reading of Bender's "Anabaptist Vision" found some confirmation in the contrast already being drawn between Anabaptism and Pietism by his colleague Robert Friedmann.[6] Friedmann acknowledged that inner experience and outward behavior were important in both movements. Yet he found the outward—actualized in the world through fellowship, suffering and mission—distinctive of Anabaptism. But Pietism's "essence" was "pure subjectivity."[7] According to Friedmann, Anabaptists emphasized working and suffering for God's kingdom (as found in the Gospels), while Pietists focused on "enjoyment" of justification (as found in Paul).[8] Friedmann sometimes separated the

---

[2]Harold Bender, *The Anabaptist Vision*, (Scottdale, Penn.: Herald, 1944), p. 13.

[3]Bender, *Anabaptist Vision*, pp. 20, 26-31, 31.

[4]Harold Bender, *These Are My People* (Scottdale, Penn.: Herald, 1962), p. 25.

[5]Harold Bender, "Who is the Lord?" in *The Lordship of Christ*, ed. C. J. Dyck (Elkhart, Ind.: Mennonite World Conference, 1962), p. 19.

[6]Bender himself did contrast the "inward experience of the grace of God" with discipleship, which was "the outward application of that grace" (*Anabaptist Vision*, p. 21). He said that Anabaptists are not pietists (ibid., p. 33) and affirmed Friedmann's "main line of interpretation" of Pietism (Robert Friedmann, *Mennonite Piety Through the Centuries* [Goshen, Ind.: Mennonite Historical Society, 1949], p. viii). For close connections between Bender and Friedmann on this, see Albert Keim, *Harold S. Bender, 1897-1962* (Scottdale, Penn.: Herald, 1998), pp. 306-31.

[7]Friedmann, *Mennonite Piety*, p. 11.

[8]Ibid., pp. 85-87.

spiritual from the practical so widely that the former seemed irrelevant.[9] Yet his reading of his own time influenced him. Friedmann believed that Pietist influence had often undermined the "outward" Mennonite focus, and he hoped to reverse that trend.

Friedmann also sought to outline historic Anabaptism's theology (though he omitted the Dutch). While sympathetic to Bender's *Anabaptist Vision*, Friedmann not only denied Anabaptism's intrinsic connection with Protestantism but proclaimed it "the only example in Church history of an 'existential Christianity.'"[10] In explaining *existential*, Friedmann puzzlingly enlisted Kierkegaard's (pietist?) notion of truth as inward subjectivity. Yet by this term Friedmann chiefly meant the "realized and practiced 'Christianity of the gospel.'"[11]

Friedmann can be read as encouraging or discouraging attempts to do contemporary theology in Anabaptist perspective. On one hand, he insisted that every religious movement, no matter how nonintellectual in appearance, has an implicit theology, and that efforts to articulate it are legitimate. On the other hand, he contrasted this implicit form so sharply with the explicit theology of most Christian tradition that many attempts at articulation would seem out of bounds.[12] Ultimately, he claimed, the difference boils down to that between "evidencing faith in life" and affirming "*simul justus et peccator.*"[13]

Friedmann styled Anabaptist theology's basic theme as the eschatological presence of God's kingdom as an existential possibility.[14] This meant that genuine discipleship is possible, as Bender said. It also entailed "an uncompromis-

---

[9]Friedmann's conclusion: "The tremendous chasm between the two consists in the fact that the Pietist feels satisfied when he experiences the personal sense of salvation and the presence of the personal God, whereas the prophetic spirit thereby only comes to the sense of committing himself to the decisive work of God and therewith desires, without any consideration for his personal feeling of happiness, to see the will of God realized for the whole world" (ibid., p. 88). For a critique of Friedmann's approach, see John Roth, "Pietism and the Anabaptist Soul." in *The Dilemma of Anabaptist Piety*, ed. Stephen Longenecker (Bridgewater, Va.: Penobscot, 1997).

[10]Robert Friedmann, *The Theology of Anabaptism* (Scottdale, Penn.: Herald, 1973), p. 27.

[11]Ibid., pp. 31, 27.

[12]Ibid., pp. 20-22, 23.

[13]That is, that a person can be "at the same time justified and a sinner," Martin Luther's formula. Friedmann apparently tied explicit theology intrinsically to this "Protestant" stance, which he rejected. Concurring with Kierkegaard that "an existential system is impossible," Friedmann claimed that for Anabaptists "Theology as a system" was "a stumbling block to discipleship" (ibid., p. 31). Anabaptism's relative lack of theology was primarily due to this fundamental incompatibility, not scarcity of learned leaders or opportunity for reflection. Friedmann also connected the implicit-explicit distinction with that between Jesus and Paul (ibid., pp. 21-22, cf. his *Mennonite Piety*, pp. 85-87).

[14]Friedmann, *Theology of Anabaptism*, p. 41.

ing ontological dualism" between church and world.[15] Friedmann further affirmed that "Anabaptists were orthodox concerning the very foundations of their faith," including classic trinitarianism and Christology. Yet Christ's exemplary life and death, rather than those doctrines, occupied the center of their Christology.[16]

So influential were Bender's and Friedmann's efforts to center historic Anabaptism and its theology around discipleship that nearly every subsequent development has interacted with them.

New Classifications

In 1952 Franklin Littell proposed another overall construal. Historic Anabaptism's basic aim was restitution of the true church, an attempted return to the purity of its origins.[17] Yet this did not engender withdrawal into separated communities but, Littell stressed, European mission efforts far more extensive than those of Protestants or Catholics.

A decade later George Williams located Anabaptism within the broader scope of the Radical Reformation, along with Spiritualists and Evangelical Rationalists. Anabaptists, in turn, were divided into three subgroups, although some individuals journeyed between them or even into another radical grouping. Evangelical Anabaptists included the pacifistic Swiss Brethren, though Williams did not grant them a normative role as did Bender. Spiritualist Anabaptists emphasized Spirit over letter, but did not go so far as Spiritualists proper, who rejected outward ceremonies like baptism (Hans Denck traveled from spiritualist Anabaptism into Spiritualism proper). Revolutionary Anabaptists included Münsterites, though Williams classified Thomas Müntzer (who did not practice believers' baptism) with the Spiritualists proper.

By "Evangelical Rationalists" Williams meant humanist-oriented intellectuals, many of whom questioned Christ's deity and the Trinity. By including them in the broader radical movement and tracing in detail their impact on the Polish Brethren, Williams brought antitrinitarianism closer to mainstream Anabaptism than had

---

[15]Ibid., p. 38. Despite the term *ontological*, Friedmann seems to mean that the distinction was of values. He asserted more strongly than Bender what Bender called an "inevitable corollary" of the church as a voluntary brotherhood (the *Anabaptist Vision*'s second theme): "the separation of the church from the world, that is nonconformity of the Christian to the worldly way of life" (Bender, *Anabaptist Vision*, p. 27).

[16]Friedmann strongly contrasted Anabaptists, who "were Trinitarians beyond doubt," with antitrinitarians such as the Polish Brethren (*Theology of Anabaptism*, pp. 53-55).

[17]Franklin Littell, *The Origins of Sectarian Protestantism*, rev. ed. (New York: Macmillan, 1964), pp. xvii, 44. The first edition was published as *The Anabaptist View of the Church* in 1952.

Friedmann or Bender.[18] Williams's overall classificatory scheme was accepted by most scholars.

Medieval Roots?

Until the 1970s interpretations were generally forward-looking: Anabaptism was the forerunner of some subsequent movement or value, such as communism, modernism or consistent evangelical Protestantism. But then many studies reversed direction, asking whether Anabaptism was more the outworking of some medieval or even patristic trend.[19]

Kenneth Davis argued that Anabaptism arose from an ascetic tradition stretching back mostly through monasticism to origins both East and West. This asceticism was basically a striving for holiness that emphasized ethics and distinctness from the world. Davis proposed that all Anabaptist theology be interpreted in light of this overarching pursuit.[20]

Davis further noted that over the centuries this ascetic tradition had assumed multiple forms, including communities of lay people who retained their marriages, families and vocations. Some of these communities were popular on the Reformation's eve. Davis asked what specific movements might have mediated this tradition to "initial Evangelical Anabaptism."[21] By this he meant, as Bender did, its Zurich form. For even though South German-Austrian Anabaptists (Hut, Denck and others) seemed more mystical, Davis did not find them differing as to religious substance. He proposed that they had derived their original beliefs from the Swiss and simply clothed them in mystical language.[22]

Davis found close similarities with Anabaptism in the Dutch Devotio Moderna

---

[18]While Williams acknowledged that "explicit opposition" to the Trinity was "largely limited to the Evangelical Rationalists," elsewhere he found frequent "alteration in the traditional formulations of the relationship of the Father to the Son" (George Williams, *The Radical Reformation*, 3rd ed. [Kirksville, Mo.: 16th Century Journal Publishers, 1992], p. xxxi). Williams cited such tendencies among Anabaptists (such as in the Christocentric unitarians Adam Pastor and Louis Haetzer [p. 15]; see pp. 433-38).

[19]In 1882 Ludwig Keller proposed that Anabaptists were successors of earlier heretical groups (Ludwig Keller, *Ein Apostle der Wiedertaeufer* [Leipzig: S. Hirzell, 1882], pp. v, 13, 30). Leonard Verduin presented this interpretation more recently (*The Reformers and Their Stepchildren* [Grand Rapids: Eerdmans, 1964], pp. 5, 16, 17, 25-30, 59-62). Albrecht Ritschl (1880) regarded Anabaptists as successors of mystical and ascetic groups, especially the Franciscan Tertiaries and monasticism. Contra Friedmann, Ritschl linked Anabaptism closely to Pietism.

[20]On ascetic tradition see Kenneth Davis, *Anabaptism and Asceticism* (Scottdale, Penn.: Herald, 1974), pp. 39-54. Davis acknowledged that this ethical emphasis was close to and sometimes intertwined with a mystical one, but he distinguished the two (p. 132). On interpreting Anabaptist theology see Davis, p. 130.

[21]Ibid., p. 32.

[22]Ibid., pp. 23, 229.

lay movement. He claimed further that the pre-1525 writings of its most famous member, the humanist Erasmus, contained "almost the whole and distinctive core of the Anabaptist synthesis."[23] Davis concluded that Anabaptism, rather being consistent evangelical Protestantism (Bender) was largely "a radicalization and Protestantization . . . of the lay-oriented, ascetic reformation of which Erasmus is the principle mediator"—and ultimately of the lengthy, "highly adaptable, Christian ascetic tradition."[24]

If Anabaptism's primary link was (backward) to Erasmus, it can be construed as quite compatible with a religious, even Catholic, humanism. Its main themes would be simplification of ritual and hierarchy, biblical exegesis over creedal formulation, freedom of the will, and ethical life based on Jesus' teachings. Discipleship still would be central. Remember, though, that Davis's Anabaptism was the Zurich variety.

What happens if another Anabaptist branch is regarded as a distinct, equally important source? Werner Packull argued that South German-Austrian Anabaptism derived not from Zurich "but from a popularized medieval mystical tradition."[25] This tradition flowed from Meister Eckhart (1260?-1328?), for whom God and the soul formed a kind of unity. Humans, then, could cooperate with God. Yet Protestants, who emphasized bondage of the will, disgreed. Mystical salvation, further, could not be divided into justification and sanctification in Protestant fashion but was one ascending movement of divinization. This process began with *Gelassenheit*, or detachment from all creatures, which brought the inner suffering sometimes called "the cross" (cf. chap. 2).[26]

As this tradition neared the Reformation,[27] sinfulness and the necessity of grace

---

[23]Ibid., p. 292. Bender did not think humanism could have been the chief influence on so biblical a group as the Zurich Anabaptists. Abraham Friesen traces the impact of Erasmus's understanding of "the Great Commission" on Zurich Anabaptism and Menno, but he grants Erasmus far greater weight in Anabaptism's formation than this strand of evidence can support (Abraham Friesen, *Erasmus, the Anabaptists, and the Great Commission* [Grand Rapids: Eerdmans, 1998], and "Present at the Inception: Menno Simons and the Beginnings of Dutch Anabaptism," *MQR* 72, no. 3 (1998).

[24]Davis, *Anabaptism and Asceticism*, pp. 292, 296. With such an emphasis on Catholic roots, Anabaptism can be read as a third Reformation force: either as quite unique, neither Catholic nor Protestant (as Walter Klaassen's popular *Anabaptism: Neither Catholic nor Protestant* [Waterloo, Ont.: Conrad Grebel, 1973] intimated) or as a both-and mixture of strengths (as Klaassen's "Sixteenth-Century Anabaptism: A Vision Valid for the Twentieth Century?" *CGR* 7, no. 3 [1989] more recently says). But even in the former interpretation Anabaptism is not as unique as Friedmann maintained.

[25]Werner Packull, *Mysticism and the Early South German-Austrian Anabaptists* (Scottdale, Penn.: Herald, 1977), p. 34.

[26]Ibid., pp. 20-26.

[27]Especially through Johannes Tauler (1300?-1361) and the anonymous fifteenth-century *German Theology* (*The Theologia Germanica of Martin Luther*, trans. Bengt Hoffman [New York: Paulist, 1980]).

received more stress, while divine-human unity became more a unity of wills than of being. Jesus increasingly became the chief exemplar of the *Gelassenheit* process until finally, with the Anabaptists, bearing the outer cross of persecution in fellowship with him became as important as the inner cross of detachment. Yet even with these changes salvation was viewed differently than in Protestantism, and discipleship was entwined more explicitly with a spiritual process than among the Swiss. Packull highlighted other differences, such as the South German-Austrian emphasis on revelation through the inner Word or Spirit in contrast to the more humanistic Swiss concentration on the outer, written Word.

The greater the role granted South Germany-Austria in Anabaptism's formation, the more broadly soteriological and the less reducible to the social-ethical it will be. Anabaptism will appear more Catholic in some (non-Erasmian) senses and yet more revolutionary (Hut).

Taking a different route, Alvin Beachy proposed that a soteriology like the one Packull found in mysticism characterized Anabaptism as a whole. Beachy studied leaders from Switzerland (Hubmaier), South Germany-Austria (Denck, Marpeck), the Netherlands (Melchior, Menno, Dirk) and a spiritualist (Caspar Schwenckfeld). He concluded that Anabaptists generally understood grace, and therefore salvation, as divinization, and showed how this shaped their views on anthropology, Christology, the sacraments, the oath, the ban and church-state relations.

Beachy defined (divinizing) grace as "God's act whereby He renews the divine image in man through the Holy Spirit and makes the believer a participant in the divine nature."[28] Yet such persons do not literally become God. While this notion is more Catholic than Protestant, it is even more Eastern Orthodox, though firm historical links between Orthodoxy and Anabaptism have never been traced.[29]

Beachy argued that Anabaptism's high behavioral expectations were rooted in this transformative notion of grace, whereas Protestant criticisms of these as works-righteousness flowed from their much less thoroughgoing concept. Beachy addressed the anthropological issues raised by Packull, especially in an appendix on medieval mysticism. He concluded that while Anabaptists affirmed human cooperation with God, they emphasized, more than the mystics, the priority and necessity of grace.[30] So far as I know, Anabaptist scholars have never seriously

---

[28] Alvin Beachy, *The Concept of Grace in the Radical Reformation* (Nieuwkoop, Netherlands: B. De Graf, 1977), p. 5.

[29] See Thomas Finger, "Anabaptism and Eastern Orthodoxy: Some Surprising Similarities?" *Journal of Ecumenical Studies* 31-32 (1994).

[30] Beachy, *Concept of Grace*, pp. 214-17.

addressed Beachy's main thesis about divinization.

If historians look back to Erasmus and monastic traditions of ascetic holiness, Anabaptism can appear more Catholic than Protestant, though still somewhat humanistic and discipleship oriented. If they look back toward mystics, Anabaptism can emerge more broadly transformative and spiritually oriented. If historians focus on divinization, this broadly Catholic background can acquire an inexplicable Orthodox hue.

Emphasis on Diversity

Packull's investigation of an Anabaptist branch other than the Swiss underscored differences between the branches. By weighting the South German-Austrians and especially the Dutch more heavily than the Swiss, Beachy arrived at a soteriology somewhat novel in Anabaptist studies. Packull's effort in particular illustrated a shift from monogenesis to polygenesis in the study of Anabaptist origins. According to the polygenesis perspective most widely accepted today, Anabaptism arose not from one main origin (Switzerland) as Bender said but from three relatively independent, significantly different ones: Switzerland, South Germany-Austria and the Netherlands.[31]

Such an approach tends to undermine the notion of a normative Anabaptism. It lends greater prominence to mystics and revolutionaries than does Swiss monogenesis (though it has discovered wider acceptance of the sword even in Switzerland).[32] Polygenesis can dilute idealization of the past by exposing greater flaws. This can challenge notions of Anabaptism's uniqueness and dishearten some who give great weight to Anabaptist distinctives like peace.[33] Recently, however, polygenesis proponents have been acknowledging significant interminglings among the different streams.[34]

While polygenesis has spread the geographical range of Anabaptist studies, a broader range of disciplines is also being employed.[35] Until about 1970 Anabaptist ideas, or theologies, were usually the focus of attention (with some exceptions, as

---

[31]James Stayer, Werner Packull and Klaus Deppermann, "From Monogenesis to Polygenesis: The Historical Discussion of Anabaptist Origins," *MQR* 49, no. 2 (1975): 83-121.

[32]See especially James Stayer, *Anabaptism and the Sword*, 2nd ed. (Lawrence, Kan.: Coronado Press, 1976).

[33]See the discussion between J. Denny Weaver ("Reading 16th-Century Anabaptism Theologically: Implications for Modern Mennonites as a Peace Church" *CGR* 16, no. 1 [1998]) and Arnold Snyder (review of *Becoming Anabaptist*, by J. Denny Weaver, *CGR* 7, no. 1 [1989]).

[34]Werner Packull, *Hutterite Beginnings* (Baltimore: Johns Hopkins University Press, 1995), pp. 8-11; Arnold Snyder, "Beyond Polygenesis: Recovering the Unity and Diversity of Anabaptist Theology," in *Essays in Anabaptist Theology*, ed. Wayne Pipkin (Elkhart, Ind.: Institute of Mennonite Studies, 1994).

[35]Werner Packull, "Between Paradigms: Anabaptist Studies at the Crossroads," *CGR* 8, no. 1 (1990).

among Marxist scholars and Troeltsch). A top-down influence of ideas on social and economic factors was assumed. Elite classes, who articulated most of the ideas, received more attention than the masses.

Historians today, however, focus more on popular culture. Reformation studies are stressing "empowerment of the common people," or "reform pushed from below."[36] Attention is being paid, for example, to connections between Anabaptism's appeal and that of the Peasants' War. Like polygenesis, this approach often uncovers highly flawed situations and behavior. It can also reinforce tendencies to minimize theology and highlight social-ethical factors. Yet it does not reduce everything to material causes, for in Reformation times, at least, ideas were clearly motives for action.

C. Arnold Snyder has recently attempted to combine the social and theological approaches while also acknowledging medieval communal and spiritual influences.[37] He accepts a polygenetic account of origins, but not the implication that three distinct theologies must emerge, since later developments need not move along the same paths. Further, differences among Anabaptists can be identified only if some shared assumptions existed.[38]

Snyder defines Anabaptists as all who practiced believers' baptism[39] and proposes that Anabaptism "centered around, and grew out of, a core of fundamental shared teachings" present in all three regions by 1526.[40] This core consisted, first, of convictions shared with all Christians—basically the ecumenical creeds. It also included beliefs shared with Protestants: antisacramentalism, anticlericalism, biblical authority and "salvation by grace through faith."[41]

Distinctive Anabaptist themes included a stronger pneumatology than the Protestants'. This was Anabaptism's sine qua non, for soteriology was its "heart and soul."[42] Further, salvation for Anabaptists "meant becoming righteous by the power of the risen Christ."[43] This involved discipleship, as Bender said, but also *Gelassenheit*, which Snyder describes as inward yielding to God and outward yielding to

---

[36]Ibid., p. 9.

[37]C. Arnold Snyder, *Anabaptist History and Theology* (Kitchener, Ont.: Pandora, 1995), pp. 15-19.

[38]Snyder, "Beyond Polygenesis," pp. 9, 10.

[39]Weaver rightly objects that Snyder should have included the Polish Brethren by this criterion. He suspects that a precommitment to trinitarian orthodoxy really underlies Snyder's omission (Weaver, "Reading 16th-Century Anabaptism Theologically," p. 43). Snyder replies that the Trinity would remain a predominant Anabaptist belief even if the Polish were included (Arnold Snyder, "Anabaptist History and Theology: History or Heresy?" *CGR* 16, no. 1 [1998]: 55).

[40]Snyder, *Anabaptist History and Theology*, p. 6.

[41]Ibid., pp. 84, 85-87.

[42]Ibid., pp. 379, 384.

[43]Ibid., p. 88.

the community.[44] Anabaptists also emphasized the eschatological outpouring of the Spirit. They sought, with varying degrees of success, to balance the interaction of Spirit and letter in revelation.

Futher, Anabaptists underlined human freedom, as Packull maintained, but only in response to grace. Finally, it was in ecclesiology that "Anabaptism came to define a separate stream of reform."[45] Anabaptists highlighted the visibility of Christ's body in a community of saints, expressed chiefly through believers' baptism and also by mutual aid, the ban, and the Lord's Supper as a memorial and communal event.

Above all, Snyder proposes that Anabaptists sought, in differing ways with varying success, to interlink the inner life with the outer, the Spirit with the letter and the individual with the community. The historian's task is not to recover one "Anabaptist vision," but, by tracing movements between these poles, to recover "Anabaptist conversations."[46]

Summary

Since subsequent chapters will develop my own reading of historic Anabaptism, I have sketched some important interpretations with which I will interact. All such interpretations are affected by one's perspectives on several important points.

1. Was there an essence or certain distinctives most basic to Anabaptism? Or can we at least find an interpretive center around which Anabaptism's other features can be arranged? Those who select Bender's discipleship (or his discipleship-community-nonviolence triad) will read Anabaptism somewhat differently than those who opt for Beachy's divinization, or striving for ascetic holiness (Davis), or the eschatological presence of God's kingdom, with its ontological dualism (Friedmann), or the interplay between the inner and the outer (Snyder). A core of common teachings (Snyder) could provide a similar center.

2. How much and in what ways should Anabaptism's distinctives be stressed, and how much its commonalities with other movements? An Anabaptism regarded as wholly unique (Friedmann) will look quite different from one exhibiting important similarities to Catholics or Protestants (Snyder) or the Orthodox (Beachy).

3. From how many sources did Anabaptism emerge, and what relative importance did each possess? Readings that prioritize Switzerland (Bender, Davis) differ from those granting at least as much significance to South Germany-Austria (Packull) and to the latter along with the Netherlands (Beachy). If Poland (Williams) is added, Christological and other issues will take on a different hue.

---

[44]Ibid., p. 89.
[45]Ibid., p. 90.
[46]Ibid., p. 97.

4. Were Anabaptism's most significant historical links to the future (modernism) or the past (certain Medieval trends)? Was Anabaptism basically tradition-breaking and forward-looking, or seeking to restore much that had been lost? This issue affects perceptions of Anabaptism's commonalities with other movements. If Anabaptists basically looked forward, they were most like traditional Protestants (Bender) and eventually perhaps liberal Protestants (Troeltsch) or even Marxists. If Anabaptists mainly looked backward, they were more like Catholics and monastic movements. If they were forward-looking, they were mostly breaking from traditional Christianity. If backward-looking, they possessed important affinities with it.

5. In explaining Anabaptism, how much should ideas be stressed, and how much socio-historical factors? This issue also affects selection of sources. If ideas are primary, publications of leaders will be highlighted. If socio-historical factors, economic, demographic and other data, court records, and testimonies will gain importance.

CONTEMPORARY APPROACHES TO THEOLOGY IN ANABAPTIST PERSPECTIVE

Just as my reading of historic Anabaptism will be influenced by the foregoing positions, my constructive theology will unfold within a broader movement to articulate a contemporary Anabaptist perspective. To indicate the issues involved, I now sketch some views with which I will interact. All writers I discuss in this section identify themselves as Anabaptist. Subsequent chapters, however, will also dialogue with current Catholic, Lutheran, Reformed, Orthodox, evangelical, liberation, feminist and other theologians.

Since I am mainly concerned with comprehensive theologizing, I will chiefly consider authors who have completed at least one work of this kind or who often addressed this task otherwise. Still, in our postmodern atmosphere, theological reflection often appears in briefer formats. Consequently, I will include Anabaptist efforts of this sort in "Postmodern Considerations" (pp. 80-91). Because most Anabaptist theologizing before 1960 considered itself evangelical, I will first present this approach (J. C. Wenger, Ronald Sider). I will then turn to the most common trend, rooted in biblical narrative (John Howard Yoder, J. Denny Weaver, Norman Kraus, James McClendon).

Other Anabaptist theologians, however, are beginning not so directly from Scripture but within some broader perspective. I will next consider four quite different efforts of this sort, emphasizing: Christian tradition (James Reimer), methodological considerations (Gordon Kaufman), social considerations (Duane Friesen) and science (Nancey Murphy with George Ellis). Finally, I will examine postmodern issues, mostly through briefer writings on (inter)textuality, Christ and culture, contemporary construction, and desire. I can hardly consider everything written in these fields but must accent those that sharpen the issues to be faced in chapters five to ten.

Evangelical Orthodoxy

Among worldwide Christian movements, one of the largest is evangelicalism. I am proposing that theology in Anabaptist perspective can contribute to such movements, especially as they face global tasks. It will be helpful, then, to ask what *evangelical* has meant and might mean in Anabaptist theology.

J. C. Wenger. In 1954, J. C. Wenger published perhaps the first Anabaptist systematic theology since Peter Riedemann's in 1545.[47] This furthered an effort, shared by Harold Bender, to link North American Mennonites with evangelicals. Before this, many Mennonites had taken fundamentalism's side in its controversy with modernism. But as some leaders adopted generally fundamentalist theologies, they wondered how to connect these with Anabaptist distinctives like pacifism.

A common solution was to compose two lists.[48] The first list included doctrines affirmed in common with conservative Protestants; the second, ethical and ecclesial principles distinctly Anabaptist. The second list did not really shape the articulation of the first. This reflected and strengthened the impression among Anabaptism's heirs and other Christians that Anabaptist contributions lay entirely in ethics.

Though Wenger affirmed Bender's Anabaptist Vision, this impacted only lightly the structure of his four-hundred-page *Introduction to Theology*, which he, like most American evangelicals, took from Protestant orthodoxy.[49] Wenger's section on

---

[47]J. C. Wenger, *Introduction to Theology* (Scottdale, Penn.: Herald, 1954).

[48]J. Denny Weaver, *Keeping Salvation Ethical* (Scottdale, Penn.: Herald, 1997), p. 24; *Anabaptist Theology in Face of Postmodernity* (Telford, Penn.: Pandora, 2000), pp. 71-93.

[49]One definition of *evangelicalism* prioritizes nineteenth-century evangelizing movements. Relatively nontheological groups like Baptists and Methodists play large roles, and the movement has a strong social orientation. According to a second definition, evangelicalism is chiefly a broadening of twentieth-century fundamentalism. Protestant orthodoxy supplies the theological framework, and the movement is largely individualistic. Protestant orthodoxy matured in sixteenth- to nineteenth-century European state church cultures and reflects a far different social perspective and placement than Anabaptism. Norman Kraus promotes the latter interpretation and contrasts evangelicalism quite sharply with Anabaptism (C. Norman Kraus, ed., *Evangelicalism and Anabaptism* [Scottdale, Penn.: Herald, 1979], pp. 39-61; "Evangelicalism: A Mennonite Critique," in *The Variety of American Evangelicalism*, ed. Donald Dayton and Robert Johnston [Downers Grove, Ill.: InterVarsity Press, 1991], pp. 184-203). I interpret evangelicalism mostly in the first way and suggest positive connections with Anabaptism (Thomas Finger, "Are Anabaptists Evangelicals?" unpublished address in Harrisonburg, Va., October 1991).

Wenger occasionally called his effort "evangelical." Though he lauded efforts of fundamentalists, or "strict evangelicals," to affirm biblical authority, he felt they emphasized written over living revelation too greatly. Wenger also chided fundamentalism for "a certain narrowness of spirit" and "a rather dull conscience on social issues" (Wenger, *Introduction to Theology*, pp. 13-14).

sanctification, however, concluded with chapters on "The Christian in Society" and "Relation to Government" informed by Anabaptism. The second list appeared in these, along with Mennonite statements on the military and on industrial relations in appendixes.

Wenger, like evangelicals, wanted to establish Scripture's entire trustworthiness as theology's foundation. Yet he located this topic not near the head of his system, as most evangelicals would do, but in the middle. Wenger first traced revelation's historical course up to "the Word made flesh," whom he contrasted with "merely verbal" revelation.[50] Only afterward did he tackle issues of inspiration. While Wenger insisted that Scripture was error free, he critiqued evangelical terms like *plenary* and *verbal* for being somewhat mechanical and neglecting the human element.[51] Here Anabaptism's Christocentrism and emphasis on active human appropriation influenced his structure and content.

At the center of his theology Wenger, not unlike Bender, placed neither ethics nor ecclesiology but "salvation through union with Christ the Lord Jesus Christ, the divine and eternal Son of God who became incarnate and by His redemptive death and glorious resurrection reconciled man to God. The concept of Christian believers being in Christ, or being united with Him, runs through the New Testament like a golden chain."[52]

Ronald Sider. Today, few writing Anabaptist theologians class themselves as evangelical—perhaps partly because that term is frequent allied, in popular parlance, with militarism. Yet as evangelicalism became more socially oriented in the 1970s, it opened up to Anabaptist influence, and few people mediated this more effectively than Ron Sider.

In 1979 Sider briefly suggested a way of combining the two outlooks. Evangelicals affirm doctrinal orthodoxy and world evangelism. Anabaptists emphasize values like peace, simplicity and concern for the poor. Both groups claim to be biblical, and their major affirmations actually are. Consequently, "If they were consistent, Evan-

---

[50]Wenger, *Introduction to Theology*, p. 150.

[51]Ibid., pp. 164-66.

[52]Ibid., p. 297. This involves faith, love, obedience (identity of will) and experiential reenactment of Christ's passion and resurrection (p. 300). While Wenger did not deny mystical experience (p. 22), neither did he emphasize the mystical as a dimension of union with Christ for fear of making emotion more central than obedience (p. 301). Obedience, though, was not merely ethical. After citing the *Anabaptist Vision*'s three principles, Wenger remarked that Anabaptists "were convinced of the centrality of divine love in redemption, and of the ability of God to infuse that same redeeming love for men into the hearts of his regenerated children. . . . The Christian life is therefore one of 'redeemed discipleship.' Union with the Lord Jesus and being filled with and controlled by His Holy Spirit produces a genuine spirituality" (pp. vi-vii).

gelicals would be Anabaptists and Anabaptists would be Evangelicals."[53]

Sider applied this to Jesus' atonement and resurrection. Anabaptists find atonement an act of love for enemies exhibited on the "horizontal" level. The righteousness that results carries "important social dimensions." Evangelicals regard atonement as expiation of God's wrath. This "vertical" element must be highlighted too, for righteousness also involves this "central forensic element."[54]

Sider, who never explicitly theologized much further on these themes, seemed to exemplify a two-lists approach. Evangelicals apparently supply the doctrines; Anabaptists the ethics. There is no real indication that if a doctrine were approached from a distinct Anabaptist perspective, it might look somewhat different than it does to evangelicals (and might entail an ethic uncomfortable to some). But might Anabaptism impact evangelicalism differently? I will suggest some possibilities. To date, however, little explicit evangelical-Anabaptist theologizing other than the two-lists variety has appeared.

The Unique Biblical Narrative

While evangelical theologies claim to be rigorously biblical, some critics, Anabaptists included, find them unduly influenced by Protestant orthodoxy, including its socially conservative tendencies. Yet most Anabaptists have been strongly biblical. Not surprisingly, then, perhaps the majority of today's Anabaptist theologians are underscoring the primacy of Scripture's categories in another way: by focusing on its distinctive narrative. Since this narrative climaxes in Jesus' story, it provides a way of emphasizing his peaceful way.

John Howard Yoder. Perhaps the first to explicitly ask how an Anabaptist perspective might affect the theological task was John Howard Yoder. In *Preface to Theology,* his class materials from the 1960s through 1981, he traced the development of Christology from the New Testament up through Chalcedon (451 C.E.). In this way he sought to illustrate, through historical precedent, how theology might function in church life.[55] Yoder drew significantly on the Biblical Theology movement of that time, which was also congenial to neo-orthodoxy.

Early Christological development showed that Jesus' significance had to be articulated differently in different contexts. Yoder, however, rejected cultural relativism. He insisted that every such interpretation must correspond with a standard.[56] The

---

[53]Ronald Sider, "Evangelicalism and the Mennonite Tradition," in *Evangelicalism and Anabaptism,* ed. C. Norman Kraus (Scottdale, Penn.: Herald, 1979), p. 149.

[54]Ibid., pp. 160, 161.

[55]John H. Yoder, *Preface to Theology* (Grand Rapids: Brazos, 2002), pp. 33-40.

[56]Ibid., pp. 92, 95, 127, 174-75.

standard is Jesus' life, death and resurrection, which form the pattern for our lives, and which Yoder sometimes called a narrative.[57] Yoder further identified "Jesus Christ is Lord" as the earliest Christian confession. By Paul's time this was functioning "something like a creed."[58] Though the Spirit kept speaking to the church, this was always in harmony with this confession and its supporting narrative.[59]

Yoder treated Christologies that converged toward the Creed of Nicea (325 C.E.) as superior to those discarded along the way. This creed, for him, rightly rejected adoptionism and supported New Testament affirmations of Christ's preexistence and role in creation.[60] Yet while this trajectory preserved some important biblical content, its ontological language moved increasingly further from Scripture's narrative form.[61] Yoder was far more critical of Chalcedon, which traveled further in this direction.[62]

In view of Nicea's terminology and its political context, Yoder wondered "whether the creed does us much good" today. Still, it "provided the best answer to an intellectual problem"—Jesus' normativity and its relation to God's uniqueness—which Christians will always have if they are biblical.[63] Radical Anabaptists, Yoder concluded, should probably not concentrate on affirming or fighting for Nicea and Chalcedon, but still less should they fight against them.[64] He noted that the creeds do not really address ethics and proposed that a contemporary Anabaptist theology include ethics in every section.

Yoder's most influential work, *The Politics of Jesus*, argued that the Jesus narrative displayed an ethic best called political.[65] He sought to show how this ethic, the path to the cross, is primary throughout the New Testament, not simply in the Synoptics, which Friedmann prioritized.[66] Yoder was rooting ethics in not universal principles but a particular historical person. Yet this, he insisted, was what the creeds intended by designating Jesus as the normative human. Yoder was affirming what the church had always said about Jesus, including his "preexistence and cosmic preeminence," and his

---

[57]Ibid., pp. 58, 110, 123-24, 379.

[58]Ibid., pp. 73, 101.

[59]Ibid., pp. 99-101, 379-80.

[60]Ibid., pp. 123-24, 139-40, 191-93.

[61]Ibid., p. 202.

[62]Ibid., pp. 212-23.

[63]Ibid., p. 204.

[64]Ibid., p. 223.

[65]By political, which comes from the Greek *polis*, meaning "city," Yoder simply meant "the structuring of relationships among men in groups" (*The Politics of Jesus* [Grand Rapids: Eerdmans, 1972], p. 50 n. 36). Many would respond that politics necessarily includes violence and therefore Jesus was not political. Yoder replied that Jesus challenged this very definition of the political—he showed that corporate life without violence is actually possible.

[66]Ibid., pp. 115-34.

perspective was "more radically Nicene and Chalcedonian than other views."[67]

Still, Yoder, who wrote in the wake of Bender's *Anabaptist Vision*, viewed "every event, text and theory" through "sharply-focused ethical glasses." These, however, could "filter out" other dimensions of meaning.[68] Though it underlined Jesus' historical humanity, did Yoder's Christology really affirm the transcendent dimensions intended in the New Testament and creeds?

Yoder, indeed, downplayed transcendent reality at times. For instance, "breaking bread together," or the Lord's Supper, simply meant that Jesus should be remembered in "ordinary partaking together of food for the body."[69] All such practices, Yoder insisted, are simply "ordinary human behavior" and can be thoroughly studied by sociology.[70] Moreover, when Yoder praised biblical and creedal Christologies, it was mostly for articulating Jesus' normativity in the language of their cultures. Yet "the last thing we should" do is to "translate into our time from theirs" concepts such as "preexistence."[71] Did Yoder mean that such transcendent concepts were simply products of outmoded, culturally relative cosmologies? Could their significance be reduced to ethical or historical affirmations today?[72]

To answer, we must recognize that Yoder's main concern was not philosophical but missional. He believed that the gospel could be adequately presented within an immanent, or historicist, framework.[73] To him this meant that the gospel's universality could be reconceived in terms of history's interconnectedness. For if all events are interconnected, then when "we report an event that occurred in our listeners' own world" and ask for their response, "what could be more universal than that?"[74] In other words, Jesus' universal significance could be expressed as his historical humanness: "in his ordinariness as villager, as rabbi, as king on a donkey, and as liber-

---

[67]Ibid., pp. 101, 105.

[68]A. James Reimer, *Mennonites and Classical Theology* (Kitchener, Ont.: Pandora, 2001), p. 296.

[69]John H. Yoder, *Body Politics* (Nashville: Discipleship Resources, 1992), p. 16.

[70]Ibid., p. 44; cf. pp. 46, 72, 77.

[71]John H. Yoder, *The Priestly Kingdom* (Notre Dame, Ind.: University of Notre Dame, 1984), p. 56.

[72]Craig Carter thinks not, but that "protecting, declaring, and unpacking the claims of classical Christology is what Yoder is about" (*The Politics of the Cross* [Grand Rapids: Brazos, 2001], p. 17; cf. pp. 23, 27). Reimer, in contrast, claims that Yoder (like Bender, Friedmann and Gordon Kaufman) espoused "an anti-metaphysical and anti-ontological world view in which human freedom and ethics are more important . . . than eternal divine truths as in classical theology"(Reimer, *Mennonites and Classical Theology*, p. 162). For fuller discussion, see Alain Epp-Weaver, "John Howard Yoder and the Creeds," *MQR* 74, no. 3 (2000); Thomas Finger, review of *The Politics of the Cross*, by Craig Carter; *Preface to Theology*, by John H. Yoder; *Mennonites and Classical Theology*, by A. James Reimer, in *Perspectives in Religious Studies* 28, no. 2 (2001); and "Did Yoder Reduce Theology to Ethics?" in *A Mind Patient and Untamed*, ed. Gayle Gerber Koontz and Ben Ollengburger (Telford, Penn.: Cascadia, 2004).

[73]Yoder, *Preface to Theology*, pp. 255-58.

[74]Yoder, *Priestly Kingdom*, p. 59.

ator on a cross" we can "express the claims which the apostolic proclaimers to Hellenism expressed in the language of preexistence and condescension."[75]

Yoder, then, intended to stress Jesus' universal relevance. He neither explicitly affirmed historicism as a philosophy nor denied divine transcendence.[76] Yet since he often reconceived issues in historical and social-ethical terms (bracketing out the transcendent), might his pioneering influence have inclined other Anabaptists toward reducing theology as a whole to these dimensions?

J. Denny Weaver. Like Yoder, J. Denny Weaver has been affected by the Anabaptist Vision. Although his own account of historic Anabaptism affirms polygenesis and candidly reports much violence, Weaver, much like Bender, concludes it with three regulative principles—discipleship, community and nonresistance. Weaver, however, derives such themes not from Anabaptism but from the Jesus story, as did Yoder.[77]

Weaver's main concern is that churches are accommodating to current culture and losing any distinctive social-ethical and especially pacifist stance. Unlike Yoder, he directs his message more to Mennonite and similar groups than to an ecumenical audience. Unlike Yoder, Bender and Wenger, he finds evangelicalism largely a foe. Weaver is also cautious about appropriating too much from other traditions, lest Anabaptism's distinct perspective be blurred.[78]

Like Yoder, Weaver is much concerned with Christology. Consistent with demar-

---

[75]Ibid., p. 62.

[76]Yet as Reimer noted, he could come close: "History is the only reality we know; we do not think about essences anymore, about substances and hypostases, about realities 'out there' having being in themselves. We think of reality as happening in personal relationships, in institutional relationships, and in the passage of time" (Yoder quoted in Reimer, *Mennonites and Classical Theology*, p. 171). Yoder recommended regarding this "historicism as philosophical stance congruent with the Bible"(*Preface to Theology*, p. 306.

[77]Snyder (review of *Becoming Anabaptist*) and Leonard Gross (review of *Becoming Anabaptist*, by J. Denny Weaver, *MQR* 63, no. 4 [1989]) critiqued Weaver for implying that he had extracted these three principles from the history he recorded, though it abounded in counterexamples (J. Denny Weaver, *Becoming Anabaptist* [Scottdale, Penn.: Herald, 1987]. Weaver acknowledged that he had drawn them from Jesus' story, not historic Anabaptism (J. Denny Weaver, "The Anabaptist Vision: A Historical or a Theological Future?" *CGR* 13, no. 1 [1995]).

[78]For different perspectives on this see J. Denny Weaver, "The General Versus the Particular: Exploring Assumptions in 20th-century Mennonite Theologizing," *CGR* 17, no. 2 (1999); cf. Weaver, *Anabaptist Theology in Face of Postmodernity*, pp. 49-70, and my article "Appropriating Other Traditions While Remaining Anabaptist" in the same journal. Weaver occasionally affirms interaction with other theologies ("Mennonites: Theology, Peace and Identity," *CGR* 6, no. 2 [1988]: 144; and "Response to A. James Reimer and Thomas Finger," *CGR* 7, no. 1 [1989]: 78), recently with Black and Womanist varieties (*Anabaptist Theology*, pp. 121-42). He recommends that we image commonalities among them as meeting points of trajectories which otherwise run in different directions. Weaver says that his main theological themes can be organized under the church's distinctness from the world, though this is ultimately Christological—the church is distinct because it is founded on Christ.

cating the church from the world, Weaver interprets Jesus' atonement in Christus Victor fashion. He regards Jesus' life and death as a conflict with evil powers, and his resurrection as triumph over them. Weaver perceives Jesus, in narrative fashion, as "bearer and representation and embodiment of the Reign of God breaking into the world."[79] But whereas the evil powers have traditionally been regarded as supernatural, Weaver's Christus Victor scheme is historicized. These powers now represent the collective ethos of social institutions. Transcendent language about God's struggle with these powers, Weaver proposes, was meant to express this struggle's ultimacy and was left dangling when ancient-medieval cosmic imagery vanished.[80]

Whereas Bender and Wenger endorsed creedal Christology, and Yoder affirmed its biblical substance (though not form), Weaver contrasts it sharply with Christus Victor. He does so, first, because Nicea and Chalcedon omit Jesus' life and teachings, so central for ethics and the struggle with evil.[81] Second, Weaver, like Yoder, critiques the creeds for substituting ontological language for biblical narrative. Third, the church from Constantine's time (313-337 C.E.) began obscuring Jesus' social-ethical stance and reducing faith to verbal confession. The creeds therefore "reflect their genesis in"[82] and were "developed" by that church.[83] Fourth, Weaver

---

[79] J. Denny Weaver, "Narrative Theology in an Anabaptist-Mennonite Context," *CGR* 12, no. 2 (1994): 173.

[80] Weaver, *Keeping Salvation Ethical*, pp. 44-45.

[81] Weaver says very little about the creeds' content but occasionally affirms that Jesus is "of God" and "of humanity" ("Mennonites: Theology, Peace and Identity," *CGR* 6, no. 2 (1988): 176). Depicting Jesus as bearer of God's reign, Weaver also calls him its "embodiment" who "incorporated" it "into his person" ("Narrative Theology," pp. 173, 175). The "presence of God in Jesus" is also "God's most complete self-manifestation in our world"("Mennonites: Theology, Peace and Identity," p. 127).Weaver can also affirm trinitarianism, as "a way of saying that the God of Israel and the God who is present in Jesus and raised him from the dead and the God who is still present for believers . . . is the same God" ("Response to A. James Reimer and Thomas Finger," *CGR* 7, no. I [1989]: 78).

[82] J. Denny Weaver, "Christus Victor, Ecclesiology, and Christology," *MQR* 68, no. 3 (1994): 278.

[83] J. Denny Weaver, "Some Theological Implications of Christus Victor," *MQR* 68, no. 4 (1994): 498; cf. Weaver, *Anabaptist Theology*, pp. 63, 68, 114; and my review of this work and McClendon's *Systematic Theology*, vol. 3, *Witness* (Nashville: Abingdon, 2000) in "Two Agendas for Baptist Theology," *Perspectives in Religious Studies* 27, no. 3 (2001). See also my review of Weaver's *Anabaptist Theology* in *Christian Scholars' Review* 30, no. I (2001). Weaver means not that they appeared de novo with Constantine, but that tendencies in their direction began earlier. I argue ("Christus Victor and the Creeds: Some Historical Considerations," *MQR* 72, no. I [1998]), however, that creeds began developing at least two centuries before Nicea among countercultural Christians who often emphasized Christus Victor. Though the creeds attained final form after Constantine, they were mainly the earlier church's product. To be sure, the Constantinian church often sought to use them the way Weaver mentions (Thomas Finger, "The Way to Nicea: Some Reflections from a Mennonite Perspective," *Journal of Ecumenical Studies* 24, no. 2 [1987]). For Weaver's other critiques of the creeds see his "Narrative Theology," pp. 176, 187; and "Response to A. James Reimer," p. 76.

regards a creedal emphasis among Anabaptists a prime instance of surrendering their distinctives and building on other foundations.[84]

Finally, creeds confined Jesus within an outmoded cosmology that emphasized a "vertical" dimension.[85] But modern cosmology has "removed the vertical dimension. . . ." This vertical emphasis involved an attempt to escape "horizontal" reality individualistically for some immutable realm.[86] Weaver, in contrast, expresses "a ready acceptance of the outlook of the scientific and technological world." God should be understood "as everywhere involved in a multidimensional historical stream." [87] Yet this does not limit God entirely to history, for Jesus' resurrection was a real event that "embodies a future consummation."[88]

Weaver not only omits the vertical dimension but apparently denies intrinsic significance to the "inner" personal realm. Mystical experiences, he believes, are shaped by environmental factors rather than shaping outward actions.[89] The nature of one's inner transformation basically depends on temperament and history.[90] Inner experience can be valid if it activates ethical behavior, but detrimental if it diverts energy from this.[91] In brief, while Weaver's christological and ethical concerns

---

[84]Weaver complains that Snyder does this by including the creeds as an Anabaptist-ecumenical common core ("Anabaptist History and Theology," p. 45; cf. C. Arnold Snyder, *Anabaptist History and Theology* [Kitchener, Ont.: Pandora, 1995], pp. 84-85, 365-66). Klaassen asserts that Anabaptists manifested "a truly massive dependence upon church tradition" and adhered to creeds because these were "massively biblically based"("Sixteenth Century Anabaptism," p. 246). Weaver finds Klaassen (and Rodney Sawatsky) now so ecumenical as to be Constantinian and ignoring pacifism ("Anabaptist Vision," pp. 79-80).

[85]J. Denny Weaver, "Perspectives on a Mennonite Theology," *CGR* 2, no. 3 (1984): 198-206; and review of *The Nature of Doctrine*, by George Lindbeck, *CGR* 3, no. 2 (1985): 191.

[86]Weaver, "Perspectives on a Mennonite Theology," pp. 194, 205-6; review of *The Nature of Doctrine*, p. 222; "Anabaptist Vision," p. 190. Weaver denies any need to add to the historical a " 'vertical mystical, ontological, sacramental, or a-historical dimension' "("Perspectives on a Mennonite Theology," p. 193; quoting Reimer, *Mennonites and Classical Theology*, p. 45). Darrol Bryant attributes this to Weaver's prior commitment to modern assumptions ("Response to J. Denny Weaver," *CGR* 3, no. 1 (1985). Weaver's strong ecclesiological and behavioral focus incline him to treat theological doctrines not as affirmations about anything transcendent but as rules describing community practices (he cites George Lindbeck's cultural linguistic understanding in support; see Weaver's review of *The Nature of Doctrine*, p. 223; "Mennonites: Theology, Peace and Identity," p. 131).

[87]Weaver, "Perspectives on a Mennonite Theology," p. 191, 207.

[88]Weaver, "Christus Victor, Nonviolence, and other Religions," in *Mennonite Theology in Face of Modernity*, ed. Alain Epp-Weaver (North Newton, Kan.: Bethel College, 1996), p. 189; Weaver, "Mennonites: Theology, Peace and Identity," p. 127.

[89]Weaver, *Becoming Anabaptist*, p. 181.

[90]Weaver, "Narrative Theology," p. 175.

[91]J. Denny Weaver, *Keeping Salvation Ethical*, p. 226, affirming Friedmann's approach to pietism. This point is developed in more detail in *Anabaptist Currents*, ed. Carl Bowman and Stephen Longenecker (Bridgewater, Va.: Penobscot, 1995), pp. 27-37. Weaver differs from Snyder, who stresses that non-

resemble Yoder's, he reduces theology's transcendent and inner dimensions more explicitly toward the historical and social-ethical.

C. Norman Kraus. Like Yoder and Weaver, C. Norman Kraus stresses that the unique Christian God is known through historical action centered on the Jesus story. Yet his useful minisystematic text *(God Our Savior)*, shaped most visibly by neo-orthodoxy, affirms that revelation is also personal. Somewhat unlike Yoder and Weaver, Kraus often avers that God can be known experientially; indeed, "the data [sic] of theology is God—the God experienced in past history, and as still experienced in the church."[92] Yet Kraus's main nemesis is Weaver's: evangelicalism or fundamentalism (cf. note 48).

Kraus speaks far more directly of God's spirituality, transcendence and personality (as "a self-conscious personal being")[93] than Weaver or Yoder. But like them, Kraus explores Christology at length. He derives his main point from biblical narrative: Jesus and God shared the same actions. Consequently, "Jesus' ministry of identification and suffering with us and for us is truly God at work." This leads Kraus to affirm, much more clearly than our two previous theologians, that Jesus is "truly God in the flesh. . . . [N]ot merely a prophet of God . . . but the presence of God among us."[94]

Yet Kraus, along with Yoder and Weaver, finds problems with the creeds. He has been criticized among Mennonites for devaluing them along with traditional Christology.[95] Kraus, however, mentions the creeds both positively and negatively.[96] He also values trinitarian doctrine for helpfully expressing how God is revealed. Nevertheless, it cannot tell us about "God's inner being,"[97] and Kraus tends to equate the Holy Spirit with Jesus' risen presence.[98]

---

violence is "a spiritual concern first and foremost" motivated by a "supernatural way of life"("Anabaptist History and Theology," p. 59). Tim Wiebe complains that Weaver *(Keeping Salvation Ethical)* omits the source for ethical living, "God's omnipotent love and grace," portrayed in the creeds (review of *Keeping Salvation Ethical,* by J. D. Weaver, *CGR* 16, no. 1 [1998]: 110).

[92]C Norman Kraus, *God Our Savior* (Scottdale, Penn.: Herald, 1991), p. 15. The "normative expression" of this revelation, as the neo-orthodox Weaver and Yoder say, is Jesus Christ.
[93]Ibid., p. 78.
[94]Ibid., p. 94.
[95]See especially Richard Kauffman, ed., *A Disciple's Christology: Appraisals of Kraus's Jesus Christ Our Lord* (Elkhart, Ind.: Institute of Mennonite Studies, 1989).
[96]Kraus, like Yoder and Weaver, regards creeds as "contextual restatements of the apostolic experiences and expressions. . . . [They are] necessary and helpful statements for their own time and place, and in some degree for other times and places" *(God Our Savior,* p. 17). He objects to attempts to universalize them, especially when assent was accomplished by coercion.
[97]Kraus, *God Our Savior,* p. 93.
[98]Ibid., pp. 35-36, 131-46.

While Kraus may appear more conservative than Yoder or Weaver, he often critiques evangelicals. Like the neo-orthodox, Kraus separates theology's personal, revelational language from those of metaphysics and historical factuality. Consequently, he places Jesus' conception, resurrection and return on different planes than empirical history.[99] Kraus critiques most evangelical views of biblical authority as overly rationalistic.

Like Yoder and Weaver, Kraus emphatically distinguishes the church from society. The church is a *"messianic change agent in history."* It is not merely an ethical community, but the *"expression of a new historical possibility 'in Christ.'* ... *[A]n anticipatory representation of the 'new order of creation' pointing to the eschaton."* Kraus emphasizes that the church *"lives and functions by the enabling power and fellowship of the Spirit."*[100] Kraus also outlines an Anabaptist spirituality.[101]

In sum, Norman Kraus highlights the church's uniqueness and social witness much like Yoder and Weaver. Yet his God is more clearly transcendent and personal, and acts inwardly as well as through outward behavior. Kraus does not reduce theology to the social-ethical realm.

James McClendon. Perhaps more thoroughly than anyone else, James McClendon has thought through what baptist theology might be.[102] His approach is more self-consciously narrative and antifoundationalist than Weaver's or Yoder's. McClendon's organizing principle is a baptist Vision, defined as "*shared awareness of the present Christian community as the primitive community and the eschatological com-*

---

[99]Ibid., pp. 26, 194-98; C. Norman Kraus, *Jesus Christ Our Lord* (Scottdale, Penn.: Herald, 1987), pp. 74-79, 88-91. This issue was central to a controversy among Mennonites around Kraus's *Jesus Christ Our Lord,* along with his alleged rejection of "high" Christology (see Kauffman, *Disciple's Christology,* and my discussion of Kraus in "From Biblical Intentions to Theological Conceptions: Some Strengths and Some Tensions in Norman Kraus' Christology," *CGR* 8, no. 1 [1990]).

[100]Kraus, *God Our Savior,* pp. 85, 164, 166 respectively, italics in original.

[101]C. Norman Kraus, "An Anabaptist Spirituality for the Twenty-first Century," *CGR* 13, no. 1 (1995); *An Intrusive Gospel?* (Downer's Grove, Ill.: InterVarsity Press, 1998), pp. 69-85.

[102]McClendon's term *baptist,* roughly synonymous with believers' church, designates "Disciples of Christ and Churches of Christ, Mennonites, Plymouth Brethren, Adventists, Russian Evangelicals, perhaps Quakers, certainly Black Baptists (who often go by other names), the (Anderson, Indiana) Church of God, Southern and British and European and American Baptists, the Church of the Brethren, perhaps some Methodists, Assemblies of God, assorted intentional communities . . . missionary affiliates of all of the above" (James McClendon, *Systematic Theology,* vol. I, *Ethics* [Nashville: Abingdon, 1986], pp. 34-35). McClendon often aligns his primary outlook with Anabaptism (see e.g., James McClendon, "Response to Stanley Hauerwas," *CGR* 16, no. 1 (1998); and his "The Radical Road One Baptist Took," *MQR* 74, no. 4 (2000). Though his background was Southern Baptist, he and his wife Nancey Murphy joined the Church of the Brethren (see his "Radical Road," and my "James McClendon's Theology Reaches Completion" *MQR* 76, no. 1 [2002]: 120-21).

munity."[103] This awareness is "mystical and immediate." Yet it conveys the significance of "narratives . . . set in another time and place" and enables people to form their identity around them.[104]

McClendon begins his *Systematic Theology* with a volume called *Ethics*—though neither to grant this subject logical priority nor reduce theology to it.[105] Instead, he aims first to discover the shape of Christian communal life, and then, in volume two, *Doctrine*, to investigate the theological teaching that "sanctions and supports" this.[106] Precisely speaking, the church's first order task is to teach what is necessary to truly be the church; theology or doctrine is a second-order clarification of this teaching's content.

McClendon's third and final volume, *Witness*, examines the culture within which churches live and pursue mission. None of the three provides a "foundation." Instead, they are "three logical levels of penetration into the data of theology." All have the same subject, goal and task, and "constitute one system, one theology."[107] Resembling the three previous authors, McClendon begins volume one insisting that "the Church is not the world."[108] Yet volume three relates these spheres more closely than the other authors do.[109]

McClendon, like Yoder, regards "Jesus Christ is Lord" as the church's basic confession.[110] This lordship, or rule, has already invaded the present, and Christian life is energized by hope for its full, future actualization. Consequently, McClendon begins *Doctrine* with eschatology.[111] He then finds that salvation intrinsically involves following Christ,[112] which Weaver stresses, but also Christ's mystical, ontological presence,[113] which Weaver largely overlooks.

---

[103]McClendon, *Systematic Theology*, 1:31, italics in original. McClendon includes in it aspects of five other candidates for this Vision: biblicism, mission, soul liberty, discipleship and community (ibid., pp. 28-35). He incorporates Bender's "Anabaptist Vision" "without confining its scope to an inward-looking community of disciples-in-waiting" (ibid., p. 32). McClendon later called his "organizing principle . . . a biblical reading strategy or 'hermeneutic' " in which Jesus' "graceful, non-violent ministry" fulfills the whole story ("Response to Stanley Hauerwas," p. 92). This is his "center" and the authentic Anabaptist Vision (ibid., p. 93).

[104]McClendon, *Systematic Theology*, 1:33, 34.

[105]Ibid., p. 42.

[106]Ibid., p. 45.

[107]Ibid.

[108]Ibid., p. 17.

[109]For a critique, see my "Two Agendas for Baptist Theology," *Perspectives in Religious Studies*, 27, no. 3 (2001): 310-11; and my "James McClendon's Theology," pp. 129-32.

[110]James McClendon, *Systematic Theology*, vol. 2, *Doctrine* (Nashville: Abingdon, 1994), p. 64.

[111]Cf. Thomas Finger, "Outlines of a Contemporary Believers' Church Eschatology: A Dialogue with James McClendon," in *Apocalypticism and Millennialism*, ed. Loren Johns (Kitchener, Ont.: Pandora, 2000).

[112]McClendon, *Systematic Theology* 2:118, 135-45.

[113]Ibid., p. 114.

McClendon's Christology, however, begins not from below, with Jesus' life, but by asking "Who is the Risen One who encounters us in worship, work, witness and Scripture?"[114] Since this One is worshiped, he must be divine.[115] Yet McClendon argues that Jesus attained this identity with God only at his resurrection.[116] He proposes that theologians think of divine and human *narratives* coming together in Jesus, not divine and human *natures,* as in the creeds. Still he finds strengths as well as weaknesses in the latter.[117]

For McClendon trinitarian doctrine validly affirms that the historical activities of the Father, Son and Spirit are each saving activities of God.[118] Since God appeared in these activities as God truly is, McClendon goes further than Kraus and allows that the Trinity tells us this much about God's inner being.[119]

McClendon's effort, like the others prioritizing the unique biblical narrative, emphasizes Jesus' story, social ethics and community. The first emphasis, for all of them, renders Jesus' peaceful way normative and brings Christology to the fore. This raises the question, How fully can these emphases be conceptualized in social-ethical terms, or must other dimensions be included? McClendon stresses God's spiritual reality and vivid, somewhat mystical presence more than Yoder, Weaver or even Kraus.

Broader Contexts

Since Anabaptism was a very distinctive historical movement, it is hardly surprising that most of its current theologians underline the particularity of their sources and approach. This suggests that Anabaptism might enrich contemporary theology most by elucidating themes of particularity and marginality.

Yet historic Anabaptists were not postmodern ethnicities delighting in their uniqueness. They aimed to restore the true, universal church. Christian theology too makes some universal claims, though recently less often. Accordingly, while today's postmodern, antifoundationalist mood can favor theologies appealing to a unique biblical narrative, other theologies seek to establish claims about ultimate reality in broader ways. Although the following approaches are quite di-

---

[114]Ibid., p. 240.

[115]Ibid., p. 245.

[116]Ibid., pp. 244-50.

[117]Ibid., pp. 274-79. Nicea rightly affirmed the risen Christ's full deity, indicating how "the very substance of God could be encountered in Christian worship and practice" (ibid., p. 253). Like Yoder, Weaver and Kraus, McClendon finds creeds valuable in their own time, but he finds their conceptuality foreign to the Gospels and inadequate for today (ibid., pp. 265, 278).

[118]Ibid., pp. 317-22.

[119]Ibid., p. 322.

verse, they share this general aim and stress it more than most current Anabaptist efforts.

A. James Reimer. Historicism, the reduction of reality to immanent, interrelated temporal processes, is regarded as a quintessential modernist project by A. James Reimer. Historicism, in Reimer's view, frees humans from transcendent restraints to shape their destiny without limit.[120] This allows stronger parties to manipulate "humanity, nature and history as objects to be controlled, and shaped."[121] Reimer insists that historicism, which Yoder urged Christians to adopt at least in mission, ultimately produces the scientifically administered totalitarian state.[122] Reimer accordingly calls for an ethic "grounded beyond itself in the very structure of reality," in "theolo;gical ontology or theological metaphysics," to limit humankind's presumption and guide it toward true justice and peace.[123]

Reimer, however, does not extol historic Anabaptism as a remedy. Rather, he finds it a prime progenitor of modernism, much as Troeltsch did. Anabaptism's optimism about human freedom and realizing God's kingdom historically, Reimer claims, display profound affinities with the modern project.[124] Many Anabaptist theologians today, he warns, are adopting modernist themes uncritically. For instance, when Yoder focuses almost wholly on the gospel's political content, he is hardly radical in an anti-ontological age.[125] Reimer insists that biblical narrative involves ontological presuppositions and that interpreters who inadequately recognize this, like Yoder and Weaver, reduce it to historicism.[126]

Reimer's antidote is classical orthodoxy. To be sure, he wants God's "universal and objective word" to sound through Scripture.[127] Yet Reimer finds no sharp distinction between the Bible's authority and the "interpretive authority of the congregation." By congregation, however, he does not means the local community, as

---

[120] A. James Reimer, *Mennonites and Classical Theology*, p. 53.

[121] Ibid., p. 56.

[122] Reimer draws on the neo-Marxist Frankfurt School, epitomized by Adorno and Horkheimer's *Dialectic of the Enlightenment* (1944), and the Canadian philosopher George Grant (see esp. Reimer, *Mennonites and Classical Theology*, pp. 21-66).

[123] Reimer, *Mennonites and Classical Theology*, p. 15.

[124] Ibid., pp. 164, 167, 245.

[125] Ibid., p. 168.

[126] Ibid., 262; cf. Harry Huebner's claim that Christian faith involves a metaphysic (which includes the Trinity), and that if this is ignored or rejected, Christian narrative becomes unintelligible. Further, this narrative requires a theological system if the church is to transmit it through generations (Harry Huebner, "Within the Limits of Story Alone?" *CGR* 13, no. 2 [1995]: 161).

[127] Reimer, *Mennonites and Classical Theology*, p. 342.

Anabaptists usually do, but the church tradition that produced the creeds.[128] Classical theology, for him, was a "necessary" development beyond Scripture.[129] It is organized under trinitarian headings, or by a creation-fall-redemption-eschatology schema. Yet Reimer, like Weaver, regards Anabaptist distinctives as basic themes, not an additional list.[130]

Reimer finds the classical Trinity relevant in several ways. It can direct environmental action by presenting God as Father, who is distinct from nature, making us accountable for it. At the same time the Trinity allows us to portray God in this "mode" as immanent in a feminine way, which keeps us from manipulating nature as dead matter.[131] Further, since Jesus is the Son, his nonviolent love is divine and therefore ethically ultimate.[132] Since the Spirit is also divine, the Spirit's activity in the church beyond the biblical text can help us "make *genuinely new judgments*" (say, regarding women in the church),[133] though always in conformity with the Son's character.[134]

However we evaluate such emphases, Reimer apparently establishes them via classical, creedal Christian tradition. But why, Weaver and others object, should this be favored by Anabaptists, who not only prioritized Scripture over this tradition but were also persecuted by many of tradition's guardians?

Perhaps Reimer's theology is rooted in something more basic: his oft-stated preference for the transcendent, premodern worldview—whether in Catholic, Lutheran, Reformed, Anabaptist or even classical Greek form—over the historicized modern one.[135] Reimer's theology consists largely in articulating such broad contrasts, often in some detail. He repeatedly "calls" for a general theological approach and sometimes outlines one; yet he just as often declines to offer "comprehensive, systematic treatments of any given doctrine."[136] Reimer even leaves his favorite doctrine, the Trinity, unthematized enough to designate its members regularly as *modes*, without addressing this term's problematic character (cf. pp. 448-49, 460-61).

Might Reimer's ultimate commitment then be to what Weaver calls theology in

---

[128]Ibid., 353; as Weaver recognizes (*Mennonites: Theology, Peace and Identity*, p. 138). Although Reimer cannot really separate Scripture and tradition, he wants "the 'scriptural tradition' " to have "precedence." He does not want any creed to be "normative in any absolute sense, or as superseding the authority of the 'scripture principle.' "

[129]Reimer, *Mennonites and Classical Theology*, pp. 201, 264.

[130]Ibid., pp. 68, 242-46.

[131]Ibid., pp. 369, 271.

[132]Ibid., p. 370.

[133]Ibid., p. 317, italics in original.

[134]Ibid., p. 347.

[135]Ibid., p. 238.

[136]Ibid., p. 321.

general, interwoven with a Greek worldview?[137] Might this theology function somewhat as a first—doctrinal—list and Anabaptist emphases as a second—ethical—list despite Reimer's disclaimers?

Nonetheless, perhaps Anabaptist theology should counter modernity and its historicism via traditional doctrines. But why then should it ground these in broad classical tradition? Moreover, how can it appeal to historic Anabaptism at all if this was basically modernity's forerunner, as Reimer reads it? If Anabaptist contributions to theology should involve classic doctrines, these will need to be established on firmer grounds and linked to historic Anabaptism in some positive way.

Excursus: Concerns About Spirituality

I have noted how many Anabaptists interpret the themes of Bender's Anabaptist Vision (discipleship, community, nonviolence) in social-ethical terms contrary to Bender's intention, and how this issue affects theologies of the unique narrative. As we consider Reimer's contrasting advocacy of a spiritual dimension, let me indicate briefly how this too expresses broadly shared concerns.

In an article widely debated among Mennonite laity as well as academics, Stephen Dintaman complains that the Anabaptist Vision, as often interpreted, casts "the language of faith into exclusively sociological and activist frameworks." This, however, cannot touch the deeper problem of human bondage.[138] The main issue, as Dintaman sees it, is whether God is a living reality or simply a symbol for moral and political values. If the former, then Anabaptist theologizing "must go beyond a commitment to 'peace' as the sole criterion of truth."[139] In fact, any attempt to perform actions of discipleship "in the strength of our own will . . . is . . . to live in unbelief."[140]

---

[137]Ben Ollenberger claims that Reimer fails to distinguish various uses of ontological language and thus cannot adequately differentiate creedal affirmations from those of a Greek worldview. Creeds, for Ollenberger, use ontological language to convey to the Hellenized mentality how the Bible's narrative outlook contradicts basic features of its worldview (cf. Thomas Finger, "Trinity, Ecology and Panentheism," *Christian Scholar's Review* 271, no. 1 [1997(b)]: 42-43). Since Reimer makes no such distinctions, he is vulnerable to criticisms that in championing creeds, he affirms Greek ontology (Ben Ollenberger, "Mennonite Theology: A Conversation Around the Creeds," *MQR* 66, no. 1 [1992]: 66-71).

[138]Stephen Dintaman, "Reading the Reactions to 'The Spiritual Poverty of the Anabaptist Vision,'" *CGR* 13, no. 1 (1995): 2, 3.

[139]Ibid., p. 9.

[140]Stephen Dintaman, "The Spiritual Poverty of the Anabaptist Vision," *CGR* 10, no. 2 (1992): 207. Perhaps the extreme statement of this tendency is Dallas Wiebe's claim that by following Jesus' ethics one can be a Mennonite and an agnostic. Interestingly, Wiebe cites Erasmus as a major source of Anabaptism ("Can a Mennonite Be an Atheist?" *CGR* 16, no. 3 (1998): 125-26.

In a similar vein Peter Erb warns that because Mennonites today support action over contemplation, they are open to full restructuring by modernity.[141] As a remedy Anabaptists should stress elements in their tradition that reflect catholic breadth. Such responses to the social-ethical understanding of the Anabaptist Vision indicate that theological discussions of this issue are not merely academic.

Gordon Kaufman. Like Reimer, Gordon Kaufman seeks a broader framework than narrative for theology. Yet while Reimer prioritizes a classical orientation, Kaufman challenges all attempts to theologize within any past perspective, whether classical, biblical or historic Anabaptist. Kaufman is much better known in academia than the other theologians covered here, except perhaps Yoder and Murphy. Kaufman does not identify his basic standpoint as Anabaptist but ponders broader methodological questions, such as how speaking of God is possible, especially in light of postmodernity.[142]

Kaufman insists that all theological concepts, including "God," are general cultural products arising from long-term collective efforts to organize and find meaning in experience.[143] This does not mean that "God" is nonsense, for it points to the deepest unity in experience. Yet it does not directly represent a being known experientially.[144] Religious experience, in fact, is more shaped by language and culture than these are by religious experience,[145] as Weaver also maintains. Theological language, therefore, is not unique but grounded in public activities and foundations.[146]

Consequently, theology cannot begin with and simply interpret language that some call God's revelation, whether this comes from a unique narrative or broad Christian tradition.

Instead, theologians should self-consciously construct their concepts, incorporating elements of their culture's worldview, a task involving much imagination.[147] By what criteria then should a God-concept be constructed today? Above all "God" should promote what is authentically human.[148] And how are people humanized? Through free exercise of historicity, a capacity to shape and reshape his-

---

[141]Peter Erb, "Contemplation and Action in the Modern World," *CGR* 9, no. 1 (1991): 12.

[142]See Gordon Kaufman, "My Life and Theological Reflection," *CGR* 20, no. 1 (2002).

[143]Gordon Kaufman, *An Essay in Theological Method* (Missoula, Mont.: Scholars Press, 1975), p. 3.

[144]Gordon Kaufman, *In Face of Mystery* (Cambridge: Harvard, 1993), p. 323.

[145]Kaufman, *Essay in Theological Method*, p. 6.

[146]Ibid., p. 8.

[147]Responsible construction today will first develop a concept of "world" by means of metaphysics, without reference to revelation (Kaufman, *Essay in Theological Method*, p. 45). Next, a God-concept will be constructed that relativizes the "world," showing it to depend on "God." Finally, theology will reconstruct its world-concept in light of its God-concept, indicating the public relevance of both (ibid., pp. 56-61).

[148]Kaufman, *Essay in Theological Method*, p. 52.

tory in light of future goals. Historicity includes responsibility, self-understanding, well-ordered freedom and concern for nonhuman reality.[149]

Yet since "God" involves all dimensions of reality, science must also help shape this concept. Kaufman proposes that "God" today refers to a serendipitous evolutionary creativity, a continuous "coming-into-being of increasing complexity, value and meaning."[150] "God," then, refers not to a being but to this world-process and its direction, which is now making life more humane.[151]

If theological language should be formed this way, is there any concept that can acquire an Anabaptist flavor? Yes, "Christ," though Kaufman applies this not only to Jesus but also includes Jesus' early community. Together they form one of those rare events that reveal bio-history's overall direction—though its real significance has emerged only in the last 150 years.[152] Concurring largely with proponents of the unique narrative, Kaufman seeks to distill "Christ's" meaning mostly from Jesus' story: basically, his announcing of God's kingdom, healing, forgiving, loving his enemies, championing the poor and social reversal.[153] Kaufman claims that cosmic christological titles in Scripture and the creeds arose not from this story but from ancient culture's interpretive framework.[154] A responsible contemporary theology then will extract Jesus' (and the early community's) story from that context and incorporate it in today's bio-historical frame.[155]

Kaufman, however, does not want to reduce "Christ's" significance to social ethics. Since the cosmic process was always moving toward humaneness, "Christ" is the revelation of "God," or what "God" always was and is doing.[156] Kaufman can employ trinitarian concepts to express how God is transcendent mystery (Father),

---

[149]Kaufman, *In Face of Mystery*, p. 130.

[150]Ibid., p. 264, cf. p. 374.

[151]Ibid., pp. 381-82. Kaufman recently acknowledged that evolutionary creativity involves much destruction and cannot be employed "abstractly . . . as a norm" ("On Thinking of God as Serendipitous Creativity," *Journal of the American Academy of Religion* 69, no. 2 [2001]: 418). Although it is indeed "the ultimate criterion of all value and meaning," it can furnish criteria for human life only in terms of "our human situatedness" within it (ibid., p. 421); only in that "sphere" of the "cosmic order" where human historicity guided by the love manifested in Jesus arose (ibid., p. 420).

[152]Kaufman, "On Thinking of God," p. 387.

[153]Kaufman, *In Face of Mystery*, pp. 382; On Thinking of God," p. 417.

[154]Kaufman, *In Face of Mystery*, p. 379.

[155]Ibid., pp. 381-82.

[156]Weaver stresses that in his Christus Victor schema, unlike in Kaufman, God is "a center of will . . . manifested in a way that is not fully contained within or described by our human ways of knowing," and that Jesus' resurrection "was some kind of real event" ("Christus Victor, Nonviolence, and other Religions," p. 189). For Reimer's views on Kaufman, see *Mennonites and Classical Theology*, pp. 138-54, and their subsequent dialogue (pp. 154-58). Reimer's initial concern for transcendence was significantly shaped by reaction to Kaufman's immanentism (esp. ibid., pp. 22-35, 37-53).

provides direction for human life (Son) and energizes all reality (Spirit).[157] Nevertheless, this God-process does not transcend history.[158]

Kaufman interacts with and incorporates contemporary conceptualities far more than the theologians mentioned so far. Yet he distills core themes congruent with a social-ethical reading of the Anabaptist Vision. Jesus, shorn of transcendent titles, becomes an ethical innovator stressing love of enemies. He is so intertwined with the early Christian community that it becomes "Christ." Reality and God are reduced to bio-historical process against Reimer's protest and more thoroughly and explicitly than by Weaver or Yoder.

Duane Friesen. Chiefly concerned with social ethics, Duane Friesen wants to overcome the sharp distinction between church and world common to proponents of the unique biblical narrative. Friesen insists that all "humans are fundamentally defined by culture." Consequently, questions about living according to Christ or culture, as if these two could be separated, are misplaced.[159] Somewhat like Reimer, he wants to draw on "the resources of the whole church catholic" and even "broader cultural wisdom."[160]

Still, Friesen is guided chiefly by the vision of an alternative society. He seeks, however, to employ it with a "balanced realism" that admits how flawed and culturally conditioned churches that promote it are.[161] To greatly influence society, moreover, churches cannot simply articulate biblical ideals but must apply them analogically and imaginatively to complex issues.[162]

Friesen locates this outlook within a comprehensive theological framework, drawing often on Kaufman. He repeatedly underscores the limitations and situatedness of all knowledge. Christian theology is "an activity of the human imagination, similar to other human cultural processes" needing to be reworked in every time and place.[163] Even the Scriptures are "imaginative interpretations in response to the . . . 'sense' of the living Spirit . . . present in the gathered community."[164] Friesen often calls Jesus his root metaphor or central symbol.

These claims raise questions about how theology could refer beyond itself, such as to some historical core. In response Friesen elaborates norms and crite-

---

[157]Kaufman, *In Face of Mystery*, p. 415.

[158]Ibid., pp. 325-28; "On Thinking of God," p. 423.

[159]Duane Friesen, "An Anabaptist Theology of Culture for a New Century," *CGR* 13, no. 1 (1995): 33, 47.

[160]Duane Friesen, *Artists, Citizens, Philosophers* (Scottdale, Penn.: Herald, 2000), pp. 34, 82.

[161]Ibid., pp. 134-39.

[162]Ibid., pp. 224-26.

[163]Ibid., pp. 68, 71.

[164]Ibid., p. 68.

ria[165] for theology and assigns Jesus' history a normativity much as do theologians of the unique narrative. Like them, he is more concerned with traditional Anabaptist issues than Kaufman.

Friesen, however, addresses some topics more thoroughly than these theologians. He not only unfolds a complex trinitarianism but calls it "essential" to the Christian "moral vision."[166] Like Kaufman, Friesen explicates "God" with reference to cosmic history and dialogues with current science.[167] Like Kaufman's "God," Friesen's is closely linked with and does not interrupt bio-history.[168] Yet Friesen's God seems more genuinely transcendent.[169] At the same time, Friesen stresses God's sacramental presence in the cosmos.[170] He devotes a chapter to "artistic imagination" and handles church sacraments, especially the Lord's Supper, more fully than other authors mentioned in this chapter.

Friesen treats the Trinity's second member as the universal Logos, the "source of all truth."[171] Christians, then, should search for truth wherever it can be found, including other religions, which Friesen considers at length.[172] Otherwise he treats Jesus almost entirely as the most complete embodiment, or vivid revelation, of "God" to us—stressing his historical particularities.[173] Similarly, *Holy Spirit* refers chiefly to the way we experience God.[174]

Friesen explicates the Trinity far more fully than Reimer. Yet it is not clear whether its second and third members are more than historical appearances, or modes, of "God." Does this Trinity, then, transcend historicism as far Reimer recommends? It is hard to tell, for Reimer too favors the term *modes*.

Nancey Murphy with George Ellis. Most twentieth-century theologians avoided science, partly due to its accelerating complexity. Anabaptist theologians generally follow suit.

---

[165]Ibid., pp. 77-82, 83-83 respectively.

[166]Ibid., p. 89.

[167]Ibid., see esp. pp. 278-85.

[168]Ibid., pp. 101-3.

[169]"The universe does not arise from itself, but is intended by God and brought into being"(ibid., p. 100). The "being" of "the entire cosmos . . . is derived from God's creating action" (p. 99). For Friesen, Sally McFague's metaphor of the world as God's body threatens to undermine God's transcendence (p. 107). Although life, according to Friesen, arose from "chance variation in the DNA molecule. . . . [T]he universe is not completely the result of chance"(p. 101). The big bang and the anthropic principle are plausible expressions of God's activity (pp. 283-85).

[170]Ibid., p. 108.

[171]Ibid., p. 257.

[172]Ibid., pp. 258-78.

[173]Ibid., pp. 99-105, 108-20. He approves Nicea and Chalcedon's intent, though not necessarily their language, to affirm "that in Jesus we find God and our humanity most fully illuminated" (pp. 108-9).

[174]Ibid., pp. 105-8, 120-25.

Kaufman and Friesen, however, in seeking a broader framework than biblical narrative, take science into account. Murphy, a Ph.D. in philosophy of science as well as theology, incorporates science much more fully into theology than other Anabaptists.[175] She also wrestles, as do Kaufman and Friesen, with broad methodological issues.

Elaborating on the situatedness and perspectival character of knowledge, Murphy rejects efforts to ground theology on secure foundations, as do Yoder and Friesen in different fashions.[176] However, she regards theology as a normative discipline with testable truth criteria. Drawing on Imre Lakatos's philosophy of science, she envisions theology as a research program.[177] Much like philosopher Alasdair McIntyre, Murphy also regards theology as a tradition or "historically extended, socially embodied argument about how best to interpret and apply the formative text(s)."[178] This fits with an Anabaptist orientation toward narrative and commu-

---

[175]Carl Keener, a Mennonite biologist, devoted several essays to this theme. For Keener, contemporary worldviews provide basic concepts and criteria for theology, somewhat as for Kaufman. Keener finds today's cosmic organicism, where all things are interrelated within an evolutionary process, "incommensurable with orthodox Christianity . . . with its implied static essences" (Carl Keener, "The Darwinian Revolution and its Implications for a Modern Anabaptist Theology," *CGR* I, no. I [1983]: 14; cf. Carl Keener, "Some Reflections on Mennonites and Postmodern Thought," *CGR* II, no. I [1993]: 54). He considers process theology most adequate for today's task. He finds Anabaptism's emphasis on freedom incompatible with an omnipotent, immutable, omniscient God. The cross is the prime revelation of divine agency and human action ("Some Reflections," p. 58) and congruent with an evolving process deity.

Citing Murphy, Keener finds nonfoundationalist epistemology "thoroughly communitarian" and consistent with Anabaptism's communal Scripture reading (57). Theology, however, should not be reduced to the "pragmatism" of following Christ, but must consider "the grandeur and sweep of the universe" ([1983]: 28). Though Weaver accepts the scientific outlook ([1984]: 191) and finds qualified value in process theology (207), he sees Keener abandoning traditional positions and reconstructing theology from scratch (190).

[176]Nancey Murphy, *Beyond Liberalism and Fundamentalism* (Valley Forge, Penn.: Trinity, 1996), pp. 85-100. Evangelicals and liberals, she claims, have usually sought such grounding: evangelicals on biblical texts and perhaps their historical referents; liberals on religious experience (ibid., pp. 11-61).

[177]Ibid., p. 101. A research program consists of a hard core, or basic theory, and also a set of auxiliary hypotheses, such as methods of observation, that check the core, theory against empirical data. When some such data are discrepant with the core, the hypotheses can be modified without abandoning the core. "A research program is a temporally extended series of complex theories whose core remains the same while the auxiliary hypotheses are successively modified, replaced, or amplified in order to account for the problematic observations." Competing theologies (research programs) can be evaluated by their "relative progress or degeneration" as they meet new challenges (ibid., p. 103).

[178]Ibid., p. 103. A tradition can be evaluated in terms of its ability "to make progress on its own terms . . . while its live competitors fail (on their own terms) to do so" (p. 109). In other words, traditions develop their own standards of rationality to deal with challenges. These standards do not always protect the tradition from all challenges but can critique it from within. Over time, some traditions can be successful in meeting challenges according to their own criteria, while others fail according to theirs (pp. 103-8).

nity, and suggests a way to establish it, rather than simply positing it, as a starting point in a relativistic postmodern atmosphere.[179] Yet it raises questions of whether such traditions can err, and whether other norms are needed if they do.[180]

Rather than stressing particular narratives or communities, however, Murphy and Quaker astronomer George Ellis argue that theology should provide genuine knowledge of transcendent reality, and about the nature and possibility of the sciences.[181] In this way theology can construct "a unified world view" and, as Reimer also urges, provide "objective grounding for morality."[182]

Unlike Kaufman, Murphy and Ellis do not fit theology into a contemporary conceptual framework so much as argue that this framework has limitations that only theology can overcome. Murphy and Ellis arrange all the natural sciences into a hierarchy in which higher levels answer questions that arise at lower ones but cannot be answered by means of the lower (e.g., some issues arising from chemical study of DNA must be answered by biology). The highest level, cosmology, still cannot answer why a universe with its regularities and specific laws exists at all.[183]

Murphy and Ellis also order the social and applied sciences hierarchically. These sciences raise questions about life's meaning that they cannot answer. Further, they actually require some answer—some concept of human life's ultimate purpose or good.[184] Murphy and Ellis contend that many social sciences actually presuppose one such answer, though usually implicitly: Human nature is conflictive. That is,

---

[179]For Murphy biblical interpreters too often seek to identify a text's meaning with or ground it on referents such as historical facts or authorial intent. But poststructuralism challenges this. Murphy proposes, instead, a focus not on the texts' referents but on their functions within early Christian communities. There these texts functioned as speech-acts, performing various roles in communal life. Their meaning then can best be grasped not by individual scholars searching for external referents but current communities seeking to live the same way ("Textual Relativism, Philosophy of Language and the Baptist Vision," in *Theology Without Foundations*, ed. Nancey Murphy, Stanley Hauerwas and Mark Nation [Nashville: Abingdon, 1998]).

Murphy takes speech-acts from J. L. Austin and incorporates the linguistic philosophies of Wittgenstein and her late husband, James McClendon. She aims in part to show how the "this is that" of McClendon's baptist vision is possible; that is, how theology can attain and then work from the "shared awareness *of the present Christian community as the primitive community and the eschatological community*" (McClendon, *Systematic Theology* I: 31, italics in original).

[180]For Murphy's answers, which also draw on MacIntyre, see "Textual Relativism," p. 106-8.

[181]Nancey Murphy and George Ellis, *On the Moral Nature of the Universe* (Minneapolis: Fortress, 1996), p. 7.

[182]Ibid., p. 1: "Theology constitutes knowledge in exactly the same sense of the term as does science." "Theological claims are confirmed on the basis of their ability to answer questions that arise within science and ethics but go beyond the purview of those disciplines alone." Yet Reimer finds this science-oriented notion of theology problematic (*Mennonites and Classical Theology*, pp. 132-37).

[183]Murphy and Ellis, *On the Moral Nature of the Universe*, p. 61.

[184]Ibid., p. 87.

these sciences presuppose an "ontology of violence."[185] Here Anabaptism becomes relevant. For it can propose an alternative value to govern all social science: "*Self-renunciation for the sake of the other is humankind's highest good.*"[186]

From where does this value arise? Murphy and Ellis root it theologically in God's self-giving character expressed decisively in Jesus' life and death. From this they draw further theological implications—for example, that God rules noncoercively, that freedom therefore is central to human nature.[187] This theological perspective also provides answers to those ultimate questions raised by natural science.[188]

In brief, while Murphy and Ellis go well beyond social ethics, they still consider nonviolent behavior, based on the Jesus narrative, as Anabaptism's main theological contribution. Yet they argue more often in scientific, social and philosophical terms than in biblical or traditional theological concepts.

Further, Murphy and Ellis maintain that the levels of reality corresponding to the higher sciences (e.g., psychology) cannot be reduced to or be entirely byproducts of lower levels (e.g., biology). Higher levels differ, however, by containing not new entities but more complex organizations of entities found at lower levels. This means, for instance, that "the seat of consciousness (and also of human spiritual or religious capacities)" is not a soul but "the human nervous system, operating in concert with the rest of the body in its environment."[189]

Further, as no soul interrupts neurological operations, God does not intervene within laws determining matter's behavior.[190] God, indeed, is nonphysical—of another metaphysical category than the cosmos.[191] Yet within the cosmos Murphy and Ellis avoid reductionism by positing higher levels of organization, not of entities.

---

[185]Ibid., pp. 111-14.

[186]Ibid., p. 119, italics in original.

[187]The cosmos's ultimate purpose, in fact, is uncoerced response to the Creator (ibid., p. 209). Nonviolence is central to morality precisely because it is noncoercion's ultimate form (p. 208). Moreover, since "self-emptying . . . is the very nature of God" (p. 194), God participates in creaturely evolutionary suffering, which is a necessary byproduct of the emergence of higher life (p. 211). Among Anabaptist theologians, Murphy and Ellis rely mainly on Yoder (pp. 178-200).

[188]Ibid., pp. 202-20.

[189]Nancey Murphy, "Nonreductive Physicalism: Philosophical Issues," in *Whatever Happened to the Soul?* ed. Warren Brown, Nancey Murphy, and H. Newton Maloney (Minneapolis: Fortress, 1998), p. 131. Murphy calls this nonreductive physicalism. It reduces higher levels to lower ones ontologically (i.e., the same entities operate on both), but not causally (higher level behavior is not wholly a product of lower), and it rejects reductive materialism. This means that religious "experiences supervene on combinations of ordinary experiences"(p. 143). Still, nonreductive physicalism needs "a theological account" in which divine action supervenes on natural and historical events to avoid reduction of religious experiences to the latter (p. 147).

[190]Murphy and Ellis, *On the Moral Nature*, p. 207; except perhaps at the quantum level, pp. 217-18.

[191]Ibid., p. 57; Murphy, "Nonreductive Physicalism," p. 148, note 41.

Postmodern Considerations

Though I am chiefly concerned with efforts at comprehensive theologizing, many considerations relevant to it appear in briefer writings. Such discourse befits postmodernity, which affects all the issues below (and clearly many above). Because Anabaptist theologians devote much attention to biblical narrative, I will first examine some articles dealing with textuality. Since Anabaptists often stress the church's distinctness, I will next explore some recent thoughts on church and world. Third, since construction is a significant postmodern issue, as Kaufman shows, I will discuss additional proposals on this theme. Finally, I will consider a postmodern theme less traditionally Anabaptist: desire.

Narrative, textuality and intertextuality. Postmodernity is often invoked to legitimate the derivation of theology from particular sources, such as biblical or Anabaptist narratives. For some, like Weaver, this implies that theology consists of socio-linguistic rules governing specific community practices and need not refer to transcendent reality, as Reimer, Murphy and Ellis think it should.

To Scott Holland such an outlook is simply a communal positivism that fails to address claims of competing communal narratives.[192] Though this outlook proclaims liberation from modernity's sovereign, individualistic self, it reverts to the premodern sovereignty of the communal self.[193] Holland argues that no pure narratives or texts exist. All texts formed by one group arise through interaction with other groups and are therefore really intertexts.

Holland is thinking not simply of other denominations' or religions' written texts but also their more mystical dimensions. Different social, ethnic and other groups also have their own stories, or texts. Ultimately Holland, not unlike Kaufman, finds all these embedded in the intertextuality of the entire human and cosmic story.[194]

Many Anabaptist women theologians are focusing on more specific contexts, those in which biblical texts are read. Since women often have felt outside the approved contextual (church) readings, they are asking how Scripture might be interpreted in light of their own experiential "texts." To do so, many employ feminist texts that critique the Bible's treatment of various issues. They read the relevant biblical texts through both feminist and Anabaptist texts. Anabaptist women often find that biblical texts viewed through these two lenses yield positive resources for addressing those issues.

For example, Dorothy Jean Weaver and Gayle Gerber Koontz consider the criticism: if women forgive their offenders, as Scripture commands, the offending behavior often

---

[192]Scott Holland, "The Problems and Prospects of a 'Sectarian Ethic' " *CGR* 10, no. 2 (1992): 165-66.
[193]Scott Holland, "Einbildungskraft," in *Mennonite Theology in Face of Modernity*, ed. Alain Epp-Weaver (North Newton, Kan.: Bethel College, 1996), pp. 246.
[194]Scott Holland, "How Do Stories Save Us?" *CGR* 12, no. 2 (1994): 144.

persists.[195] They respond that forgiving one who hurts you is central to Christian behavior, especially in Anabaptist perspective. Yet, they add, if this takes place in communities of accountability—another Anabaptist theme—offenders can be disciplined and the needs of the offended met.[196] Here feminist and Anabaptist texts do not literally correct biblical texts but open up dimensions of the latter that are often distorted or missed.

Similarly, Mary Schertz and Rachel Reesor respond to objections that emphasis on Jesus' suffering legitimates suffering in general.[197] Both reply that Jesus' suffering was willingly chosen and that similar experiences will likely befall anyone who opposes evil. Yet while such suffering is acceptable (though not desirable), biblical texts, like feminist texts, insist that suffering in general and specifically suffering from oppression are not. Schertz, Reesor, D. J. Weaver and Gerber Koontz represent the approach to biblical narrative most common among Anabaptists today. Mary Anne Hildebrand, however, believes that emphasis on Jesus' death wrongly sanctions suffering, and we need new myths, stories and symbols.[198]

Such investigations raise the question, To what extent are revelation and authority located in biblical texts or in interpreting communities?[199] Lydia Harder finds such phrasing oversimplified. For it invites us to picture texts as objects over against ourselves as interpreting subjects. Texts, however, reach us through intervening historical patterns of interpretation. These developed within authority structures that often excluded women and other marginalized groups. Perhaps then these channels

---

[195]See Dorothy Jean Weaver, "On Imitating God and Outwitting Satan," *MQR* 68, no. 2 (1994); and Gayle Gerber Koontz, "As We Forgive Others: Forgiveness and Feminist Pain," *MQR* 68, no. 2 (1994).

[196]Gerber Koontz previously recommended "creative revisioning" of biblical texts through artistic and historical imagination ("The Trajectory of Scripture and Feminist Conviction," *CGR* 5, no. 3 [1987]: 206). She did not regard authority as an intrinsic property of these texts, for then interpretation would involve "violent" subordination. Yet Scripture, she also stressed, must critique contemporary convictions (p. 213) and interpretation must avoid endless subjectivity (p. 216). Gerber Koontz balanced these concerns by regarding authority as "functional," as freely evoking consent, and therefore "non-violent," because it appeals to our imagination, mind and heart, and "rings true to our deepest capacity for truth and goodness" (p. 215). She also advocated "serious engagement" with texts by reading them within communities, which must include diversity.

[197]See Mary Schertz, "God's Cross and Women's Questions," *MQR* 68, no. 2 (1994); and Rachel Reesor, "Atonement: Mystery and Metaphorical Language," *MQR* 68, no. 2 (1994).

[198]Mary Anne Hildebrand, "Domestic Violence: A Challenge to Mennonite Faith and Peace Theology," *CGR* 10, no. 1 (1992): 79. Articles by D. J. Weaver, Gerber Koontz, Schertz and Reesor come from the second Anabaptist "Women Doing Theology" conference in Bluffton, Ohio (collected in *MQR* 68, no. 2 [1994]). Hildebrand's article emerged from the first conference in Waterloo, Ontario (papers in *CGR* 10, no. 1 [1992]). A third conference was held in Winnipeg (see *CGR* 14, no. 2 [1996]), and a fourth in 1997 in North Newton, Kansas (papers were unavailable, even to participants). These conferences considered not only prose texts but also poetry, story, music and dance.

are clogged by far-reaching distortions of Scripture that arose to establish and keep these authorities in power.[200]

Consequently, feminism should teach us to question not only particular texts but also the channels through which we hear all texts. Harder generally affirms a current shift of attention away from a text's referents (e.g., historical events, beliefs) toward the way language shapes a community's interpretation of it.[201] Nadine Pence Frantz adds that any written text is a reworking of previous texts. Many voices and meaning levels are present within it. It is appropriate then that many people be involved in interpreting it.[202] Women's lives, in fact, are also texts; theology involves bringing God's presence in them to expression, much as interpretation does for a written text.[203]

Such an emphasis is not only feminist. Many historic Anabaptists insisted that whole communities, including illiterate and marginal people, interpret the Bible together. Nonetheless, this foregrounding of interpreting communities, where various life texts encounter biblical texts, presses the issue of where biblical authority is found. For Pence Frantz interpreters participate in " 'authoring' the text's voice"; this means that one "must be authored by the text as much as one authors it."[204] For Harder "the function of a text in a social context is part of its meaning" and interpretation continues the author's creative work.[205]

Other Anabaptist women, however, question this slant. Jo-Ann Martens claims

---

[199]Katie Funk-Wiebe reported some uncertainty at the first conference about what really constituted the "text" and what the role of experience was. In her perception, though, the women always went from text to experience ("Reflections on the Conference 'In a Mennonite Voice: Women Doing Theology,' " *CGR* 10, no. 2 [1992]: 211-12). They did not want to destroy the church and the Bible (p. 211). In Funk-Wiebe's view the "source of authority" should be "the self-revelation of God through the scriptures within the context of the body of Christ" (p. 213).

[200]Lydia Harder, *Obedience, Suspicion and the Gospel of Mark* (Waterloo, Ont.: Wilfred Laurier University Press, 1998), pp. 1-21, 53-56, 145-50.

[201]Lydia Harder, "Biblical Interpretation: A Praxis of Discipleship?" *CGR* 10, no. 1 (1992): 25; cf. Murphy's notion of biblical texts as speech acts operating in early Christian life, best apprehended within current communities seeking to live as they did (note 178). Harder adds, not unlike Kaufman, that we belong to language far more than it belongs to us. For "the notion of objectivity is becoming more and more suspect." We probably cannot apprehend "reality in a direct, unmediated way. . . . [W]hat we name reality is constituted through the interpretations that, through argument and discussion, have gained the status of truth or fact at this point in history" ("Postmodern Suspicion and Imagination," *MQR* 71, no. 2 [1997]: 270).

[202]Nadine Pence Frantz, "The (Inter)Textuality of Our Lives: An Anabaptist Feminist Hermeneutic," *CGR* 14, no. 2 (1996): 132-39.

[203]Ibid., p. 141.

[204]Ibid., p. 136.

[205]Harder, "Biblical Interpretation," p. 25.

that for Harder language can refer only to one's social context; it cannot stretch beyond this to reveal something really new.[206] Interpretation's goal, however, is not to continue the authors' work but to transcend our own horizon and come to understand the author's intent; through this we encounter God.[207] Sheila Klassen-Wiebe contrasts the traditional search for one main meaning in a text to Pence Frantz's stress on multiple meanings and current interactions of texts. Klassen-Wiebe wonders how the latter task would proceed.[208] How, for instance, do we decide what community does the interpreting? How are dissenting voices evaluated?[209]

Harder and Pence Frantz, however, apparently do not mean to shift authority chiefly to interpreting communities. Harder recommends suspicion toward texts and their customary readings, and creative attempts at new readings. But she intends these to unmask traditional distortions so that communities can return "again and again to the biblical texts for" their "identity" and "criteria for truth"—and to obey them.[210] Pence Frantz also stresses that in believers' churches, understanding texts is inseparable from obeying them. This implies a basic trust in and receptivity to the canonical writings.[211]

In a tradition that valorizes biblical narrative, it might seem that theologians can derive their views straightforwardly from its texts. But the voices just raised do not find it so simple. For every text is an intertext: its meaning emerges through encounter with other texts, whether of religious bodies, secular movements or readers' lives. Some of these can help unlock Scripture's meaning. Yet still other texts have locked much of it in. Historic Anabaptists well knew that the biblical narrative had been distorted by and needed to be retrieved from Western culture's metanarrative.

This suggests that today's Anabaptist theologians might approach Scripture by putting questions to it in light of historic Anabaptist texts, with their multiple voices. In this way marginalized voices can emerge, sensitizing theologians to other efforts, past and present, to raise them. Biblical interpretation might begin from a variety of "impression points" (Harder's term), originating in texts addressed to the Bible or within the Bible itself. These can open up some portions of Scripture as keys to the whole.[212] To be sure, external texts can be read into or superimposed

---

[206]Jo-Anne Martens, "Response to Lydia Harder," *CGR* 10, no. 2 (1992): 219-20.

[207]Ibid., pp. 217-18.

[208]Sheila Klassen-Wiebe, "Response to Nadine Pence Frantz," *CGR* 14, no. 3 (1996): 200.

[209]Ibid., p. 292.

[210]Lydia Harder, *Obedience, Suspicion and the Gospel of Mark* (Waterloo, Ont.: Wilfred Laurier University Press, 1998), p. 56.

[211]Nadine Pence Frantz, "Theological Hermeneutics: Christian Feminist Biblical Interpretation and the Believers' Church Tradition" (Ph.D. diss., University of Chicago, 1992), pp. 148-53; 205-12.

[212]Harder, "Biblical Interpretation," p. 26.

on the Bible. Yet in response to Anabaptist and other current texts, the biblical texts themselves might yield unsuspected resources.

Church and world. Interest in texts other than the Bible is intertwined with interest in social contexts other than Anabaptist churches. According to John Roth, Yoder sharply contrasted following either the Anabaptist Vision or current culture. But for Roth, continual tension between the two is the fabric of Christian life.[213] Scott Holland's interest in non-Christian texts is partly sparked by his conviction that God dwells not only in churches but also in "the public square."[214] We have also noticed how for Duane Friesen all people are intrinsically shaped by society, so that Christ and culture cannot be cleanly separated.

Critique of the church's attempted separation from society is also fueled by feelings of suffocation under its behavioral conformity and moral discipline. Holland calls Anabaptism a superego religion that stifles individuals.[215] Melanie May theologizes out of her "angry and anguished experience of the tyranny of disciplined community."[216] Her first step toward healing was to take back the life she thought she owed the church, with its exhortations to self-sacrifice.[217] Anabaptist Vision advocates often regard individualism as society's major problem and community the solution. May deconstructs the disciplined community ideal and proposes that "the 20th century may be characterized by the tyranny of community."[218]

Elaine Swartzentruber investigates the Anabaptist church body using clues from Michel Foucault, not by "searching the scriptures or the old Anabaptist texts."[219] She questions Bender's equation of this body with Christ's transcendent body. Swartzentruber contends that this theological claim was an attempt to remove the church from the fray of power, violence, loss and desire, and to deny its wounds, bro-

---

[213]John Roth, "Living Between the Times: The 'Anabaptist Vision' and Mennonite Reality," *MQR* 69, no. 3 (1995): 328, 330.

[214]Scott Holland, "Anabaptism as Public Theology," *CGR* 11, no. 3 (1993): 279.

[215]Scott Holland, "The Resurrection of the Soul in the Anabaptist Body," in *The Believers Church: A Voluntary Church*, ed. William Brackney (Kitchener, Ont.: Pandora, 1998), p. 3, referring to Dintaman ("Spiritual Poverty of the Anabaptist Vision") positively, though Dintaman regards retrieval of a more traditional perspective, which Holland also finds somewhat stifling, as part of the solution.

[216]Melanie May, "The Pleasure of Our Lives as Text," *CGR* 10, no. 1 (1992): 32.

[217]Ibid., pp. 35, 43-44.

[218]Ibid., p. 38; in contrast, e.g., to Kraus: "In American society today, the unquestioned assumption is that the individual takes precedence over the group. Freedom means individual independence" (C. Norman Kraus, *The Community of the Spirit* [Scottdale, Penn.: Herald, 1993], p. 31). "The presuppositions of humanistic individualism provide the working definitions and assumptions of modern Western society" (p. 35). Kraus, however, does not devalue individuality, but develops a biblical, community-related notion of it (pp. 33-56).

[219]Elaine Swartzentruber, "Marking and Remarking the Body of Christ: Toward a Postmodern Mennonite Ecclesiology," *MQR* 71, no. 2 (1997): 246.

kenness and scars.[220] The church must be more honestly appraised. For this, how-ever, we require neither a "transcendent authority" nor a "theological . . . space of otherness." We need instead "a theory and practice of how to live as faithful and just disciples of Christ implicated in the power relations of the world."[221]

We have seen how champions of the uniqueness of biblical narrative and of communities formed by it appeal to postmodernity—by citing its valorization of particularity. Yet postmodernists often focus on particularity to illumine the con-crete social shaping, with all its flaws, of texts, interpretations and communities that claim them. For the voices just raised, postmodernity provides tools to unmask Anabaptist idealizations of its own separatist and internally oppressive tendencies.

These voices critique theology for simply elaborating idealized statements about the church, even biblical ones. For theology must ask whether these ideals function in practice to mask the church's very deviations from them. Yet to hear the relevant questions theologians must listen—especially to marginalized people within the church and beyond. This recalls our postmodern biblical critics' claim: for texts to truly be heard church structures through which they have been inter-preted must be identified and critiqued by the same two audiences.

If these voices are even partially on target, theological texts can be written only through dialogue with and critique from other texts and social contexts. This, how-ever, raises the question, Can the latter provide norms for theology equal or supe-rior to biblical narrative?

Contemporary construction. This question leads back to Kaufman's claim that all the-ology is constructed by means of concepts circulating widely in the current culture. Kaufman is granting epistemological priority to the interpretive context over Scrip-ture and to culture over the church. Further, if construction can only employ con-temporary concepts, the present will have priority over the past.

Ted Grimsrud sketches a neo-Mennonite outlook that he spots among many cur-rent Mennonites and considers a legitimate option.[222] Neo-Mennonites insist that

---

[220]Ibid., pp. 261-62; polygenesis historiography, by more carefully investigating Anabaptism's varied and of-ten stained origins, began the deconstruction of this ideal (p. 262); cf. Bender, "Who Is the Lord?" p. 19.

[221]Swartzentruber, "Marking and Remarking," pp. 262-63. Nonetheless, Swartzentruber may not be wholly rejecting the notion of Christ's transcendent body but stressing the need to make it visible "not by erasing the lines of productive power that constitute its materiality but by marking and re-marking that body for our times"(p. 263). Though she emphasizes community, Swartzentruber cri-tiques some current theological idealizations of it; though she employs many postmodern tools, she critiques various aspects of postmodernity (see Elaine Swartzentruber, *They Were All Together and Had Everything in Common: Subjectivity and Community in Modern and Postmodern Theologies* (Ph.D. diss., At-lanta: Emory University, 1999).

[222]Ted Grimsrud, "Mennonite Theology and Historical Consciousness," in *Mennonite Theology in Face of Modernity*, ed. Alain Epp-Weaver (North Newton, Kans.: Bethel College, 1996), p. 138.

"*no* formulation can help but be a contemporary construct." They find even Reimer's retrieval of classical themes "every bit as much a late twentieth-century formulation" as anything from Kaufman. Grimsrud stresses that doctrines like the Trinity, Christ's deity and biblical inspiration emerge from "past constructs." Quite understandably then neo-Mennonites can "affirm God *without* positing 'Classical' notions of Transcendence, Eternity, and Ontology." Consequently, such persons will have "much greater interest in . . . spirituality and ethics than classical creeds and dogmatics."[223]

For neo-Mennonites "the central criterion for *our* theology is that it be meaningful for *us*, and that it address *our* reality." Grimsrud believes that they need to see the Bible in "a constructive, non-authoritarian" way that they can connect to their lives as "a conversation partner which helps us in *our* construction, which emerges through *our* experience . . . not an authority-over." In conclusion, Grimsrud affirms that the reality into which Jesus and Paul tapped is "fully accessible to us when we listen first to God via our own hearts."[224] I find it difficult to ascertain to what extent Grimsrud is representing the neo-Mennonite position or his own.[225]

Elsewhere Grimsrud maintains that theology has "a normative aspect." It does not simply describe "what people in congregations happen to believe."[226] Still, its "starting point" is "congregational life," for theology "emerges from and directly addresses historical existence."[227] Grimsrud identifies four sources, though none are "authorities to be prioritized."[228] One is the Bible, whose "message of God's healing love provides the core content for all Christian theology." However, it provides not a "supreme authority for specific decisions" but a common language and orientation toward life.[229]

Mennonite history provides a second source. Later eras are more important than historic Anabaptism, for they "formed present-day Mennonite identity more."[230] Three main transitions occurred, from (1) adult to child baptism, (2) ag-

---

[223]Ibid., pp. 150, 140, 151, 140, respectively.

[224]Ibid., pp. 152, 154, 155, respectively.

[225]The previous sentence, Grimsrud indicated to me, would reflect his view if paraphrased: he "concludes that present-day Christians are able to access the same Holy Spirit as Jesus and Paul did" (letter, January 23, 2003). Grimsrud called this essay "mostly descriptive," adding that if he was "advocating anything, it is simply that in-house theologians and everyone else should be aware" of how neo-Mennonites think. While I appreciate this clarification, I still find Grimsrud italicizing terms like *present experience* often, both in this article and the one below, which expresses his own position. I still find it hard to tell which emphases in the first, "mostly descriptive" article are only descriptive.

[226]Ted Grimsrud, "Constructing a Mennonite Theology in a Congregational Setting," *Mennonite Life* 52, no. 1 (1997): 31.

[227]Ibid., p. 35, cf. p. 30. He expresses great indebtedness to Kaufman, such as for the notion that "theology is always an act of construction rather than 'hermeneutics' "(ibid., p. 31, citing Kaufman).

[228]Ibid., p. 31.

gressive evangelism to seeking toleration, and (3) open membership to ethnicity. Grimsrud believes these attempts at new understandings in new contexts should be appreciated, but he mentions no criteria for evaluating them. Grimsrud lists present-experience life as theology's third source. It should be a shaped by the fourth: eschatological hope that God will bring "wholeness for all of creation."[231]

In his congregational theology Grimsrud apparently allots Scripture and tradition greater roles than neo-Mennonites do. But while Scripture's message of "God's healing love" provides theology's "core content," I still find relationships among Grimsrud's four sources vague. While he does not construct theology entirely from present experience, might experience still exercise important normative functions?

Daniel Liechty views language and hence theological concepts as wholly human artifacts, constituted by reference to other language, not anything transcending it. Consequently, Liechty suggests, God language is wish fulfillment. We can have no assurance that God exists.[232] Apparently, though, language can still elucidate a universal human structure that shows how wishes arise.

Liechty proposes that God concepts are symbols for values that humans strive for but will never fully attain.[233] These values, we hope, will overcome our fear of death.[234] We can strive toward either positive values (transcendence, creativity and love), which involve self-giving for others and accepting death's inevitability; or negative values, which deny death and seek power over others. In this sense the con-

---

[229]Ibid., p. 32. Grimsrud is reflecting on how Scripture functioned in congregations he pastored. Perhaps, then, denial that it provides a "supreme authority" simply summarizes what happened there. He does affirm that "the Bible's message" provides theology's "core content." (He develops this elsewhere as "God's healing strategy" in *God's Healing Strategy* [Telford, Penn.: Pandora, 2000], esp. pp. 23-25). But does Scripture play any other normative role? Grimsrud's relevant remarks are often either-or polarities: e.g., the Bible's "commonality with our lives" is opposed to "direct revelation of timeless truths which relieve us of the responsibility to seek faithfulness in new ways in our contexts"(ibid.). Does this imply rejection of any biblical norms transcending the present? For me, Grimsrud's assumptions and methodology are too unclear to tell.

[230]Grimsrud, "Constructing a Mennonite Theology," p. 32.

[231]Ibid., p. 34.

[232]Though we also cannot be sure that God does not exist (Daniel Liechty, *Theology in Postliberal Perspective* [Philadelphia: Trinity Press International, 1990], p. 33). Liechty is taking to the extreme the claim that theological affirmations cannot refer to non-communal reality but only to how communities function (Daniel Liechty, "The Seamless Robe of Human Experience," in *Mennonite Theology in Face of Modernity*, ed. Alain Epp-Weaver [North Newton, Kans.: Bethel College, 1996], p. 84; cf. Weaver's similar affirmation *[Nature of Doctrine]* and reference to Lindbeck [George Lindbeck, *The Nature of Doctrine* (Philadelphia: Westminster, 1984)]). Liechty can ascribe the validity of these affirmations to communal affirmation ("Seamless Robe of Human Experience," p. 90), but also their authority to the author (*Theology in Postliberal Perspective*, p. xi).

[233]Liechty, *Theology in Postliberal Perspective*, pp. 6-8; "The Seamless Robe of Human Experience," p. 85.

[234]Liechty, *Theology in Postliberal Perspective*, p. 9.

test between nonviolence and violence is most basic for humans. Consequently, the "truth of any particular construct of God" will depend on which of these it promotes—that is, on its capacity for forming humanizing values (as for Kaufman).[235]

Jesus best actualized positive values, including opposing oppression, championing the poor and accepting death. Christians and churches, then, should work together on ethical grounds, following Jesus' example—but not doctrinal grounds, since Christological doctrines involve transcendent claims.[236] Nonviolent discipleship is indeed Anabaptism's "defining characteristic." Yet given postmodern sensibilities, this will involve not legalistic implementation of Jesus' teachings but becoming more like him "in spirit, mind, attitude, deed"—and apparently for Liechty now—"in communion with God."[237]

But insofar as theology cannot transcend human culture, the Christian community must be its main object. Yet while Liechty stresses today's culture, he could, in 1996 at least, call the community's "historical memory" theology's "basic content." Theologians could help bring its values into the present. By retrieving pacifism, mutual aid and community spirituality, Leichty claimed, his theology was Mennonite or Anabaptist.[238]

Liechty, however, is increasingly impressed by postmodernity "as a style of consciousness," a "conglomerate" of notions about "how one navigates or negotiates action" in a world largely formed through visual imagery that transgresses and interfuses modern notions of self, time and place.[239] This world will not be reached through writing prized by modern consciousness: "well-honed, terse, and linear presentation of data leading to a well-defined conclusion."[240] To this postmodern setting, moreover, historic Anabaptism's contribution is "In the strictest sense . . . none." Nevertheless, Anabaptist spirituality can yield several "ethically-oriented" themes: nonviolent discipleship, faith's corporate nature and, surprisingly, "*The immediacy of the human relationship with God*."[241]

---

[235]Ibid., p. 33.

[236]Ibid., p. 63; Daniel Liechty, "Communication Technology and the Development of Consciousness: Reframing the Discussion of Anabaptists and Postmodernity," *CGR* 18, no. 1 (2000), pp. 41-42.

[237]Ibid., pp. 43, 42.

[238]Liechty, "The Seamless Robe of Human Experience," pp. 84, 89.

[239]Liechty, "Communication Technology," pp. 28, 35. Such a consciousness is appearing in a person "who from a very young age, upon awakening, habitually puts on cyberlenses to keep connected throughout the day with an entire virtual world of interactive information and stimulation." This consciousness assumes a nonlinear logic, "a protean sense of identity that easily moves with changes in names, life narratives and even gender." It is able "to 'ride astride' many different areas of stimulation at once, and an almost frightening melding of mind with machine" (ibid., pp. 35-36).

[240]Ibid., p. 33.

[241]Ibid., pp. 40, 41.

In pressing postmodernity's historicist, anthropocentric and ethical sensibilities to an extreme, Liechty seeks to construct theology in terms of such cultural notions and criteria. At least initially he reduced theology to social-ethical dimensions more fully than Yoder, Weaver or Kaufman. Apparently, however, a God "ever and always present to the believer" has returned to today's historical world.[242] Nonetheless, though Liechty, Grimsrud and Kaufman occasionally reach toward the past, I find it unclear how they can really transcend the present.

Desire. When Anabaptists deal with postmodern issues, their tendency to reduce theology to ethics and community still abounds. But some recent thinkers link this predilection with Anabaptist elitism, judgmentalism and social isolation. Scott Holland and Melanie May want theology to transcend narrow, communal-ethical exclusivism and energize the church's spiritual and social mission. But in the postmodern present, traditional notions of transcendence collapse into cultural constructions of the past. Where then can transcendence be found?

Holland turns from the intellectual and practical (doctrine and ethics) toward the affective. The soul's language, he claims, is first of all poetic. Theology is at best third-order explanation.[243] Holland insists that the aesthetic dimension prominent in Scripture and worship must be central in Christian life. Yet he often conceptualizes this dualistically, maintaining, for instance, that the path to the Infinite is desire and *eros*, not knowledge and *gnosis*.[244] Holland strongly privileges "the id of Desire" and the aesthetic in general. He argues, however, that these are not individualistic. They can arouse passion for others and their welfare, energizing social critique and promoting justice in the "public square."[245]

May, having rejected the stifling disciplined community ideal, stresses attunement to "lifegiving energy coursing through my body, mind, and heart in relation to the world pulsing all around." This makes her life a text touching others.[246] May valorizes her body's wisdom, and especially pleasure, for it "conflicts with cultural canons. Shocks and shakes up. Unsettles foundations and founding assumptions." Pleasure, however, "Cannot be captured conceptually. It blazes and burns itself out

---

[242]Ibid., p. 41.

[243]Holland, "Einbildungskraft," p. 8.

[244]Scott Holland, "Theology Is a Kind of Writing: The Emergence of Poetics," *MQR* 71, no. 2 (1997): 229. Yet he claims he resists modern divisions between poets and philosophers (ibid., p. 230). Theology is not poetry but metafigural assessment of imaginative figures (p. 229).

[245]Gerald Biesecker-Mast proposes, arguing somewhat differently, that the Anabaptist emphasis on bodily obedience can overcome the usual split between ethics and desire, and foster an ethics valuing the latter (Gerald Biesecker-Mast, "Spiritual Knowledge, Carnal Obedience, and Anabaptist Discipleship" *MQR* 71, no. 2 (1997): 215-16.

[246]May, "Pleasure of Our Lives as Text," p. 33. Hence, her theme too is intertextuality (see Nadine Pence Frantz, "Response to Melanie A. May," *CGR* 10, no. 2 [1992]).

in an instant. Ecstatic. . . . No more shoulds; no more shame."[247]

Still, however deeply impacted by experience, theology employs words. Where do these come from? May, like Holland, suggests imagination, and writes "theopoetics."[248] She finds imagination not merely subjective but "appreciation and acceptance of reality." Imagination, further, is "an invitation to epiphany. A revelation. And revelation is not closed or completed. Imagination is not bound to texts and traditions."[249]

If theological awareness is embedded in our bodies, God might be also. May stresses "divinity deep in our flesh-and-blood wisdom" through which "We give birth to a new reality."[250] Several other Mennonite women express similar visions. Rosalee Bender celebrates "Godbecoming"—those "changes occurring in all of creation" of which we are part.[251] Godbecoming is especially "an image which the people of the periphery incarnate," for their spirituality is a resistance whose site is the body.[252] This means that today we can perceive crucifixion occurring in capitalism's exploitation of bodies,[253] resurrection in new sites occupied by women's bodies[254] and incarnation in "Godbecoming located with us in history."[255]

While the focus on desire seems quite different from the call for spirituality or classical doctrines (Dintaman, Reimer), its proponents sometimes see themselves more faithful to traditional themes than Anabaptist Vision advocates. May calls her theology Christological and trinitarian.[256] She critiques Anabaptism's deficient sense of grace.[257] Holland can stress "a personal savior who redeems by grace through faith, not by ethics and discipleship."[258] Holland grounds his theology,

---

[247]May, "Pleasure of Our Lives as Text," p. 34; *Pleasure* means not "plaisir that comforts and is legitimated as culture" but *jouissance* (cf. Roland Barthes). See her fuller treatment of the body's wisdom (*The Body Knows* [New York: Continuum, 1995]). May critiques Kaufman's emphasis on construction for assuming that nature is a passive surface on which this social activity can be imposed (ibid., pp. 102, 110 n. 3; cf. p. 23).

[248]May, *The Body Knows*, p. 24, cf. p. 74.

[249]May, "Pleasure of Our Lives as Text," pp. 45, 46.

[250]Ibid., p. 47.

[251]Rosalee Bender, "Locating Ourselves in 'Godbecoming,' " *CGR* 10, no. 1 (1992): 56.

[252]Ibid., p. 55.

[253]Ibid., p. 57.

[254]Ibid., p. 58.

[255]Bender, "Locating Ourselves in 'Godbecoming,' " p. 58. Barbara Weiler affirms panentheism, especially as taught by Matthew Fox (Barbara Weiler, "Response to Veronica Dyck," *CGR* 14, no. 3 (1996): 296-301). Ruth Krall stresses the interconnectedness of all things and invites us to accept ongoing revelation in history and culture (Ruth Krall, "Anger and an Anabaptist Feminist Interpretation," *CGR* 14, no. 2 (1996): 151). These views are somewhat different.

[256]May, *The Body Knows*, p. 41.

[257]Ibid., p. 117 n. 7.

somewhat like Friesen, in "the sacramental nature of the universe."[259] He protests reducing the Lord's Supper to a human-communal process that fails to convey Mystery, to point toward the Other.[260]

The appeal to body-based desire, then, not only highlights faith's experiential, emotional and aesthetic dimensions, which theology must always reflect. It also provides some sort of transcendent apprehended with some degree of immediacy and certainty, which at least partially escapes the relativities of social location and the intellect's limitations.[261] Desire engenders passion, which can overflow the strict standards and social isolation of many Anabaptist communities. It finds commonality with expressions of Mystery in other "texts" like churches, religions and public life.

Overall, desire provides a contemporary possibility for conceiving that linking of inner spiritual life with the outer material world that Snyder finds central to Anabaptism.[262] It also offers a rare critique of the "community" theme lauded by Anabaptists, especially proponents of the unique biblical narrative. Yet does this approach point to a truly transcendent reality, or rather to some vitalistic, historical flow? Can it provide criteria for distinguishing among desire's promptings, and for establishing credible, alternative doctrines and ethics?

Summary

Just as my readings of historic Anabaptism will be influenced by others in that field, so my constructive theology will interact with the views and themes just sketched.

---

[258]Holland, "Einbildungskraft," p. 6.

[259]Ibid., p. 148 n.

[260]Scott Holland, review of *The Lord's Supper in Anabaptism*, by John Rempel, *CGR* 12, no. 1 (1994): 103-6; cf. "Even the Postmodern Story has a Body: Narrative, Poetry and Ritual," in *The Presence of Transcendence*, ed. Lieven Boeve and John Ries (Leuven, Belgium: Peeters, 2001). Still, this Other often lurks and works beyond "the Cathedral." "Theos in moments of kairos, refuses the logos of orthodoxy" and "enters history and the human soul not through established formulas . . . but through a heretical revolution of transgression, excess and gift"(Scott Holland, "When Bloch Pointed to the Cages Outside the Cathedral," in *Anabaptists and Postmodernity*, ed. Susan Biesecker-Mast and Gerald Biesecker-Mast [Telford, Penn.: Pandora, 2000], p. 152).

[261]Holland may not endorse immediate, veridical awareness of the divine. The "quiet voices" in each person are socially and linguistically constituted (Scott Holland, "Mennonites on Hauerwas, Hauerwas on Mennonites," *CGR* 13, no. 2 [1995]: 147), and God's presence is never unmediated (ibid., p. 148). Phil Stoltzfus, however, claims that Holland presents the aesthetic realm as simple "sensual immediacy," overlooking more complex interrelations with faith, thought and culture (Phil Stoltzfus, "Performative Envisioning," *CGR* 16, no. 3 [1998]: 80). In a sensually saturated culture Holland's emphasis can be interpreted as "Epicurean pleasure" and be commodified, as are most kinds of vivid experience (ibid., p. 82).

[262]Snyder, *Anabaptist History and Theology*.

Let me briefly identify, as I did in summarizing the historiography, some major issues they raise.

1. What is theology's starting point? Scripture in general, as evangelicals affirm (Wenger, Sider)? Or Scripture's unique narrative, centered on Jesus' story, the option selected by more Anabaptists than any other? Does narrative, however, simply mean rehearsal of past events, or at times those events brought to life through experience—as in McClendon's baptist vision or Kraus's focus on God as experienced? Further, might experience be broadened to include affectivity, especially desire (May, Holland)? And might the ethics derived from narrative at times provide as functional a starting point as the narrative itself (possibly Yoder, Weaver)?

Or might theology begin with classic Christian tradition? While only Reimer selects this explicitly, Sider and Wenger (and Bender) probably prioritize Protestant tradition. Or might theology possibly begin with general epistemological considerations, as for those influenced by postmodernity, and for Kaufman, with his focus on contemporary construction? Construction, as employed by Grimsrud and Liechty, can also render the contemporary Christian community a theological starting point. And might not community implicitly exercise a similar function for Yoder and J. D. Weaver, or for Harder and Pence Frantz, who stress communal biblical hermeneutic? Finally, scientific considerations can strongly affect the scope of theological questions and the form of their answers (Murphy, Ellis, Kaufman).

2. By stressing the social situatedness of knowledge, postmodernity questions most of the above starting points. How can theology—indeed, can theology—reach beyond its immediate context to appropriate any of them? Postmodernity also challenges idealizations of the church and its biblical, ethical and theological affirmations. It unmasks ways in which these hide or justify the concrete social shaping, with all its flaws, of texts, affirmations and communities (Harder, Swartzentruber, May, Holland).

Postmodernity favors beginning from and highlighting particularities of biblical narrative and of Anabaptist and other marginalized communities. Yet how can these—indeed, can these—carry universal relevance? Postmodernity questions whether any theology can make universal affirmations. But if none can, can churches really share a common global mission?

3. What is theology's main referent or primary concern? The options can be specified in light of polarities, or dynamisms such as transcendent/historical, spirit/matter, inner/outer and spiritual/social-ethical. Is theology's main referent God (Reimer), "God" (Kaufman, Friesen), or communal practices (Liechty, Swartzentruber; possibly Weaver, Yoder)? All Anabaptists stress historical life and ethics. Social ethics is regarded as Anabaptist theology's main contribution by thinkers so diverse as Sider, Yoder, Weaver, Friesen, Kaufman, Swartzentruber,

Liechty, Murphy and Ellis. Greater stress falls on the spiritual in Wenger, Dintaman, McClendon, Kraus, Holland, May and especially Reimer.

But how might spiritual reality be conceived today? Via classical ontology (Reimer), largely as Holy Spirit (Kraus), the Spirit with the risen Christ (McClendon), as Mystery (Kaufman, Friesen)? Via organizational levels (Murphy, Ellis),
as aroused by desire (Holland, May)? Snyder finds efforts to balance such polarities central to historic Anabaptism. Yet some historiography inclines toward the
social side themes (Bender, Friedmann, Stayer), some toward the spiritual (Packull, Beachy).

4. What is the role of other Christian theologies? Should Anabaptist theologians, in Weaver's words, adopt a theology-in-general and a second Anabaptist,
largely ethical list (Wenger, Sider, possibly Reimer)? Should they derive significant
content from broader methodologies (Kaufman, Friesen, Murphy, Ellis, Swartzentruber, Liechty, Holland, May), or seek to place all content in an Anabaptist framework (Yoder, J. D. Weaver, McClendon, Kraus, Grimsrud), or directly engage an
other approach, as many Anabaptist women engage feminism? This issue echoes the
relative importance of Anabaptist distinctives and commonalities with other movements in historiography.

More particularly, should Anabaptists affirm the historic creeds (Reimer,
Wenger, Sider), critique them (Weaver, Kaufman) or elaborate their strengths and
weaknesses (Yoder, Kraus, McClendon, Friesen)?

5. How can explication of Anabaptism's implicit theology contribute to the life
and mission of all churches in a world (1) enriched both by postmodernity's valuing of particularities and modernity's enhancement of communication through
globalization, and (2) threatened by postmodern fragmentation and globalization's
increasingly hegemonic domination.

4

SOME MAIN ASSUMPTIONS

Anabaptist theologians today travel along multiple paths. The variety of discoveries, insights and proposals is rich indeed. Yet readers may feel a bit overwhelmed: so many orientations label themselves Anabaptist that it can be difficult to discern what the term means and to evaluate the multiple conflicting claims.

To help clarify such confusions, the present work will attempt to identify its own assumptions, methods, norms and aims. This will not render it most worthy of the Anabaptist imprimatur. I simply seek to describe my particular path in hopes that some others will sketch theirs more clearly. Diverse theologies need not always clash but can enrich and balance each other. This will more likely occur when reasons for differences in scope, content and conclusions can be identified and evaluated.

To help readers follow my path as it interweaves many others, I will first set forth some main assumptions. I realize that by listing them now, I may create the impression that I simply assumed them before beginning research, and then imposed them on the data.

However, good research, and indeed thinking in general, seldom move in straight-line fashion: either from general premises, like my assumptions, to particular data (deduction), or from data to general conclusions (induction). Instead, thinking and research involve crisscrossing interplay among assumptions, data and many sorts of generalization.[1] This process, of course, is partly guided by various reasoning patterns and assumptions. Yet the thinker is often not explicitly aware of these. One's assumptions and reasoning methods are frequently modified, supplemented, discarded or even discovered during the actual process.

---

[1]Cf. Nancey Murphy, *Beyond Liberalism and Fundamentalism* (Valley Forge, Penn.:Trinity, 1996), pp. 11-35, 85-109.

In contrast to this (chronological) process, clear communication of thought by an author requires a more structured (logical) presentation. The major assumptions discovered and refined through research and reasoning play important roles in forming this structure. Consequently, the final written product can be better understood and evaluated if it distinguishes these assumptions from its particular data and arguments.

It is to help readers understand and evaluate what follows that I state my assumptions now. These assumptions did not provide an unquestioned (chronological) starting point but were revised, expanded, narrowed, intuited, sometimes even discovered (chronologically) in the manner just described. Only afterward have I (logically) articulated them and placed them here. Their validity rests on their success or failure in my overall task, including the handling of particular data.

THE GENERAL NATURE OF THEOLOGY

I. I define *theology*, generally following James McClendon, as the discovery, understanding and transformation of the basic convictions of religious communities, and relating these convictions coherently to each other and to whatever else exists.[2] It is often said that theology deals with beliefs. Beliefs frequently connote clearly understood intellectual affirmations. Convictions, however, are orientations toward life that shape a person's or group's every attitude and action. They cannot be relinquished without that person or group becoming very different at their roots.

Some convictions, of course, may also be beliefs. For instance, someone might consciously affirm that "good is stronger than evil" and regularly act on that basis in face of evil. Nevertheless, people who never think about this notion or often doubt it or even deny it intellectually may also act that way whenever the chips are down. By so doing they show that their lives are really guided by this conviction, even if they have never articulated it.[3] When such convictions are not explicit, they operate like what Robert Friedmann calls implicit theologies. As he argues, religious groups that have little explicit theology are nonetheless shaped by implicit convictions—otherwise they would never act as they do.

Theology then consists largely in rendering implicit convictions explicit, yet not by simply discovering and then merely stating what a religious community already assumes. Theology also transforms or critically revises the community's affirma-

---

[2]Cf. James McClendon, *Systematic Theology*, vol. I, *Ethics* (Nashville: Abingdon, 1986), p. 23.

[3]People may also affirm beliefs consciously but contradict them in their actions, indicating that these are not really convictions. Theology asks whether stated beliefs are really functioning as convictions, and if not, what unstated convictions are really operating. It aims to bring explicit verbalizations into better correspondence with actual implicit orientations.

tions in light of the community's most basic norms, challenges from its culture and interaction among these.

2. Christian theology is a task of the church, undertaken to guide its worship, fellowship and mission. It is not a public task erected on general cultural understandings of religious concepts (as Gordon Kaufman claims).

3. Nonetheless, the church cannot be cleanly separated from the world, though Anabaptists have sometimes attempted this. Theology is always in dialogue with its cultural context (Duane Friesen), including the academic sphere. Theology tests the church's current beliefs and often revises them through conversation with its culture (see 17 on pp. 100-101). Anabaptists should not only celebrate their distinctives but also recognize how preoccupation with distinctives can encourage narrowness, exclusivity and a false sense of superiority (Scott Holland, Melanie May, Elaine Swartzentruber).

4. Since theology articulates norms and visions to guide the church, these will often critique present beliefs and practices. Description of these ideals, however, should never imply that churches or individuals have attained them and thereby legitimate current situations and mask their shortcomings (Swartzentruber, May, Holland, Lydia Harder).

5. At the church's center is a kerygma, or revelatory claim, about specific historical events and their meanings which, when appropriated, are the source of its life (esp. affirmed by John Yoder, J. Denny Weaver, Norman Kraus, James McClendon).[4] Basic kerygmatic themes were well expressed in the earliest Christian confessions.[5] This kerygma is not simply a recital of events but also an active, divine communication of their significance (stressed by McClendon and Kraus). These

---

[4]C. H. Dodd found the kerygma expressed narratively in Acts 2:14-39; 3:23-26; 4:10-12; 5:30-32; 10:26-40; 13:17-41. He validated its primitive character by evidence that it was presupposed by Paul (Rom 1:1; 2:16; 8:34; 10:8-9; 14:9; 1 Cor 1:23; 2:2-5; 15:1-7; Gal 1:3-4; 3:1; 4:6; 1 Thess 1:10). Dodd found its broad emphases congruent with Mark 1:15. The kerygma announced, basically, that God's promises to Israel had been fulfilled in the ministry, death and resurrection of Jesus, who would return as final Judge. The boundary had been crossed between the old age (out of which Jesus delivered us) and new age (begun with his resurrection and ascension). Jesus was now Lord of the cosmos, though this would be manifest only at his return. Jesus was raised through God's Spirit, who was poured out on those repent and believe (*The Apostolic Preaching and Its Developments* [New York: Harper, 1964]: 7-35). The kerygma closed with the promise of forgiveness and salvation to those who responded (cf. Thomas Finger, *Christian Theology: An Eschatological Approach* [Scottdale, Penn.: Herald, 1985], 1:35-40, 120-25). In my theology the kerygma's significance is illuminated by its communal and missional matrix (esp. Acts 2–3).

[5]Oscar Cullmann found the core of the earliest confessions in "Jesus Christ is Lord" (*The Earliest Christian Confessions* [London: Lutterworth, 1949]). These identified Jesus as the fulfillment of Israel's messianic hopes, and even more as present, reigning cosmic Lord. This Lordship was inseparable from his subjection of the powers. It entailed his return, though this was not always explicitly confessed.

events form a narrative centering around Jesus of Nazareth.[6] When this past is appropriated in the present, the life so mediated flows toward the future.

6. Postmodernity challenges the preceding claim. It asks how data and convictions found in any one culture or historical setting can be significant for others, and whether they can inform more general valid affirmations. For if we apprehend everything through contemporary, culturally constructed frameworks, how can former or different contemporary cultures speak to us in their own voices? Won't such data be restructured so thoroughly by our frameworks that we cannot perceive what they meant or mean? And if they are, this data apparently cannot really challenge or transform today's basic cultural outlook, or be incorporated into affirmations that transcend some or even all cultures. (Kaufman, Daniel Liechty and Ted Grimsrud's neo-Mennonites, by foregrounding contemporary construction, raise this issue acutely.)

My response, basically, is that even these critiques of general affirmations tacitly employ several themselves. Postmodernists who stress gaps between cultures often do so to affirm the integrity of each—especially to enable marginalized cultures to be heard in their own voices, and not be drowned out by established majorities. This effort rightly includes the unmasking of alleged universal "truths" that really promote the interests of some cultures over others. However, this entire task involves the tacit assumption that each culture, and ultimately each person, has integrity—has something to contribute to others if allowed to speak in its authentic voice. Since this assumption is all-inclusive, it's universal.

To encourage such contributions many postmodernists valorize free, uncoerced conversation among cultures. Such conversations, however, implicitly presuppose that people in one culture can indeed learn something new from another. In other words, if such conversation is possible, one's cultural starting point cannot wholly shape and determine what one perceives in others. To believe that cultures can learn from each other and to encourage this, one must presuppose that knowledge is not wholly conditioned and limited by one's own culture. In fact, one could not even ask whether knowledge is so conditioned unless one were already aware of other cultures and some of their genuine differences. Moreover, one could not even rec-

---

No more than the kerygma did confessions simply list events. Confession was elicited by the Spirit in worship and also in public where it implied that "Caesar is not Lord," and brought persecution. Dodd's kerygma and Cullmann's confessions formed the historical baseline for Yoder's early Christology (*Preface to Theology: Christology and Theological Method* [Grand Rapids: Brazos, 2002], pp. 54-57, 71-78).

[6]I understand the biblical narrative to be rooted in actual historical events, and yet it also conveys the meaning of those events. While event and meaning can be distinguished to some degree, I find attempts to separate them artificial.

ognize one's culture as different from others without some general criteria, which cannot be solely the product of any one, and which enable them to be compared.[7]

This also means that significant new things can be discovered about events, ideas and values from previous cultures and time periods. We can move beyond the present and hear the past in its own voice (Jo-Ann Martens, cf. Sheila Klassen-Wiebe). Still, our cultural location will shape and limit all efforts to know the past. So will our intentions for utilizing such knowledge in the present and future. Fully accurate knowledge of the past can only be pursued as a (not fully attainable) goal. This issue will receive further consideration, especially in connection with the universality of theological affirmations (see "Contemporary Appropriations" on pp. 230-32, 280-83).

7. The life communicated through the kerygma is conveyed ultimately by the Holy Spirit and involves an irreducible spiritual dimension. Yet it is mediated by social factors, psychological factors such as the imagination and intellect, and physical ones, such as the body with its desires (May, Holland, Rosalee Bender). This life, however, is not wholly reducible to any or all of these mediating channels.

8. All authentic Christian living and thinking moves back and forth among three poles. They appropriate the events at their origin, whose significance they seek to actualize in the present and which press toward further, future actualization.

9. The events and meanings associated with Jesus, which are crystallized in the church's kerygma, carry authority for its present and future. They provide criteria and norms for evaluating and guiding action and thought in the present and for envisioning the future.

10. This process involves thought. Appropriating the foundational events requires some learning. Actualizing their significance necessitates some knowledge of the present context along with creative thinking about this context's relation to the past events and the significance of both for the future. Such thought includes imagination and is partly shaped by the body and its desires (May, Holland). Imagination, desire and the life- and thought-forms of the context can provide sources for theology and material about which theology reflects. However, none of these provide norms for determining the truth of theological affirmations (cf. 17 on pp. 100-101).

11. Such thinking is often elicited by some present "impression point" (Harder) in light of which the past is consulted. Since this thinking is rooted in the

---

[7]Cf. Thomas Finger, "Confessing Truth in a Pluralistic World," in *Practicing Truth*, ed. David Shenk and Linford Stutzman (Scottdale, Penn.: Herald, 1999); " 'Universal Truths?': Should Anabaptist Theologians Seek to Articulate Them?" in *Anabaptists and Postmodernity*, ed. Susan Biesecker-Mast and Gerald Biesecker-Mast (Telford, Penn.: Pandora, 2000).

church's overall life and directed toward future action, it involves much reflection on practice.[8] Texts or events from the past also initiate this process. Yet in all cases, whatever elicits thought is ultimately received and perceived in light of the Jesus story transmitted through the church's history. Accordingly, while reflection may "start from" experience (chronologically), it is always initially shaped (logically) by this history, including its theological dimensions, and at least implicitly directed toward the future.

12. Despite significant differences among past and present conceptualities, our ability to identify and differentiate among them indicates that some significant connections exist between our thought world and previous ones. These all cannot be such distinct constructions as Kaufman, Liechty and Grimsrud's neo-Mennonites often imply. Words like *God*, for instance, involve histories too lengthy to be constructed entirely afresh, except quite arbitrarily. Christian theology's true meanings "for *us*," for "*our* reality,"[9] are in continuity with its authentic past meanings. When past texts are explored in light of present texts and contexts, their own significance need not remain obscure. On the contrary, previously unrecognized meanings of the former can be discovered this way, as Anabaptist women theologians often stress. Nonetheless, such explorations can also project current views into the past and must aim to avoid this by truly hearing the latter (cf. point 16 on p. 100).

13. The kerygmatic events involved conflict between God's goodness and the evil in the world. That conflict still continues. Consequently, it is crucial for current and future well-being that these events and their interpretations be recovered and their significance be actualized today and tomorrow.

14. Since the founding events and interpretations had to be communicated widely, written accounts of them became indispensable. Much diversity exists among these accounts, showing that such events could be transmitted and interpreted in multiple ways. Most such writings, however, also excluded other interpretations as false and as opposing them in the basic conflict between good and evil. Such struggles eventually necessitated that interpretations within a given range be acknowledged as authoritative and distinguished from others that were not. Consequently, a faith rooted in historical events and interpretations and intended for future generations found a collection of authoritative writings (canon) indispensable.

15. In my theology, then, the Bible provides the ultimate norm for evaluating

---

[8]*Practice* is a more general term than *praxis*, which, as usually defined, involves movement toward some sociopolitical option. While all theological thinking has sociopolitical implications, it is not always aimed directly toward them.

[9]Grimsrud, "Mennonite Theology and Historical Consciousness," p. 52.

historic Anabaptism and the current context, and for guiding the future. However, diversities among canonical writings require that they be read according to some pattern (hermeneutic) to function authoritatively. The canon is structured along the lines of a narrative stretching from creation to consummation, centered on Jesus' life, death and resurrection. This narrative provides the interpretive pattern. But precisely speaking, the Bible as canon—not the narrative somehow abstracted from it—is the ultimate norm.[10]

Since genuine knowledge of historical particularity is possible, theology should seek to hear the biblical authors' intentions as accurately as possible and interconnect them hermeneutically in line with the canonical framework—as an ultimate, though never fully attainable, goal.

16. Biblical authority includes the recognition that most writings include a range of meanings, reflecting many voices (Pence Frantz, Harder). Different valid meanings will be discovered in varying socio-historical contexts, often as people address questions shaped by current life forms and conceptualities to the texts. Such meanings come alive through the Holy Spirit, guiding the church toward the future. In this sense the texts' living authority becomes actual through contemporary appropriation.

Yet neither the church nor its traditions nor particular interpreting communities nor experiences and conceptualities addressed to the texts or the Spirit as distinct from the texts provide final norms for theology. Dorothy Jean Weaver, Gayle Gerber Koontz, Mary Schertz and Rachel Reesor show how the texts themselves, approached both as authoritative and in light of current issues, can yield numerous new meanings.

17. Since theology is always pursued within a cultural context, this context provides guidance and standards of a sort.[11] Since theology must make sense to people, a context's language, thought and life forms provide standards of intelligibility. Since theology must address at least some crucial issues in its setting, such issues help provide standards of relevance. Further, these thought and life forms provide sources for theology, material theology reflects on. In face of a culture's "texts" (Holland), that is, theology, cannot simply repeat past expressions of its kerygma but must be intelligible and relevant to that culture. If it is not, theology obscures

---

[10]I will sometimes refer to it as "Scripture"—singular. Since this term means a canon or collection, it entails that diversities among writings are important (cf. Finger, *Christian Theology: An Eschatological Approach*, 1:214-17).

[11]I once spoke of a contextual norm (ibid., p. 54). But this could create the impression that it functioned on the same level as my biblical norm to determine theology's truth, as Donald Bloesch objected (see *A Theology of Word and Spirit* [Downers Grove, Ill.: InterVarsity Press, 1992], p. 117, esp. 302 n. 46).

the kerygma's present and future vitality.

Yet some thought and life forms in any context conflict with the kerygma. The context cannot, therefore, provide norms to determine the truth of theological affirmations. Only Scripture provides theology's overall norm (read intracanonically, centering on the narrative climaxing in Jesus). Theology then must indeed "construct new conceptualities" for wrestling with current issues. This, however, does not equal constructing new meanings determined by contemporary thought and life forms (Kaufman, Grimsrud's neo-Mennonites), for the meanings theology seeks to express stretch from the past through the present into the future.

18. Challenges to articulate the kerygma anew also arose in past cultures. Many past responses crystallized into theological traditions. These shape today's hearing of the kerygma, even if people are unaware of them. Interaction with other traditions also shapes any one tradition, including Anabaptism, though people may again be ignorant of this. All traditions contain significant insights into the kerygma, which theology should appropriate if possible. This requires acquaintance with these traditions and their development amidst other cultural contexts and traditions. All such traditions, though, also distort the kerygma in ways that theology should critique. Some valuable critiques, however, have already appeared in other traditions, although they often come to us as affirmations (e.g., the priesthood of all believers). To appropriate these, theology must again appreciate the contexts where they developed.

Any Christian theology, then, involves intertextual shaping through other Christian traditions. The way any tradition expresses its distinctives arose, and arises, in part from disagreements with others. On the other hand, any Christian tradition also agrees with others at points. To explicate only a tradition's distinctives or commonalities with others yields an incomplete and distorted picture. My theology, then, will dialogue with both the differences and similarities found in other Christian texts, and will seek to dilute neither.[12]

APPROACH TO HISTORIC ANABAPTISM

1. Historic Anabaptist emphases entail at least implicit theological themes amenable to fuller intellectual explication (Friedmann).

2. In accord with most current historiography, historic Anabaptism will refer to all groups who practiced believers' baptism in the Reformation era (more precisely, 1525-1575). During this time the bodies that survived (Swiss Brethren, Hutterites, Mennonites) journeyed from radical beginnings to highly organized bodies,

---

[12]Cf. Thomas Finger, "Appropriating Other Traditions While Remaining Anabaptist," *CGR* 17, no 2 (1999).

actualizing a broad range of Anabaptist possibilities. The latter date (1575) also allows for formation of the Polish Brethren, who practiced believers' baptism though they did not finally survive. This fate, however, renders them no less significant an expression of historic Anabaptism. While Anabaptism is often associated with this particular time frame, its relative brevity is also congruent with limitations of my competence and of space in this volume. Other time frames might lead to somewhat different theologies in Anabaptist perspective.

3. I organize my presentation of historic (and current) Anabaptism around a general theme: the coming of the new creation in three inseparable dimensions: personal, communal and missional (see introduction to part two, pp. 105-7). However, I represent neither this nor any other features as Anabaptism's definitive characteristics or essence. Moreover, even when distinctives of any historical movement are identified, it never possesses them in the sense that it would remain basically the same if all other features were removed or varied. The shape of a historical movement involves both features distinct to it and commonalities it shares with others (cf. point 18 on p. 101; contra Robert Friedmann, who finds Anabaptism unique).[13] A movement's distinctives, however, can configure it as a whole, including its shared features, in unusual, even unique ways.

4. I adopt a polygenetic understanding of origins: that Anabaptism arose from three largely distinct sources—Swiss, South German-Austrian, Dutch—and a relatively distinct fourth one—Polish, with some Italian provenance. I also acknowledge early crossfertilizations among the first three. I will seek to give each of these three roughly equal consideration. Yet South Germany-Austria produced the greatest quantity and variety of theological writing, the Netherlands less and Switzerland least. For this reason, the space allotted to each stream will often vary, though their relative importance will not. Polish Anabaptism will be closely examined only in reference to Christology and the Trinity. Other identifications and weightings of sources might lead to somewhat different theologies in Anabaptist perspective.

5. Recognizing Anabaptism's largely peasant-artisan character, I refer to occasional writings and popular sources when I can. I take serious account of social, economic and political factors. However, longer or collected writings of well-known leaders will furnish the most extensive resources for exploring Anabaptist theology. I highlight these mostly because of my subject matter, not a strong preference for ideas over socio-historical factors.

CONTEMPORARY CONTEXT AND AUDIENCE
1. I write chiefly for Western, mostly North American audiences, where church mem-

---

[13]Robert Friedmann, *The Theology of Anabaptism* (Scottdale, Penn.: Herald, 1973), p. 27.

bers are becoming more highly educated and most church leaders possess graduate degrees. For Anabaptist insights to be accessible in such a culture, they can usefully be presented in a somewhat comprehensive, interconnected manner, in dialogue with dominant cultural conceptualities. This can be in a form shaped by interaction with the Western systematic tradition. Yet this is by no means the only useful form. I only propose that it can be helpful, in light of the factors just mentioned.

2. At the same time I aim to convey to these audiences insights from an oppressed, marginalized tradition. By using an academic format to express perspectives and sensitivities not often found in such works, I hope to draw readers toward involvement with people from less privileged locations.

3. I deem articulation of Anabaptist and similar movements' theologies crucial for the churches' global mission. A postmodern outlook is opening many churches to the unexpectedly rich resources of marginalized traditions. These can help churches assist the numerous marginalized peoples threatened by increasingly powerful expressions of modernity, especially globalization (cf. chap. I). Yet while appreciating this postmodern opportunity, I find it important to critique its fragmenting tendencies. While critical of modernity's tendencies toward economic and cultural domination, I appreciate its potential for enhancing global communication and understanding.

4. Numerous churches today have educated leaders who do some teaching. Many of these, along with many laity, receive education in settings where questions about what is truly Anabaptist and how to communicate this are explored. These inquiries are informed by historical and (more recently) theological research. Yet much of this material is somewhat disconnected and can be confusing. This volume is intended to lessen that confusion so Anabaptist insights might be better perceived and communicated. It is aimed chiefly at people researching these areas and those who have studied or are studying them. The overall goal, however, is that through them these insights might be more effectively taught and incarnated in congregations.

5. Many leaders and educated members of other churches explore similar questions about their own communions. In our ecumenical era this often leads to interest in other traditions. Such people can gain much from an Anabaptist perspective. I try to show how Anabaptist insights can illumine issues of concern to evangelicals, mainline ecumenicals, Catholics, Protestants and Orthodox. I hope that my "sectarian" tradition can make significant ecumenical contributions.

6. The locus of my theologizing is the worshiping, fellowshiping church in mission, and it is primarily intended to affect this arena (cf. point 2 on p. 96). However, many traditions that I engage are also shaped by academia. I also hope that it will contribute to and be enriched by discussions there, especially since academia is now quite interested in particular and minority traditions.

7. I consider the question of whether some reality transcends the historical process, which modernity tends to deny but to which postmodernity is more open,
crucial today (cf. chap. I, excursus). Most theologians today affirm such a reality
and that it exceeds the sum total of matter-energy and its interactions.[14] For many,
this reality is also intrinsically connected with some features of the universe and always has been. Traditionally, though, divine transcendence has meant that whatever
is uniquely characteristic of God as God, or "by nature," is not intrinsically connected with or dependent on anything else.[15] To discuss this issue I will use "ontological distinction" to indicate this differentiation of God from matter-energy and
whatever else there might be.

Christian theologians usually have also maintained that God created all other
realities and interacts with them by grace. I will use "ontological barrier" to indicate the view that God acts on other realities and Spirit acts on matter-energy, only
externally, or at a distance.[16] I will use "ontological transformation" to indicate the
contrasting view that God directly touches and alters some other realities and that
Spirit alters matter-energy internally. Ontological transformation, however, is by
God (or by Spirit)—not into God (or Spirit). That is, even in so close a relationship the ontological distinction between God and all else remains. Though ontology can mean many things, including descriptions of the being of all kinds of realities, I will use it mostly in this limited way.[17]

---

[14]I use *matter-energy* because the cosmos's ultimate components, in science today, exhibit features of both.
"Energy," so used, is as physical as matter, not something transcending it; cf. pp. 252-254, 419-21.

[15]Advocates of the first view differentiate it from pantheism, which means that God *(theos)* equals the
sum total of reality, or is everything *(pan)*. They usually call it panentheism, meaning that God is in
(en) everything. Literally translated, panentheism could describe the second view also, since its God
is omnipresent by grace. Today, however, panentheism nearly always indicates the first view (for discussion of it in Sally McFague, Rosemary Ruether, process theology and others, see Thomas Finger,
Self, Earth and Society [Downers Grove, Ill.: InterVarsity Press, 1997], pp. 168-92, 305-12; and "Trinity, Ecology and Panentheism," *Christian Scholar's Review* 271, no. I [1997]).

[16]*Spirit* will be defined more precisely in chapter eight. The "ontological barrier" will become important in chapter six.

[17]In chapter eight, however, *ontological* will often refer to God's being. Chapter seven will use *ontological*
to mean what is the case in contrast to *epistemological*, meaning what we know. I will also mention an
ontology of violence since Nancey Murphy and George Ellis use it often (*On the Moral Nature of the
Universe* [Minneapolis: Fortress, 1996], taken from John Millbank), though *ontology* means something somewhat different there. Murphy and Ellis apparently affirm divine transcendence in my
sense (God "exists in a totally different order of reality or being" [ibid., p. 57, cf. pp. 6-7]). But I
am unsure about Murphy's "ontological" reduction of higher levels to lower ones ("Nonreductive
Physicalism: Philosophical Issues," in *Whatever Happened to the Soul?* ed. Warren Brown Murphy and H.
Newton Maloney [Minneapolis: Fortress, 1998], p. 131; cf. chap. 3 n. 187 on p. 79).

PART II

THE COMING OF THE
NEW CREATION

I am proposing that the relatively little-known Anabaptist movement can provide significant resources for many theological issues facing churches today. While Anabaptism's contributions to Christian ethics have often been appreciated, most people, even among Anabaptism's heirs, assume that its strengths lie only there. I argue, however, that these ethics are shaped and fortified by a profound implicit theology only beginning to be explored. If the convictions comprising this theology can be explicated, they will, I believe, enrich not only similar, historically marginalized churches but also mainstream communions. Such a theology can help all churches address both postmodern trends toward particularity and modern trends toward globalization.

Several theologians have begun this task, and a variety of interesting insights and proposals have emerged. Yet some confusion exists over what *Anabaptist* means, and there is some disagreement over how theology should be done. To help clarify these issues I identified several of my own assumptions and procedures (cf. chap. 4), and will compare them with my fellow travelers'. Like some of them I begin from a kerygma, or revelatory claim, about particular historical events and their meanings found in the biblical narrative centering around Jesus. Scripture, understood as a canon structured in line with this narrative, provides my ultimate theological norm.

Were I to jump from Scripture to the present, however, I would leave historic Anabaptism's important role unclear. To avoid this I devote the first halves of the next six chapters, or sections of them, to my reading of historic Anabaptism, that is, its Swiss, South German-Austrian, Dutch and Polish expressions from 1525-1575. I organize historic and current Anabaptist thought around an interpretive center: The coming of the new creation in three inseparable dimensions—personal, communal and missional. Though I will not treat this as Anabaptism's essence, let me briefly explain why I choose it over other plausible options.

Many Anabaptists opt for discipleship (often understood to include community and nonviolence, the other two components of Harold Bender's Anabaptist Vision). Discipleship, however, is often understood largely in social-ethical terms, omitting the transcendent aspects that Bender himself took for granted (cf. chap. 3). Another possibility is the kingdom of God, which Jesus made his ministry's main theme. *Kingdom* is more comprehensive than discipleship. Yet its use also often privileges the sociopolitical dimension, minimizing the personal, transcendent and environmental. *Peace,* understood as shalom, can remedy this, for it involves humankind's relationships with not only each other but also God and nonhuman nature. Yet current Anabaptist parlance often reduces peace to one essential Christian social practice.

Though each term properly understood could designate Anabaptism's interpretive center, all sometimes connote reductions of theology toward social ethics. Since I intend to examine this trend, I sought another comprehensive notion. Chapter two showed how Anabaptists highlighted total transformation of life. Their concerns were broadly soteriological.[1] Transformation, further, affected not simply individuals or even churches, for both were aspects of a cosmic, eschatological alteration. To designate this, *creation* sounded preferable to *kingdom* or *peace.* Since this transformation sharply opposed the present situation, it was radically new. And although it was not yet complete, it was already operating with great dynamism, or coming. I am aware that it may seem strange to select so comprehensive a theme for Anabaptism since it is often regarded as "separatist."

To underscore this comprehensiveness I will try to show how the coming of the new creation inseparably intertwines three dimensions that Christians today often separate: the personal, communal and missional. Paradoxically, to stress that historic Anabaptists did not separate them, I will begin with these distinctions and then show how they break down when applied to Anabaptism. Were I investigating these realities from a different cultural context, I might not conceptualize them this way.

I will begin with a chapter on each of these dimensions (chaps. 5-7) and relegate eschatology to its usual position: the end (chap. 10). From there it will help me

---

[1] C. Arnold Snyder, *Anabaptist History and Theology* (Kitchener, Ont.: Pandora, 1995), p. 384. Robert Friedmann, however, maintained that " 'soteriology' . . . cannot be a major theme in Anabaptist thought." Yet he was using this term quite narrowly, for the individual concern to "escape eternal damnation" or "find a gracious God" (*The Theology of Anabaptism* [Scottdale, Penn.: Herald, 1973], p. 78).

review the whole and indicate more fully how this coming can shape all loci in Anabaptist theology.

My threefold distinction, even if provisional, requires beginning with one dimension. Very good reasons can be given for each. I have opted for whatever best promotes descriptive clarity. This I believe will be a narrative sequence running from personal conversion through communal involvement into missional practice (which, of course, leads to further conversions and communal involvements). Historic Anabaptism involved a radical challenge to and disjunction from the status quo. I can best portray this by beginning from the anguish and conflict that most people experienced as they entered the movement.

This personal starting point could, of course, render my theology overly individualistic. I will seek to avoid this by repeatedly indicating that conversion is to a community, that personal experience occurs within this context and that all this spills over into mission (which again calls for personal transformation in communities).

Chapter five explores the new creation's personal dimension, in dialogue with current ecumenical discussion on justification and divinization. Chapter six covers the communal dimension under four headings: baptism, the Lord's Supper, discipline, and economic sharing, considering liberation theology as well as ecumenical perspectives. Chapter seven approaches the new creation's missional dimension, focusing on the kerygma's universality in conversation with postmodernity and Gordon Kaufman; and the church-world relationship, interacting with current Anabaptist approaches found in Duane Friesen, Norman Kraus and "conflict transformation."

Part two, then, considers those concrete, experiential transformative processes to which historic Anabaptists devoted most attention. In this sense Anabaptists lent these a certain priority. However, we will find that participation in these processes was intrinsically shaped by convictions on themes found in formal theology. To accurately explicate Anabaptism's implicit theology these must also be treated. Part three considers three components of this convictional framework: Christology, anthropology and eschatology (chaps. 8-10).

5

THE PERSONAL DIMENSION

Some current Anabaptist theologies that stress social ethical aspects of Christian life grant little space to the personal. They rightly fear that in our individualistic culture the former could get lost. To avoid this they underplay those inward and spiritual concerns that characterize evangelicals more than "ecumenicals." Historic Anabaptism, however, would never have arisen had not the new creation's call aroused profound inner struggle and transformation, which continued within those who took up their crosses in response. Contemporary theology in Anabaptist perspective must find ways to affirm this while simultaneously linking it with the new creation's communal and missional dimensions.

In Reformation times the personal dimension came to the fore in disputes about justification by faith. Today scholars debate how well such language can express the Anabaptist orientation, then or now. Robert Friedmann found "A forensic view of grace, in which the sinner is . . . undeservedly justified . . . simply unacceptable" to Anabaptists.[1] A more nuanced scholar like Arnold Snyder can assert that historic Anabaptists "never talked about being 'justified by faith.' "[2] Yet Snyder's investigations show that they often linked justification words with faith terms. Apparently his point is that Anabaptists critiqued Protestant talk of "faith alone" and sharp separations of faith or righteousness from works of a transformed life.[3]

---

[1]Robert Friedmann, *The Theology of Anabaptism* (Scottdale, Penn.: Herald, 1973), p. 91.

[2]C. Arnold Snyder, *From Anabaptist Seed* (Kitchener, Ont.: Pandora, 1999), p. 19.

[3]E.g., C. Arnold Snyder, *Anabaptist History and Theology* (Kitchener, Ont.: Pandora, 1995), pp. 44, 87, 371-72. The first of Hubmaier's "18 Theses Concerning the Christian Life" ran: "Faith alone makes us righteous before God." The third thesis, however, showed what kind of faith Hubmaier meant: it "cannot be idle, but must break forth . . . in all sorts of works of brotherly love" (*Balthasar Hubmaier,* ed. Wayne Pipkin and John Yoder [Scottdale, Penn.: Herald, 1989], p. 32). Precisely speaking, Hubmaier wrote this before becoming Anabaptist. But even if Snyder is somehow technically correct, I find his flat assertion misleading.

However, might the Anabaptists' fairly frequent use of justification language have expressed not simply their response to others but also their own outlook to some extent? Were such Anabaptist texts shaped not just externally but also to some degree internally? I suggest that we search for Anabaptist understandings by employing justification language as an exploratory framework. We can begin, that is, by asking where Anabaptists did and did not approximate it. If we find that this vocabulary did not always best conceptualize their deepest apprehensions, we can move beyond it, to search for more uniquely Anabaptist understandings. (On this topic I am proposing that we discover historic Anabaptist distinctives by beginning from yet going beyond commonalities shared with other traditions.)

Considering justification may also help Anabaptists contribute to contemporary theology. After centuries of division evangelicals and Catholics are finding convergences on this theme, while Catholics and Lutherans have signed a joint declaration on justification. Historic Anabaptists appeared to affirm sometimes Catholic, sometimes Protestant, sometimes quite differing views on this topic. But what if this diversity did not express confusion but an implicit soteriology that integrated some of the conflicting emphases? If it were explicated, might it contribute to today's discussion?

In hope that it might I will interact with these conversations as I construct my own soteriology (see "Contemporary Appropriations," pp. 132-56). By then, however, it will be clear that Anabaptist understandings of personal salvation involve another notion, divinization. Though this appeared in medieval Catholicism, it was, and is, more prominent in Eastern Orthodoxy. (It is also found, less thematized, in marginalized traditions such as Pentecostal and Quaker.) For now, to prepare our provisional investigative framework I will briefly sketch the original Catholic-Protestant controversy over justification (quite generally, though I am well aware of nuances and exceptions).

THE REFORMATION DEBATE

Medieval Catholics spoke of twofold justification. A person was justified in the first sense at baptism, usually as an infant. There God bestowed forgiveness of sins and a saving relationship that would last eternally if the person always kept it. As people matured, however, they broke this relationship through committing mortal sin. Nevertheless, God might grant justification again—justification of the first kind—though only through the sacrament of penance. In this first justification, God accepted people who were not yet fully righteous.

Catholicism affirmed, however, that God's ultimate purpose was to make people fully righteous. When they attained this, they were justified in the second sense. When did this occur? For a few saintly people, at death or perhaps even before. But clearly most were not fully righteous at death. Some were under mortal sin and eternally lost, but the rest had been justified in the first sense (through baptism and, usually, penance). When would they attain the second justification?

To express it positively, they attain the second justification when they obtain full righteousness. This process was conceptualized as acquiring merit through good works. But this had a reverse side, which was often stressed more strongly: purgation from all sin. For most people this required a lengthy stay in purgatory. Though this process was really sanctifying, in popular presentations purgatory often appeared about like hell.

Catholic theology considered justification mostly in connection with penance. According to Thomas Aquinas (1225-1274) justification, from God's standpoint beyond time, was a single act of grace. God simultaneously bestowed forgiveness, repentance (turning from sin) and faith (turning to God). In the experience of penitent adults, however, this spread out into various acts of repentance and faith over time.[4] And while justification was initially received by faith, Catholics believed that faith is increasingly formed by love.

True faith then would produce good works. Accordingly, justification for Catholics was a process. It was received by faith but also involved acts of repentance and loving works, until people finally became fully righteous. Justification, accordingly, could be increased.

Medieval Catholics expected that in a truly penitent person evidence of formation by love and true righteousness would appear. Penance, accordingly, also was usually a process, including many penitent acts. Absolution came only at the end, reuniting penitents with the church and justifying them (in the first sense) once again. Consequently, the preceding acts could be called preparation for justification.

Yet medieval Catholics often viewed penance as they did purgatory: in negative, punitive ways. The acts involved—theoretically, righteous acts formed by love flowing from grace—they called satisfactions. Priests often prescribed specific satisfactions that were humiliating and severe. It was easy for penitents, and really all Christians, to suppose that such works were required to earn God's grace—a notion strengthened by the concept of merit.

Though this was not official church doctrine,[5] the Protestant Reformers complained that justification by works was the prevailing teaching. The apparent neces-

---

[4] Aquinas *Summa Theologica* pt. 2.1, Q.113aa.2-8; cf. Q.114a.5.

[5] According to the official teaching, from the Second Council of Orange (529 C.E.), repentance and good works were possible only when God initiated, guided and energized the entire process (*The Church Teaches: Documents of the Church in English Translation*, ed. John Clarkson et al. [St. Louis: B. Herder, 1955], pp. 225-29).

sity of acquiring merit enough and a character righteous enough to earn justification instilled great anxiety. To relieve this the Reformers insisted that justification arises solely from God's initiative, from grace. To underline this they insisted that justification is received only by faith. And to foreground faith's receptive character, they often opposed it, rhetorically, to all works.[6] They could stress justification "by faith alone" and deny that justifying faith was formed by love since loving behavior involved human work.[7] Preparation for justification too was out since this seemed to imply earning it by works.

To highlight God's initiative the Reformers often conceptualized justification in legal terms: God declared or reckoned people righteous; God imputed righteousness to them. The Reformers meant to deny that justification was based on or given as a reward for any righteousness acquired by humans. Yet this conceptuality could make justification appear wholly abstract—simply a divine decision without affect on human life since it did not alter the sinner's actual righteousness or lack thereof.

The Reformers did affirm that all who are truly justified would perform good works and become more righteous. Yet they insisted on the sharp theological distinction between justification, or imputation of righteousness, as God's act and the increase of righteousness in justified persons, which involved human activity and was eventually called sanctification. Justification itself could never be increased.

Protestants usually prioritized justification and faith over sanctification and works. To accent this Martin Luther declared that a justified person is "righteous and a sinner at the same time" (simul justus et peccator). Many understood this to mean that a faith decision by itself guarantees salvation regardless of how the person lives. This attitude sometimes reappeared much later in evangelicalism.

In brief, Protestants stressed salvation's divine and spiritual origin but could minimize its human and ethical dimensions. Yet they were reacting against Catholics who focused so much on the human-ethical that they seemed to place salvation on that level. Perhaps this was partly because Catholics emphasized justification's future goal and thus tended to view it as a process. Protestants, however, focused on justification's origin; this could make it seem like a punctiliar event.

As we explore Anabaptist understandings of the new creation's personal dimension, the issues just sketched will provide an initial framework for asking what they thought. This framework will also alert us to expressions that do not fit or in which

---

[6]Yet they taught that true faith produces good works, and responded to objections that they did not (e.g., The Augsburg Confession, arts. 6, 20).

[7]E.g., Robert Kolb and Timothy Wengert, eds., The Book of Concord (Minneapolis: Fortress, 2000), pp. 138-39.

Catholic or Protestant emphases were differently configured. (I must, of course, often speak quite generally, not stopping for variations and exceptions.)

HISTORIC ANABAPTIST PERSPECTIVES

All my historical sections will begin with Switzerland, where Anabaptism first arose. The Bender school prioritized the Swiss as normative, somewhat Protestantized Anabaptism (see "Contemporary Approaches to Historic Anabaptism" on pp. 48-50). By surveying Swiss views first and then comparing them with other Anabaptists sources, we can gain some sense of the contrast between Bender's approach and those that allot differing weights to the others.

Few extant Swiss writings besides Hubmaier's address theological issues in depth. Bender, however, minimized Hubmaier.[8] Yet if Hubmaier is eliminated, little detailed information on Swiss Anabaptist theology remains. This makes it easier to suppose, as Bender apparently did, that because the Swiss were biblical they must have developed a "consistent evangelical Protestantism."[9]

Switzerland

In 1524 Conrad Grebel and his friends voiced a common complaint against the perceived consequences of justification by faith alone: "Every man wants to be saved by superficial faith, without fruits of faith . . . without love and hope, without right Christian practices." But one will be saved, they protested, only if "he lives his faith."[10] Does this mean that works were necessary, as causes, for salvation? An early selection of biblical texts that circulated among the Swiss, which Grebel likely helped compile, suggests not. It began with verses showing that faith "alone saves and is only given from heaven."[11]

Still, Anabaptists underscored changed conduct so strongly that Protestants accused them making it salvation's cause.[12] Felix Mantz insisted that baptism was

---

[8]Probably because Hubmaier endorsed some use of the sword. Hubmaier did write some important mature works during his final year, in Moravia (Pipkin and Yoder, ed., *Balthasar Hubmaier*, pp. 339-562). Yet his Anabaptist convictions were forged in the Swiss milieu, where he composed at least thirteen works, including his *Entire Summa of the Christian Life* (ibid., pp. 83-89) and major treatments of baptism (pp. 95-49, 167-233, 275-95). Most main Hubmaier citations in this chapter come from Swiss works. In this and subsequent chapters I will indicate where Hubmaier's Moravian writings express important differences. Otherwise, I will treat Hubmaier citations as consistent, for my purposes, with his views developed among the Swiss.

[9]Harold Bender, *The Anabaptist Vision* (Scottdale, Penn.: Herald, 1944), p. 13.

[10]Conrad Grebel and Friends, "Letters to Thomas Muentzer," in *Spiritual and Anabaptist Writers*, ed. George Williams and Angel Mergal (Philadelphia: Westminster Press, 1957), pp. 74, 80.

[11]Leland Harder, ed., *The Sources of Swiss Anabaptism* (Scottdale, Penn.: Herald, 1985), p. 427.

[12]Ibid., p. 317.

only for those who reformed, forsook evil deeds and did "righteous works from a changed heart."[13] Similarly, "the heaven of eternal joys" was purchased "whenever a person brings forth genuine fruits of repentance." Still it is not clear that such works were primary causes: for this "heaven" was purchased "through grace" and "obtained for him by Christ."[14]

Hubmaier outlined the personal salvation process comprehensively. It arose from the missional impetus of the new creation's coming, usually through preaching. It commenced with deep despair over sin. The biblical law, heard according to its letter, revealed that "there is no health in us but rather poison, wounds and all impurity."[15] But then Christ, the living Physician, leads us to repentance. We surrender as much as a wounded person can, and his healing gradually enables us to follow his teaching. Hubmaier stressed that we could not do this of ourselves but only in God's grace and power. Christ now lives in us and is our life.[16]

Hubmaier often depicted this process as rebirth through the Spirit,[17] the incorruptible Seed, or the divine Word that makes us "turn green, grow, blossom, and bring forth fruit."[18] As Alvin Beachy maintains, this was not legal language or even justification language, but language of "ontological transformation." By this Beachy means, as I will throughout this volume, not transformation of human reality into another kind of reality (divine) but transformation by divine reality of those who remain fully human.[19]

Since we are employing justification language as an exploratory framework, however, let us ask whether Hubmaier utilized it as well. Like the Protestants he

---

[13]Ibid., p. 313; cf. pp. 415, 521.

[14]Thieleman J. van Braght, ed., *The Bloody Theater, or, Martyrs' Mirror* (Scottdale, Penn.: Herald, 1950), p. 415.

[15]Pipkin and Yoder, *Balthasar Hubmaier*, pp. 84; cf. pp. 85, 100, 102, 144. Robert Friedmann claimed that such a struggle was foreign to Anabaptists: "They did not start with the crushing awareness of being lost sinners but . . . with the glorious experience of regeneration" (*Theology of Anabaptism*, p. 78). All Anabaptists covered here contradict this assertion. In his positive account of grace Friedman leaned, quite unhistorically, on two Quakers and a French existentialist (ibid., p. 95).

[16]Pipkin and Yoder, *Balthasar Hubmaier*, pp. 84-86.

[17]Ibid., pp. 100, 147; cf. pp. 238, 431. His main texts were Jn 3:5; Jas 1:18; 1 Pet 1:3.

[18]Ibid., p. 85; cf. pp. 145, 236, 243, 337, 445.

[19]Alvin Beachy, *The Concept of Grace in the Radical Reformation* (Nieuwkoop, Netherlands: B. De Graf, 1977), p. 72, cf. "Contemporary Approaches to Historic Anabaptism" in chapter three and my use of *ontological* (point 7 in "Contemporary Context and Audience" in chap. 4). He believes that Schiemer and Marpeck's emphasis on ontological transformation derived from Hubmaier (ibid., p. 73), whose anthropology provided the normative model through which medieval mystical anthropology influenced Anabaptism, especially in South Germany (p. 202). While these other Anabaptists utilized Hubmaier's conceptuality, I argue that ontological and mystical influences arose mainly in South Germany-Austria.

occasionally used legal concepts. For instance, since our righteousness before conversion "is corrupt and reproachable," the "foreign righteousness" of Jesus, who fulfilled the "righteousness demanded by the law," must intervene.[20] Justification comes through Jesus' death, regarded as objective payment and satisfaction for sin.[21] Hubmaier, however, also attributed atonement to his resurrection.[22]

Hubmaier could also assert, as previously mentioned, that "Faith alone makes us righteous before God." Yet he immediately defined faith in way that could not be opposed to works: "faith cannot be idle, but must break forth in gratitude toward God and in all sorts of works of brotherly love."[23] Faith was not simply acceptance of a legal judgment, as Protestants might say, but a dynamism that produced fruits of the Spirit through love, as Catholics especially stressed.[24] Consequently, like Catholics, Hubmaier insisted Christians should fulfill God's commands. This was an essential feature of personal salvation.

In his post-Swiss writings Hubmaier could even call this "easy,"[25] for (ontological) rebirth through the Word and Spirit renders our wills as free as Adam's.[26] Yet Hubmaier usually portrayed the Christian walk, beset by persecution, as "the cross"[27]—as taking up our crosses, like Jesus, to "fulfill Christ's suffering in his body" that we might "inherit eternal life."[28] This process, which Bender called discipleship, included that walk toward holiness foregrounded by Kenneth Davis (see pp. 51-52). But in the context of justification debates, it raises the question whether the works involved are necessary, as causes, for salvation.

Hubmaier sometimes seemed to answer yes. Through obedience our bodily members must become instruments "of righteousness that they might become holy and might reach that goal . . . eternal life."[29] He could employ penance terminology: anyone who sins must "make compensation . . . for his transgression against the divine righteousness."[30] Since this would lead to recovery of one's lost righteousness and since obedience increased one's faith and love, Davis argues that works were causes of final justification, as for Catholics (not simply

[20]Pipkin and Yoder, *Balthasar Hubmaier*, p. 106, cf. p. 110.

[21]Ibid., p. 115; cf. pp. 236, 347, 348, 399.

[22]Ibid., pp. 86, 100, 115, 134; cf. pp. 344, 349.

[23]Ibid., p. 32.

[24]Ibid., pp. 32, 517, 526; cf. pp. 87, 348.

[25]Ibid., p. 400.

[26]Ibid., pp. 361, 439, 464. On greater optimism in his later anthropology, see the first sections of chaps. 7 and 9.

[27]Ibid., pp. 86; cf. pp. 39, 297, 304, 364, 529.

[28]Ibid., p. 560; cf. pp. 344, 364.

[29]Ibid., p. 373.

[30]Ibid., p. 537; cf. p. 544.

evidence of being justified, as for Protestants).[31] Yet Hubmaier acknowledged that "weaknesses and imperfections constantly are intermingled with" a Christian's acts,[32] so that they are "not at all just before the face of God."[33]

Such works then cannot produce a perfection that would justify us. Instead, as Protestants stressed, God has already granted perfection in Christ and "will not reckon" our imperfections "to our eternal condemnation."[34] And though God will finally reward our works, this will flow from "pure grace." We should never call such works merits, nor God's rewards payments.[35] Neither did "compensation" mean equivalent payment for Hubmaier.[36]

For Hubmaier, then, like Protestants, justifying righteousness was apparently granted through the response of faith. Salvation began, again as for Protestants, with conviction of sin, usually induced by preaching. Yet its main content was neither forgiveness nor imputed righteousness. Hubmaier was more concerned to stress, like Catholics, that any genuine faith "must break forth in . . . all sorts of works of brotherly love," and also the importance of living by Jesus' commands.

Neither, however, is Hubmaier's soteriology best described as stressing something like Catholic final justification. Salvation, instead, was most centrally ontological transformation (of human beings by, but not into, divine being). This was directly bestowed by the Word, often identified with Christ, and the Spirit. This differed from the usual Catholic experience of gradual growth through moral development and sacrament. Still, this transformation was not instantaneous, even though Hubmaier could imply this by, say, calling discipleship "easy." But other

---

[31]Kenneth Davis, *Anabaptism and Asceticism* (Scottdale, Penn.: Herald, 1974), pp. 181, 182. Though Hubmaier insisted that salvation was by grace, Davis finds works "more than evidential" and "so fused with grace as to become almost identical with grace"(p. 181). He concludes that Hubmaier, like the preceding monastic tradition, "saw salvation and forgiveness the product of this total process of becoming holy"(p. 143).

[32]Pipkin and Yoder, *Balthasar Hubmaier*, p. 402.

[33]Ibid., p. 519, cf. pp. 489, 497. Still, some phrases may seem to imply the opposite: e.g., the Seed makes us "free and whole again by a new law so that absolutely nothing damning is any longer in us"(p. 445). Hubmaier acknowledged, however, that "sin or weakness" still affects our acts. He meant that it is "no longer . . . poisonous or damning . . . if we do not follow it wantonly" (p. 446).

[34]Ibid., p. 402, cf. pp. 144-45, 148.

[35]Ibid., p. 361.

[36]Hubmaier's remarks on penance appeared in his "Apology to Ferdinand," where he sought the largest possible common ground with Catholicism. Still, *compensation*, for Hubmaier, meant only "remorse, sorrow, and repentance" (ibid., p. 537). He cited his writings on the ban, which mentioned only general repentance, not penitential acts of saving contrition (pp. 373-85, 410-25). I mainly refer to Hubmaier's post-Swiss writings because most passages enlisted to support his "Catholic" soteriology were penned then. If he countered "Catholic" notions in these later writings, it is highly likely that his soteriology was never really "Catholic" (cf. note 8 of this chap.).

statements, and especially his own poignant history—several recantations and finally his anguished though courageous martyrdom (cf. chap. 2)—show how incomplete and open to further growth this transformation was. Still, Hubmaier's lofty call to discipleship arose neither from Protestant soteriology nor "Catholic optimism," but from a salvation experienced holistically as a new birth or new creation.

South Germany-Austria

The Anabaptism that emerged from the relatively independent source of South Germany-Austria bore clear traces of medieval mysticism. According to Davis this mysticism merely provided a different linguistic vehicle for expressing what Swiss Anabaptists meant.[37] Werner Packull, however, finds it far more formative of this second stream and discrepant with "consistent evangelical Protestantism."[38] This mysticism, with its identifiable soteriology, appears in the earliest Anabaptists considered here (Hans Hut, Hans Denck, Leonhard Schiemer and Hans Schlaffer). We will see to what extent it can be traced forward through Peter Riedemann and Pilgram Marpeck.

Earliest years. This mystical process, according to Hut, drew one into the divine trinitarian dynamic and could best be explained through a tripartite schema.[39]

First, consider the work of God the Father, who can be known through the "Gospel of all Creatures."[40] Lower creatures exist for the sake of higher ones. Many plants and animals fulfill their destiny through being killed and consumed by humans. Similarly, humans attain their destiny through a crucifixion experience that purges and prepares them for communion with God. All creatures participate in this process that points to God, especially as crucified Son.

Second, consider the work of this Son, or Word (Denck). It uproots all inordi-

---

[37]Davis, *Anabaptism and Asceticism*, p. 229.

[38]Werner Packull, *Mysticism and the Early South German-Austrian Anabaptists* (Scottdale, Penn.: Herald, 1977). Cf. sec. one of chap. 3.

[39]Hans Hut, "Ein christlich Unterrich, wie goettliche Geschrift vergleicht und geurteilen solle werden," in *Glaubenzeugnisse oberdeutscher Taufgesinnter* (= Quellen und Forschungen zur Reformationsgeschichte), ed. Lydia Mueller (Leipzig: M. Heinsius Nachfolger, 1938), 20:34.

[40]Ibid., pp. 28-32; Hans Hut, "On the Mystery of Baptism," in *Early Anabaptist Spirituality*, ed. Daniel Liechty (New York: Paulist Press, 1994), pp. 71-72; Hans Schlaffer, "Instructions on Beginning a True Christian Life," in *Early Anabaptist Spirituality*, ed. Daniel Liechty (New York: Paulist, 1994), pp. 99-109, esp. 100-103 (more fully elaborated in sec. one of chap. 7). God could also be known through the Word or Lamb in everyone's heart (Hans Denck, "Whether God Is the Cause of Evil," in *Spiritual and Anabaptist Writers*, ed. George Williams and Angel Mergal [Philadelphia: Westminster Press, 1957], pp. 86-111, esp. 95, 98); Schiemer added the Law (Leonhard Schiemer, "Three Kinds of Grace," in *Early Anabaptist Spirituality*, ed. Daniel Liechty [New York: Paulist Press, 1994], pp. 85-87).

nate attachments (physical, emotional or social) that tie us to creatures. This feels like that tearing away or cutting that animals undergo when humans prepare them for food. "God must take us from that which is creaturely and take us naked and pure into the second birth."[41] We feel abandoned by all creatures, even God, and descend into hell.[42] The appropriate attitude is *Gelassenheit:* yielding to God's work and yielding up those objects and relationships we tend to grasp.[43]

This work of God the Son was often called "crucifixion with Christ." For although Christ suffered for our sins historically, he "does not keep me from sin unless he suffers in me." And unless Christ dies in me, I will not go to heaven with him.[44] This was also expressed eucharistically: through consuming Christ's flesh and blood, at the deepest level, we are "incorporated into Christ's flesh, life, suffering, and death, and become partakers of it. Only in this way do we participate in his resurrection and the glory of his kingdom."[45]

In the earlier mystical tradition this crucifixion was chiefly an inner process, though imitation of Jesus' life was sometimes recommended. South German-Austrian Anabaptists, however, often experienced such crucifying experiences in their outward lives—when, as expressions of the new creation's missional coming, their witness and lifestyle aroused severe persecution. They began insisting that this coming, on the personal level, involved not only internal crucifixion but also following "in the footsteps of Christ and his elect in the school of affliction."[46]

This sounds somewhat like Swiss discipleship, which also flowed from inner transformation. Yet the accent on mystical participation in Christ's life and "conception, birth, death and resurrection in us" was specifically South German-Austrian.[47] Suffering with or participating in Christ was also communal. It occurred in his body, the church.[48] Release from creaturely attachments involved sharing goods there,[49] and renouncing "injustice in our way of living and our misuse of the creatures" everywhere.[50]

[41]Schiemer, "Three Kinds of Grace," p. 91.

[42]Hut, "Ein christlich Unterrich," p. 35.

[43]Walter Klaassen, " 'Gelassenheit' and Creation," *CGR* 9, no. 1 (1991).

[44]Schiemer, "Three Kinds of Grace," pp. 34-35.

[45]Hans Schlaffer, *Selections,* in *Spiritual Life in Anabaptism,* ed. Cornelius Dyck (Scottdale, Penn.: Herald, 1995), p. 205.

[46]Hut, "On the Mystery of Baptism," p. 65.

[47]Schiemer, "Three Kinds of Grace," p. 90.

[48]Hut, "On the Mystery of Baptism," p. 75.

[49]Ibid., p. 72; Schiemer, "Three Kinds of Grace," p. 92.

[50]Hut "On the Mystery of Baptism," p. 70; cf. Hans Denck, *The Spiritual Legacy of Hans Denck,* ed. Clarence Bauman (Leiden: E. J. Brill, 1991), pp. 67, 95, 157; Klaassen, " 'Gelassenheit' and Creation."

Justification terminology could also express this work of God the Son, or Word. It referred mostly to the process of becoming righteous and its final goal, as in Catholicism. Like the Swiss, South German-Austrians critiqued those who wanted to be justified simply by a faith profession, especially for avoiding the suffering that eventually destroys sin.[51]

Yet for Hut the justification process still began with faith, which was God's work in us, for "no person can justify himself." What followed, however, was no legal declaration but "the baptism of affliction which God has shown and worked . . . to which the person is subjected as justification."[52] This suffering often involved fear that God would desert one, or be unfaithful—though this really arose from one's habitual unfaithfulness to God.[53] Eventually, however, God's faithfulness would be revealed to our faith.[54] This would then "be conformed to the faith of God and united with Christ."[55]

Despite God's priority and our receptivity in this process, the human transformation involved prompts the question put to the Swiss: were works necessary, as causes, for salvation? Various statements by Schlaffer and Hut might imply this. Yet their immediate contexts attributed the primary work to God.[56] Schiemer, however, so strongly stressed response to God through creation and to Jesus' call to take up the cross that such acts apparently played some causative role in justification.[57]

Denck also sounded more Catholic. He could equate righteousness and being

---

[51]Hans Schlaffer, "Instructions on Beginning," pp. 104; Hut, "On the Mystery of Baptism," pp. 64-66, 73, 75-77.

[52]Hut, "On the Mystery of Baptism," p. 73.

[53]Scheimer, "Three Kinds of Grace," p. 91.

[54]Hut, "On the Mystery of Baptism," p. 76.

[55]Ibid., p. 75; cf. Hans Schlaffer, "Ein kurzer Unterricht zum Anfang eines recht chrislichen Lebens," in *Glaubenzeugnisse oberdeutscher Taufgesinnter* (= Quellen und Forschungen zur Reformationsgeschichte), ed. Lydia Mueller (Leipzig: M. Heinsius Nachfolger, 1938), 20:95.

[56]E.g., Schlaffer paralleled justification with "making us worthy for the honor and glory" of God's kingdom; yet he stressed "that God (and not we ourselves) works in us for our justification" ("Instructions on Beginning," p. 102). Hut declared that "the Law of the Father" would eventually "be perfected in us," but added that this would occur "through Christ" at the climax of a process where God's initiative was often stressed. Packull finds that Hut carefully avoided late Medieval semi-Pelagianism. Still, "on no account" did he teach a passive righteousness like Luther's (Werner Packull, *Mysticism and the Early South German-Austrian Anabaptists* [Scottdale, Penn.: Herald, 1977], p. 76).

[57]God enlightens all people, who can snuff this out, respond sleepily or "set their hearts on" God with "all diligence . . . " (Schreiner, "Three Kinds of Grace," p. 89). God will draw the latter onward, but the Spirit will be "given only to those who have taken up the cross and seek the Lord." Justification, indeed, will be God's work, for it "cannot take place outside of Christ, who through his conception, birth, death, and resurrection in us . . . is our righteousness" (p. 90). Yet human preparation seems to be not simply a response to grace, but also to play some distinct causal role.

justified with fulfilling the law;[58] every body member must fulfill the law as perfectly as the Head.[59] Like Hubmaier, Denck could mention merit, reward and making full satisfaction for any infraction.[60] Yet this mystical author's meaning was often other than first appeared. Denck, for instance, reduced the law to loving God alone; when the Spirit wrote this law on hearts, people needed not worry about its prescriptions and satisfactions.[61]

Righteousness, moreover, basically meant restoring what belonged to God. Those who yielded themselves fully to God, then, were righteous.[62] They could do this by following the Word's inner prompting, which calls everyone to do so. Did their works then play a causal role in making them righteous? Denck sought to deny this by differentiating the Word's activity from ours. The Word works in us but is not of us.[63] Responding to it is really to cease working and let God work.[64] Merits and rewards resulted from this. They were really gifts of grace, as Hubmaier said.[65]

Is yielding to God, then, actually exercising faith (Protestant), or is it "working" in the Catholic sense? We probably cannot force Denck to answer in these terms. To be sure, he stressed human transformation, like Catholics, and could use their concepts to do so. Yet he also used Protestant language to avoid objections. Ultimately, Denck endorsed neither, for he viewed salvation quite differently: as divinization.

A Protestant theme found in Hubmaier also appeared in this Anabaptist stream. Though justification here usually meant (Catholic) final justification, authentic faith that responded to the preached Word "will be counted to the person as jus-

---

[58]Denck, *Spiritual Legacy of Hans Denck*, p. 109.

[59]Ibid., p. 131.

[60]Ibid., p. 141. Penance "must be as hard on the flesh as the breaking was easy . . . as much as was taken from the Law and God must thereby be restored." Christ's making satisfaction was pioneering "the Way which no person could find. . . . Whoever does not walk the Way does not come to life." (Making, or "made satisfaction" is the usual translation of *genug gethon*. Bauman, however, translates it literally as "done enough" [Clarence Bauman, ed., *The Spiritual Legacy of Hans Denck* (Leiden: E. J. Brill, 1991), pp. 132, 133]). Jesus "fulfilled the Law, not that he wished to exempt us from it, but to give us an example for following him." Whoever says they cannot keep the law denies that Christ has come in the flesh (ibid., p. 143).

[61]Denck, *Spiritual Legacy of Hans Denck*, pp. 145, 151-55, 191-95.

[62]Ibid., pp. 189, 193-95. Jesus did this most thoroughly and was thus the most righteous of all. Therefore we receive "righteousness out of grace" from him (p. 97, cf. pp. 185-87). As to whether this meant more than being strengthened by his example, see the first sec. of chap. 8.

[63]Ibid., p. 87.

[64]Ibid., pp. 89-91, 111-17. We cannot come to God ourselves but must lose ourselves and suffer God, or the Word, to bring us (pp. 225, 229).

[65]Pipkin and Yoder, eds., *Balthasar Hubmaier* (Scottdale, Penn.: Herald, 1989), pp. 141-43, 253-55.

tification until . . . that person is justified and made pure through the cross."[66] That is, God also reckons us as righteous, through grace, as we walk the saving path, while we still sin.

Although early South German-Austrians focused overwhelmingly on the second divine, crucifying work of the Son (or Word), they finally reached a third work, the Spirit's filling of comfort and joy.[67] They called it resurrection, being newborn, being led out of hell. It became evident that the entire process, while definitely including ethical following of Jesus, involved that thorough transformation that Beachy calls divinization.[68]

Divinization, of course, can be a problematic term. People who use it sometimes speak as if it dissolved our humanity. Schiemer, for instance, could say that we were created not to remain "as humans [*der Mensch*], but . . . to become godly, divinized."[69] He added that "the creaturely [*die Creatur*]" is a covering obscuring the divine light in us and "must be removed."[70] Yet the first expression hardly seems literal, for this divinization was "true human rest [*menschlichen Rue*]."[71] In the latter context Schiemer affirmed the body's resurrection and exclaimed that true awareness of God would involve "a pure joy . . . that would surge through my body," making it "wholly immortal and glorified." "The creaturely [*die Creatur*]," then, likely meant creatures as objects of human grasping along with that grasping—not the created nature of humans or any other beings.[72]

---

[66]Hut, "On the Mystery of Baptism," p. 75; cf. p. 73. Sin will not be reckoned when it is not done *"mit Lust"* (Hut, "Ein christlich Unterrich," p. 36). God counts people who are moving in the right direction among the perfected (Denck, *Spiritual Legacy of Hans Denck*, pp. 229-31). Through faith that suffers we will be reckoned as just even while we are imperfect (Schlaffer, "Ein kurzer Unterrich," p. 95).

[67]E.g., Schiemer, "Three Kinds of Grace," pp. 93-94.

[68]Denck, *Spiritual Legacy of Hans Denck*, p. 101; cf. pp. 65, 87, 93.

[69]Leonhard Schiemer, "Ein epistl an die gemain zu Rottenburg darin huebsche erklearungen der 12 hauptsteuck unseres christlichen glaubens begriffen sein" in *Glaubenzeugnisse oberdeutscher Taufgesinnter* (= Quellen und Forschungen zur Reformationsgeschichte), ed. Lydia Mueller (Leipzig: M. Heinsius Nachfolger, 1938), 20:44-58, esp. p. 49; cf. Leonhard Schiemer, "The Apostles' Creed: An Interpretation," in *Spiritual Life in Anabaptism*, ed. Cornelius Dyck (Scottdale, Penn.: Herald, 1995), p. 32.

[70]Leonhard Schiemer, "Leinharten Schiemers epistl an die gmain Gottes zu Rottenburg, geschrieben 1527, von dreierlie gnadt," in *Glaubenzeugnisse oberdeutscher Taufgesinnter* (= Quellen und Forschungen zur Reformationsgeschichte), ed. Lydia Mueller (Leipzig: M. Heinsius Nachfolger, 1938), 20:58-71, esp. p. 67.

[71]Schiemer, "Ein epistl an die gemain," p. 49.

[72]Schiemer, "Leinharten Schiemers epistl an die gmain," p. 67. Liechty, however, translates *"die cCreatur"* as "our creaturely nature" (Daniel Liechty, ed., *Early Anabaptist Spirituality* [New York: Paulist Press, 1994], p. 92), and Klaassen, as "the creatures" (Walter Klaassen, ed., *Anabaptism in Outline* [Scottdale, Penn.: Herald, 1981], p. 55). Schiemer affirmed bodily resurrection elsewhere (Schiemer, "The Apostles' Creed," p. 35), and also that God hates sin, but not the creatures God made (Schiemer,

Among early South German-Austrian Anabaptists, then, we do find justification terminology—with connotations less Protestant than Catholic. Yet while some such terminology could often convey Swiss views fairly well, here it was largely adapted in response to Protestant emphases and potential objections to express a somewhat different soteriology. South German-Austrians, like the Swiss, also foregrounded following Jesus' nonviolent way amidst savage persecution. Yet they conceived this explicitly as the necessary outward expression of an inward, mystical participation in his incarnation, life and death, and ultimately his divinizing resurrection.

For these Anabaptists, then, mysticism was hardly a mere vocabulary for expressing Swiss theology (Davis). On the contrary, their theology was inherently mystical (Packull) and they sometimes borrowed other vocabularies, such as justification, to express it.

Continuing themes? The four men just considered were dead by February 1528. Did their soteriology really comprise an ongoing Anabaptist orientation? Denck transitioned into spiritualism during his lifetime, and Buenderline and Entfelder took this trend further. Another line, descending from Schlaffer and possibly Schiemer, soon mingled with Swiss currents and became more sectarian and evangelical, less apocalyptic and mystical.[73] However, the mystical orientation's effect can best be discerned by searching for it among those distinct Anabaptist groups that emerged from the earlier stream: the Hutterites and Pilgramites.

1. Hutterites included among their ancestors Hut, Schiemer and Schlaffer, all of whom advocated community of goods. Their coleader from 1542-1556, Peter Riedemann, maintained that God is reflected in creation but that humans misuse creatures, seizing them for their selfish purposes.[74] Sin, therefore, is not only disobedience,[75] but originates in grasping what is not ours.[76] To come to God, then, one must surrender all that one has misappropriated. This involved that painful inner detachment from creaturely things long accented in South German-Austrian mysticism.

"Ein Epistl an die Gemain," p. 46). Hut mentioned that in being baptized as new creatures, "all sin and human characteristics [menschlicher aigenschaft]" must be washed away ("On the Mystery of Baptism," p. 78 ["Ein christlich Unterrich," p. 25]). But the context shows that, like Schiemer and many earlier Rhineland mystics, Hut was critiquing inordinate attachment to creaturely realities, not creatures or human characteristics themselves.

[73]Packull, *Mysticism*, pp. 148-54.

[74]Peter Riedemann, *Peter Riedemann's Hutterite Confession of Faith*, ed. John Friesen (Scottdale, Penn.: Herald, 1999), pp. 63.

[75]Ibid., p. 92.

[76]Peter Rideman, *Confession of Faith* (Rifton, N.Y.: Plough, 1970), p. 58 (cf. chap. 2 n. 32).

Hutterites extended this misappropriation to include all private property. People could use creatures appropriately only through sharing them communally.[77] Inner *Gelassenheit*, that is, became outward not only in personal Jesus-like behavior but also in structured communal forms. Through such communities the new creation began reshaping the physical earth.

The new creation's missional impulse sent Hutterites out of their communities to call others through preaching that, like Hubmaier's, focused on personal sinfulness and divine judgment, eliciting remorse and repentance.[78] Preaching often utilized South German-Austrian mystical motifs, such as dying to sin through participation in Christ's death, by which a "person's surrendered will interweaves itself with the divine will in such a way that the divine will and the human will become one."[79] Such persons were also grafted into the risen Christ, becoming "one with him in mind, in his very character and nature, so that they become one plant and organism . . . one substance and essence."[80] Organic and personal divinization language abounded in Riedemann's theology.

Riedemann seldom used *justification* terminology. Like Protestants, though, he affirmed God's initiative in salvation.[81] He denied justification by works, for "all our deeds, as far as they are our deeds, are nothing but sin and unrighteousness."[82] Further, faith was clearly God's gift. Yet faith grasped not simply a justifying declaration but "the invisible, one and only, mighty God, making us close to God and at one with him, and able to partake of his nature and character." Clearly, such a faith will produce works. It will make people "resemble God in his nature, living in God's righteousness, ardent in God's love, and observing his commandments."[83]

Riedemann seldom mentioned *righteousness* and did not connect it with imputation. Instead, it was divine and dynamic: "Christ is our righteousness and goodness, because he himself demonstrates and accomplishes in us the justification and goodness that make us beloved of God and pleasing to him."[84] In this rare appearance justification most resembled (Catholic) final justification—which Christ would pronounce at the last judgment.[85]

---

[77]Riedemann, *Peter Riedemann's Hutterite Confession*, pp. 94, 119-20, 134; Peter Walpot, "True Yieldedness and the Christian Community of Goods," in *Early Anabaptist Spirituality*, ed. Daniel Liechty (New York: Paulist Press, 1994), pp. 138-96.

[78]Riedemann, *Peter Riedemann's Hutterite Confession*, pp. 95-96, 174-78.

[79]Ibid., p. 179.

[80]Ibid., p. 97.

[81]Ibid., pp. 67-68, 84-85, 100-101, 112-13, 166-67, 174-75, 178, 208.

[82]Ibid., p. 75.

[83]Ibid., p. 84; cf. pp. 61, 85, 97, 116-17, 178-79, 196-97.

[84]Ibid., pp. 74-75.

[85]Ibid., pp. 72-73.

As in his forerunners, justification terminology connected Riedemann's soteriology with Protestant concerns, but it often sounded more Catholic. Salvation, however, was again basically divinization. But while Riedemann's predecessors foregrounded painful participation in Jesus' life and death, Riedemann more often celebrated the risen One, who offered thorough transformation through participation in his nature and character. Yet this character clearly included Jesus' earthly comportment.[86] For Hutterites this implied rejection not only of war but also, going beyond most other Anabaptists, of war taxes.[87]

To be sure, divinization soteriology can seem to ignore finite limitations, arousing unrealistic expectations. Perhaps Riedemann hinted at this by defining God's image in humans as spirit, "not flesh and blood," so that temporal things are "alien to our true nature."[88] Yet this conceptual definition clashed with the thoroughgoing transformation of bodies, communities and environments by divine energies in his Hutterite vision.

2. Pilgram Marpeck emphasized justification more than other South German-Austrians, in ways recalling Hubmaier. *Righteousness* sometimes meant God's standard for final judgment.[89] As with Protestants, Marpeck called Jesus' death a righteousness that God accepts in place of our sin.[90] Yet Marpeck connected justification chiefly with Jesus' resurrection.[91] It conveyed righteousness too vitally to call it "reckoned": Marpeck applied this term only to Old Testament saints, for whom Christ's righteousness was a future hope.[92]

Like Catholics and Riedemann, Marpeck affirmed that we will be justified through Christ's righteousness working in us.[93] Christ also fulfills the law in us.[94] With Hubmaier and Denck, Marpeck expected salvation to finally involve rewards, though only as God's gifts.[95] While faith was God's gift, it did not receive some-

---

[86]Ibid., pp. 132-37, 217-24.

[87]Ibid., pp. 225-27; cf. "Church and World" on p. 289.

[88]*Peter Riedemann's Hutterite Confession of Faith*, ed. John Friesen (Scottdale, Penn.: Herald, 1999), pp. 89, 120; cf. chap. 10.

[89]Pilgam Marpeck, *The Writings of Pilgram Marpeck*, ed. and trans. William Klassen and Walter Klaassen (Scottdale, Penn.: Herald, 1978), pp. 324, 325, 531.

[90]Ibid., pp. 154, 175, 432, 433, 439.

[91]Marpeck called Jesus' resurrection "the highest article of our faith" (ibid., p. 92; cf. pp. 91, 94, 100, 101, 122, 134, 137, 233, 453).

[92]Ibid., pp. 109, 117.

[93]Ibid., p. 324.

[94]Ibid., pp. 320, 343. He appeared to mean, like Denck, that love fulfills all commands (pp. 315, 327, 343); perfect legal rectitude might not have been meant. Similarly, Marpeck spoke of the Spirit's work in us as the basis on which we are forgiven (pp. 422, 469, 470-71, 525), and of salvation depending on love of neighbor (p. 54) and of grace making us worthy of praise (p. 536).

[95]Ibid., pp. 552-53.

thing imputed but the Spirit, through whom Christ lives in our hearts.[96] Marpeck's language was often ontological: faith received life from the seed of the Word,[97] as for Hubmaier; through faith God entered into us and we into God,[98] as for Riedemann. True faith, accordingly, was love in action. It could not help but manifest itself in works,[99] as Hubmaier and Riedemann insisted.

Marpeck drew something from the South German-Austrian mystical stream, including traces of the "Gospel of all Creatures." He portrayed a conversion struggle where one feels "completely forsaken of all creatures in heaven and earth."[100] He also called this "the baptism of tribulation in Christ,"[101] which persisted in some way until death.[102] Like Hubmaier and Martin Luther, however, Marpeck also referred to being "shattered, beaten and broken by the law."[103] All this was rooted in divine grace—yet it prepared one for more grace.[104]

As for other South German-Austrians, salvation was essentially divinization, vividly expressed in Marpeck's more mystical writings.[105] For example: the divine Word issues forth from the Father's mouth and "kisses the hearts of the faithful," so that "the divine nature of the children of God is conceived and born from this love of the Word, the imperishable seed." Such experiences, however, were not individualistic, for God's Spirit brings those so conceived to the church, through which they are born.[106]

Neither were they basically inner, for only as we "pattern ourselves after" Jesus do we "more fully partake of the divine nature."[107] On this path, with its persecution, "revenge is no longer permitted . . . for, through patience the Spirit can now

---

[96]Ibid., pp. 53, 83, 89, 126, 128.

[97]Ibid., p. 399.

[98]Ibid., p. 529.

[99]Ibid., p. 53.

[100]Ibid., p. 489, cf. p. 251.

[101]Ibid., p. 116.

[102]Ibid., pp. 63, 211; see also his references to "the German theology" (J. Loserth, *Pilgram Marbecks Antwort auf Kaspar Schwenckfeld's Beurteilung des Buches der Bundesbezeugung von 1542* [Vienna: Carl Fromme, 1929], pp. 48, 53, 213-15, 259, 266-69).

[103]Marpeck, *Writings of Pilgram Marpeck*, pp. 127; cf. pp. 134-35, 315, 439-40.

[104]Ibid., pp. 485-497. He sometimes said that faith precedes repentance (pp. 89, 93); cf. repentance in Menno and Dirk and note 128 on p. 128.

[105]Strangely, Alvin Beachy denies this (Alvin Beachy, *The Concept of Grace in the Radical Reformation* [Nieuwkoop, Netherlands: B. De Graf, 1977], p. 29). Yet the specific terminology of partaking in the divine nature (2 Pet 1:4) appeared three times in Marpeck's earliest writing (Marpeck, *Writings of Pilgram Marpeck*, pp. 62, 63, 66) and at least twenty times elsewhere. Such references only provide a window into the numerous functions of divinization for Marpeck.

[106]Marpeck, p. 393; cf. pp. 474-75.

[107]Ibid., p. 62.

more powerfully overcome enemies."[108] This process was not merely ethical, for it drew people directly into the trinitarian dynamic.[109] Yet Marpeck cautioned, more clearly than his predecessors, we remain fully human and are never absorbed into God.[110]

The Netherlands

Melchior Hoffman. Initially preaching as a Lutheran, Melchior Hoffman warned of imminent eschatological judgment against those who trusted in works. He taught, like Protestants, that salvation began by accepting Jesus' substitutionary suffering for sin, through faith granted by grace.[111] Yet even in early days he connected this with being slain by the gospel and descending into hell or the wilderness of the deity. There *Gelassenheit* wrought detachment from the "world," one's works and one's ego. Thereby one was wholly drawn into God, or divinized, to perfectly will God's will. Hoffman and South-German Austrians drank from the same mystical stream, though he stressed more rapid divinization and irrevocable loss of salvation through one major sin.[112]

In mid 1529 Hoffman visited Strasbourg. He found little affinity with Swiss Anabaptists or Pilgramites, but much with prophetic circles around the late Hut's disciples and the legacy of the late Denck. The latter especially persuaded Hoffman that all humans share some awareness of God[113] and that salvation involves their cooperation. He accommodated these to his earlier views by teaching a twofold justification.

Though Catholics also taught two justifications, Hoffman's first occurred at neither baptism nor penance, but the aforementioned acceptance of Jesus' sacrifice. This freed the will, bound by original sin, to undertake the wilderness struggle leading toward the second justification, which required many good deeds.[114] Final

---

[108]Ibid., p. 63, cf. p. 438.

[109]Ibid., pp. 420-21, 435-36, 440-41.

[110]Ibid., p. 531.

[111]According to Klaus Deppermann, before 1530 Hoffman believed that grace preceded faith. Afterward Hoffman maintained that although God's saving Word is a gift, accepting it is up to us. Since all Hoffman's writings but one exist only in Dutch and are very difficult to obtain, I will largely follow Deppermann's understanding (see Klaus Deppermann, *Melchior Hofmann* [Edinburgh: T & T Clark, 1987]).

[112]Ibid., pp. 82-84, cf. p. 240. Contact with Russian Orthodoxy was another possible source of Hoffman's divinization theme. Since Orthodoxy had split with Rome, he considered it apostolic (p. 249). Hoffman endorsed its Eucharist and identified it with the church at Philadelphia (Rev 3:8-13).

[113]Ibid., pp. 223-24.

[114]Ibid., pp. 190, 265, 237. Justification by faith made justification by works not superfluous but possible (p. 300); "faith cannot make one justified if one does not bring in therewith his fruits"(Melchior Hoffman, "The Ordinance of God," in *Spiritual and Anabaptist Writers,* ed. George Williams and Angel Mergal [Philadelphia: Westminster Press, 1957], p. 201).

judgment, as Catholics often insisted, was according to works, not faith.[115] Still, Hoffman included a Protestant qualification found in Hubmaier and most early South German-Austrians. For those on this path Christ's sacrifice had already obtained forgiveness for weaknesses (though not major sins).[116]

The mystical orientation still predominated Hoffman's soteriology, however. Not unlike Marpeck, he called the gospel "the kiss rich in joys from the mouth of the Bridegroom" to whom he urged "complete, voluntary, and loving surrender" as a bride.[117] This union was intimately experienced in the Lord's Supper, where the bride "is completely naked and resigned . . . completely wedded by the grace of God."[118] Hoffman's chief aim was "to call upon everyone to be a perfected, spiritual man."[119]

Perfecting could be swift because the new creation or true kingdom of God "is given here and now" and will be fully present soon. This appealed especially to the oppressed, for the rich and the rulers would soon be overthrown, and equality and sharing would pervade the new creation. Yet it also encouraged unrealistically high hopes of transformation, even spiritualization. The perfected, moreover, had supposedly transcended the external or written Word. Consequently, "fantasies, dreams, revelations, and visions daily occurred."[120] Hoffman claimed that his apostles were perfected.[121] Jan Matthijs's apostles boasted of invulnerability—and were soon tortured to death.[122]

Menno Simons and Dirk Philips. Dutch Anabaptism was transformed from a revolutionary, visionary, antinomian exuberance into a pacifist, biblicist, disciplined institution by Menno Simons and Dirk Philips. Like all Anabaptists these two found the new creation invading the personal realm when the preached Word was received through faith—which was God's gift,[123] since salvation was only by grace,[124] But as for most Protestants, Hubmaier and sometimes Marpeck this Word had two com-

---

[115]Hoffman, "Ordinance of God," pp. 193-94.

[116]Deppermann, *Melchior Hoffman*, p. 234.

[117]Hoffman, "Ordinance of God," pp. 186, 187.

[118]"There the old Adam is put off completely. . . . He is crucified and dead . . . so that the sinful seed brings forth its fruit no more . . . and . . . there is nothing more that is blameworthy to be found" (ibid., p. 191).

[119]Depermann, *Melchior Hoffman*, p. 240.

[120]Obbe Philips, "A Confession," in *Spiritual and Anabaptist Writers*, ed. George Williams and Angel Mergal (Philadelphia: Westminster Press, 1957), p. 213.

[121]Hoffman, "Ordinance of God," pp. 188, 190.

[122]Philips, "A Confession," pp. 216-19; cf. chap. 2.

[123]Menno Simons, *The Complete Works of Menno Simons*, ed. J. C. Wenger (Scottdale, Penn.: Herald, 1956), p. 116.

[124]Ibid., pp. 396-97, 545, 566.

ponents. First came the law with its conviction of sin, engendering a tumultuous repentance struggle.[125]

Beachy argues that for Dutch Anabaptists the law did not simply prepare for grace by pushing hearers to despair, as Protestants said it did. Rather the law actually drove out sin, rendering hearers worthy of forgiveness.[126] But if so, response to the law would be a kind of work, not a movement of faith. Menno and Dirk could indeed stress repentance so strongly that it sounded like a work necessary for receiving grace.[127] However, the contexts in which they enunciated the law-grace dynamic prioritized the latter, and they insisted that both were apprehended through faith. Their overall view, so far as I can see, does not differ sharply from other Anabaptists', though their harsh emphasis might have induced some people to attempt repentance as a work.[128]

In receiving the Word's second component, grace, faith grasped a content expressed more often in Protestant fashion than by any other Anabaptist considered here.[129] Righteousness frequently meant God's legal standard[130] and Christ's righteousness, his life and death, which fulfilled that law or paid its penalties.[131] Menno

---

[125]Ibid., p. 329; Dirk Philips, *The Writings of Dirk Philips*, ed. Cornelius Dyck, William Keeney and Alvin Beachy (Scottdale, Penn.: Herald, 1992), pp. 207-8.

[126]Alvin Beachy, *The Concept of Grace in the Radical Reformation* (Nieuwkoop, Netherlands: B. De Graf, 1977), pp. 17-20.

[127]Without knowledge of sin and fear of the Lord "no one can be justified"(Philips, *Writings*, p. 359). Menno, referring to John the Baptist (Lk 3:8), affirmed "a penitence possessed of power and works," and that "without it no one can receive grace." (Simons, *Complete Works*, pp. 111, 112, cf. pp. 54, 92, 337). For the influence of late medieval penance on Menno, see Sjouke Voolstra, "True Penitence: The Core of Menno Simons' Theology," *MQR* 62, no. 3 (1988); and Marjan Blok, "Discipleship in Menno Simons' Dat Fundament," in *Menno Simons: A Reappraisal*, ed. Gerald Brunk (Harrisonburg, Va.: Eastern Mennonite College, 1992).

[128]Menno especially could appear to specify that experience of repentance must precede faith, as when treating these in this order in his "Foundation of Christian Doctrine" (*Complete Works*, pp. 110-16). This seems contrary to his view that law and grace are both received by faith. Yet Menno prefaced both treatments by extolling "The Day of Grace" (pp. 108-10). Calvin critiqued Anabaptists for making repentance into a work that earns faith (much as he thought Catholics treated penance). Calvin insisted that repentance could not occur unless faith, even if somewhat unconsciously, first assured one of God's grace (John Calvin, *Institutes of the Christian Religion* (Philadelphia: Westminster, 1960), pp. 592-95, cf. pp. 606-7). Apparently, Marpeck generally agreed with Calvin (see p. 125 n. 104).

[129]For Menno one had to believe in Jesus' sacrifice and reconciliation "as certain and true" (Simons, *Complete Works*, p. 336). For Dirk, faith certified not only this but also "all of God's words and excepts none" because "all of God's words are as active as fire" (Philips, *Writings of Dirk Philips*, p. 260).

[130]Simons, *Complete Works*, pp. 306, 341, 439; Philips, *Writings of Dirk Philips*, pp. 256-57.

[131]Simons, *Complete Works*, pp. 428-29, 506, 818, 1053; Philips, *Writings of Dirk Philips*, pp. 68, 162, 165, 362.

insisted that we cannot attain "the original righteousness required in the commandments" because "our works are always mixed with imperfection and weakness." Consequently, only Jesus could be our "eternal righteousness, reconciliation, and propitiation with the Father."[132]

In such phrases and in affirming that lingering imperfections are forgiven by Christ's continuing intercession,[133] justification was the reckoning of something we do not have. Menno repeatedly denied that salvation comes through works, rather than Jesus' "innocent flesh *and* blood" sacrificed "once" on the cross.[134] In this Menno appeared, contra Beachy, not too distant from Lutherans, whom he critiqued for claiming that "faith alone saves, without any assistance by works."[135]

Dirk also maintained that God does not reckon continuing perfections as sins[136]—as did Hubmaier, Hoffman and most early South German-Austrians. Yet Dirk gave two reasons for this: because Jesus "paid our debt with his bitter sufferings" and because Jesus has "given us out of grace all that he has" and is "one with us and we with him."[137] Stated otherwise, we are "justified through the imputation *and* sharing of His righteousness."[138] Dirk, that is, affirmed justification both by (Protestant) imputed righteousness and (Catholic) righteousness of character, attained through participation in Christ's active righteousness,[139] flowing from his resurrection.[140] Despite dissimilarities between Dirk and Hoffman, both taught some kind of twofold justification, unlike Menno.

Regarding faith, Menno sometimes treated it—like Schiemer, Hut and Schlaffer—as a response to God's faithfulness and also to Jesus' faithfulness in his saving work.[141] Despite their Protestant tendencies, neither Dutch leader really portrayed faith as reception of a declaration. Faith most often was the channel through which the Holy Spirit incorporated people into Christ and his life, death and resurrection. Their frequent use of justification terminology notwithstanding, Menno and Dirk, like South German-Austrians and Hoffman, regarded salvation ultimately as divinization. They could stress, therefore, that faith joined us with this "true divine

---

[132]Simons, *Complete Works*, p. 654.

[133]Ibid., pp. 336, 506, 827.

[134]Ibid., p. 506, cf. p. 760.

[135]Ibid., p. 333.

[136]Philips, *Writings of Dirk Philips*, p. 243, 248.

[137]Ibid., p. 285.

[138]Ibid., p. 78, italics added.

[139]Ibid., pp. 313, 316, 367.

[140]Ibid., p. 75, cf. p. 82.

[141]For Jesus' own faith, or faithfulness, see Simons, *Complete Works*, pp. 54, 59, 441. For the human response of faithfulness, see ibid., pp. 348-49, 398, 492, 620; cf. Philips, *Writings of Dirk Philips*, pp. 164, 607-8.

righteousness"; it made us "participants in the divine nature."[142]

This renewal occurred through participation in trinitarian dynamics, as for Riedemann and Marpeck.[143] Humans were born again, or anew, "out of [uit]" the Father through Christ and the Spirit.[144] Yet this did not communicate God's essence, as did the eternal Word's birth "from [van]" the Father. This distinction helped Dirk and Menno insist, like Marpeck—and somewhat unlike Hoffman—that humans would always remain creatures.[145] Menno strongly contrasted this birth out of the divine nature with our original birth out of corrupt human nature.[146]

Divinization, further, was not only an inner process. For "whoever has become a partaker of the divine character, the being of Jesus Christ and the power and character of the Holy Spirit, conforms himself to the image of Jesus Christ in all submission, obedience and righteousness."[147] Paradoxically, we attain divinization by seeking to "follow and emulate" Christ, not "according to his divine nature . . . but according to his life and conversation here on earth, shown forth among men in works and deeds as an example set forth before us to follow so that we thereby might become partakers of His nature in the Spirit."[148] On the other hand, this process involved participation in Jesus' flesh, which was of a more perfect kind than ours (see chaps. 6-8).

Menno and Dirk managed to interweave divinization, which soared toward unrealistic heights in Hoffman and the Münsterites, with the tasks of discipleship and daily life. Recoiling from earlier excesses, the later Dutch structured divinization into fairly strict ethical and communal frameworks. They were certainly seek-

---

[142]Philips, *Writings of Dirk Philips*, p. 69; cf. pp. 78, 79, 122-23.

[143]E.g., "The heavenly Father generates or bears the new creature, but the Word of the heavenly Father is the seed out of which the new creature is born and the Holy Spirit renews, sanctifies, and keeps the new creature in a divine nature" (ibid., p. 296; cf. "The Trinity" on pp. 433-38).

[144]Ibid., pp. 294-99.

[145]We "do not become identical in nature and person itself to what God and Christ are. Oh no! The creature will never become the Creator and flesh will never become the eternal Spirit itself which God is." Instead, "believers become gods and children of the most high through . . . participation and fellowship of the divine nature. . . . They will be purified as God, shine as God shines, and live as God lives eternally" (ibid., p. 145). The Dutch contrast between birth directly "from [van]" God and human rebirth "out of [uit]" God is strikingly similar to the Orthodox contrast between identity with the divine essence (which Christ and the Spirit alone share) and renewal by divine energies (see discussion of ontological transformation language pp. 148-50).

[146]Simons, *Complete Works*, pp. 53-62, 139, 439. E.g., through being "renewed, regenerated . . . through this incorruptible seed, namely the living Word of God" one is "clothed with the same power from above, baptized with the Holy Ghost, and so united and mingled with God that he becomes a partaker of the divine nature and is made conformable to the image of His Son" (ibid., p. 58).

[147]Philips, *Writings of Dirk Philips*, p. 294.

[148]Simons, *Complete Works*, p. 55.

ing to interconnect Spirit with matter and the inner with the outer, much as South German-Austrians. Yet we can ask whether they set their ideals too high. They expected people born from the divine nature, who participated in Christ's exalted flesh, to maintain a continuous holy, even if not perfect, walk. Frequent failures led to multiple regulations and ugly disciplinary procedures (cf. chap two). This high, harsh moralism could portray even repentance and therefore personal salvation much like a work.

Summary

I began investigating the new creation's personal dimension in light of sixteenth-century justification controversies. These issues proved to have some significance for Anabaptists, especially the Swiss, Marpeck and the Dutch (above all, Menno). Like Protestants, all Anabaptists affirmed that salvation originates from God's initiative and is basically apprehended through faith. Many Anabaptists granted further that God accepts imperfect persons when they begin their faith walk.

Like Catholics, however, Anabaptists were most concerned about salvation's goal (righteous character) and the process leading to it. They sought to conceive faith as an activity that intrinsically produced works. To this end, many stressed that faith unites people directly with the risen Christ. Yet such a union involved ontological transformation. At this point the faith-works question, raised within the justification framework, led beyond it to Anabaptism's primary soteriological notion: divinization.[149] Among the Swiss, though, salvation was not considered quite so thoroughgoing as divinization implies and is best called simply "ontological transformation."

These terms, however, can suggest that people actually become God (or a divine being) rather than remaining human and being deeply transformed by God. They can foster unrealistic expectations by minimizing or ignoring human limitations. Some Anabaptists succumbed to this, especially in the Netherlands up to Münster. Most Anabaptists, however, avoided it because their ontological transformation was intrinsically patterned. It reflected Jesus' life, death and resurrection—*christomorphically*. Divinization was shaped by—even as it reshaped— the finite world, including suffering and death. Anabaptists traveled this journey *inwardly*, through spiritual participation in Christ, and simultaneously *outwardly* along the path through the material world opened by his life and death. They

---

[149]Friedmann considered Beachy's divinization thesis (Friedmann, *Theology of Anabaptism*, p. 93). He wondered whether Beachy meant by "ontological" what he meant by "existential." Yet he noted that Beachy meant "divinization" in the Johannine sense, which he regarded as "hardly a genuine Anabaptist term."

traversed it not separately but communally and missionally.

Discipleship then was indeed essential to Anabaptism.[150] Yet the term is too one-sidedly "outward" to designate salvation's personal dimension. The further today's reduction of theology to social-ethical dimensions proceeds the less it reflects historic Anabaptism. Beachy and Packull are largely correct in fore-grounding divinization and mysticism—but only as christomorphically patterned. My reading emerges from granting Swiss, South German-Austrian and Dutch sources roughly equal weight. Anabaptism's patterned divinization and mysticism exhibited greater continuity with medieval trends than those prefiguring modernity. In this personal dimension Anabaptism displayed significant commonalities with Catholicism, some with Protestantism and some (inexplicably) with Orthodoxy—yet in configurations distinct from the general orientations of any.

CONTEMPORARY APPROPRIATIONS

Having marshaled resources from historic Anabaptism, how might they help today's churches deal with matters of personal salvation? To explore this we can employ justification issues as an exploratory framework, for these are resurfacing in ecumenical conversation. I will first outline some themes in current Catholic-evangelical and Catholic-Lutheran justification dialogues. I will then address some questions they raise, as well as others from the earlier sections of this chapter, to Scripture, the chief source and sole norm of my theology. Biblical texts involve several levels of meaning. Consequently, when issues are put to texts from different perspectives, they can bring obscured levels to light, as Anabaptist women especially stress.[151] My marginalized tradition will supply the primary perspective, or lens, for discovering and highlighting biblical themes.

Current Anabaptist theologians seldom consider justification. Perhaps it is still widely but tacitly assumed that discipleship and justification belong on two lists (J. D. Weaver), the former being the Anabaptist concern, the latter quite foreign.[152] J. C. Wenger devoted seven pages to justification but interpreted it in Protestant orthodox fashion with little development.[153] Presumably an evangeli-

---

[150]Cf. Bender, "Contemporary Approaches to Historic Anabaptism" on pp. 48-50, as well as the introduction to part two, p. 105.

[151]Regarding this see "Contemporary Approaches to Theology in Anabaptist Perspective" (pp. 80-84) and point 16 (p. 100).

[152]E.g., Friedmann, *Theology of Anabaptism*, pp. 21-22; Robert Friedmann, *Mennonite Piety Through the Centuries* (Goshen, Ind.: Mennonite Historical Society, 1949), pp. 85-87.

[153]J. C. Wenger, *Introduction to Theology* (Scottdale, Penn.: Herald, 1954), pp. 284-90.

cal approach like Ron Sider's would consider justification. John Yoder suggested some social implications of this doctrine.[154] James McClendon touches justification but briefly as one of several images.[155] He builds soteriology around "Salvation as Revolution" and "Following Jesus."[156] I find no real mention of justification in Norman Kraus's minisystematic,[157] and little or none in other theologians discussed in chapter three. To learn how the current discussion of this theme might contribute to Anabaptist theology and vice versa, I must engage ecumenical and evangelical partners.

Justification, however, will simply provide our initial framework. Once again it will point us beyond itself toward more distinctly Anabaptists ways of conceiving personal salvation.

Current Dialogues

Catholic-evangelical. While evangelicals and Catholics have often been enemies in America, in 1997 "The Gift of Salvation," a document signed by some leaders in both camps, affirmed that they can jointly bear witness to this gift despite "some persistent and serious difference."[158]

All signers, echoing the Reformers, agree that justification is "not earned by any good works or merits of our own; it is entirely God's gift." This is because "God, on the basis of Christ's righteousness alone, declares us to be no longer his rebellious enemies but his forgiven friends, and by virtue of this declaration it is so." Justification, further, is "received through faith," which is likewise God's gift. "Alone" is not added, though the signers believe they are expressing "what the Reformation traditions have meant by . . . faith alone."[159]

Echoing Catholic tradition, the signers add that faith is "an act of the whole person . . . issuing in a changed life." This is "a life of discipleship . . . in obedience to Jesus." In justification we also receive "the Holy Spirit, through whom the love of God is poured forth in our hearts." Justified sinners, therefore, have not only been saved but are being saved and will be saved.

Although this document calls justification a "declaration," it acknowledges need for further discussion about "imputed" and "transformative" righteousness—as well as "merit" and "reward." Yet while "The Gift of Salvation" does not speak for any church, and though it has aroused some evangelical op-

---

[154]John H. Yoder, *The Politics of Jesus* (Grand Rapids: Eerdmans, 1972), pp. 215-32.

[155]James McClendon, *Systematic Theology*, vol. 2, *Doctrine* (Nashville: Abingdon, 1994), pp. 110-13.

[156]Ibid., pp. 105-22; 135-45; cf. pp. 117-21.

[157]C. Norman Kraus, *God Our Savior* (Scottdale, Penn.: Herald, 1991).

[158]"The Gift of Salvation," *Christianity Today*, December 8, 1997, p. 35.

[159]Ibid., p. 36.

position,[160] it expresses a noteworthy convergence between a more individualistic, conversionistc theology stressing divine initiative and a more communal, ethical theology stressing human response.

Catholic-Lutheran. Since justification is often thought to be the root of sixteenth-century church division, it is more remarkable that the Vatican and the Lutheran World Federation signed a "Joint Declaration on the Doctrine of Justification" in October 1999. Together they affirm that "all persons depend completely on the saving grace of God for their salvation."[161]

Sounding quite Lutheran the declaration insists that "Through Christ alone are we justified, when we receive this salvation in faith"—though "alone" is not added—and that "Faith is itself God's gift." No works that precede or follow justification can be regarded as its basis.[162]

The declaration also affirms, with Catholics, that people "cooperate" with God, although this too is "an effect of grace." Moreover, "good works . . . contribute to growth in grace," though these are also God's gifts. This is because faith that justifies is "active through love," and "renewal of one's way of life . . . necessarily results from justification." Without this "faith does not exist."[163]

What makes this convergence possible? Perhaps primarily the common understanding, central also among historic Anabaptists, that through faith we "share in Christ . . . the saving presence of God himself," for Christ "is present in faith."[164] Faith unites us with Christ's "death and resurrection." This incorpo-

---

[160]"The Gift of Salvation" is a theological articulation of some convergences affirmed in the 1994 statement "Evangelicals and Catholics Together." These convergences were among those critiqued by the "Alliance of Confessing Evangelicals" in its 1996 "Cambridge Declaration" and its 1998 "An Appeal to Fellow Evangelicals." The former insists that "Christ's righteousness is imputed to us as the only satisfaction of God's perfect justice" and does not rest on "any merit to be found in us, or . . . infusion of Christ's righteousness in us" (Alliance of Confessing Evangelicals, "The Cambridge Declaration," Thesis 4, April 20, 1996, <www.alliancenet.org/partner/Article_Display_Page/0,,PTID307086|CHID560462|CIID1411364,00.html>). The latter finds "irreconcilable differences" between the Protestant claim that God justifies believers by imputing Christ's righteousness to them and the Catholic claim that God saves by infusing with Christ's righteousness through a process that requires human cooperation (Alliance of Confessing Evangelicals, "An Appeal to Fellow Evangelicals" 17, <www.alliancenet.org/CC/article/0,,PTID307086|CHID560462|CIID1415576,00.html>). See also Donald Bloesch, "An Evangelical Response," and Jeffrey Gros, "A Catholic Response," in *Christianity Today*, October 7, 1996.

[161]*Joint Declaration on the Doctrine of Justification in Ecumenical Proposals* (Chicago: Evangelical Lutheran Church in America, 1996), art. 19. It took three years for the declaration to be printed, made available for worldwide discussion and adopted by both churches.

[162]Ibid., arts. 16, 25, 27.

[163]Ibid., arts. 20, 38, 12, 26.

[164]Ibid., arts. 22, 26, cf. p. 27.

rates us into the historical and present "work of the triune God." When people share in Christ like this, God, as Lutherans stress, "no longer imputes to them their sin"; yet God also, as Catholics insist, "through the Holy Spirit effects in them an active love."[165] This cannot help but lead to good works—as Anabaptists repeatedly maintained.

When the Lutheran World Federation finally adopted this declaration (in June 1998, after twenty-five years of discussion) the Vatican still raised three reservations. Though these did not finally prevent official approval, they indicate continuing differences.

First, the Joint Declaration mentions "mere passive" justification.[166] The Vatican found that inconsistent with the belief that justification involves a "new creation" that enables one to cooperate with grace.[167] Since Catholics believe that justification enables cooperation, they can affirm that good works are "also the fruit of man" even though initiated entirely by God.[168] Lutherans seemed to be underplaying the "interior transformation" that occurs in justification.[169] Some Lutherans, however, protested this continuing Catholic accent on cooperation, identifying it as the reason why the declaration had not affirmed "faith alone."[170]

Second, since humans, for Catholics, can cooperate in justification, they can also lose it through mortal sin. For Catholics this necessitates the sacrament of reconciliation (penance) through which "the sinner can be justified anew."[171] The declaration, however, only mentions receiving peace and forgiveness through this sacrament. The Vatican found this too weak.[172]

Third, Catholics objected, as Anabaptists once had, to the Lutheran notion found in the declaration that persons can be totally righteous and sinners simul-

---

[165]Ibid., art. 11, cf. pp. 10, 34, 15, 25.

[166]Ibid., art. 21.

[167]The declaration also says that "grace in justification remains independent of human cooperation" (art. 24). The Vatican could accept this only if it meant that God's gifts of grace do not "depend" or are not based on human works, "but not in the sense that justification can take place without human cooperation" ("Official Catholic Response to Joint Declaration," *Origins* 28, no. 8 [1998]: 131). Catholics still want to talk about merit and reward. The declaration affirms this so long as they are understood, with Hubmaier and Denck, as gifts of grace (*Joint Declaration*, art. 38).

[168]"Official Catholic Response," p. 131.

[169]Ibid., pp. 130-31.

[170]For these and other objections raised mainly by German theology professors, see "JDDJ: A Critical Evaluation," *Lutheran Commentator* 11, no. 5 (1998).

[171]"Official Catholic Response," p. 131.

[172]*Joint Declaration*, art. 30; "Official Catholic Response," p. 131.

taneously *(simul justus et peccator)*.[173] To call such persons sinners seemed to deny
that inner transformation really occurs.[174]

A continuing issue. Today many evangelicals and Lutherans agree that justification
produces an "interior transformation," or "new creation," and its resultant good
works. Yet Catholics tend to include these within justification itself. Many Protestants, however, still seem hesitant to include these in justification—even while insisting that they necessarily result from it. Why does this difference, which echoes
the sixteenth-century debates, persist?

Apparently because many Protestants still wish to stress, above all, salvation's origin in God's initiative. To accomplish this they still find it crucial to distinguish
God's activity clearly from all human actions. Consequently, if justification is God's
act, human acts cannot really be included in it. Accordingly, while God's justifying
act always produces human righteousness, many Protestants still find it crucial to
distinguish these two sharply.

Most Catholics, however, still stress personal salvation's goal: righteous character, which matures through a process. For them justification designates this process
well, for righteousness is part of its meaning. Consequently, Protestant talk of justification can still seem artificial. For how can the term for a truly renewing act exclude those whom it renews—omit their interior "new creation?"

In short, divine and human action still tend to seem so dissimilar, for Protestants,
that the two must be conceptualized quite differently; whereas human action, for
Catholics, still tends to seem so unlike what Protestants think it is that they must conceptualize it quite differently from them. While divine and human activity are surely
very different, it is still difficult to avoid conceptualizing them as incompatible, competing forces, one of which must be diluted or misrepresented to affirm the other.

An Anabaptist Response

In light of historic Anabaptism several observations can be raised about the aforementioned dialogues which will sharpen our eyes for Scripture.[175]

1. While the joint declaration often roots justification in Jesus' death and resurrection, it barely mentions his life.[176] Anabaptists, however, stressed salvific partic-

---

[173]*Joint Declaration*, art. 29.

[174]"Official Catholic Response," p. 130. The Vatican also felt that too great a difference remained between
    the Lutheran understanding of justification as the criterion for theology as a whole, while Catholics regard
    it as one of several important criteria (*Joint Declaration*, art. 18; "Official Catholic Response," pp. 130-31).

[175]In addition, the joint declaration often connects justification with baptism which, in practice, usu-
    ally means infant baptism. I will treat this in chap. 6.

[176]The declaration refers only once to Jesus' "teaching and example" (in art. 31, which locates Jesus'
    saving efficacy in this death and resurrection).

ipation (both inner and outer) in all three. Might justification, in Scripture, also be rooted in Jesus' life and include participation in it?

2. The lengthy discussions of good works and righteous character, in justification discussions both past and present, hardly mention the kinds of works and character involved. Anabaptists ask: What shape does the justified life take? What sorts of acts are righteous? Anabaptists suspect that broad discussions of righteousness-in-general may obscure discipleship's demands.[177] Does justification really appear in Scripture without reference to ethical, communal and social behaviors?

3. Justification, in the twentieth century as in the sixteenth, almost always refers to the individual. Anabaptists instinctively wonder: Could so prominent a biblical theme really lack social, perhaps even cosmic, dimensions?

4. Historic Anabaptists employed justification language less often than that of ontological transformation. They depicted this transformation more often in organic than legal terms. Might some controversies and limitations associated with justification concepts—especially the continuing impasse between accenting divine initiation or human transformation—be overcome by greater use of ontological transformation language?

From biblical materials I will construct a contemporary soteriology (provisionally distinguishing salvation's personal from its communal and missional dimensions). I will articulate some of its themes in justification concepts, then others in ontological transformation language, and finally, briefly summarize this section.

Biblical considerations. I will approach the texts from the perspective opened up by historic Anabaptism. To help in this I will take my bearings from biblical scholars who seek to relinquish Western theological grids and consider themes like "righteousness" and "faith(fulness)" afresh in their original contexts.

1. Old Testament. Here *righteousness* (*sedeq/sedaqà*) "has a cosmic orientation of great breadth" much like *shalom:* a "peace" that includes universal harmony and prosperity.[178] This dimension appears in declarations like: "Righteousness and jus-

---

[177] The declaration avers only once that social-ethical issues must be connected with justification, some day (art. 43). Only once does it admonish Christians "to bring forth works of love" (art. 37) or point to Jesus' teaching and example as "a standard of conduct for the justified" (art. 31). The Catholic-evangelical dialogue, however, stresses somewhat more "a life of discipleship . . . in obedience to Jesus" ("The Gift of Salvation," p. 36).

[178] John Reumann, *Righteousness in the New Testament* (Philadelphia: Fortress, 1982), p. 14. This volume probably presents most exhaustively and lucidly the biblical materials informing current Catholic-Lutheran conversations (H. George Anderson, T. Austin Murphy and Joseph Burgess, eds., *Justification by Faith: Lutherans and Catholics in Dialogue VII* (Minneapolis: Augsburg Press, 1985). For my fuller exposition, see Thomas Finger, *Christian Theology: An Eschatological Approach* (Scottdale, Penn.: Herald, 1989), pp. 174-90; idem, "An Anabaptist Perspective on Justification," in *Justification and Sanctification in the Traditions of the Reformation*, ed. M. Opecensky and P. Reamond (Geneva: World Alliance of Reformed

tice are the foundation of your throne; / steadfast love and faithfulness go before you" (Ps 89:14). Or more fully:

> Steadfast love and faithfulness will meet;
>> righteousness and peace [šālôm] will kiss each other.
> Faithfulness will spring up from the ground,
>> and righteousness will look down from the sky.
> The Lord will give what is good,
>> and our land will yield its increase.
> Righteousness will go before him,
>> and will make a path for his steps. (Ps 85:10-13; cf. 97:2, 6; 99:4)

Second, *ṣqd* terms are connected with covenant-making, so that Yahweh's "righteous deeds" often express "fidelity to the covenant and to creation, a rightful, creative power that will in the future establish justice anew."[179] Because God's covenant people were often oppressed, *righteousness* in this sense frequently denotes their deliverance, the defeat of God's foes (Judg 5:11; Ps 9:4-6) and also the people's vindication through these acts. Third, *ṣdq* can refer to Yahweh's own self-vindication or manifestation as righteous (Ex 9:27; Jer 12:1).

Righteousness became especially crucial in the biblical narrative after Judah's captivity. This righteous deliverance then became an eschatological hope that God would finally "judge the world with righteousness, and the peoples with his truth."[180] Especially in "second Isaiah," *ṣdq* terms come to express salvation itself in all its dimensions. Here one finds what some Protestant scholars call courtroom scenes, where Yahweh summons the covenant peoples' enemies "to judgment, recites the acts of past beneficence and the current accusations, and then calls on the witnesses to the covenant in both earth and heaven."[181]

In these trials *ṣdq* terms occur in challenges to the gods of Israel's enemies: will they "be proved right?" (Is 43:26); can their witnesses "justify them?"(Is 43:9). No, for it will finally be said of Yahweh alone that "He is right!" (Is 41:26). For Yahweh declares, "From my mouth has gone forth in righteousness a word that shall not return: 'To me every knee shall bow, every tongue shall swear' "(Is 45:23). When this happens the eschatological "glory of the Lord shall be revealed, and all people shall see it together" (Is 40:5).

Churches, 1999). Reumann, I argue, pays insufficient attention to some significant meanings and subordinates them too fully to the traditional justification framework (ibid., pp. 51-62).

[179] Reumann, *Righteousness in the New Testamant*, p. 18.

[180] Ps 96:13. The Hebrew word for "truth," *ʾemûnâ*, is sometimes translated "faithfulness"; cf. Ps 98:9, Is 62:1-2; Alfred Jepsen, *"aman, emunah, amen, emeth,"* in *Theological Dictionary of the Old Testament*, ed. G. Johannes Botterweck and Helmer Ringgren (Grand Rapids: Eerdmans, 1974), 1:292-323.

[181] Reumann, *Righteousness in the New Testamant*, p. 16 n. 20; 199.

At the same time the "vindication" *(sedeq)* of God's people will shine out "like the dawn, / and her salvation like a burning torch. / The nations shall see your vindication *[sedeq]*, / and all the kings your glory " (Is 62:1-2, cf. Is 60:1-3). Here a fourth meaning of *righteousness* emerges: energy that will renew and pervade human communities and nature.[182]

In the Old Testament then *righteousness* refers less often to human character than to its source in Yahweh's cosmic rule, deliverance, eschatological self-manifestation and renewal. Similarly, the main word for "faith," *'emûnâ*, throughout the biblical narrative refers most often to God's faithfulness to the covenant, its people and creation. *'Emûnâ* is often paralleled with *hesed* ("steadfast love").[183] But in contrast to God's faith (fulness), humans are often faithless (e.g., Num 14:11; Deut 1:32, 9:23; Ps 78:8, 32, 37). Those few whom *'mn* words describe respond faithfully to Yahweh over a long walk — like Abraham, to whom believing God was "reckoned . . . as righteousness" (Gen 15:6; cf. Rom 4:16-22).

2. New Testament. According to many scholars the New Testament is pervaded by the conviction that the biblical narrative has attained its climax: the promised eschatological salvation has arrived and will soon be consummated on a cosmic scale. Applied to justification this meant that the judgment of God's enemies, deliverance and establishment of God's people, and divine self-vindication had already occurred through Jesus and would soon be consummated through him.

Various scholars argue that God's self-vindication is proclaimed in Romans, the *locus classicus* of justification teaching.[184] Here we find imagery of a cosmic trial, recalling second Isaiah. God is accused of faithlessness to the Jewish people and their promised salvation. But Paul exclaims, "let God be proved true. . . . 'So that you

---

[182]Is 32:15-18; 54:14-15; 58:8; Joel 2:23. The "justified" person can then sing that God "has covered me with the robe of righteousness, / as a bridegroom decks himself with a garland, / and as a bride adorns herself with jewels. / For as the earth brings forth its shoots, / and as a garden causes what is sown in it to spring up, / so the Lord God will cause righteousness and praise to spring up before all nations!" (Is 61:10-11).

[183]As in Ps 85:10; 89:14. This is the theme of Ps 89 (esp. 1-2, 14, 24, 33, 49); cf. Ps 35:5-10, 40:9-10.

[184]Space limits restrict me to Romans. My more detailed biblical methodology would first search for earlier kerygmatic expressions of the aforementioned Old Testament themes (briefly sketched in note 188 below). Still, if these themes are central in Romans, they would likely be significant elsewhere. On Romans interpretation, see esp. Manfred Brauch, "Perspectives on 'God's Righteousness' in Recent German Discussion," in *Paul and Palestinian Judaism*, ed. E. P. Sanders (Philadelphia: Fortress, 1977), pp. 523-42; Ernst Käsemann, " 'The Righteousness of God' in Paul," in *New Testament Questions of Today* (Philadelphia: Fortress, 1969), pp. 168-82; and Käsemann, *Commentary on Romans* (Grand Rapids: Eerdmans, 1980), esp. pp. 77-85; Christian Mueller, *Gottes Gerechtigkeit und Gottes Volk* (Göttingen: Vandenhoeck & Rupprecht, 1964), esp. pp. 49-51, 57-65; Peter Stuhlmacher, *Gottes Gerechtigkeit bei Paulus* (Göttingen: Vandenhoeck & Rupprecht, 1965), esp. pp. 84-91, 113-46, 203-7; and Finger, *Christian Theology*, 2:184-86.

may be justified in your words, and prevail in your judging' "(Rom 3:4). Paul is announcing that God's "truthfulness" (Rom 3:7), which is virtually equivalent to God's "faithfulness" *(pistis)* (Rom 3:3) and "righteousness" *(dikaiosynē)* (Rom 3:5), has already triumphed in eschatological glory (Rom 3:7).

Righteousness here means "fidelity to the covenant," as it often is in the Old Testament, but now expanded to all creation. Romans 3:1-8 in particular shows that "Righteousness/justification has a cosmic side. . . . This emphasis is utterly necessary alongside the individualistic emphasis (so dear to much later interpretation)."[185] But how has righteousness triumphed?

The world, which accuses God of faithlessness (Rom 3:3), has been charged with being under sin's power (Rom 3:9) and condemned under God's law (Rom 3:19). Humans, not God, are shown to be unrighteous (Rom 3:4, 10-18). But this is not all. God's righteousness has been revealed in a way transcending the condemning law (Rom 1:17; 3:21). This is through "faith of Jesus Christ *[pistis Iēsou Christou]*" (3:22). This phrase is usually translated: "faith in Jesus Christ." Yet it much more likely means the "faithfulness of Jesus Christ."[186]

Paul emphasizes that Jesus' cross was a demonstration or "proof *[endeixis]*," through Jesus' faithfulness, of God's righteousness (Rom 3:25, 26).[187] Yet not only his death but also his resurrection was "for our justification" (Rom 4:25).[188] Fur-

---

[185]Reumann, *Righteousness in the New Testament*, pp. 73-74. Reumann finds this emphasis also in Rom 1:17 (p. 65). Joseph Fitzmeyer finds this text speaking of "God's victory over a real world" (as quoted in ibid., p. 211). Yet though he stresses justification's corporate dimensions, Fitzmeyer claims that it concerns only the human world.

[186]The most extensive and influential argument is probably Richard Hays, *The Faith of Jesus Christ*, 2nd ed. (Grand Rapids: Eerdmans, 2002). For a dissenting view, see James Dunn, *The Theology of Paul the Apostle* (Grand Rapids: Eerdmans, 1998), pp. 379-85. Two basic reasons for preferring "faithfulness of Jesus Christ" are (1) Paul would be excessively redundant (even for him!) if *pistis* (faith) always meant human faith, esp. in Rom 3:22; Gal 3:16. Yet if *pistis Iēsou* is translated "faithfulness of Jesus" here and elsewhere (Rom 3:25, 26; Gal 2:16, 20; Phil 3:9), much emphasis on human faith remains; (2) since Paul underlines human inability to attain justification and dependence on God's initiative, why would he stress the human side every time he used the phrase, never the divine (cf. Finger, *Christian Theology*, 2:186-89)?

[187]Rom 3:25 says that God put forth Christ "as a sacrifice of atonement" and follows with the words, "through *pistis* in his blood" (see NIV). Most translations render this an atoning sacrifice, "effective through [human] faith" (e.g., NRSV). But Paul more likely means that Christ became a sacrifice "through his faithfulness," expressed or actualized "in" shedding "his blood." Jesus' death, in other words, was the utmost actualization and expression of God's faithfulness.

[188]Reumann thinks this comes from the pre-Pauline kerygma (*Righteousness in the New Testament*, p. 78) as did I Tim 3:16, which declared Jesus "revealed in the flesh, / vindicated in the Spirit." *Vindicated*, or "justified *[edikaiōthē]*," here refers to Jesus' resurrection, showing him "to be 'in the right.' This means eschatological victory in the 'lawsuit' of God and Christ against the world" (ibid., p. 30). Reumann also finds early formulations in I Pet 3:18, where "made alive in the Spirit" may indicate

ther, justification terminology describes those who respond to that resurrection (Rom 10:6-10). Those who "receive the abundance of grace and the free gift of righteousness [will] exercise dominion in life through . . . Jesus Christ." For "just as sin exercised dominion in death," grace will "exercise dominion through righteousness to bring eternal life" (Rom 5:17, 21).

This righteousness works ethically, in opposition to sin. Yet sin and righteousness are also corporate (i.e., more than human) energies in which humans participate (Rom 6:12-22). The struggle between this pair is closely paralleled by struggles between the suprahuman powers of death and life (Rom 5) and of flesh and Spirit (Rom 8). Through these conflicts the Spirit renews not only human bodies (Rom 8:10-11) but also the nonhuman creation (Rom 8:18-25). Christians still suffer. Yet being justified by the risen Christ (Rom 8:33-34), they will never be separated from him, for he has already conquered all cosmic powers (Rom 8:35-39).

Given the dynamism of the righteousness involved in justification, faith that appropriates it cannot be passive. Instead, Abraham's long walk of faithfulness provides its paradigmatic expression (Rom 4:16-25). And Jesus' faithfulness, though it is also God's, involves the "obedience" normative for humans.[189] Faith(fulness) then must involve works of some kind.[190] Yet faith is hardly based on works, for Abraham was completely guided by God's promise and dependent on God's power.

In this reading of Romans, justification terminology carries much of the meaning of their Old Testament antecedents. Righteousness, the triumph of God's faithfulness, is a cosmic power. It reveals itself in defeat of God's enemies,[191] deliverance of God's people and divine self-manifestation. It renews human persons and communities along with nonhuman nature. Faith is chiefly faithfulness: first God's

---

the same (p. 29), and I Cor 1.30, where the expression Jesus became "our righteousness from God" is "but a short step" from being " 'declared righteous, being vindicated by God,' at the resurrection" (p. 31). For Stuhlmacher, Christ in this verse is "the pardoning demonstration of God's fidelity to his covenant" (quoted in Reumann, p. 32). From such early fragments, Reumann concludes (and I agree): "justification . . . has to do not only with the passion, death, blood, and expiation but also the resurrection and exaltation as vindication of the Righteous one" (p. 40).

[189]Rom 5:19, also Phil 2:8; Heb 5:8-9. Hays argues that "obedience" is central to what Romans means by "the faithfulness of Jesus" (*Faith of Jesus Christ*, pp. 16-67).

[190]In Galatians where Paul introduces justification, "works," when mentioned negatively, are always "works of the law" (excepting "works of the flesh" [Gal 5:19]). Paul's first three negative references to "works" in Romans are also to "works of the law" (Rom 3:20, 27, 28). In the rest of Romans, then, "works" seems to be shorthand for the latter (esp. Rom 4:2, 6). Paul precedes all this by affirming final judgment according to works (Rom 2:6, 7, 15; cf. Gal 5:6, 6:4). He is not against works in general but only a particular kind.

[191]These enemies include humanity as a whole (Rom 5:10), who are defeated in God's judgment on their sin (Rom 1:18; 3:9-19), and cosmic forces of evil (Rom 8:38-39), including death, sin, law and the flesh, dealt with in Rom 5, 6, 7 and 8 respectively.

through Jesus, then as human response to this and complete dependence on it. And a trial is surely held, though not in a courtroom among legal declarations but in history itself among forces that claim to govern it.

Theological construction. This third section of the present chapter ("Contemporary Appropriations") first sketched current ecumenical dialogues on justification and then considered them through historic Anabaptist lenses. So viewed, three main Anabaptist emphases were missing: (1) Jesus' life, (2) salvation's ethical aspects and (3) salvation's corporate dimensions. Anabaptism also prompted the question of whether ontological transformation language might help resolve some impasses, especially between divine initiative and human transformation. I then trained these historic lenses, sharpened through interaction with current ecumenical issues, on Scripture, seeking hitherto obscured levels of meaning. I am ready to construct a contemporary soteriology in light of my findings.

I will first employ justification terminology to conceptualize the three issues just mentioned and several others that they prompt. Then I will shift to ontological transformation vocabulary as shaped by the historic Anabaptist theme: christomorphic divinization.

1. In justification perspective.

• *Jesus' life and teachings.* For the Catholic-Lutheran "Joint Declaration on the Doctrine of Justification," justification involves participation in Christ and his righteousness. Yet while this declaration stresses Jesus' death and resurrection, it scarcely mentions his life (following most sixteenth-century treatments).

For historic Anabaptists also, inward or spiritual participation in Christ's righteousness, including his cross and resurrection, was essential to salvation and often expressed in justification language. But this involved Christ's whole journey toward the cross. Inwardly, this journey was experienced as continuing crucifixion of sinful inclinations (or of inordinate creaturely attachments, especially in South Germany-Austria). Yet this inner path was inseparable from walking Jesus' way outwardly, in obedience and suffering, in tension with the "world."

Biblically, the triumph of God's long-term faithfulness is central to righteousness. This, however, was actualized through "the faithfulness of Jesus Christ." Jesus' entire path of obedience (Rom 5:19; cf. Phil 2:8, Heb 5:8) then must be included in his righteousness. Consequently, participation in Christ's righteousness must include living in accord with his life and teachings, inwardly in intention and outwardly in action.

Though the "faithfulness of Jesus" can turn theology's attention toward human activity, it hardly diminishes the divine initiative. Rather, it magnifies it. The traditional translation of this phrase *(pistis Iēsou)* as "faith in Jesus" draws attention to the human response and away from the events that elicit it. The strategy of reiterating faith alone to highlight God's priority can instead lead to a subjectivism devoid of external referent. The divine initiative is greatly magnified if Jesus' justifying faithfulness is our faith's object and is also intrinsic to God's self-manifestation and self-vindication.

• *Ethical dimensions.* If the overall "faithfulness of Jesus Christ" becomes central in justification theology, human faith can no longer lead to a vague righteousness-in-general. Instead, truly justifying faith will energize behavior formed by Jesus' life and teachings—which can be called discipleship—with their social as well as personal implications.[192] And if the Christ whom we receive by faith and experience spiritually is the one who leads us along this path, the faith-works split at the heart of justification controversy can be overcome.

• *Corporate dimensions.* Historic Anabaptism leads one to suspect that justification has corporate dimensions. Yet Anabaptists did not connect justification vocabulary with these dimensions as often as they connected it with participation in Jesus' life. Still, Anabaptists lenses can help theology perceive that biblical righteousness includes God's faithfulness to the whole creation. God manifested this climatically through Jesus' resurrection (as well as his life and death), which released a righteousness that renews all things. Since we are justified through this cosmic act (e.g., Rom 4:24-25), justification cannot really be conceived individualistically.

Justification enlivens justified people with an energy that raises the dead and brings a whole new creation. This new creation already affects all dimensions of our world and draws us into mission that announces and extends it.

This cosmic dimension was intimated when Anabaptists identified righteousness with eschatological judgment (Riedemann, Marpeck), and justification with God's persisting faithfulness (Hut, Schiemer, Schlaffer, Menno) and Jesus' resurrection (Hubmaier, Marpeck, Dirk). It emerged most vividly in their expectation of an imminent cosmic transformation that would correspond with God's self-manifestation and their own vindication (chap. 10). Biblical justification themes were central in this expectation, even if this was not often expressed by justification vocabulary. Anabaptist justification language, then, at least implied corporate dimensions, for even when its direct referent was an individual, this was but one expression of the eschaton's holistic present and future arrival. The next two chapters will make this clearer, by reconnecting the new creation's personal with its

---

[192]See Yoder's development of justification's ethical dimensions, starting with Galatians 2 (John H. Yoder, *The Politics of Jesus* [Grand Rapids: Eerdmans, 1972], pp. 215-32).

communal and missional dimensions.

• *Eschatology.* Since the historic Anabaptist orientation toward justification is helpfully clarified from its eschatological vantage point, a contemporary Anabaptist theology can ask whether justification itself might best be viewed eschatologically.

The divine and human sides of justification are different enough that efforts to describe one adequately seem inadequate, almost inevitably, to describe the other. To emphasize divine initiative, Protestants often conceive the righteousness that God bestows in verbal or legal terms like *reckoned, declared* or *imputed.* But these can seem to hover in the air, remote from the concrete lives of justified persons.

Conversely, to describe the human side adequately, Catholics often employ ethically laden terms like "preparation for" justification and "merit." But these can seem not only remote from God's initiating grace but also contradictory to it. Similarly, Protestant designations of the human side, like *sinner* (as in Luther's "simultaneously righteous and a sinner *[simul justus et peccator]*"), while in a sense accurate, hardly describe the earthly human reality adequately and risk placing it in flat contradiction to God's action and our ("righteous") spiritual state.

Since the human and divine sides are so different, theological efforts to describe justification may always involve paradox.[193] But might conceptuality be found that does not describe each side so differently (as do, say, the legal and ethical) and in ways that can easily sound contradictory?

Eschatological lenses help one recognize that the justification paradox is largely temporal. In Romans, justification words express both a completed act (Rom 3–4) and an ongoing, future-oriented process (Rom 5–6).[194] Romans 3–6 as a whole is eschatological. Perhaps, then, the paradox could be expressed as follows: When the new creation's call awakens us, and we respond in faith to God's faithfulness in Jesus, we already begin participating in the new creation's dynamic righteousness. It already transforms us. Nevertheless, we are far from fully righteous. We will be so only when the new creation pervades everything, at God's final self-manifesta-

---

[193]The Greek words combined to form *paradox (para* and *doxa)* indicate something that is "against the appearance," or a seeming contradiction. Many important theological doctrines assert that two realities which seem vastly different and even contradictory in our experience (such as divine foreordination and human freedom) are actually compatible, though in a way we can never fully comprehend. Such seeming contradications, or paradoxes, are quite different from real contradictions.

[194]The words translated "to justify" *(dikaioō)* and "justification" *(dikaiōma, dikaiōsis)* as well as those translated "righteous" *(dikaios)* and "righteousness" *(dikaiosynē)* come from the stem *dikaio-*. This questions attempts to sharply separate the first two—as legal—for the last two—as ethical.

tion and vindication, which will also manifest and vindicate our true selves (cf. Rom 8:19-24, which includes the creation).[195]

Conceived this way, the righteousness that God bestows by grace, and in which we participate, is very real. It has been won, manifested and poured out through Jesus' life, death and resurrection. This righteousness is already actual and active, though this is more evident from God's standpoint, which beholds us and the creation in light of what we will become. God treats us as righteous because we already participate in this divinely established righteousness, by grace alone, and not on the basis of our own still imperfect righteousness.

Conceived eschatologically, righteousness characterizes both God's initiative, character and act, and also our concrete, earthly reality. To be sure, the relationship between God's righteousness, which is already active and fully real, and creaturely righteousness, which is not yet fully actualized and real, is paradoxical. The contrast is great enough that these two often *seem* contradictory. But by employing one basic conceptuality rather than two, and conceiving the difference in temporal-eschatological terms, this approach is less likely to present divine initiative and human response as competing, incompatible forces, one of which must be diluted or misrepresented to affirm the other. It is more likely to portray the justification dynamic as a genuine paradox, not a puzzling contradiction.

Anabaptists undertook discipleship neither to obtain justification nor simply to obey Jesus' teachings, but from just such an eschatological apprehension (cf. chap. 10). They could attempt discipleship because God's new creation was already present. They could endure terrible opposition and their own shortcomings because it was not yet fully present—yet they kept going because it surely would be.

• *Basis and content.* Justification theology, however, has not ignored the temporal features of divine and human righteousness. It has connected them in ways that involve, or seem to involve, different temporal phases. Protestants, to stress salvation's origin, typically imply that justification was an initial divine act, followed by a series of acts shaped by human volition called sanctification. Catholics, to stress salvation's goal, also call justification a divine act but typically imply that it occurred first in baptism and will occur a second time in the future, culminat-

---

[195] According to Paul Althaus, Luther himself viewed righteousness as something that "exists in the present and at the same time is still coming in the future" (Paul Althaus, *The Theology of Martin Luther* [Philadelphia: Fortress, 1966], p. 236). In Luther's own words: "We are *not yet* made righteous— yet we are *already* made righteous, but our righteousness still rests on *hope*" (ibid., p. 237, italics added). This is one reason why Luther, in contrast to some Anabaptist readings of him, could affirm that God would never "declare man to be righteous if he did not also intend to make a new man out of him" (ibid., p. 236).

ing in a series of acts shaped by human volition.

As long as divine and human action occupy different temporal phases, however, the problematic disjunction between them persists. For Protestants, who sharply distinguish the phases, justification can be seen as solely God's act, and sanctification as solely our act—a human work that we can perform to earn holiness. For Catholics, who interconnect the phases, human acts which lead toward final justification "increase" justification. These acts can be seen as necessary causes of, or partial contributors to, God's justifying act.

But the eschatological reading, to which historic Anabaptism alerts us, can help theology avoid these opposing misconceptions, which arise from assigning justification to a specific temporal phase. To be sure, the eschatological "already" might appear to be equivalent to one temporal phase (the present) and the "not yet" to another phase (the future). But their relation is paradoxical: both God's actual, final reign and also movement toward its consummation characterize every moment since Jesus' resurrection. The consummation's "not yet" does not mean that the new creation is only partly present; rather, the new creation is everywhere present—precisely as continually coming. That which is coming is "already" everywhere present—as dynamically arriving.

Now the same New Testament justification (*dik-*) words that express both features of the eschatological paradox—a completed, fully realized act and an ongoing, future-oriented process—also designate both divine and human activities.[196] New Testament justification language, that is, describes not only God's acts but also ours. Further, their interconnection is a feature of the eschatological paradox.

This interconnection, illumined by historic Anabaptism's eschatological lens, suggests that contemporary theology might use justification terminology for both divine and human activities rather than introducing another term (such as *sanctification*). This should indicate that these activities are not different phases of a temporal process. Rather than two temporal phases, let us distinguish two permanent but paradoxical features of justification: basis and content.

This would enable theology to insist, as Protestants do, that the basis comes entirely from God. The basis includes the events of Jesus' history, the kerygma's power that communicates them and the Spirit's freeing of persons to respond. These are strictly divine acts, initiated and actualized apart from human response. They also include the presence or indwelling of the risen Christ, whom justifying faith directly grasps. This is what makes faith intrinsically transformative and productive of good works according to historic Anabaptists and today's Lutherans and Cath-

---

[196]Cf. n. 203.

olics. Though faith that receives Christ involves human activity, he is present through a divine activity which belongs to justification's basis.[197] The activities included in justification's basis are also eschatological: the last judgment, final resurrection, Spirit's outpouring, God's dwelling among creatures. Though these events have not yet occurred in the final, fullest sense, they have already occurred in the most decisive sense—through Jesus' faithfulness—and are dynamically invading the present.[198]

Viewed in terms of its basis, justification arises entirely from the divine righteousness. Humans can do nothing to alter or increase this basis. The source, direction and energy underlying any act expressing this righteousness, however long after people enter the salvation process, are already present in Christ's historical and indwelling righteousness, effectuated by his Spirit.[199]

Justification's content, however, consists in the human acts and states arising in response to and dependence on this basis. Viewed in terms of its content—and *only* in this way—the righteousness involved in justification alters and increases, as Catholics maintain, for it is dynamic and transformative. How could it be otherwise if this biblical righteousness is an energy of the new creation's coming?

Nonetheless, however profound and wide-ranging such salvific renewal might be, its basis never alters. No personal, social or environmental transformations, however extensive, add to or alter Jesus' life or death, his resurrected presence or the

---

[197]This notion can also claim Lutheran support. According to Althaus, Luther taught that "our heart itself becomes righteous, not only because it is accepted as such through the imputation of Christ's righteousness" but also "because God's Holy Spirit is poured into the heart and he brings love and new obedience with him" (Althaus, *Theology of Martin Luther*, p. 234). "Luther sees the essence of justifying faith in the fact that it grasps Christ" (p. 230). Many current Lutheran theologians agree that for Luther, Christ himself, and thus his righteousness, were present in faith; see esp. the "New Finnish Interpretation" epitomized by Tuomo Mannermaa (*Union with Christ*, ed. Carl Braaten and Robert Jenson [Grand Rapids: Eerdmans, 1998]). In a similar way, Gerhard Forde shows how Lutheran theology can avoid the justification-sanctification schema with its temporal connotations (Gerhard O. Forde, "Christian Life," *Christian Dogmatics*, ed. Carl Braaten and Robert Jenson [Philadelphia: Fortress, 1984], 2:395-444). Divinization can also be found in Lutheranism to some extent (see John Meyendorff and Robert Tobias, eds., *Salvation in Christ: A Lutheran-Orthodox Dialogue* [Minneapolis: Augsburg, 1992]).

[198]These notions can also be derived from a Christus Victor understanding of Jesus' saving work (Cf. chap. 8, pp. 349-65; cf. Finger, *Christian Theology*, 1:317-67; 2:184-90).

[199]Since precise distinctions are important to many people, let me try another phrasing. Although we are justified when we respond in faith to the revelation and actualization of God's faithfulness in Jesus, through which we already begin participating in the new creation's dynamic righteousness, we are not justified because of any change which that participation brings in us. We are justified because of the saving events of Jesus' history, the kerygma's power, the Spirit's freeing and Christ's indwelling, which are all acts of divine grace; because God has grasped us and indwells us, not because of any subjective changes produced by this.

Spirit's initiative. Perhaps most importantly, salvific transformations occur only when people rely wholly on that basis and nothing else—only when they renounce all tendencies to act autonomously but thank God for acceptance and forgiveness and draw on God's eschatological presence as the source of all activity. Justification's content can increase only when people repeatedly return to that basis: repeatedly renounce efforts at autonomy and receive divine grace anew.

2. In ontological transformation perspective. This chapter has approached personal salvation from the angle of justification first to lead us into historic Anabaptism and then to see whether some Anabaptist insights might contribute to current ecumenical discussion of this theme. In that first, historical task, the justification framework finally led us beyond itself to historic Anabaptism's primary soteriological motif: christomorphic divinization. Now, having formulated some Anabaptist insights in current justification discourse, we will see whether these can also be expressed, perhaps more satisfactorily, in ontological transformation language.

I will again begin by approaching Scripture through the perspective opened up, or the "lens" provided, by historic Anabaptism. Since historic Anabaptism drew our attention to divinization, I will ask whether, or in what ways, that theme appears in the Bible. But *divinization* can be a fuzzy term. To focus on Scripture, then, my Anabaptist lens needs "polishing." That is, I need a more precise understanding of *divinization*. Although Catholics (and sometimes some Protestants) use this term, it is most prominent in Eastern Orthodoxy. I will, accordingly, first dialogue with that tradition to polish my lens and then turn it toward the Bible.

• *Divinization in Eastern Orthodoxy.* Divinization and the broader term "ontological transformation," by which I designate Swiss Anabaptist soteriology, can appear to mean transformation *into* God rather than *by* God while remaining fully human. Marpeck and Dirk explicitly rejected this understanding.[200] Other Christian theologies have denied it by defining divinization as becoming by grace what God is by nature. This distinguishes God from creatures by making divine action, and divine being insofar as it initiates that action, prior. Yet if we become all that God is, we will apparently be omnipotent, omniscient and omnipresent (for starters). This is hard to square with truly remaining creatures. Such expectations can encourage unrealistic behavior, as displayed by some Anabaptists (notably Hoffman and the Münsterites).

The above definition appears in Eastern Orthodoxy.[201] This tradition, however,

---

[200]Marpeck, *Writings of Pilgram Marpeck,* p. 531; Philips, *Writings of Dirk Philips,* p. 145.

[201]E.g., Maximus the Confessor could say that "All that God is, except for an identity in ousia, one becomes when one is deified by grace" (quoted in Pelikan, *Spirit of Eastern Christendom,* p. 267).

also insists that God's essence will remain forever transcendent, beyond our being and knowledge.[202] Gregory Palamas (1296-1359) elucidated this by differentiating God's essence from God's energies, which act directly on us. This strikingly recalls Menno and Dirk's distinction between the eternal Word's birth "from [*van*]" God, which conveys God's essence, and our new birth "out of [*uit*]" God, which does not. In Orthodox and most historic Anabaptist theologies, humans will never become or know God's essence, yet they are transformed by the energies' direct operation on them.[203]

For example, the divine righteousness that renews us (Rom 5–6) is not some force created by God, however sublime. It is God's very own action on, in and through us. This righteousness is not simply judicial, ethical or social; it also draws us into direct communion with God, with its unimaginable closeness and transformative potential. Divine energies are not impersonal forces but God's own direct, personal action.

Though Orthodoxy has sometimes inclined toward spiritualism, it has often stressed christomorphism: "participation in Christ's death and resurrection . . . extends dynamically to cover all the phases and forms of human existence. The crucified body of Christ . . . teaches [us] how to share in the virtues and sufferings of him who was crucified; it shows [us] the way of love, humility, obedience, mortification of the passions, and, in general, of life according to God's will."[204] The first passion to be crucified is avarice, or grasping after earthly possessions, much as among South German-Austrian Anabaptists. The emerging "deified humanity . . . does not in any way lose its human characteristics. . . . [T]hese characteristics become even more real and authentic by contact with the divine model

---

[202]Catholic theology, in contrast, traditionally understands eternal life as the beatific vision, or beholding God's essence (Aquinas *Summa Theologica* pt. 3, sup. Q. 96) and that God is presently in all creatures "by essence" (pt. I, Q. 8.a.3).

[203]For Palamas, direct experience of God was of God's own, or uncreated, grace. His opponent, Barlaam, insisted that this must be indirect or through created channels (Jaroslav Pelikan, *The Spirit of Eastern Christendom (600-1700)* [Chicago: University of Chicago Press, 1974], pp. 254-70; John Meyendorff, *Byzantine Theology* [New York: Fordham University Press, 1983], pp. 76-78, 164; for much greater detail see John Meyendorff, *St. Gregory Palamas and Orthodox Spirituality* [Crestwood, N.Y.: St. Vladimir's Press, 1998]). Speaking very generally, Orthodoxy has affirmed Palamas's emphasis on uncreated grace, and Catholicism has affirmed Barlaam's on created grace.

[204]Georgios Mantzaridis, *The Deification of Man* (Crestwood, N.Y.: St. Vladimir's Seminary Press, 1984), pp. 64-65, describing Palamas's view. Here "The crucified body of Christ" refers chiefly to the Eucharist. This may appear quite different from Anabaptism (but see "The Lord's Supper," on pp. 184-208); cf. Panayiotis Nellas, *Deification in Christ* (Crestwood, NY: St. Vladimir's Seminary Press, 1997), pp. 135-39.

[Christ] according to which they were created."[205]

In sum, Orthodoxy's concept of divine energies can help Anabaptist theology characterize divinization and ontological transformation as not becoming a different, divine being, but as renewal of our thoroughly human being by the divine Being's direct action or touch. Christomorphism can help Anabaptists insist that this occurs through earthly following of and increasing conformity to Jesus and his way.

• *Biblical considerations.* Is something like this historic Anabaptist notion, now sharpened by Orthodoxy, found in Scripture? Precise theological language of divinization appears only in 2 Peter 1:4, which Anabaptists often cited: we are becoming "participants of the divine nature." But something quite similar is conveyed by the Anabaptists' foremost biblical image, the new birth: we are born from the Word of truth (Jas 1:18), from imperishable seed through the living Word (1 Pet 1:23), through Jesus' resurrection (1 Pet 1:3-4), "from above . . . of water and Spirit" (Jn 3:3, 5). Birth seems to indicate impartation of something of divine reality itself.

The Bible also attributes such a direct transformation to the Holy Spirit's work in and among us. This can operate below conscious levels (Rom 8:26-27; cf. Gal 4:6; 1 Cor 2:9-11). God's Spirit makes our bodies, personal and corporate, God's own temple (1 Cor 3:16-17; 6:17, 19; cf. 1 Cor 12:13; Eph 2:18, 22). The Spirit liberates us and transforms us into the divine glory (2 Cor 3:17-18; Rom 8:13-22, 1 Pet 4:13-14).

Paul often spoke of Christ in a similar way: as being in us (Col 1:27; Gal 2:20; 4:19) and of our being in Christ.[206] This "in" was no static position but dynamic inward participation in Jesus' crucifixion and resurrection, expressed outwardly in a life like his.[207] Paul could beautifully express this indwelling as trinitarian (Eph 1:7-14, 17-23; 3:14-21). It involved "a mystical sense of the divine presence of Christ"; yet not only within individuals, for being in or with Christ "cannot be fully enacted except as a 'with others' and 'with creation.' "[208]

The Johannine writings expressed the same realities. Christians "abide" in

---

[205]Meyendorff, *Byzantine Theology*, p. 164. Yet Orthodoxy can differ on what authentic human characteristics are. Humanity's fall can be so damaging that our present bodies and social forms are not God's original creations but garments of skins (Nellas, *Deification in Christ*, pp. 43-91, cf. Gen 3:21). These can include cities, industries and the arts, as well as two sexes and marriage (Nellas, *Deification in Christ*, pp. 86-89, 73, 76). The human body itself, however, is not a garment of skin.

[206]Esp. 1 Cor 1:30; 2 Cor 5:17; Eph 2:5-6, 21-22; Col 2:9-13; 2 Tim 2:11-12.

[207]Esp. 2 Cor 4:10-11; Rom 6:3-13; 8:10-11, 16-17; Phil 3:8-11; Col 2:6-7, 20. "Paul's sense of the mystical Christ functioned in his ethical life as resource and inspiration" (Dunn, *Theology of Paul*, p. 411).

[208]Ibid., pp. 401, 404.

Christ (1 Jn 2:6; 3:6; 4:15), as branches in a vine (Jn 15) and in his teaching, in which we have both Father and Son (1 Jn 2:24 ; 2 Jn 9, cf. 1 Jn 4:14). We abide in the Son (1 Jn 5:20) and in the Son and Spirit (1 Jn 2:27; 3:24). Conversely, the Son is in us (1 Jn 5:9-12) as living water (Jn 4:13-14; 7:37-38) and living bread (Jn 6:35, 50-58). This indwelling prompts us to act with and for others as Jesus did for us (Jn 15:12-13; 1 Jn 3:16-17; 4:9-11; 5:1-3). We are also "born" of the Spirit (Jn 3:3-8), of the Son (1 Jn 2:29) and of God (1 Jn 3:9; 4:7, 12; 5: 1, 18). Moreover, the Son and Father dwell in each other (Jn 14:10-11), and Christians dwell in both (Jn 14:20-23; 17:22-23), so that salvation involves participation in the trinitarian dynamic (Jn 14:16-17; 15:26; 16:13-16).

For various New Testament writers, then, salvation involved God's direct, personal transforming action within and among individuals. This was often depicted christomorphically: as participating inwardly and living outwardly in accord with Jesus' death and resurrection. Yet few texts can be stretched to suggest that Christians actually become divine—in essence. The process they portray, however, can aptly be called "transformation by divine energies"—of our thoroughly human existence through concrete, earthly activities.

- *Reviewing the saving process.* Through the historic Anabaptist "lens" of christomorphic divinization, sharpened in dialogue with Orthodoxy, texts expressing that theme have been found in Scripture. How might some contemporary justification issues look if refocused through this lens?

Justification theology seeks to interrelate divine initiation and human transformation in many nuanced ways. Yet difficulties keep arising, largely because God's action is still conceived mainly in one language, usually the legal, but human transformation mainly in another, usually the ethical. If a legal declaration initiates the process (Protestant), it still seems somewhat unconnected with the ethical life, and God can appear distant from the latter. If the declaration climaxes the ethical life (Catholic), legal concepts like merit tend to be superimposed on this life. Here too God, regarded chiefly as Judge, often appears distant from this life, standing over against it critically, measuring it by legal criteria. Within a justification framework, a basis-content interplay might better resolve these tensions, as I have suggested.

But what if theology conceives them within a divinization framework, whose language is mostly personal or organic? These languages can highlight divine initiative. No creature could be born unless another, quite independently of and prior to its efforts, conceived and brought it to birth. No branch could grow and bear fruit unless it arose from and was continually nourished by the root. Moreover, divinization, by definition, originates from God and continually draws from and remains dependent on God's energies.[209]

Divinization language can also emphasize human transformation. Anything born is intended to grow. Anything planted is intended to bear fruit. No yawning gap opens between this transformation and its divine initiation or culmination. The progenitor, of course, is distinct from the offspring and the cause of their existence. Yet loving parents and healthy plants produce offspring for the very purpose of nurturing their growth. Christian growth is better conceived as a response to and devotion toward a caring, disciplining parent than as a judge or legal declaration.

Organic language can also stress the urgency and difficulties of growth, the dangers which beset it, and the negative consequences of stagnation (e.g., as withering, drying up, being broken off and burned [Mt 13:30; Jn 15:6; Rom 11:17-21]). Moreover, if divinization is christomorphic, its personal language will often be ethical. Ethics, however, will not be guided chiefly by imperatives, rules or even traditions, but will express and shape personal, communal and spiritual relationships.

Still, legal language has a role in theology. Scripture surely speaks of God as Judge and of rewards and punishments. Yet theology, I propose, can best express the biblical sense of these notions if its legal terms are shaped by divinization's personal and organic framework. I have shown that in Scripture justification's legal terminology draws little from courtroom proceedings, and refers to historical "verdicts" of triumph, deliverance and defeat, of personal vindication and self-manifestation. The righteousness manifested in these "trials" also operates organically, renewing persons, communities and creation.

Nevertheless, organic language can sometimes blur important distinctions. For instance, personal salvation, if conceptualized entirely in organic terms, could appear to be one smooth, seamless process. The importance of decisive actions, such as turning from "the world" to Christ, could be missed. For these, legal concepts, like change of status, which have sharper edges, are appropriate. How might some other justification themes look if expressed in christomorphic divinization language?

• *Merits and rewards.* Merits and rewards can be ways of affirming that justified persons really do become holy and pleasing to God.[210] This conceptuality, however,

---

[209] A clear Creator-creature distinction, however, must be maintained. Birth could imply some ontological continuity between them; germination, more so because root and branches are parts of the same plant. This can be countered by observing that offspring, human and animal, can exist quite independently of parents, as can leaves, fruit, grain, etc., apart from original roots.

[210] E.g., Karl Rahner, "The Comfort of Time," in *Theological Investigations III* (Baltimore: Helicon, 1967).

values and evaluates actions in terms of what they earn. For Catholics, of course, the entire process is initiated by and sustained by grace. But how fittingly can the terminology of evaluation and acquisition represent the movement of grace?

Might not this process be better expressed in organic language, where growth naturally produces fruit? Or in personal terms, where maturation develops character and draws one into deeper relations with others? Indeed, won't the reward or eschatological culmination of the process consist in a fulness of these relationships, permeated by divine energies (where the creation bears rich fruits; cf. chap. 10)? If God's gracious movement in and among us brings loving relationships to maturity, wouldn't the entire process be better conceived in terms of growth or gift rather than switching languages at the end to insist that merits and rewards are God's gifts (as in Catholic tradition, Hubmaier, Denck and the "Joint Declaration on the Doctrine of Justification")?

• *Preparation for justification.* If justification is entirely a legal declaration pronounced solely by God, notions of preparation for it will also be evaluated legally, as efforts to earn what only God can grant. Catholics again seek to avoid this implication by insisting that such preparation, traditionally occurring in penance, is possible only for people "awakened and assisted by [God's] grace."[211] Preparation reflects a widespread Christian experience: of repenting and altering one's behavior as much as possible as steps that seem necessary before experiencing salvation.

An Anabaptist perspective favors transposing such experiences from the legal evaluative framework into the organic framework of birth. If personal salvation is a new birth, one would expect it to arrive through struggle—through wrenching away from a dark, enveloping environment into the dazzling, initially discomfiting light of a new world. Recall that for Anabaptists (mainly in South Germany-Austria) inordinate creaturely attachments were virtually organic roots in the soul. *Gelassenheit* involved tearing them up so that the Spirit could graft persons into Christ, making them "one plant and organism with him."[212]

Birth, however, is initiated by the parent. The newborn, by struggling in the pro-

---

[211]Council of Trent, "Decree on Justification," article 5, in *The Church Teaches: Documents of the Church in English Translation*, ed. John Clarkson et al. (St. Louis: B. Herder, 1955), pp. 230-47. Trent rooted the penitential process in a divine call. Mortal sinners "do not merit" this, for "without God's grace" they "could not take one step toward" justification. Through penitential acts assisted by grace they could regain (first) justification through penance (ibid., cf. art. 14). As they move on toward final justification, Christ's "strength always precedes, accompanies, and follows the good works of the justified and without it the good works cannot be . . . meritorious"(art. 16).

[212]Riedemann, *Peter Riedemann's Hutterite Confession*, p. 97. Of course birth does not parallel conversion at every point (neither do legal or any other processes). In conversion the previous "dark" environment is sinful. Tearing away from it involves volition.

cess, is not "earning" birth but simply going through what birth from one environment into another involves—though this is, of course, "necessary" for being born. To be sure, historic Anabaptists experienced this transition intensely. The Dutch could occasionally make repentance sound like a work. Yet when they addressed the issue explicitly, Anabaptists (except perhaps Denck and Schiemer) attributed the new birth's initiation and continuation to God. Their organic, divinization language could stress this initiative, yet also human response, in terms other than earning. (New birth, however, need not always be experienced so intensely, especially when it occurs in more stable environments.)

• *Faith alone? Or formed by love?* For Catholics justification is received by faith. Yet with adults this normally culminates a grace-initiated process (of penance for first justification, of sanctification for final justification). During this process, faith will be formed by love. But love is formed by works of love. To Protestant Reformers, then, faith formed by love meant a faith supplemented by works to make one worthy of justification. The Reformers agreed that true faith acts through love (Gal 5:6). Yet to stress that justification is sheer gift bestowed on the ungodly and unloving, they insisted that it was received by sheer faith, unformed by any virtues—by faith alone.

But what if salvation originates when the Word "kisses" hearts and "the divine nature . . . is conceived and born from the love of the Word?"[213] What if faith is "knowledge of God's mercy," conviction that one "has a gracious, kind, and merciful God?"[214] Then it sounds strange to speak as if faith could act alone, apparently unattracted by God's love, unshaped by apprehension of it, without receiving it, without being informed by it in acts toward others. Theology must deny that faith has to be supplemented by loving acts to earn justification. But to do so it need not intimate that faith's own acts and apprehensions are or sometimes can be isolated from love.

If birth and divinization language can affirm the divine initiative, theology in Anabaptist perspective has no reason to separate faith and love. To be born of God is to be renewed by God's love. Faith that receives or joins one to the risen Christ receives Christ's love. Yet such love is not a human work but a divine gift. Still, true faith is shaped by it from the start. This is why it will inevitably produce works of love.[215] To imply that it might not can drive a wedge between life's inward and out-

---

[213]Marpeck, *Writings of Pilgram Marpeck*, p. 393.

[214]Hubmaier, *Balthasar Hubmaier*, pp. 32, 85.

[215]Cf. Trent's "Decree on Justification": "In the very act of being justified . . . a man receives through Jesus Christ, to whom he is joined, the infused gifts of faith, hope, and charity. For faith without hope and charity neither perfectly unites a man with Christ nor makes him a living member of his body" (art. 7). Lutherans now agree: we trust in God's promise "by justifying faith, which includes hope in God and love for him. Such a faith is active in love and thus the Christian cannot and should not remain without works" ("Joint Declaration on the Doctrine of Justification," 25).

ward dimensions and between religion and everyday existence.

• *Righteousness as "reckoned."* Since this notion is applied to people who act unrighteously, it is easily critiqued as a legal fiction, unrelated to the real world. Yet Hubmaier, Hut, Denck, Schlaffer, Menno and Dirk all affirmed that God accepts flawed people as they pursue the saving path, not counting their sins against them. Here they agreed with the Reformers: people cannot undertake that journey unless they feel accepted or justified by God while still imperfect.

This theological concept is taken from *logizomai,* the New Testament word usually translated "reckon," especially in Romans 4. *Logizomai* can mean commercial or legal calculating, such as assigning a number or criminal case to one list or another. From this, Protestants inferred that it meant ascribing a legal verdict or standing to people regardless of their moral state. Yet in the New Testament, *logizomai* more often means considering something in a general way. Frequently, this involves seeing it far differently than most people normally do, from the perspective of God's saving acts.[216]

Thus in reckoning us righteous, God does not simply place us in a legal category. God regards us, deals with us, from a different standpoint than our shortcomings deserve. This paradox can be well expressed eschatologically. We are reckoned righteous because we already participate in the new creation's righteousness. Not, however, because our imperfect righteousness merits this verdict but because we exist within that righteousness which God has established and placed us by grace. God views us and the whole creation from this perspective, despite all contrary appearances. Biblically, this is entirely compatible with being not yet fully righteous.

Theology can speak, alternatively, of being reckoned righteous in view of justification's basis, of that righteousness flowing through God's Spirit from Jesus' life, death and resurrection, in which we participate by grace. Or more briefly, as historic Anabaptists and today's Lutherans and Catholics affirm, we participate in the risen Christ himself, with whom the Spirit unites us through justifying faith. God reckons us righteous because (on the basis) of this One in whom we participate through grace, not the imperfect righteousness (or content) we derive from it.

This notion, however, is really ontological, a participation in renewing divine reality. Not accidentally this is central, even in my Anabaptist justification theology. For I have been considering justification, ultimately, through the lens of christo-

---

[216]Esp. in Romans itself (6:11; 8:18, 36), and 1 Cor 4:1; 2 Cor 10:7 (cf. vv. 2, 11) and Heb 11:19, which contrast how things look from ordinary and eschatological perspectives. For a traditional Protestant interpretation of *logizomai,* see these Romans passages in John Murray, *The Epistle to the Romans,* 2 vols. (Grand Rapids: Eerdmans, 1959).

morphic divinization. This notion of ontological participation, though basically personal and organic, best explains for me justification's paradoxes: how faith always produce works (because it participates in Christ's active righteousness), and how God's initiation brings about human transformation (because it births us into the same).

Summary. Today, as both globalization and pluralism raise new challenges for worldwide Christian witness and mission, some issues that have divided churches most painfully are being seriously reconsidered. Catholics dialogue with both ecumenical and evangelical Protestants over justification, an issue at salvation's heart. I have tried to show that the historically marginalized Anabaptist tradition can contribute much to these discussions. Not only does its implicit soteriology resonate with many recent convergences, Anabaptism can also suggest ways of incorporating (1) Jesus' life and teachings, (2) ethics and (3) social and cosmic perspectives into the justification drama, and also of conceiving its paradoxes in terms of (4) eschatology and (5) what I call basis and content.

For Anabaptists, however, salvation is more characteristically ontological transformation, even divinization in the sense of transformation by divine energies of our thoroughly human existence on a christomorphic pattern. It is transformation *by* God or Being, not *into* them. A similar emphasis exists among the Orthodox. Divinization also appears in Catholicism and, in less explicit form, among some Protestants, particularly Quakers, Wesleyans and Pentecostals. If Anabaptists can suggest ways of linking justification and divinization, these could be soteriologically relevant to most churches around the globe.

Were not justification so significant in my Western context, currently and historically, I might have developed my soteriology more directly from christomorphic divinization. But to communicate within this context, I seek chiefly to show how such a divinization might illumine some issues often discussed under justification: (1) divine initiation and human transformation, (2) merits and rewards, (3) preparation for salvation, (4) faith and love, and (5) the reckoning of righteousness.

Anabaptism's contributions to justification theology expand it well beyond the personal realm. Its christomorphism shapes not only inward, spiritual experience but also outward, social behavior. The new creation's personal dimension can be distinguished only provisionally from its communal and missional dimensions. The next two chapters will reconnect it with them.

6

THE COMMUNAL DIMENSION

The coming of the new creation in three intertwined dimensions—personal, communal and missional—can be usefully regarded as Anabaptism's central theme. Chapter five, for discussion purposes, loosened the personal dimension from the other two. Today, as globalization continues modernity's dissolution of communal solidarities and relationships, it separates countless individuals from any sense of connectedness. Many turn toward religion for personal meaning. The resultant, wide-ranging quest for spirituality connects at points with the Anabaptist notion of divinization.

In Anabaptism, however, we repeatedly found this personal dimension pointing back toward the communal. It is worth noticing, then, that today's spiritual search is also shaped by a postmodern interest in particular groups, identities and values. Many seekers long for meaningful community as well as spiritual satisfaction. Perhaps the personal and communal dimensions of contemporary experience are more related than they often seem.

The Anabaptist focus is quite concrete, concerned largely with specific practices. To apprehend the new creation's communal dimension, then, I will investigate four practices central to historic Anabaptist communities—baptism, Lord's Supper, discipline and economic sharing—and then make some generalizations.[1] Among these, the two less obviously ecclesial, discipline and sharing, were more distinctly Anabaptist. Anabaptism's particular communal understanding might emerge most clearly by beginning with these. Nevertheless, for several reasons, I will start with baptism, followed by the Supper, discipline and sharing.

---

[1]Snyder lists just these four as essential to historic Anabaptism's ecclesiological core, both early and late (C. Arnold Snyder, *Anabaptist History and Theology* [Kitchener, Ont.: Pandora, 1995], pp. 90-93, 373-74).

First, the connection between the personal and communal dimensions emerged most visibly in historic Anabaptism's insistence that conversion lead to baptism—even if it cost one's life. This, by definition, distinguished Anabaptists from other religious groups. Since baptism incorporated one into the church, personal faith was initially, necessarily and therefore intrinsically actualized in a communal context. Moreover, the communities' continuing call to believers' baptism propelled them into mission and thereby a unique relationship with society (cf. chap. 7).

Second, I earlier decided that part two's abundant material might be most comprehensible if arranged somewhat narratively (moving from personal to communal to missional). This sequence will be clearest if I link the personal dimension first to the practice which joined it with the communal: baptism.

Third, historic Anabaptists often presented baptism as the foundation for discipline, and the Supper as a time to exercise it as well as the basis for economic sharing. That is, their two distinctive practices, they claimed, emerged naturally from two ceremonies that all Christians affirm. Anabaptism then can be connected with current ecclesiology by beginning from commonalities most comprehensible to others (under baptism and the Supper) and then elaborating distinctives, which become increasingly evident under discipline and economic sharing.

Contemporary Anabaptist theologies provide a fourth reason for this order. They repeatedly highlight the church and several broad themes foreshadowed by discipline and economic sharing, such as ethical character and community. This emphasis arises partly from missional concerns—to reach a generation hungry for community yet often negative toward institutional religion. But perhaps for this reason, few such theologians say much about baptism and the Supper.

Norman Kraus, for instance, scarcely mentions them in his minisystematic or his book on the church.[2] Among those few who consider these two ceremonies, John Yoder, at one pole, calls them simply "ordinary human behavior." They are "not mysterious" and can be thoroughly studied by sociology.[3] At the other pole, James McClendon, while emphasizing their ethical meanings,[4] integrates baptism

---

[2] Kraus's first work devotes about a page to sacraments overall (C. Norman Kraus, *God Our Savior* [Scottdale, Penn.: Herald, 1991], pp. 177-78, cf. p. 167). His second work allots around a page to baptism and mentions the Supper in passing (*The Community of the Spirit* [Scottdale, Penn.: Herald, 1993], pp. 29, 110, 111). Worship receives two paragraphs in Kraus (*God Our Savior*, p. 179) but no thematic treatment in *The Community of the Spirit*.

[3] John H. Yoder, *Body Politics* (Nashville: Discipleship Resources, 1992), p. 44; but see pp. 62-63, 231-32. Yoder's procedure resembles mine in that he examines practices (binding and loosing, breaking bread, baptism, the fullness of Christ and the rule of Paul) and lets generalizations emerge inductively.

[4] James McClendon, *Systematic Theology*, vol. 1, *Ethics* (Nashville: Abingdon, 1986), pp. 214-19, 255-59.

and the Supper into a theology of worship, considered as Spirit-enabled response to the risen Lord's initiative.[5]

More recently, Scott Holland is exploring his themes of body and desire in the context of ritual, particularly the Supper.[6] Duane Friesen is developing a broad concept of sacrament (see pp. 75-77). He insists, atypically among Anabaptists, that any church who wants to be "a new society," to be "transformed rather than conformed to distorted and false values must concern itself with ritual."[7] Friesen outlines five sets of focal practices. This notion is mainly sociological: he groups baptism and the Supper under rituals of moral formation.[8] These, however, include a transcendent dimension missing in Yoder, whose other contributions Friesen classes under process practices.[9]

Perhaps Holland and Friesen herald a new trend. Still, most current Anabaptists approach the church in sociological, political and ethical terms largely omitting practices that make it church. This reflects a welcome transition from Anabaptist isolation into serious cultural engagement. Yet it tends to reduce not only theology but even the church to social-ethical dimensions. Is this really the best way to convey Anabaptism's communal insights to the wider world?

This chapter will often suggest otherwise. The new creation could hardly have taken visible form among historic Anabaptists, against extraordinary opposition, had their concern been merely behavioral, had they not felt unified and strengthened by Spiritual experiences and forces unique to churches. Today, many who search for community also hunger for spiritual reality, despite their suspicion of formal religion. Can churches best serve them by promoting social groupings and agendas lacking the depth of true Christian communities?

---

[5]James McClendon, *Systematic Theology*, vol. 2, *Doctrine* (Nashville: Abingdon, 1994), pp. 373-416.

[6]Esp. Scott Holland, "Even the Postmodern Story Has a Body," in *The Presence of Transcendence: Thinking 'Sacrament' in a Postmodern Age*, ed. Lieven Boeve and John Ries (Leuven, Belgium: Peeters, 2001). Concern with spirituality among Anabaptists (see pp. 72-73) is increasing along with attention to worship, especially the Supper. A new Mennonite journal devoted its first two issues to spirituality and communion (*Vision* 1, no. 1 [2000] and 2, no. 1 [2001]). Reimer critiques historic Anabaptists for antisacramentalism (e.g., A. James Reimer, *Mennonites and Classical Theology* [Kitchener, Ont.: Pandora, 2001], pp. 162, 327, 592n. 35) and favors classical theology's greater sacramental awareness. Yet he never treats sacramentality or sacraments at any length, so far as I can discover.

[7]Duane Friesen, *Artists, Citizens, Philosophers* (Scottdale, Penn.: Herald, 2000), p. 142.

[8]Ibid., pp. 141-55.

[9]Ibid., pp. 155-61. Rituals of moral formation also include sabbath, prayer and singing. Process practices are discernment, reconciliation and recognition of gifts; the first approximates Yoder's binding and loosing; the second, discipline; the third combines Yoder's fullness of Christ and rule of Paul. Friesen also includes pastoral care practices (ibid., pp. 161-62), and practices of service to the wider community (pp. 163-66).

160   A CONTEMPORARY ANABAPTIST THEOLOGY

Current Anabaptist theology's relative neglect of ecclesial themes like baptism and the Lord's Supper then provides a fourth reason for considering these first, and discipline and economic sharing afterward. This order, however, is only methodological, like that of chapters five to seven (personal to communal to missional). It could perhaps direct the church away from today's world. Chapter six, however, will continually point toward engagement with the world, leading into chapter seven.

In constructing contemporary Anabaptist views of baptism and the Supper, I will continue the interaction with mainline approaches begun in chapter five—here, especially with Catholics. Then I will shift toward minority traditions. Under "Discipline" I will consider Anabaptist contributions to the current field of "conflict transformation"; and under "Economic Sharing" I will look at Latin American liberation theology. I will close with several inductive generalizations. Even though this chapter is lengthy, it omits several important areas (e.g., ministry, worship). It can only begin to explore Anabaptist ecclesiology. Hopefully colleagues will help me complete the task.

BAPTISM

Since various denominations practice believers' baptism today, some specific arguments by which Anabaptists originally promoted it are well known. Though these are still important, their familiarity can hinder new insights. To facilitate fresh consideration I will mainly investigate Anabaptist perceptions of baptism's broadest horizons and implications. To be sure, historic Anabaptists often concentrated explicitly on specific texts and practices. Yet they deeply apprehended baptism's overall significance for the church (Littell). I will, accordingly, probe this more implicit level of reflection, asking what it might yield for churches today.

Unlike the justification theme (chap. 5), believers' baptism was not partially shared by historic Anabaptists with their opponents. Therefore, I will not employ some other baptismal view as a "lens" to help discover Anabaptism's outlook, as I did with justification. I will search more directly for Anabaptist distinctives. Yet these will prove surprisingly relevant to ecumenical discussion today.

Historic Anabaptist Perspectives

Switzerland. The Swiss were first to foreground, as all Anabaptists soon did, biblical texts that apparently taught that conversion always occurs in a specific order: first comes preaching or teaching, then faith, then baptism only after these. Anabaptists based this chiefly on Jesus' instructions in Matthew 28:19-20 and Mark 16:15-16, and on conversion accounts in Acts. Since children could not follow this pattern,

Anabaptists also argued that New Testament households that were baptized did not include children.[10]

Anabaptists, including the Swiss, probably mentioned 1 Peter 3:21 most often. Here baptism brings salvation as the *eperōtēma:* the appeal to God for or perhaps the pledge to God of a good conscience through Jesus' resurrection. In either rendering, baptism's salvific character is connected with a conscious attitude. Anabaptists also frequently foregrounded Colossians 2:11-13: in Christ

> you were circumcised with a spiritual circumcision, by putting off the body of the flesh in the circumcision of Christ; when you were buried with him in baptism, you were also raised with him through faith in the power of God. . . . [W]hen you were dead in trespasses and the uncircumcision of your flesh, God made you alive together with him.

Citing this text Zwingli was the first of many Reformers to argue extensively that baptism was the successor of Hebrew circumcision and could therefore be performed on infants to signify their inclusion in a covenant and its promises.[11] Hubmaier replied, as many Anabaptists would, that circumcision functions here not as parallel with baptism's outer form but as a figure for its inner, spiritual reality, which transpires "through faith."[12]

Hubmaier, like Felix Mantz and later Anabaptists, also highlighted Romans 6:3-11, which treats baptism as participation in Jesus' death and resurrection.[13] Again like most Anabaptists, Hubmaier often mentioned being born of water and the Spirit (Jn 3:3-8). And like them, he applied it and other new-birth texts to the

---

[10]Acts 16:15, 33; 1 Cor 1:16 (cf. note 108). Matthew 28:19-20 instructs the disciples to "make disciples of all nations, baptizing them . . . and teaching them." Hubmaier interpreted "make disciples [*mathēteusate*]" as teaching, and the three activities as consecutive: teach, then baptize, then teach further. Zwingli countered that the first was a general term, and the next two (baptize, teach) were its components, to be performed in that order (*Balthasar Hubmaier*, ed. Wayne Pipkin and John H. Yoder [Scottdale, Penn.: Herald, 1989], pp. 198-200; Ulrich Zwingli, *Of Baptism*, trans. Geoffrey Bromiley, The Library of Christian Classics 24 [Philadelphia: Westminster, 1953], pp. 141-44). Both readings are possible. Mark 16:15-16 might better support belief before baptism, but it was not originally part of that Gospel. Though faith generally precedes baptism in Acts, episodes involving households do not indicate whether young children were included. However, Hubmaier insisted that his basic argument would hold if no text explicitly placed faith before baptism (*Balthasar Hubmaier*, p. 135).

[11]Roland Armour, *Anabaptist Baptism* (Scottdale, Penn.: Herald, 1966), pp. 36-37.

[12]Hubmaier, *Balthasar Hubmaier*, pp. 186-88; cf. Michael Sattler, *The Legacy of Michael Sattler*, ed. John H. Yoder (Scottdale, Penn.: Herald, 1973), pp. 167-75. Further, he at least implied that if baptism paralleled circumcision, it would merely look forward to forgiveness and Christ's presence, like other Old Testament ceremonies. But baptism celebrates present forgiveness and a risen Christ (Hubmaier, *Balthasar Hubmaier*, pp. 188, 102-4). See also note 42 in this chapter.

[13]Felix Mantz, as cited in Leland Harder, ed., *The Sources of Swiss Anabaptism* (Scottdale, Penn.: Herald, 1985), p. 313.

Spirit baptism that must precede valid water baptism (Jn 1:12-13; 1 Pet 1:23-25; Jas 1:18).

Though Anabaptists discussed many other passages (Hubmaier sought to be exhaustive), their basic point was that all these described baptism as a reality that necessarily involves conscious appropriation. The three chief epistle texts (1 Pet 3:21; Col 2:11-13; Rom 6:3-11) stressed participation in Jesus' resurrection. Anabaptists believed that transforming communion with the risen Jesus simply must be conscious and chosen. They experienced this at the core of personal salvation: in their conversion struggles and continuing participation in Jesus' life, death and resurrection (cf. chap. 5).

Hubmaier also insisted that inward faith saves only if expressed outwardly, in public profession.[14] Authentic faith would lead to confession and baptism into a church, including commitment to live by Jesus' way through the triune God's power.[15] This was not because the water or ceremony was salvific, but because genuine faith intrinsically produces good works.[16] Among these works, baptism, which Jesus directly commanded, was extremely important. Baptism further was an outward sign not simply of the baptizand's faith but also, as Yoder maintains, of a new people forming, free from former social divisions.[17]

Nonetheless, Hubmaier did not consistently maintain this basic insight: that the inner and spiritual must be expressed through the outward and material. Like Zwingli, Hubmaier felt that the two were quite different and that the latter might not fittingly reflect the former.[18] Consequently, Hubmaier often insisted on outward forms not because they were intrinsically appropriate, but simply because God commanded them.[19]

Baptism incorporated one into the church not only by public identification with it but also because, for Grebel and Hubmaier, it involved voluntary submission to the power of the keys: the church's authority to "admonish, punish, ban, and reaccept."[20] Discipline was also an essential mark of the true church, necessary for its very survival. Nonetheless, baptism submitted one to the keys not as an alien force,

---

[14]Hubmaier, *Balthasar Hubmaier*, pp. 178, 188, 293, 352. His basic text was Romans 10:9-10 (p. 193). Mantz also conceived baptism as an outer expression of an inner cleansing (Harder, *Sources in Swiss Anabaptism*, p. 313).

[15]Hubmaier, *Balthasar Hubmaier*, pp. 85-86.

[16]Ibid., pp. 32, 87, 348, 528; cf. "Historic Anabaptist Perspectives," pp. 115-16.

[17]Yoder, *Body Politics*, pp. 28-35.

[18]Armour, *Anabaptist Baptism*, p. 32.

[19]Hubmaier, *Balthasar Hubmaier*, pp. 125-26, 280, 292, 350.

[20]Ibid., p. 127, cf. pp. 85-86, 239, 389, 413-15; Conrad Grebel and Friends, "Letters to Thomas Müntzer," in *Spiritual and Anabaptist Writers*, ed. George Williams and Angel Mergal (Philadelphia: Westminster Press, 1957), p. 80.

for it granted authority to participate in exercising the keys and all other church functions.[21]

Baptizands submitted themselves (at least ideally) not to a controlling institution but a body where they had a function and voice. This resulted fittingly from participating in their own baptisms, not receiving them passively from an institution. Indeed, Hubmaier could affirm more broadly that "the church is built on our own faith . . . not we on the faith of the church."[22] This could imply, however, that the church was a merely human institution.

*South Germany-Austria.*1. Earliest years. By baptism Hubmaier usually meant water baptism. Yet he also mentioned three phases of baptism: of the Spirit, water and blood.[23] The first was the internal, often painful process that brings one to faith. The second was the public ceremony, valid only if it bore witness to the first. The third was "daily mortification of the flesh" brought on largely by following Jesus in the world, culminating in martyrdom or deathbed.[24]

This understanding of baptism as spanning the Christian life was expanded by early South German-Austrians and connected with the *Gelassenheit* process (cf. chap. 5). For Hans Hut, for instance, water baptism was simply the sign—a prefiguring, preparation, model—of true baptism in Christ. The "real essence and power of baptism" was that water of tribulation which swallows one in Jesus' death but finally makes one clean—or justified.[25]

While Hut often depicted this baptism, mostly attributed to the Spirit, as following water baptism, Hans Schlaffer apparently placed the latter first.[26] Yet this difference was not so much a contradiction as an indication that baptism of the Spirit, like justification, designated not a specific salvific phase but a continuing process. Nonetheless, water baptism did mark a particular stage; it should not occur until Spirit baptism had at least worked repentance. But afterward, the Spirit's continued cleansing merged somewhat into the baptism of blood, though the latter referred chiefly to mortification through conflict with the "world."

As they extended baptism through the life process, South German-Austrians be-

[21]Hubmaier, *Balthasar Hubmaier,* p. 389.

[22]Ibid., p. 247.

[23]Ibid., pp. 189, 226-27, 301, 349-50; cf. I Jn 5:8. Grebel spoke of being "baptized in anguish and affliction, tribulation, persecution, suffering and death" through which one mortifies one's "spiritual enemies" ("Letters to Thomas Muntzer," p. 80).

[24]Hubmaier, *Balthasar Hubmaier,* p. 350.

[25]Hans Hut, "On the Mystery of Baptism," in *Early Anabaptist Spirituality,* ed. Daniel Liechty (New York: Paulist Press, 1994), pp. 73, 78.

[26]Hans Schlaffer, *Selections,* in *Spiritual Life in Anabaptism,* ed. Cornelius Dyck (Scottdale, Penn.: Herald, 1995), p. 201.

gan presenting Jesus' own adult baptism as our precedent. (Mantz also had in Switzerland.)[27] Leonhard Schiemer cited it as evidence that baptism involved yielding and obedience to the Father that only the Spirit could bring.[28] For Schlaffer this episode indicated that baptism was for the mature and led, through the Spirit, to conflict with evil.[29] For Hut, Jesus showed that baptism was a lifelong struggle with evil, perfected only at death.[30] By presenting baptism as a continuing process shaped by Jesus' way, including his adult water baptism, South German-Austrians treated the latter as an important outward sign of incorporation into that divinizing participation, both inner and outer, in Jesus' life, death and resurrection at salvation's heart (cf. chap. 5).

This participation, however, was not individualistic. Experiencing baptismal suffering as participation in Christ involved becoming one with him and others in his corporate body.[31] This cleared out a space where Christ could live and which could expand, preparing humankind to be God's dwelling.[32] Baptism also provided a sign of acceptance into a covenanted community of those who, detached from creaturely desires, shared life and material goods.[33] As for Hubmaier, baptism also incorporated people as active participants into church discipline and teaching.[34]

Moreover, since baptism continued through life, the water ceremony provided a sign that one would finally complete "true baptism"—a sign that one belonged, despite imminent eschatological catastrophe, to a community that would endure to the end.[35] It was a mark enabling those so destined to recognize each other. Baptism testified to God's faithfulness[36] and convinced them that

---

[27] Harder, *Sources of Swiss Anabaptism*, p. 314.

[28] Leonhard Schiemer, "Three Kinds of Grace," in *Early Anabaptist Spirituality*, ed. Daniel Liechty (New York: Paulist Press, 1994), p. 95. He followed the three-stage process more precisely, identifying the first with this total yielding through the Spirit (even though it involved water baptism for Jesus). Then water baptism outwardly sealed an inward covenant. Baptism of blood apparently was simply martyrdom, which Schiemer himself faced (pp. 95-97).

[29] Schlaffer, *Selections*, p. 107.

[30] Hut, "On the Mystery of Baptism," p. 78.

[31] Ibid.

[32] Ibid., pp. 79, 76, 78.

[33] Baptism as the sign of a covenant, not only of individuals with God (1 Pet 3:21) but also among individuals in a church, came originally from Hans Denck (Armour, *Anabaptist Baptism*, p. 63). However, Denck eventually decided that "External baptism is not required for salvation" (Hans Denck, *The Spiritual Legacy of Hans Denck*, ed. Clarence Bauman [Leiden: E. J. Brill, 1991], p. 63) and therewith left Anabaptism.

[34] Hans Schlaffer, "Instructions on Beginning a True Christian Life," in *Early Anabaptist Spirituality*, ed. Daniel Liechty (New York: Paulist, 1994), p. 108; Hans Schlaffer, "Ein kurzer Unterrich zum Anfang eines recht chrislichen Lebens," in *Glaubenzeugnisse oberdeutscher Taufgesinnter* (= Quellen und Forschungen zur Reformationsgeschichte), ed. Lydia Mueller (Leipzig: M. Heinsius Nachfolger, 1938), 20:95.

[35] Hut, "On the Mystery of Baptism," p. 73.

[36] Armour, *Anabaptist Baptism*, pp. 90-91.

they were participating in history's climax.[37]

2. Peter Riedemann. Some creative thoughts about baptism were contributed by Peter Riedemann. For this discussion, however, it is only significant that he, like Hubmaier, connected baptism with the church's key of forgiveness,[38] and that he placed baptism of water before baptism of Spirit.[39]

3. Pilgram Marpeck. All Anabaptists insisted that inner, Spirit baptism and outer, water baptism must give expression to each other because inward and outward participation in Jesus' life, death and resurrection were interconnected generally in the new creation's coming (chap. 5). Often, however, their rationale was simply that the water rite was commanded. Pilgrim Marpeck's foremost contribution was to provide deeper, christological roots for this intertwining.

Marpeck reaffirmed many previous themes. Baptism, as Hubmaier said, was public witness before the church, and faith the base on which the church was built.[40] Baptism is three-phased, beginning with the Spirit's inner work; water designated not only the subsequent ceremony but also continuing tribulation which culminated in blood.[41] Baptism is participation in Jesus' death and resurrection. Our baptismal tribulation, like Jesus', should begin with voluntary baptism and follow his way to the cross.[42]

---

[37]Ibid., p. 107. Schlaffer claimed that in the last dangerous days God was erecting a holy community made known to the world through baptism (Schlaffer, "Ein kurzer Unterrich," p. 95; cf. Dirk Philips, *The Writings of Dirk Philips*, ed. Cornelius Dyck, William Keeney, and Alvin Beachy (Scottdale, Penn.: Herald, 1992), pp. 239, 250, 297, 377, 381, 424). Baptism could also be understood as a guarantee of protection (Armour, *Anabaptist Baptism*, pp. 87-88, cf. Rev 7:3-4).

[38]Peter Riedemann, *Peter Riedemann's Hutterite Confession of Faith*, ed. John Friesen (Scottdale, Penn.: Herald, 1999), p. 111.

[39]Ibid., p. 108. The notion of rebirth entailed that, while all children are born into Adam's nature, baptism witnesses to birth into God's nature through faith. Accordingly, only those so born should receive it (pp. 109-10). Faith's chief exemplar was Mary, in whom Christ was born solely through faith in the angel's word (pp. 102, 110). Unlike other Anabaptists, Riedemann noted a parallel with circumcision: since it was applied only to those born into Abraham's household, which could hardly be before they were born, baptism is not for those not yet born into Christ's house (p. 110; cf. p. 193).

[40]Pilgram Marpeck, *The Writings of Pilgram Marpeck*, ed. and trans. William Klassen and Walter Klaassen (Scottdale, Penn.: Herald, 1978), pp. 249, 234.

[41]Ibid., pp. 138-39, 145-46, 435.

[42]Ibid., pp. 139-40, 201. He also widened the difference between circumcision and baptism by sharply contrasting their respective covenants (see William Klassen, *Covenant and Community: The Life, Writings and Hermeneutics of Pilgram Marpeck* [Grand Rapids: Eerdmans, 1968]). The old covenant placed people under the law, driving them to wrestle with sin (Marpeck, *Writings of Pilgram Marpeck*, pp. 110, 125). It could not grant forgiveness; at most it promised forgiveness in the future (ibid., pp. 117-18). Under the new covenant, however, one receives the Spirit, poured out only at Jesus' resurrection, and is born from "the seed of the Word . . . that comes from God's nature" (ibid., p. 240). See also note 12 in this chapter.

Marpeck critiqued spiritualists for seeking a communion with God higher than anything mediated by human words or earthly objects. He considered this an expression of humanity's chief sinful tendency, straining to rise above itself on its own. Paradoxically, such attempts imprisoned the human spirit under the flesh. This spirit was raised back over the flesh, into contact with God's Spirit, only through Jesus' lifelong obedience to God.[43] For Marpeck, the church with its physical actions, structures and sacraments continued this incarnational process. People had to return to God not only through inner communion with Jesus but also through his flesh: through participation in those outer church activities that extended that flesh. Submitting to these reversed the sin of denying human limitations. Water baptism then was necessary because it alone formed the material channel for expressing that humility through which whole selves enter into communion with God's Spirit. This, of course, meant entering humbly into communion with each other. Participation in Christ's continuing incarnation was a corporate venture.

The four Anabaptist practices—baptism, Lord's Supper, discipline and economic sharing—were intrinsic to church life not simply because God commanded them. They were essential for whole persons to submit themselves humbly to God and each other, and to be indwelt by God. These actions, however, were not simply human but were also rooted in God's triune dynamism. In a sacrament like baptism, the Son was enacting externally, through its form, what the Father, as Spirit, was simultaneously performing internally in the baptizand.[44] This triune interaction interwove water with Spirit and baptizands, body and spirit, into the divinizing dynamic. This was the reason why baptism, following Jesus' command, employed the triune formula.[45]

Marpeck called the inner-outer correspondences forms of cowitness. Not only did the Son's outer work cowitness with the Spirit's inner activity, the baptizand's inner confession of a good conscience cowitnessed with the rite's material form and what Scripture said about baptism. Outward washing cowitnessed with inner burial with Christ.[46] The water cowitnessed with the Spirit.[47] But infant baptism, for Marpeck, was mere outward action of water without inward Spirit action;[48] spiritualists committed the reverse error.[49]

---

[43]Marpeck, *Writings of Pilgram Marpeck*, pp. 76-80.
[44]Ibid., p. 195. Though his awkward language could seem to identify the Father with the Spirit at times, trinitarianism was basic to his theology (see "The Trinity" in chap. 8).
[45]Mt 28:19-20; ibid.
[46]Ibid., p. 197.
[47]Ibid., p. 143.
[48]Ibid., p. 111.
[49]Ibid., pp. 195-96.

The Netherlands. 1. Melchior Hoffman. After hearing and surrendering to the gospel, Melchior Hoffman's converts struggled through a spiritual wilderness, and there they betrothed themselves publicly to Christ through baptism.[50] The old Adam was utterly slain in this wilderness, and the new Adam was put on through baptism. Here, apparently, all inner struggle ceased, for the baptized "remain absolutely and fully in the good pleasure, spirit, mood, and will of the Lord Jesus." Yet despite this lofty portrait of salvific progress, Hoffman occasionally warned that one must endure to the end to be saved and that disobedience and banning were possible.[51]

Like early South German-Austrians, Hoffman portrayed Jesus' own baptism as exemplary. At the Jordan, Jesus "covenants and betroths, yea, offers himself, his whole self, to his Heavenly Father" as we must to him.[52] Through this he was "detached," as we must be, "from his own will and, through God's covenant, absorbed into the will of the exalted Father" and guided by the Spirit — though this immediately aroused conflict with Satan.[53]

As among early South German-Austrians, baptism also functioned as an eschatological sign. It assured one of belonging to the community that would prevail, and perhaps hinted that one might be invulnerable. After Hoffman's imprisonment, Jan Matthijs exploited this kind of confidence to rally Dutch Anabaptists to Münster.

2. Menno Simons and Dirk Philips. As congregations began to form in the aftermath of the Münster delusion, Dutch views of baptism understandably became more modest. Baptism still marked the church as God's distinct people. Yet Menno Simons and Dirk Philips did not grant it as intrinsic a role in establishing congregations as the Swiss and some South German-Austrians did—as entailing acceptance of congregational authority, yet granting baptizands a share in it. Instead, Dirk stressed that only duly authorized leaders could baptize.[54]

Like other Anabaptists the later Dutch presented Jesus' baptism as the model for ours.[55] But baptism as a three-phased, lifelong process disappeared; the blood connected with baptism became that shed on the cross.[56] *Baptism* almost always de-

---

[50]Melchior Hoffman, "The Ordinance of God," in *Spiritual and Anabaptist Writers*, ed. George Williams and Angel Mergal (Philadelphia: Westminster Press, 1957), pp. 186-87.

[51]Ibid., pp. 190, 191, 196.

[52]Ibid., p. 189.

[53]Ibid., p. 190.

[54]Dirk Philips, *The Writings of Dirk Philips*, ed. Cornelius Dyck, William Keeney and Alvin Beachy (Scottdale, Penn.: Herald, 1992), pp. 72, 300.

[55]Menno Simons, *The Complete Works of Menno Simons*, ed. J. C. Wenger (Scottdale, Penn.: Herald, 1956), pp. 120-21, 141; Philips, *Writings of Dirk Philips*, pp. 106-7.

[56]Philips, *Writings of Dirk Philips*, pp. 80, 328.

noted a church ceremony. The coupling inner conversion with outer rite was still underlined. Yet the later Dutch promoted this ceremony not because it fittingly expressed the spiritual through the material but simply, and even more strenuously than Hubmaier, because God command it.[57]

Menno and Dirk, of course, were affirming the general Anabaptist principle that genuine inward faith leads to outward works.[58] Yet they could insist on baptism, just as they insisted on repentance (chap. 5), in ways that seemed to base salvation on it. Menno, for instance, declared that in baptism "we bury our sinful flesh and take unto ourselves a new life, seal and confess our faith, testify to the new birth and a good conscience, and enter into the obedience of Jesus."[59] Baptism was sounding more like something humans do, less like a witness to what God does.

Though Menno did connect divinization language with inner baptism,[60] he said little about the outer rite's spiritual meaning. Dirk more often discussed water baptism's significance, associating it with washing,[61] drowning fleshly lusts[62] and burial and resurrection with Jesus.[63] Yet as baptism became a more exclusively outward mark of the church, its meanings were shrinking to features of a ceremony.

Children in the church. Rather than detailing Anabaptist arguments against infant baptism, I have sketched baptism's broader meanings for life in the church. Yet these frequently leave the impression that children played no part in this. To fill out the Anabaptists' understanding of community, we must ask how they answered an unavoidable question: how are unbaptized children related to God?

Hubmaier sometimes professed ignorance.[64] He was certain that children are born in sin and under wrath.[65] Yet he also said that they are innocent and that Christ loves them.[66] He hoped for God's mercy on them.

Anabaptists commonly taught, however, that children were in God's safe-keeping until they intentionally sin. This was sometimes based simply on Jesus' acceptance of them (e.g., Mt 19:13-15). This could lead to regarding children as wholly

---

[57]Ibid., pp. 72, 300, 366-67. Menno and Dirk insisted that every word of God must be obeyed (ibid., pp. 73, 108; Simons, *Complete Works*, p. 126, cf. pp. 124-25, 235-37, 244).

[58]Simons, *Complete Works*, pp. 266, 272.

[59]Ibid., p. 302.

[60]Simons, *Complete Works*, p. 139. While Menno and Dirk believed that the Spirit's work must precede water baptism (e.g., Philips, *Writings of Dirk Philips*, p. 72), the Spirit more often sealed or otherwise accompanied the latter (Philips, *Writings of Dirk Philips*, p. 95; Simons, *Complete Works*, p. 243).

[61]Philips, *Writings of Dirk Philips*, pp. 78-79; Eph 5:26; Tit 3.

[62]Ibid., p. 81; I Pet 3:20-21.

[63]Ibid., p. 75; Col 2:11-12; Rom 6:3-7.

[64]Hubmaier, *Balthasar Hubmaier*, pp. 140-41, 203-4.

[65]Ibid., pp. 218, 284.

[66]Ibid., pp. 284, 141, 291.

innocent, as "born with the purity of creation."[67] Moreover, since sin (like salvation) must involve voluntary action, infants could not really bear guilt for it. Nonetheless, most Anabaptists thought that though children were affected by sin, they were cleansed through Christ's atonement.[68]

Consequently, since all children somehow participated in salvation, children of Christians certainly did. The later Dutch expressly included them in the church.[69] Marpeck reported that infants were ceremonially commended to the church's and their parents' care.[70] In sum, Anabaptist children certainly participated in salvation and the church, though quite differently from those capable of mature decision.

Summary. Because historic Anabaptist baptism was unique in its day, I have been looking mainly for its distinctive features. Many sprung from the conviction that the new creation's coming involved a radical turning from the "world" to Christ.[71] Though rooted in grace, so crucial a decision was by definition a conscious faith response. Though inward, it intrinsically engendered outward activity. Anabaptists argued that Scripture consistently presented water baptism as the initial, public, outward expression of the new birth, or of inward Spirit baptism, or of participation in Jesus' death and resurrection (esp. Rom 6:3-11; Col 2:11-13; I Pet 3:21) whose form was derived from his own life.

Since this turning from the "world" was toward a communal reality, the outward expression united persons with it. For some Anabaptists baptism constituted all members both subjects and agents of discipline. Anabaptist faith then, while personal in inner motivation (as among evangelicals today), was corporate in its context and much of its content (as among ecumenicals). It was personal, but not at all individualistic. It drew people into communities that overcame class antagonisms. These included children in ways suitable for those not ready for major choices.

Anabaptists could present the outer, water rite simply as a divine command or as a rigid requirement (Menno, Dirk, sometimes Hubmaier). Marpeck, however,

---

[67]Marpeck, *Writings of Pilgram Marpeck*, p. 246, cf. pp. 128, 139, 252, 257; Schlaffer, "Ein kurzer Unterrich," pp. 100-101.

[68]Grebel, "Letters to Thomas Müntzer," p. 81; Klassen and Klaassen, *Writings of Pilgram Marpeck*, p. 337; Simons, *Complete Works*, p. 131; Philips, *Writings of Dirk Philips*, pp. 91-92.

[69]Children of Christians "are saved, holy and pure, pleasing to God, under the covenant and in His church" (Simons, *Complete Works*, p. 133). Dirk could even say that they "are already washed and baptized with the blood of Jesus Christ which saves their souls," although "the sign of baptism they shall receive at the appointed time, on the confession of their faith" (Philips, *Writings of Dirk Philips*, p. 106).

[70]Marpeck, *Writings of Pilgram Marpeck*, pp. 147, 242.

[71]For the distinction between the "world" and the world (no quotation marks), see "Contemporary Appropriations" on pp. 310-11, 314-16.

expressed a rationale consistent with their overall outlook. Baptism involved co-witness among all the following realities: inner faith and the outer ceremony, a spiritual reality and its material expression, individual and congregational commitment, and even among trinitarian persons. Rejection of infant baptism followed cogently from perception of that rite as only outer.

In the three dimensions found in all but the Dutch—Spirit, water and blood—baptism covered the whole Christian life. (The Dutch viewed life much the same, but not under the baptismal motif.) The Anabaptist emphasis on voluntary baptism could imply that the church itself was the product of human decisions (esp. Hubmaier). Anabaptists highlighted the divine initiative, however, by insisting that a valid water ceremony must witness to the Spirit's prior work. In other respects the three baptisms were not really phases but interrelated aspects of the salvation process.

A community composed of persons taking such a dangerous public stand, involving such costly interpersonal commitment, was quite conscious of its distinction from the "world," and ready to call others away from it (Littell). Baptism overflowed into a missionary calling to baptism and into distinctive church-world relationships shaped by that call (chap. 7).

Contemporary Appropriations

Although individualism is widespread today, many people long for meaningful involvement in groups. Sociologically, baptism resembles other process by which people begin participating in groups. Some persons join organizations through dramatic decisions or conversions (say, from alcoholism). Others find group identity gradually, through increased involvement in ethnic, special interest or religious solidarities. Transitions of the first kind typify historic Anabaptism and current evangelical movements. The second has characterized most ecumenical churches.

Today, however, Anabaptism's historic ecumenical foes—Lutherans, Reformed and especially Roman Catholics—are rethinking this issue. They recognize that infant baptism was more congenial in traditional state church societies, where children would be raised in congregations and exposed to their teachings. But today most churches are minorities in cultures often hostile or indifferent. Babies baptized perfunctorily often disappear from church.

All communions recognize that to thrive today, they must be somewhat like believers' churches in the past. Their members must be deeply committed and show this by their lives. Ecumenical communions acknowledge that they must reconsider how people first become part of the church, for Christians are made, not born.[72]

---

[72]Frank Senn, *Stewardship of the Mysteries* (New York: Paulist Press, 1999), p. 34.

Might Anabaptists, then, enrich ecumenical discussion from their distinctive standpoint? At first glance, it might not seem so. Ecumenists often call for churches to unite by affirming a common baptism. Their major document, *Baptism, Eucharist and Ministry,* flatly asserts: "Any practice which might be interpreted as 're-baptism' must be avoided."[73] Wouldn't believers' baptism churches be perceived as opposing church unity? To promote unity, shouldn't they accept all baptisms performed in other churches?

Reconsideration. Around mid-twentieth century, several prominent Reformed theologians, including Karl and Markus Barth, began promoting believers' baptism.[74] Today, some mainline churches offer the options of either the infant or believers' rite.[75] Others oppose indiscriminant baptism and limit the infant ceremony to committed church families. This, they claim, (re)connects baptism with faith, for children are baptized into the faith of their parents and the church. Finally, many churches have given greater importance to confirmation, when individuals (usually adolescents) profess their faith and commitment to the church, and receive laying on of hands for reception of the Spirit.

Since at least the 1960s, however, other directions have been encouraged by historical research.[76] Most scholars now concur that baptism in East and West, until at least the fourth century, was normally performed on catechumens.[77] Persons became catechumens by forsaking negative behaviors and affirming their desire to join the church. From then on they were regarded as actually part of it. A two to three year catechumenate not only included teaching but also involvement in most aspects of church life except the Eucharist.

Catechumens were usually baptized in a joyous, churchwide Easter celebration that included the water rite, laying on of hands for reception of the Spirit (which later became confirmation) and admission to the Eucharist. These three components gradually separated into different ceremonies in the West, though they still coincide in the Orthodox East.

Influenced by such research many ecumenical churches are reconsidering some

---

[73]*Baptism, Eucharist and Ministry,* Faith & Order Paper 111 (Geneva: World Council of Churches, 1982), art. 13.

[74]Dale Moody, *Baptism: Foundation for Christian Unity* (Philadelphia: Westminster Press, 1967), pp. 50-55.

[75]E.g., Jürgen Moltmann, *The Church in the Power of the Spirit* (New York: Harper & Row, 1977), pp. 240-42.

[76]For baptism in particular, see Maxwell Johnson, ed., *Living Water, Sealing Spirit* (Collegeville, Minn.: Liturgical Press, 1995), pp. 11-34. For confirmation, see ibid., pp. 148-59, 202-58; and Aidan Kavanagh, *Confirmation* (New York: Pueblo, 1988).

[77]Disagreement exists over how early and widely infant baptism was practiced. Few scholars, however, question that the pattern described here was standard, or that New Testament baptism was mainly of adult converts. For several baptisms of families in the New Testament, see note 105 of this chap.

Anabaptist themes with a seriousness that invites dialogue. Most now stress that baptism, not a subsequent first communion or confirmation, is the true entrance into the church. Although the historical research has influenced Protestants, Catholics have probably reflected on it most deeply, especially in light of Vatican II's increased emphasis on the laity and on sacraments as performed by the whole church.[78]

I. Catholic developments. At least three main viewpoints, or "schools," can be identified in current discussions.[79] According to an environmentalist school, the church is a society that reverses original sin's orientation. This society includes children, since it forms them into its milieu. Infants can receive baptism if parents are ready to raise them in this setting, but it can be postponed if they are not. A corresponding practice school argues that many paths to faith exist, and infant or adult baptism can be appropriate for different people. However, a mature adulthood school has attracted most attention. It maintains that believers' baptism is the norm and that this is affirmed, even if only implicitly, in the official Catholic Rite of Christian Initiation of Adults.[80]

Proponents of this third view generally agree that the New Testament presents a basic pattern or order that provides "common ground for all the multivalent practices."[81] This order leads from proclamation to faith to baptism (with the Spirit involved in all three) and then to a community life of teaching, breaking bread, fellowship, prayer and witness. All this comprises "a whole new ethic and way of life" in "a community so new and different that conventional social analogues can hardly be used to describe it."[82]

Advocates then affirm that Vatican II derived a "norm of baptism" from "the New Testament doctrine of conversion." Though the Vatican Council expressed this diffusely, it essentially described baptism as a "solemn sacramental initiation done especially at the paschal vigil and preceded by a catechumenate of serious content and considerable duration."[83] This means that infant baptism is abnormal—but in the sense of less than ideal, not impermissible.[84]

---

[78]Walter Abbott, ed., *The Documents of Vatican II* (New York: Guild, 1966), pp. 25-37, 56-65, 137-82, 489-521.

[79]Johnson, ed., *Living Water*, pp. 335-42, 345-48, 329-35.

[80]Ibid., pp. 329-35. The Rite of Christian Initiation of Adults was first published by the Vatican in 1972. For issues of practical implementation, see Thomas Morris, *The RCIA: Transforming the Church*, rev. ed. (New York: Paulist, 1997).

[81]Aidan Kavanagh, *The Shape of Baptism* (Collegeville, Minn.: Liturgical Press, 1978), p. 23.

[82]Ibid., pp. 22, 30.

[83]Ibid., p. 109.

[84]While "neither scripture nor tradition . . . support infant baptism as the pastoral norm," they "clearly support the practice as a benign abnormality in the life of a community whose ministry regularly focuses on the evangelization, catechesis, and initiation of adults of faith." Infant baptism can be "a modest manifestation of God's love for all ages and of the stunning liberality of his grace" (ibid., p. 110).

Baptism is a trinitarian reality in which the water rite incorporates people into the Son's mission. Confirmation, which should immediately follow, communicates the Spirit's outpouring. Baptism then leads to the Eucharist, and the Eucharist in turn sustains baptism. "From this premier sacramental union flows all the Church's life."[85]

Catholics who encourage adult baptism hope that their church will become more like a believers' church.[86] They want evangelism and catechesis to become regular activities. They want whole congregations to be involved in the catechumenate and catechumens to make regular members aware of the need for continuing repentance and conversion.[87] Such Catholics envision baptism as a public declaration of the baptizands' commitment to the church and the church's commitment to them.[88] Baptism incorporates everyone into the one priesthood of Christ so that when a few are ordained later, this can only be to exercise particular functions.[89]

Aidan Kavanagh maintains that Rome now has two initiatory theories. These express two visions of the church. The infant theory fits a Christendom model where large numbers receive Catholic instruction, supported by the state. But the adult theory "does not presuppose the state." It arose "not only without recourse to state benevolence but often in opposition to its pretensions."[90]

On this mature adulthood theory baptism is "anti-structural." Given Western society's post-Christian character, Kavanagh hopes it will eventually win out. This would mean that "the days of evangelization through social structures sustained by a sympathetic state are numbered. . . . [T]he days of a practical correlation between Church and civil society are over."[91]

2. *Protestant developments.* Partly in response to the historic Anabaptist critique, many Protestant communions developed confirmation into the major occasion for affirming mature faith. Yet today most mainline Protestants, influenced by the historical research that is challenging Catholics, regard baptism as the one initiatory sacrament that includes, at least ideally, confirmation and first communion. They also promote baptism as the basis for church unity.

Lutheran, Episcopal and Methodist liturgies present baptism as a covenant. They highlight God's initiative in establishing it. Infant baptism is legitimated because it purportedly illustrates this: Since infants, who cannot respond, receive bap-

---

[85]Ibid., pp. 147, 122.
[86]Johnson, *Living Water*, pp. 331, 349, 379, 381.
[87]Kavanagh, *Shape of Baptism*, pp. 112-14.
[88]Johnson, *Living Water*, p. 271.
[89]Ibid., pp. 267-68.
[90]Kavanagh, *Shape of Baptism*, p. 197.
[91]Ibid., pp. 197-98; cf. Senn, *Stewardship of the Mysteries*, p. 170.

tism, salvation must depend utterly on God, not on us.[92] Yet baptism is not simply an individual or clerical rite. Participation by church members is encouraged. Baptizands are committed to the church universal as well as the local congregation, while the congregation commits itself to care for creation.

Since baptism is now the sole initiatory sacrament, confirmation can no longer be that later bestowal of the Spirit that completes baptism. Yet Lutherans, Episcopalians, Methodists and Presbyterians still retain confirmation or something like it—though as one of several reaffirmations of baptism that are encouraged but not strictly required. Catechesis often occurs before the first reaffirmation, though patterns and timings of instruction vary.[93]

The rationale for baptism as the single initiating sacrament is clear in Lutheranism. For Luther, the whole Christian life involved daily drowning with Adam and rising with Christ. Consequently baptism is *"the* sacramental sign under which all Christian life is lived."[94] Faith is involved in the sense that baptism is into the church's faith. Yet individual sin and salvation are not so much in focus today as communal and environmental restoration.[95] Nevertheless, American Lutherans often find it difficult to scale down confirmation, for it has long been their ceremony for profession of faith.

3. Summary. Historical research has helped bring many Catholics and ecumenical Protestants to affirm one initiatory sacrament—baptism—and theoret-

---

[92]E.g., Johnson, *Living Water*, p. 280. Kurt Stasiak presents a Catholic argument for infant baptism on the grounds that it highlights God's initiative and that the child "is a sacrament of that radical openness" we all must have toward God (*Return to Grace: A Theology for Infant Baptism* [Collegeville, Minn.: Liturgical, 1996], pp. 107, 123).

[93]For Lutheran, Episcopal, Methodist and Presbyterian practices, see Johnson, ed., *Living Water*, pp. 284-88, 292-309; Richard Osmer, *Confirmation: Presbyterian Practices in Ecumenical Perspective* (Louisville: Geneva, 1996), pp. 93-98, 104-2, 148-60; Gerald Austin, *Anointing with the Spirit* (New York: Pueblo, 1985), pp. 65-96. For a current Presbyterian proposal for confirmation, see Osmer, *Confirmation*, pp. 162-228. For a Catholic overview, see Austin, *Anointing with the Spirit*, pp. 125-50. Since baptism involves first communion, some Protestants argue that infants should be communed, as they are in Orthodoxy. But when Protestants baptize infants, regular eucharistic participation is usually deferred, even though it often recommences before confirmation/reaffirmation. When Lutherans sought to forbid infant communion in 1978, much controversy resulted (Senn, *Stewardship of the Mysteries*, p. 156). For Lutheran discussion see Johnson, *Living Water*, pp. 350-51, 358-64, and Senn, *Stewardship of the Mysteries*, pp. 155-70. Infant communion was strongly supported in a World Council of Churches study (Geiko Mueller-Farenholz, ed., *And Do Not Hinder Them: An Ecumenical Plea for the Admission of Children to the Eucharist*, Faith & Order Paper 109 (Geneva: World Council of Churches, 1982).

[94]Luther, as quoted in Osmer, *Confirmation*, p. 70. "The sacrament of baptism, even in respect to its sign, is not the matter of a moment, but continues for all time. Although its administration is soon over, yet the thing it signifies continues until we die, nay, until we rise at the last day. For as long as we live we are continually doing that which our baptism signifies—we die and rise again" (ibid., p. 231).

[95]Johnson, *Living Water*, p. 308.

ically at least to emphasize confirmation less. These churches are performing more believers' baptisms. Yet infant baptism is still far more common and stands in some tension with the new views and the widely recognized need for mature profession of faith in a post-Christian world. The multiplicity of proposals for conducting and interconnecting first communion, catechesis and confirmation/ affirmation indicate the importance of such a profession and uncertainty about how to celebrate it.

An Anabaptist response. Two different paths could be taken in response to today's ecumenical discussions. Anabaptists could affirm the call for church unity on the basis of a common baptism. Since this involves acknowledging all baptisms performed in other churches, this approach would likely endorse infant baptism. Anabaptist theology could also ponder current discussion from its distinctive vantage point and identify those who raise similar concerns. It could then reexamine baptismal theology in dialogue with them. Two such concerns are the importance of (1) one initiatory sacrament, and (2) mature, ritual faith confession. To explore these I will first turn to Scripture, my theology's chief source and sole norm. I will view it through lenses provided by historic Anabaptism now sharpened by interaction with current, mostly Catholic, scholars.

1. Biblical considerations. Despite frequent citations of Matthew 28:19-20 by Anabaptists, I do not find it necessarily mandating that preaching, faith and baptism always occur in that order. Nevertheless, scholars like Kavanagh assert that New Testament "proclamation . . . always precedes baptism"[96]—it does seem clear that this was the standard pattern.

In fact, we find, perhaps surprisingly, that current New Testament scholars largely agree with Anabaptist readings. Favorite Anabaptism texts represented reception of baptism as a very intentional, conscious act (esp. Rom 6:3-11; Col 2:11-13, 1 Pet 3:21). Scholars generally concur that Scripture (1) repeatedly links baptism with faith[97] and teaches that baptism (2) incorporates people into a community very different from the "world,"[98] (3) is into Christ, and that (4) the Spirit is baptism's agent.

---

[96]Kavanagh, *Shape of Baptism*, pp. 20-21, cf. pp. 22-23. "While the possibility that infant baptism was also practiced in the apostolic age cannot be excluded, baptism upon personal profession of faith is the most clearly attested pattern in the New Testament documents" (*Baptism, Eucharist and Ministry*, art. 11).

[97]In addition to historical accounts in Acts, esp. Gal 3:26-27; Eph 1:13; 5:26; Col 2:12; Heb 10:22; cf. *Baptism, Eucharist, and Ministry*, arts. 8-10: the four points in this paragraph are clearly affirmed in this document. For fuller discussion of biblical texts, see G. R. Beasley-Murray, *Baptism in the New Testament* (London: Macmillan, 1962), pp. 266-75.

[98]Jn 3:3-5; Acts 2:38-42; 1 Cor 6:9-11; Gal 3:27-28; Eph 4:28-32; Col 2:11-12; 3:7-11; Tit 3:3-7; cf. *Baptism, Eucharist, and Ministry*, arts. 2, 4, 7.

A few texts on the last theme, by themselves, do not clearly indicate conscious appropriation (I Cor 6:11; Tit 3:5). And the Spirit, indeed, often works on unconscious levels (including in infants). Still, God's Spirit, in the New Testament, far more often energizes conscious, willed activity, including faith.[99]

Yet while scholars broadly agree about the New Testament, it deals mostly with first generation Christians. It is virtually silent on how their children entered the church. Is it possible that some New Testament baptismal meanings could be extended, in quite different situations, to include infants? Might some metaphors—say, rebirth, being washed or sealing—be "quite compatible" with infant baptism, since these are "passively undergone rather than actively undertaken"?[100]

Rebirth or new birth, however, was the Anabaptists' chief metaphor for salvation. They repeatedly described it arising from the preached Word, initiating a vividly conscious baptism of the Spirit, vastly different from the old birth.[101] Rebirth, I have argued, can express human activity's role in salvation (pp. 153-54). In Scripture it is far too active to convey passive reception.

Three baptismal uses of being washed connect it also with conscious appropriation.[102] Yet two others that were recently mentioned, which highlight the Spirit's agency, may not. Titus 3:5-7 attributes salvation and apparently justification to

---

[99]Mk 1:8-11 and pars.; Jn 3:5-8; Acts 2:38; 10:44-48; 19:5-6; I Cor 10:2-4; 12:13; cf. *Baptism, Eucharist, and Ministry*, art. 5; Beasley-Murray, *Baptism in the New Testament*, pp. 275-79. For Kavanagh, the New Testament "water bath is a function of the Spirit" (*Shape of Baptism*, p. 25). Sealing by the Spirit almost certainly refers to baptism (see note 100 and Beasley-Murray, *Baptism in the New Testament*, pp. 171-77).

[100]Frederick Bauerschmidt, "Baptism in the Diaspora," in *On Baptism: Mennonite-Catholic Theological Colloquium, 2001-2002*, ed. Gerald Sehlabach (Kitchener, Ont.: Pandora, 2004), p. 8. In Eph 4:30, "being marked with a seal" may appear passive. Yet this almost certainly refers to Eph 1:13, where the seal was received through faith. In 2 Cor 1:22, Paul and his companions receive a seal through an anointing, along with the Spirit in their hearts, apparently for their ministry. While sealing may seem to connote passive reception, in the New Testament it often does not (e.g., Jn 3:33; 6:27; Rom 4:11; I Cor 9:2), though it probably does in Rev 7. Though I differ with Bauerschmidt at several points, I find his essay the best Catholic interaction with the Anabaptist position so far. A major premise is that "The church is a distinctive social order that is set apart from the world to be the instrument of the world's salvation" (ibid., p. 14).

[101]Jn 3:3-8; Jas 1:18; I Pet 2:23-25; cf. Jn 1:12-13.

[102]Clearly in Acts 22:16. Heb 10:22 encourages readers to approach God "with our hearts sprinkled clean;" yet also, immediately preceding this, "with a true heart in full assurance of faith." It seems difficult to separate out "sprinkled" as passively received, especially since it is "from an evil conscience," which presumably would not vanish apart from some active process. In Eph 5:26 Christ gives himself for the church "to make her holy by cleansing her with the washing of water." Yet this is also "by the word," and since cleansing's goal is eschatological perfection (Eph 5:27), "washing" probably refers to a continuing, active process.

"the washing of rebirth and renewal by the Holy Spirit." First Corinthians 6:11 simply states, without mentioning any mode of appropriation, that readers were washed, sanctified and justified in the Spirit and the Lord Jesus' name.[103] Some will argue that choice is implied in such events since they also conveyed justification and sanctification.[104] These passages, of course, do not deny that choice is involved. But neither do they teach this.[105] Perhaps these two texts provide some basis for extending baptismal washing beyond conscious reception of it.

The third commonly affirmed New Testament theme is that baptism is into Christ. In favorite Anabaptists texts this is into his death and resurrection.[106] Participation in Christ is also central to justification—for Anabaptists, Scripture, and today's ecumenical discussion. For all these, this participation is in his death and resurrection. But Anabaptist theology, I propose, should add "in and according to his life pattern" (cf. pp. 142-43). Now if participation in Jesus' earthly way is intrinsic to salvation, might our way begin, as his did, with believers' baptism? Might not baptism into Christ be not only into his death and resurrection, but also into his life, and appropriately modeled after his own baptism?

Although many Anabaptists invoked Jesus' adult baptism as a basis for ours,[107]

---

[103] *Washing* might have another passive usage if Rev 1:5 portrays us as "washed *[lousanti]* from our sins" rather than the preferred reading, "loosed *[lusanti]*." Jesus' washing of the disciples' feet (Jn 13:1-11) graphically portrays cleansing as passively received. While Tit 3:5 does mention "rebirth *[palingenesias]*," I find this too slim a basis for extending this general motif to include passive reception, given its very active meaning elsewhere in the New Testament.

[104] As does Beasley-Murray, *Baptism in the New Testament,* pp. 162-67, 209-16; cf. my previous interaction with Bauerschmidt ("Initial response" in *On Baptism,* pp. 26-28), where I took this approach. Though I still find it quite plausible, I am seeking to consider these texts as do those who do not assume conscious appropriation.

[105] Similarly, New Testament reports of baptisms of households indicate neither that children were baptized nor that they were not (Acts 16:15, 33; 1 Cor 1:16). Like the two washing text, they, by themselves, raise a slight possibility of infant baptism in New Testament times.

[106] Rom 6:3-11; Col 2:11-3; 1 Pet 3:21; also 1 Cor 10:2-4; 12:12-13, Gal 3:26-28; cf. Eph 4:5; cf. *Baptism, Eucharist, and Ministry,* arts. 3, 6.

[107] Moreover, "Shortly after the apostolic period Jesus' baptism was the primary paradigm for Christian baptism until the 4th century" (Bauerschmidt, "Baptism in the Diaspora"). Orthodoxy also cites Jesus' baptism as a basis for the rite (Alexander Schmemman, *Of Water and the Spirit* [Crestwood, N.Y.: St. Vladmir's Seminary Press, 1995], pp. 41-43, 47-51). It envisions Jesus being baptized into his own coming tribulation, or blood, which eventually issued in others taking up his messianic ministry (Johnson, ed., *Living Water,* pp. 263-64; for a Catholic appropriation, see Kilian McDonnell, *The Baptism of Jesus in the Jordan* [Collegeville, Minn.: Liturgical Press, 1996]). Jesus' reference to his own death as "baptism" provided the basis for regarding baptism as dying with him (Mk 10:38; Lk 12:50; Kavanagh, *Shape of Baptism,* pp. 14-15). Anabaptists certainly had precedent for connecting the baptisms of water and blood.

I cannot see that this by itself mandates believers' baptism,[108] for discipleship is not copying Jesus in every detail. Nonetheless, this foregrounding of Jesus' practice corresponds with overall New Testament teachings on not only baptism, but also justification and divinization.

Finally, New Testament baptism into Christ often includes incorporation into a community transcending social divisions (1 Cor 12:12-13; Gal 3:26-28; Col 2:11-13; 3:9-11; cf. Eph 3:3-5). Anabaptists can stress that baptism into Christ, like participation in Christ's righteousness (see chap. 5), has an intrinsic social dimension.

2. Theological construction. While New Testament evidence strongly supports believers' baptism, remember that it does not address children. Accordingly, even though New Testament metaphors (except possibly washing) cannot really stretch to include infants, it is still important to ask whether broad ecclesiological considerations might.

Today, one such consideration is missiological. Christians often work together despite baptismal differences, and few unchurched people are interested in these. Might not a theology that aims to serve churches in effect drop this issue? Might it, following many current Anabaptist theologians, focus on broader features of community, not specific ecclesial ones? In particular, might believers' churches accept other churches' baptisms, as many ecumenists recommend, to better unite with them in expressing a distinct, countercultural witness in a rapidly globalizing world? Let me respond in light of three ecclesiological themes which are also broadly theological.

- *The inner and the outer.* The question of baptism's form is sacramental: a question of to what extent and how specifically inward spiritual grace need be expressed in outward, material forms. We have seen that in its personal dimension the new creation involves the intertwining of inner and outer. Here the outward is expressed mostly in everyday activity. But does this mean that ceremonial, or more specifically sacramental, forms are unimportant or perhaps infinitely variable?

This chapter, hopefully, will increasingly show that in Anabaptism and Scripture they are not, for Christian communal life is not simply doing things together. Above all, it means belonging, through deep commitment, to a historic church community involving worship, remembrance and spiritual nurture. Wherever commitment, belonging and history are important, forms of incorporation provide crucial indicators of what commitment and communal life itself really mean—for

---

[108]Although Jesus provides human behavior's norm, theology cannot conclude that every aspect of his life is normative for us. Some features of Jesus' mission, e.g., climactically embodying God's righteousness and faithfulness, were uniquely his (see "An Anabaptist Response," pp. 142-43, 146-48).

the individual, the community and outsiders. If these actions also intend to point to a reality transcending the community, it is even more important that they symbolize all this appropriately.[109]

But how might Anabaptist theology communicate this to people today who search for spirituality and community but dislike institutions? I recommend by gently but realistically insisting that true community is really incompatible with modern notions of uncircumscribed freedom. Community requires acceptance of definite limitations—letting one's life be shaped by very specific persons and ways of doing things. And since entrance into community involves acceptance of specific behaviors, it is fittingly marked by a specific ceremonial activity.

Anabaptists, like current ecumenical churches, find this entrance important enough that a single initiatory sacrament should render it and the nature of the church being entered visible. But how might this sacrament, baptism, best express that interaction of inner and outer so central to church life? Like historic Anabaptists, I find that infant baptism does this poorly, for the initiate is hardly aware of what happens. Of course, the inward dimension is expressed by others who commit themselves to the initiate's nurture. But this also occurs in believers' baptism—and is enhanced because the initiate shares in a mutual commitment.

Believers' baptism also portrays membership not only as submission to or reception into an institution—but also, since it involves inward, conscious choice, as taking an active role. Infant baptism can hardly express that interplay between individual freedom and corporate identity central to ecclesial existence.[110] Neither does it symbolize that interaction of divine grace and human response woven through all Christian life. To be sure, infant baptism is often defended as a symbol of God's initiative, for its recipients are passive and helpless. Yet human activity— of a finite, often flawed church—is surely involved.[111] Might not such baptisms less

---

[109]To indicate that baptism points beyond itself, McClendon calls it a sign, rather than a symbol, which, for him, is simply an "emblem of some thought, emotion, or experience" (*Systematic Theology* 2: 388). McClendon names baptism, the Lord's Supper and preaching "remembering signs." These point beyond themselves to historic signs, which include the biblical narrative's main events and even creation itself (pp. 381-406).

[110]While baptism "presupposes the dignity and responsibility of the individual person before God," it is not like joining "a club or community organization." It "arises out of the power of the gospel" and bestows a new corporate identity (Duane Friesen, *Artists, Citizens, Philosophers* [Scottdale, Penn.: Herald, 2000], pp. 143, 142). Believers' baptism seems to better symbolize full involvement of all members, which nearly all churches today promote. Infant baptism can symbolize inscription into hierarchical structures at the expense of participation flowing from conscious commitment.

[111]I owe this point to Heidi Yoder. I am somewhat surprised that Catholics, Orthodox and liberal Protestants, who advocate some degree of human freedom, find it unnecessary for baptizands. Here they seem closer to Lutheran and Reformed positions.

aptly symbolize God's priority over humans than the institution's priority over individuals?

Every sacrament has human components. Divine initiative is properly symbolized not by sacraments that allegedly eliminate these, but by those which properly relate the divine and human. The issue is not whether the divine is prior—it is—but how it interconnects with the human, both personal and corporate.

Admittedly, believers' baptisms today often overplay the baptizands' experiences and decisions. Precisely because Anabaptists and their successors stress concrete commitment, they can appear to base baptism on human subjectivity, as Hubmaier could. This raises the common objection that believers' baptism is rooted in "the emerging modern concept of the person as an autonomous individual" that makes each "self the source of its values and its own identity."[112]

To rectify this, baptisms of water must witness more clearly to their divine origin, baptism of the Spirit. It must also be evident that the individual's decision, which they celebrate, involves acceptance of the community's values and of limitations that accompany committed participation.

In overall church life, however, Anabaptists have tended to exaggerate not the baptizand's subjective preferences but communal demands for conformity, as May and Holland protest.[113] Yoder may inadvertently encourage this. While rightly treating baptism as the sign of a new people bridging social divisions, he denies that it is a product of individual, "inward believing."[114] In our individualistic era, many seekers for spiritual satisfaction may find believers' baptism not too subjective but too demanding of commitment and self-limitation. Might not infant baptism, where baptizands make no commitments, at times allow more room for living by subjective values and preferences?

• *Church and "world."* The new creation's coming involves a decisive turning from the "world" to a community energized by and seeking to embody that creation. Which form of the initiatory sacrament makes most visible that turning and the church as the body of those turned? Again, it clearly seems, one which celebrates and actualizes deliberate movement away from the "world" through burial with Christ and toward the new creation through resurrection with him.[115]

It is often objected, however, that many people first enter the church in in-

---

[112]Johnson, ed., *Living Water,* p. 377.

[113]See "An Anabaptist Response," pp. 84-85.

[114]Yoder, *Body Politics,* pp. 28-35.

[115]Cf. Friesen, *Artist, Citizens, Philosophers,* p. 145.

fancy, are nurtured by it and eventually commit themselves to it. Doesn't believers' baptism exclude such children from the church? On the contrary, Anabaptist churches have a broadly sacramental way of accepting them. The arrival of children and the commitment of Christian parents and congregations to nurture them can be celebrated in dedication ceremonies, as already occurred in Marpeck's day.[116]

Nevertheless, countless children who enter the church through infant baptism or dedication never join. Many react negatively, and multitudes drift away. The question is not whether two ways of coming into the church—as children or through mature decision—should be marked in broadly sacramental ways. The real questions are: Which best expresses (1) what true initiation into the community of the new creation is, and (2) what that community itself really is?

Ecumenical churches still perform baptism, the initiating sacrament, mostly on infants. Yet Protestant ecumenicals cannot avoid giving sacramental importance to ceremonies, like confirmation, which acknowledge the church's distinctive character and mission, and commit people to it.[117] At this moment, then, I think Anabaptists can best contribute to others by asking, gently, whether their own positions might not point toward aligning confession with baptism: toward making these *together* the distinctive initiating sacrament (as believers' baptism). Might this best attain their aim of making the nature of Christian commitment, the church, and its significance for the world as visible as possible? Many features now associated with infant baptism could retain sacramental significance by incorporating them into dedication.

- *Salvation of children.* For many people this proposal will raise the question of how or whether children are saved. In response, most historic Anabaptists pointed to a universal aspect of Jesus' atonement: his "act of righteousness leads to justification and life for all" (Rom 5:18); "as all die in Adam, so all will be made alive in Christ"

---

[116]Marpeck, *Writings of Pilgram Marpeck*, pp. 147, 242. Anabaptists more often distinguish between what is appropriate to childhood and adulthood than many infant baptism proponents, such as Stasiak, who regards childhood openness as ideal for all ages (*Return to Grace*, pp. 115-25). Unbaptized children are no less part of Anabaptist churches than they are of their families. Inability to earn income does not make them lesser family members. It only affects their roles. Children do not receive baptism or drivers' licenses for much the same reason: they are not ready. If, when they become mature enough to choose for or against Christ, they remain unbaptized, they can be treated much as catechumens so long as they are involved in church and headed toward baptism. Such persons are indeed included in the church, though with fewer participatory privileges and responsibilities than full members.

[117]I employ the traditional distinction between sacraments, which convey grace regularly and are essential to the church, and sacramentals, other rites that can convey grace but are not essential.

(I Cor 15:22). These texts, I believe, include everyone in salvation in some sense.[118] Yet such an affirmation, I propose, can be drawn from Anabaptist soteriology another way.

Salvation involves inward and outward participation in Jesus' life. Jesus' earthly life was not simply exemplary but a phase of the process by which he brought humankind back to God. As Marpeck best expressed it, Jesus walked the path assigned to Adam (see "The Work of Jesus Christ" on pp. 341-43). Yet Jesus remained in constant relationship with God. This brought humankind, in his person, back into divinizing relationship with God. Adults participate in this relationship when the risen Jesus draws them through faith into his life, death and resurrection, reorienting them toward God.

Since Jesus was fully human, he also passed through infancy and childhood in communion with God. He brought the whole span of human life into it. Since adults participate in that saving process in the way appropriate to them (faith), can we not assume that young children also do in a manner suitable for them?[119]

• *Benign abnormality?* Catholics who find believers' baptism normative call infant baptism abnormal. This, however, does not mean infant baptism is invalid, for it can still have benign results.[120] Even if Anabaptists cannot accept infant baptism, can they find some benign features in this rite?

Anabaptists insist that true inward faith produces outward works. Many adults baptized as infants manifest both. Some want to join Anabaptists congregations. What should these congregations do? I recommend that they teach these persons the meaning of believers' baptism and invite them to receive it as a premier outward expression of their faith. Some such individuals, however, consider their infant baptism sufficient. Many Anabaptist congregations receive them without believers' baptism. So would I. Why? Because such people have been appropriating by faith some meanings expressed, however imperfectly but still benignly, in their infant baptisms. Although that rite for them was outward, with-

---

[118]They say more than that Christ's atonement is sufficient for all (as do Jn 3:16; I Jn 2:2). *All* might simply mean some people from all nations (Rev 7:9). But this is unlikely since atonement's scope is parallel with the universal effect of Adam's sin. Both verses, in context, point toward the future (cf. Rom 5:17, 19; I Cor 15:23-24). Yet the notion that they apply to all beyond death (universalism) conflicts with many other texts (cf. Thomas Finger, *Christian Theology: An Eschatological Approach* [Scottdale, Penn.: Herald, 1985], 1:148-53). The context refers to the present at least as much: sin is already defeated and eternal life already here for all (cf. Rom 5:15-16; I Cor 15:20-21). If this is not true of all adults now, and will not be for everyone in the next life, to whom does it pertain but children?

[119]cf. Johnson, *Living Water*, p. 395.

[120]Kavanagh, *Shape of Baptism*, p. 110.

out inward faith significance, its meanings are coming alive inwardly for them. Some of those meanings, of course, might have been appropriated by that congregation. Such appropriation by the church that receives baptizands is, indeed, crucial to baptism. But by itself, it cannot constitute baptism's inward side. For this involves mutual appropriation, commitment and reception by baptizand and congregation.[121] Still, some people so baptized do appropriate baptism's meanings inwardly later on. When they wish to join a church, they are ready for mutual commitment and reception through an outward rite.

A membership rite other than believers' water baptism will not carry that sacrament's full meaning. Yet if the candidate's inward appropriation and outward commitment are genuine, such a rite will express much of its significance. It will still symbolize and actualize Christian commitment's outer, corporate character, which Anabaptists especially should make visible. Yet inward appropriation of baptism is deeply personal and equally important. Requiring believers' baptism of persons who understand it and desire outward commitment, but still find their infant baptism sufficient, can smother baptism's personal significance under demands for communal conformity, as Anabaptists sometimes have. I advise then that (only) such persons be received without that specific rite.[122]

Ecumenically, this does not entail accepting all baptisms of all churches. Anabaptists should still affirm believers' baptism's values. Yet this perspective can increase their understanding of other Christians who manifest faith's fruits and believe they are appropriating their infant baptism benignly or savingly.

3. Summary. Very briefly, baptism interlinks some main features of the new creation. Through baptism these cowitness to each other. Baptism itself, in fact, is an interlinking, three-phased process of Spirit, water and blood. It provides the initial link between the new creation's personal and communal dimensions. Baptism of water links the individual with the community, and inner baptism of the Spirit with outer, public expression. Baptism incorporates a person into the community's in-

---

[121]Infants can be incorporated into the church's faith in the sense of its nurturing context, which includes its beliefs and traditions. This should occur through a sacramental dedication. The church's faith can guide children toward their own faith, which will appropriate some features of the church's faith. Yet faith, as decisive reception of the risen Christ along with elements of the church's faith, is quite different than this passive incorporation.

[122]More fully, since infant baptism can express or point toward some baptismal meanings, and since some of its subjects appropriate these later and consider it sufficient, I propose that in today's context, for these subjects only, a membership rite with inner, outer, personal and communal meanings, though not water, will express baptism's meaning adequately—yet imperfectly—and better than a water rite suppressing the inner, personal sides. McClendon, somewhat differently, recommends that believers' baptism churches consider the infant rite imperfect and "repair" or "regularize" rather than discard it (*Systematic Theology* 2:395-96).

terrelated practices, most directly discipline, and also the Lord's Supper and economic sharing. Performed in the triune name, baptism is energized by and witnesses to God's own interactivity, or cowitness (see "The Trinity" on pp. 424-25, 431-34, 439-40). By bestowing material form on both the baptizand's and the community's faith, believers' baptism provides fuller sacramental union of the inner and outer than the infant rite.

Believers' baptism sacramentalizes not only allegiance to the new creation but also the decisive breaking of another link—of allegiance to the old creation, or the "world." This nevertheless does not isolate the individual or community from the world. It leads them to form links with it through mission (cf. chap. 7). In our day of globalization yet fragmentation, believers' baptism can help churches make a distinctive communal way of life visible and offer authentic involvement in it.

THE LORD'S SUPPER

Though current Anabaptist theologians say little about baptism, they allot perhaps less space to the Supper.[123] Yoder tends to reduce its meaning, like baptism's, to social dimensions. Jesus, he claims, introduced no ceremony but simply made his followers' "ordinary partaking together of food" his memorial.[124] Holland, however, questions whether one can move so directly "from text to ethical action" as narrative theologies often assume.[125] Doesn't narrative language rather desire dramatic performance, desire to spill over into "prayer, the liturgy, the hymn, the homily, the Eucharist—the performance of doxology"? And can't these draw one, rather than away from the world, further "into productive public life," opening "one who eats and drinks to another hunger, a holy desire . . . a eucharistic eros toward the world"?[126]

McClendon, who stresses narratives, finds a variety of them intersecting in the Supper. Yet this meal, for him, not only remembers Jesus, but through it the risen Jesus also re-members us with each other and himself.[127] Friesen, who calls the Supper the "central ritual of the Christian faith," stresses the economic significance of its sharing of food. Yet this must also point " 'beyond' ordinary profane life" and

---

[123]Rempel illustrates and critiques this tendency (John Rempel, *The Lord's Supper in Anabaptism* [Scottdale, Penn.: Herald, 1993] pp. 205-10, 220-26). For recent attempts to redress it, see Dale Stoffer ed., *The Lord's Supper: Believers Church Perspectives* (Scottdale, Penn.: Herald, 1997).

[124]Yoder, *Body Politics*, p. 16.

[125]Holland, "Even the Postmodern Story," p. 240.

[126]Ibid., pp. 246, 241, 251-52.

[127]"The major narratives tell of forgiveness ('blood shed for forgiveness of sin') . . . solidarity ('my body') . . . thanksgiving . . . ('giving thanks, he broke it')" and the eschatological banquet "('until he comes')" (McClendon, *Systematic Theology* 2:401; cf. *Systematic Theology* 1:214-19).

participate in a "world of sacred meaning."[128] Friesen and McClendon, then, while underscoring economic and narrative functions like Yoder, point far more clearly to their sacramental intersection with spiritual reality. Holland adds that these physical features are not thinglike signs. They are enactments, performances, actions that typify the church's overall worship life. For Holland these also evoke transcendence, but apparently it is inherently material.[129]

Even if today's Anabaptists often marginalize the Lord's Supper, historic Anabaptists found its right practice essential to any true church. We must ask then what roles it played in their communal life and whether, with sensitivity to our current context, these should be reconsidered. Wouldn't today's disinterest in institutional religion point toward minimizing the Supper? But alternatively, might not the postmodern valorization of particular communities and of symbolic and ritual expressions over cognitive ones point toward highlighting it?

To discover historic Anabaptist perspectives I will begin with, and thereby test, a common claim: that Anabaptists understood the Supper largely as a memorial of Jesus' death.[130] In Reformation times, Zwingli championed this outlook.

Zwingli protested the Catholic teaching that the substance of Jesus' body and blood was directly present in the bread and wine (whose substance was transformed, or transubstantiated, into the former). Along with Anabaptists and all other Reformers, Zwingli also critiqued Rome's practice of allowing only its priests to perform the Mass. They all protested that this practice, combined with transubstantiation, allowed Rome to claim that it possessed Christ and controlled his presence. They all perceived the Mass as an illegitimate instrument of power—a source of multiple oppressive claims, ecclesiastical and sociopolitical.

Luther, however, still stressed that Christ was present in, with and under the Supper's elements, though he rejected transubstantiation. But for Zwingli, matter and spirit were so different that matter could not contain spirit but only point to it. Almost all notions of Christ's presence seemed too crudely material. The elements, however, could point to something—Jesus' death—and help us remember it. In a secondary sense, moreover, the congregation could be called Christ's body.

Severe as disagreements between sixteenth-century Catholics and Protestants were, we found their heirs converging on justification (cf. chap. 5) and baptism. Since Catholics are also rethinking the Supper, I will dialogue with them again in

---

[128]Friesen, *Artisans, Citizens, Philosophers*, pp. 122, 146.

[129]E.g., "The very structure of reason itself comes from the details of our embodiment. . . . [R]eason is not in any way a transcendent feature of the universe" (George Lakoff and Mark Johnson, *Philosophy in the Flesh* [New York: Basic Books, 1999], p. 4, as approvingly quoted in Holland, "Even the Postmodern Story," p. 243).

[130]E.g., Snyder, *Anabaptist History*, pp. 85, 93.

constructing my own view. I will propose that here also the allegedly nontheological, nonsacramental Anabaptist tradition can contribute to ecumenical discussion.
In latter sections of this chapter, however, I will turn toward minority and postmodern concerns.

Historic Anabaptist Perspectives

Switzerland. Anabaptists here, despite sharp disagreement with Zwingli over baptism, generally affirmed his memorialism. They agreed that Jesus' body, which is
now in heaven, cannot be in or transformed into bread.[131] With Zwingli they could
call the worshiping congregation Christ's body on earth. Did they also view the
Supper, like him, as mainly a memorial?

Conrad Grebel insisted, as all Anabaptists would, that Communion bread is
simply bread. Yet when received in faith, it was also "the body of Christ and the
incorporation with Christ and the brethren." When used this way, the bread
showed "that we are truly one bread and one body";[132] or in Schleitheim's words,
"made one loaf."[133] Significantly, the "inner" meaning of this "Supper of Fellowship" was not simply experiential but a communal bonding, as it would be for
Hubmaier.[134] This Supper called to mind "the covenant of the cross" and the need
to suffer for Christ's sake and the brethren,[135] or as Schleitheim said, to give our
lives for them as Jesus gave his life for us.[136] For Anabaptists, who communed in
secret for fear of government authorities, this was not merely figurative. They might
soon be discovered and dragged off to martyrdom. The original Supper's atmosphere was recreated almost literally.

Though Grebel insisted on celebrating the Supper with extreme simplicity, he
advocated doing so "much and often," as Sattler did.[137] Yet since it would not really
be the Lord's Supper without love, Grebel and Schleithem expected church discipline to be exercised beforehand to ensure that this inner reality was present.[138]

I. Balthasar Hubmaier foregrounded the remembrance of Jesus, who shed his
blood for forgiveness, which also led participants to give their bodies and blood for
each other. The bread, as many Anabaptists would say, symbolized the congrega-

---

[131]E.g., Michael Sattler, *The Legacy of Michael Sattler,* ed. John Howard Yoder (Scottdale, Penn.: Herald,
    1973), p. 71.
[132]Grebel, "Letters to Thomas Müntzer," p. 76.
[133]Sattler, *Legacy of Michael Sattler,* p. 37.
[134]Hubmaier, *Balthasar Hubmaier,* p. 76.
[135]Grebel, "Letters to Thomas Müntzer," p. 76.
[136]Sattler, *Legacy of Michael Sattler,* p. 45.
[137]Grebel, "Letters to Thomas Müntzer," p. 77; Sattler, *Legacy of Michael Sattler,* pp. 45, 62.
[138]Grebel, "Letters to Thomas Müntzer," p. 77; Sattler, *Legacy of Michael Sattler,* pp. 37.

tional unity possible only when individual "grains" renounced their separateness to be kneaded and baked into one loaf.[139] By virtue of this public body-and-blood commitment, the Supper, like baptism, formed a bond with God and others unto death.[140] It presupposed baptismal submission to and participation in communal authority, which was often exercised before the Supper.[141] It included willingness to share material goods.[142] It was a sacrament, by which Hubmaier meant chiefly a pledge, though one fulfillable only "in the grace and power of the suffering and the blood shed" by Jesus.[143]

As for Grebel, the bread for Hubmaier was simply bread. Yet as it was "offered, broken, taken, and eaten" it was "the body of Christ in remembrance."[144] That is, as church members shared the bread, and thereby their lives, with each other, it became the vehicle through which Jesus' broken historical body was remembered and the world affected by the salvation it brought. But this meant that the congregation itself, as Zwingli also affirmed, became Christ's body on earth. Moreover, through its active remembrance and pledge to share, the congregation became the Supper's main agent—even its primal sacramental reality.[145] For the Supper has to do "completely and exclusively with fraternal love."[146]

Hubmaier believed that God's Spirit was active in the Supper, as in all phases of baptism.[147] He said that the Supper satisfied a spiritual hunger and thirst.[148] Yet having located Jesus' body in heaven, like Zwingli, he hardly ever mentioned Christ's own presence in the Supper, or the Supper as spiritual communion with him.[149] Hubmaier indeed affirmed Christ's deity. Yet he seldom mentioned it being active in Communion or in any earthly way save the preached Word. Outside preaching, Christ existed in two largely disconnected forms: in heaven, and as largely synonymous with his body on earth, the church.

Hubmaier stressed the Supper's communal dimension and its expression through concrete, outward ethical activity. He also believed that the Spirit oper-

---

[139]Hubmaier, *Balthasar Hubmaier*, pp. 75, 334.

[140]Ibid., p. 70.

[141]Ibid., p. 127, cf. p. 416.

[142]Ibid., pp. 88, 402.

[143]Ibid., pp. 391, 397-398, 403-6.

[144]Ibid., p. 324.

[145]Rempel, *Lord's Supper*, pp. 48, 64-65.

[146]Hubmaier, *Balthasar Hubmaier*, p. 399.

[147]Ibid., p. 398.

[148]Ibid., pp. 333, 394-97.

[149]Hubmaier's communion service included a prayer to Jesus to abide with them and extolled "brotherly love and communion in God the Father, the Son, and the Holy Ghost." He mentioned eating Christ "spiritually and in faith" (ibid., pp. 395, 399, 407).

ated inwardly. Yet as with baptism, he provided no clear theological rationale for these interconnections. At the same time he disengaged the Supper from the risen Christ, constituting the community as its main agent, even its primary sacramental reality. This would pave the way for reducing it, as experience of the Spirit faded, to an expression of social-ethical commitment inspired by an historical example.[150]

2. I am employing a common historical claim as an investigative hypothesis: that Anabaptists understood the Supper largely as a memorial of Jesus' death. So far the memorial aspect has surely been underscored. Yet even among the Swiss we spot another motif, resembling a secondary Zwinglian theme (the congregation as Christ's earthly body), perhaps becoming primary among Anabaptists: the Supper as communal expression of love and mutual, costly commitment.

South Germany-Austria. Since the first leaders barely established congregations before their deaths, most of what we know about the Supper here reflects later communities.

I. Hans Schlaffer, as previously noted, connected the Supper with that saving process that he and his colleagues also called baptism. Consuming Christ's flesh and blood was God's work in us, incorporating us through faith "into Christ's flesh, life, suffering, and death" as "partakers of it."[151] We consume his body largely by dedicating our bodies to his commands. If we are persecuted for this, we finally shed Christ's blood, not ours. For Schlaffer, eucharistic reality clearly transcended recollection of Jesus' death and indeed any and all ceremonies. Yet it also included that ritual in which, as Hubmaier emphasized, we remember how Jesus gave his body for us and are called to give our bodies for each other, and "become one body and one bread, drinking from one cup."[152] Since Schlaffer strongly stressed such sharing, which, as for Hubmaier, included the economic, he perhaps implicitly regarded the community itself as a sacrament.[153]

Hans Denck foregrounded the spiritual dimension. Through consuming the "invisible bread," one dies in Christ, while through the "invisible cup" one "be-

---

[150]Rempel, while recognizing this possibility, believes that Hubmaier desired "not a reducing of spiritual reality to the human" but to assert "that the ethical is the mode of the spiritual." He sought "an innovative way of speaking about spiritual reality as external" (Rempel, *Lord's Supper,* pp. 81, 89). However, Rempel adds that the incarnation, for Hubmaier and Dirk, was a temporary mode of divine presence, not so much extended as replaced by the Spirit. Another reason for emphasizing human over divine action was that Hubmaier grounded the Supper in love more than faith—but baptism more in faith than love (Hubmaier, *Balthasar Hubmaier,* p. 407; Rempel, *Lord's Supper,* p. 65).

[151]Schlaffer, *Selections,* p. 205.

[152]Ibid., pp. 206, 205.

[153]Stephen Boyd, "Community as Sacrament in the Theology of Hans Schlaffer," in *Anabaptism Revisited,* ed. Walter Klaassen (Scottdale, Penn.: Herald, 1992).

comes deified through the love of God while God becomes incarnate in him."[154] Eventually this inward reality so overrode the outward ceremony that Denck rejected the latter's necessity and became, in effect, a spiritualist.

2. Sounding like the Swiss, Peter Riedemann called communion bread simply bread. He critiqued all notions, Lutheran and Catholic, of Christ actually being in the elements and of consuming his body and blood.[155] Such assertions drew South German-Austrian Anabaptism's most serious charge: worshiping the creature rather than the Creator.

For the Hutterite leader the Supper was also a sign of something. But here he differed from the Swiss. The Swiss could affirm the bread, with its many grains, symbolized how individuals had "become one plant, one living organism and body of Christ, holding to him in one Spirit."[156] But for Riedemann this indicated, further, that Christ had planted them all "into the true divine nature and character";[157] grafted them "into the divine promise and made [them] one with his divine nature and body."[158] The Supper recalled, of course, that Jesus had obtained this through his death, but also that participants keep growing in him only by taking on his suffering or sharing the likeness of that death.[159]

Riedemann did not assert that the Supper or its elements directly convey divinizing participation in Christ (as in the Catholic *ex operere operato*). Yet in this ceremony, whose symbols conveyed it so vividly, something of this surely occurred. The Hutterite Supper involved spiritual participation of a different kind, in a Christ much more directly present, than among the Swiss Brethren. Yet this participation was also communal, much as for the Swiss. The meal was a sign of "fellowship in Christ's body" where all "declare themselves with all the others, to be of one mind, one heart, and one spirit with Christ."[160] It was hardly accidental that Riedemann

---

[154]Denck, *Spiritual Legacy of Hans Denck*, pp. 20-21, 65.

[155]Riedemann, *Peter Riedemann's Hutterite Confession*, pp. 113-15, 199-201. He also mentioned that Jesus could not be in the elements because he was at the Father's right hand—but not as a major argument.

[156]Ibid., p. 116.

[157]Peter Rideman, *Confession of Faith* (Rifton, N.Y.: Plough, 1970), p. 192. This translation renders more exactly the original "goettlichen Art und Natur" (*Rechenschaft unserer Religion, Lehr und Glaubens, von den Brüdern, so man die Hutterischen nennt* [1565; reprint, Wiltshire, England: Verlag der Hutterischen Brueder, 1938], p. 210) than Friesen's "divine nature" (Riedemann, *Peter Riedemann's Hutterite Confession*, p. 202). Anabaptists sometimes employed Christ's divine "nature" and "character" almost as synonyms, perhaps to indicate that divinization involved transformation of both.

[158]Riedemann, *Peter Riedemann's Hutterite Confession*, p. 203.

[159]Ibid., pp. 116, 117, 202, 203.

[160]Ibid., pp. 117-18.

followed these remarks on the Supper with a chapter on community of goods.[161]

3. As the leader of an early community in Moravia, Gabriel Ascherham was banned by the Hutterites in 1533. He envisioned a closer connection of the elements with the Supper's spiritual dimension. Ascherham favored spiritual reality over the material. Yet he affirmed that God's work in the former realm brings matter into harmony with it.[162] Ascherham, like Zwingli and most Anabaptists, understood the body in the Supper to be the gathered community. Yet the Supper also drew people into divinizing union with Christ. In this the elements played so vital a role that they "were not ordinary bread or wine but a 'sanctified and separated bread and wine.' "[163] Accordingly, Ascherham treated the elements and the ceremony with a reverence that Hutterites found too Catholic.

4. For all Anabaptists the Supper's inward reality, like that of baptism and the entire salvation process, had to be expressed outwardly and communally. However, John Rempel points out that most also assumed, intellectually, much like Zwingli, that an ontological barrier separated spirit and matter.[164] This meant not simply that an ontological distinction existed between spirit and matter, which Catholics and Lutherans also affirmed, but that the former could not be embodied or directly conveyed or expressed through the latter. Once such a barrier was presupposed, Zwingli's claim seemed obvious: Christ could not be in the elements. But this created a further problem. What connection could these elements have with the risen Jesus? Once again Pilgram Marpeck approached this issue, as he did Spirit-matter relationships in baptism and church life, in a more profoundly theological manner than others.

Marpeck began by insisting that the Supper, like baptism, was not a thing but an activity. We should consider, therefore, not the elements' nature but their overall function.[165] Marpeck, like Hubmaier, also defined a sacrament as a pledge, but developed the notion further.[166] This meant, for him, that its material form was a gift through which the Giver pledged faithfulness and love. If this material form was received with a corresponding commitment, it became the seal of a covenant.[167]

---

[161]Ibid., pp. 119-22.

[162]Werner Packull, *Hutterite Beginnings* (Baltimore: Johns Hopkins University Press, 1995), pp. 124, 129.

[163]Ibid., p. 296.

[164]Rempel, *Lord's Supper*, p. 29.

[165]Marpeck, *Writings of Pilgram Marpeck*, pp. 170-71, 269, 277, 283; J. Loserth, *Pilgram Marbecks Antwort auf Kaspar Schwenckfeld's Beurteilung des Buches der Bundesbezeugung von 1542* (Vienna: Carl Fromme, 1929), pp. 453-56, 465.

[166]Marpeck, *Writings of Pilgram Marpeck*, p. 169; Loserth, *Pilgram Marbecks Antwort*, pp. 92-93.

[167]Marpeck, *Writings of Pilgram Marpeck*, pp. 169-72.

As mentioned in the section on baptism, humans, body and spirit, are brought into contact with God's Spirit only through Jesus. Jesus had reconnected these in his own physical, human life and continued the process through the church, which extended his humanity. Accordingly, Jesus' humanity, whether in his own history, the church, or one of its rites, was no mere external sign pointing to a very different internal reality. It belonged to the essence of God's saving activity, that movement of faithfulness and love toward us through Son and Spirit that penetrates and transforms body and soul.

Consequently, when communion bread, though it physically remains bread, functions in this continuing saving drama, Marpeck did not simply call it a sign, which could be separated from the sacrament's essence, for the elements function outwardly, as did Jesus' historical humanity, to mediate the Spirit to us inwardly. In authentic sacraments God worked outwardly as Son, through its physical features, and simultaneously, inwardly as Spirit. Through the overall sacramental activity, that is, these divine persons cowitnessed to each other, as did the participants' inner experiences with the outward actions (see p. 166).

This led Marpeck to a surprising conclusion: The communion elements were so intrinsic to this process that they became "no longer signs, but are one essence in Christ, according to the inner and outer being."[168] To be sure, they neither altered chemically nor actually became Christ's blood and body. Yet through this unique function they became, somewhat like Ascherham's "sanctified and separated bread and wine," essential, indispensable components of this divine-human interaction.

In this way, Marpeck sought to answer why the Supper's material features are inseparable from its spiritual reality. Why can't the Supper consist simply of the invisible bread and cup (Denck) or ethical and communal commitment (Hubmaier's tendency)? Because the Supper is an activity—is itself an intertwining of spirit and matter. Its material features then cannot simply point to spiritual reality but must participate in it. Its spiritual reality cannot simply be experienced internally but must express and mediate itself through matter. No ontological barrier between spirit and matter exists.

The Spiritualist Caspar Schwenckfeld, however, protested. Jesus' risen body was so glorified that communion with him could be purely spiritual. Though Marpeck lacked theological training, he found this issue so crucial that he kept trying to re-

---

[168]Ibid., p. 195; cf. pp. 196, 197; Loserth, *Pilgram Marbecks Antwort*, pp. 114, 121, 124, 127, 456, 458. "Not the element . . . but the activity . . . not water, bread and wine . . . but baptism and the Supper" are "one essence with the inner" (Loserth, *Pilgram Marbecks Antwort*, p. 137). As Blough points out, "essence *(wesen)*" here cannot mean simply identity of substance, but must include simultaneity of action (Neal Blough, *Christologie Anabaptiste* [Geneva: Labor et Fides, 1984], pp. 158-59).

fine his thoughts—sometimes awkwardly. To appreciate his mature views, we must glance at this convoluted process.

Initially Marpeck proposed that the Supper communicated Jesus' unglorified body, in which he walked the human path and was crucified. By this partaking of Jesus' body, Marpeck evidently meant hearing the gospel of Jesus' atoning death conveyed through the Supper's crucial memorial function. Jesus, then, was present in the communication and actualization of the effects of his historic work, not wholly unlike Hubmaier said. The church also extended this unglorified body.[169] It participated in Christ largely by sharing his sufferings, which became present through the communion symbols of his death.

However, Marpeck also wanted to affirm, like Schwenckfeld, that the risen Jesus, not simply effects of his historic work, was with us in the Supper. Yet with Zwingli, Marpeck believed that Jesus' glorified body was in heaven. To resolve this apparent conundrum, Marpeck eventually proposed that Jesus was present only in his divine nature. Hubmaier had said this, but at the cost of rendering Jesus virtually absent. Marpeck, however, sought to conceive Jesus' presence dynamically. To do so he often equated Jesus' deity with the Holy Spirit (citing 2 Cor 3:17). Yet Marpeck also insisted that Jesus' divine and human natures are united in heaven.[170] This led, finally, to the conclusion that this one Jesus, with his two natures, was somehow present in the Supper "through his divine power as Holy Spirit, and nevertheless with his body, flesh and blood, he remains wholly undivided in heaven."[171]

Marpeck apparently concocted an exceedingly awkward Christology. Jesus seemingly existed in four forms: as unglorified body on earth, as Holy Spirit in the Supper, and yet in both natures in heaven and also, somehow, in the Supper. Marpeck, at times, apparently collapsed Jesus' divine nature into the Spirit. Jesus' human nature was present in the Supper, though his glorified body was not.

Remember that Marpeck, despite his profound intuitions, was not trained theologically. But despite this he wrestled more than any other Anabaptist to articulate

---

[169]Loserth, *Pilgram Marbecks Antwort*, pp. 481-82, 123, 134.

[170]Ibid., p. 485.

[171]Ibid., p. 515. As he developed this notion Marpeck spoke much less of Jesus' unglorified humanity. He began dividing Christ's human nature not into glorified and unglorified bodies but into physical features (confined to heaven) and spiritual features (subsumed under the Spirit's work) (Rempel, *Lord's Supper*, p. 119). Marpeck was endeavoring to conceptualize how Jesus could be really present—but not physically—and how his mortal self could be received—but only spiritually (ibid., pp. 112-13). (Perhaps, however, he implied a more physical understanding of the bread from heaven [Jn 6], when he connected it to "the pure flesh and blood of the virgin Mary" [Marpeck, *Writings of Pilgram Marpeck*, p. 447; cf. p. 83; Loserth, *Pilgram Marbecks Antwort*, p. 484]).

many insights in dialogue with classical theology. Perhaps his convoluted concepts will yield meaning if we ask what he intended to say with them.

Perhaps partaking of Jesus' unglorified body meant that the Lord whose active presence we experience is the same one who suffered humanly. Maybe this was a way of denying that his resurrection, as Schwenckfeld seemed to say, distanced him from our very human struggles. Perhaps Marpeck often equated Christ's deity with the Holy Spirit to affirm that Jesus was present in power, though not substantially. This would also counter any impression that Jesus was, in effect, absent, as he seemed to be for Hubmaier. If so, the Spirit would not really be Christ's divine nature but the active, divine medium through which he is with us; or the cowitness flowing from Christ and back to him who draws us into the divinizing trinitarian dynamic.[172]

Perchance it was, again, to deny Christ's substantial presence that Marpeck located his body in heaven. Yet perhaps he added that Christ's natures are united there and also somehow in the Supper to assert that we experience the one Jesus—both crucified and risen, human and divine.[173]

Despite his rarefied speculations, Marpeck repeatedly portrayed the Supper as a communal event where many grains became one loaf.[174] Participants gave themselves for each other, as Jesus had for them, and pledged to love even their enemies.[175] This mutual giving included material goods, though this was not to be coerced, as Marpeck felt it was among the Hutterites.[176] Each person's readiness could be assured, as among the Swiss, by performing discipline beforehand. Through the Supper each participant's heart was revealed to the others.[177] They cowitnessed to each other while the physical actions and elements and the divine persons themselves cowitnessed to it all.

5. When we turn from Switzerland to South Germany-Austria, our guiding hypothesis—Anabaptists understood the Supper largely as a memorial of Jesus' death—becomes more questionable. Another dimension, the communal, perhaps already chief among the Swiss, was also quite pronounced among the South Germans-Austrians. And a third dimension emerges: participation in Christ, which was surely communal, but also spiritual in a divinizing sense foreign to Switzerland.

---

[172]Marpeck, *Writings of Pilgram Marpeck*, pp. 194-98, 522; cf. pp. 432-38 below.

[173]Cf. Marpeck's Christology, pp. 375-81 below.

[174]Marpeck, *Writings of Pilgram Marpeck*, pp. 267, 280.

[175]Ibid., pp. 249, 267, 270, 275; Loserth, *Pilgram Marbecks Antwort*, 439, 442. Footwashing symbolized this very appropriately, though it is unclear whether he recommended its literal practice (Marpeck, *Writings of Pilgram Marpeck*, p. 264).

[176]Marpeck, *Writings of Pilgram Marpeck*, pp. 279-81.

[177]Ibid., pp. 112, 275-76, 296-97, 340.

What will we now find, if I grant Anabaptism's third main branch roughly equal weight?

The Netherlands. For the Dutch, like the Swiss, communion bread was simply bread. Yet they underlined its memorial function less often. More frequently, somewhat like South German-Austrians, they highlighted participation in Christ's flesh and blood—but strongly flavored by their distinctive Christology. Though they insisted that Jesus' flesh and blood were fully human, these had originated not from Mary but from a unique divine act. When resurrected they were quite ethereal and apprehended spiritually.[178]

I. Melchior Hoffman portrayed the Supper through the same nuptial imagery that he depicted personal salvation (cf. chap. 5). The human bride received Christ the Bridegroom "physically," although this was "through belief." Thereby "the bodily Christ, who sits at the right hand of God, is in truth bodily her own and . . . she is bodily his, yea with flesh and blood."[179] While such language sounded Lutheran or Catholic, Christ's body was the spiritualized one, and the bride's bodily participation indicated her utter, divinizing commitment.[180] Hoffman, like Riedemann, accused Lutherans, who called the bread Christ's body, of idolatry.

Melchior pictured the earthly bread as an engagement ring, not a thing *in which* Christ was present but an instrument or means of expression *through which* he gave himself. Bread and wine functioned not directly as body and blood but as channels through which "the Bridegroom and the outpouring of his blood is one with" the bride's. "She is in him and, again, he is in her, and they together are thus one body, one flesh, one spirit, and one passion."[181] A similar nuptial portrayal of the Supper as divinizing communion appears in Eastern Orthodoxy.[182]

---

[178]Cf. pp. 39, 384-87. Conversations with Schwenckfeld in Strasbourg formed one source of Hoffman's Christology (Klaus Deppermann, *Melchior Hoffmann* [Edinburgh: T & T Clark, 1987], pp. 213-17). For Hoffman, however, Jesus' glorified body retained spatial location and physical features to some (minimal) extent. Schwenckfeld eventually regarded it as infinite and no longer creaturely (Rempel, *Lord's Supper,* pp. 109ff., esp. in contrast to Marpeck).

[179]Hoffman, "Ordinance of God," p. 194.

[180]Jesus' Passover words did not refer to the bread but meant that "through the bread and belief in the Word [the disciples] should receive the body which sat by them there, that that same body should be their own which would be burned at the cross. And . . . that theirs also was the physical blood which would be poured out at the cross" (ibid., p. 195). Jesus apparently was referring to future spiritual partaking that would so incorporate his heavenly body into theirs that both could suffer together in martyrdom (by fire, as Anabaptists often underwent).

[181]Ibid., p. 194.

[182]In the eucharist Christ "has bound us to Himself and united us, as the bridegroom unites the bride to himself, through communion of this Blood, becoming one flesh with us" (Gregory Palamas, as quoted in Georgios Mantzaridis, *The Deification of Man* [Crestwood, N.Y.: St. Vladimir's Seminary

Extending this imagery, Hoffman could call the congregation Jesus' body and "the fellowship of his blood."[183] Yet unlike the Swiss or South German-Austrians, he said little about the Supper's communal and memorial dimensions but highlighted its personal and spiritual aspects.[184]

2. In seeking to stabilize Dutch Anabaptism after Münster, Menno Simons and Dirk Philips explained the Lord's Supper in a more balanced way, as having three main functions: remembering Jesus' death; expressing communal love, unity and peace; and communing spiritually with Christ's flesh and blood.[185] Menno occasionally employed joyous nuptial imagery, recalling Hoffman.[186]

Menno and Dirk repeatedly portrayed the church as Christ's bride, the new Eve, flesh of his flesh and bone of his bone. Christ's own flesh imparted divinization, perhaps more nearly in the sense of making people divine than of transforming them by divine energies, as among South German-Austrians. For since Jesus' flesh originated from the Word, and not Mary, he was never of our flesh. Nevertheless we, especially through the church, could be of his.[187] The true church, that is, possessed a spiritual, even divine nature.[188]

In such a church the Supper was crucial. It provided a chief means of partaking of Jesus' heavenly flesh and being released from solidarity with Adam's corrupt seed.[189] Though both Dutch leaders insisted that Jesus' body is in heaven,[190] this did not place his reality far beyond us, as for Hubmaier. The imperishable inner person could partake spiritually of Christ's imperishable body and blood.[191]

Though this spiritualizing tendency fostered high behavioral expectations and strict discipline (see pp. 216-19), it did not foster individualism. For Menno and Dirk, like all Anabaptists, also underlined the Supper's communal functions. For them also the bread symbolized that communicants (grains) must be kneaded to-

---

Press, 1984], p. 53). The bread as ring also appeared in the Dutch sacramentarian Cornelius Hoen (Deppermann, *Melchior Hoffman*, p. 147). Zwingli also portrayed the bread as a ring, but of a deceased husband, reminding one of him (ibid., p. 148).

[183]Hoffman, "Ordinance of God," p. 197.

[184]Snyder, however, claims that Hoffman's main eucharistic writing (Hoffman, "Ordinance of God," pp. 184-203) expressed the common Anabaptist notion of a "Supper of unity (understood in a memorial sense)" (C. Arnold Snyder, *Anabaptist History and Theology*, rev. student ed. [Kitchener, Ont.: Pandora, 1997], p. 211.

[185]Simons, *Complete Works*, p. 515; Philips, *Writings of Dirk Philips*, pp. 122-23, cf. p. 112.

[186]Simons, *Complete Works*, p. 148, cf. pp. 221, 343, cf. Philips, *Writings of Dirk Philips*, pp. 340-41, 483.

[187]Simons, *Complete Works*, pp. 772, 829, 867; Philips, *Writings of Dirk Philips*, pp. 361-62.

[188]Simons, *Complete Works*, pp. 273-74, 650; Philips, *Writings of Dirk Philips*, p. 415.

[189]Simons, *Complete Works*, p. 439; Philips, *Writings of Dirk Philips*, pp.122-23, 414-15, cf. pp. 361-62.

[190]Simons, *Complete Works*, p. 153; Philips, *Writings of Dirk Philips*, pp. 117-20.

[191]Simons, *Complete Works*, pp. 153-54; Philips, *Writings of Dirk Philips*, pp. 114-15.

gether. This, as for nearly all Anabaptists, involved willingness to share goods.[192] In such ways, the unity of the community of the new creation was expressed through concrete, outer forms.

But what theological rationale did the later Dutch provide for the sacramental linking of spiritual and material, individual and community? Mostly, as we noted with baptism, they simply insisted that God commanded these rites. Whether they make intrinsic sense or not, they must be performed "to exercise our faith and to show our obedience." We "dare not depart one hair's breadth from . . . all things whatsoever the Lord has commanded."[193]

Nevertheless, since Jesus' risen body, however etherialized, still transformed people, the Dutch could connect him more directly with the Supper than Hubmaier. Jesus united believers, as his body, to himself as head and poured his life into them. Thus when the Supper was rightly practiced, Jesus was in their midst. More precisely, Jesus was in and among them through the Spirit,[194] as he was for Riedemann and Marpeck.

In the end, though, the ontological barrier remained. Material signs, for Dirk at least, could neither participate in nor mediate spiritual reality. They could merely point toward it and away from themselves.[195] Consequently, though the later Dutch joined the risen Christ's spiritual, inward reality more closely with the Supper's physical, outward ritual than Hubmaier, exalted communion with Christ's heavenly flesh still intersected rather obliquely with eating earthly bread.

Summary. Having investigated historic Anabaptism in light of the hypothesis that they understood the Lord's Supper largely as a memorial of Jesus' death, I conclude:

1. While all Anabaptists indeed regarded the Supper as a memorial, this was not their chief emphasis. A communal dimension was more distinctly Anabaptist. It was at least as important in each of Anabaptism's three branches and certainly overall. Participation in Christ, while communal and experienced by the Swiss in this sense, took on a third, spiritual dimension more significant than memorialism in the other two branches.

2. Through its communal dimension, the Supper was interconnected with numerous aspects of everyday life—most conspicuously, economic sharing. These links, enhanced by the Supper's intrinsic connection to baptism and discipline, gave existence in the new creation a sacramental quality. Due to its centrality in this, the Supper might well be called a sacrament. Yet its Swiss form, by prioritizing human

---

[192]Simons, *Complete Works*, p. 146; Philips, *Writings of Dirk Philips*, pp. 121, 123.

[193]Simons, *Complete Works*, pp. 133, 349; cf. Philips, *Writings of Dirk Philips*, pp. 461, 465.

[194]Philips, *Writings of Dirk Philips*, pp. 121, 131, 120, 126-27.

[195]Rempel, *Lord's Supper*, pp. 175, 186; note 165.

over divine agency, could function more as a social-ethical practice than a sacrament.

3. The Anabaptist(-Zwinglian) intellectual presupposition that an ontological barrier prevented spirit from being embodied or conveyed through matter contradicted this lived sacramentality. Quite likely, then, when Anabaptists employed concepts that apparently denied Christ's presence (e.g., the bread is only bread) it was mostly to deny the notions of presence they knew, because these seemed too crudely material (transubstantiation and Luther's "in, with, under"). Nevertheless, Anabaptists very often affirmed Christ's presence through the Spirit. Except for Marpeck, however, they found no concept for expressing this but "spiritual." This left a problematic spirit-matter gap in most of their eucharistic theologies, which was largely bridged in practice.

4. Especially since they experienced Christ communally, and not simply in the elements, Anabaptists implicitly understood the Supper as an activity. For the memorialist Hubmaier Christ's body became present as the bread was "offered, broken, taken, and eaten."[196] For the spiritualizing Hoffman the bread, like a wedding ring, functioned as a channel for Christ's self-giving. Consequently, Marpeck's claim that the elements, considered in their function of conveying Christ's presence and uniting his body, belonged to the Supper's essence provides a plausible conceptualization of Anabaptist sensibility. Historic Anabaptism's implicit awareness of the Supper as an activity can help contemporary theology explicate the connections of its spiritual and material dimensions.

Contemporary Appropriations

While baptism incorporates people into the community of the new creation, the Lord's Supper provides continuing nurture and solidarity. Although a bread and wine rite might seem anachronistic today, appreciation for symbols and the role of ceremonies in shaping groups has increased over the last few decades. Symbols and rites are congenial with postmodern sensibilities and reactions against modernity's cognitive and technological representations of reality. Many evangelical, baptist and other marginalized churches are rethinking their rather barren worship lives, while most ecumenical communions are becoming more eucharistic and liturgical. Ecumenists not only promote baptism as a basis of unity but also encourage concelebration of the Supper. Perhaps the time is ripe for Anabaptists to consider the Lord's Supper as seriously as their founders did.

Historic Anabaptist views, like Protestant views, were partly shaped by reactions against the Roman Mass. Especially since Vatican II, however, Catholics have

---

[196]Hubmaier, *Balthasar Hubmaier*, p. 324.

been rethinking the Mass and Protestant criticism of it, much as they have baptism and justification. Since Anabaptist theology today seldom considers the Lord's Supper, I think it can gain much from this critical reevaluation "from inside."

Catholic Developments

I. The communal dimension. Sixteenth-century Anabaptists and others complained that the clergy controlled the Mass while laity played little part. Vatican II, however, proclaimed that in liturgy "full and active participation by all the people is the aim to be considered before all else."[197] To be sure, priests, through ordination, are still "marked with a special character" that enables them to preside over and perfect the Eucharist.[198] Nonetheless, current Catholic theology often calls the church community as a whole the Supper's true celebrant. (Though it sometimes grants this, ultimately, to the risen Christ.)

As the entire congregation's act, the Supper includes many "horizontal" expressions, as was true among historic Anabaptists. Jesus' sacrifice elicits participants' "loving self-gift to their fellow humans." By sharing in this "covenant meal . . . they are pledging their 'being for' one another."[199] The Eucharist is a "public symbol" through which "communities develop a sense of inner coherence and of public identity."[200] Since sacraments are performed by and happen to communities, theology cannot start with individuals to understand them.[201] Many Catholic theologians now call the church itself the primary sacrament.

Yet this communal orientation sometimes seems to reduce sacramental reality to the horizontal, human level, much as Hubmaier's theology did. It can be said that "the church assembled to celebrate is Christ. The real mystery is that we are sacred."[202] We ourselves then "constitute the whole sacrifice;" "any liturgical celebration is in its total thrust 'horizontal.' "[203] Even more, "our image of God is not complete until a fourth has been added to the three of the trinity . . . ourselves, the body of Christ."[204] But if so, sacraments are actions the congregation performs, not something it receives, "something we do rather than something that is done to us."[205]

---

[197] Abbott, ed., *Documents of Vatican II*, p. 144.

[198] Ibid., p. 535.

[199] Bernard Cooke, *Sacraments and Sacramentality* (Mystic, Conn.: Twenty-Third, 1983), p. 108.

[200] David Power, *The Eucharistic Mystery* (New York: Crossroad, 1995), p. 296.

[201] Tad Guzie, *The Book of Sacramental Basics* (New York: Paulist, 1981), p. 99.

[202] Ibid., p. 62.

[203] Tad Guzie, *Jesus and the Eucharist* (New York: Paulist, 1974), p. 155; Guzie, *Book of Sacramental Basics*, p. 62.

[204] Guzie, *Book of Sacramental Basics*, p. 70.

[205] Ibid., pp. 31-32.

Some Catholic theologians, however, counter this humanistic tendency by identifying Christ, not the church, as the primary sacrament. For his taking flesh and blood was God's original self-communication through matter.[206] From this perspective the church and its ceremonies are sacramental not because it performs them but only insofar as these continue Jesus' historic mediation of Spirit through matter.[207] The risen Jesus is the Supper's initiator and ultimate celebrant (or its basis), however much communal activity comprises its content.[208] This outlook seems similar to Marpeck's.[209]

2. Transignification. Anabaptists and Protestants critiqued the Mass for not only its priestly orientation but also its theory of how Christ was present: transubstantiation. Many protested that the claim that the actual substance of Christ's body and blood existed under the accidents of bread and wine fostered worship of these elements, or idolatry. Today, however, Catholic theologians commonly assert, as many Anabaptists did, that sacraments are not things but actions. To search for Christ's presence by asking how he is located in the elements is to pose the wrong question.[210]

Some Catholics call Christ's relationship to the elements transignification.[211] It is generally agreed that on the physical level "nothing happens to the bread and

---

[206]Kenan Osborne, *Sacramental Theology* (New York: Paulist, 1988), p. 84. On whether Jesus or the church is primary sacrament, see ibid., pp. 10ff., 69-89; cf. Cooke, *Sacraments and Sacramentality*, p. 234. The notion of sacraments rests on "the principle that matter is good, that material things . . . are . . . capable of acting as the instrument or vehicle of the Holy Spirit. This principle is an immediate corollary of the Incarnation wherein the 'Word became flesh,' the visible instrument of the Triune God. . . . Christ is in effect the sacrament par excellence" (Paul Palmer, ed., *Sacraments and Worship* [New York: Longmans, Green, 1957], p. vii). Karl Barth sought to counter Catholic emphasis on the church by calling Christ in his incarnation "the one and only sacrament" to which the church can only "attest." (Karl Barth, *Church Dogmatics* 4.2 [Edinburgh: T & T Clark, 1969], p. 55). Anabaptists intimated this by arguing that sacraments cannot communicate grace directly because Christ alone is the true sign of grace (e.g., Philips, *Writings of Dirk Philips*, pp. 102-3).

[207]Osborne, *Sacramental Theology*, p. 98; Power, *Eucharistic Mystery*, p. 169.

[208]On basis and content see pp. 145-48.

[209]Cf. McClendon, *Systematic Theology* 2:401-2.

[210]Older Catholic theology conceived Christ's presence on the model of efficient causality: the words of institution affected the elements that affected the communicants, much as one physical phenomenon affects another. Today, eucharistic causality is often conceived as symbolic (Guzie, *Jesus and the Eucharist*, pp. 103-27; Guzie, *Book of Sacramental Basics*, pp. 38-51; Cooke, *Sacraments and Sacramentality*, pp. 42-55; Power, *Eucharistic Mystery*, pp. 270-81 [differently than McClendon, note 109]). A symbol points toward and participates in some other reality. Since the elements function as symbols in the Supper, it is hardly strange that they should draw us into Christ's presence. Many Catholics now conceive this causality also as personal address and response.

[211]For transignification's history, see Powers, *Eucharistic Theology*, pp. 111-79.

wine."[212] But while their substance does not change, their significance—their function as signs, their role in signifying something—does. Rather than simply providing nourishment, as they ordinarily do, the elements become vehicles through which the risen Lord imparts his presence and through which communicants express their devotion back to him and toward each other.

Recent discussions of this sometimes employ the wedding-ring analogy,[213] as did Hoffman (and the Orthodox monk Gregory Palamas [see note 182]). When given to express and seal lifelong love and commitment, a ring signifies and simultaneously communicates something quite different than it does in a store window. Similarly, when Christ employs bread and wine to bestow his risen presence—so marked by his human sufferings that we can share in them—might one say that these elements "are" his body and blood?

Various Catholic theologians answer yes and maintain, following Rome, that any change in signification must rest on an ontological change in the elements.[214] For if Christ really gives himself through the bread, it must not only symbolize him but somehow also be him, and "no longer simply bread in its ultimate reality."[215] Some Catholics interpret ontological change more modestly, as a limit concept: a way of simply affirming that something more than transignifying action, communal participation or anything we know of is involved.[216] In any case, current Catholic theologians find Jesus present throughout the entire service with its many actions.

Some Catholics also call change in the elements transfinalization.[217] They envision bread, wine and all the eucharistic actions being caught up into the kind of final unity with God that will someday pervade all energy and matter. In this way eucharistic transformation affects not only humans but begins permeating all creation. The new creation, which is not yet fully here, becomes present already in a special way.[218] The Spirit's action in the Supper then is largely eschatological. By uniting creatures with their Creator it inspires and draws them toward the day when this communion will be complete. The Spirit working in and among communicants rather than mere human energy is the source of their participation.[219]

---

[212]Guzie, *Jesus and the Eucharist*, p. 113.

[213]Powers, *Eucharistic Theology*, pp. 166-67.

[214]Pope Paul VI, *Mysterium Fidei* (London: Catholic Truth Society, 1965), sec. 46, cf. secs. 11, 14.

[215]Powers, *Eucharistic Theology*, pp. 173, 146, cf. pp. 144, 153, 176.

[216]Power, *Eucharistic Mystery*, pp. 275, 294, 320.

[217]Powers, *Eucharistic Theology*, pp. 115-6, 131-39.

[218]Much as in my understanding of justification; see pp. 144-45.

[219]Power, *Eucharistic Mystery*, pp. 302-3.

3. The memorial dimension. Anabaptists and others critiqued Catholicism for submerging the memory of Jesus' past saving sacrifice under a flood of current cultic sacrifices. Many Catholic theologians today, however, underline the importance of memory in conveying religious reality. They often do so by highlighting story or narrative. Jesus' death communicates salvation not as a punctiliar event but only as incorporated into a narrative extending from the past, and then transmitted to new generations through that expanding narrative tradition.[220] The original Supper, a covenant in Jesus' blood, pointed back to Yahweh's faithfulness to Israel, and subsequent memorials of it recall, celebrate and make present God's faithfulness through the generations.[221] Salvation that is experienced in a community involves this making present of the power of the past.

4. The social dimension. While Anabaptists and others saw the Mass as an expression of ecclesiastical and social power, current Catholic theologians often highlight its implications for social reversal and renewal.[222] The Supper recalls a person executed by military and political powers that feared his advocacy of the oppressed.[223] It memorializes Jesus' nonviolent response.

Bread and wine recall the ordinary labor and the social and economic processes needed to produce and distribute them.[224] As products of the earth they witness to our interconnectedness with it and our need to use it wisely. Providing refreshment and nourishment, the elements bring to mind those who lack them. By welcoming all without distinction, the Supper overcomes barriers of status, ethnicity, wealth and class. It portrays "an alternative humanity in which God's Spirit works, overcoming the death-dealing forces abroad in the world."[225]

An Anabaptist response. If we consider the Lord's Supper through the lenses provided by historic Anabaptism and current Catholic theology, what contributions

---

[220]Ibid., pp. 304-16; Guzie, *Jesus and the Eucharist*, pp. 78-87; and *Book of Sacramental Basics*, pp. 11-23.

[221]Power, *Eucharistic Mystery*, pp. 44, 298, 308-9. While this narrative affirms some purpose for history, it leaves room for darkness and mystery, for at its center God is known through suffering (pp. 307-16). Further, by "its very stress on time . . . narrative allows for the absence of what it represents" (p. 306). The Supper's memorial dimension, then, communicates a God absent as well as present, though absence points forward to fuller eschatological presence (pp. 315-16; cf. Donald Gray, "The Real Absence: A Note on the Eucharist," in *Living Bread, Saving Cup*, ed. Kevin Seasoltz (Collegeville, Minn.: Liturgical, 1987).

[222]Cooke, *Sacraments and Sacramentality*, pp. 168-212; James Empereur and Christopher Kiesling, *The Liturgy That Does Justice* (Collegeville, Minn.: Liturgical Press, 1990), pp. 109-30.

[223]Bernard Cooke, *The Future of Eucharist* (New York: Paulist, 1997), p. 26; Power, *Eucharistic Mystery*, p. 309.

[224]Philippe Rouillard, "From Human Meal to Eucharist," in *Living Bread, Saving Cup*, ed. Kevin Seasoltz (Collegeville, Minn.: Liturgical, 1987).

[225]Power, *Eucharistic Mystery*, p. 28.

might a contemporary theology in Anabaptist perspective make?[226] I will consider biblical texts as I construct my response.

I. The communal and social dimensions. These would surely be highlighted. First Corinthians 11:17-33 clearly depicts communion occurring in the context of full meals where social and economic equality were requisite for it to truly be the Lord's Supper (I Cor 11:20-22). First Corinthians 10 calls the Supper a mutual sharing or participation *(koinōnia)* in Christ's body and blood, where the one bread shows that all present are one body (I Cor 10:16-21).

The importance of the meal calls attention to meals as occasions and symbols of fellowship throughout the Bible. Beginning with Isaiah 25:6-9, the eschatological destruction of death, revitalization of nature and fellowship among all peoples is envisioned as a great banquet. In this light Jesus' meals with the marginalized appear as inbreakings of God's end-time kingdom. Given the function of ancient meals in solidifying family, ethnic and class groupings, Jesus' commensality challenged all social divisions at the core.[227] Since these occasions looked forward to the eschaton, it is hardly surprising that Jesus' resurrection appearances also included meals with him (Lk 24:13-35, Jn 21:4-14, Acts 10:41).

Jesus' practice continued in essence when the earliest church, gathered from many nations, began "breaking bread" and worshiping together (Acts 2:42, 46). They soon shared possessions and meals in common (Acts 4:32-37, 6:1-6). Though some scholars regard this communal sharing as the exception in early church life, this interpretive trend can be traced to the Reformers' rejection of the Anabaptist emphasis on these texts.[228] Among Jews and Gentiles at that time, fellowship was most fully expressed by eating together, often accompanied by worship of a god. Since most early Christians were poor, eating together would also have often involved sharing what food each one had—one of their few possessions.[229]

---

[226]See Stoffer, *Lord's Supper*, esp. the findings of a Believers' Church Conference on the Lord's Supper (pp. 285-88) and my "Proposed Theses for a Believers Church Theology of the Lord's Supper" (pp. 256-60; cf. Thomas Finger, *Christian Theology* [Scottdale, Penn.: Herald, 1989], I:331-42).

[227]A major theme of John Dominic Crossan, *The Historical Jesus* (San Francisco: Harper, 1991). While I disagree with much of Crossan's and the Jesus Seminar's theology, I find them on target here. For my reading of them see Thomas Finger, *Self, Earth and Society* (Downers Grove, Ill.: InterVarsity Press, 1997), pp. 227-58.

[228]Lareta Finger, *An Investigation of Communal Meals in Acts 2:42-47 and 6:1-6* (Ph. D. diss., Northwestern University: 1997), pp. 11-64.

[229]Ibid., pp. 121-218, cf. Lareta Finger, "Social Implications of the Lord's Supper in the Early Church," in *The Lord's Supper*, ed. Dale Stoffer (Scottdale, Penn.: Herald, 1997); Ben Witherington III, "Making a Meal of It: The Lord's Supper in Its First-century Social Setting," in *The Lord's Supper: Believers Church Perspectives*, ed. Dale Stoffer (Scottdale, Penn.: Herald, 1997). Sharing goods, or at least food, seems assumed by 2 Thess 3:10, where the community could withhold food from any-

Of course, remembrances of Jesus' death and celebrations of his resurrection varied in New Testament times. Yet good evidence exists that both often occurred together in the context of a full meal (which, after all, the Last Supper was). Here sharing of goods was at least symbolized and often to some extent practiced as an expression of present eschatological reality and hope for its fuller coming.[230]

Accordingly, my contemporary Anabaptist theology recommends restoring the full meal context to the Supper, sometimes literally, otherwise by increasing the consciousness and gestures of sharing (e.g., passing the loaf and cup to each other).[231] The link between Jesus' giving his life for us and our giving our lives and possessions is implied by the Supper, even though stated most explicitly in Scripture apart from it (1 Jn 3:16-17). To be authentic, mutual sharing among participants should express and lead to overcoming social and economic dispar-ities within congregations—and beyond them, for Jesus gives his flesh for the world (Jn 6:33, 51).

Authentic sharing of bread and wine, common products of labor and sources of nourishment (e.g., Ps 104:14-15), will arouse desire to extend the sufficiency they represent to those deprived of them, as Friesen and current Catholics stress. Since nonhuman creation participates in eschatological fullness through such labor, gen-uine Communion will flow into care for all creatures. This can be highlighted by celebrating the Supper with many symbols and reminders of creation, rather than in the barest and briefest (Zwinglian) way.

These communal meanings surely render the Lord's Supper more than a partic-ular ceremony of a traditional institution. Nonetheless, if these meanings alone are foregrounded, the community can come to be regarded as the Supper's main agent,

---

one who did not work (cf. 1 Thess 4:9-12). The form of this command suggests that it may have been passed on from other Christian communal situations (Robert Jewett, "Tenement Churches and Communal Meals in the Early Church," *Biblical Research* 38 [1993]; Robert Jewett, *Paul the Apostle to America* [Louisville: Westminster John Knox, 1994], pp. 82-83). Rom 13:8-10 may reflect similar economic sharing in connection with a love feast (Robert Jewett, "Are There Allusions to the Love Feast in Romans 13:8-10?" in *Common Life in the Early Church*, ed. Julian Hills [Harrisburg, Penn.: Trinity Press, 1998]). The Qumran community shared meals and possessions.

[230]Eschatological reference appears in Jesus' words about drinking wine anew in the kingdom (Mt 26:29; Mk 14:25; Lk 22:18) and in the 1 Corinthians instruction to "proclaim the Lord's death until he comes" (1 Cor 11:26). These texts do not mean "do this until then" but "do this in ex-pectation of what will come then."

[231]The Church of the Brethren and the Brethren Church, which have Anabaptist roots, traditionally celebrate Communion in the context of a full meal and foot washing (Stoffer, *Lord's Supper*, pp. 157-68, 185-92). Dirk regarded foot washing as an ordinance (Philips, *Writings of Dirk Philips*, pp. 367-68, cf. pp. 178, 301, 376). Marpeck extolled it as symbol, but perhaps not a practice (Marpeck, *Writings of Pilgram Marpeck*, p. 264). I recommend that foot washing sometimes accompany the Sup-per. It can be considered as sacramental (cf. note 117).

even its subject. We have seen how this occurred in Hubmaier's theology, and among recent Catholics who claim that we do the sacraments, that the assembled church is Christ. The latter, understandably, are reacting against hierarchical tendencies, as Hubmaier did, and also seeking to reach contemporary people. Yet if the Supper's transcendent, mysterious dimensions disappear, will more than a (post)modern, communalistic humanism be left?[232]

2. The memorial dimension. If this is understood as transmitted through narrative, Anabaptist theologians could say much about it. Yet only McClendon portrays the Supper as an intersection of narratives.[233] He treats it (along with baptism and prophetic preaching) as a remembering sign of God's saving acts, which he calls historic signs, and therefore an occasion for pondering the entire story of God's people.[234] This enables Jesus' cross to be remembered not simply as a distant event with perhaps one purpose (e.g., forgiveness) but as a focal point illuminating the histories that precede and follow it. In this way not only the cross but also many dimensions of those narratives which shape communities and character can be actualized through the Supper.

The memorial dimension, as some Catholics point out, also facilitates remembrance of and response to the concrete social-ethical features of Jesus' death: his nonviolent yet prophetic response to state and military power; his identification with the lowest, most marginalized persons and groups; his self-giving servanthood, contrasted with common sociopolitical practices (Lk 22:24-28), and symbolized by washing feet (Jn 13:1-20). To facilitate this I recommend that Jesus' historic cross be remembered in every celebration, at least through the words of institution.

Given the Supper's narrative richness, it is surprising that Anabaptist theologians who stress story and ethical-communal formation scarcely mention it, save McClendon, Yoder and Friesen. Since few of them touch baptism either, one wonders whether they are tending in this case to reduce not transcendent reality but the church to social-ethical dimensions? Are they adequately considering the ecclesial aspects of Christian communities, as did historic Anabaptists who found a proper baptism and Supper essential to the church's existence? Despite their laudable desire to connect Christian life with social-ethical issues and champion countercultural communities, is this really the best way to reach a spiritually hungry society?

Perhaps neglect of these ecclesial features also rests on another assumption: that

---

[232]This potential humanistic reduction arises, in part, from frequent identifications of freedom with the modern notion of autonomy (Guzie, *Jesus and the Eucharist*, p. 136; Cooke, *Sacraments and Sacramentality*, p. 12; Power, *Eucharistic Mystery*, p. 136). This chapter proposes that true freedom flourishes in relationships and communities where it is limited and shaped by others. Chapter nine will expand on this.

[233]McClendon, *Systematic Theology* 2: 401-2.

[234]Ibid., pp. 381-85, esp. 404, 406.

narrative is best embodied directly in ethical activity and need not be expressed or mediated through symbol, drama or ritual.[235] Anabaptist theology must consider this, however.

3. Transignification. The memorial dimension, like the communal, carries multiple social-ethical implications. Yet it too can be understood as the product of human agency—of efforts at remembering and replicating the cross. However, divine agency and presence in the Supper are affirmed especially in John 6, which depicts Jesus bestowing his flesh, and recipients abiding in him as he abides in the Father, sharing in divine life (Jn 6:56-57). "Participation" *(koinōnia)* in Christ's flesh and blood indicates something similar, with more explicit communal implications (I Cor 10:16-21). The cry "Maranatha!" invoked or celebrated Christ's personal presence in very early Christian suppers.[236]

But to apprehend the manner of this presence, we must remember that the Last Supper and its early successors were meals and involved dramatic actions. Anabaptists as dissimilar as Hubmaier, Marpeck and Hoffman regarded the Supper chiefly as an action. Its main symbols, as Marpeck perceived, were really *breaking* bread and *sharing* the cup.[237] Jesus said, "This *[touto]* is my body that is for you. Do this *[touto]* in remembrance of me," and in parallel fashion, "This *[touto]* cup is the new covenant in my blood. Do this *[touto]* . . . in remembrance of me" (I Cor 11:24-25). In asking how Jesus is present, Catholic and Lutheran theologians traditionally supposed that the first *this* referred to the bread, and the third *this* to the wine; that is, Jesus identified his body and blood with two substances or things.

But if we visualize the original meal as an activity, we envision Jesus breaking the bread and passing the cup as he speaks. When he says "this" the first time, he may not mean the bread itself but the action of breaking it. Similarly, the third *this* may indicate not the cup but the sharing of it. Clearly, when Jesus says "this" the second and fourth times—in "do *this*"—he does mean actions. But perhaps *this* in all four cases points to actions. If so, Jesus' "body" and "blood" would indicate not things (bread and wine) but his activity of self-giving—through bread and wine when they are shared in his memory.[238]

Even if one questions this exegesis, it seems harmonious with the Supper's early

---

[235]As Holland complains, "Even the Postmodern Story," p. 240.

[236]I Cor 16:22; cf. Rev 22:20; see Oscar Cullmann, *Early Christian Worship* (London: SCM Press, 1953), pp. 12-14; and his *The Christology of the New Testament* (Philadelphia: Westminster, 1959), pp. 208-13.

[237]Loserth, *Pilgram Marbecks Antwort*, p. 137; also Guzie, *Book of Sacramental Basics*, p. 34.

[238]Guzie, *Book of Sacramental Basics*, p. 34; Vernard Eller, *In Place of Sacraments* (Grand Rapids: Eerdmans, 1972), pp. 87-90, 106-9; Graydon Snyder, "The Text and Syntax of Ignatius Pros Ephesious 20:2c," *Vigilae Christianae* 22 (1968): 11; cf. Finger, *Christian Theology*, 1:349-342.

setting of a full meal marked by sharing. There Jesus' presence would have been experienced throughout the event, not merely in two foods. Nonetheless, since bread and wine played a special role, prefaced by specific words, his presence was distinctly focused through them. But rather than actually being him, they functioned as instruments or symbols through which he conveyed himself. In this very special role their significance, their signifying function, certainly changed from their more ordinary uses, as Gabriel Ascherham recognized. To emphasize today that something unique and wonderful is happening through this activity, I find it helpful to speak of a change (trans-) in signification.

Bread and wine, when received in faith, are so intrinsic to the special way the risen Christ becomes present that a contemporary Anabaptist theology can include them, following Marpeck, in the Supper's essence. But since the Supper is an activity, its essence consists not in things but actions without which it could not be what it is. The elements are essentially Christ's body and blood, not as things identical with him but as means indispensable to this special manner of self-impartation. *Is* can indicate not only something's composition but also what it becomes, how it operates, "in its ultimate reality."[239] In this sense, something is what it does.

Given the eschatological anticipation pervading the New Testament and Anabaptist Suppers,[240] transfinalization can also find place in contemporary Anabaptist theology. It can indicate that Christ is present already in the eucharistic actions and thus their elements in the way that will someday pervade creaturely reality. The physical actions and elements, that is, point not only to the risen Jesus but also toward his future and ours.[241] Thereby they also point outward toward the new creation's cosmic horizons with their environmental implications.

The paradox that Christ is already present in our world transforming matter es-

---

[239]Power, *Eucharistic Mystery*, p. 146. McClendon apparently concurs. If we present bread to the risen Lord, he asks, is it not his? "And if he returns it to us each in the words first used long ago . . . (1 Cor 11:24) is it not rightfully his bread, his body, that we then receive?" (*Systematic Theology* 2: 402).

Yoder, in contrast, interprets "is" at least as literally as transubstantiation when he reduces breaking bread to "economic sharing," "an economic act" without remainder (*Body Politics*, pp. 20, 21, 44). Yoder does speak of God acting "in, with, and under" the Supper's human actions (p. 1), and of God occasionally enabling these (p. 9), but he much more often identifies the two (e.g., "The community's action is God's action" [p. 3]). Yet I do not find him ascribing any content to God's action that differentiates it from the human. What then can his "God" references really mean? Despite Yoder's ecumenical interests he flatly denies that the New Testament can shed "any light on . . . much later eucharistic controversies" (p. 15). As usual, Yoder discovers profound social meanings where others often do not. Yet he treats all "sacramental" approaches pejoratively. Eller exhibits much the same attitude but provides some valuable Anabaptist insights (*In Place of Sacraments*).

[240]Friedmann, *Theology of Anabaptism*, pp. 139-40.

[241]McClendon, *Systematic Theology* 2: 405.

chatologically but that matter is not yet fully transformed is fittingly expressed by specific sacraments that actualize and symbolize this transformation more fully than other Christian activities. Such sacraments indicate that the new creation is truly present but not yet equally everywhere: present at some points, from which it spreads toward others. Eucharistic sharing, to use Yoder's words, will indeed enhance the participants' "ordinary partaking together of food."[242] Yet the Supper can hardly be generalized and reduced to this, as he implies. For through distinct sacraments general sacramental awareness of God's presence is very often enhanced.

Finally, a practical question: In presenting an element in the Supper, is it best to say, This is the body (or blood) of Christ? If recipients are likely to construe this as a quasi-empirical assertion, probably not. But if otherwise, probably so. *Is* language, if associated more with the action than the thing, can fittingly invite one to expect Christ to be present without limit.[243] Literalistic misunderstanding can be further avoided by stressing, with historic Anabaptists, that Christ is only present through the Spirit.[244]

4. Summary. Throughout their history Anabaptists have seldom been considered sacramental, by themselves or others. Zwinglian plainness has greatly shaped their worship, along with Hubmaier's "real absence" (from all but the preached Word) of the risen Christ. Most current Anabaptist theologians reinforce this impression by neglecting baptism and the Supper, while Yoder, who does not, reduces these further than Hubmaier to social-ethical dimensions. Yet if *sacramental* means expression of invisible, spiritual grace through visible, material channels, Anabaptists appear quite sacramental so far.

I am locating the Lord's Supper not on Anabaptism's periphery but as central to its continuing nurture. This Supper's communal dimension symbolizes and energizes social-ethical practices while its memorial dimension connects these with biblical narrative. Its dramatic, ritual character indicates that new creation sacramentality also involves aesthetic and physical actions. Biblical narrative affects the world not by being translated directly into ethics but only as it touches and trans-

---

[242]Yoder, *Body Politics,* p. 16.

[243]I am perhaps employing *is* somewhat as Power does "ontological change": as a limit concept (*Eucharistic Mystery,* pp. 275, 294, 320). But Power seems to use it somewhat apophatically: to affirm that more happens than we can know or describe. For me, *is* also functions as an invitation to expect more, even much more, than we know. I am not sure this is best called "ontological."

[244]Calvin expressed this in a helpful way, often regarded as midway between Zwingli and Luther. Since the Spirit "truly unites things separated in space," "Christ's flesh, separated from us by such a great distance penetrates to us" (John Calvin, *Institutes of the Christian Religion* [Philadelphia: Westminster Press, 1960], p. 1370). Therefore, "from the very substance of his flesh Christ breathes his very life into us—even though Christ's flesh itself does not enter into us" (p. 1404).

forms psychological and physical life as well.[245]

Perhaps my outlook could be called "communal presence." Yet this label could be understood largely in horizontal, social fashion, á la Hubmaier. Christ's presence, as experienced by Dutch and South German-Austrian Anabaptists (as well as Lutherans and Catholics), is also personal or real. The memorial function, underlined by all Anabaptists and Reformed, is crucial too. The Eucharist, in my view, conveys Jesus' real, communal and memorial presence as a primary manifestation of grace birthing the new creation in visible communal form.

Clearer emphasis on the two sacraments common to nearly all churches might facilitate Anabaptist dialogue with traditional, ecumenical communions—yet challenge them with these rites' radical implications. (Though Catholics especially are way ahead in this!) By highlighting such implications Anabaptists might also encourage marginalized communions to take sacraments more seriously.

Life today is profoundly shaped by the apprehension of reality driving much globalization, which is materialistic, quantified, linear, literalistic, imageless. Yet most people resent its depersonalizing character and consequences. Ours is also a media-saturated age. People increasingly appreciate images, symbols, rituals and the ways these identify unique groups. If churches portray the Supper not as a static institutional identity marker but as central to a rich, dramatic, symbolic communal life, they may appeal to many people—probably far more than by styling the church as simply a social-ethical community.

However, even if many spiritually searching persons might find the Eucharist and perhaps baptism appealing, what about those apparently more demanding, more distinctly Anabaptist practices—discipline and economic sharing?

DISCIPLINE

Historically, churches have usually exercised some kind of discipline. In today's individualistic and relativistic culture, however, most mainline churches and other communions have diminished its practice. In contrast, some evangelical groups are gaining popularity by emphasizing clear behavioral boundaries.

Much Catholic discipline occurs under the sacrament traditionally called "penance," but now "reconciliation." Reformation Protestants and Anabaptists complained that penance, much like the Mass, granted priests inordinate power: in this case, to retain and absolve sins. Catholics also enacted some disciplinary penalties through the state, notably excommunication, inflicted on many Anabaptists through gruesome executions. Zwingli entrusted much church discipline to magis-

---

[245]Holland, "Even the Postmodern Story."

trates by treating them as elders of congregations. The consistory in Calvin's Geneva, composed mostly of church officials, determined exacting behavioral standards enforced by city government.

Anabaptists were even more concerned that the new creation transform behavior. They insisted, though, that this be nurtured and regulated by churches alone. Discipline was no distinct social or ethical concern, but it was to be integrated into sacramental life. Submission to and exercise of discipline were entailed in the baptismal vow.[246] And it was often practiced along with the Supper. Many Anabaptists regarded discipline as a third practice necessary for restoring the church.

Today, Anabaptist theologians foreground behavioral transformation in communal contexts, and the accountability that it requires. Though they derive this from the historic practice of discipline, they, like theologians of other churches, seldom discuss it. Yoder, however, treats discipline, or binding and loosing, as something of a paradigm for all church practices, including baptism and the Supper (breaking bread). Yet he reduces the first, much like the latter two, mostly to social-ethical dimensions.

McClendon and Friesen also consider discipline, but largely as an aspect of communal discernment of God's will.[247] They are wary of discipline's tendency, among Anabaptists, to encourage legalism over holiness, domination over servanthood, conformity over initiative, mediocrity over creativity, condemnation over empathy and repression of bodily energies over their transformation. When May, Holland and Swartzentruber complain of Anabaptist rigidity, such uses of discipline are in view. They find these often linked with an artificial sense of superiority over and an unrealistic sense of separation from the "world."

Since historic Anabaptists developed discipline in unusual directions, I will not utilize some contemporaneous view as a "lens" to discover its contours, but instead I will search more directly for these, as I did with baptism. To this point, my constructive dialogue has been mostly with mainline churches that operate internationally in our globalizing era. But now, after glancing briefly at current Catholicism's sacrament of reconciliation, I will turn toward marginalized, minority traditions. I will also begin bringing the broad social potential of church practices more to the

---

[246]Expressed explicitly by Hubmaier (*Balthasar Hubmaier*, p. 389) and Schlaffer ("Instructions on Beginning," p. 108; "Ein kurzer Unterricht," p. 95) and indirectly by Riedemann (*Peter Riedemann's Hutterite Confession*, pp. 111, 153-154), but perhaps not among the Dutch.

[247]McClendon, *Systematic Theology* 2: 142-44, 343, 478-82, cf. McClendon, *Systematic Theology* I: 227-28. Friesen distinguishes discernment from discipline, which he designates by the current Catholic term *reconciliation* (*Artists, Citizens, Philosophers*, pp. 156-60). Both authors treat discipline more or less as a negative moment or occasional outcome of discernment. Yoder distinguishes *discernment* from *discipline*, calling discernment the "Rule of Paul" (*Body Politics*).

fore, leading into chapter seven. My constructive view of discipline will engage a social practice emanating in part from Anabaptism itself: conflict transformation. Some postmodern issues will arise. Then under the "Economic Sharing" section I will explore Latin American liberation theology.

Historic Anabaptist Perspectives

From the beginning, Anabaptist discipline was fostered by a striving for ascetic holiness, but not by this alone.[248] Advocates of various dubious practices, including violent revolution, were calling themselves Anabaptists. Anabaptist congregations felt it necessary to dispute with and often exclude such persons. Tight discipline was also encouraged by the need for cohesion and secrecy amid rampant persecution.

Switzerland. From early on, discipline was based on the baptismal commitment and utilized to ensure love and unity at the Supper.[249] Even though observers reported daily excommunications when Anabaptism spread into St. Gall, Anabaptists exhorted their congregations to discipline with compassion and humility.[250] They contrasted their approach to deviations with the coercive, violent measures employed by governments and churches that called on them.[251] However, at least by the time of Schleitheim, discipline was connected with a sharp dualism between "believing and unbelieving" people, between "the world and those who are [come] out of the world . . . and none will have part with the other."[252]

Hubmaier grounded both submission to and participation in exercising discipline in the baptismal covenant. Like Grebel, he regarded discipline as essential preparation for the Supper. Yet Hubmaier educed an additional basis for discipline, the power of the keys—Jesus' assurance that whatever his disciples bound or loosed on earth would be bound or loosed in heaven (Mt 16:19; 18:18-20; Jn 20:21-23). More precisely, the church employed "the key of admitting and loosing" in baptism and "the key of excluding, binding, and locking away" before the Supper.[253] Discipline was as necessary as either sacrament to a true church. For Jesus had "assigned all his authority to the holy Christian church"—the very same authority he had exercised on earth.[254] The church, then, really could forgive and condemn, so

---

[248]Kenneth Davis, *Anabaptism and Asceticism* (Scottdale, Penn.: Herald, 1974).

[249]Leland Harder, ed., *The Sources of Swiss Anabaptism* (Scottdale, Penn.: Herald, 1985), p. 355; Grebel, "Letters to Thomas Müntzer," p. 77; and Schleitheim [Sattler, *Legacy of Michael Sattler*, p. 37]).

[250]Harder, *Sources of Swiss Anabaptism*, p. 382; Sattler, *Legacy of Michael Sattler*, pp. 23, 44.

[251]Grebel, "Letters to Thomas Müntzer," p. 80; Sattler, *Legacy of Michael Sattler*, p. 23; Harder, *Sources of Swiss Anabaptism*, pp. 345, 514.

[252]Sattler, *Legacy of Michael Sattler*, p. 38.

[253]Hubmaier, *Balthasar Hubmaier*, p. 175, cf. pp. 413-14.

[254]Ibid., pp. 415, 371, 411-14.

that no salvation existed outside it.[255]

Jesus no longer exercised this authority for the same reason that he could not be present in the Supper: he was in heaven. The church had to be the agent and subject of each.[256] In both ways the church tended to become Christ insofar as he was active in this world (though he was directly present in the preached Word). The church could also seem to be a merely human institution, for "the church is built on our faith and affirmation, not we on the faith of the church."[257]

But why should churches discipline and ban? First, because "human beings are by nature" so "evil and vicious" that we must sometimes "cut off the corrupt and stinking flesh together with the poisoned and unclean members, so that the entire body might not thereby be deformed, shamed, and destroyed."[258] This rhetoric echoed Hubmaier's appraisal of the individual's body. Even after conversion it will remain "entirely worthless and hopeless unto death. It is not . . . capable of anything other than sin, striving against God."[259] Perhaps partly for this reason Hubmaier advised churches not to worry about being overly harsh, for their admonition "proceeds from such inner, heartfelt and fervent love" that anyone who rejects it "must be a most ignorant, wild and godless monster."[260]

Discipline and bannings were also salutary because they frightened the remaining members away from sin.[261] This maintained the purity of the church's witness to the world. Discipline also exposed those who claimed to have faith but did not perform the works that true faith energizes.[262] Finally, banning could even be productive for those banned: sometimes this drastic measure alone could induce them to examine their sins and repent.[263]

For Hubmaier, as for all Anabaptists, disciplinary procedure was classically outlined by Jesus in Matthew 18:15-18. Anyone who felt sinned against or noticed other members at odds should seek to reconcile things through individual conversation. To fail to do this was to participate in their sins. God could wonderfully reconcile enormous conflicts in this way.[264] But if individual dialogue failed, several more members should help. Within these first two steps, which constituted admo-

---

[255]Ibid., pp. 239, 371.
[256]Ibid., pp. 371, 411, 415.
[257]Ibid., p. 247; cf. p. 163 above.
[258]Ibid., p. 374, cf. pp. 376-77.
[259]Ibid., p. 433. Though he ascribed this to "the flesh" here, flesh was nearly equivalent to "body," which Hubmaier called an "essential substance" (pp. 429-32).
[260]Ibid., p. 380.
[261]Ibid., pp. 353, 411.
[262]Ibid., pp. 376, 383.
[263]Ibid., pp. 354, 380.
[264]Ibid., pp. 379-82.

nition, forgiveness (from Christ via the keys) was possible as often as one sincerely repented.[265] Those who admonished were to do so lovingly, mindful of their own susceptibility to sin.

If these steps failed, however, the congregation had to become involved. Those who could not be reconciled through this third step were banned in a fourth step, apparently before the Lord's Supper. This exclusion from the only ark of salvation—back into the realm of the "world," flesh and devil—was literally Christ's judgment to eternal condemnation.[266] Sometimes, when gross public sins occurred, it had to be performed swiftly, without the first two steps, to preserve the church's witness.[267] But even then the church hoped that the excommunicated would repent, reform and return.

Hubmaier stipulated that no church member should speak, greet, eat or conduct business with banned persons.[268] Yet they should not hate such individuals or drive them away—just avoid them.[269] Of course, if excommunicants experienced some calamity, church members should aid them, as they should enemies, Jews and pagans. But while Christians should normally exercise friendliness and loving works toward the last three groups, they should not toward the banned.[270]

South Germany-Austria. Given their brief ministries, early leaders had little opportunity to consider discipline. Hans Schlaffer envisioned the church as a bride without spot or wrinkle and baptism as an indication of readiness to participate in discipline.[271] Leonhard Schiemer connected "brotherly discipline" and Hans Hut probably connected baptism with the community's power to bind and loose.[272] Schiemer mentioned the community releasing people from sin.[273]

I. Hutterites, who formed through mutual banning among leaders and groups (cf. chap. 2), contrasted the church's purity with the "world's" evil at least as strongly as the Schleitheim Confession. Ever since Adam, they believed, God had worked mainly at separating a unique, holy people from the wicked.[274] Echoing the

[265]Ibid., p. 239.
[266]Ibid., pp. 416-17.
[267]Ibid., pp. 377-78.
[268]Ibid., pp. 353, 417.
[269]Ibid., pp. 418.
[270]Ibid., p. 419.
[271]Schlaffer, "Instructions on Beginning," p. 108.
[272]Schiemer, "Three Kinds of Grace," p. 92; Hut mentioned "baptism as a covenant of acceptance before the Christian community" and being received into it in close connection with Jesus' words that "what is bound on earth will be bound in heaven" ("On the Mystery of Baptism," p. 72).
[273]Schiemer, "Three Kinds of Grace," p. 93.
[274]Riedemann, *Peter Riedemann's Hutterite Confession,* pp. 159-80.

Dutch, they insisted that the church participated so fully in Christ's divine nature that true members must think like him.[275]

This concern, however, was not bluntly separatist. It would help the church become a "lantern of righteousness" filled with divine light to be "held up to the whole world, so that . . . people may learn and see and know the way of life."[276] Hutterite missionary zeal was extraordinary.

Hutterites agreed with Hubmaier that Christ had given the church the keys, that whomever it excluded or forgave received eternal damnation or salvation, and that apart from the church there was no salvation.[277] Riedemann briefly connected the power of these keys with baptism and affirmed that it was given to the whole church.[278] He portrayed discipline as a basic dynamic of church life. All members "admonish one another, warning and rebuking each other persistently."[279] Hutterite communities, however, were hierarchical. Ulrich Stadler assigned the chief disciplinary role to deacons and insisted that congregations unanimously support their decisions.[280]

According to Riedemann, people who sinned without premeditation, but "through weakness of the flesh," were forgiven—yet they were also refused the kiss of peace for a time to humble them. Riedemann mentioned neither Matthew 18's four steps nor, at any length, redemptive possibilities like those associated with the first three. He jumped immediately to "major sins." Their perpetrators were swiftly banned without admonition, as probably occurred at times in Hubmaier's circles.[281]

Riedemann's Hutterites, apparently like Hubmaier's followers, had no fellowship with banned persons. This seemingly entailed no meals. Unfortunately, details regarding marital or other contacts are lacking. Excommunicants received differing degrees of discipline, which perhaps included penitential practices, according to the gravity of their sins. They were not readmitted until they evidenced "a truly repentant life" for some time. Then, since their first entrance into the church via the keys was through a sign, baptism, readmission by the same keys involved another: laying on of hands.[282]

---

[275]Ibid., p. 77; cf. Ulrich Stadler, "Cherished Instructions on Sin, Excommunication, and the Community of Goods," in *Spiritual and Anabaptist Writers*, ed. George Williams and Angel Mergal (Philadelphia: Westminster Press, 1957), p. 277.

[276]Riedemann, *Peter Riedemann's Hutterite Confession*, pp. 77-78.

[277]Ibid., p. 81.

[278]Ibid., pp. 111, 81.

[279]Ibid., pp. 152-53.

[280]Stadler, "Cherished Instructions on Sin," p. 276.

[281]Riedemann, *Peter Riedemann's Hutterite Confession*, p. 153.

[282]Ibid., pp. 153-54.

Though the serious Hutterite discipline appears somewhat moderated in Riedemann's account, it was far less so in Stadler's. Stadler also exhorted people to "mortification," based on a dim view of the body like Hubmaier's.[283] Riedemann's perspective on the body was also surprisingly pessimistic.[284] Hutterites apparently correlated strict discipline, like Hubmaier, with a negative view of corporeality.

2. Pilgram Marpeck also believed that all baptized persons share the authority to bind and loose, and that the ban should be administered before the Supper.[285] Unlike the Swiss and Hutterites, however, he stressed that the Spirit is really the one who retains or forgives sin and that the church judges rightly only under Christ's active sovereignty.[286] Further, Marpeck extolled a virtue seldom prioritized by other Anabaptists: patience. Marpeck rooted this in God's patience exercised toward us when Christ patiently took on human sufferings. Marpeck no doubt experienced this through the Spirit toward himself.[287] Yet he noticed that when church members struggled with sin, others tended to react quickly and harshly. Their intent was to ward off future sin. But Marpeck protested that they often ran ahead of the Spirit's patient work.[288]

Marpeck concurred with all Anabaptists that the church must appraise the "fruits" of its members' lives. Yet he complained, especially against the Swiss, that it often judged by "blossoms or leaves." That is, when negative behavior appeared, people assumed that a person would become worse and worse—bearing "evil fruit." However, Marpeck cautioned, negative signs might well indicate that the Spirit is at work internally. Despite sickly blossoms or leaves, a plant might eventually bear ripe fruit; despite beautiful leaves or blossoms, the fruit might be rotten.[289]

Marpeck's concern, as with baptism and the Lord's Supper, was that the church's outer actions—here its disciplinary measures—cowitness with the Spirit's inner work just as the Spirit cowitnessed with Son and Father.[290] When the church ran ahead of the Spirit, it tended to impose the law or a burden of ironclad prohibitions on people. Yet this could only frighten, stifle and sadden someone wrestling with the Spirit of grace.[291]

Why did Marpeck draw attention to a lengthy fruit-bearing process? Because

---

[283]Stadler, "Cherished Instruction," pp. 281, 283, 284.
[284]See pp. 238, 479-81 and chap. 9 below.
[285]Marpeck, *Writings of Pilgram Marpeck*, pp. 112, 275-76, 296-97.
[286]Ibid., pp. 334, 336, 415-16, 472.
[287]Ibid., pp. 354-55, 359-60, 446-47.
[288]Ibid., pp. 333, 324-25.
[289]Ibid., pp. 325, 334, 344-52.
[290]Ibid., pp. 423-25.
[291]Ibid., pp. 313, 315, 327-29, 358.

his anthropology differed from that of the Hutterites and Swiss. They perceived the human body as largely or wholly hostile to the divine Spirit—no doubt presupposing some ontological barrier between them.[292] The body could not really be transformed but had to be ceaselessly resisted and subjugated. No wonder those Anabaptist bodies interpreted sickly "leaves" as the eruption of entirely negative forces requiring speedy suppression.

Marpeck's alternate view flowed from his Christology. Since Jesus' human corporeality was not opposed to divine Spirit but was designed to be its vehicle, so is ours—though it had risen up over our spirits, blocking their communion with God's Spirit.[293] Consequently, though sin now operates in and through our flesh, flesh itself is not sin.[294] Jesus returned the human spirit to its rightful position over the flesh, and because Christians live in communion with him, their spirit-flesh interaction is being healed according to his pattern. Since Marpeck believed that Jesus was very patient with us, he was unperturbed by the time the healing took in us.[295]

Still, Marpeck thought that evil fruit also could mature in the church. Then the church was not to "run behind" God's Spirit but ban.[296] Marpeck even placed his Swiss correspondents outside the true church![297] Yet he devoted less attention to banning's mechanics than they or the Hutterites did. He said little about conduct toward the banned, save that it, like all discipline, should aim toward their improvement.[298]

In about 1540 Marpeck's community revised a proto-Hutterite Discipline from 1529. The earlier code simply declared that whoever "leads a disorderly life . . . shall be punished" publicly or privately, depending on their offence. In contrast, the Pilgramites insisted that

> Diligent attention is to be paid in each case of transgression be it secret or open, large or small, one warning or more, how the person is dealt with according to gentleness and sharpness, patience and impatience. For correction and excommunication must be distinguished according to the actual circumstances. . . . The power of Christ is

---

[292]Cf. p. 195 above.

[293]Marpeck, *Writings of Pilgram Marpeck*, pp. 79, 76.

[294]Ibid., p. 108.

[295]Overall, Marpeck was optimistic about the church. Its members were children of God the Father, conceived through the Spirit, "of one flesh, one bone, one blood" with Christ and possessing "the divine nature and manner" (ibid., p. 396). Birthed and nurtured through this triunity, they could not really be separated (p. 523). Marpeck extolled this corporate dwelling of believers in the triune dynamism and of it in them (pp. 435-36, 440-44).

[296]Ibid., pp. 325-26, 344, 424.

[297]Ibid., pp. 366-68.

[298]Ibid., pp. 275-76.

not a power to destroy or to exercise tyranny, but to improve.[299]

The Netherlands. 1. Melchior Hoffman, with his lofty expectations of divinization, sometimes spoke as if true Christians never sinned.[300] Yet perhaps inconsistently he insisted that some serious postbaptismal sins make forgiveness impossible.[301] Perhaps even less consistently, in the midst of extolling the Supper as
complete marital union, Hoffman acknowledged that the bride could commit
adultery, be divorced (after three warnings) and delivered to Satan's kingdom—
but even after that turn back and be betrothed again.[302] Melchior at first promoted
egalitarian congregations. Later he endorsed hierarchical leadership where pastors
could ban unilaterally.[303]

2. Menno Simons and Dirk Philips could hardly build a credible church after Münster without eliminating some people prone to violence and other excesses. Their concern about this, however, was heightened by their notion of
the true church as heavenly and spotless, sharing Christ's mind so fully that its
members could disagree neither with him nor each other.[304] Dirk, much like
Riedemann, maintained that God from the beginning had separated true believers from the "world."[305] Menno regarded the "world" as anti-Christ's
realm, and with Dirk, Hubmaier and Hutterites, he denied salvation outside
the true congregation.[306]

Dirk once acknowledged that the church, with its human members, is composed
of "two different substances," Adam's as well Christ's.[307] For the Dutch, however,
Adamic "flesh" and Christ's divine nature were even more opposed ethically than
matter and spirit were ontologically. Adamic nature could not be transformed
gradually by the Spirit, for it remained permanently hostile. Consequently, when
people's behavior differed from group norms, Dutch leaders could only conclude
that they had turned back wholly to "the flesh."

Unlike the Swiss, the Dutch neither derived discipline explicitly from baptism

[299]Packull, *Hutterite Beginnings*, p. 307-8, cf. pp. 33-53.
[300]Hoffman, "Ordinance of God," pp. 189-91.
[301]Ibid., pp. 199-200.
[302]Ibid., pp. 196-97.
[303]Deppermann, *Melchior Hoffman*, p. 266. The church as a whole was led by apostles, below whom
came prophets, pastors, then congregational members (p. 265). Hoffman, however, opposed the
confessions involved in Catholic penance for allotting priests, who alone pronounced absolution,
too much power. Menno also contrasted true penance with Catholic confession (*Complete Works*, pp.
382-83).
[304]Philips, *Writings of Dirk Philips*, pp. 246, 311-12; Simons, *Complete Works*, pp. 409-10, 738.
[305]Philips, *Writings of Dirk Philips*, p. 242.
[306]Simons, *Complete Works*, p. 967; Philips, *Writings of Dirk Philips*, pp. 81, 596.
[307]Philips, *Writings of Dirk Philips*, p. 415.

nor linked it tightly with the Supper. Yet they insisted that all three were necessary. While they occasionally based discipline on the power of the keys,[308]
Menno regarded the key of binding as essentially the threatening and condemning law, and the key of loosing as the freeing news of grace—and both as dimensions of the preached Word.[309] In including or excluding people, then, either at
first or later on the church was simply extending the basic gospel of grace or
judgment.

Like the Swiss the later Dutch located disciplinary authority in the congregation, though they granted its leaders greater powers. But whereas Hubmaier believed that Christ, whose body was in heaven, had given the church all disciplinary
authority, the Dutch insisted, like Marpeck, that the living Christ, through his
Spirit, administered discipline—as he did the Supper—and that they were simply
his messengers.[310]

Discipline was valued mainly for avoiding "worldly" contamination. It also kept
the congregation's witness clear.[311] Further, discipline shamed and chastened one's
Adamic flesh in order to save one's spirit.[312] On one level, discipline meant daily
activities of mutual instructing, admonishing, comforting and reproving.[313] One
should confront a brother soon after he errs, though with gentleness; if he repents
at this first disciplinary step, one should wholly forgive.[314]

Yet as time passed, Menno and Dirk increasingly applied the first three disciplinary steps only to offences committed through "weakness." Both leaders eventually insisted, apparently more stringently than Hubmaier or Hutterites, on immediately banning "all offensively carnal sinners, such as fornicators, adulterers,
drunkards, etc." The basic reason, apparently, was that the divinizing Spirit-
Adamic flesh gap now seemed so wide that such persons must be "no longer flesh
of Christ's flesh, and members of his Holy body, seeing they are so carnal and
devilish that they have made themselves into dogs and swine and . . . children of
the devil."[315]

---

[308]Simons, *Complete Works*, pp. 469, 991; Philips, *Writings of Dirk Philips*, p. 369.

[309]Simons, *Complete Works*, pp. 989-90, cf. pp. 127-29 above.

[310]Simons, *Complete Works*, pp. 469, 992; Philips, *Writings of Dirk Philips*, pp. 369-70.

[311]Philips, *Writings of Dirk Philips*, pp. 246, 600; Simons, *Complete Works*, pp. 458, 969.

[312]Philips, *Writings of Dirk Philips*, pp. 246, 581, 600, 614.

[313]Simons, *Complete Works*, p. 733; Philips, *Writings of Dirk Philips*, p. 515.

[314]Simons, *Complete Works*, pp. 412, 980-81; cf. Philips, *Writings of Dirk Philips*, pp. 243, 247-48.

[315]Simons, *Complete Works*, p. 975, cf. Philips, *Writings of Dirk Philips*, p. 247. Menno also argued that
such sins are usually premeditated (*Complete Works*, p. 982); if everyone had three chances to repent,
hypocrites would coast through the first two with no intent of changing (p. 976). He added that
public sins call for public rebuke (p. 981) and that swift excommunication's shock value would
more likely induce repentance (p. 975). By 1558 Menno concluded that interpersonal offenses

Though Menno was initially more lenient, he eventually taught with Dirk, and as Hubmaier had, that church members should neither eat, greet nor do business with excommunicants.[316] Yet both leaders agreed on helping excommunicants in times of great need. The Dutch, somewhat uniquely, emphasized that such shunning induces shame.[317] They considered shame essential for true repentance, though this had to be evidenced by behavioral reform.[318] Here, as in describing initial repentance (chap. 5) and baptism, the Dutch came closest among Anabaptists to implying that works must precede grace.

Particularly controversial was the extension of shunning to marriage, forbidding even spouse and family to live with an excommunicant. In the 1554 Wismar Articles, Dirk, Menno and other leaders required individual consideration of such cases, respecting the consciences of those involved.[319] Dirk, however, soon denounced all exceptions to strict shunning. Reluctantly, Menno eventually agreed—perhaps fearing the ban himself.[320]

---

could be admonished three times, heretics or sectarians once or twice, and "an open, offensive, sensual sinner" not at all (p. 982; for his responses to those insisting on three admonitions, see pp. 1043-45, 1060-63). Yet in 1554 Menno divulged that he sometimes worked "a whole year or two" with persons who were eventually banned (p. 729). All along he advocated finding procedures neither too harsh nor too lenient.

[316]In 1550 Menno allowed occasional or necessary business contacts with banned persons, though not regular commercial associations (Simons, *Complete Works*, pp. 474-75, 481-82). Though he forbade the Christian kiss of peace with them, he encouraged an informal "good morning" and the like (p. 479). At about that time Dirk granted much less leeway on business dealings and greetings (Philips, *Writings of Dirk Philips*, pp. 613-14). Menno also urged providing "temporal necessities" for banned family members. Some other Dutch were recommending that excommunicants themselves not be avoided "but only their false doctrines and offensive lives." Others favored exclusion only from practices like the Supper and kiss of peace (Simons, *Complete Works*, p. 457).

[317]Simons, *Complete Works*, pp. 414, 458, 470, 724; Philips, *Writings of Dirk Philips*, pp. 369, 613.

[318]Simons, *Complete Works*, pp. 412, 468, 977, 992; Philips, *Writings of Dirk Philips*, p. 247.

[319]Simons, *Complete Works*, p. 1041. Wismar also affirmed banning persons who married "outside the congregation" but allowed their return if they manifested "a proper Christian life." Just before his death, however, Dirk insisted that marriage to one outside the church places a person in sin's realm (Philips, *Writings of Dirk Philips*, p. 565); return was impermissible unless the spouse also was converted (p. 573).

[320]Menno's statements on marital shunning were inconsistent, even in his last years (Snyder, *Anabaptist History*, pp. 339-47). Yet as this embattled leader waxed increasingly pessimistic about "sinners" and harsh toward opponents, he kept claiming that he had always obeyed God's exact words, and had never changed his mind. Menno advocated flexibility and concern for the weak in 1550 (Simons, *Complete Works*, p. 479) and still in 1556, critiquing the best-known attempt to ban one who refused marital shunning, Swaen Rutgers (Simons, *Complete Works*, p. 1051). Yet in 1558 he insisted on rigid shunning, referring to nearly three hundred couples who had not observed it and fallen away (Simons, *Complete Works*, pp. 970-74). That same year, however, Menno opposed separating those wishing to care for their children, unable to remain celibate or whose faith would not be hindered by

These quarrels helped foment the Waterlanders' departure in 1556 and subsequent bannings among Flemings and Frisians, and between Swiss and Dutch (see chap two). Even Dirk was excommunicated by some.[321] Damaging as Dutch banning became, Menno countered that it outshone that which other churches inflicted on Mennonites: the wheel and gallows.[322]

To be sure, if Dutch Anabaptism was to survive Münsterite and other aberrations, along with savage persecution, some degree of uniformity and accountability had to be ensured. But as extremely high behavioral expectations met disappointment, they were not significantly modified. Instead, the Dutch imposed more severe strictures on the flesh.[323] They were surely seeking to unite inner spirituality with outward behavior, like all Anabaptists—but in a way that could drive the two further apart.

Summary. If genuine faith produces good works (cf. chap. 5) and the new creation takes visible communal form contrasting sharply with the old's, certain behaviors will express this while others will not. Still, unless this creation arrives instantaneously, its behaviors will involve some developmental process, requiring structure, nurture and discipline of some sort. Yet much as discipline today often connotes the restrictive and punitive aspects of growth, most historic Anabaptists underlined these when considering disciplinary processes. In searching for distinctive features of their outlook, we noticed that discipline included many positive features of personal and interpersonal development. Anabaptists surely stressed these in practice, particularly when applying Matthew 18's first three steps. Distinctive also, however, was the increasing prominence of the dreaded fourth step, especially among the Hutterites and later Dutch. Why?

Perhaps because Anabaptist efforts to interconnect Spirit with matter, and inner reality with outer, encountered a significant obstacle. Anabaptists joined these fairly well in baptism, insisting that inward, personal baptism of the Spirit be completed through outward, communal baptism of water, which in turn expressed and witnessed to the former. Greater difficulties arose with the Lord's Supper. The assumption that an ontological barrier prevented matter from embodying spirit

---

their excommunicated mate (p. 1061). Accused in 1556 of changing his views, Menno bitterly countered "that none under heaven can practice his faith while living with his apostate consort" (pp. 1002, 1007).

[321]Philips, *Writings of Dirk Philips,* pp. 468-551.

[322]Simons, *Complete Works,* p. 402.

[323]Using the nuptial imagery common among Dutch Anabaptists, Dirk and Menno often claimed that a Christian's marriage to Christ, actualized in the church, must precede any earthly marriage tie. Menno could frame the issue as "whether spiritual love has to yield to carnal love" (Simons, *Complete Works,* p. 971).

pushed Anabaptists to either separate the risen Christ from the physical rite (in Switzerland) or call his presence purely spiritual.

Daily behavior expressed the new creation's sacramentality more comprehensively. Yet here the ontological barrier raised greater obstacles. The body, for most Anabaptists, was so incorrigible that it could express the Spirit only when restricted by multiple rules. As a result it often seemed that Anabaptist bodies, individual and corporate, were being not so much transformed by as clashing with God's Spirit to the detriment of both.[324]

We can admire Anabaptism's intense quest for holiness and appreciate the historical necessity for tight communal solidarity. Yet with discipline it is obvious that theology in Anabaptist perspective cannot simplistically take historic Anabaptism as its norm but must evaluate it by other criteria.

Contemporary Appropriations

It is not only Anabaptist practices that raise questions about discipline. Few people today, despite the widespread hunger for community, are interested in commitments and criteria that would regulate their behavior. The current interest in spirituality is often driven, unconsciously, by a consumer mentality, seeking ever more varied pleasures without limit. Yet on the other hand, many searchers also seek to escape domination by impersonal institutions, a possibility that increases with globalization. Life today is threatened by not only individualism but also what May calls "the tyranny of the community."[325]

In both historical and contemporary perspective, then, discipline appears more controversial than baptism or the Supper. I will, accordingly, first address Scripture with these historical and contemporary issues in mind, to see what it says about this topic. Following this, I will briefly consider two concepts that might better express this third church practice: reconciliation and discipling. Then I will explore, at greater length, a contemporary movement affecting church and society that is indebted to this practice: conflict transformation. Finally, I will construct my own theology.

Biblical considerations. It can hardly be doubted that Scripture encourages, even commands, pursuit of holiness. Jesus taught a righteousness exceeding even the Pharisees', permeating hearts as well as outward actions—of being "perfect"

---

[324]Snyder adds that the Anabaptist groups that survived sought to be "above all, 'without spot or wrinkle.' . . . It was the divine Christ, not the incarnate Christ, that inspired the Anabaptist tradition of the 'Body of Christ;' consequently, it was above all divine purity, not human growth, that was expected to be 'incarnated' by believers" (*Anabaptist History*, p. 362; cf. Swartzentruber's critique of Anabaptist ecclesiology [pp. 84-85 above]).

[325]Melanie May, "The Pleasure of Our Lives as Text," *CGR* 10, no. 1 (1992): 38.

(teleios) as was his Father (e.g., Mt 5:20, 22, 28, 48). Anabaptists, by rightly insisting that Jesus meant such teachings to be obeyed, could imply that these were prescriptions, or legal conditions, for entering God's kingdom. Instead, they were descriptions of how people who received the gift of God's kingdom, or righteousness, could live.[326] Since this righteousness was already present, Jesus' teachings could be followed, but since it was not yet wholly present, they could be followed ever more fully and still keep pointing toward yet greater fullness. True obedience was not flawless and instantaneous but sincere and maturing.

Obedience, or holiness, could hardly be individualistic, for most virtues involved were relational. The New Testament often encourages Christians, for example, to be clothed

> with compassion, kindness, humility, meekness, and patience. Bear with one another and, if anyone has a complaint against another, forgive each other. . . . Above all, clothe yourselves with love, which binds everything together in perfect harmony. . . . [T]each and admonish one another in all wisdom; and with gratitude in your hearts sing psalms, hymns, and spiritual songs. (Col 3:12-14, 16; cf. Eph 4:25–5:20)

Such virtues are actualized through a process, the growth of all members toward unity and the maturity of Christ (Eph 4:11-16, cf. 2 Cor 3:18). Yet this harmony cannot be attained without painful struggle against behaviors and attitudes that clash with it. This involves internal and external crucifixion as well as resurrection with Christ (e.g., Phil 3:10-16; Heb 12:1-2; 1 Pet 4:1-2, 12-14). And as Marpeck recognized, patience is essential.[327] Paradoxically, only through humility that is not and appears not triumphant but weak and perplexed does Jesus' resurrection life become active and visible (2 Cor 4:7-12).

Nonetheless, in so difficult a growth process, certain behaviors had to be eliminated—and sometimes individuals,[328] though only by people exercising caution

---

[326]Robert Guelich, *The Sermon on the Mount* (Waco, Tex.: Word, 1982), esp. pp. 109-11, 157-74, 234-37. While "perfect" *(teleios)* has moral dimensions, it points chiefly to the wholeness possible in this new relationship with God and others (p. 236).

[327]E.g., Lk 8:15; Rom 5:3-4; 8:24-25; Eph 4:2-3; Col 1:11; Heb 10:35-36; Jas 1:3-4; Rev 1:9; 13:10.

[328]Historic Anabaptists most often cited 1 Cor 5:11: Do not even eat with a member "who is sexually immoral or greedy, or is an idolater, reviler, drunkard, or robber." This admonition followed the delivery of an extreme offender "to Satan," though still "that his spirit may be saved in the day of the Lord" (1 Cor 5:5). But since the Corinthians struggled with extreme immorality, I find generalizations of such exhortations problematic. Four other texts seemed to demand avoidance. Three, however, need not mean more than Do not let some persons keep teaching or disputing (Rom 16:17; Tit 3:9-10; 2 Jn 10-11). The fourth, 2 Thess 3:6, concerned a community practicing some economic sharing. Members were urged to stand aloof from *(stellō)* other members living in idleness. These particular circumstances raise problems for generalizing this admonition also (see also Jn 15:2, 6; Rom 11:15).

and humility (Gal 6:1-2). As historic Anabaptists recognized, the clearest procedure for this appears in Matthew 18:15-18. They understood it, along with John
20:21-23 and the keys of Matthew 16:18-19, to equate the church's decisions with
God's decisions. Consequently, they claimed as great authority for their excommunications and exclusivity for their churches as did Catholics.

Recent developments. Since *discipline* accentuates the negative features of this process,
several other terms should be considered.

1. Reconciliation. Catholics traditionally identified the sacrament most connected with this process by the negative term *penance.* Not surprisingly, penalties,
satisfactions and purgation often took center stage.[329] In 1975 this rite was revised
under the overarching theme "reconciliation," to indicate that it deals mostly with
bringing together people who differ. This means that the whole church is continually involved in a conversion and reconciliation process of which this sacrament is
but one expression (cf. Eph 4:11-17). The church and its leaders, then, do not
stand outside and simply evaluate this movement but are also subject to it.[330] Some
members may be excluded from the Eucharist or other activities for a time to undergo repentance and conversion anew. Yet emphasis falls on their restoration,
which is not simply terminated with their reinstatement but celebrated as a reunion
among the church's members.

Jesus' work is aptly called *reconciliation* (Rom 5:10; 2 Cor 5:17-21; Eph 2:16),
through which God is reconciling "to himself all things, whether on earth or in
heaven" (Col 1:20). I will adopt this term to designate the overarching framework
within which discipline occurs.

2. Discipling. In Anabaptist circles Marlin Jeschke suggests that *discipling* better
describes the process traditionally called discipline.[331] Discipling, of course, means
training in discipleship, and *disciple (mathētēs)* in Scripture means "one who learns."
Discipling aptly combines the serious commitment and continual growth that
characterize biblical holiness or righteousness.

I have not chosen discipleship for my theology's interpretive center, despite
Bender's advocacy, for *discipleship* cannot, I believe, express the totality of God's
transforming work as well as *new creation.* Further, many Anabaptists use *discipleship*
to highlight outward, human, social-ethical activity while underplaying inward, divine and ecclesial reality. But for me, Christian life involves both outer and inner
participation in Jesus' way—or christomorphic divinization (cf. chap. 5)—within
a community entered through inner (Spirit) and outer (water) baptism, and nur-

---

[329]See pp. 111-12 above.
[330]James Dallen, *The Reconciling Community* (New York: Pueblo, 1986), pp. 258-60.
[331]Marlin Jeschke, *Discipling the Brother* (Scottdale, Penn.: Herald, 1973).

tured through the Spirit by Christ's presence in the Lord's Supper. Within this framework, *discipling* expresses well the mutual, ongoing learning, growth, struggle and occasional failure marking the corporate walk toward holiness on Jesus' path. I will use *discipling* for what tradition called "discipline."

Conflict transformation. Despite earlier aberrations in Anabaptist discipling, enough of its meaning endured for some later Anabaptists to draw on it and become widely recognized contributors to this practice, which extends far beyond the church.[332] Conflict transformation emerged out of differing activities such as labor negotiations, international peacemaking, crisis counseling and out-of-court settlements.[333] It still operates in these and similar arenas. Anabaptists in this field can provide concrete suggestions as to what discipling might mean today, when few people seem interested in the rules, structures and penalties connoted by discipline.

I will first show how the most crucial text, Matthew 18:15-20, can be read in light of conflict transformation experience. Then I will briefly probe some suggested theological foundations for this practice. These will take us a bit beyond the church and raise some postmodern issues in preparation for chapter seven.

I. John Paul Lederach, a recognized leader in conflict transformation, proposes reconciliation as the overarching theological rationale for this practice.[334] He guides us through Matthew 18:15-20 in four steps but shows why these often are not really followed today. Perhaps Anabaptism's previous difficulties arose for much the same reasons. Jesus began (step I): "If another member of the church sins against you, go and point out the fault when the two of you are alone. If the member listens to you, you have regained that one" (Mt 18:15).

This verse, and thus the subsequent steps, might seem to concern only very personal offenses against oneself. Menno, who wanted to avoid the first three steps for all disputes, interpreted it that way.[335] Yet similar texts show that Jesus intended this procedure for all significant conflicts.[336]

In reality, Lederach points out, Christians frequently avoid this step: when disturbed by someone's actions they often first find others who will support their viewpoint. Why? Because if I first contact a person "alone," I must face my own resentments, assumptions and anxieties. Further, I will have to really listen to the

---

[332]W. Scott Thompson and Kenneth Jensen eds., *Approaches to Peace* (Washington, D.C.: United States Institute of Peace, 1988), p. 306.

[333]Ibid., pp. 299-332; I. William Zartman and J. Lewis Rasmussen, eds., *Peacemaking in International Conflict* (Washington, D.C.: United States Institute of Peace, 1997), pp. 51-77.

[334]John Paul Lederach, *The Journey Toward Reconciliation* (Scottdale, Penn.: Herald, 1999).

[335]Simons, *Complete Works,* pp. 979-82.

[336]Mt 5:23-24; 7:3-5; cf. Gal 6:1; Jas 5:19-20; moreover, "against you" is missing from some important early manuscripts of Mt 18:15.

other's perspective. What I might first have intended as a simple criticism will often become an extended dialogue. This may well alter my outlook as well as the other's.[337]

Next, Jesus said (step 2): "If you are not listened to, take one or two others along with you, so that every word may be confirmed by the evidence of two or three witnesses" (Mt 18:16). Though it might seem at first that these persons are simply to confirm the other's guilt, listening to "every word" means pondering everything all parties say. These persons, if not chosen just to reinforce the original complaint, can help create space where the two individuals can become more transparent and gain new insights. This will likely expand discussion beyond than the original issue. All parties will become involved with and accountable to the whole community.[338]

However, Jesus continued (step 3): "If the member refuses to listen to them, tell it to the church" (Mt 18:17). This does not mean, for Lederach, that the original "offender" is brought to trial but that the whole congregation must now help work toward resolution. In this process, church leaders must find creative ways of incorporating various people.[339] The church, the herald of reconciliation (cf. 2 Cor 5:17-21), is now challenged to work out reconciliation, "the transformation of people and their relationships," in its midst.[340]

Nevertheless (step 4), "If the offender refuses to listen even to the church, let such a one be to you as a Gentile and a tax collector" (Mt 18:17). Most Anabaptists thought that Jesus here commanded shunning. From this, controversies about eating, doing business or living conjugally with banned persons arose. Lederach, however, interprets behavior toward Gentiles and tax collectors by Jesus' practice: "Jesus ate with them."[341] Therefore, when disputing parties must go different ways, he advises the church to "Maintain relational and emotional contact" with those who leave. Eating together can especially foster "non-anxious presence" and "vulnerable transparency," which might yet lead to reconciliation—still the goal.[342]

Lederach notes that these four steps precede what Anabaptists thought of as referring to the keys: whatever you bind or loose on earth will be bound or loosed in heaven (Mt 18:18; cf. Mt 16:19). Yet he proposes that, seen in context, these words refer mainly not to the final decision but to the entire process. They do not mean that God sanctions every church decision but that God becomes present, that

---

[337]Lederach, *Journey Toward Reconciliation*, pp. 123-28.
[338]Ibid., pp. 128-30.
[339]Ibid., p. 132.
[340]Ibid., p. 131.
[341]Ibid., p. 134.
[342]Ibid., p. 135.

heaven and earth (the spiritual and the material) come together, as churches wrestle through this process.[343]

Lederach is asking, in light of conflict transformation experience, how Matthew 18 might actually work today. Among Anabaptists "discipline" often initiated a series of accusations leading to legal sentence or acquittal. Yet Lederach shows how it can also create space for people to be open and vulnerable, to learn from each other, better understand themselves and thereby participate in the church's continuing task of reconciliation. But this requires humility and patience. Often these come hardest to people who overestimate their own sanctification or fear facing their own lack of it. Anabaptists have not always been immune to these tendencies.

Lederach reiterates that reconciliation of all things is God's major work. The church's mission is to align itself with what God is already doing. This "happens through the incarnation, the way in which Word becomes flesh."[344] All this is embodied in God's Son, who enables us to see, hear and interact with God's reconciling love made present.[345]

2. As Anabaptists pursue such a mission through conflict transformation far beyond the church, what, in this postmodern era, might be their theological rationale? Ronald Kraybill proposes that such work (he calls it peacebuilding) is inherently religious. Peacebuilders, that is, cannot really function without overall hopes and goals.

Kraybill is guided by a vision of *shalom*, the Old Testament term often translated "peace." It includes well-being and harmonious relations among all humans and other creatures.[346] Kraybill also maintains that every religion is a social construction. Shalom then "is socially constituted through the processes by which people erect structures of meaning to interact with and ultimately create the world they live in."[347]

Kraybill proposes that peacebuilding's main goal is transformation.[348] This includes empowerment, which increases "peoples' sense of strength and ability to

---

[343]Ibid., pp. 138-40.

[344]Ibid., p. 160.

[345]Ibid., p. 161.

[346]Ronald Kraybill, *Peacebuilders in Zimbabwe: An Anabaptist Paradigm for Conflict Transformation* (Ph. D. diss.: University of Capetown, 1996), pp. 108-35. He derives this almost entirely from the Old Testament, highlighting its notions of salvation and justice (pp. 26-28). This allows him to define *shalom* mainly in a social (and environmental) way, omitting the New Testament term for "peace" *[eirēnē]*, which often includes the personal and spiritual (Jn 14:27; Rom 14:17; Phil 4:7; Col 3:15-16). *Eirēnē*, though, is multifaceted and frequently includes the social as well. Its inclusion would not contradict Kraybill's account of shalom but enrich it. Kraybill's work, the only extensive theology of conflict transformation I know, is a doctoral dissertation which he graciously let me use.

[347]Ibid., p. 140, cf. pp. 14-15.

[348]Ibid., pp. 19, 42-62.

take control of their situation," to formulate goals, consider options, solve problems and "make conscious, reflective decisions." As these capacities increase, people experience greater "self-worth, security, self-determination, and autonomy."[349]

Transformation also includes guidance by moral norms. But which ones should be followed? Kraybill answers that only the parties involved in a conflict can decide this and that "the quest for universal norms is increasingly recognized as fruitless."[350]

Kraybill proposes, further, that peacebuilders can learn "what is 'real' " from the experiences and aspirations of people who are vulnerable and on society's margins. Peacebuilders should generally favor their causes, for history works in a transformative way in which visions for leading society beyond the control of current dominant forces emerge from these margins.[351]

Kraybill also insists that shalom cannot be pursued apart from communities where people share a common vision and are mutually accountable.[352] Such communities, as McClendon and others stress, must be rooted in narratives, including a master story, and be involved in a spiritual journey.[353] People cannot really build peace until they experience love and reconciliation in such communities. These communities will be characterized by storytelling, discernment practices, political engagement, universal loyalty, continuing transformation, critical thinking and commitment to foundational issues.[354]

Kraybill's theology, like Lederach's, is shaped by experiences with Anabaptist communities and their visions. Yet Kraybill also makes postmodern claims: All religions are social constructions; communities must determine their own moral values. Kraybill also outlines understandings of human actualization and historical transformation. How might these notions affect discipling and its implications today in the world at large and within churches?

An Anabaptist response. Guided by Scripture I will focus on the lifelong growth process of discipling within communities, promoting God's reconciling work whose goal can be called shalom. How might Anabaptist insights help extend this communal dimension of the new creation to people who long for spiritual and relational fulfillment but resist traditional institutions and disciplinary rules? How might these insights help churches extend this reality, which requires not only flexibility and openness to God's Spirit but also clear identities rooted in deep com-

---

[349]Ibid., p. 44.
[350]Ibid., p. 56.
[351]Ibid., pp. 66-67.
[352]Ibid., p. 136.
[353]Ibid., pp. 140, 145-46.
[354]Ibid., pp. 141-42, 147-49.

mitments?

1. The keys. Anabaptist exclusivity and rigidity, which May, Holland and Swartzentruber critique, owed much to the assumption that because the church possessed the keys of binding and loosing, its acceptance and rejection equaled God's eternal verdicts of salvation and damnation. Yet if reexamined within the biblical horizon sketched above, the keys can provide another comprehensive way of conceiving the new creation's communal, sacramental dimension.

Let's focus, as Scripture does, on the overall discipling process, not chiefly on legal rules and sanctions. In this light it seems quite plausible that binding and loosing (Mt 18:18) refer to the entire preceding process, not simply its definitive decisions. In other words, as Lederach says, heaven and earth (or, in my terms, the spiritual and material, the inner and outer) begin corresponding as people work at reconciliation. But this hardly means that every decision can claim divine sanction, here or in Matthew 16:19.

Historic Anabaptists also derived the keys from John 20:21-23. Here Jesus told his disciples, "As the Father has sent me, so I send you." Then after breathing the Spirit on them, he said, if you forgive or retain anyone's sins, it will be so. But what was Jesus doing within the overall context? As Marlin Jeschke points out, he was endowing the disciples to continue his basic mission: to proclaim God's judgment and forgiveness. This occurs in many ways, including evangelism.[355] We recall that Menno equated the keys of binding and loosing with these two dimensions of the preached Word.[356]

In giving the church the keys Jesus bestowed the power to bring God's judging and forgiving words alive, to impact and transform people. It is not surprising that John associated this with giving the Spirit, as did Marpeck.[357] This gift is awesome: the capacity to render God's words living and actual. Yet it hardly entails that every word uttered in preaching, evangelism or deliberations about behavior is directly God's. To be sure, God often acts incisively through such human words. But many of these, even when uttered in reliance on God's Spirit, are imperfect. Some may partially obscure God's will. Other human words can badly distort it if they lack the Spirit's inner guidance.

Accordingly, although Jesus bestowed the gift of proclaiming God's Word effectively on the church, he hardly meant that whenever the church says so, God affirms every pronouncement. No word, indeed, can be expressive of the keys that does not at a minimum correspond with Scripture's overall intent and God's on-

---

[355]Marlin Jeschke, *Discipling the Brother* (Scottdale, Penn.: Herald, 1973), pp. 48-49.
[356]Simons, *Complete Works*, pp. 989-93.
[357]Marpeck, *Writings of Pilgram Marpeck*, pp. 334, 336.

going reconciliation.

If the keys, then, refer not to specific, authoritative, saving and damning pronouncements but the church's general announcement of judgment and forgiveness, they can provide a sacramental framework for the whole life of discipleship. For the "power of the keys," as recognized in Catholicism's sacramental renewal, "is first exercised in preaching baptismal forgiveness," which many Catholic theologians prefer for adults. Continuing repentance (penance) flows from this action of the keys, "expressing and renewing the paschal mystery that is complete in the eucharist," a corporate celebration.[358] Jeschke connects such a process with the Lord's Supper in Anabaptist fashion: the Supper is a confessional act declaring our forgiveness and commitment to each other.[359] The keys, that is, provide another way of understanding how the three practices discussed so far participate in God's continuing reconciling work and give it sacramental form.

The keys also help theology perceive church life as a single movement of repentance, reconciliation and renewal. But if it is, conflicts and sinful acts cannot be foreign to it. Discipling, in other words, will consist in not unwavering reflection of Jesus' perfection but gradual transformation with many highs and lows, as we find in Scripture. We need not fear that sins and conflicts always indicate capitulation to evil, as many Anabaptists did. For if Christian behavior is not only already righteous but also not yet fully righteous, such phenomena will often accompany a transforming struggle, as Marpeck understood.

This emphasis on gradual growth implies a view of the body different from most historic Anabaptists' and much like Marpeck's. Human bodies, even when contaminated by sin, cannot be irreversibly warped toward evil and away from God. If God intends to manifest the new creation through bodies, they must be redeemable and transformable. It is no accident that May, Holland, Swartzentruber and Rosalee Bender, who critique Anabaptist discipline, connect it with repression of bodies and their desires, and promote the latters' liberation and expression. They rightly challenge theology to unmask legitimations of this repression by church structures, even (perhaps especially) when they employ Scripture. Theology can promote all this, however, without elevating body-based pleasure or desire to quasi-revelatory status.[360]

In witnessing to God's judgment and forgiveness churches must embody not only Jesus' lofty commands but also his deep concern for those who stray. Inner and outer participation in Jesus' way involves both. Patience, as Marpeck recog-

---

[358]Dallen, *Reconciling Community*, p. 257.

[359]Jeschke, *Discipling the Brother*, pp. 106-7.

[360]See pts. 7 and 16 on pp. 98, 100 and chap. 9 for fuller discussion.

nized, is essential as we companion each other in this—and possible because it flows from Jesus' historic and continuing love.

Such an attitude neither condones nor ignores sin. The keys, the announcement of divine judgment and forgiveness, arise from the kerygma which reports a decisive historical conflict between good and evil, and proclaims that evil is already defeated.[361] Through the keys, baptism sacramentalizes a sharp turn from the old creation, dominated by sin and evil, to the new, ruled by righteousness and life (Rom 5:8–6:23). Nonetheless, evil is not yet destroyed. Sin keeps seeking to reassert its reign. To keep participating in the new creation, then, baptizands must continue turning from sin. This process must continue to become visible, via the keys, through the Lord's Supper and especially discipling, where real struggle with and forgiveness of sin, and therefore active sin to some extent, will be evident.

2. Boundaries. Transformation into Christ's image (2 Cor 3:18) or measure (Eph 4:7), or participation in his way, is compatible with a variety of lifestyles but not all. No one, moreover, can be truly shaped by a basic pattern without rejecting contrary ones. Further, if the church "lantern" does not clearly reflect some beams of righteousness, people will not "learn to see and know the way of life."[362] Still, decisions about where and how to draw lines, especially in pluralistic societies, are excruciating. I offer but one suggestion.

When peoples' actions conflict with Jesus' way, remember that Christian behavior always involves growth and struggle with evil. The best question then is usually: In what direction are they heading? If they basically mean to continue along that path, their errors can often be regarded as indications of genuine struggle, occasions for providing companionship and teaching and facilitating growth. It is crucial, though, that those who give admonition and guidance be open to receiving it (Gal 6:1-2). For discipling's main aim, as all Anabaptists affirmed in theory, is for all members to move toward maturity by helping each other. Matthew 18's first three steps should receive greatest attention by far.

Nonetheless, some people may persistently head back toward the old creation's patterns. If a church means to be clear about its vision and to be a fellowship of continuing repentance, renewal and reconciliation, authenticity eventually requires following Matthew 18 to its fourth step—telling such persons that they really do not belong. Hopefully the contrast between such persons' aims and the church's would become so evident that they would not feel bitterly rejected but simply not wish to remain.

In rare cases, however, people may sin seriously and obviously enough to bring

---

[361]See pt. 13 on p. 99 above.
[362]Riedemann, *Peter Riedemann's Hutterite Confession*, p. 78.

the church into immediate public disrepute. Even then I recommend that churches not proceed immediately to Matthew 18's final step, as later Dutch Anabaptists increasingly did. Churches can probably address the problem and clarify their stance through measures that still allow offenders to receive the church's ministries, which they may need more than ever, as long as they are willing.

Those who leave, however, should be regarded as not simply under God's judgment but also, like all people, as potential recipients of forgiveness and grace.[363] If they wish, the church should maintain relational and emotional contact with them.[364] In what ways? That depends, as does the form of all church practices, on what facilitates and makes visible the church's nature and mission. In this case, the church must express positive behaviors that the new creation makes possible, its disapproval of behaviors that oppose this, and patience and concern for those who struggle within it and outside.

3. Postmodern considerations. Even when congregations agree on behavioral boundaries, or norms, good discipling will apply these sensitively. The New Testament, indeed, is more concerned with the discipling process than legal decisions and sanctions. Many churches today, however, are influenced by postmodern assumptions. These make it plausible to suppose that all values involved in the process are determined by the members, and that the church and its faith themselves are simply social constructions. Indeed, Hubmaier perhaps foreshadowed this. Kraybill's theology of conflict transformation includes such statements. How compatible are these notions with biblical discipling?

Conflicts often erupt among parties who clutch opposing beliefs tightly. Understandably, conflict transformers encourage them to begin considering these not as absolutes but their particular perspectives. And if Matthew 18 is to function as Lederach rightly reads it, all participants must be willing to rethink their assumptions and values.

But is this willingness the same as regarding all values and beliefs as "simply ours" (Gordon Kaufman)? Does it imply that all religious affirmations are contemporary human constructions, as Kaufman, Ted Grimsrud's neo-Mennonites and often Dan Liechty maintain?[365] Yoder perhaps suggests something similar when he begins his discussion of church practices with binding and loosing. This phrase, found in some favorite Anabaptist texts (Mt 16:19; 18:15-20; Jn 20:21-23), allows him to take the common activities of dialogue and decision as his model for ecclesial practice rather than, say, the ritual and symbolism of baptism or the Sup-

---

[363]Jeschke, *Discipling the Brother*, pp. 102-23.
[364]Lederach, *Journey Toward Reconciliation*, p. 135.
[365]See pp. 57-93 above.

per. Yoder once mentions binding and loosing being "guided and enabled by God's own presence." Still, he finds it "not very different from" the "social science" of conflict resolution.[366] Then, as noted above, he reduces baptism to a sign of cross-cultural inclusion and the Lord's Supper to ordinary meals. Nevertheless, some small space for the Spirit to transcend human interaction apparently remains.[367]

Despite his desire to be biblical, Yoder develops ecclesiology largely from contemporary concepts, much like Kaufman, neo-Mennonites and Liechty. And if religious affirmations, as they say, can only be constructed from today's thought world, might not any historic belief or value be dismissed—including Matthew 18—especially if it seems to generate conflict? Why not exchange any that seem undesirable for better constructions?

The answer depends largely on how that central Anabaptist notion, community, is understood.[368] If the communities that disciple are simply contemporary communities, it is hard to see how norms and values can emerge from anywhere but their experience. *Community*, however, can also mean a historically continuous body literally constituted, in large part, by narratives and traditions. Members of such communities can articulate faith and shape practice only in light of something beyond themselves. They cannot simply create norms and values. Further, if their master story carries universal implications, so will their beliefs.

Anabaptists, despite many shortcomings, have long sought to derive discipleship's norms chiefly from Jesus' life, death and resurrection and their radical, counter-cultural implications. Behavior guided by this radicality will conflict with some behaviors in all societies and also with some among Christians, for they are partially shaped by their societies. Now if congregations, as they wrestle with deep differences, believe that they must create values that foster reconciliation, this radical model may often lose priority. For while it is compatible with various lifestyles, it simply does exclude many others. Appeals to it often seem, initially, to create rather than resolve conflict.

More generally, if congregations suppose that knowledge and values can only be

---

[366]Yoder, *Body Politics*, pp. 9, 11.

[367]"The point at which the divine empowerment is crucial" is "trusting the Spirit's leading in contextual application." Through this we can be "guided and enabled by God's own presence" (ibid., p. 9; cf. note 3). However, Yoder apparently stresses the community's creative role over values transmitted by tradition. For the "dialogical reconciling process must come first. Only then must we turn to talk of the set of standards that this process enforces" (p. 6). "The Christian community is equipped not with a code but with decision-making potential" (p. 8), even though "substantial prescriptions," such as care for the needy, are somehow involved (p. 9).

[368]Cf. Thomas Finger, " 'Universal Truths?': Should Anabaptist Theologians Seek to Articulate Them?" in *Anabaptists and Postmodernity*, ed. Susan Biesecker-Mast and Gerald Biesecker-Mast (Telford, Penn.: Pandora, 2000), pp. 80-82.

contemporary constructions, it is hard to see how they could be guided by anything transcending their culture or how they could offer their members or society anything but some variant of a current value or belief system. For if construction can only incorporate contemporary concepts and values, it must select among these for its guiding theme(s). How then could churches guide their decisions by a truly distinct option: the vantage point and lifestyle of a new creation? How could they make any such option visible to others—not simply some version of the old?

The theologies recently mentioned are indeed governed largely by current cultural notions—often conspicuously modern ones, such as Kaufman's bio-history and Liechty's anthropological striving toward transcendence, creativity and love. Yoder, in replacing the sacraments' symbolic and transcendent references with ethical ones, makes a typically modern move.

Kraybill also includes modern concepts and values among conflict transformation's goals: people should "take control of their situations," should increase their sense of "self-worth, security, self-determination, and autonomy."[369] Kraybill's notion of historical transformation beginning from society's margins also reflects a recent outlook. However, Kraybill also grants narratives a key role in forming communities and their values. Perhaps, then, his theology is not a current construct in all respects. (Since Kraybill takes us beyond the church into mission, I will consider him again in the next chapter.)

In critiquing contemporary construction, I do not mean to imply that theology or churches should seek isolation from their cultural contexts, as Anabaptists sometimes have. Churches are always in dialogue with their cultures; their practices and theologies are always shaped by them.[370] I propose, though, that the source and meanings of their beliefs and practices originate from beyond these contexts. I will explain and seek to support this claim, hotly contested by many postmodernists, under the kerygma's universal and missional implications.[371]

In brief: discipling and reconciliation require much humility and flexibility, much willingness to reconsider and change. Only so will discipling further authentic growth, not stifle it, as has much rigid Anabaptist discipline. Yet authentic divinization is christomorphic. Discipling, then, follows a pattern and operates within a framework. It is shaped by values not simply constructed in the present but flowing from the biblical narrative.

4. Summary. In Anabaptist and biblical perspective the Christian community manifests the new creation's sacramentality in baptism, the Lord's Supper and ev-

---

[369]Kraybill, *Peacebuilders in Zimbabwe*, p. 44.
[370]See pt. 3 on p. 96 above.
[371]See pp. 316-19 below.

eryday behavior. A new link among these three activities has emerged: the keys, the power not of judicial exclusion and inclusion but of rendering God's judging and forgiving words living and actual.

Anabaptists, however, have often treated the new creation's behavioral possibilities, with their significant social implications, as not good but sorrowful news. They have often focused on failures, punitive corrective measures and the worst-case outcome—the ban. To many people today, behavioral expectations will also seem bad news. They may find community attractive but resist anything that connotes the rigidity and impersonality experienced in too many institutions and processes.

Discipline, however, can be called, more positively, discipling, which intrinsically includes lows as well as highs. Discipling occurs within the framework of God's reconciling work that involves all church members. Everyone, at times, receives as well as gives admonition and help. In Anabaptist perspective this two-sided participation flows from the baptismal vow.

Through discipling, the whole church grows into Christ's image, which includes his patience as well as his moral perfection. The church then must manifest not only divine judgment but also forgiveness—which cannot be seen unless people actually stumble and are restored, actually disagree and then reconcile. This growth of Christ's body transforms individual bodies, although historic Anabaptists often denied this in effect by treating bodies as incorrigible. A positive view of discipling requires a positive view of the body.[372]

Discipling fosters not only holiness but also humility—willingness to change, reconsider, admit mistakes. Current conflict transformation practices, which owe much to Anabaptist roots, can help greatly in this. Yet the ultimate values guiding discipling are not constructed by participants, as transformation theories may imply. They are rooted in biblical narrative and expressed most fully in Jesus' history.

To be sure, even so positive and patient a process may seem overly restrictive to many today. At this point, I believe, Anabaptists can best contribute to theology by gently insisting that true community simply does involve commitments, limitations and accountability. It is incompatible with uncircumscribed, individualistic freedom. Anabaptists can best aid churches by underlining what many of them recognize: they will hardly extend the new creation, or even survive, unless they themselves are true communities, expressing clear identities and united by deep commitments.[373] This will be more evident as we consider economic sharing and then the church's missional role in making visible the new creation (chap. 7).

---

[372]Cf. chap. 9.
[373]See esp. pp. 178-79.

ECONOMIC SHARING

Among historic Anabaptists the new creation's sacramentality spread beyond baptism and the Lord's Supper into daily behavior in another way. Its effect on work, commerce and possessions carried broad socioeconomic implications. As we enter this realm, we move beyond what is often considered ecclesiology. Yet economic sharing (along with the preceding three practices) marked all historic Anabaptist churches initially and also later, though much else changed.[374]

In approaching sharing, we recall that Anabaptism emerged from history's underside as a largely peasant-artisan phenomenon. Social and economic factors are crucial for comprehending this practice. Anabaptism's social vision affirmed and radicalized many ideals that met disaster in the Peasants' War. These harked back to medieval communal practices far more than they pointed forward toward the distant modern world.

James Stayer notes that the peasant movements based their demands on Scripture and presented themselves as earnestly Christian.[375] Stayer suggests that for peasants and artisans, measures like tithe and tax relief, abolition of usury, selection of their own pastors and free access to meadows, rivers and woods constituted the Reformation's main meaning.[376] As many Lutheran and Reformed leaders became distant from lower classes, and the Peasants' War failed, Anabaptists alone still treasured these ideals. Stayer finds Hutterite communalism the "institutionalized, flourishing culmination of the commoners' Reformation of 1525."[377] Given the importance of these socioeconomic factors, they will provide the primary lens through which I will explore historic Anabaptist understandings of this practice.

Current Anabaptist theologians often discuss social and economic justice. When they do, economic sharing is in the historic background, much as is discipline (discipling) in their treatments of accountability and other corporate behaviors. Nonetheless, as with this chapter's other three practices, current Anabaptist theologians say little about sharing in particular. Only Kraus, so far as I know, handles it somewhat directly.[378]

Similar themes, however, are emerging in a recent movement from the underside:

---

[374]Snyder, *Anabaptist History*, pp. 93, 374.

[375]James Stayer, *The German Peasants' War and the Anabaptist Community of Goods* (Montreal: McGill-Queen's University Press, 1991), p. 88.

[376]Ibid., p. 43. Though these demands reflected medieval common law, whose privileges peasants were losing, peasants were shifting their basis somewhat toward divine law, which offered more transformative possibilities (pp. 4, 37-38). In these matters, as in the spiritualities that affected it, Anabaptism more often looked "backward" historically than forward to modern democratic movements.

[377]Ibid., p. 158.

[378]Kraus, *Community of the Spirit*, pp. 140-44; cf. Kraus, *God Our Savior*, p. 151.

liberation theology, particularly in Latin America. Through it, the outlook of many marginalized churches is finding a voice. Liberation theologies challenge many assumptions and features of globalization. As globalization increasingly imprints all cultures and societies churches everywhere, especially mainstream communions with worldwide constituencies and ministries, should consider these critiques,. Liberation theology and Anabaptism will interact dynamically as I construct my contemporary theological perspective.

Historic Anabaptist Perspectives

Switzerland. Like discipling, economic sharing spread early and widely here. The pastors of the first rural congregations around Zurich to protest the compulsory ecclesiastical tithe soon helped launch Anabaptism.[379] Conrad Grebel backed their cause and urged Thomas Müntzer to be supported not by interests and tithes, but his congregation.[380] Many proto-Anabaptists critiqued usury, especially through a Zurich Bible study in 1523.[381]

The first Anabaptist congregation at Zollikon (early 1525) immediately practiced "community of temporal goods . . . broke the locks off their doors, chests, and cellars, and ate food and drink in good fellowship without discrimination."[382] A congregational Order circulating with the Schleitheim Confession (early 1527) affirmed that no member "shall have anything of his own, but rather, as the Christians in the time of the apostles held all in common, and especially stored up a common fund, from which aid can be given to the poor . . . and . . . permit no brother to be in need."[383] This Order shaped a discipline adopted by the Hutterites (1529) and a later Pilgramite Order (1540). In such matters, Swiss Anabaptism provided a formative, quickly spreading influence.[384]

Though Grebel, Mantz and Blaurock apparently advocated something like the Swiss Order, when put on trial they denied teaching a community of goods. Evidently this was to dissociate themselves from the forcible confiscations and redistributions of the Peasants' War,[385] and from accusations that Anabaptists shared

---

[379]Harder, *Sources of Swiss Anabaptism*, pp. 208-10, 437; cf. pp. 17-21 above.

[380]Grebel, "Letters to Thomas Müntzer," pp. 220, 78.

[381]Harder, *Sources of Swiss Anabaptism*, pp. 203-6.

[382]Ibid., p. 345, cf. p. 410.

[383]Sattler, *Legacy of Michael Sattler*, p. 45.

[384]Packull, *Hutterite Beginnings*, p. 53.

[385]Stayer, *German Peasants' War*, pp. 97-99; Harder, *Sources of Swiss Anabaptism*, pp. 436-40. Hans Kruesi reportedly affirmed at his execution that "All things should be held in common" (Harder, *Sources of Swiss Anabaptism*, p. 425, cf. Stayer, *German Peasants' War*, p. 65). See also Joerg Tucher's statement that everyone should work yet hold things in common, and the trial testimony of three others against compulsory sharing (Stayer, *German Peasants' War*, pp. 104-5).

wives as well as goods. Meanwhile, as Hubmaier was converting Waldshut, he opposed the tithe, proclaimed that forests, streams and meadows should be free to all,
and helped peasant leaders compose a list of such demands.

Hubmaier, stressed that the Lord's Supper, in recalling how Jesus gave his life
for us, called participants to give "body, life, property, and blood" for each other.[386]
Hubmaier told the wealthy lords of Nicholsburg, Moravia, that cross-bearing and
obedience extended to sacrificing their goods and giving up their bodies and
lives.[387] When Zwingli accused him of promoting a community of goods, however,
he replied more moderately that Christians are but "stewards and distributors" of
their possessions. They should always aid the needy, but never "take what belongs
to the other and make it common."[388] Christians should even pay exorbitant tithes,
though those who exacted them were wrong.[389] Hubmaier, and increasingly the
Swiss Brethren, advocated what we might call mutual aid rather than a full community of goods.

South Germany-Austria. I. While the Discipline adopted by the Hutterites in 1529
was influenced by the Swiss Order, Anabaptists here rooted economic sharing in
their distinctive *Gelassenheit* spirituality. Sin, which involves ultimate attachment to
creatures rather than the Creator, not only distorts and inflames our inner desires
but also leads to exploitation of nonhuman nature, and to conflicts over accumulation and defense of wealth. Salvation, then, involves painful crucifixion of these
attachments, including surrender of material possessions.

Hans Hut taught that Christians were justified and purified "inwardly from
greed and lust, outwardly from injustice . . . and our misuse of creatures."[390] Baptism especially expressed love to the brethren "with . . . life and goods."[391] Hut's
converts established a common purse to aid the poor.[392] The proto-Hutterite Discipline assumed such a purse, which was managed by the leaders. When put on trial,
Hut and his followers conceded that some converts had sold fields and distributed
the proceeds. Yet, they protested, Hut had merely asked those with more than
enough to help the needy. No one had been pressured to such actions.[393] According

---

[386]Hubmaier, *Balthasar Hubmaier,* p. 88, cf. p. 397.

[387]Ibid., p. 170.

[388]Ibid., pp. 183, cf. p. 152.

[389]Ibid., pp. 304-5.

[390]Hut, "On the Mystery of Baptism," p. 70, cf. Denck, *Spiritual Legacy of Hans Denck,* p. 97.

[391]Hut, "On the Mystery of Baptism," p. 72.

[392]Stayer, *German Peasants' War,* p. 59.

[393]Ambrosius Spittelmaier explained that Christians should use houses, fields and trade implements,
     but that none should say that any of these was "mine," for "Everything is ours" (ibid., p. 115). In
     1527-1528 Augsburg Anabaptists practiced mutual aid, gave to the poor and hosted traveling

to one disciple, however, Hut secretly taught that when God finally called Anabaptists to take the sword, they would make all goods common.[394]

Leonhard Schiemer insisted that converts separate from all that is not of Christ and hold all God's gifts—teaching and understanding as well as goods—in common.[395] For Hans Schlaffer, as for Hubmaier, the Supper indicated that as Jesus gave himself for us, we must give "goods, body and life" for each other.[396]

2. Economic sharing was so central to Hutterites that Jacob Hutter asked new converts to contribute to a common purse and surrender surplus cash to a common treasury.[397] The Hutterite evangel called people to this immediate sharing and also future communal life in Moravia.[398]

Hutterites wed inner yielding of creaturely attachments most intimately to outer surrender of possessions. For Ulrich Stadler, true *Gelassenheit* was "to yield and dispose oneself with goods and chattels in the service of the saints."[399] Peter Walpot underlined this inner-outer correspondence by exclaiming that if spiritual communion could exist without community of goods, baptism of the Spirit would be adequate without baptism of water, and bread and wine not needed for the Lord's Supper. Walpot elaborated on how baptism and the Supper expressed full community.[400]

Peter Riedemann taught that creatures had been made "to teach and to lead people to God."[401] Resources that no one could control, such as air and sun, showed that all things were made for everyone.[402] But since nonhuman creatures

---

preachers (p. 121). In the Tyrol, Wolfgang Brandhuber asked all converts to disclose their wealth but to share common purses only in households, "the largest practicable sphere of Christian community of goods" (p. 122).

[394]Ibid., p. 114. When tried in 1533, most members of the Sorga congregation in central Germany said that Christians should devote their property to God, though not necessarily make it common, and should never take goods from anyone, although several favored exceptions in very needy situations. For members of the neighboring Berka congregation, everything should be held in common and goods could be seized in dire circumstances (p. 118).

[395]Schiemer, "Three Kinds of Grace," p. 92; cf. Leonhard Schiemer, "The Apostles' Creed: An Interpretation," in *Spiritual Life in Anabaptism*, ed. Cornelius Dyck (Scottdale, Penn.: Herald, 1995), p. 39.

[396]Schlaffer, *Selections*, p. 205.

[397]Packull, *Hutterite Beginnings*, pp. 201, 204.

[398]Stayer, *German Peasants' War*, p. 148.

[399]Ulrich Stadler, "Cherished Instructions on Sin, Excommunication, and the Community of Goods," in *Spiritual and Anabaptist Writers*, ed. George Williams and Angel Mergal (Philadelphia: Westminster Press, 1957), p. 284, cf. p. 279.

[400]Peter Walpot, "True Yieldedness and the Christian Community of Goods," in *Early Anabaptist Spirituality*, ed. Daniel Liechty (New York: Paulist Press, 1994), pp. 188, 169-70.

[401]Riedemann, *Peter Riedemann's Hutterite Confession*, p. 62.

[402]Ibid., p. 120; cf. Stadler, "Cherished Instructions on Sin," p. 278.

had fallen victim to "unjust acquisition"[403]—by being viewed simply as actual or potential possessions—they now led people away from God. Sin had originated in wrong taking.[404] Because humans had seized what they should have left, they had become "accustomed to accumulating things and hardened in doing so."[405] Walpot added that those who desired possessions were possessed—by their own desires.[406]

Riedemann continued that since God is spiritual, we fall away from God when we cling to materiality.[407] We can return only by turning our hearts toward God and emptying them of all else. This entails giving up "acquiring things and holding property."[408] Christ would then lead us from love of creatures back to the Father.[409] Only then could we be filled by God, that power which "pours itself into believing souls," transforming us to become like itself.[410]

Yet even though God is spiritual, God's gifts are both spiritual and material.[411] Salvation, accordingly, also involved using the latter as God intended: sharing them with others. For Hutterites, salvation was so intertwined with transforming creation that one expects Riedemann to add: humans too are essentially spiritual and material. But surprisingly, he conceived God's image in humankind as "not flesh and blood but spirit," so that the "temporal . . . is alien to our true nature."[412] Apparently, a conceptual ontological barrier between spirit and matter overrode a deep Hutterite intuition: spirit can express itself through and transform matter so genuinely that every aspect of ourselves and our lives must come into harmony with matter.[413]

Riedemann provided another rationale for communal sharing. God "the Father has nothing for himself, but everything he has, he has in the Son." The Son likewise has everything with the Father. The Son, further, gives all this to people

---

[403]Riedemann, *Peter Riedemann's Hutterite Confession*, p. 63.

[404]Rideman, *Confession of Faith*, p. 58; see p. 33, n. 32; cf. Walpot, "True Yieldedness," p. 152.

[405]Riedemann, *Peter Riedemann's Hutterite Confession*, p. 119.

[406]Walpot, "True Yieldedness," p. 196.

[407]Riedemann, *Peter Riedemann's Hutterite Confession*, pp. 119-21.

[408]Ibid., p. 120.

[409]Walpot, "True Yieldedness," p. 152.

[410]After God's power "poureth itself into believing souls," he adds, it "maketh us like, similar and conformable to itself" (Rideman, *Confession of Faith*, p. 16). Though Friesen omits this (John Friesen, ed., *Peter Riedemann's Hutterite Confession of Faith* [Scottdale, Penn.: Herald, 1999], p. 60), it is preferable, since the original reads: "macht uns ihr aehnlich und gemaess und gleichforming" (Riedemann, *Rechenschaft unserer Religion*).

[411]Riedemann, *Peter Riedemann's Hutterite Confession*, p. 121.

[412]Ibid., pp. 89, 120.

[413]Cf. chap. 9.

who dwell in him. Hence "they are one with the Son as the Son is one with the Father," and his people are one with each other. This too implied that Christians should possess nothing for themselves but share all things.[414]

In the highly structured Hutterite communities, economic activity, like discipline, was governed by leaders. Ordinary members could neither buy nor sell.[415] No Hutterite could be a merchant, purchasing and then selling something at a profit. For this made things "more expensive for the poor; it is stealing bread from their mouths and forcing them to become nothing but slaves to the rich."[416]

Since the Hutterites emerged from a mutual banning process, it is not surprising that those who left critiqued them. Gabriel Ascherham protested that they had lost *Gelassenheit's* true meaning: humble, empty waiting on God, followed by gracious filling. No one had commanded the first Christians to share goods; they did so spontaneously in response to God's kingdom.[417] But Hutterites, Ascherham complained, had replaced this Spirit-led unity with legalistic conformity.[418] They induced people to buy the kingdom by handing over their goods. Yet "salvation does not lie in good works but in the grace of God." Jesus' death alone releases from sin. Though Ascherham promoted communal living, he believed that Hutterites had exchanged inward, spiritual motivation for outward, material legalism.[419]

3. Soon after his conversion Pilgram Marpeck visited Moravia. There he was commissioned, perhaps by the first communal group at Austerlitz, under Jacob Wiedemann.[420] Soon after arriving in Strasbourg Pilgram, despite his upper-class background, sought to aid Anabaptist refugees and identified with those victimized by usury and struggling for economic viability. He advocated a community of goods.[421] Marpeck later named usury and avarice the root of idolatry. He reproved those who controlled international purse strings, through whom "many hundreds of thousands of people . . . are betrayed, sold, and bought by their loans, finance, and usury." They did so to preserve earthly pomp and honor, but against them James cried, "Howl and weep, you rich."[422]

Marpeck connected the fellowship of the Lord's Supper with economic sharing,

[414]Ibid., p. 80, cf. p. 119.

[415]Stayer, *German Peasants' War*, p. 146; Stadler, "Cherished Instructions on Sin," p. 281.

[416]Riedemann, *Peter Riedemann's Hutterite Confession*, p. 149.

[417]Packull, *Hutterite Beginnings*, p. 126.

[418]Ibid., p. 128.

[419]Ibid., p. 129.

[420]Ibid., pp. 135-38.

[421]Ibid., p. 51.

[422]Marpeck, *Writings of Pilgram Marpeck*, pp. 344, 449-50.

though less often than with discipline.[423] Like Ascherham he found Hutterite practices coercive, contra the first Christian community's spontaneity. As in his critique
of Swiss banning, Marpeck contrasted such legalism with the freedom of love.[424]
But when he approached the Hutterites about this, he was perhaps even less successful than with the Swiss.

Basically, Marpeck advocated mutual aid: Christians could control their possessions, yet they must regard these as belonging not to them but "to God and the
needy." In reality all their material goods were communal since Christians offer everything they have "by the heart" to God.[425] The Order adopted by Pilgram's congregation, developed from the early Swiss Order and the proto-Hutterite Discipline, directed that offerings for the poor be taken at every service as a "voluntary
expression of compassion."[426]

The Netherlands. 1. In Melchior Hoffman's pre-Anabaptist mission in Livonia, he
inveighed against usury. In its cities he helped organize minority, non-German
peasants who were fleeing dire economic conditions.[427] In 1525 they and he were
at the center of a widespread riot that helped oust Catholic leaders and usher in
the Reformation. But in 1526 Hoffman accused a magistrate of embezzlement and
was sent packing.[428] Though he apparently had no consistent political aims, Hoffman surfaced surprisingly often at scenes of social unrest. Later in the Netherlands
Melchior instructed his apostles to surrender all property.[429] Most of his converts
were artisans, and many refused to pay usury.[430] Their fortunes declined considerably after 1530 when Britain halted its abundant wool exports to the Dutch, and
the Danes closed all ports to them.

2. As increasing poverty stalked the savagely persecuted Melchiorites, astounding
tidings reached them: Anabaptists had assumed governance of a city to the west, Münster, through normal political channels. Preachers were being elected by their own congregations. This miracle demonstrated that God's final judgment was to emanate from
Münster, which would be safe from not only Catholic but also divine wrath. Beleaguered saints who journeyed there would share Münster's wealth, for non-Anabaptist
citizens were leaving lands and houses behind. All this would be shared in common.

For Bernhard Rothmann, Münster's theologian, the solidarity experienced in

---

[423]Ibid., p. 280.
[424]Ibid., pp. 278-79, cf. p. 51.
[425]Ibid., p. 279.
[426]Packull, *Hutterite Beginnigns*, p. 313.
[427]Deppermann, *Melchior Hoffman*, pp. 55-60.
[428]Ibid., p. 83.
[429]Ibid., p. 237.
[430]Stayer, *German Peasants' War*, p. 133.

the Lord's Supper entailed a community of goods.[431] As the Münster program unfolded, he reported that

> everything which has served the purposes of self-seeking and private property, such as buying and selling, working for money, taking interest and practicing usury . . . eating and drinking the sweat of the poor (that is, making one's own people and fellow-creatures work so that one can grow fat) . . . are abolished amongst us by the power of love and community.[432]

All money, jewels and precious metals were collected by Jan Matthijs. Many houses and much property were confiscated and deeds destroyed. Moveable possessions were placed in public storage. Cloisters were plundered and then used to house newcomers. Deacons preserved and distributed all goods (including those of immigrants), procured food and supervised common meals.[433] Still, patriarchal households remained the primary units of production and consumption, and former property owners retained disproportionate political power.[434]

After Jan van Leyden assumed control, much food and clothing was collected from these households. Some community wealth was diverted to glorify his kingly splendor. More spacious homes were divided into quarters for newcomers. Polygamy was introduced. Before the German princes' siege closed off all communication, the government purchased what food it could. Finally wartime rationing was instituted, supervised by the deacons.[435] This grandiose communal experiment, of course, terminated in a horrendous bloodbath. Thereafter, any mention of community of goods was linked with it throughout the Netherlands.

3. Menno Simons and Dirk Philips, as they sought to rebuild a respectable church, repeatedly denied that Anabaptists held goods—or wives—in common.[436] Nonetheless, they both exhorted their followers "to serve your neighbor . . . with possessions, houses and lands . . . with the fruit of your toil and travail, with your blood if need be."[437]

---

[431] Bernhard Rothmann, *Bekentnisse van beyden Sacramenten*, in *Zwei Schriften den münsterischen Wiedertäufers Bernhard Rothmann*, ed. Heinrich Detmer and Robert Krumbholz (Dortmund, 1904).

[432] Bernhard Rothmann, quoted in *Anabaptism in Outline*, ed. Walter Klaassen (Scottdale, Penn.: Herald, 1981), p. 234.

[433] Stayer, *German Peasants' War*, pp. 134-35.

[434] Ibid., pp. 136, 130.

[435] Ibid., pp. 136-38.

[436] Simons, *Complete Works*, pp. 545, 558, 560.

[437] Ibid., p. 139, cf. pp. 185, 199, 369, 398, 558, 731. Dirk considered sharing a feature of an ordinance: brotherly love (Philips, *Writings of Dirk Philips*, pp. 371-72). Both claimed that in contrast with state churches, they cared for all their neighbors economically, and none needed to beg (Simons, *Complete Works*, p. 558; Philips, *Writings of Dirk Philips*, pp. 371-72).

While many Mennonites, like Melchiorites, were artisans, Menno seemed quite familiar with the lower classes' economic burdens. He excoriated rulers who "tax and toll, grasp and grab" and "suck the very marrow from the bones of the poor."[438] He urged people with servants, in contrast to usual practices, to "Give them decent support and their earned pay and do not dock their wages. . . . [I]f they are weak and sick, assist and serve them. Get someone else to serve in their place without loss to them until the Lord takes them or restores them to health."[439] Menno also denounced merchants who "cheat the people, and strip them of their possessions; they sell, lend, and secure the needy at large profit and usury." Yet unlike the Hutterites, he allowed that a Christian might be a merchant, as some Mennonites apparently were.[440]

Dirk added that the Lord's Supper leads participants to regard all Christian need as common and to aid one another.[441] Like Riedemann, Dirk noted that the Father and Son share "the same divine nature . . . do all things together, and have all things together in common."[442]

In short, Dutch Mennonites were reticent to speak much of economic sharing, mostly due to past abuses, it seems. It is unlikely that they practiced full community of goods. Yet the necessity of frequent sharing, or mutual aid, was apparently unquestioned, especially since so many of them suffered deprivation.

Summary. All Anabaptists assumed that Christian love entailed some significant sharing of possessions among themselves as well as aiding the needy in general. Economic sharing was not simply a social-ethical practice but often an implication of the Lord's Supper, and sometimes of baptism. If new creation sacramentality was truly transforming and united people, it had to impinge directly on that most concrete, often most resistant, department of daily life: the things we own, the ways we use them and how we acquire them.

Having viewed this practice through a socioeconomic lens, it is evident that sharing, among persecuted, relatively poor people whose livelihoods were often threatened, was no mere utopian ideal. It was frequently quite practical, even necessary, and regarded favorably among lower classes. It echoed medieval peasant ideals far more loudly than it forecasted socialism or communism. Had economic sharing been practiced widely, it would have greatly influenced society as a whole.

In South Germany-Austria early leaders and later communitarians treated sur-

---

[438]Simons, *Complete Works*, p. 367; cf. pp. 286, 359, 520, 526, 603.
[439]Ibid., pp. 365-66; cf. pp. 212-14, 529.
[440]Ibid., p. 368.
[441]Philips, *Writings of Dirk Philips*, p. 123.
[442]Ibid., p. 157.

render of goods and pooling of resources as the consistent outer expression of the inner crucifixion of earthly attachments and union with the risen Christ. Sharing incorporated the materiality of human and nonhuman creatures into the Spirit's birthing of the new creation.

Early Swiss Anabaptists, like these South German-Austrians, often practiced full community of goods, though families remained in their lands and dwellings. But among Swiss Brethren, Pilgramites and Mennonites this evolved into mutual aid. Such a shift surely involved reaction against the forcible confiscations of the Peasants' War and Münster, and the perceived legalism of Hutterite communities of production and consumption. Whether it also signified a shift from early Anabaptist radicalism to the moderation of more established communities I find difficult to assess. I find Hutterite communalism not *the* "culmination of the commoners' Reformation of 1525"[443] but *an* authentic culmination or valid expression.

Contemporary Appropriations

If the new creation's coming involves sharing of possessions in its communal dimension, then in a world of vast economic inequality and poverty churches seeking to embody and extend this coming must be instances and signs of a different order. Not only will individual Christians share wealth, churches as bodies will often cross economic lines, conveying a distinct message about the role of material goods in life.

As globalization rapidly increases wealth for some and poverty for others, economic issues become more pressing for church life and mission. Many churches recognize this and are addressing poverty in various ways. The most challenging theological analysis comes from Latin American liberation theology, especially its claim that churches should exercise a preferential option for the poor. This challenge is especially pertinent for Anabaptists. Liberationists (most of whom are Catholic) insist that Jesus' history and teachings should be normative in theology. In addition, their "base ecclesial communities" are nonhierarchical, local gatherings, mostly of lower-class people.

As liberationists theologize from this marginalized vantage point, they raise issues discussed by Anabaptists, especially women, about Scripture. As Lydia Harder, Nadine Pence Frantz and others stress, biblical texts harbor various levels and dimensions of meaning.[444] The church, however, usually leaves biblical interpretation to a small, homogeneous elite. These elite typically perceive certain

---

[443]Stayer, *German Peasants' War*, p. 158.
[444]See pp. 80-84.

strands of meaning in texts that become standard interpretations. However, people who approach Scripture from other social, economic and gendered perspectives discern other dimensions of meaning. But so long as marginalized people are absent from the church's hermeneutical venture, these dimensions will remain largely hidden.

Liberation theologians explore Scripture from history and society's underside. This, they claim, yields novel and crucial insights, particularly into Jesus and the church. Anabaptists can gain much by reviewing economic sharing from this perspective. With the aid of this and historic Anabaptist lenses, we will appraise Jesus' biblical, normative significance for the church and current economic issues. How can this challenge from the margins enhance our understanding of the church's sacramentality and help all churches address globalization?

The Church of the poor. Vatican II's nonhierarchical definition of the church as the "people of God" lies, in a general way, behind the "church of the poor" theme.[445] Basically, it means that people conform to the risen Christ not through general sorts of believing and acting but only by following the concrete demands and practices of the crucified Lord.[446] Jesus then cannot simply be the object of our faith; his faithfulness, his human walk and his experience of God must also provide the "structural model" for ours.[447] This walk involves not only ethical formation but also participation in Jesus' resurrection—in life's ultimate triumph over death. Though liberation theology is often alleged to abandon the spiritual for the political, it is producing rich spiritualities.[448]

Liberation theologians believe that God's historical work advances through the poor, as does Ron Kraybill. The poor must provide its "structural channel." A church of the poor will not simply be for them but "formed on the basis of the poor." They will not be a mere part of it but its center, "the principle of its structure, organization, and mission."[449] The "entire Church should migrate to the periphery and share in the powerlessness of the poor, at the feet of the crucified God."[450] Liberationists, like many historic Anabaptists, affirm that this comportment is essential to keeping in God's will.[451]

Liberation theology has also been influenced by a Marxist outlook on history.

---

[445] *The Documents of Vatican II*, ed. Walter Abbott (New York: Guild, 1966), pp. 29-30.

[446] Jon Sobrino, *The True Church and the Poor* (Maryknoll, N.Y.: Orbis, 1984), p. 89.

[447] Ibid., pp. 128-29.

[448] Gustavo Gutiérrez, *We Drink from Our Own Wells* (Maryknoll, N.Y.: Orbis, 1984); Jon Sobrino, *Spirituality of Liberation* (Maryknoll, N.Y.: Orbis, 1988).

[449] Sobrino, *True Church*, p. 93.

[450] Ibid., p. 98.

[451] Ibid., p. 137.

This "process of popular self-liberation is deeply, securely irreversible."[452] The common people increasingly become agents of their own history and construct new societies.[453] The church must help them create "objective conditions" for initiating "the struggle for their rights" and "begin actually to take power."[454]

To dismiss liberation theology as baptized Marxism, however, is to overlook how often economic aims are intrinsic to spiritual movements among lower classes, as Anabaptism well illustrates.[455] Moreover, liberation theologians often caution against reducing everything to historical process.[456] Ultimately it is God's word that enters history, opens it up and "charges it with futurity."[457]

1. The preferential option for the poor. Most broadly, poverty means death: "unjust death, the premature death of the poor, physical death."[458] Poverty also includes cultural death: lack of education, social identity and meaningful traditions. What bearing does Jesus have on all this?

Biblical supports for the preferential option for the poor come mostly from the Synoptic Gospels. There the "poor" denoted economically marginalized people as well as those despised by society, including publicans and sinners.[459] The "poor" *(ptōxos)* almost always meant a social class. The frequent contrast between the "poor" and the "rich" confirms this.[460]

Liberationists find Jesus' preferential option clearest in (1) his "inaugural address" in Luke 4:18-19, which announced "good news to the poor"; (2) his beatitude "Blessed are you who are poor, for yours is the kingdom of God!" balanced with "But woe to you who are rich, for you have received your consolation!" (Lk 6:20, 24); (3) the evidence he gave for his messiahship, including that "the poor have the good news brought to them" (Lk 7:22; Mt 11:5)

Further, Jesus often denounced the behavior of oppressing groups. From a mar-

---

[452]Gustavo Gutiérrez, *The Power of the Poor in History* (Maryknoll, N.Y.: Orbis, 1983), p. 82.

[453]Ibid., p. 150.

[454]Ibid., p. 97. "Humankind constructs itself and attains a real awareness of its own being; it liberates itself in the acquisition of genuine freedom which through work transforms the world and educates the human species. For Hegel, 'world history is the progression of the awareness of freedom.' . . . Thus human nature gradually takes hold of the reins of its own destiny. It looks ahead and turns toward a society in which it will be free of all alienation and servitude" (Gustavo Gutiérrez, *A Theology of Liberation* [Maryknoll, N.Y.: Orbis, 1973], p. 19).

[455]Cf. Gutiérrez, *Power of the Poor*, pp. 94, 98.

[456]Sobrino, *True Church*, p. 158.

[457]Gutiérrez, *Power of the Poor*, p. 83.

[458]James Nickoloff, ed., *Gustavo Gutiérrez: Essential Writings* (Minneapolis: Fortress, 1996), p. 144.

[459]Jon Sobrino, *Jesus in Latin America* (Maryknoll, N.Y.: Orbis, 1987), pp. 80-81.

[460]Ibid.; Jon Sobrino and Ignacio Ellacuria, eds., *Systematic Theology* (Maryknoll, N.Y.: Orbis, 1996), p. 28.

ginalized vantage point, Jesus' expressed or implied perspective on social conflicts can be recognized as that of the oppressed. Many of his actions signified solidarity with the poor, such as meals with various undesirables. He also conveyed this through parables about who is and is not invited, and his preference for sinners, not the righteous.[461] Even more, Jesus himself took on the condition of the poor, becoming the Servant whom Isaiah prophesied (see esp. Is 42:1-7).

Since the poor were a class, Jesus' "good news" can be clarified from a marginalized perspective by considering how they must have understood it.[462] Good news for poor people, liberationists claim, always involves economic betterment and social liberation. Since the poor hear many empty promises, words will not suffice. Real material transformation then must be involved.[463] This includes unmasking and transforming the roots of oppression.[464] Today this means that the poor to whom this gospel comes are "the proletariat," struggling for their "most basic rights."[465]

Liberation theologians deny idealizing the poor, for these include good and bad persons.[466] They ascribe the gospel's coming to the poor to God's initiative: God's choice to work through certain people despite their desert or lack of it.[467] If we resist this preferential option, we really want God's choice to be based on human worth, not sheer grace.

2. Consequences for the church. What can this appraisal of Jesus, through liberation theology's lens, tell us about the church and especially its economic relevance? Liberationists often extol the church of the poor as "a newness in substance and a historical break from other ways of being the Church."[468] Yet these mostly Catholic theologians do not mean a distinct community marked by pursuit of holiness, as Anabaptists did. The church of the poor rather is "the true way of being a church in Jesus" and "the structural means of approximating" this amid other elements in the church as a whole.[469] Hierarchy still has its place,[470] although more egalitarian base communities are the church of the poor's distinct expression.

From their vantage point the poor throw new light on some basic features of the

---

[461]Sobrino and Ellacuria, *Systematic Theology*, pp. 29-30.

[462]Sobrino, *Jesus in Latin America*, p. 142; Jon Sobrino, *Jesus the Liberator* (Maryknoll, N.Y.: Orbis, 1993), p. 79.

[463]Sobrino, *Jesus the Liberator*, p. 87.

[464]Sobrino, *Jesus in Latin America*, p. 142.

[465]Gutiérrez, *Theology of Liberation*, p. 301.

[466]Nickoloff, *Gustavo Gutiérrez*, p. 146.

[467]Sobrino, *True Church*, p. 139; Sobrino, *Jesus in Latin America*, p. 83; Gutiérrez, *Power of the Poor*, p. 95; Nickoloff, *Gustavo Gutiérrez*, p. 146.

[468]Sobrino, *True Church*, p. 84.

[469]Ibid., pp. 123-24, 135.

[470]Ibid., pp. 103-4.

church. Consider the traditional four marks: unity, holiness, catholicity (universality) and apostolicity. Since mutual help comes naturally to those struggling for survival, the poor can help the whole church realize that unity is not simply uniformity in doctrine or jurisdiction. It must involve sharing each other's burdens, which are often economic.[471] Nonetheless, since God sides with the poor and opposes their degradation, the poor also push the church to attain doctrinal unity: it cannot allow "pluralism in the ultimate understanding of God, Christ, the kingdom, grace, and sin."[472]

Perhaps above all, the church, for liberationists, is an eschatological sacrament, a material expression of that future that God desires for all humankind. But to be so, it must be holy. (As Riedemann put it, the church is "a lantern of righteousness, in which the light of grace is held up to the whole world, so . . . people may learn to see and know the way of life.")[473] The poor help the church realize that holiness involves not simply sacraments and spirituality but also concrete behavioral patterns, both personal and communal, both ecclesial and social. Unlike Anabaptists, however, holy living for liberation theologians distinguishes "not so much between true churches and false churches as between various degrees of realization of the church." Still, "the church of the poor is truer" because in it "the holiness of the Servant of Yahweh" shines more fully.[474]

The poor also teach that catholicity cannot be attained by accepting every cause and person but only through partisanship for causes that God favors.[475] To be truly universal, then, the church must exclude what God opposes—a theme Anabaptists underscored.

Finally, the church will be truly apostolic not merely by claiming apostolic succession but only by continuing the apostles' mission. From their vantage point the poor can show the church that mission brings the true good news only when it transforms their circumstances.[476] But then the poor will not only be evangelized. As they communicate their experiences to the church, they will evangelize it.[477]

If the church enters the world of the poor, conversion's meaning will also become more vivid. The poor's otherness and circumstances will raise unsettling

---

[471]Ibid., pp. 103, 115.

[472]Ibid., pp. 102.

[473]Riedemann, *Peter Riedemann's Hutterite Confession*, pp. 77-78.

[474]Sobrino, *Jesus in Latin America*, p. 110. God's holiness is not simply "being separated from the profane, in his inaccessibility and mystery," but more "the unconditional character of his Yes and No to the world as he draws near," God's continuing Yes of love and grace, and No to sin (p. 107).

[475]Sobrino, *True Church*, p. 111.

[476]Gustavo Gutiérrez, *The Truth Shall Make You Free* (Maryknoll, N.Y.: Orbis, 1990), p. 7.

[477]Sobrino, *True Church*, p. 121; Gutiérrez, *Power of the Poor*, p. 110; cf. Aidan Kavanagh, *The Shape of Baptism* (Collegeville, Minn.: Liturgical Press, 1978), pp. 112-14.

questions about one's self-identity. Circumstances so contrary to what God desires will render sin's nature and God's No to it graphically evident. In poverty's midst, one's status as sinner will become plain. Further, the poor's liberation will appear as God's Yes to the world.[478] In all the above ways, experiences of the poor can provide the church a new way of knowing reality. Kraybill recommends such a way to conflict transformers.

Ultimately, a church shaped by the poor will take up Jesus' servant mission, his mission of self-emptying, or *kenōsis* (Phil 2:3-11). The church will be poor not by idealizing its most oppressed members' condition, for the Bible condemns poverty of this kind. Nor will its poverty be simply an inner, spiritual openness before God, though this will be important. The church will be poor primarily in that the whole church will take on poverty voluntarily, in solidarity with those struggling against poverty of the first kind.[479]

An Anabaptist response. 1. Agreements. How congruent is Anabaptist economic sharing with this church of the poor? Anabaptists today can agree that Jesus' life, death and resurrection provide the pattern for all relationships with God and each other. Jesus' orientation, further, can certainly be called a *kenōsis*, or self-emptying, which includes taking on the poor's condition. The main *kenōsis* text stresses that he did not come only in "human form" but also "the form of a slave," which led to the cross (Phil 2:6-8). Slaves and most of those crucified were from the "poor" *(ptōkos)*, usually as both economically deprived and socially marginalized.

This classic christological passage corresponds with another that extols "the generous act [grace] of our Lord Jesus Christ, that though he was rich, yet for your sakes he became poor, so that by his poverty you might become rich" (2 Cor 8:9). These two texts envision Jesus' life course as do the Synoptics, where his favor toward the poor involved sharing their circumstances and arousing opposition, which hastened his death.

Jesus, moreover, demonstrated some kind of partiality toward people who were poor, both economically and sociologically. This is clear in numerous parables and sayings that evidence understanding of and sympathy for their situation; it is also clear in the three texts most often cited by liberationists (Lk 4:18-19; 6:20, 24; 7:22). It is perhaps most evident in the Synoptics' frequent treatment of "poor" and "rich" as opposed classes.[480] Neither Jesus nor the New Testament writers utter a truly positive word about wealth.[481] Riches seriously threaten to turn one's

---

[478]Sobrino, *True Church*, p. 145.

[479]Gutiérrez, *Theology of Liberation*, pp. 291-302.

[481]I find it inaccurate, however, to include, as does Sobrino, "publicans," who were agents of oppression,

heart from God, much as South German-Austrian Anabaptists insisted.

All these texts show that the new creation's coming claims not only one's inner self but also one's possessions. The first Christians immediately drew this implication (Acts 2:43-47; 4:32-37; 6:1-6). So did Paul by making a collection for needs of fellow Christians central to his mission.[482] This sharing can take various forms, such as total community of consumption early in Acts[483] or total community of production and consumption, as among Hutterites. In the New Testament as in historic Anabaptism, sharing was intrinsic to the church, at least as mutual aid, regarding possessions as not ours but God's gifts at the disposal of fellow Christians and the needy in general, and regarding ourselves as stewards, to distribute these material goods as God's Spirit directs. In light of New Testament practices, which embodied the new creation's coming, we will likely be directed to share generously, even sacrificially, and often.

2. Some differences.

- *The preferential option for the poor.* From an Anabaptist perspective, Jesus' earnest call to everyone to repent and turn toward God's kingdom (esp. Mk 1:15) seems somewhat missing from the liberationist reading. While the new creation for Anabaptists was indisputably communal, their foregrounding of the personally experienced baptisms of Spirit, water and blood meant that the new community could only be entered through definitive decision.

Moreover, Jesus warned that God's kingdom comes as judgment for all who reject it, whatever their social class.[484] As his ministry proceeded, opposition

---

and all other "sinners" indiscriminately among the poor (*Jesus in Latin America*, pp. 80-81). While Jesus surely called publicans like Matthew (Mt 9:9) and Zacchaeus (Lk 19:1-10) to align with the poor, his conspicuous friendliness toward such bitter enemies of this class, which his followers were to share, modifies liberation theology's close identification of God's favored people with that class.

[481]Jesus was surely concerned about inner attitudes that wealth and its pursuit can arouse, not riches simply as material objects. Yet his uniformly negative approach apparently meant that the latter would almost inevitably arouse the former (for biblical detail, see my *Christian Theology* [Scottdale, Penn.: Herald, 1985], 1:284-88). The Gospels' most positive statements about wealth indicate that it might sometimes be used to honor Jesus (Mt 26:6-13; 27:57 and pars.). The most positive New Testament statement elsewhere admonishes the wealthy "to be rich in good works, generous, and ready to share" (1 Tim 6:18). Though this may not mean surrendering all their wealth, they are warned not "to set their hopes on the uncertainty of riches" (1 Tim 6:17); desire to become wealthy is sharply condemned (1 Tim 6:7-10).

[482]Acts 20:4 (this group accompanying Paul was also taking the collection from Gentile churches to Jewish churches in Jerusalem); 24:17; Rom 15:25-27; 1 Cor 16:1-4; 2 Cor 8–9; Gal 2:10. Some of Paul's converts were wealthy and aided the church (e.g. Lydia [Acts 16:14-16], Philemon). But the majority could not. This discrepancy could raise barriers to unity—graphically so at the Lord's Supper (1 Cor 11:20-22).

[483]See pp. 202-4 above.

mounted. Finally, at the cross the whole society rejected Jesus and his kingdom. To be sure, different groups did so differently. Religious and Roman leaders attacked Jesus directly. His disciples fled. The masses acquiesced to it all. Nonetheless, the Gospel stories of Jesus' total abandonment correspond with the book of Romans's verdict that everyone came under God's judgment in this episode, which amounted to eschatological defeat of all God's enemies (Rom 3:5-20).[485]

The necessity of conversion and the certainty of judgment for all persons from all classes means that God prefers no class—in the sense of sanctioning all its aims as a social group. Theology then cannot argue that because the poor as a class desire economic betterment and because they understand "good news" to include this, therefore God's kingdom must always bring economic betterment.[486] If God brings the kingdom, we cannot deduce its character in this way, for God's gracious initiatives involve many surprises.

To be sure, when liberationists adopt a marginalized vantage point, they provide significant insights about the poor. Their concept of preferential option, however, construes the poor not only as a class but more specifically as the proletariat pursuing an irreversible history of self-liberation. This construal does not arise inevitably from their Latin American vantage point. It arose long ago from a European metanarrative that conflicts with the biblical metanarrative at important points.

Still, liberation theology shows that Jesus was partial to the poor in some sense. What sense? Construed within the biblical narrative, especially Jesus' link with the prophets, his critique of wealth implies the rich are by far more responsible for the problems stemming from pursuit and defense of wealth. Since the rich also control societal structures that perpetuate these, God holds them more responsible. Since many resulting injustices disproportionately affect the poor, God is more sympathetic to them, to the extent that their afflictions arise from these.

Further, since God's kingdom rechannels wealth, any authentic church today will reach in some way across class lines. Wealthy, socially dominant people must begin associating with (not merely aiding) the deprived and marginalized. Notice,

---

[484]E.g., Jesus pronounced final judgment on cities that rejected him (Mt 11:20-24) and people who rejected his call (Mk 8:34-38 and pars.). He often forecast future judgment (Mk 13 and pars.; Lk 19:41-44; 20:9-18 and pars.; 23:28-31). John the Baptist also associated salvation or judgment with the kingdom's coming (Mt 3:1-11; Lk 3:1-7).

[485]See "An Anabaptist Response" on pp. 139-42 above.

[486]Cf. Sobrino, *Jesus in Latin America*, p. 142; Sobrino, *Jesus the Liberator*, p. 79. I critique this pattern of argument, not its conclusion. However, I wonder about the way this conclusion is often stated. If God's kingdom is allowed to flourish, it will surely better the poor economically. Yet the kingdom often meets opposition that worsens its adherents' economic status for some time. Might Sobrino's formulation lead readers to expect that the good news will always improve the poor's economic situation?

however, that this "good news" tends to sound much better to the latter (who have much to gain from it) than to the former (who have much to lose). I propose that the poor are preferred in this sense: they are more likely to hear the kerygma as good news and more predisposed to respond.

• *Consequences for the church.* The more that churches genuinely include and learn from the poor, the further will they "migrate to the periphery and share in the powerlessness of the poor, at the feet of the crucified God."[487] The more churches advocate the poor's genuine causes, the more likely will they experience persecution, powerlessness and poverty.[488] The church's four marks will be enhanced, and conversions through involvement with the poor will multiply, much as Sobrino says. An authentic church will be not simply *for* but also *of* the poor in the sense that the poor and their concerns will be integral to its life and mission.

Still, since I find Scripture preferring the poor as a class only in the sense recently mentioned, I would call the poor neither the church's center nor "the principle of its organization, structure, and mission" or the "basis" on which it is formed.[489] The church's unity and catholicity involve, most basically, drawing together people from all classes, races, nations and other particularities.[490] None can claim this kind of centrality—including Westerners, whites or males. A contemporary theology in Anabaptist perspective can underscore and amplify liberation theology's vision of economic reversal at the church's heart, yet without allotting any one group—the poor, the hierarchy or the state—unique privileged status.[491]

3. Summary. Economic sharing makes it evident that the new creation's sacramentality, in its communal expression, involves not only major rituals (baptism and Lord's Supper), essential as they are, and interactive discipling merely in a general sense but interaction across economic, social, ethnic and other class lines, taking material shape in the most basic ways people acquire and use possessions. Since all forms of these basic activities are increasingly affected by globalization, churches that express Jesus' concerns about wealth and poverty will often wrestle with economic and social matters.

---

[487]Sobrino, *True Church*, p. 98.

[488]Ibid., p. 137.

[489]Ibid., p. 93.

[490]Though this is a major ecclesiological theme, I cannot develop it here; see e.g., Acts 2:5-8; Gal 3:27-28; Eph 2:12-19; Col 3:11; Rev 5:9-10; 7:9. Its economic dimension was highlighted by Paul's collection (see note 483, cf. Finger, *Christian Theology*, 2:255-58, 268).

[491]Sobrino links the poors' unique position to the privileging of certain structures in Catholicism (*True Church*, p. 95). This recalls, for Anabaptists, how sixteenth-century church hierarchies sanctioned the state. Anabaptists objected that no social entity that included people simply by birth or position could play a privileged role in that new creation.

Membership in such churches, however, will involve commitments that many in our individualistic, consumer-oriented societies find too demanding. Others, however, troubled by enormous discrepancies in wealth and privilege, and the strength of globalizing forces shaping them, might welcome the alternatives these communities offer. Many who long for significant relationships will also find such congregations attractive.

Anabaptist contributions to ecclesiology cannot disguise the costliness—figurative and literal—of real church membership. Yet Anabaptists should hardly valorize commitment, sacrifice and lofty behavior in themselves. Rather they should emphasize the patience and companionship involved in discipling, the joy and beauty of ritual and symbolic expression, the freedom of release from economic anxiety, and the richness available in cross-class, crosscultural relationships. Above all, Anabaptists should stress that this rich, varied human and material existence is initiated, indwelt and energized by the divine Spirit.

Churches that aim toward such things will function as an eschatological sacrament. They will begin to embody, through their economic sharing, discipling, Supper and baptism, something of what God desires for all humanity. The more they do, the more meaningfully will they speak to the world. In other words, these features of the new creation's communal dimension will find expression through its missional dimension.

ECCLESIOLOGICAL THEMES

This chapter is not a comprehensive ecclesiology. It covers but four essential practices. A complete treatment would include others, like worship, ministry and polity. Other Anabaptist theologians, I hope, will help me explore these. My focus on practices reflects historic Anabaptism's concern with concrete activities. Yet this was not inconsistent with broader generalizations. I will, then, venture some contemporary ones. (More comprehensive investigations, of course, might modify or supplement these.)

1. The content and orientation of Anabaptist faith are largely communal. Faith's most direct object, of course, is the risen Christ. Anabaptists stress conversion (chap. 5) and mission (chap. 7), as do evangelicals. Anabaptist theologians can affirm these without endorsing, even when critiquing, various features of evangelicalism today. Conversion, however, intrinsically leads to baptism and its communal commitments. Faith is hardly individualistic, even though it is deeply personal. Turning to Christ is inseparable from turning to his community and participating in its corporate walk in his life, death and resurrection. Authentic faith, by its very nature, not only produces good works (chap. 5) but also transforms individuals and shapes communities. These, all the while, offer this distinct way of life to others

(chap. 7).

2. In the most basic sense Anabaptist communities are deeply sacramental. The transcendent, risen Christ, their foundation and source, forms them inwardly through the Holy Spirit. This simultaneously energizes them to express his life, death and resurrection outwardly in the material world. Historic Anabaptists envisioned the church itself much as a sacrament.[492] Since this church heralds the new creation's fullness, Anabaptists can call it, with liberation theologians, an eschatological sacrament: a visible, present sign of what God finally desires for all humanity. However, since Jesus initiated this Spirit-matter intertwining, his incarnation can be called the primordial sacrament. Sacramentality implies the basic goodness of matter-energy, including human bodies (contra many historic Anabaptists), however distorted by sin.

This sacramentality is expressed most comprehensively as members disciple each other according to Jesus' pattern, which includes sharing possessions. Discipling is a corporate journey within God's overall reconciling mission toward increasingly Christlike character, which includes patience and moral perfection.

Through this reconciling process, matter-energy is already being transformed eschatologically by God's Spirit. Clearly, however, it is not yet fully transformed, nor is most of life. At times during this journey, then, it is important and fitting that this "already," or presence, be expressed through specific sacraments (baptism and Lord's Supper) and to a lesser extent sacramentals (e.g., infant dedication, footwashing), which actualize it more regularly than other actions. This specificity fittingly symbolizes that the new creation's presence is authentic—but also limited.[493] Sacraments and sacramentals mediate this presence not of themselves but only as vehicles of God's grace, and because of Jesus' promise.

Both ritual, symbolic expressions (esp. baptism and the Supper) and behavioral expressions (esp. discipling and sharing) are essential to the new creation's communal sacramentality. Each complements, evokes and strengthens the other. All are activities. But since they by definition incorporate and transform material phenomena, the latter are intrinsic to them. When certain material elements function regularly in specific rituals (esp. bread, wine, water), they are not simply signs pointing to something else, but they belong to that ritual's essence. That is, they are essential to that sacramental activity, though their material essence does not alter (Marpeck). Incor-

---

[492]Snyder, *Anabaptist History*, pp. 361-64.

[493]Because Christ's fullness is both present and absent from our world, we may expect his presence more regularly through baptism and the Supper than elsewhere. Christ, of course, is not entirely absent anywhere. Nonetheless, his saving presence operates more dynamically at some points than others. Though this can happen beyond these two sacraments, his presence is more regularly connected with them, when celebrated in faith, than with other circumstances or rites.

poration of these elements symbolizes and indicates that the broader realm of matter-energy participates in the new creation's spiritual transformation.

3. Anabaptist community life is a mutual interactivity among diverse participants. This is perhaps most evident in economic sharing, which draws together people from different economic and other classes, and influences all of life by affecting how we acquire and use possessions. The mutuality evident in sharing characterizes the entire discipling journey, including decision-making and organization (covered by theology under ministry and polity). Differences among members must be highly respected. Yet these ultimately promote broader, richer unity. The freedom of each is most enhanced, paradoxically, by interactivity, which necessarily includes limitation. This discipling and sharing are symbolized, actualized and strengthened by believers' baptism, through which one becomes subject to and an acting subject in discipline, and the Lord's Supper, where sharing in the crucified and risen Jesus' life energizes sharing of goods and lives.

4. The church community is the historic community rooted in biblical narrative. While Anabaptist communities stress extensive mutual participation in decision-making, they do not ultimately create their own norms and structures. These originate from the kerygma centered around Jesus, whose history provides their norms, passed down through preceding generations. Communities receive the kerygma through Christ's Spirit, the continuing Source of their life who energizes all their activities, including decisions, guiding them toward the future.[494] True Christian communities today *are* this historic community in its present expressions. They are intrinsically connected with past eras, not products of an era so different that they must construct their own norms and structures from its materials.

5. Anabaptist communities are distinctive, especially in contrast to the "world." Their initiating sacrament, believers' baptism, by symbolizing and actualizing a turn toward the new creation, entails a sharp turn from the old creation, or the "world." The christomorphism of other Anabaptist practices, with their divinizing function, contrasts notably with any era's lifestyle. This gives Anabaptists something in common with other marginalized communions. At the same time they share many features with mainline communions. I recommend then that Anabaptist ecclesiology seriously explore both kinds of commonalities, yet in light of their own distinctives precisely to contribute most helpfully to most churches. Nevertheless, Anabaptist communities are linked with the "world" through the new creation's mission. To fully appreciate the distinctives of new creation communities, we must next consider their role in this.

---

[494]See pt. 5 on pp. 96-97 above.

7

THE MISSIONAL DIMENSION

Since the new creation's personal, communal and missional dimensions are inter-twined, I could have begun with the last. I could have stressed that mission launched the call for conversion and baptism, and those countercultural communities that arose from them. I might have recalled how, by involving all members in mission, sixteenth-century Anabaptist communities differed greatly from Protestants and Catholics.[1] I am proceeding in the opposite direction only to provide descriptive, narrative clarity.

The new creation's missional dimension is as central to its coming as the other two. Chapter six implied this by calling the church an eschatological sacrament. The church, that is, makes God's desires for all people visible as its members live and work among them.

To what kind of world is the church to be a sacrament today? A world increasingly drawn together by globalization, with its unprecedented potential for cross-cultural understanding but also its intensification of modern trends like unrestrained capitalism and Western hegemony.[2] These tend to impose homogeneous superstructures and values on all societies, and thereby subordinate most weaker nations, and weaker classes and cultures in all nations. If the new creation's coming crosses economic and social lines, churches that extend it will have special concern for these groups.[3] Church mission can learn much from postmodernity's appreciation of their particularities. At the same time, missions can appreciate the potential of globalization's sophisticated telecommunications for extending the kerygma.

---

[1] See Franklin Littell, *The Origins of Sectarian Protestantism*, rev. ed. (New York: Macmillan, 1964).

[2] Again, I critique capitalism only insofar as its pursuit of production, profit and consumption is unrestrained by political, cultural or other forces. When moderated by these, such pursuits can produce some positive results.

[3] See pp. 243-52.

But here a paradox emerges. Christian missions have understood their kerygma to be universal. For over two centuries, however, missions have been aided by and sometimes aided modern, Western socioeconomic forces aiming toward world domination, and touting their own values as universal. Today, as yesterday, most dominated cultures are non-Western. Many are strongly shaped by non-Christian religions. To extend the new creation Christian missions must appreciate their particularities. Can missions do so if they keep stressing the kerygma's universality? Can they stress it, especially through media that speed globalization, without strengthening modern, Western hegemony?

To be an eschatological sacrament, to embody God's desires for the world and call people toward them, the church must also be distinct from this world. Historic Anabaptists sought to be distinct. They urged people to turn decisively from the old creation to the new. An Anabaptist theology that draws on this history then must consider evangelism. I will do so, first focusing on that crucial contemporary issue, the universality of Christian truth claims. Many current Anabaptist theologians ponder this issue and other aspects of mission despite their frequent silence on church practices. I will develop my view in dialogue with the challenge raised to universal Christian affirmations by Gordon Kaufman and others, like Paul Knitter and John Hick, who promote a pluralistic theology of religions. Postmodern concerns like those in chapter six will be further explored.

Although historic Anabaptists called people away from the "world," that very task created contacts with governments, economies and whole societies. Anabaptism's distinctive communal vision challenged contemporary leaders and lifestyles. Accordingly, an Anabaptist mission theology must ask how the church's efforts to be distinct are related to and affected by the broader society. The second section of this chapter will consider these interactions. I will dialogue with several of the many Anabaptists addressing these issues: Duane Friesen, Norman Kraus and, once again, Ron Kraybill and "conflict transformation." I will close with several brief conclusions.

In considering evangelism, a contemporary Anabaptist theology will interact with evangelicalism by way of challenge and critique as well as affirmation. By doing so from somewhat outside the evangelical mainstream, Anabaptists can invite ecumenical churches to consider evangelism from a different perspective. This perspective will include many social concerns pursued by ecumenical missions (and increasingly by evangelicals). As globalization affects all spheres of life, missions must articulate global perspectives on multiple issues and yet appreciate the particularities of numerous societies and religions. Perhaps both aims can be attained by learning much from marginalized churches while developing a broad cultural and global outlook, as do mainline communions.

EVANGELISM

To explore historic Anabaptist understandings of evangelism, we must consult not only leaders' writings but also popular sources. Evangelism was largely undertaken by peasants or artisans, mostly illiterate, whose circumstances greatly influenced their methods. To discover these we must consider numerous court records and opponents' complaints, and also Anabaptist narratives, songs, and lists of biblical texts used in mission. I will be viewing historic Anabaptist evangelism, then, through the lens provided by its broad social context, much as I viewed economic sharing (see pp. 234-52).

I will also approach it in light of a current issue: the universality of the kerygma and Christian truth claims. Though this was somewhat peripheral at that time both lenses, perhaps unexpectedly, will occasionally direct us to the same phenomena. They will provide historical resources, first, for briefly sketching a contemporary approach to evangelism, and second, addressing universality mainly as raised in today's pluralistic theology of religions.

Historic Anabaptist Perspectives

Among biblical texts, Matthew 28:19-20 and Mark 16:15-16 loomed largest for Anabaptist evangelists. These not only prescribed an apparent sequence—preaching, faith and only afterward baptism—but also mandated the Great Commission. Infant baptism was administered to almost every European, and it had cemented church-state ties for over a millennium. Anabaptist evangelists then challenged every aspect of the current social order, even if not often explicitly in their message.

Switzerland. Within days of the first baptisms in Zurich, Anabaptists evangelized the neighboring village of Zollikon. "There water was prepared and if anyone desired baptism they poured a panful of water on his head in the name of the Father, Son, and Holy Spirit." Immediately, as mentioned in chapter six, converts "also . . . practice[d] community of temporal goods" and "broke the locks off their doors, chests, and cellars."[4] They also "assumed the apostolic office . . . to follow Christ when he said, 'Go ye into all the world, etc.' [Mk 16:15]. They ran beyond the city gate into the outlying villages, regions, and market towns to preach there."[5] Grebel, Mantz, Blaurock and others soon baptized multitudes in many places. Yet governments swiftly sought to repress them.[6]

When the Schleitheim Confession began circulating, plans for widespread European mission were attached. Michael Sattler, who was apprehended carrying

---

[4]Leland Harder, ed, *The Sources of Swiss Anabaptism* (Scottdale, Penn.: Herald, 1985), p. 345.
[5]Ibid., p. 423.
[6]Cf. chap. 2.

these, remarked at his trial that if he believed in war, he would join the Turks, who were then poised to conquer Christendom. For Turks knew "nothing of the Christian faith." They were not nearly so hostile to true Christianity as his captors, "who boast of Christ, but still persecute the faithful witnesses of Christ."[7] Anabaptists, who hailed mostly from society's despised lower ranks and were cruelly ostracized, often shared Sattler's sentiment: those most opposed to the gospel were not "the heathen" but people and societies who falsely claimed to follow it.

I. General features of both Swiss and South German-Austrian evangelism can be gleaned from popular sources. Although reforming ideas were circulated rapidly by that fairly recent invention, the printing press, Protestants and Catholics controlled most of these by 1525. Anabaptists had to rely largely on older communication methods, some handwritten but most oral. (Here again, as in their mystical and communal sensitivities, Anabaptists were more oriented toward medieval trends than toward the Enlightenment.) Most people were exposed to Anabaptist tracts and the Bible orally, read aloud by the few who were literate in the vernacular, though even they lacked cultured education. Illiterate hearers absorbed these ideas, memorized many Scriptures and passed these on to each other.[8]

Though all church members normally evangelized, select individuals were also commissioned for mission, and baptizing was reserved for church leaders quite early.[9] Anabaptists often sought out family members first, then neighbors. They frequently discussed issues at social gatherings and invited people to Bible studies.[10] Anabaptist ideas were also shared with coworkers, especially among craftspeople.[11]

Whereas the authorities often watched suspected male leaders, women could usually share their faith unnoticed through daily contacts with merchants, friends and family. Though fairly little is known about individual Anabaptist women, this grassroots movement likely owed its spread and sustenance at least as much to women as men.[12]

Since persecution often forced Anabaptists from their homes, the faith was also spread by those compelled to wander. And since Anabaptists thought they were reviving the early church's apostolate, specially commissioned persons following stra-

---

[7]Michael Sattler, *The Legacy of Michael Sattler*, ed. John Howard Yoder (Scottdale, Penn.: Herald, 1973), pp. 72-73.

[8]C. Arnold Snyder, *Anabaptist History and Theology* (Kitchener, Ont.: Pandora, 1995), pp. 100-104.

[9]Wilbert Shenk, ed., *Anabaptism and Mission* (Scottdale, Penn.: Herald, 1984), pp. 61-65, 72-74.

[10]Ibid., pp. 74-77.

[11]Snyder, *Anabaptist History*, pp. 104-7; Shenk, *Anabaptism and Mission*, pp. 77-79; cf. chap. 2.

[12]Snyder, *Anabaptist History*, pp. 108-11; Shenk, *Anabaptism and Mission*, pp. 79-80. The most comprehensive source is C. Arnold Snyder and Lydia A. Huebert Hecht, *Profiles of Anabaptist Women* (Waterloo, Ont.: Wilfred Laurier University Press, 1996). One gruesome indication of womens' importance is the large number martyred.

tegic itineraries also appeared on the roads. They often went by threes: a minister of the Word doing most preaching, a lay brother, and a minister of needs addressing economic and other difficulties frequent among the lower classes.[13] Husbands usually, but not always, traveled without their wives. Teaching was frequently organized around lists of biblical texts and also the Lord's Prayer and the Apostles' Creed, which most hearers knew by heart.[14] Persecution was so severe that of the roughly sixty who attended the mission-oriented Martyrs' Synod in Augsburg in August 1527 only two or three lived to 1530.

2. Balthasar Hubmaier outlined how many Anabaptists understood evangelistic preaching. First, it convinced people through the Law that "there is no health in us . . . neither help, comfort, nor medicine." One "must despair of himself and lose heart."[15] But then the living Jesus, whom Hubmaier called the Samaritan, led one to repentance. Jesus "softens his pain and drives it away," presenting himself as the only "reconciler, intercessor, mediator, and peacemaker toward God." This living Word enlivened the sinner, who "comes to himself, becomes joyful, and henceforth surrenders himself entirely to the physician" as much as a wounded person can.[16] Public confession, baptism and the way of the cross followed. Hubmaier, at least in earlier writings, stressed human helplessness in conversion.

Later, however, Hubmaier perhaps granted converts some limited capacity to turn toward God. This issue is important for missions today. Some such capacity might make salvation possible apart from Jesus, perhaps in other religions. Hubmaier's perspective appeared mainly in his anthropology.[17]

The person was composed of three substances. At humankind's fall, the body or flesh had turned wholly away from God; it was irredeemable in this life, which necessitated rigor in discipline. The soul had turned toward the flesh and became entirely incapable of knowing or choosing good. The spirit, however, still turned wholly toward God.[18] Lodged in the spirit the desire to do right still existed in everyone, Jews and heathen included.[19] Nonetheless, the spirit was so captive to soul and flesh that it could only cry out to God like a prisoner, with unspeakable groaning.[20]

---

[13]Shenk, *Anabaptism and Mission*, p. 65.

[14]Snyder, *Anabaptist History*, pp. 106-7.

[15]Balthasar Hubmaier, *Balthasar Hubmaier*, ed. Wayne Pipkin and John H. Yoder (Scottdale, Penn.: Herald, 1989), p. 84.

[16]Ibid., pp. 84-85.

[17]For a detailed discussion, cf. chap. 9.

[18]Hubmaier, *Balthasar Hubmaier*, pp. 433-44.

[19]Ibid., p. 436.

[20]Ibid., p. 438. Hubmaier equated body with flesh so often that they can be treated as equivalent unless context indicates otherwise.

Hubmaier also attributed this "power for willing what is right" to God's image in us.[21] His later writings called this "image and inbreathing of God . . . the source of conscience" in Jews and pagans. It was captive but "as a live spark covered with cold ashes" that "will steam if heavenly water is poured on it."[22] Humans then, even under sin, could will the good and long for God. Nonetheless, as I will argue, they could not by themselves find God.[23]

Despite this, Hubmaier assured readers that God would satisfy those who sincerely "hunger and thirst after righteousness and want gladly to do good," even if they knew of God only through creation. Did this mean that people beyond the kerygma's hearing could receive salvation? Hubmaier averred that God would send such seekers "ambassadors and epistles." While he apparently was thinking mainly of the Christian variety, he allowed that if these did not reach such persons, angels would.[24] Might this ever occur through other religions? For Hubmaier, salvation was only bestowed by the living Word, which was (or at least directly expressed) the risen Jesus, through the Spirit.[25] Further, Hubmaier apparently traced any ability to respond to God to Jesus' death and resurrection.[26] Jesus, then, was the only, or universal, Savior in reality (or ontologically). Nonetheless, the spirit or conscience in adherents of all faiths longed for God and willed the good. It might be consistent with these claims to affirm that where Jesus was unknown (epistemologically), salvation could sometimes have been apprehended through some features of other religions. Hubmaier, so far as I know, neither affirmed nor denied this.

South Germany-Austria. I. Anabaptism was introduced here through the vigorous, far-flung preaching missions initiated and largely organized by Hans Hut, who was propelled by eschatological urgency. Baptism was mainly understood as the elects' final sealing. Otherwise, evangelism functioned much as among the Swiss. Evangelists like Schiemer and Schlaffer spread quickly into the Tyrol, but they modulated the eschatology.

Early leaders implied more strongly than Anabaptists elsewhere that salvation might be possible apart from knowledge of Jesus. This was linked with a tendency to prioritize revelation through the Spirit over the biblical letter. The latter was conditioned by peasant/artisan reaction against the monopoly that educated persons claimed on Scriptural interpretation. Even literate Anabaptists everywhere shared this bias and castigated "the scholars" for seeking to control and pervert biblical revelation.

---

[21] Ibid., p. 437.

[22] Ibid., p. 360.

[23] Cf. chap. 9.

[24] Ibid., p. 437.

[25] See pp. 367-69.

[26] Hubmaier, *Balthasar Hubmaier,* pp. 359-60, cf. p. 446; but cf. chap. 9.

• The inner Word revealed God more directly for Hans Denck than outer, biblical words. Yet this divine Word *in* us was not *of* us and came to the fore only through the painful, mystical *Gelassenheit* process of relinquishing creaturely attachments.[27]

Denck identified this Word with an image common to early South German-Austrians: the Lamb which had suffered from time's beginning and would until its end.[28] This inner Word, or Lamb, proclaimed God's will to everyone, pagans and Jews included.[29] Yet if the inner Word worked in everybody, perhaps Jesus was not the Word in a unique sense but simply a man who yielded to it more fully than others. If so, knowledge of him would not be strictly necessary for salvation (epistemologically). Neither would the written word; illiteracy would be no disadvantage. Jesus, moreover, would not be the only (universal) Savior, even ontologically. Salvation might well be available through other religions.

Denck found evangelistic preaching about the earthly Jesus helpful. But he critiqued Protestants, who regarded it as necessary, for seeking Christ "solely in the flesh."[30] This elevation of the inner salvation process over its outward, historical mediation eventually led Denck to Spiritualism.

• Though he was an avid preacher, Leonhard Schiemer maintained that everyone could know God through the Word's internal presence (Jn 1:1-5). Its basic content

---

[27]Hans Denck, *The Spiritual Legacy of Hans Denck*, ed. Clarence Bauman (Leiden: E. J. Brill, 1991), pp. 87-93, 221-25.

[28]Ibid., pp. 89-91, 225; cf. 1 Pet 1:19-20. See Hans Hut, "On the Mystery of Baptism," in *Early Anabaptist Spirituality*, ed. Daniel Liechty (New York: Paulist Press, 1994), pp. 73, 75; Leonhard Schiemer, "Ein epistl an die gemain zu Rottenburg darin huebsche erklearungen der 12 hauptsteuck unseres christlichen glaubens begriffen sein," in *Glaubenzeugnisse oberdeutscher Taufgesinnter* (= Quellen und Forschungen zur Reformationsgeschichte), ed. Lydia Mueller (Leipzig: M. Heinsius Nachfolger, 1938), 20:55; Leonhard Schiemer, "The Apostles' Creed: An Interpretation," in *Spiritual Life in Anabaptism*, ed. Cornelius Dyck (Scottdale, Penn.: Herald, 1995), p. 38; Hans Schlaffer, "Ein kurzer Unterrich zum Anfang eines recht chrislichen Lebens," in *Glaubenzeugnisse oberdeutscher Taufgesinnter* (= Quellen und Forschungen zur Reformationsgeschichte), ed. Lydia Mueller (Leipzig: M. Heinsius Nachfolger, 1938), 20:96; Hans Schlaffer, "Instructions on Beginning a True Christian Life," in *Early Anabaptist Spirituality*, ed. Daniel Liechty (New York: Paulist, 1994), p. 103; *Selections*, in *Spiritual Life in Anabaptism*, ed. Cornelius Dyck (Scottdale, Penn.: Herald, 1995), p. 203.

[29]Denck considered the objection that Paul preached not of an inner Word but "Christ crucified and raised from the dead." Denck nonetheless identified Paul's message with the call to love God alone and detach oneself from creatures—the true inward death and resurrection, which existed in Jewish hearts. The difference between Paul's message and Moses', and between both theirs and what other people knew of God, was "only external" (Denck, *Spiritual Legacy of Hans Denck*, p. 95). Schlaffer once affirmed that from the perspective of Christ known according to the Spirit, not the flesh, anyone who lives according to God's will, whether Jew, Turk or heathen, is incorporated into the breadth of God's love ("Ein kurzer Unterrich," p. 96).

[30]Denck, *Spiritual Legacy of Hans Denck*, p. 95.

corresponded to Moses' external law and the law written on all hearts.[31] God was known through conscience and also creation.[32] However, Schiemer regarded these avenues not simply as human capacities but as God's gift, or first grace.

People could respond by snuffing out this awareness, by half-heeding it sleepily or else by setting their hearts on God's Word. The last response involved hearing much preaching, asking questions and prayer.[33] Such persons alone experienced God's second grace, which Schiemer called the cross. This was essentially the mystical experience of Christ's "conception, birth, death and resurrection in us."[34] These were followed by a third grace: joy after suffering.[35]

Though Schiemer affirmed that Jesus suffered historically for us, he mainly emphasized that Jesus must suffer in us.[36] Like Denck, Schiemer critiqued Lutherans for knowing Jesus "only according to the flesh," for wanting him to dwell only among, but not in, us.[37] Moreover, knowledge of the earthly Jesus was not essential for the first grace, which could be received through conscience and creation. When Schiemer said that only those who heard preaching received the second grace, did he mean that such knowledge was essential? Or was he merely reporting how evangelism worked in his experience? Might the second grace have been available at times apart from this knowledge since it was mainly a mystical process? I find his extant writings too brief to support a definitive answer.

• The "Gospel of all Creatures," which stemmed from medieval mystical roots, was perhaps early South German-Austrian Anabaptism's most distinctive feature.[38] For Hubmaier and Schiemer, God could be known through the created order. But this normally led to a more specific, converting encounter with the biblical Word. They only hinted at the possibility of salvation apart from this. Denck went further: the Word could convey Jesus' saving death and resurrection inwardly, apart from Scripture. According to the "Gospel of all Creatures," all

---

[31]Leonhard Schiemer, "Three Kinds of Grace," in *Early Anabaptist Spirituality*, ed. Daniel Liechty (New York: Paulist Press, 1994), pp. 85-86; cf. Rom 2:14-16.

[32]Ibid., p. 88; Schiemer, "Ein epistl an die gemain," p. 49; "Apostles' Creed," p. 32.

[33]Schiemer, "Three Kinds of Grace," pp. 85-90. Here Schiemer, like Hubmaier, depicted the soul standing between the flesh and the spirit, and Christ the physician bringing souls to life through the Word (pp. 87-88). Beachy believes that Schiemer derived his overall views from Hubmaier (Alvin Beachy, *The Concept of Grace in the Radical Reformation* [Nieuwkoop, Netherlands: B. De Graf, 1977], p. 68). I question this, because Schiemer's notion of the first grace was far more fully developed.

[34]Schiemer, "Three Kinds of Grace," p. 90; cf. chap. 5.

[35]Ibid., pp. 93-97.

[36]Schiemer, "Apostles' Creed," pp. 34-35.

[37]Schiemer, "Three Kinds of Grace," pp. 84-85.

[38]Cf. Gordon Rupp, "Thomas Müntzer, Hans Hut and the 'Gospel of all Creatures,' " *Bulletin of the John Rylands Library* 43 (1960-1961).

this could be apprehended outwardly, from nature.

For Hans Schlaffer, the entire Bible declared nothing other than this Gospel.[39] Hans Hut identified it with Christ crucified in all his members. Hut maintained that it was known before Moses, in Old Testament law and through heathen commandments and rituals that were "almost the same."[40]

Hut and Schlaffer insisted that this Gospel could be clear to illiterate peasants, simply from their daily tasks. But scholars, they claimed, were blind both to it and Scripture, which they perverted. Peasants know well that plants and animals attain their destiny by letting humans uproot, slaughter, pluck, cut and cook them to prepare them to fulfill human purposes.[41] This can teach ordinary people that they attain their destiny only by letting God prepare them for divinization by plucking up and shearing away all creaturely attachments. Hut and Schlaffer also called this emptying and eventual filling "dying and rising with Christ."

They did not mean, however, that all peasants inferred this from daily activities. Inordinate attachments bound them too, even if less than the rich. Consequently, this "Gospel of all Creatures" often had to be preached. When early South German-Austrians mentioned proclaiming the gospel, this was often part of what they meant. For Schlaffer, at least, this Gospel frequently provided a starting point: the first witness, which led to the second, Scripture, and then the third, Christ.[42]

The "Gospel of all Creatures" provided another way for illiterate persons, and even those who never heard of Jesus, to experience salvation. This did not mean that people attained this through their own efforts, for God's initiative and the need for grace were stressed.[43] But perhaps Hut and Schlaffer implied, somewhat like Denck, that Jesus himself was not this divine initiator but only "an example of one upon whom the baptism of tribulation is richly poured out."[44] If so, Christian claims about Jesus as Savior could not have been true for everyone, or universally.[45]

2. Though Anabaptist evangelism spread swiftly into the Tyrol through Schi-

---

[39]Schlaffer, "Ein kurzer Unterrich," p. 95.

[40]Hut, "On the Mystery of Baptism," p. 71.

[41]Ibid., pp. 67-72; Schlaffer, "Instructions on Beginning," pp. 100-03; Schiemer, "Apostles' Creed," p. 32.

[42]Schlaffer, "Instructions on Beginning," pp. 100-9; "Ein kurzer Unterrich," pp. 94-96.

[43]Esp. Schlaffer, "Ein kurzer Unterrich," pp. 94; Schlaffer, "Instructions on Beginning," p. 100; *Selections*, pp. 198-201.

[44]Hut, "On the Mystery of Baptism," p. 73.

[45]"The Person of Jesus Christ" (pp. 365-421 below) will show that this may have been Hut's view, but not Schlaffer's. Beachy concludes that early South German-Austrian Anabaptists did not root the first level of grace soteriologically (in God's activity) but anthropologically (in created human nature [*Concept of Grace*, p. 68]).

emer, Schlaffer and others, intense persecution made it nearly impossible to establish congregations. Before long the evangel included a call to Moravia, where true Christian life (communal living) alone seemed possible. This economic dimension was so integral to salvation that evangelists often asked coverts to share their wealth from the start.[46]

One might suppose that Hutterites, who foregrounded church-world separation more than other Anabaptists, deemphasized evangelism. Yet the very purpose of separating and then reorganizing life communally was to let the new creation shine most brightly, attracting the maximum number of people.[47]

Often at Easter (without interruption from 1560-1590), Hutterite evangelists were commissioned for mission throughout much of Europe until autumn. Riedemann's *Confession* provided their theological basis. Families separated with intense prayer and apprehension, for sometimes only 20 percent returned. Missionaries dealt creatively with enormous transportation problems, for converts had to be spirited back to Moravia (somewhat as slaves were on America's Underground Railroad). Though Ascherham, Marpeck and others critiqued Hutterites for rigidity, they absorbed numerous families from widely varied regions and backgrounds every year.

Like his South German-Austrian predecessors, Riedemann, who spent about seven years in mission (much of it in prison), viewed all creatures as vehicles through which humans should learn of God. Yet while Hutterite evangelists must have used natural illustrations, Riedemann added that creation by itself, due to human misuse, now leads people away from God.[48] The salvation process then could not be read off from nature as in the "Gospel of all Creatures." Though Hutterite evangelists dealt mostly with lower-class people, Riedemann never hinted that salvation was available, even epistemologically, apart from preaching about Jesus, who was humankind's sole Savior ontologically.

Hutterite evangelists first warned of coming judgment,[49] moving hearers to remorse and repentance, and then to the comforting gospel.[50] This law-gospel approach resembled Hubmaier's, Menno's and Dirk's, though it added the call to financial sharing and travel to Moravia.

3. While little is known about the outreach of Pilgramite communities, Pilgram Marpeck's early writings championed witnessing to the whole world in the last

---

[46]See p. 237.

[47]Peter Riedemann, *Peter Riedemann's Hutterite Confession of Faith* (Scottdale, Penn.: Herald, 1999), pp. 77-78.

[48]Riedemann, *Peter Riedemann's Hutterite Confession*, pp. 62-63, 87, 119-20; cf. "Economic Sharing" on pp. 237-38.

[49]Shenk, *Anabaptism and Mission*, pp. 107, 118.

[50]Riedemann, *Peter Riedemann's Hutterite Confession*, pp. 95-101, 174-75, 178, 184-85.

days.[51] Many of his Spiritualist opponents claimed that the Great Commission had ceased with the apostles. Pilgram protested that they opposed evangelism of the heathen just as the "world" did.[52]

Marpeck countered that preaching was the outer means through which inner spiritual reality was mediated. Much as Jesus' physical ministry was necessary for reconnecting humans with God's Spirit (perhaps Marpeck differed here from early South German-Austrians) preaching about him was crucial for salvation.[53] Marpeck critiqued his opponents for devaluing all external, visible witness; this, for him, alone led to the invisible.[54] Marpeck regarded the church's works and worship as light (or material cowitnesses) through which God's Spirit streamed out to the world.[55]

Marpeck understood evangelistic preaching much like Hubmaier and the Hutterites.[56] Vestiges of the "Gospel of all Creatures" also appeared: God had designed creatures to be our apostles and teachers,[57] but human disobedience had corrupted them.[58] Sin involved idolatrous love of creatures.[59] Repentance included descent into the depths of forsakenness by them all.[60]

Though Marpeck always underlined the importance of preaching and the earthly Jesus, he gradually elaborated a theology of natural revelation as well. All humans, he said, possess a general awareness of what is socially and ethically right.[61] Old Testamemt law also taught this.[62] Such awareness involved a "natural piety" that was "zealous about the good, even after the divine nature, which all men have in them by nature,"[63] even though it also can spawn "all manner of idolatry."[64]

---

[51]Pilgram Marpeck, *The Writings of Pilgram Marpeck,* ed. and trans. William Klassen and Walter Klaassen (Scottdale, Penn.: Herald, 1978), p. 48.

[52]Ibid., pp. 57, 87.

[53]Ibid., p. 60.

[54]Ibid., pp. 56-57; cf. Rom 1:19-20.

[55]Marpeck, *Writings of Pilgram Marpeck,* p. 423.

[56]Ibid., pp. 416, 484-97.

[57]Ibid., pp. 56, 112, 138.

[58]Ibid., p. 113.

[59]Ibid., pp. 111, 414, 479.

[60]Ibid., p. 489. Marpeck asserted, somewhat confusingly, that "Carnal reason . . . has no right to use the witness of the creatures to the gospel," and yet that "carnal man . . . must first, by means of the creatures, be led into a knowledge of God" (ibid., pp. 352-353). "Carnal reason" apparently meant thought independent of revelation, as in philosophy. The second statement evidently referred to the way revelation is mediated through creatures, as in parables.

[61]Ibid., p. 341.

[62]J. Loserth, *Pilgram Marbecks Antwort auf Kaspar Schwenckfeld's Beurteilung des Buches der Bundesbezeugung von 1542* (Vienna: Carl Fromme, 1929), p. 219.

[63]Marpeck, *Writings of Pilgram Marpeck,* p. 511.

[64]Ibid., p. 479.

This natural awareness, like the law, could operate as a first grace, á la Schiemer. It could induce repentance and awareness of God's wrath. But it could also arouse hope in the promise of forgiveness and in this way include one in salvation.[65] Marpeck believed that Old Testament saints were saved in this way.[66] Adherents of other religions could also be saved since this salvation was initially promised to Adam and Eve.[67] Marpeck considered as saved people in his day who had repented through the law but had not yet entered the church.[68]

Marpeck eventually identified this natural awareness of good and of sin with terms like the *breath, light, love* and *law* originally infused into Adam.[69] Echoing Schiemer, he remarked that some people extinguish it, others let it shine half-way and still others let it shine fully, producing virtues like love, wisdom and fear of God. These virtues, though, operated on the human, or natural plane. Supernatural, divinizing virtues were bestowed by the Holy Spirit and depended on knowledge of and faith in Christ.[70] Salvation on both levels, however, was bestowed by the triune God and therefore through Christ as the sole Savior, ontologically.

What might this mean for people who never heard of Jesus, and were separated from him epistemologically? In 1531 Marpeck wrote that before the Gentile Cornelius heard Peter preach (Acts 10), "the light, the Word and the natural law" struggled in him as "in all men." Still, while God "accepted" Cornelius, his prayer was "not pleasing to God," for he was still under "the curse of the natural law."[71] Sometime between 1547 and 1561, however, Pilgram affirmed more clearly that even before Cornelius received the Spirit through preaching, he was saved by hope in the promise.[72] Today Marpeck would apparently suggest that non-Christians who allow the natural light to shine fully are received and saved by God even though they have not yet experienced the divinizing renewal possible only through explicit faith in Jesus.

The Netherlands. Anabaptism here, as in South Germany-Austria, sprung from evangelistic zeal and calls with specific apocalyptic content.[73] For Melchior Hoffman, all humanity was under Satan's dominion. Consequently, his announcement of judgment and call for conversion, like Jan Matthijs's, were harsh. Yet Hoffman

---

[65]Ibid., pp. 114, 120, 364, 440, 512.
[66]Ibid., pp. 118, 123, 439-40.
[67]Ibid., pp. 114-15, 123, 222; cf. Gen 3:15.
[68]Marpeck, *Writings of Pilgram Marpeck*, pp. 470-71.
[69]Loserth, *Pilgram Marbecks Antwort*, pp. 219, 222.
[70]Ibid., p. 222.
[71]Marpeck, *Writings of Pilgram Marpeck*, p. 102.
[72]Loserth, *Pilgram Marbecks Antwort*, p. 131.
[73]See chaps. 2 and 3.

also thought that Jesus' atonement had restored human freedom. Consequently, those who heard could "lead themselves out of the realm of Satan."[74] Following the Münster tragedy, evangelism by no means ceased. Leenaert Bouwens, for example, baptized 10,378 persons between 1551 and 1582.

I. "The Spiritual Resurrection" (1536) and "The New Birth" (1537), Menno Simons's early writings, were evangelistic messages.[75] His *Foundation of Christian Doctrine* (1539) commenced by proclaiming "The Day of Grace."[76] After this, however, Menno aimed mostly at consolidating and defending a credible church. Yet his writings continued to advocate evangelism and reflected communities much involved in it.

Evangelism included proclaiming "the terrifying law" and "the comforting gospel," as for Hubmaier, Hutterites and Marpeck, but with more stress on active repentance, as among the earlier Dutch. Though the eschatological urgency of repentance was still stressed, eschatological predictions disappeared. Menno fervently desired that God's name be acknowledged everywhere.[77] He envisioned the church, like Riedemann and Marpeck, as God's light to the nations.[78] Menno believed that when his followers shunned other churches, they exposed the latter's flaws and might bring them to repentance.[79]

Menno repeatedly asked for safe conduct to engage opponents in open debate. But he also defended the Mennonite refusal to hold public meetings for fear of persecution. Being almost always denied safe public opportunities, Menno's followers nonetheless preached

> as much as possible, both by day and by night, in houses and in fields, in forests and wastes, hither and yon, at home or abroad, in prisons and in dungeons, in water and fire, on the scaffold and on the wheel, before lords and princes, through mouth and pen, with possessions and blood, with life and death.[80]

Martyrdom (which literally means "witness") certainly spread the evangel, as

---

[74]According to Deppermann, Hoffman also developed something of a natural theology. Conscience and the heavens revealed God to everyone, who would be judged by their responses to the light they had (Klaus Deppermann, *Melchior Hofmann* [Edinburgh: T & T Clark, 1987], p. 225, cf. p. 247). I lack the resources to investigate this matter and regrettably cannot include it in this historical examination.

[75]Menno Simons, *The Complete Works of Menno Simons*, ed. J. C. Wenger (Scottdale, Penn.: Herald, 1956), pp. 53-62, 89-102.

[76]Ibid., pp. 108-10.

[77]Ibid., pp. 311, 319, 425, 490, 636, 964.

[78]Ibid., pp. 326, 527, 549, 965-66, 985.

[79]Ibid., p. 720.

[80]Ibid., p. 633.

numerous testimonies indicate.[81] Much like Sattler, Menno called false Christians "more unbelieving, blinder, more hardened, and worse than Turks, Tartars, or any other far away heathen."[82] Yet Menno never implied, to my knowledge, that salvation was available to the latter through another ontological source or even another epistemological route than Jesus.

Beachy suggests that Menno and Dirk might have presupposed, with Hoffman, that Jesus' atonement restored everyone's free will.[83] This could account for their tendency to sometimes advocate human responsibility to the border of works righteousness.[84] Yet I find little to either substantiate this or indicate that for Menno such freedom might have helped people to salvation apart from Christ.

Still, Menno often assumed that reason should lead toward God—although wrong use of it could oppose faith. He repeatedly appealed to "reasonable readers" and often to the natural law that taught all people to care for their fellows.[85] On this basis Menno exhorted rulers to just treatment of their subjects.[86] Menno, moreover, sometimes grounded arguments on rational considerations[87] and built cases for peace, love and civil rights on them.[88] God's love and character, he maintained, were evident in creation.[89] He said that God gave humankind the divine Word first through the natural law, then though Moses and the prophets, and finally in his Son.[90] But perhaps Menno's repeated frustration at being misunderstood and persecuted testified, paradoxically, that people are seldom guided by reason.

For Menno, then, as for Marpeck, reason might teach morality and justice on a natural plane. Yet I find no indication that this could lead, for Menno, to a kind of salvation, as Marpeck claimed.

2. Exhibiting less explicit concern for mission, Dirk Philips's followers nevertheless prayed for their neighbor's salvation with fiery hearts.[91] They preached law and gospel much as Menno did.[92] Dirk was particularly concerned about false prophets. He therefore elaborated on the marks of genuine ones, and on how

---

[81]Esp. Thieleman van Braght, *The Bloody Theater or Martyrs Mirror* (Scottdale, Penn.: Herald, 1950).
[82]Simons, *Complete Works*, p. 384, cf. p. 481.
[83]Beachy, *Concept of Grace*, p. 69.
[84]Cf. chap. 5.
[85]Simons, *Complete Works*, pp. 586-87, 631, 985.
[86]Ibid., pp. 285, 359, 385, 500, 546.
[87]Ibid., pp. 134, 136, 143, 215.
[88]Ibid., pp. 190, 338, 1012.
[89]Ibid., pp. 143, 145, 215, 968.
[90]Ibid., pp. 305-6.
[91]Dirk Philips, *The Writings of Dirk Philips*, ed. Cornelius Dyck, William Keeney, and Alvin Beachy (Scottdale, Penn.: Herald, 1992), pp. 86, 132, 600, 616.
[92]Ibid., p. 207-8.

churches should call preachers.[93] Like Menno, he justified clandestine evangelism.[94]

Unlike Menno, Dirk seldom appealed to reason. He depicted it more frequently as opposed to the Word.[95] Somewhat like Marpeck, Dirk believed that Adam and Eve had "accepted with genuine faith the gracious promise of the gospel." Going beyond Marpeck, Dirk attributed this to "the power and enlightenment of the Holy Spirit" through which they were "born anew out of" God.[96] In the same way, Abel had become "a member of the Christian church,"[97] as had some heathen like Abimelech, Job and "many others" who "do by nature the work of the law . . . written on their hearts."[98]

These people had not received salvation through Jesus epistemologically. Yet Dirk was not hinting at an ontological source other than the triune God. He normally insisted that people could not grasp God's promise without the Holy Spirit[99] and even more that Jesus was the only way into God's congregation.[100] He rejected Sebastian Franck's assertion that God's true congregation was scattered, invisibly, among Jews, heathen and Turks as well as Christians.[101] Evangelism, for Dirk, included taking universal Christian claims to Jews, Turks and heathen.[102] Dirk protested that God's congregation must be visible, as did Anabaptists in general, and that one cannot enter it without knowing something about God, presumably through evangelism.[103]

Overall, while Dirk acknowledged the epistemological possibility of salvation apart from hearing about Jesus, I do not find that it affected his evangelism. Dirk warned against accepting any wisdom, even if it came through creation, which was not ultimately "taught and commanded" by Christ.[104]

Summary. Anabaptism owed its origin to mission, in which evangelism played an indispensable role. Texts cited most often to support believers' baptism also com-

---

[93]Ibid., pp. 198-217.
[94]Ibid., pp. 226-36.
[95]Ibid., pp. 101, 112, 158, 266.
[96]Ibid., p. 353.
[97]Ibid.
[98]Ibid., p. 355, cf. Rom 2:14-16. Since such persons, for Marpeck, were saved through processes on the natural plane, he did not include them in the church. The church began, for him, only with Jesus' resurrection and outpouring of the divinizing Spirit. Since Dirk attributed this earlier and wider salvation to God's Spirit, he included its beneficiaries in God's congregation, which by then included the church but began with the angels (Philips, *Writings of Dirk Philips*, p. 350-57).
[99]Ibid., pp. 358, 362.
[100]Ibid., pp. 380, 413.
[101]Ibid., p. 463.
[102]Ibid., p. 228.
[103]Ibid., pp. 463, 465.
[104]Ibid., p. 450.

manded teaching and preaching to all nations (Mt 28:20; Mk 16:15-16). Anabaptists felt, far more strongly than most Protestants, that they were reviving this apostolic ministry, propelled by eschatological urgency. Evangelism included calls to personal conversion, often on a law-gospel pattern. Yet these simultaneously enjoined corporate accountability and usually economic sharing. As the next section will show, issuing and receiving such calls affected all spheres of society.

Still, Anabaptism was primarily a lower-class movement. It aimed not at transforming rulers but at ecclesial and communal ideals congenial to artisans and peasants. The kerygma spread mainly through family, neighborhood and vocational networks along unsophisticated but well-organized oral channels.

Anabaptists stressed the verbally proclaimed biblical Word. Did they also hint at other routes to salvation and perhaps implicitly question the universality of Christian claims? Four leaders mentioned channels that could at least prepare persons for the kerygma.

For Schiemer the unwritten law, operating inwardly through conscience and outwardly through creation, originated ultimately from the Word (Jn 1:1-5) and could bring one to this point. Hubmaier was confident that even though no one on their own could really practice righteousness, God would come to all who longed for it—by extrabiblical means if necessary. Dirk allowed that the Spirit had renewed many who followed the inner law before Jesus (Rom 2:14-16) and thus apart from him epistemologically. Yet he insisted on preaching Jesus as the universal and therefore ontological Savior to Jews, Turks and heathen. Marpeck went further. An incomplete kind of salvation involving repentance and hope for Christ's fulness could result from openness to God's breath or light or natural law infused into everyone. This implied that this salvation could be mediated epistemologically by features of other religions. So perhaps could those salvific operations mentioned by Schiemer, Hubmaier and Dirk. Yet for none of these four did any such thing qualify the affirmation of Christ as universal, ontological Savior.

Some early South German-Austrians, however, mentioned channels other than biblical preaching that might bring full salvation.[105] For Denck it was the Word indwelling everyone; for Hut and Schlaffer especially, it was the crucifixion-resurrection process visible in the "Gospel of all Creatures." In both, Jesus could be regarded simply as one who made salvation visible, perhaps supremely so. But then he would be an epistemological, not the ontological, source of salvation. Christian affirmations about him would not be universally true. Full salvation would very likely be available through other religions.

---

[105]On Hoffman, see p. 267 n. 74.

Contemporary Appropriations

Traditionally, Christian mission articulated its broad, global vision around universal claims: most centrally, Jesus as sole Savior and Lord. Western imperialism, however, similarly justified itself as the promoter of universal values (e.g., democracy). As globalization extends the reach of dominant economic forces today, these frequently make such claims (e.g., about free markets). Can Anabaptists, who rejected Europe's monolithic church-state cultures but found favor in society's alienated segments,[106] help churches communicate a global message that respects the particularities of many peoples, especially marginalized ones? If so, will it convey universal affirmations?

To dilute evangelism's imperialistic potential, many current Anabaptist theologians highlight not the kerygma's universality but its particularity. James McClendon treats each religion as "a set of powerful practices."[107] Doctrines are efforts to explain the significance of these particular practices, and they cannot be abstracted from them. This means, for example, that neither judgment nor salvation has any general meaning applicable to people outside Christian communities.[108] McClendon wants to encourage communication across religious lines and avoid relativism.[109] Yet it is somewhat unclear how Christian affirmations can transcend the particularities of their communities.[110]

Duane Friesen begins differently. Christ as Logos transcends all religions but is

---

[106]Cf. Shenk, *Anabaptism and Mission*, pp. 194-95.

[107]James McClendon, *Systematic Theology*, vol. 2, *Doctrine* (Nashville: Abingdon, 1994), p. 421.

[108]James McClendon, *Systematic Theology*, vol. 3, *Witness* (Nashville: Abingdon, 2000), pp. 422-23. In mission, Christians will proclaim Jesus as Lord of all. Yet of others they can say no more than "they need Jesus" (p. 423). McClendon draws on George Lindbeck's cultural linguistic theory where doctrines describe and regulate community life (George Lindbeck, *The Nature of Doctrine* [Philadelphia: Westminster, 1984]). Weaver, who also appropriates Lindbeck, envisions religions as trajectories (J. Denny Weaver, Review of *The Nature of Doctrine*, by George Lindbeck, *CGR* 3, no. 2 (1985): 223; "Mennonites: Theology, Peace and Identity" *CGR* 6, no. 2 [1988]: 131). They intersect at various points, which makes dialogue and cooperation possible (J. Denny Weaver, "Christus Victor, Nonviolence, and Other Religions," in *Mennonite Theology in Face of Modernity*, ed. Alain Epp-Weaver [North Newton, Kans.: Bethel College, 1996], pp. 195-203). Yet they cannot be compared or evaluated by objective criteria. Still, the truth of Christian claims can be validated by "the presence in history of people and of communities shaped by the claims" (p. 202).

[109]McClendon, *Systematic Theology* 3: 51-52, 297-300, 350.

[110]McClendon's last volume considers Christian witness comprehensively. He speaks less of religions pluralistically, as practices, and more of religion quite generally (e.g., of "Religion as Culture," ibid., pp. 65-97). Perhaps this shift indicates, implicitly, the difficulty of maintaining a pluralistic approach consistently (cf. Thomas Finger, "Two Agendas for Baptist Theology," *Perspectives in Religious Studies* 27, no. 3 [2001]: 310-311; "James McClendon's Theology Reaches Completion," *MQR* 76, no. 1 [2002]: 126-27).

also the source of significant truth in each. In view of this commonality, Friesen promotes dialogue among religions and eventually cooperation.[111] Like McClendon, Friesen downplays doctrines.[112] The church should begin by confessing its own particularity and that of the Jesus story.[113] Nonetheless, it can recommend this paradigm to others on more general grounds since criteria exist for evaluating narratives and religious traditions.[114]

John Yoder affirms the lordship of Jesus and his way. This lordship leads him to expect God to be working among people of other faiths. But rather than following, in mission, some theory of how this happens, Yoder recommends interacting with and learning from them on all levels of life. This should allow the most relevant similarities and differences to emerge and provide direction for continuing discussion, cooperation, and witness.[115]

Among Anabaptists, Gordon Kaufman addresses issues of pluralism, postmodernity and truth most fully. I will develop my own view in dialogue with him and other pluralistic theologians of religions. (I will consider Norman Kraus in the next section.) However, evangelism is many-faceted, and I am exploring these issues in light of its actual practice. To keep them there I will first propose several features to mark a contemporary evangelism in Anabaptist perspective. I cannot support these, biblically or otherwise, due to space limitations.

General features of evangelism. People turn to God in many ways and situations. I am not implying that this turning must involve explicit recognition of all the following features. Since evangelism adapts itself to each situation, every feature does not need to be explicitly included in all communications. I mean

---

[111]Duane Friesen, *Artists, Citizens, Philosophers* (Scottdale, Penn.: Herald, 2000), pp. 257, 261-64.

[112]"The key relationship" among religions consists not in a "set of truths, beliefs or dogmas. Christians do not relate to religions as intellectual constructs or symbolic systems, but to people" (ibid., p. 261). Although "the Christian vision also provides a standard of judgment about what is valid or authentic," Christians should not engage others "about speculative truths concerned with metaphysical claims about the universe" but "about how one lives" (p. 276). "Truth grows out of a relational process between people" (p. 262).

[113]Ibid., p. 265.

[114]These are "adequacy, interpretive power, coherence, and the practical implications for personal and social life" (ibid., p. 272). Friesen develops these in explicit contrast to Lindbeck's approach (pp. 81-84). He acknowledges that they are somewhat imprecise and that no one can evaluate paradigms with complete objectivity (pp. 271-73).

[115]Though Yoder developed no theory of mission, Gayle Gerber Koontz helpfully culls some general themes from his many relevant remarks (Gayle Gerber Koontz, "Evangelical Peace Theology and Religious Pluralism: Particularity in Perspective" *CGR* 14, no. 1 [1996]). See also Yoder's appropriation of postmodern and historicist orientations in mission (pp. 62-63; Thomas Finger, "Did Yoder Reduce Theology to Ethics?" in *A Mind Patient and Untamed,* ed. Gayle Gerber Koontz and Ben Ollengburger [Telford, Penn.: Cascadia, 2004], pp. 318-39).

only that each feature should be integral to the overall evangelistic message and enterprise and that conversion should involve openness, even if quite implicit, to each.

1. Evangelism's main task is transmission of the kerygma by communities of the new creation to those who belong to no such community. Centering around Jesus the kerygma communicates historical events and their significance, and invites people to appropriate the life they convey. The kerygma emerges from and calls people into not only present Christian communities but mainly into the historic Christian community that, through its activities and traditions, has extended the kerygma from the past and propels it toward the future.[116]

2. Evangelism is a task of the whole church.[117] Since the kerygma is not mere verbal information but a speech act energized by the Spirit's drawing power, it often comes most alive amid the friendships, service and sharing of ordinary Christians. These are expressions of the new creation's coming—of the evangel's very content. The kerygma assumes many verbal forms besides preaching, and within many contexts besides special events or meetings. Not every Christian need be an evangelist per se. Nonetheless, select individuals should be commissioned for evangelism, and specific evangelistic events or processes can be fruitful.

3. Evangelism seeks to elicit the decisive, personal turning from the old creation to the new. It calls for personal faith in and surrender to the risen Christ who, as the living Word, is evangelism's primary agent through the Holy Spirit. This turning, however, occurs in many ways. It need not always include severe emotional struggle or a specific conversion experience, although these were common among historic Anabaptists.[118] However, evangelism that calls people simply to church membership or social involvement is neither biblical nor Anabaptist.

4. This personal turning intrinsically involves turning toward the communities and lifestyles of the new creation. Faith in the risen Christ through the Holy Spirit involves incorporation into the communities and the discipling processes they energize. Evangelism that calls people to an individual salvation alone is neither bib-

---

[116]Cf. pt. 5 on pp. 96-97.

[117]Cf. McClendon, *Systematic Theology* 2: 419, 450.

[118]Contra Robert Friedmann's amazing assertion that historic Anabaptists "did not start with the crushing awareness of being lost sinners but began rather with the glorious experience of regeneration or spiritual rebirth" (*The Theology of Anabaptism* [Scottdale, Penn.: Herald, 1973], p. 78). Friedmann also alleged that "Anabaptist sources in the introspective area" describing grace or regeneration "are almost nonexistent" (p. 95). He then sought to develop an Anabaptist theology of grace from two late-seventeenth-century Quakers and a French Catholic existentialist, Gabriel Marcel.

lical nor Anabaptist.[119]

5. Personal turning toward the new creation intrinsically involves turning away from various activities, associations, attitudes and behaviors of the old creation. Evangelism that implies that people can participate in salvation without critically examining and rejecting patterns opposed to it is neither biblical nor Anabaptist.[120]

6. This does not mean that converts should avoid engagement with society or simply seek to be different, as Anabaptists sometimes have.[121] Evangelism, which is done by converts, engages people through activities of many kinds and must be sensitive to and appreciative of cultural particularities. Many particularities are not evil but simply patterns through which reality is perceived and intentions actively expressed. For the kerygma to be the dynamism that it truly is, the church must convey it through these patterns.[122]

7. Salvation, or divinization, bestowed by the risen Christ and received through faith in him, involves continuing participation in his life, death and resurrection (through the Spirit and with the Father, within the community). Evangelism that promises simply pardon and resurrection joy is neither biblical nor Anabaptist. Neither is evangelism that simply calls one to the way of the cross, obedience and suffering.

8. Congregations whose membership comes entirely from Christian families seldom apprehend evangelism's full challenge, vitality and importance. They usually gain this only through people coming for the first time into the church. Congregations will likely share the kerygma little unless they share this experience of first-generation Christians. This means that coming from a non-Christian background to Christian faith "is an essential part of that faith."[123] That is, this missional activity of the new creation is so essential to the new creation's communities that without it they may cease to be its true communities.

---

[119]I do not mean that no individually understood conversion could ever be valid. Individualistic evangelism, however, should not be standard practice. Similarly, though God might reach people through calls to church membership or social involvement alone (pt. 3) or calls that omit critique of negative patterns (pt. 5), these too should not be standard.

[120]On confrontation in Anabaptist mission, see Takashi Yamada, "The Anabaptist Vision and Our World Mission (II)," in *Anabaptism and Mission*, ed. Wilbert Shenk (Scottdale, Penn.: Herald, 1984), pp. 189-93. On the counter-cultural character of the churches it calls forth, see Larry Miller, "The Church as a Messianic Society," in *The Transfiguration of Mission*, ed. Wilbert Shenk (Scottdale, Penn.: Herald, 1993), pp. 136-49.

[121]Cf. Scott Holland, Melanie May and Elaine Swartzentruber.

[122]Cf. pt. 3 on p. 96.

[123]Robert Ramseyer, "The Anabaptist Mission and our World Mission (I)," in *Anabaptism and Mission*, ed. Wilbert Shenk (Scottdale, Penn.: Herald, 1984). He actually writes "non-Anabaptist background" and "Anabaptist faith" (p. 179, cf. p. 121). Recall how some Catholic theologians promote believers' baptism to revitalize congregations in this way (p. 173).

Religious pluralism. Having investigated historic Anabaptist evangelism through the lenses provided by its social context and the issue of universal affirmations, I will sharpen the second by considering how it is configured in today's pluralistic theology of religions. I first show how pluralistic theologians, especially Kaufman, handle such affirmations and ponder some critical responses. Then I will develop my own views on universal affirmations, ways to salvation and evangelism's central affirmation.

I. General approaches to the relationship between Christianity and other religions today face the criticism that Christianity's universal truth claims are impossible in theory and imperialistic in practice. Exclusivism responds by reaffirming that Jesus Christ is salvation's only source (ontologically) and further that knowledge of and commitment to him are necessary for salvation (epistemologically). Exclusivists usually allow that all cultures are aware of God through other channels. Yet they find these insufficient for salvation.

Inclusivism also holds that Jesus is salvation's sole source ontologically—but not always epistemologically. That is, God always draws people to salvation through Christ. However, some people experience this drawing but do not know that it comes through him. A *modest* inclusivism affirms that some people in non-Christian religions (or perhaps no religion) receive salvation, but this kind of inclusivism is reluctant to speculate how many, in what religions or by what means.[124] *Strong* inclusivism, however, treats all religions, or some aspects of them, as regular channels of salvation.[125]

With postmodernity, a pluralistic theology of religions is emerging and sharply critiquing Christianity's universal claims.[126] It accepts the findings of much comparative religion: religions are vastly different and in many important respects incommensurable. Pluralists conclude that no religion can be qualita-

---

[124]See John Sanders, *No Other Name* (Grand Rapids: Eerdmans, 1992); Calvin Shenk, *Who Do You Say that I Am?* (Scottdale, Penn.: Herald, 1993), pp. 34-73. For a briefer treatment see Thomas Finger, "Jesus Christ and Religious Pluralism," *Catalyst* 25, no. 3 (1999). Modest inclusivism is affirmed in Clark Pinnock, *A Wideness in God's Mercy* (Grand Rapids: Zondervan, 1992); Clark Pinnock et al., *The Openness of God* (Downers Grove, Ill.: InterVarsity Press, 1992); and John Sanders, *What About Those Who Have Never Heard?* (Downers Grove, Ill.: InterVarsity Press, 1995).

[125]Strong inclusivism appeared in early twentieth-century treatments of other religions as less perfect expressions of what Christianity expressed most fully (cf. Paul Knitter, *No Other Name?* [Maryknoll, N.Y.: Orbis, 1985], pp. 37-71). Karl Rahner inspired another form in the 1960s, arguing that all religions are vehicles of salvation, and many of their adherents are anonymous Christians ("The Comfort of Time," in *Theological Investigations III* [Baltimore: Helicon, 1967], pp. 120-44).

[126]The classic manifesto is probably John Hick and Paul Knitter, eds., *The Myth of Christian Uniqueness* (Maryknoll, N.Y.: Orbis, 1987). These editors remain among pluralism's chief proponents. Gavin D'Costa collects essays contrasting with and dissenting from those in the former volume (*Christian Uniqueness Reconsidered* [Maryknoll, N.Y.: Orbis, 1990]).

tively or universally superior to others (exclusivism). Nor can some religions be parallels or inferior versions of others (strong inclusivism). Differences among faiths, which fuel economic and military conflicts as well as religious, are very real. As globalization multiplies contacts among religions, these conflicts increase. In response, pluralists, who highlight diversity, also seek to promote positive relations among religions.

2. Kaufman's theology is congenial with religious pluralism. All religious beliefs are "creations of human imagination" that are "simply ours."[127] Religions were constructed over many centuries to help diverse peoples organize and find meaning in their worlds. Religions are dissimilar because they originated in different settings. According to Kaufman all major belief systems contradict each other (though each is coherent if its premises are accepted). To find grounds for positive relationships among religions, we cannot begin by accepting the claims of any.[128]

However, since each religion is a way of grappling with the world to attain human ends, a criterion for evaluating them and promoting cooperation can be suggested: humanization. Religious claims, that is, can be affirmed to the degree that they further what is authentically human.[129] In assessing them theology should avoid "talk of another world and of other realities that are more important" than this one since this "distracts us from this massive effort for a more humane order." Kaufman, more transparently than other Anabaptist theologians, reduces theology's content to material and social-ethical reality.[130]

Kaufman believes, nonetheless, that the "God" concept can usefully guide the humanizing process. When properly reconstructed, "God" can function as a symbol of goodness to which everyone should be devoted and which people everywhere can share. It therefore transcends the most common alternative for guiding human life: rational self-interest.[131] Further, if God is represented by "Christ" (that is, Jesus and his immediate historical effects), then attributes like self-giving and reconciliation, even among enemies, are added to the general God concept, and they

---

[127]Hick and Knitter, *Myth of Christian Uniqueness*, pp. 8, 12.

[128]Gordon Kaufman, *God—Mystery—Diversity* (Minneapolis: Fortress, 1996), p. 35. Kaufman contends that if Christians affirm specific beliefs like Christ's deity, they imply the superiority of their religion. But this is "neither appropriate nor useful." All religions need to work together to find more humane ways of living. Kaufman sharply contrasts affirming basic truth(s), which he calls making "claim for ourselves or our truth against our neighbors," with undertaking a "ministry of reconciliation," which requires loving and accepting "our neighbors as ourselves" (pp. 38-39).

[129]Gordon Kaufman, *In Face of Mystery* (Cambridge: Harvard, 1993), p. 130, cf. pp. 73-74 in this book.

[130]People are humanized through historicity: their capacity to shape and reshape their settings in light of future goals. Historicity includes responsibility, self-understanding, well-ordered freedom and concern for nonhuman reality (Kaufman, *In Face of Mystery*, p. 130).

[131]Kaufman, *God—Mystery—Diversity*, pp. 26-28.

also supplement general notions of humanization.

Kaufman plays off Jesus' death, which expresses love and self-sacrifice, against stories of his resurrection, which have provided a basis for triumphalism and imperialism. This happened, in his view, because early Christians combined stories of Jesus with their ancient concept of God as omnipotent and personal.[132] Reconstruction according to the humanistic criterion, however, renders God a bio-historical force promoting egalitarian values.

Humanization is more than a criterion for constructing particular beliefs. It involves an assumption about history as a whole: that it is moving in a humanizing direction. This movement, further, is toward one interdependent world. Humanization, that is, works against the kind of independence among cultures valorized by postmoderns. It levels down each religion's uniqueness so that religious pluralism "increasingly exists within and is formed by the powerful movement everywhere toward modernization."[133]

Kaufman concedes that this view of history is "largely descendant from western religions and cultural traditions."[134] It "grows out of modern Western historical thinking."[135] In other words, it has been intertwined with Western imperialism. Kaufman insists, though, that today this global movement toward humanization can press onward, freed from this connection.[136]

This outlook that emphasizes the religions' irreducible diversity, then, does not simply appreciate each one's uniqueness. It evaluates them all by its humanistic norm. It critiques Hindu beliefs in karma and reincarnation, for instance, for fatalistically opposing humanizing change. Kaufman lauds government efforts at "building a new secular India"[137] even while acknowledging that challenging such beliefs "is to ask people to give up their very being, their sense of identity . . . their history . . . to live in a different world than the one they have regarded for generations as the real world."[138] Kaufman also critiques Pure Land Buddhism's devaluation of historical life for its transitory character.[139]

In sum, while Kaufman, like other pluralists, finds numerous differences among religions incommensurable, he proposes an ethical criterion for reconstructing them all and grounding interfaith cooperation. The "God" concept that emerges, however, is shaped by a "Christ" image derived from Jesus' life and death. Its main

---

[132]Kaufman, *In Face of Mystery*, pp. 377-82; *God—Mystery—Diversity*, pp. 114-15.

[133]Kaufman, *God—Mystery—Diversity*, p. 34.

[134]Ibid., p. 35.

[135]Hick and Knitter, *Myth of Christian Uniqueness*, p. 14.

[136]Kaufman, *God—Mystery—Diversity*, p. 33.

[137]Ibid., p. 32, cf. *In Face of Mystery*, pp. 135-36.

[138]Kaufman, *God—Mystery—Diversity*, p. 221.

[139]Ibid., p. 159.

features—servanthood, love for enemies, advocacy for the oppressed—resemble those of most Anabaptist theologies.[140]

Kaufman, in other words, preserves something of Christianity's uniqueness by dropping its transcendent claims but proposing that its "Christ" image can modify somewhat the general values guiding humanization.[141] This raises questions about other Anabaptist theologies whose content is largely a social-ethical lifestyle rooted in Jesus' ministry and death. What could an evangelism derived from them offer? Would it be more or other than Kaufman allows?

Further, if their content is mostly this lifestyle, can these theologies address Kaufman's broader claims: for example, that "God" denotes no transcendent reality but a bio-historical force? If they cannot, would they be implying that such issues are irrelevant to Christian life and mission? Can such theologies, further, engage other religions' transcendent claims? Or will they imply, by default, that mission should ignore such issues and champion social causes?[142]

3. At least three of Kaufman's major tendencies appear in many other pluralistic theologies of religion. First, after rejecting the universality of religious claims, they evaluate them all by universal social-ethical criteria.

Paul Knitter, for example, proposes liberating praxis as a criterion: "The fundamental option for the poor and nonpersons."[143] Yet he wants to avoid the criticism that he is proposing some "preestablished absolutist or definitive position."[144] Accordingly, Knitter insists that praxis is no " 'foundation' . . . or sure-fire criterion of judgment, but . . . an approach, context, a starting point that will be further clarified as it clarifies and creates new common ground."[145] In other words, if liberation becomes a main theme in interfaith dialogue, as he hopes, different parties will discuss the way they understand it. They need not all agree at the outset.

Let me trace this process further. If religions are going to work together for lib-

---

[140]Kaufman, *In Face of Mystery*, p. 382; *God—Mystery—Diversity*, pp. 116-17.

[141]Salvation in many New Testament texts is "nothing else than the special quality human life will take on" in the Christian community (Kaufman, *God—Mystery—Diversity*, p. 122, citing 2 Cor 5:17-20; Gal 5:16, 20-23; I Jn 4:7-8). On "God," see Kaufman, *In Face of Mystery*, pp. 325-28; and pp. 73-74 above). Friesen seeks to appropriate many of Kaufman's themes without being as reductionistic (esp. *Artists, Citizens, Philosophers*, pp. 64-77, 139-41).

[142]Note J. D. Weaver's characterization of "the church's mission": to "symbolize and witness to the presence in the world of the social dimension of the gospel" (J. D. Weaver, *Anabaptist Theology in Face of Postmodernity*, [Telford, Penn.: Pandora, 2000], p. 154). Still, such theologies might differ from Kaufman's by insisting that Jesus' pattern cannot supplement, but contradicts or radically revises, humanistic ideals, as Weaver and Yoder apparently maintain.

[143]Hick and Knitter, *Myth of Christian Uniqueness*, p. 186; cf. pp. 235-36).

[144]Hick and Knitter, *Myth of Christian Uniqueness*, p. 181.

[145]Ibid., p. 186.

eration, or Kaufman's humanization, they will sooner or later have to agree on some things—about, say, what a "nonperson" is. Yet they will not be able to do so without coming to agree on or at least sharing an implicit assumption about what a "person" is.

In other words, it will impossible for several religions to cooperate unless they agree, at least implicitly, on certain ethical goals and the ontological convictions intrinsic to them. And it will be impossible for all religions to do so cooperate unless they can agree, implicitly or explicitly, on some such universal goals and convictions.[146] Briefly stated: if religions renounce their universal religious claims, they will still have to affirm some other kind of universal claims together if they wish to work together.

A second tendency in Kaufman and many other pluralistic theologians is to pinpoint some historical trend originating from the West as the one to bring all religions and cultures together. John Hick, for instance, believes that modern science and technology, along with freedom, equality and democracy, arose in the West.[147] Though he does not suppose that they had to emerge there, they nonetheless initiated trends whose global effects "must be . . . progressive secularization of both thought and society."[148] Today this process, with its considerable potentials and perils, is reshaping all religions and cultures. We can now see that these transformations are "part of a universal soteriological process" available through all religions and offering "the possibility of a limitlessly better existence."[149]

For supporting Western imperialism Hick, Kaufman and other pluralists sharply critique the missionary affirmation of Christ's universal lordship. Yet here again it is clear that when they reject universal religious claims they substitute other universal affirmations for them. In this case, despite their apparent appreciation of religious and cultural diversity and critique of imperialism, their universal is precisely the spread of Western ideas and forces. This is far more modern than postmodern.

Further, critics of pluralism complain that interfaith dialogues arranged by pluralists actually occur among Westernized intellectuals who have rejected their own faiths' important particularities and whose language is academia. Critics protest that when religions surrender their distinctive beliefs in order to cooperate, they

---

[146]Knitter wrestles further with postmodernity's critique of universality and his own preference for liberative praxis (*One Earth, Many Religions* [Maryknoll, N.Y.: Orbis, 1995], pp. 38-53, 73-96). He argues that universal agreement is quite needed to guide environmental activity, for all the earth's eco-systems interact with each other (pp. 118-35). Knitter proposes "Eco-human well-being" as "a universal criterion for truth" (p. 124).

[147]Hick and Knitter, *Myth of Christian Uniqueness*, p. 25.

[148]Ibid., p. 26.

[149]John Hick, *An Interpretation of Religions* (London: Macmillan, 1989), p. 380.

level significant differences and shield themselves from meaningful encounters with genuine others.

If so, these dialogues take place not in the world marked by real inequalities but in one of "global media and information networks, international agencies and multinational corporations."[150] Such discourse systematically incorporates and dissolves all oppositional spaces, such as those occupied by the truly poor, traditional and uneducated.[151] It employs a homogeneous logic that "irons out the heterogeneous precisely by subsuming it under the categories of comprehensive and totalizing global and world theologies." In this way, such dialogue "sedately but ruthlessly domesticates the other—any other—in the name of world ecumenism and the realization of a 'limitlessly better possibility.' "[152]

Third, when Kaufman and other pluralists replace religious norms with social-ethical ones, this very effort can be traced to the imperializing Western mentality. According to John Millbank, religions differ over social and political practices as much as anything else. To suppose that a-theological spaces for social cooperation can be found within religions is to assume "that a common secular realm of human aspiration, relatively free from mythical and metaphysical elaborations, has always been latent with the religious traditions" and also to assume the modern distinction between politics and religion.[153]

Sociopolitical agreement among religions, however, is usually a product of secularization. It "nearly always betokens the triumph of Western attitudes and a general dilution of traditional belief."[154] This only occurs when religion is subordinated to "the universal sway of the liberal state and the capitalistic market."[155]

An Anabaptist response. To sharpen focus on the role of universal affirmations in evangelism, I have viewed it through the critical lens provided by pluralistic theologians of religion. Yet they have not weakened but strengthened the plausibility and value of such affirmations. For even as they seek to appreciate religious particularities, globalizing trends are drawing all religions together. To address the issues

---

[150]Kenneth Surin, "A Politics of Speech," in *Christian Uniqueness Reconsidered*, ed. Gavin D'Costa (Maryknoll, N.Y.: Orbis, 1990), p. 201.

[151]Ibid., p. 195.

[152]Hick, quoted in ibid., pp. 210, 200. Kaufman critiques Hick's approach as a form of monism ("Religious Diversity and Religious Truth," in *God, Truth and Reality: Essays in Honour of John Hick*, ed. Arvind Sharma [New York: St. Martin's Press, 1993]). Duane Friesen, responding to Hick's *Interpretation of Religions*, faults Hick for treating all faiths as partial manifestations of a "universal concept of 'the Real' " (*Artists, Citizens, Philosophers*, p. 265).

[153]John Millbank, "The End of Dialogue," in *Christian Uniqueness Reconsidered*, ed. Gavin D'Costa (Maryknoll, N.Y.: Orbis, 1990), p. 182.

[154]Ibid., p. 184.

[155]Ibid., p. 179.

that arise, these pluralists find that they must replace the religious universals they discard with social and ethical ones.

Since the issue of universal affirmations is usually argued philosophically, I will address it first this way. Then, turning to Scripture, I will consider the issue of different paths to salvation. I will close with what I find to be evangelism's central affirmation.

1. In light of the particularities that shape knowledge and values in any culture, many postmodernists ask: Can people from different cultures really affirm common, or even universal, beliefs and values?[156] Let us consider this in light of the increasing interconnections and corresponding tensions emerging among all peoples through globalization. These make it crucial to work together toward goals like worldwide justice and peace. But this will be impossible unless the parties involved generally agree, or are working toward agreement, on what justice and peace are. If such universal values are not sought and acted on, destructive global forces, like environmental destruction, will surge on largely unchecked.

Global interconnectedness shows that all people indeed have certain things in common. They share common aspirations and face common threats. If we believe or hope that some such aspirations can be attained and threats avoided, we must suppose that universal agreement (or convergence toward it) on basic, important values is at least possible. Such values involve convictions or beliefs about the way things really are.

Universal affirmations, or agreements, then must exist at least as goals worth striving for, however difficult it may be to state any adequately at present. People who work toward them must presuppose (even if not consciously), as a condition of the possibility of even attempting this, that universal agreement on some important values and beliefs might some day be attained.

This becomes clearer when we consider the kind of interchange that would lead toward this. The best global agreements would benefit everyone, everywhere, in the best possible way. Such agreements, however, could not be reached unless people from all social, cultural, racial and gender groups were able to engage in free, uncoerced dialogue on the issues. Postmodernists laud few ideals as highly as such open conversation.[157] To be sure, as long as the old creation lingers, this ideal will

---

[156]Cf. pt. 6 on pp. 97-98 above.

[157]Valorized by Kaufman, *In Face of Mystery*, pp. 64-69; *God—Mystery—Diversity*, pp. 197-201. See also William Placher, *Unapologetic Theology* (Louisville: Westminster/John Knox, 1989), pp. 105-22; Richard Bernstein, *Beyond Objectivism and Relativism* (Philadelphia: University of Pennsylvania, 1988), pp. 171-231; and Thomas Finger, "Confessing Truth in a Pluralistic World," in *Practicing Truth: Confident Witness in Our Pluralistic World*, ed. David Shenk and Linford Stutzman {Scottdale, Penn.: Herald, 1999), pp. 208-12; " 'Universal Truths?': Should Anabaptist Theologians Seek to Articulate

not be fully attained. Nonetheless, those who seek the best attainable agreements among as many people as possible will be guided by it, even if tacitly, as the goal to increasingly approximate.

To strive toward it, however, people must assume, even if only implicitly, that certain rights belong to every potential participant. In other words, every person is valuable and has the right to respected and heard. The assumption that such rights and dignity belong to everyone—that these are *universal* truths—is a necessary, even if unrecognized, condition of the possibility of such conversations occurring.

Further, when people anywhere converse genuinely, they will be agreeing, even if tacitly, on certain criteria for truth. That is, if you present views different from mine, I must be open to the possibility that you might give reasons for them which accord with truth criteria that I accept and thus would prompt me to alter my views. You also must be tacitly acknowledging truth criteria that would call you to change if I presented adequate reasons. Fruitful conversation can continue only if all parties either accept or are seeking, perhaps without recognizing it, some criteria in light of which they could agree.

Now expand such conversations to include all voices needed to reach the best agreements on global issues. All participants would need to at least search for universal criteria in light of which they all could agree. To be sure, no actual process will attain this fully. Nevertheless, this ideal remains the goal that genuine efforts at common agreement will approximate. In other words, acknowledgment that universal truth criteria and truths might be found is a condition of the possibility of such conversations occurring.[158]

Notice that I characterize universal affirmations not as foundations for conversation, that is, not as convictions on which people must agree before they begin. Instead, they are goals of dialogue and thought—what people must work toward and seek to discover if they wish to really understand one other. Universal affirmations, in other words, are eschatological; though they are not yet fully articulated, many are already expressed well enough that people can begin operating by them and through them be drawn toward the future.

In theology, all genuine universal affirmations have this character. Though they seek to express reality as well as possible in the present, they are open to fuller, fu-

---

Them?" in *Anabaptists and Postmodernity*, ed. Susan Biesecker-Mast and Gerald Biesecker-Mast (Telford, Penn.: Pandora, 2000), pp. 82-85.

[158]This general line of critique of relativism can be found in Jürgen Habermas; see Bernstein, *Beyond Objectivism*, pp. 182-97; and Stephen White, *The Recent Work of Jürgen Habermas* (New York: Cambridge University Press, 1988), pp. 22-24, 40-65.

ture clarification, confirmation or disconfirmation. They do not seek to freeze the meanings of their founding kerygmatic events in the present but to channel them from the past toward the future.[159] In this way theological affirmations do not simply describe reality. By pointing forward and transmitting a dynamism forward, they, like evangelistic affirmations, participate in changing it.

In light of postmodern challenges, I am considering the theoretical issue of whether universal affirmations are possible. However, the practical missional question—whether attempts to make them are imperialistic—has been in the background. I respond: to counter imperialism and other global evils and affirm the value of all particular cultures, the possibility of such affirmations must be presupposed and steps toward making them must be taken. We have seen pluralistic theologians reject universal Christian assertions to avoid supporting Western imperialism—but then replace them not only with other universals but ones which endorse Western cultural expansion in a new religious guise. A theology concerned with global mission cannot avoid attempts to frame universal affirmations. But it must derive them differently.

2. If people everywhere can aspire toward universal affirmations, we now ask, Might they share some common awareness of God? Might such an awareness be salvific? And in any case, What bearing would it have on universal evangelistic affirmations?

Nearly all historic Anabaptists agreed that an internal or external law of nature, conscience or some similar source bestowed common ethical and social sensitivity on everyone. Some Anabaptists believed that positive response to this source could lead toward or even into salvation.

The biblical text they cited most was Romans 2:14-16: what the Jewish law requires is written on all Gentile hearts, and some who follow it will be "excused" at the final judgment. John 1:4, which calls the Word "the light of all people," also appeared frequently, especially in Denck. Other oft-mentioned passages identified some aspects of God known through nature: eternal power and deity (Rom 1:20), glory and creative skill (Ps 19:1-4), God's providence, experienced through nature's abundance (Acts 14:17), the One in whom "we live and move and have our being" (Acts 17:28). Let me add that Proverbs and Ecclesiastes, which contain sayings paralleled in other ancient Near Eastern literature, indicate that various moral and religious truths are somewhat widely known.

Citing such passages, some Christian theologies have articulated a fairly specific body of natural law, allegedly known by everyone, and sanctioned it as a basis for civil law and also theology. Many such theologies, however, add that salvific aware-

---

[159]Cf. pt. 8 p. 98.

ness of God must be bestowed by supernatural grace.[160] However, it is difficult to extract specific contents from texts like those above. While they affirm that all people possess some God-awareness along with ethical and social values, they leave open the possibility that the content of these might vary, perhaps widely, in different persons and cultures.[161]

Moreover, Scripture most often portrays general human God-awareness as seriously distorted (e.g., Rom 3:11; 2 Cor 4:4, Eph 2:1-3). And though such awareness might indeed come through other religions, the Bible regards these mostly as perversions.[162]

It appears, then, that while Scripture affirms some kind of universal God and social-ethical awareness apart from knowledge of Jesus, it provides no warrant for designating specific religions or moral codes, or aspects of them, as regular, salvific paths to God. In other words, I find no real biblical basis for strong inclusivism, for maintaining, for example, that the Word's internal work (Denck), the "Gospel of all Creatures" or natural awareness of good (Marpeck) regularly provide channels to salvation.

On the other hand, the Bible portrays God- and social-ethical consciousness as widespread enough that God might occasionally draw people toward or into salvation through them. Scripture, of course, does not guarantee that this happens. Once again, most texts that affirm this consciousness stress that most people do not follow it (Jn 1:10-11; Acts 14:11-18; 17:22-34; Rom 1:18-23; 2:14-16). Yet all this seems compatible with modest inclusivism: God bestows salvation through other means than specific confession of Jesus, although theology cannot specify these.

Modest inclusivism is supported by texts affirming God's will that all people be saved.[163] From these one can argue that if God desires everyone's salvation and many never hear of Jesus or only a distorted version of him,[164] won't God provide them some other (epistemological) channel to salvation, as Hubmaier apparently

---

[160]Preeminently, Catholic theology, beginning with Aquinas (1225-1274). Menno employed natural law as a technical term. So did Marpeck, along with the natural-supernatural distinction.

[161]Cf. Thomas Finger, *Christian Theology* (Scottdale, Penn.: Herald, 1985), 1:248-55.

[162]E.g., Ps 96:5; Is 45:20-21, I Thess 1:9. The issue becomes more complex with Jews, who possess much of the same revelation as Christians. Many Old Testament saints who knew only part of it attained salvation of some kind. Judaism, then, might possibly provide some discernible channels toward salvation (cf. McClendon, *Systematic Theology* 2: 360-65; Friesen, *Artists, Citizens, Philosophers*, pp. 273-74).

[163]E.g., Jn 12:31; 2 Cor 5:15; 2 Pet 3:9; cf. Sanders, *What About Those*, pp. 21-55.

[164]Theologians often discuss those who have never heard. But what of those to whom Jesus is drastically misrepresented? Aren't those who are, say, enslaved in Jesus' name but know nothing else significant about him at least as unreached? Might they, when they oppose what they think is Christian, be closer to Jesus than those who badly represent him? Sattler and Menno found the impression of Jesus conveyed by false Christians more misleading than no impression, which characterized "the Turks."

insisted? The logic sounds cogent. But are there biblical indications that this actually occurs?

If biblical narrative points toward Jesus, then people like Abraham, Sarah and Moses attained a salvation derived ultimately from him. Yet while these looked forward to God's promise of salvation (Heb 11), they could hardly have known specifics about Jesus. Within the Bible, then, a significant group appears whose salvation flowed from Jesus ontologically, even though they attained it, epistemologically, apart from explicit faith in his historical existence. This group included some beyond Israel, such as Melchizedek (Gen 14:18-20; Heb 7:17), the widow in Elijah's time (1 Kings 17) and Naaman (2 Kings 5).

In light of this major biblical theme and of God's universal salvific will, I find it valid to assume that salvation is bestowed, at least occasionally, on some people apart from specific confession of Jesus of Nazareth.[165]

To be sure, this (universal) theological affirmation is vague. Human curiosity presses on: how does this actually happen? Through what religions, beliefs, actions, rituals will it most likely occur? Anabaptists, indeed, identified some possibilities: natural law or conscience (Schiemer, Marpeck, Dirk, perhaps Hubmaier); inwardly, through the Word (Denck); outwardly, through a Gospel of the creatures (Hut, Schlaffer). Channels like these at times operate through other religions. But I see no way to specify, even very generally, how and when God might use which.

The main point, in biblical and Anabaptist perspective, is that God always wills to save and works in some way in all cultures. Christian mission, then, should be sensitive to every culture and its particularities, to discern where God might already be working, as Yoder recommends. Further answers as to how this might occur can be gleaned only as postmodernists stress: from involvement in specific contexts, and not extended much beyond them. If anyone wants to know more, become involved in mission and go look!

3. Theology can affirm (universally) that all people possess some God awareness and that God works through this in various ways, salvifically at times. This means that evangelism is best done by whole communities involved in the lives of particular cultures and includes dialogue through which they learn from and wit-

---

[165]Some forms of exclusivism make this possible for people who never hear of Jesus during their lives. According to one, most often found in Catholicism, Jesus appears to everyone at death (see Sanders, *No Other Name*, pp. 164-67). For this I find no biblical support. Another, popular in Eastern Orthodoxy, grants all people a chance to decide at Jesus' return, when they are raised. While I have not explored this view, it could perhaps be supported by eschatological considerations (cf. John Meyendorff, *Byzantine Theology* [New York: Fordham, 1983], p. 222; Sanders *No Other Name*, pp. 177-214; Thomas Finger, "Response to Miroslav Volf: 'The Final Reconciliation,' " presentation to the Evangelical Theology Group, American Academy of Religion [Boston: November 20, 1999]).

ness to others (McClendon, Friesen, Yoder). Evangelism will normally begin not with universal affirmations, however valid, but by searching for clues of God's prior activity. This process, however, will be guided by and include direct expression of the kerygma.

While I have argued that universal affirmations are possible, even unavoidable, I have said little about evangelistic claims themselves or whether they might function imperialistically. Might announcing Jesus as sole Savior and Lord portray him as a super emperor, sanctioning earthly rulers and systems, as Kaufman complains? Obviously, mission's links with Western and other kinds of domination show that it can.

Nevertheless, any genuine call to turn decisively to the new creation implicitly critiques all ideologies dominating the old creation, especially imperialistic ones. Anabaptist evangelism can largely affirm postmodern criticisms of imperialism. Perhaps surprisingly, this is evident in that very phrase that has functioned so objectionably: Jesus Christ is Lord. It originally summarized the earliest Christians' faith.[166] When understood in light of Jesus' actual history, a sharp contrast emerges between his lordship and all others (cf. I Cor 8:5-6).

Jesus' lordship can be called kenotic: the lordship of one who

emptied *[ekenōsen]* himself,
　taking the form of a slave,
　being born in human likeness.
And . . .
　humbled himself
　and became obedient to the point of death—
　even death on a cross. (Phil 2:7-8)

It is the lordship of one who became a servant, who poured himself out, even for his enemies (Rom 5:10), of one who identified with the humble and downtrodden, who implacably opposed the forces of pride, violence, injustice and inequality. It is a lordship that does not domineer over its subjects but gives itself utterly for their sakes (Mk 10:42-45).

Consequently, this Lord is opposed to all oppressive cultural, political and ideological forces that claim universal or ultimate allegiance. To come under Jesus' lordship is to be liberated from all claims of these would-be lords. To accept this universal Truth is to reject the appalling spectrum of dominations that dress themselves up as universal truths; it is to receive the God who became a self-giving servant; and, indwelt by love, it is to become ourselves such servants to others,

---

[166]Rom 10:9; I Cor 8:6; Phil 2:9-11. Cullmann identified these and found early affirmations of Jesus as Son of God virtually equivalent (Acts 8:37; Rom 1:14; Heb 4:14; I Jn 4:15; see Oscar Cullmann, *The Earliest Christian Confessions* [London: Lutterworth, 1949]).

through lifestyles that challenge all oppressive powers. To celebrate postmodern particularity to the point of neglecting this Truth's universal critique of these powers (e.g., unrestrained consumerism) is to facilitate their full sway.

Since a theology stressing divine kenosis promotes such a lifestyle, it need not, to counter globalization's imperialistic dynamisms, reject transcendent religious affirmations and search elsewhere for some notion of "humanization" or "liberation." Jesus' servantlike path provides a rich, though paradoxical, "structural model" for true humanization.[167] This paradigm cannot really be derived from bio-history and then adding Jesus at the end. Bio-history, with its pervasive evolutionary conflict, is not really supplemented or heightened but largely reversed by Jesus' way.[168]

Such a lordship, moreover, enables true cultural pluralism to flourish. By destroying the absolutist pretensions of all national, ethnic or social values and institutions, it frees many of them to be what they truly are: admirable, valuable, finite expressions of different human particularities. Desacralized in this way, they can still help specific peoples form their identities, though without sharply opposing others', and even offer enrichment to others.[169]

Because humility and servanthood are central to this lordship, it cannot be imposed on top of cultures by leaders. Its dynamism circulates within them through communities who live and work there, along lines of contact and dialogue with other ordinary folks in ordinary activities. To express and witness to this kenotic lordship, these communities must appreciate their culture's particularities and seek to discern God's work in its midst. They will indeed verbalize the kerygma, but sensitively, realizing that it can be misheard many ways, especially given its historic ties with imperialism. Rightly expressed and heard, this kenotic universal will forbid rather than encourage bigotry and discrimination against different beliefs and practices.

Some theologians, however, suggest that this kenosis notion is not uniquely Christian but might help unite religions. Masao Abe, a Buddhist, affirms the classic kenosis text (Phil 2:5-11) for expressing "a complete abnegation of Christ as the Son of God. . . [T]he Son of God abandoned his divine substance. . . . Christ's kenosis signifies . . . a radical and total self-abnegation of the Son of God."[170] Sim-

---

[167]Jon Sobrino, *The True Church and the Poor* (Maryknoll, N.Y.: Orbis, 1984), pp. 128-29.

[168]For my critique of deriving Christian ethics more or less from evolutionary history, see Thomas Finger, *Self, Earth and Society* (Downers Grove, Ill.: InterVarsity Press, 1997), pp. 158-92 (covering Rosemary Ruether, Sallie McFague, Jay McDaniel, John Cobb, Charles Birch, Teilhard de Chardin, Matthew Fox, Thomas Berry and Brian Swimme).

[169]See esp. C. Shenk, *Who Do You Say that I Am?*

[170]John Cobb and Christopher Ives, eds., *The Emptying God* (Maryknoll, N.Y.: Orbis, 1990), pp. 9-10; cf. Paul Knitter and Roger Corliss, eds., *Buddhist Emptiness and Christian Trinity* (New York: Paulist Press, 1990).

ilarly, Kaufman likens Jesus' weakness, or suffering on the cross, to the Buddhist *sunyata* (often translated "emptiness"). Both cross and *sunyata* convey "that which is utterly unsubstantial, that which does not maintain itself successfully through time and is thus not a 'thing' or 'substance,' that which . . . sacrifices itself to its context and to that beyond itself" as the ultimate point of reference.[171]

These interpretations, however, evaporate the rich paradox at the heart of Philippians 2:5-11. Its hymnic structure descends from the heights of deity, with Christ "in the form of God" (v. 6) to the lowest possible abasement, "even death on a cross" (v. 8) and then back to the cosmos' apex: "God highly exalted him and gave him the name that is above every name" (v. 9).[172]

Such celebrations of Jesus' resurrection do not replace a humble man with some tyrannical emperor symbol, as Kaufman charges. Instead, they present an exceedingly rich, unfathomable paradox. The very eternal deity became the execrated slave. Yet this was hardly "complete abnegation" of his divinity or becoming "utterly unsubstantial." For he remained the same One, so that the humility of the cross is now the most significant power in the cosmos.

Such a reading calls people, just as paradoxically, to a servanthood not of passivity and self-denigration but of proactive witness for justice and peace. This is energized by the Spirit who raised Jesus and who, through the kerygma, sets people on this path.[173] In contrast, while I admire Masao Abe's wrestling with the kenosis text, his construal and Kaufman's are far too one-sided. They absorb any transcendent, personal deity into the world. But if the world is no longer challenged by a truly divine Other, it is difficult to see how this text can elicit a discipleship that strongly challenges the status quo.

4. In summary, since the new creation is distinct from the old, it will, in its missional dimension, call people to a distinct way of life. Evangelism highlights this distinctiveness, with its call to turn decisively from the old to the new. The old creation is dominated by allegiance to finite institutions, peoples and values that falsely claim ultimate, universally valid lordship. Evangelism has been co-opted by some of these at times, most notably by modern, Western values and movements, many of them now extended through globalization.

The new creation will be good news for all people only if it provides alternative

---

[171]Kaufman, *God—Mystery—Diversity*, p. 149.

[172]McClendon, *Systematic Theology* 2: 266-69; Nancey Murphy and George Ellis, *On the Moral Nature of the Universe* (Minneapolis: Fortress, 1996), pp. 176-78; and perhaps John Howard Yoder, *Preface to Theology* (Grand Rapids: Brazos, 2002), pp. 80-88, interpret "form of God" as God's image, which Adam possessed; it indicates Jesus' humanity, not prehuman divine status. For careful exegesis, see pp. 402-6 below.

[173]McClendon, *Systematic Theology* 2:432-34.

values and transforming energy of worldwide or universal range. Its evangelists, accordingly, will express universal affirmations as well as they can, realizing that these always point toward the eschatological future. If church mission fails to provide these and simply affirms cultural particularities, the dominion of spurious universals over all particular peoples will increase. Their power will be unmasked and broken only by a radically different universal power, identified by the affirmation: "Jesus Christ is Lord."

Jesus' lordship is radically different because it is kenotic. Churches cannot represent this in any culture without respecting that culture's particularities, learning from it dialogically and searching for indications of the new creation's activity, as Yoder proposes. They will verbalize the kerygma, with its universal claims, as intelligibly and concretely as possible. Evangelism will not be detachedly spiritual but another sacramental embodiment of divine reality through physical activities.[174]

In other words, mission's call to distinctness, through evangelism, will be heard only as mission involves itself in society—as it makes contact with many social structures, activities and leaders, and the new creation affects them more broadly. How might Anabaptist theology, as it seeks to assist mission, illumine this wider interaction?

CHURCH AND WORLD

The first section of this chapter, "Evangelism," proposed that a mission theology that draws on historic Anabaptism must consider evangelism. The theology developed there highlighted evangelism and conversion, as do today's evangelicals. To be sure, it devoted greater attention to community formation and behavioral transformation than some. Still, it may seem that this theology, like many evangelical ones, dealt far less with social transformation, a major concern of ecumenicals.

Indeed, Anabaptists have often stressed distinctness from the world in social affairs. Initially, severe persecution was clearly a reason. But if we look more closely, might historic Anabaptist attitudes display some variety? I will explore the issue chiefly through the lens of this question. Whatever the results, however, historic Anabaptism does not provide my theological norm. I will then turn to Scripture to determine how an Anabaptist mission theology might address today's social, economic and political megaforces, including those driving and opposing globalization. I will chiefly ask whether theology can identify some basic patterns in such church-world interaction.

---

[174]Cf. Neal Blough, "Messianic Mission and Ethics," in *The Transfiguration of Mission*, ed. Wilbert Shenk (Scottdale, Penn.: Herald, 1993), pp. 187, 189.

Over the last half century Anabaptists have been increasingly involved in society. I will construct my view with the help of three: Norman Kraus, who connects church-world concerns with those of evangelism; Duane Friesen, who is perhaps investigating the most facets of this issue in the greatest depth; and to help draw these reflections together, once again I will examine Ron Kraybill's theology of conflict transformation.[175]

Historic Anabaptist Perspectives

Anabaptists probably shook sociopolitical life most palpably by forming illegal churches and refusing to participate in violence. If they did not consider these direct challenges to the social order, governments surely did. Anabaptists were usually persecuted for treason, not heresy. Their outlook on society appeared most often in encounters with and discussions of the state, particularly its lethal power, the sword. Since these were recorded in trials, letters and other popular sources, I will consult them as well as Anabaptist leaders' writings.

Switzerland. I. Anabaptism's rise challenged the state. By protesting the tithe and asking to appoint their own pastors, Simon Stumpf's and Wilhelm Reublin's rural congregations challenged the Zurich government, which controlled both.[176] Conrad Grebel opposed Zurich's rulers on tithes, protested usury and reportedly threatened council members with destruction if they hindered the gospel.[177] In late 1523 he, Stumpf and Felix Mantz proposed formation of a pure state church. They expected most citizens to join and elect a new council to rule collaboratively with the church.[178] Only when they perceived that Zwingli was entrusting church reform to an unregenerate council did they abandon this hope and form a separated church.[179]

---

[175]Cf. pp. 225-26 above.

[176]Cf. chap. 2. Stumpf may not yet have embraced pacifism, for the Zurich Council charged him with inciting self-defensive action and iconoclasm (James Stayer, *Anabaptism and the Sword*, 2nd ed. [Lawrence, Kan.: Coronado Press, 1976], p. xii; Leland Harder, ed., *The Sources of Swiss Anabaptism* [Scottdale, Penn.: Herald, 1985], p. 233). According to Zwingli, Stumpf advocated killing priests (Harder, *Sources of Swiss Anabaptism*, p. 437). At about this time Zwingli opposed interest and usury (ibid., p. 217), and favored sharing goods (ibid., p. 210): views of the state like those Anabaptists would adopt.

[177]Harder, *Sources of Swiss Anabaptism*, pp. 203, 220, 227, 177.

[178]Ibid., pp. 276-77.

[179]When Stumpf protested at the Second Disputation (October 1523) that Zwingli was entrusting the council with abolishing the Mass but had no authority to do so, Zwingli answered that he was not. The council would not "decide about God's word" but only "the most appropriate way for this to be done without an uproar." When Stumpf declared that he would "teach and act against" any decision contrary to God's, Zwingli replied that he would too (ibid., p. 242).

As Anabaptism radiated out from Zurich, varied attitudes toward government emerged. When St. Gall allowed preaching and baptism, Grebel may have hoped that its rulers, headed by his brother-in-law Vadian, would officially establish Anabaptism. (He may have entertained similar goals for Schaffhausen.)[180] Yet Vadian soon adopted Zwingli's hard line.[181] Elsewhere, Anabaptism spread in close connection with peasant unrest. Peasants pledged to protect Reublin, Johannes Broetli and Hans Kruesi by arms. At Hallau, where most citizens accepted baptism, an assembly refused to pay tithes and troops cooperated with peasant armies.[182] At least through 1525, various Anabaptist approaches to the state and sword were circulating.

During that year, however, Anabaptists were often accused of seeking to abolish government, denying that Christians could be a rulers and sedition.[183] While rejecting the first and third charges, they accepted the second. The sharp church-state distinction which this implied crystallized in the Schleitheim Confession's dualism between "the world and those who are come out of the world," neither of which "will have part with the other."[184] This meant that the sword could only be "an ordering of God outside the perfection of Christ."[185] Though it protected the good, wielding it was completely opposed to Jesus' way and impossible for Christians. Christians, in fact, should avoid all "disputes and strife about worldly matters," especially legal ones, and taking civil oaths. Their citizenship was not in the world but in heaven; they judged things by the Spirit, not the flesh.[186] Accordingly, even though Michael Sattler could call the judges who tried him "servants of God," he could not accept the validity of any legal process.[187]

Despite the varied approaches to the state in Swiss proto- and early Anabaptism, Schleitheim's dualism soon became normative.

2. Balthasar Hubmaier meanwhile was guiding an Anabaptist reformation in Waldshut, one of only three locales where Anabaptism came to power legally—along with Nicholsburg, Moravia, where Hubmaier also would preside, and Münster. Hubmaier promoted peasant political aims and welcomed the protection provided Waldshut by peasant and Zurich militias.[188] Unlike other Anabaptists, save

---

[180]Stayer, *Anabaptism and the Sword,* p. xxii.

[181]Harder, *Sources of Swiss Anabaptism,* pp. 359-76, 378-85.

[182]Stayer, *Anabaptism and the Sword,* p. 109-10.

[183]Harder, *Sources of Swiss Anabaptism,* pp. 345, 375, 340, 387, 437-39.

[184]Sattler, *Legacy of Michael Sattler,* p. 38; cf. chap. 2.

[185]Ibid., p. 39.

[186]Ibid., pp. 40-42, 70, cf. p. 38.

[187]Ibid., pp. 70, 74.

[188]Cf. chap. 2. Jacob Gross, however, left Waldshut because he refused to support peasant armies. Yet later at Strasbourg he stood guard and carried a spear, though he refused to kill (Stayer, *Anabaptism and the Sword,* pp. 107-8, 186).

revolutionaries, Hubmaier defended government's use of the sword.

His deepest reason was perhaps soteriological. Whereas salvation for almost all non-Swiss Anabaptists involved divinization, Hubmaier insisted that "we become members of Christ in faith, not in nature."[189] While most Anabaptists thought that their true citizenship, consequently, was in heaven, Hubmaier countered that the kingdom of the world "clings to us until death," so that "we are stuck in it right up to our ears."[190] This was largely because the flesh remained so opposed to God that sometimes even Christians needed the discipline connected with the sword.[191]

In other words, despite his strong ethical emphasis, Hubmaier did not believe in so thorough a personal transformation as most other Anabaptists. This apparently allowed him to accept more people for baptism and to suppose, like Grebel and Stumpf early on, that they might become a majority in a state and participate in its government. Significantly, many proto-Hutterites who rejected his ministry in Nicholsburg complained that he allowed too many unprepared people into the congregation.

While Hubmaier was less optimistic than most Anabaptists about the ordinary Christian's transformation, he was more optimistic about rulers' possibilities. Christian officials were able to punish without hatred, but only from love, though with sad hearts.[192] Christians should not avoid governing, for they make the best rulers—though they should not seek this difficult task.[193] Christians could also be judges and enforce verdicts, even though they should not sue.[194] Christians should fight when governments ask, though wars of conquest are wrong.[195]

Although Austria executed Hubmaier for sedition at Waldshut, he normally stressed great deference to authorities. Obedience to them was pledged in his Lord's Supper ritual.[196] Hubmaier could encourage Christians to suffer under oppressive governments as their cross or punishment for their sins.[197] He often denounced rebellion and distanced himself from Hut's revolutionary tendencies.[198] Yet Hubmaier also implied that bad governments might in some cases be legitimately deposed.[199] Like many other Anabaptists and Reformers, he often critiqued unjust rulers.

Given his practice at Waldshut and Nicholsburg, Hubmaier doubtless pro-

---

[189]Hubmaier, *Balthasar Hubmaier,* p. 519.

[190]Ibid., p. 497.

[191]Ibid., p. 519, cf. pp. 433-34; cf. pp. 211-12 above.

[192]Ibid., pp. 511, 515, 518.

[193]Ibid., pp. 98, 152, 498, 510, 517.

[194]Ibid., pp. 502-3, 507.

[195]Ibid., p. 517.

[196]Ibid., p. 403.

[197]Ibid., pp. 304, 506.

[198]Ibid., p. 560.

[199]Ibid., p. 521.

moted some church-state cooperation. He regarded God's Word as authoritative over the latter.[200] Yet he also distinguished their spheres, as did many other Anabaptists and Reformers, by allotting temporal affairs to the state and the soul to the church.[201] The state existed chiefly to protect the good and punish the evil—though it could, when necessary, claim citizens' lives and goods.[202]

Yet Hubmaier could also insist that "the world . . . hates life and light and loves darkness" and that the "kingdom of this world" is one of "sin, death and hell."[203] His own experience bitterly testified that governments usually served this kingdom. To be sure, Hubmaier promoted far more Christian participation in government, and implicitly other spheres of society, than the Swiss after Schleitheim. Yet he still admitted some sharp conflict between the church and the "world."

South Germany-Austria. I. Hubmaier sought to assure Ferdinand of Austria that his politics diverged sharply from Hans Hut's.[204] Hut appealed to the social hopes and thirst for vengeance aroused by the Peasants' War. Though he professed, at his trial, that he had taught obedience to government (and his converts backed him up), Hut had also allowed that when Christ returned to slay the wicked, Christians could unsheathe their swords. Hut also affirmed that Christians could be rulers and, in that capacity, employ lethal force.[205]

Hut's vision of the new creation involved sweeping social transformations. Humans, released from creaturely attachments through sharing in Jesus' crucifixion, would be freed "from injustice . . . and our misuse of the creatures."[206] Lust for possessions, the major source of inequality, poverty and strife, would be uprooted this way. Hut's converts implemented this immediately through sharing possessions—though this, he claimed at his trial, was voluntary, not mandated. The baptized were to live nonviolently in covenanted fellowships until Christ's return. Hut, however, apparently thought this too imminent to consider whether churches might have long-term relationships to the world.

---

[200]Ibid., p. 43.

[201]Ibid., pp. 519, 559.

[202]Ibid., pp. 522, 558.

[203]Ibid., pp. 86, 496-97.

[204]Ibid., p. 560.

[205]Stayer, *Anabaptism and the Sword*, pp. 154-58. Hut also taught (he claimed at his trial) that God did not forbid taking oaths or perhaps even some forms of military service. But I find the latter statement vague (Christian Meyer, ed., *Zur Geschichte der Widertaeufer in Oberschwaben, Teil I. Die Anfaenge der Wiedertaeufertum in Augsburg, in Zeitschrift des Historischen Vereins fuer Schwaben und Neuberg I* (1874), pp. 227-28; cf. Deppermann, *Melchior Hoffman*, p. 202; and pp. 521-23, note 53. Influenced somewhat by Hut, Anabaptists in Esslingen, central Germany, mixed pacifist and nonpacifist concerns from 1527-1544 (Stayer, *Anabaptism and the Sword*, pp. 159-61).

[206]Hut, "On the Mystery of Baptism," p. 70.

Hans Denck's remarks were occasional and perhaps paradoxical. He sometimes indicated that no Christian could use force or rule and sometimes that perhaps a Christian might.[207] Denck critiqued both poor and rich for grasping after wealth rather than preparing their hearts through *Gelassenheit* for Christ's filling.

Hans Schlaffer conceded that a rare ruler, through special grace, might become Christian. But he did not indicate whether such a person might continue governing.[208] Schlaffer acknowledged that some taxes were for the common good.[209] Like Hubmaier he insisted that political power extends only to bodies, not souls, and to punishing evil and protecting good. Apparently unlike Hubmaier, he added that it is unneeded in Christ's kingdom, where social distinctions cease.[210]

Leonhard Schiemer sharply contrasted allegiance to Christ as Lord with the allegiance most people grant to earthly lords.[211] He critiqued nobles who fleeced the poor mercilessly, supported by false prophets who promised forgiveness without repentance.[212] Schiemer and Schlaffer seem to have separated the church and whatever social transformation it heralds rather sharply from worldly government and society, but less so than the Schleitheim Swiss.

2. Peter Riedemann viewed government more negatively, even though he affirmed that God instituted it out of grace to preserve humankind and that the more obedient one is to it (with certain exceptions to be noted) the more obedient one is to God.[213] In general, however, Riedemann bifurcated state from church by regarding the first as the product of God's wrath and curse. Since Christ redeemed people from these, his followers had nothing to do with the state.[214]

Clearly, then, no Christian could be a ruler,[215] as Schleitheim also said. Rulers could become Christians only by divesting themselves of their glory as Christ did,

---

[207]Denck, *Spiritual Legacy of Hans Denck*, pp. 199-201; Stayer, *Anabaptism and the Sword*, pp. 148-50.

[208]Schlaffer, "Instructions on Beginning," p. 106; contra Stayer, who infers from this remark that Schlaffer "believed that Christian government was possible, if unusual" (*Anabaptism and the Sword*, p. 58).

[209]Schlaffer, *Selections*, p. 199.

[210]Schlaffer, "Instructions on Beginning," pp. 106, 109.

[211]Schiemer, "Three Kinds of Grace," p. 93.

[212]Schiemer, "Apostles' Creed," p. 215.

[213]Riedemann, *Peter Riedemann's Hutterite Confession*, pp. 130-31, 213.

[214]Ibid., pp. 130, 133, 223, 225. Though government was appointed by God the Father, "it must remain in Christ. Otherwise, the Son would be against the Father" (ibid., p. 220). Luther identified the Son's way with God's proper work, which was nonviolent. But by separating it from God's alien work, which included the sword, he allowed Christians to wield the latter. Riedemann sought to avoid that implication but allowed that the Father appoints some things "in Christ" and others "apart from Christ" (ibid.).

[215]Ibid., pp. 133, 223.

thereby ceasing to cleave to created things. This would involve renouncing their offices, for when Christ works in people, "he causes them to do nothing but what he himself did . . . on earth."[216]

Riedemann detected a certain appropriate logic underlying government's institution and operations. Since humans turned from God to the flesh, God allowed the flesh, through government, to rule them. Further, when a people became very wicked, God gave it very wicked rulers—and conversely gave very wicked rulers very wicked peoples—so that they destroyed each other.[217] Though subjects should not rebel against evil rulers, God allowed this to happen to punish rulers for their sins, especially when they became imperialistic.[218]

Like most Anabaptists, Hutterites neither took oaths nor went to court; Christians should suffer wrong rather than sue.[219] Yet more than most Anabaptists, Riedemann allowed obedience to authorities to be qualified when they exercised not God's office but their own, particularly when they transgressed conscience, which is responsible to God alone.[220]

This meant that Christians should resist not only decrees harming the church, as all Anabaptists affirmed, but also taxes for war, which most Anabaptists denied.[221] Riedemann further distinguished annual taxes, which should be paid, from ad hoc levies for greedy purposes, which should not. Christians need not submit to governments' "every whim," but give only what is truly due. This did not, however, sanction withholding legitimate taxes because they were badly spent.[222]

Though Hutterites withdrew further from society than other Anabaptists, this hardly distanced them from social and economic questions. Their project of an alternative, self-sufficient community demanded very creative thinking about these issues. Hutterites sought to serve their neighbors—whether fellow communalists or outsiders—by making all variety of useful things. They became self-sufficient in clothing (but avoided ostentatious styles). While they declined to manufacture weapons, they produced knives and axes, though they acknowledged that these could be misused.[223]

Hutterites had neither inns nor innkeepers. Yet they offered hospitality to all

---

[216]Ibid., pp. 133-34, 217-18, 222.

[217]Ibid., pp. 131-32.

[218]Ibid., pp. 216, 226.

[219]Ibid., pp. 138-43, 204-12.

[220]Ibid., pp. 130-31, 225.

[221]Ibid., pp. 110, 225.

[222]Ibid., pp. 136, 227; Rom 13:7.

[223]Ibid., pp. 137-38.

travelers who asked.[224] They rejected trading—that is, buying and then selling for profit—arguing that it made things more expensive for the poor.[225] Instead, Hutterites worked with their hands, and their products were in high demand in surrounding areas. While they were often accused of withdrawing from society, they were seeking to forge a "polity for the whole world."[226]

3. A wealthy political and industrial leader before his conversion and a highly competent city engineer afterward, Pilgram Marpeck provided a different church-world model. Soon after his conversion Marpeck probably visited the Hutterites. A tract sometimes thought to be proto-Hutterite probably came from him. It identified inordinate grasping for earthly goods with the origin of property, and the desire to protect property with the origin of government. It concluded that people who ask the state to protect their property must assist it in guarding all property by force.[227]

We have seen how Pilgram sought to aid the refugees in Strasbourg without government approval (chap. 2). Yet while he often criticized the state, he mainly meant to deny its authority over the church, not to exclude all Christians from it.[228] He must have taken oaths required for civil service in Strasbourg and elsewhere,[229] even though disagreement over other oaths and city defense provoked his banishment.[230]

Marpeck affirmed some common Anabaptist principles: for example, Christ alone, and no magistrate, is ruler and lord; government authority extends only to earthly matters, not Christ's kingdom, whose members have citizenship in heaven.[231] Echoing Riedemann, he called rulers unclean vessels of wrath.[232]

Yet as already intimated, Marpeck was less dualistic than the Hutterites or Schleitheim. He maintained that rulers possessed a wisdom for their office that citizens

[224]Ibid., pp. 149-50.

[225]Ibid., p. 149.

[226]Ulrich Stadler, "Cherished Instructions on Sin, Excommunication, and the Community of Goods," in *Spiritual and Anabaptist Writers*, ed. George Williams and Angel Mergal (Philadelphia: Westminster Press, 1957), p. 278.

[227]Pilgram Marpeck, "Exposé of the Babylonian Whore," in *Later Writings by Pilgram Marpeck and His Circle*, ed. Walter Klaassen, Werner Packull, and John Rempel, trans. Walter Klaassen (Kitchener, Ont.: Pandora, 1999), pp. 30-31. For discussion of the authorship of the "Exposé," see pp. 22-23; Stayer, *Anabaptism and the Sword*, pp. 171-72; Werner Packull, *Mysticism and the Early South German-Austrian Anabaptists* (Scottdale, Penn.: Herald, 1977), pp. 150-51; "Research Note: Pilgram Marpeck's Uncovering of the Babylonian Whore and Other Anonymous Anabaptist Tracts," *MQR* 67, no. 3 (1993); *Hutterite Beginnings* (Baltimore: Johns Hopkins University Press, 1995), pp. 136-37.

[228]Marpeck, *Writings of Pilgram Marpeck*, pp. 151, 539-41; Stayer, *Anabaptism and the Sword*, pp. 178-79.

[229]Stephen Boyd, *Pilgram Marpeck* (Durham, N.C.: Duke University Press, 1992), p. 53; cf. pp. 56, 58, 93, 112, 137, 142, 164.

[230]Marpeck, *Writings of Pilgram Marpeck*, p. 306.

[231]Ibid., pp. 149-52, 538-39.

[232]Ibid., p. 446.

of heaven lacked and should not seek to emulate.[233] Government, further, had been established not simply to "restrain evil and protect the good" but, more subtly, to mediate between them in a fashion that promoted rest and peace.[234] Stephen Boyd suggests that Marpeck "endorsed a critical participation in the use of force."[235] Stayer includes "perhaps even police and military service, short of taking" life.[236] However, while Marpeck affirmed Christian participation in government's socially beneficial functions, I find no real evidence that he included coercive ones.

So far, our search for different Anabaptist understandings of the church-world relationship has found Schleitheim and the Hutterites sharply separating the two. The earliest Swiss, Hubmaier and Marpeck, however, all proposed different models, and the earliest South German-Austrians perhaps hinted at others.

The Netherlands. I. Like all Anabaptists, Melchior Hoffman initially taught that the sword existed to punish evil. It had no authority over the church, which followed Jesus' suffering way.[237] Yet Hoffman, with his apocalyptic preoccupations, expected things to change soon. He introduced a theme not found so far, except somewhat in Hubmaier, which Dutch Anabaptism never fully renounced: the pious magistrate who would further the Christian cause. Such a ruler might outlaw false religion if necessary and even hold church membership.[238]

Such magistrates figured in Hoffman's various apocalyptic schemes. For instance, the Holy Roman Empire, the dragon that granted the pope power (cf. Rev 13), would attack the saints, but two pious kings would protect them.[239] The persecuted saints would gather in an elect city—Strasbourg for Hoffman, Münster for later Melchiorites—whose magistrates would play a similar role. Anabaptists would dig trenches and stand guard duty but not fight.[240]

Overall, Hoffman affirmed a general church-state separation and nonretaliatory suffering. Yet Melchiorites focused not on governments' precise relationships with the church, but on what end-time roles each one might play—especially, which one might champion the saints?

During imprisonment in Strasbourg, Hoffman briefly endorsed the notion that after Christians had been persecuted, a Christian military victory would initiate an

---

[233]Ibid., p. 558.

[234]Ibid., pp. 537-38.

[235]Boyd, *Pilgrim Marpeck*, p. 163.

[236]Stayer, *Anabaptism and the Sword*, p. 167.

[237]Ibid., pp. 214-15.

[238]Ibid., pp. 215-16; Deppermann, *Melchior Hoffman*, pp. 263-64.

[239]Stayer, *Anabaptism and the Sword*, p. 219, cf. Deppermann, *Melchior Hoffman*, p. 264.

[240]Deppermann, *Melchior Hoffman*, p. 161.

earthly theocratic interregnum to precede Christ's return.[241] Though he soon dropped this idea, it temporarily supported the Münster effort to bring in God's kingdom violently. Even Hut, who envisioned Christians eventually unsheathing the sword, had postponed this until the parousia.

2. Münster was the third, and last, city where Anabaptists assumed power through legal channels (after Hubmaier's Waldshut and Nicholsburg). This granted its leaders the right, according to Hoffman's theology (and, it would seem, most Anabaptists') to wield the sword. When the Catholic bishop's troops threatened, Münster's leaders argued that they were legitimately resisting the tyranny of a higher government, for it had besieged a lesser one without granting it the requisite hearing.[242] After Jan Matthijs's death, however, eschatological rationales overwhelmed political ones as Jan van Leyden proclaimed a new government from God, not men.[243]

Initially, Münster Anabaptists felt ambivalent about taking arms. Before city leaders were baptized and became bona fide Anabaptists (January 4, 1534), they wielded weapons against forces sent to exile them (on November 5, 1533). Afterward, however, Anabaptists assumed that they would not fight but suffer. Only after prophets exhorted them to arms and the Anabaptist faction took power legally (February 23, 1534) did they ready the city militarily.[244]

Their main justification became an eschatological rereading of biblical narrative.[245] According to Bernard Rothmann, the Gospel Age was now past. In the Age now dawning, Jesus would reign on earth with his saints. Jesus, however, would be not the David who inaugurated this reign but the Solomon who would rule in peace after the eschatological David—Jan van Leyden, of course—conquered Jesus' enemies (cf. chap. 10).

Münsterites endeavored to implement a biblical vision of social harmony and equality. Yet van Leyden's dictatorship became a reign of terror, meting out executions even for questionable attitudes.[246] This effort to actualize God's kingdom almost instantaneously, resembling Melchiorite expectations for divinization

---

[241]Ibid., p. 257.

[242]Stayer, *Anabaptism and the Sword*, p. xvii, 235. The bishop replied, however, that rebaptism had been illegal in the Empire since the late fourth century.

[243]Ibid., p. 237.

[244]Ibid., pp. 229-33.

[245]Ibid., pp. 239-52.

[246]The twelve elders through whom Jan supposedly ruled first decreed as capital crimes blasphemy; disrespect for government, parents or household heads; adultery and fornication; avarice; theft; fraud; lying; gossiping; quarrelsomeness and sedition. Shortly afterward Jan added perverting Scripture, false prophecy, military indiscipline, rebellion, desertion and unsubstantial accusations (ibid., pp. 259-60).

(chap. 5) and aided by the sword in opposition to the "world," reaped unimaginable disaster.[247]

3. Even before he left the priesthood, Menno Simons sharply criticized Münsterite violence, arguing that since Christians follow Jesus' way, they could never use the sword.[248] Menno denounced the identification of David with a mere man (Jan van Leyden) and Solomon with Jesus, and assigning the kingdom's violent inauguration to the first but its peaceful rule to the second. For Jesus was both true David and true Solomon. He alone would both defeat his earthly enemies and establish lasting peace.[249]

While Jesus' way and violence remained opposed for Menno, he also retained the hope, perhaps inconsistently, that rare Christian magistrates might rule justly and promote true religion. Menno and probably Dirk retained this Melchiorite outlook, which somewhat resembled the more optimistic perspective among some early Swiss and Hubmaier.[250] (Denck, Schlaffer and Marpeck possibly hoped for Christian rulers, but Marpeck, at least, did not believe they should promote religion.)

Menno's "Foundation of Christian Doctrine," written in 1539, four years after his conversion, exhorted magistrates to be "not persecutors but followers of Christ" so that they would not be ashamed of their office at the judgment.[251] But like other Anabaptists Menno stressed that they were lords only over earthly affairs, whereas Christ alone was Lord over souls.[252] The only sword for promoting God's kingdom was the Word.[253]

Nevertheless, Menno also encouraged rulers to "assist and favor" the true religion, guided by this Word.[254] He further implored them to "dismiss the blind and false teachers . . . who disgrace and blaspheme the Almighty Majesty of God with the teachings of Antichrist and with their hellish, beastly living."[255] However, his

---

[247]Surprisingly, similar expectations survived even Münster (ibid., pp. 283-97). In addition, David Joris and other Melchiorites who emigrated to the Rhineland revived a stance like Hoffman's, minus eschatological details. They revered authority and affirmed the possibility of Christian rulers, but separated government's earthly sphere from the church's heavenly one. Some speculated that a war might be just if it satisfied certain criteria (pp. 300-305).

[248]Simons, *Complete Works*, pp. 44-45.

[249]Ibid., pp. 34-43, 46-50.

[250]Given Dirk's working relationship with Menno, their views on government were probably similar, though evidence for Dirk's is scarce (cf. Stayer, *Anabaptism and the Sword*, p. 321).

[251]Simons, *Complete Works*, p.106.

[252]Ibid., pp. 119-20.

[253]Ibid., p. 175, cf. p. 44.

[254]Ibid., p. 191.

[255]Simons, quoted in Stayer, *Anabaptism and the Sword*, p. 317.

revised "Foundation" of 1558 added that true religion should be enforced "by reasonable means, that is, without tyranny and bloodshed" so that God's kingdom could be enlarged and protected "without force, violence and blood."[256] These alterations suggest that in 1539 Menno might have approved, or at least not clearly rejected, promotion of religion by state force. But by 1556 he had concluded that Christian rulers should never shed blood, implying that government could execute its legitimate functions through relatively peaceful means.[257]

In any case, Menno never dropped the notion that rulers could be Christians and should favor the true faith. He never ceased addressing rulers and church leaders. According to Stayer, he wavered between withdrawing from the world and at least hoping for its transformation, and never became completely nonresistant, though Mennonites did after his death.[258]

Despite Menno's frequent pleas that rulers be guided at least by reason, he repeatedly complained that "The pitiful moaning and misery of the wretched men does not reach your ears. The sweat of the poor we find in your houses, and the innocent blood on your hands. Their gifts and presents are received to pervert judgment."[259] His hopes for Christian magistrates notwithstanding, Menno's writings witnessed that rulers and societies they governed nearly always opposed Anabaptists viciously.

The slightly positive Dutch attitude toward government shaped stands on additional issues a bit differently from other Anabaptists'. The Wismar Articles (1554) allowed carrying weapons while traveling, and apparently on guard duty.[260] Though Menno condemned going to court, Wismar approved "demanding payment, at law, of just indebtedness" so long as "no wickedness results therefrom."[261] While Menno, and especially Dirk, often opposed God's kingdom to the world, Menno insisted, unlike Hutterites, that business relations with the latter were necessary to avoid destitution.[262] Menno indicated that his followers paid all taxes and tolls. Some governmental functions, like providing roads, were obviously legitimate. Yet like most Anabaptists, he refused to take public oaths.[263]

Summary. Anabaptist understandings of the church-world relationship were

---

[256]Simons, *Complete Works,* p. 193.

[257]Ibid., pp. 920-22. In 1542 Menno also asked magistrates to help him obstruct false teachers, though nonviolently (ibid., p. 362). In 1552 he remarked that every Christian must walk as Christ did, "whether he be an emperor or king" (p. 553). These three affirmations apparently implied that such persons could be Christians without renouncing their offices.

[258]Stayer, *Anabaptism and the Sword,* pp. 318-19.

[259]Simons, *Complete Works,* p. 195.

[260]Ibid., p. 1042.

[261]Ibid., pp. 213, 658, 1042.

[262]Ibid., p. 474.

[263]Ibid., pp. 518, 521, 922-24.

chiefly shaped by painful encounters with the state's coercive force, which seemed opposite of Jesus' peaceful way. Not surprisingly, these severely marginalized people strongly contrasted church and world. However, I have searched for variations within this general outlook, and several have emerged.

At one end of the spectrum the Schleitheim Confession and the Hutterites considered the church antithetical to the world and its governments, and apparently its main institutions and behaviors. Christians could participate directly in none of the latter. Nonetheless, governments were instituted by God. They deserved obedience except when they contradicted faith, and Christian behavior was to be exemplary everywhere. Among these contradictions Hutterites included war taxes and allowed selective rejection of exorbitant fiscal demands. Their own communities, however, were virtually alternative states, whose farms and industries benefited surrounding regions.

Moving toward the spectrum's center: Hoffman, Menno, probably Dirk, and maybe Schlaffer and Denck hoped for rare pious rulers. These would promote true religion and (at least for Menno) conduct civic affairs by reason. They might even join the church—depending mostly, it seems, on whether governing could be separated from violence. Church and world overlapped slightly, permitting restrained Christian participation in business, legal and some other affairs. Christians might gain some modest foothold in the social order.

Marpeck suggested another model: Christian participation in society's and government's service functions but avoidance of coercive ones.

Moving away from the center, Hubmaier allowed Christians to exercise various political and social functions, including the sword. The state would support but have no authority over the church. Very early on, some Swiss Anabaptists perhaps granted the state some ecclesiastical function, for they envisioned a thoroughly reformed state church. Quite soon, however, any Anabaptist state church proved impossible.

At the spectrum's far end, the new creation's missional impetus seemed to call not only for new persons and communities but also overthrow of governments—whether to promote peasant demands (some early Swiss), assist Christ's return (Hut) or prepare the way for it (Münster). Christians or Christ would establish and govern wholly different societies. Disastrous outcomes vetoed this approach. Yet it showed how central peasant-artisan visions of equality and justice were.

While historic Anabaptists perceived church-world conflicts more sharply than have most Christians, different relational patterns emerged within this broad outlook. A similar variety of options, then, can be considered in Anabaptist theologies today.

Contemporary Appropriations

It is understandable why marginalized Anabaptists often attributed the intense opposition they experienced to a single systemic entity, the "world." In today's postmodern climate, however, Christian groups often focus on specific audiences and
problems. Ministries proliferate in response to them. Churches sometimes seem to
exist simply to meet pressing but highly varied personal and social needs. But even
though everything in our globalizing era seems to change swiftly, might something
more systemic shape the maladies that arise? That is, can theology still speak of
something broader, perhaps even universal, like the "world"? Might theology identify some of its basic features and of the church's interaction with it? Or can any
such knowledge only be gleaned from mission involvement in specific settings, and
not generalized much further—like discernment of God's salvific work in non-
Christian contexts?

In any case, it is important for mission to ask how the new creation's coming,
which energizes the church and flows out through it, might be related whatever else
exists in its environment.[264] As the church seeks to be an eschatological sacrament,
might the new creation be operating elsewhere, apart from its mission? If so, how
might mission identify and link up with this? Or are all other structures and processes unilaterally opposed to mission? These questions are not simply theoretical.
Missionary practice is often shaped by perceptions about which features in its setting oppose God and which belong to life as God wills it. If these issues are not
decided explicitly, they will be decided implicitly anyway.

We recall that "Anabaptist Vision" advocates accent the church's distinctness
from all else. Yoder promoted this outlook, and Denny Weaver seeks to perpetuate it. In contrast, May, Swartzentruber and Holland complain that this vision
unrealistically exempts Anabaptists from the flaws and limitations of their concrete situatedness. Holland insists that God also dwells in "the public square"

---

[264]Theologians often discuss this under H. Richard Niebuhr's rubric "Christ and Culture." But as Yoder noted, this schema tends to treat culture as autonomous, capable of existing apart from Christ
(John H. Yoder, "How H. Richard Niebuhr Reasoned: A Critique of *Christ and Culture*," in *Authentic
Transformation*, ed. Glen Stassen, D. M. Yeager and John H. Yoder [Nashville: Abingdon, 1996], p.
55). Moreover, "culture" lumps all human activities together, implying that culture is monolithic
and must be accepted or rejected as a whole (ibid., pp. 37, 54; cf. Friesen, *Artists, Citizens, Philosophers*,
pp. 43-63). Niebuhr relegated Anabaptists, who opposed many aspects of their era's culture, to his
"Christ against Culture" category (H. Richard Niebuhr, *Christ and Culture* [New York: Harper &
Row, 1951], pp. 45-82). But Niebuhr missed what Yoder found Anabaptists doing: discriminating
among various cultural activities, accepting some but rejecting others ("How H. Richard Niebuhr
Reasoned," pp. 54, 69, 71). They renounced culture's supposed autonomy as demonic (ibid., pp.
68-69). Even Hutterites were hardly against culture, for they reconstructed much of it in light of
Christ.

and that church texts always interact with other written, historical and social texts.[265] Having examined these relationships through the historic Anabaptist lens, I now call on three Anabaptists who are considering them in detail to help me sharpen it.

Contemporary Anabaptist Approaches. I. C. Norman Kraus raises many issues considered in the "Evangelism" section of this chapter, but in the broader context of culture. Though many postmoderns might object, Kraus believes that mission involves spiritual intervention in culture that humans cannot control.[266] Yet he also respects postmodern critiques of Western imperialism's influence on mission. He asks how claims about the uniqueness of Christ and the church can be dissociated from claims of Western superiority.

Mission's goal, for Kraus, is to transform individuals and cultures according to the patterns of the kingdom Jesus announced.[267] This cannot be reduced to social-ethical dimensions.[268] Kraus recommends a kind of transformation called "catalytic": one that releases, without altering, potentialities already present in cultures from obstacles that inhibit their development.[269] By working catalytically, mission seeks to be unintrusive.[270] If it suggests innovations, it presents these as completions and perfections of the cultures where it works.[271] This approach assumes that tendencies working toward God's kingdom are operating widely beyond the church.

Kraus apparently does not anticipate many clashes between authentic Christian mission and other religions. He prefers dialogue to proclamation, for in dialogue non-Christian partners retain their identities and aim at "voluntary human community on its highest possible moral and spiritual level," which need not involve conversion.[272] Kraus expects that since God is working everywhere, "the message

---

[265]Cf. pt. 3 on p. 96 above.

[266]C. Norman Kraus, *An Intrusive Gospel?* (Downers Grove, Ill.: InterVarsity Press, 1998), pp. 56, 49.

[267]Ibid., p. 42, cf. p. 56. Mission's aim is "penetration of the culture with the spirit of Christ . . . not simply the rescue of individuals from it" (ibid., pp. 106-7, cf. p. 54). Though Kraus says little about evangelism or forming churches, he calls "verbal ministries," which include "witness," integral to mission (p. 107). Yet he also describes witness as "sharing an evangelical life rather than preaching evangelical doctrine" (p. 34). Kraus acknowledges that mission normally begins with individuals (p. 62) and works through communities living out alternatives to the status quo (p. 73). Yet, as seen in chap. 4, Kraus says little about churches and their practices.

[268]Mission connects people with transcendent reality and integrates inner reality with outer (ibid., p. 80). Kraus redraws "lines between the spiritual and the social-physical" (p. 14, see esp. pp. 69-91).

[269]Ibid., p. 44.

[270]Ibid., p. 59.

[271]Ibid., pp. 60-61.

[272]Ibid., p. 45.

of Jesus will be self-authenticating when it is presented in word and deed."[273]

To consider how God might be working broadly toward the kingdom, let's revisit the topic of non-Christian religions. Kraus regards all religions, Christianity included, as *"relative human responses to the light of God."*[274] Although religions are quite different, they all manifest a "human substratum of common religiosity."[275] For this reason, mission should not erode the religious bases of premodern societies.[276] Kraus further bridges differences between Christianity and other faiths by stressing that all involve imperfect human, culturally relative elements. Though Christ (despite postmodernity) is normative, Christianity (á la postmodernity) is not, and it often reflects Western features and shortcomings.[277]

Kraus finds God savingly present in other religions with a regularity I would call strong inclusivism.[278] Like many historic Anabaptists, Kraus affirms that Jesus was "the historical focus of the light that has shown . . . from the beginning" (cf. Jn 1:4). For him this means that Jesus, rather than originating salvation, climaxed the many ways God had bestowed it.[279]

Kraus further identifies saving faith, in Paul, with a "secret longing and action for righteousness," "a sincere will to do God's will," so that faith is present wherever God's law is honored.[280] Paul sought to introduce "a transforming dynamic into the religious and cultural pluralism of the first-century world without pitting one religion against another," which mission should emulate.[281]

---

[273]Ibid., p. 127. He often criticizes evangelicals for promoting conversion "as strictly an individual, theocentric change" in practice, even if not in theory (ibid., p. 53; cf. his evangelical paradigm, pp. 54-55).

[274]Ibid., p. 124, italics in original.

[275]Ibid., p. 83.

[276]Ibid., p. 37.

[277]Kraus's criticisms of Christianity's cultural forms counter Anabaptist tendencies to idealize the church and separate it from society. Yet they also weaken Anabaptist insistence that salvation involves incorporation in congregations. This can suggest that people can participate adequately in the new creation through any religion or none if they follow kingdom values.

[278]"All people . . . have the same access to God" through the "way that has been disclosed through Jesus," though they may not know of him (ibid., p. 116, cf. p. 127). Kraus also deduces, from the fact "that *there is only one God, who is the loving God of all humankind,*" that God cannot offer salvation "to only *part* of that race" (p. 119, italics in original).

[279]Ibid., pp. 116, 126-27.

[280]Ibid., pp. 115-16. Here "faith" is largely unhooked from and is no longer the response to "the faithfulness of Jesus Christ" (cf. p. 141). I do not find Paul identifying faith *(pistis)* with honoring God's law (though Gentiles who follow it inwardly might escape judgment [Rom 2:14-16]. Kraus seems to downplay the triumph of God's righteousness through Jesus in favor of a general, ethically oriented religiosity (cf. note 342 below).

[281]Ibid., p. 127.

Norman Kraus finds the new creation operating in somewhat parallel ways in the church and in all cultures and religions. Still, he wants to stress a radical turning from the old creation in Anabaptist fashion:[282] specifically, from violence, self-seeking, fatalistic traditions, hierarchical structures and superstition.[283] Kraus ascribes these opposing tendencies to "principalities and powers."

For Kraus, these forces are not actual beings but "social, ideological, systemic, institutional" forces that control cultures. He believes that humans created culture but that these forces took on lives of their own. They now seek to win our ultimate allegiance, usurping the lordship belonging only to Jesus. Yet these powers are not essentially demonic. Mission seeks to intervene where these powers operate and redeem them by proclaiming "God's original intention for them."[284]

Consequently, while Kraus finds evil powers quite active in the old creation, they also seem open to movement toward God's kingdom, as are cultures and religions in general, though the powers resist it more strongly. The historic Anabaptist conflict between the church and the "world" is modified by the notion that all realms outside the church, including forces apparently most opposed to it, possess potentialities for growth toward God, which are being actualized to some degree.

2. Duane Friesen challenges Anabaptist church-world dualism by considering creation, a theme Anabaptists seldom have touched. Drawing on Kaufman, Friesen describes all culture as a human construction. Humankind's culture-forming activity is God's image in us, an aspect of God's good creation.[285] Culture, or society, is not a given structure but an ongoing process that continues today. Much like Kraus, Friesen interprets the New Testament principalities and powers as the most fundamental social structures humans create. They are inherently good but also fallen and in need of and capable of transformation or redemption.[286]

Since humans, by definition, create and are shaped by culture, Christians cannot really withdraw from society. They can only choose among differing ways and visions of living in it. Friesen recommends that Christians regard themselves as exiles in the midst of society. They necessarily act within its structures and processes but

---

[282]Ibid., pp. 99-102.

[283]Ibid., pp. 73-76.

[284]Ibid., pp. 96-98.

[285]Humans "are co-creators with God. They literally construct their world" (Duane Friesen, *Christian Peacemaking and International Conflict* [Scottdale, Penn.: Herald, 1986], p. 58; cf. *Artists, Citizens, Philosophers*, pp. 55-56). Friesen adopts Kaufman's definition of the image of God "in terms of man's creating himself through history," that is, his "continuously creating himself," or "historicity" (*Christian Peacemaking*, p. 61, cf. 226; cf. Gordon Kaufman, *Systematic Theology* [New York: Scribner's, 1968], p. 343). Culture's main aim is to promote the common good (Friesen, *Christian Peacemaking*, p. 105; *Artists, Citizens, Philosophers*, p. 235).

[286]Friesen, *Artists, Citizens, Philosophers*, pp. 121-22.

seek to do so quite differently than most.[287] Churches can affect broader structures by drawing analogies from their vision of God's kingdom to suggest how other institutions and activities might function.[288]

Kraus helped us consider the church-world issue in light of non-Western societies and non-Christian religions. Friesen can help us ponder that point at which Anabaptism clashed, and apparently still clashes, most sharply with all societies: its way of peace.

Friesen acknowledges that forming and maintaining social institutions involves coercion.[289] He finds various forms of it legitimate. Yet Friesen seeks to distinguish them from violence, which he defines as "violations of the person."[290] Coercion then is acceptable when it does not harm people in their basic personhood but "initiates a process that can lead to the restoration of human beings and eventually to reconciliation." This can include "police use of physical force that is properly restrained and aims to protect and preserve the life of both the community and the criminal" and to enforce just laws.[291]

For Friesen, as for Ron Kraybill, the ultimate goal of humankind's culture-creating activity is peace, in the Old Testament sense of *shalom*. Yet Anabaptism's heirs have often understood peace as absence of conflict and therefore largely withdrawal. To counter this Friesen insists that true peace includes justice. Peacemakers then must further humanity's continuing construction of society by helping to create just institutions.[292] Friesen acknowledges, however, that historic Anabaptists did not anticipate much institutional change but mainly witnessed to peaceful ways they expected society to reject.[293]

In Scripture, justice consists in ensuring that the basic needs necessary for everyone to live holistic material, social and spiritual lives are met.[294] Accordingly, re-

---

[287]Ibid., pp. 23-42. He also calls this dual citizenship: "To be a Christian is to live on a boundary, a citizen of two societies. . . . shaped by membership in two different sociological structures: the nation-state and the church" (ibid., p. 211).

[288]Ibid., pp. 224-26.

[289]Social existence involves being limited by others and their decisions, including past ones (Friesen, *Christian Peacemaking*, p. 61). Friesen equates coercion not with violence but its Latin root: being "pressed together, shaped, structured into behavior that coordinates with others" (p. 60).

[290]Ibid., p. 152.

[291]Ibid., p. 153.

[292]Ibid., p. 60.

[293]Ibid., p. 26.

[294]Ibid., pp. 111-12. Friesen grounds this in biblical affirmations that earth's resources belong to everyone and on the worth of each person (ibid., p. 112, 115, 117, 119). Though Friesen says that Christian ethics should be based on biblical narrative and contribute distinctively Christian themes to public debate (pp. 105-8, cf. *Artists, Citizens, Philosophers*, pp. 77-84), his discussion of justice seems to be based more on general principles (*Christian Peacemaking*, pp. 109-22; on restorative justice see *Artists, Citizens, Philosophers*, pp. 246-47).

dress of inequalities is at its core.[295] And since being fully human involves constructing one's world, redress is best accomplished through "self-realization," or "people gaining increasing control over their environment and their destiny."[296] Friesen, in other words, favors "development as 'the process by which both persons and societies come to realize the full potential of human life in a context of social justice, with an emphasis on self-reliance.' "[297] Such language echoes liberation theologies and Kraybill's theology of conflict transformation.[298]

Yet because each person has intrinsic worth, the route to justice must be nonviolent—though it can involve moderate coercion. Yoder argued that nonviolent activists cannot aim for effectiveness in our violent world; they must simply live by Jesus' peaceful way without worrying about results. Friesen concedes that Yoder rightly identified this as the usual historic Anabaptist approach. Friesen responds, however, that to even choose one action over another, one must have some idea how each will turn out.[299] Yet this kind of thinking hardly disqualifies nonviolence, for it often provides effective social strategies, especially for avoiding the horrendous costs of wars. Friesen therefore urges Christians to promote nonviolent strategies in public debate.[300]

The same is advocated by Nancey Murphy and George Ellis who, as mentioned, regard theology as knowledge "in exactly the same sense" as science.[301] They propose that all human sciences should be governed by ethical affirmations, the chief of these being *"Self-renunciation for the sake of the other is humankind's highest good."*[302]

Against objections that such ethics cannot be practiced in the real world, Murphy and Ellis argue that many social sciences are in fact governed by a less plausible ontology of violence.[303] They adduce empirical evidence that their kenotic ethic provides more effective approaches to law, economics, business, government and other fields.[304] While Murphy and Ellis admit that their evidence is sometimes thin, they insist, like Friesen and Kraus, that Anabaptist principles are

---

[295]Friesen, *Christian Peacemaking*, p. 112.

[296]Friesen quoting Edgar Stoesz with approval in *Christian Peacemaking*, p. 140.

[297]Friesen quoting Merrill Ewert with approval in *Christian Peacemaking*, p. 140.

[298]Friesen, *Christian Peacemaking*, p. 83.

[299]Ibid., pp. 154-56.

[300]Ibid., pp. 168-72.

[301]Nancey Murphy and George Ellis, *On the Moral Nature of the Universe* (Minneapolis: Fortress, 1996), p. 7; cf. pp. 76-78 above.

[302]Ibid., p. 118, italics in original.

[303]Ibid., pp. 111-14.

[304]Ibid., pp. 122-72.

the most effective for society as a whole.[305]

For Friesen, Murphy and Ellis, then, the new creation's missional dimension involves much participation in the public square. The church itself, by seeking to live in the light of this creation, provides "a powerful political alternative" to current social structures.[306]

However, since the powers structuring society are human constructions—though they have acquired a momentum of their own—and Christ is now their Lord, Christians can also help restructure or transform these powers more directly.[307] Murphy, Ellis, Kraus and Yoder also regard the powers' redemption as a mission task.[308] Murphy and Ellis, however, challenge the claim that culture is a purely human construction. Such a view, they point out, undergirded Enlightenment attempts at unrestricted dominion over property, nature and all else.[309]

To redeem the powers and guide culture toward *shalom*, Friesen recommends practices with Anabaptist roots, such as victim-offender reconciliation and conflict transformation. He adds that these "must become institutionalized" and become "available to the larger community."[310] Friesen is also greatly concerned about international war and offers numerous suggestions for influencing public policy on this.[311]

Friesen, like Kraus, says little about evangelism or forming churches. Yet both find spirituality essential for Christian peacemaking. Friesen emphasizes crucifixion of creaturely attachments much like South German-Austrian Anabaptists.[312] Unlike many current Anabaptist theologians, Friesen devotes attention to life within the church, especially worship, prayer and the Lord's Supper.[313]

3. Anabaptists today are influencing the world beyond the church through the practice of conflict transformation. To round off this discussion of current Anabaptist theologians, I will integrate several of Ron Kraybill's emphases into it.

---

[305]Friesen, though, acknowledges that "empirical demonstration is partial and inconclusive." Faith in Jesus' resurrection and the future it portends is the ultimate reason for following Anabaptist principles (*Christian Peacemaking*, p. 169).

[306]Ibid., p. 92.

[307]Ibid., pp. 90-91, 93, 109.

[308]Murphy and Ellis, *On the Moral Nature of the Universe*, p. 190; Friesen, *Christian Peacemaking*, p. 157.

[309]Murphy and Ellis, *On the Moral Nature of the Universe*, pp. 112-13.

[310]Friesen, *Christian Peacemaking*, p. 210, cf. pp. 199-201.

[311]Ibid., pp. 212-14, cf. pp. 131-41.

[312]Ibid., pp. 229-36, cf. Kraus, *Intrusive Gospel*, p. 86.

[313]On worship see esp. Friesen, *Christian Peacemaking*, p. 245; *Artists, Citizens, Philosophers*, pp. 187-88. On prayer see Friesen, *Christian Peacemaking*, pp. 236-38; *Artists, Citizens, Philosophers*, pp. 151-53. On the Lord's Supper see Friesen, *Christian Peacemaking*, pp. 100-101, 246-47; *Artists, Citizens, Philosophers*, pp. 145-49.

First, Kraus and Friesen regard the nonchurch world neither as a fixed "ordering . . . outside the perfection of Christ" (cf. Schleitheim) nor as essentially dominated by coercive government, but as a multifaceted, evolving process of human construction. Its potentialities surge toward self-determination, justice and equality, especially for oppressed peoples, and ultimately toward God's shalom, or kingdom. Similarly, Kraybill recommends that conflict transformation be guided by the notion that history moves toward greater "exercise of free choice and the practice of new possibility."[314] Paths toward this emerge among people on its margins.[315]

Historic Anabaptists, however, tended to think of the new creation as present at one mobile point—the church, with its evangelistic call and those responding— and to expect it to triumph suddenly everywhere at Jesus' return. How will we evaluate the notion that tendencies toward the new creation are developing more gradually and globally outside the church? Could such trends really connect with the church at that point where differences often seem sharpest: Jesus' way of peace?

Second, our Anabaptist theologians propose that the new creation comes to light through not only evangelism but also other than Christian discourse. Friesen, Murphy and Ellis recommend participation in public-policy debate. Kraus endorses dialogue where non-Christians retain their identities and all partners seek to develop moral and spiritual community. Kraybill promotes transformative dialogue where moral norms are determined by participants.[316]

How will we evaluate whether the new creation might be dawning through concerns shared by non-Christians and advanced with little or no use of Christian vocabulary? Might our authors be baptizing some merely human drive toward self-creation, especially if they call not only culture but also all religions human constructions?[317] Or when they call theology "an activity of the human imagination similar to other human cultural processes"?[318] Might Christian faith viewed in ways so congenial to postmodernity be but one human construction evolving along with others?

Construction raises a third issue. Are principalities and powers no more than collective human creations acquiring a momentum of their own? If so, can they finally be redeemed? Further, if they can be redeemed through human reconstruc-

---

[314]Ronald Kraybill, *Peacebuilders in Zimbabwe* (Ph. D. diss., University of Capetown, 1996), p. 44.

[315]Cf. Friesen's support for "self-realization," or "people gaining increasing control over their environment and their destiny" (*Christian Peacemaking*, p. 140) with Kraybill's approval of "empowerment," which increases "peoples' sense of strength and ability to take control of their situation" and "make conscious, reflective decisions" (Kraybill, *Peacebuilders in Zimbabwe*, p. 44).

[316]Kraybill, *Peacebuilders in Zimbabwe*, p. 56; cf. pp. 63-64, 74-75, 85, 119.

[317]Ibid., pp. 14-15, 140.

[318]Friesen, *Artists, Citizens, Philosophers*, p. 68.

tion, how does the spiritual dimension of this process, affirmed by Kraus, Friesen and Kraybill, figure in?

An Anabaptist approach. As church mission affects sociopolitical life, an arena especially important to ecumenicals, can theology assist it by identifying some broad realm that does not (yet) acknowledge Christ's lordship? As churches seek to be eschatological sacraments, can theology perhaps sketch such a realm's major features and guidelines for interacting with it? Or do such generalizations transgress epistemological limits, as postmodernists are quick to ask?

Historic Anabaptists designated some such reality and often called it "world." Turning the lens they provide on Scripture, we find that it too calls it the "world" *(kosmos)*. New Testament usage of *kosmos*, however, seems ambiguous. On one hand, it included the totality of physical and social environments humans live in. In this use *world* denoted, rather neutrally, the basic structures and processes that shape human life, or more positively, God's good creation, or more positively yet, the object of God's love (e.g., Jn 3:16-19; 2 Cor 5:19; 1 Jn 4:14). Yet *kosmos* also designated the collectivity of behaviors, values and institutions that oppose God (e.g., Jn 17:9-19; 1 Cor 1:21; 1 Jn 2:16).

This dual usage may seem contradictory. Yet many church-world issues can be addressed by untangling it. Let me, then, explore *kosmos's* negative usage, which I have been designating by the "world" all along, and then its more positive uses, which I have indicated by the world. For each use I will consider the basic biblical materials and then their mission implications.

1. The "world." In this function *kosmos* was not really a place or thing but the dynamic collective momentum of many forces or a way of being. It was from "world" in this sense that historic Anabaptists turned. I have been using it synonymously with "old creation." The opposition from the "world" Anabaptists experienced defies imagination.

For New Testament writers this "world" was ruled by demonic forces. John called the chief of these "the Prince of this world" (Jn 12:31; 14:30; 16:11). Titles like Satan, the devil, Belial and others also denoted this supreme evil entity. Intertwined cosmic forces, such as sin, death and flesh (esp. Rom 5–8) were likewise named as wholly opposed to God. Hostile spiritual powers with broad though more specific jurisdictions were designated in quasi-political style as thrones, dominions, principalities and powers.[319] "Elemental spirits" *(stoicheia)* designated re-

---

[319]Thrones *(thronoi)*, dominions *(kyriotētes)*, principalities *(archai)* and powers *(exousiai)* appear in Col 1:16. *Archai, exousiai* and *kyriotētes* along with *dynameis* (also translated "powers") are found in Eph 1:21. *Archai* could designate political rulers and was related to *archōn*, or "prince," as in "prince of this world." *Exousiai* and *thronoi* could also denote earthly rulers, and *kyriotētes*, earthly

ligious entities with a somewhat political flavor (Gal 4:3, 9; Col 2:8, 20). More localized demons influenced individuals and groups, especially in the gospels.

Although the forces indicated by these words deeply affected human behavior, New Testament writers envisioned them as more than human. For instance, while a "principality" *(archōn)* might work through and even largely control a human ruler (also called *archōn*), the latter was only its instrument. Moreover these powers did not simply trouble individuals psychically. They also permeated the "social, ideological, systemic, institutional" aspects of culture (Kraus).[320] These biblical data raise three theological questions:

- *Are the powers spiritual?* Or are they these corporate structures themselves: that is, human constructions insofar as they have acquired a negative momentum of their own (Kraus, Friesen)? From my Anabaptist perspective this question can be addressed by considering again the basic process of salvation, or christomorphic divinization: participation in Jesus' life, death and resurrection.

This process originated in Jesus' own history, which involved intense conflict with evil powers. The Gospels portray Jesus being opposed by demons and the devil but also by Israel's religious leaders, Roman political forces, and inner human lusts and fears. The Gospels show how all these collaborated to defeat Jesus.[321] Since the last three forces worked together, might language about the demonic simply be a dramatic way of picturing the opposition of these and other human forces?

The Gospels also portray Jesus confronting these powers through a power that transcended human reality. His initial conflict with Satan arose immediately from his baptismal reception of God's Spirit, who impelled him into the wilderness and then back into Galilee (Mt 3:16—4:1; Mk 1:12; Lk 4:14, 18). Jesus' exorcisms were manifestations of the comprehensive victory of God's kingdom over Satan's, wrought by this divine Spirit (Mt 12:28 // Lk 11:20). When the religious and

---

Thrones *(thronoi)*, dominions *(kyriotētes)*, principalities *(archai)* and powers *(exousiai)* appear in Col 1:16. *Archai, exousiai* and *kyriotētes* along with *dynameis* (also translated "powers") are found in Eph 1:21. *Archai* could designate political rulers and was related to *archōn*, or "prince," as in "prince of this world." *Exousiai* and *thronoi* could also denote earthly rulers, and *kyriotētes*, earthly authority. *Archai* and *exousiai* appear together in Eph 3:10; 6:12; Col 2:10, 15; and Tit 3:1; and both with *dynameis* in 1 Cor 15:24. *Dynameis* is also found with *archai* in Rom 8:38 and with *exousiai* in 1 Pet 3:22, and alone in Mt 24:29 and pars. *Dynameis, thronoi* and *exousiai* occur together in Rev 13:2. I have only listed usages directly connected with the demonic. Much debate swirls around whether others might also imply this dimension.

[320]These powers were similar to the gods of the nations in the Old Testament as further elaborated in the intertestamental period. These gods represented and embodied their nations' social and cultural values and functions (Finger, *Christian Theology*, 2:147-51).

[321]See pp. 355-57 below. Finger, *Christian Theology*, 1:291-98.

political powers in service of Satan's kingdom executed Jesus, he triumphed over them through the same resurrecting Spirit (Rom 8:11; I Tim 3:16; I Pet 3:18).

Briefly said, the Gospels (and many Epistles) present Jesus' saving work climaxing in the unique divine act of resurrection and also accomplished all along through the power of the Spirit who raised him. The Gospels represent humankind's bondage to the powers as so severe that God alone could have released us.

If the powers, though, are simply human forces, why would direct divine action be necessary? Couldn't the conflict have been waged and won on a human level? But if God alone could have confronted these forces effectively, must not this powerful demonic opposition have transcended humanly constructed reality in some significant way? The battle must have been fought not only on the human plane but in this dimension too.

The same conclusion follows from considering salvation's continuing character: participation in Jesus' way through the divinizing energy of God's Spirit. Why would this transcendent dimension be so basic if this transformation and everything opposing it functioned solely on the human level? If the Spirit actualizes Jesus' life, death and resurrection in the church and its mission in some significant way, wouldn't the kind of spiritual conflict he experienced be involved?

Our consideration of the church's missional interaction with the "world" is leading back toward a recurring Anabaptist theme: the transformation of matter-energy by Spirit. Today spiritual reality is often conceived, within modernity's immanent framework, as the inner ethos or momentum of human forces. These are often reduced, in turn, to matter-energy. But does this adequately express what spiritual transformation meant in historic Anabaptism or Scripture? Can this transformation be reconceptualized as realignment among forces on the human, perhaps ultimately material, plane as some current Anabaptist theologians propose?

These questions, arising as we finish exploring Anabaptism's salvific center (part 2) are leading into some ontological issues involved in its convictional framework (part 3). More explicit discussion must await fuller examination of the spiritual conflict in Jesus' mission and what this entails about his divine reality (chap. 8). For now, I simply affirm that in view of the transcendent dimension of that conflict and the kind of salvation it brings, the powers that oppose salvation cannot be wholly reduced to human or material levels.

• *Are the powers personal?* If the powers transcend human construction, are they volitional beings? In Scripture they operate mysteriously enough that the answer must be paradoxical. On one hand, these powers work to depersonalize structures and individuals. Thus they can hardly be personal in the full sense. Nonetheless, their operation (in both Scripture and historic Anabaptism) was clearly intentional—whether frightening and destabilizing or uncannily covert. This makes it misleading to regard them as wholly structural and impersonal. For this can easily imply that if we knew enough sociology and psychology, we could control them. This would again overlook the biblical theme that struggle against them, at its deepest level, is spiritual. Perhaps then these forces can only be designated as both depersonalizing and yet somehow personal.

• *Are the powers being redeemed (as Kraus, Friesen, Murphy, Ellis and Yoder maintain)?* Only one biblical text comes close to affirming this clearly: "through [Jesus] God was pleased to reconcile to himself all things, whether on earth or in heaven" (Col 1:20); these included thrones, dominions, rulers and powers.[322] Elsewhere in Scripture, the evil forces seem implacably opposed to God. Historic Anabaptists certainly experienced the "world" this sense. Yet if we take Colossians 1:20 seriously, reconciliation must affect the powers some way. What way?

If this reconciliation means full redemption of the powers, fairly clear signs of the redemption of some should have appeared over the last two millennia. Theologians, indeed, have often identified historical movements as just such signs: Christianization of the Roman Empire, hegemony of the Roman Catholic Church, the Protestant Reformation, divine rule of monarchs, democratic revolutions against monarchs, prosperity of the Christian West, liberation movements against Western dominance. Anabaptists suffered horribly from such alignments of political states with God's Catholic or Protestant purposes. Modernity also identifies certain trends with history's forward momentum: science, technology, capitalism, socialism, democracy, globalization and others. Postmodernists rightly object that all such trends, religious or secular, harbor dark sides, and that such grandiose claims are ideological masks designed to justify and extend their power.

Of course, some such movements have accomplished good things. Some, at

---

[322]Col 1:16. Other passages are sometimes cited (esp. Oscar Cullmann, *Christ and Time* [Philadelphia: Westminster Press, 1964], pp. 191-210). In Eph 3:10 the church makes God's wisdom known to such powers. Yet awareness of this wisdom need not involve conversion to it. According to Phil 2:10-11 every tongue everywhere will confess Jesus as Lord (cf. Rev 5:13). Yet *every* need not mean "every creature which ever existed" (which would imply universalism) but can indicate individuals from every significant created grouping (cf. Finger, *Christian Theology*, 1:148-53). However, this text probably envisions the Last Judgment, where both the redeemed and condemned will acknowledge Jesus. Finally, Heb 1:13-14 calls angels "serving spirits," and some argue that all suprahuman entities are included in this category. But given the many names for such beings, this generalization hardly holds.

times and in certain respects, have even helped further God's redeeming work. Early church mission, for instance, was occasionally aided by Roman law (e.g., Acts 18:12-16; 19:35-41; 25:10-12). Yet this legal structure did not operate in increasingly redeemed fashion; centuries later, for instance, it helped abrogate many traditional rights of Germanic lower classes, sparking the Peasants' War. I find no historical evidence that any power itself—any ideology, institution, social structure—has been predominantly aligned with redemption or is on the way to being so.

The notion of fully or largely redeeming such powers resembles strong inclusivism in relation to non-Christian religions. Much as strong inclusivists regard other faiths as regular channels of Christ's saving work, "redeeming the powers" rhetoric can attribute a similar function to social movements, structures and ideologies. But does this not risk sacralizing them along with their flaws?

Is the notion of redeeming the powers, then, valueless for mission practice? Not entirely. For the one clear text on it (Col 1:20) implies something like modest inclusivism. That is, reconciliation, or the new creation, does influence such powers (such as Roman law). Some of them at times promote values consistent with that creation in fragmentary ways, though they will oppose it in other ways. Theology, however, cannot provide general guidelines for discerning how this occurs. It should instead recommend a sort of postmodern modesty. For while theology can affirm that the forces comprising the "world" oppose mission globally, it cannot tell in advance how God might interact with them in specific contexts. This can be discerned only through mission involvement in such settings.[323]

Further, assurance that reconciliation does touch these powers encourages Christians to search for its activity among them. This legitimates hopes for occasional "pious magistrates" or political structures or social movements that will sometimes operate justly, as Menno entertained, along with Dirk, Hoffman, some early Swiss, Hubmaier and possibly Schlaffer and Denck.

So far I have considered that arena where mission operates only insofar as it is permeated by the "world": systemic opposition to God under the powers' rule. Even in this respect it is not as uniformly opposed to the church as Schleitheim and the Hutterites claimed. Perhaps the second use of *kosmos* can tell us more.

2. The world. The "world's" opposition seems so strong that one wonders how Anabaptists could insist on actualizing the new creation in everyday life on this earth. This can be clarified by the other New Testament use of *world* (*kosmos*). It normally signified the universe, but usually with earthly structures and processes

---

[323]Cf. pt. 3 on pp. 285-88 above.

shaping human life in the foreground.[324] New Testament writers often employed *aiōn*, or "age," almost synonymously with *kosmos*.[325] Whereas *kosmos* might connote a fixed spatial structure, *aiōn* indicated a time span where change occurs. The New Testament mentioned several ages. When *aiōn* was used synonymously with *kosmos*, it meant the present era, distinguished from "the age to come," or culmination of God's purposes.[326] *Kosmos*, similarly, seldom included this future dimension.[327] Whereas "new creation" terms often indicated both this reality's presence and its future coming, *kosmos* and *aiōn* referred mainly to past and present reality, not their consummation.

The *kosmos*, further, was the object of God's salvation and love (Jn 3:16-19; 2 Cor 5:19; I Jn 4:14). It also formed the arena where mission announced and inaugurated this salvation (Mt 26:13; Rom 1:8; Col 1:6). As object and arena of God's saving love, *kosmos* and its structures were not inherently flawed but directly willed by God, even if not intrinsically everlasting. Theology, then, can use *world* to denote the universe as God created it, and pronounced "very good" (Gen 1:31), particularly those features and processes necessary for humans to exist and flourish. I have been using *world* in this sense synonymously with the original creation.

The world then forms a common stage on which humankind's movement toward God's purposes is acted out—but also its rebellion. Rebellion takes collective form, seeking to become a "world" unto itself. The comprehensiveness of both world and "world" indicates why turning toward God cannot simply be inward, spiritual or individualistic. People must also turn outwardly, away from one collective way of life and toward another way, or new creation, with material form. People who so turn, however, cannot exit the stage. We cannot, as Friesen insists, choose

---

[324]Roughly synonymous with the meaning of *kosmos*, both the Old Testament and New Testament express positively God's sovereignty over all created things: Ps 8:6; Is 44:24; I Cor 8:4-6; Phil 3:21; Heb 1:2; I Pet 4:7. This included principalities and powers (Col 1:16-17, 20; Eph 1:10).

[325]E.g., Mt 28:20; I Cor 7:33; I Tim 6:17; Tit 2:12; Heb 9:26. Such parallelism is also evident in *aiōn*'s frequent negative use in the sense of the "world" (e.g., Mk 4:19; Rom 12:2; I Cor 2:6-8; 3:18-19 [paralleled with *kosmos*]; 2 Tim 4:10).

[326]For *aiōn* as the present age differentiated from the age to come, see Mt 12:32; Mk 10:30; Lk 18:30; 20:34-35; Eph 1:21; Heb 6:5 (numerous references simply to "this age" also imply this distinction). For plural uses of *aiōn* see I Cor 10:11; Eph 3:9; I Tim 1:17; Heb 1:2 (synonym for "all things"); 11:3.

[327]Though Sasse claims that the New Testament avoided this entirely (Hermann Sasse, "κοσμέω κτλ.," in *Theological Dictionary of the New Testament*, ed. Gerhard Kittel [Grand Rapids: Eerdmans, 1965], 3:885), Paul referred to *kosmos* eschatologically in Rom 4:13 and Rom 11:12, 15. Salvation prepared from, or before, "the foundation of the world" (Mt 25:34; Eph 1:4; I Pet 1:20; Rev 13:8, 17:8), or the lamb slain from thence (Rev 13:8), indicate that God designed the *kosmos* in view of and directed it toward the consummation.

between living in society or not but only among different ways of living in it.

Since God endowed humans with creative capacities, the world is also a process, or age, and also resembles a plot line, which humans can develop in many directions. In its basic intended direction this process is "very good." Consequently, the original creation's structures, processes and goals cannot be vastly different than the new creation's. New as the new creation is, it does not abolish life's basic structures. It fulfills their potentialities, even if its consummation will somehow transcend them.[328] The world (process), that is, was aimed toward peace, in the full-orbed sense of shalom, which includes justice, and involved the creation of conditions requisite for everyone's material, social and spiritual development (Friesen, Kraybill).

To this point I largely agree with Friesen, Kraus and Kraybill. Yet I wonder: how adequately can this process be referred to as human construction? Can societies, cultures, even the evil powers, be sufficiently described by that term? Murphy and Ellis point out the modern origins of this notion: an effort to justify unlimited rights to wholly reshape nature and society.[329] Melanie May complains that construction tacitly assumes that nature is a mere passive surface on which limitless social configurations can be imposed.[330]

• *Culture as human construction?* For Friesen, justice furthers humanity's task of social construction by helping people gain "increasing control over their environment" and attain "self-realization."[331] For Kraybill, peacebuilding enhances peoples' "strength and ability to take control of their situation" and increase their "self-worth, self-determination and autonomy."[332] Such discourse owes its origins to the modern project of reshaping nature and society without reliance on or interference from tradition or transcendent reality. In a postmodern atmosphere this discourse is frequently adopted by or on behalf of particular, often marginalized groups seeking to express and further forge their identities.

While the world surely involves creative processes, when construction, "self-realization" and "taking control" are continuously valorized, it can appear that societies are simply whatever people decide they should be. Societies can seem to be wholly uncircumscribed by any constant features or limitations. To be sure, human creativity is far-reaching and surprising. Its constants and limitations cannot be defined exactly.

---

[328] For a fuller discussion, cf. chap. 10.

[329] Murphy and Ellis, *Moral Nature of the Universe,* pp. 112-13.

[330] Melanie May, *The Body Knows* (New York: Continuum, 1995), pp. 102, 110n. 3; cf. p. 23.

[331] Friesen, *Christian Peacemaking,* p. 140.

[332] Kraybill, *Peacebuilders in Zimbabwe,* p. 44. Though Kraus uses such language less often, I find it echoed at times, e.g., when he calls dialogue's aim "voluntary human community on its highest possible moral and spiritual level" attainable apart from Christian commitment (Kraus, *Intrusive Gospel,* p. 45).

Nonetheless, biblical creation texts also underline human finitude, not least by portraying the disastrous consequences of pursuing wisdom and immortality on our own, and social construction beyond finite limits.[333] Today, environmental problems should make it evident human societies depend on and are quite limited and shaped by ecosystems.[334] Moreover, human activity as God designed it is not autonomous but responsive to God's call and guided by God's purposes, character and Spirit.

The second meaning of *world*, then, affirms human cultural creativity. I recommend that mission encourages this creativity. Ways of doing so, however, should vary significantly in different contexts. When the discourse of "self-realization" and "taking control" appears in self-help books and financial-success recipes in prosperous societies, it plays on desires for prestige, accumulation and dominion, which ultimately fuel globalization. It tends to implicitly presuppose the notion explicit in the Greek concept of *kosmos* as opposed to the biblical one: reality as a self-contained whole governed by an immanent law, open toward neither a transcendent Creator nor transformation in a future age.[335] For many people today this whole is a biological process culminating in autonomous human construction, inseparable from an ontology of violence (cf. Murphy and Ellis).

Friesen, Kraybill and Kraus mean to avoid this interpretation. However, their frequent references to religions as human constructions render them vulnerable to it, and their notions of divine transcendence, in my view, are not developed fully enough to overcome this.[336] Kaufman, I find, follows the logic of valorizing human

---

[333]Gen 3; 11:1-9. God, of course, intended humans to attain wisdom, immortality and the kind of unity and cultural accomplishment indicated in Gen 11. Sin does not occur in seeking these but in doing so apart from dependence on God, which involves accepting finite limits. Pentecost, where the Spirit crossed all language barriers, began to reverse Babel's effects in God's way (Acts 2:5-13).

[334]None of our authors, of course, denies this. Friesen, e.g., defines culture as "the world of meanings created by humans" but "within the matrices of biological existence." Our "relationship to the earth is an integral component of an adequate cultural vision" (*Artists, Citizens, Philosophers*, pp. 56-57). I only propose that they prioritize human creativity too far over biological and other contexts and limitations, and ultimately over God's transcendent creativity.

[335]Sasse, "*kosmos*," 3:873-74.

[336]I also find this in their denial of transcendent, spiritual reality to the powers. Friesen, however, discusses transcendence at length. He treats all views of God as human constructions, following Kaufman (ibid., pp. 65, 68-70), and stresses God's immanence, often as ground of being (Tillich). This God "does not intervene in the universe" (p. 101); life arose from "chance variation in the DNA molecule" (p. 100). Still, Friesen critiques panentheism and the model of the world as God's body (McFague). He wants to affirm transcendence in the sense of God's independence of creation, which safeguards the latter's distinct integrity (p. 107). I share this aim but question whether Friesen's primary concepts can attain it. Since Kraus speaks less of construction, I will discuss his view of transcendence in chap. 8 .

construction more consistently and rejects any transcendent spiritual reality.[337] My Anabaptist theology recommends that mission mute construction discourse in highly developed societies, at least among middle and upper classes. I recommend that creativity be inspired, rather, by Jesus' alternative pattern and consist in efforts to actualize it.

Nevertheless, people who view themselves as pawns of fate or society, who despair of ever altering their circumstances, can hear discourse of construction and self-determination quite differently. Appeals to control their destiny can render the kerygma's hope concrete and spark the creative potentialities bestowed on everyone in the world (process). Mission, then, can employ such discourse among them, though I recommend finding more biblical terms.

Here is the main question: Is construction language meant to resound within the horizon of the new creation's gracious coming, or to stand on its own? For example, when parties in conflict are advised to devise their own norms (Kraybill), are they being encouraged to grapple creatively with their preconceptions and actual situation in overall reliance on God's grace, or to construct values and lifestyles entirely by themselves?

For Kraybill, like liberation theologians, clues to God's work can be found among people on society's margins, for history advances through their experiences and aspirations. We can therefore learn "what is 'real' " from them.[338] Anabaptists can indeed regard such people as preferred, in the sense that the kerygma more often appears as good news to them than to others.[339] Yet Kraybill, like Latin American liberationists, apparently refers to a metanarrative that arose neither from biblical narrative nor directly from experiences of the marginalized, but in nineteenth-century Europe. Most theologians who utilize it are seeking to identify a historical movement as the spearhead of the world process. Perhaps Kraybill means to avoid this by granting biblical narrative and the communities formed by it some priority.[340]

In actual practice Anabaptist-style mission will normally learn much about God's historical work from marginalized people. For as mission actualizes the new creation's social and economic dimensions, it will often find itself among them. Through involvement in such contexts, the church may gain significant historical understanding. Such knowledge, however, will be largely local and contextual, like insight into the powers' redemption and God's salvific work beyond the church. It will not warrant a

---

[337]Kaufman, *In Face of Mystery*, pp. 325-28; Walter Kaufman, "On Thinking of God as Serendipitous Creativity," *Journal of the American Academy of Religion* 69, no. 2 (2001): 423.

[338]Kraybill, *Peacebuilders in Zimbabwe*, pp. 66-67.

[339]Cf. pp. 249-51 above.

[340]Ibid., pp. 136-49.

universal affirmation that history advances mainly through its margins.

• *Visible alternatives.* Since the new creation actualizes the original creation's, or the world's, aims, Anabaptist principles, insofar as they are biblical, will actually be best for society in its basic intent, as Murphy, Ellis, Friesen and Kraus maintain. Nonetheless, historic Anabaptists portrayed the "world's" opposition to this process more darkly, and I have too, though to a lesser extent. To clarify these differences, I will begin where the new creation seems to contrast most widely with all societies: Jesus' way of peace.

Though Friesen affirms Jesus' kingdom vision as normative, he also considers this issue from a standpoint that I find somewhat incompatible with it: human construction of society, emerging from biological evolution. Friesen proposes that coercion is intrinsic to all civilizations. He finds coercion acceptable if it does not violate personhood and initiates processes that can foster restoration and reconciliation. Police force is acceptable if it is restrained, enforces just laws and aims to protect and preserve both community and criminal.[341]

I agree that some forms of coercion are unavoidable. Toddlers must be prevented from rushing into busy streets; people wholly out of control must be restrained from harm. Yet I am uneasy about sanctioning police force, in actual practice, in the names of restoration, reconciliation or protection of society and of offenders from themselves. Police often justify oppressive procedures in just such terms and additional procedures that prevent the public from detecting this. In many oppressed countries police are, or are worse than, the army.

I want to begin consistently from Jesus, noting that his teachings were addressed to a colonized people and central to his overall way of dealing with oppressors and ending Israel's exile.[342] Jesus' teachings concretized the meaning of his message: God's kingdom is at hand! When you are wronged, he counseled, and feel the natural urge to retaliate—stop! Since God's kingdom is at hand, search for a better, more creative response. I find Jesus' outlook best capsulized not by terms like nonviolence but by Paul: "Do not repay anyone evil for evil. . . . [B]ut overcome evil with good."[343]

Paul added that Jesus not only taught this way, he traveled it in his reconciling work. Jesus manifested God's love most fully by dying for us while we were God's

---

[341]Friesen, *Christian Peacemaking*, pp. 152-53.

[342]See esp. N. T. Wright, *Jesus and the Victory of God* (Minneapolis: Fortress, 1996).

[343]Rom 12:17, 21. *Nonviolence* only indicates what Christians should not do. *Nonviolent resistance* names something they should do (mainly reactive) and how not to do it. By themselves, these terms hardly epitomize Jesus' courageous, proactive orientation. *Pacifism* could epitomize Jesus' stance—if understood comprehensively as shalom. But *pacifism* has acquired many, often discrepant, connotations— not least of an "ism" separable from Jesus, or if not from Jesus, from full participation in his life, death and resurrection. (I thank David Lukens for clarifying my thoughts on these points.)

enemies (Rom 5:10). In mission, then, Christians not only seek to communicate and live by Jesus' teachings, they do so as people who, at some level, have rebelled violently against God. But rather than executing us, as would have been just, God absorbed the awful consequences of our violence. When churches face situations that seem to require violence (such as preventing crime), let them first recall that they witness to this kind of love and to the new creation, which pervade all of life. Let them then search not for pacifist formulas but, guided by Scripture and God's Spirit, for creative responses springing from this love.

Such responses, made in light of the new creation, will indeed be consonant with ways that the original creation still operates in societies. This approach differs, however, from attempts to begin with the original creation and then assume that certain features, like coercion, belong to it and must continue in the new. Theology, instead, should begin from the new creation. Only principles consistent with it should be perceived as indications of the original creation or world. Principles inconsistent with it should be treated as indications of the old creation or "world." From this standpoint, perhaps, limited coercion or police action might at times be appropriate. Yet churches will be extremely reticent to endorse, say, police practice broadly.

Perhaps Friesen would agree somewhat. From Jesus' reconciling work, however, I recently adduced another conclusion: the "world" is not simply the world, or human construction, gone awry. The horrendous, death-dealing effects of, say, war and gaps between rich and poor arise not only from collective human momentum. They also reflect a malevolent intentionality that transcends and works through this momentum. What implications might this carry for mission?

Like Kraus, I previously recommended that mission, when it enters a culture, search for signs of God's prior activity. Yet I would less often expect obstacles to the kerygma to be removed "unobtrusively," the culture's created potentials to emerge catalytically, or Jesus' message to appear "self-authenticating when presented in word and deed."[344] Neither would I expect to find genuine faith wherever God's law was sincerely honored.[345] Reverence for law perhaps more often leads away from God.[346]

---

[344]Kraus, *Intrusive Gospel*, p. 127. Since any culture's created potentialities (original creation) exist somehow within it, I might affirm *catalytic's* literal meaning: removing whatever obstructs them. Yet I expect these to be more intertwined with and twisted by the old creation, and less often unobtrusively extractable, than I understand Kraus to mean.

[345]Ibid., p. 116.

[346]I also question whether Paul sought to introduce "a transforming dynamic into the religious and cultural pluralism of the first-century world without pitting one religion against another" (ibid., p. 127). Paul, of course, sought not to replace "Judaism" with "Christianity" but to proclaim Jesus as Israel's Messiah. Paul also found links between his proclamation and Gentile religions (e.g., Acts 14:15-17, 17:22-31). Yet he considered most of the latter idolatry, superseded by Jesus' advent (e.g., Acts 17:31-34).

Given the "world's" opposition, I would expect the church to affect the public realm not so much by furthering ongoing trends or institutions as by making alternative forms of social life visible. For the powers spread a kind of systemic blindness over society. Their influence also permeates society with inequality, dishonesty, injustice and an ontology of violence. Since people constantly experience such things, they assume that reality necessarily operates like this. They will suppose that other ways are not really possible—unless they see these lived out.[347]

The church's main social task, then, is to embody alternative approaches to race relations, violent conflict, poverty and other issues—as an eschatological sacrament. Through these, societies become aware of new, transformative possibilities. Since Jesus denounced injustice and actively promoted shalom, this might involve marshaling collective moral force to oppose current practices—so long as positive alternatives, in the long run, receive more attention. There is no telling how far alternative approaches might spread. For the world is open to reconciling influences, at times, and so are various powers governing the "world." For these reasons direct participation in social structures is also possible. But whatever the approach, missional announcement of the new creation's peace and justice will hardly be credible apart from communal efforts to visibly embody these.

Since new creation principles are best for society in its original intent, Christians should advocate them in public discussion whenever possible. Since many dimensions of life are not explicitly religious, such interchanges need not always employ Christian vocabulary. Menno's appeals to reason implied such an outlook. So did Schiemer and Marpeck's notions of a natural law teaching common social principles. Though the contents of such awareness cannot be specified exactly, Christians can anticipate some agreement with others on various social aims.

Anabaptist practices, accordingly, should "become institutionalized" and "available to the larger community" when possible.[348] That community, however, will often find these practices too idealistic. Churches then will more often recommend analogies of them to society.[349] Anabaptists can join others in promoting specific proposals that fall short of their ideals if these improve situations by approximating those ideals more closely (e.g., true application of just war criteria can limit aggression). Churches, however, should not endorse such proposals in ways that imply that these have God's full blessing.

My view excludes the extreme dualism of Schleitheim and the Hutterites. It is congenial with hopes for occasional just rulers and processes, as entertained by

---

[347]Cf. Finger, *Christian Theology*, 2:287-88.
[348]Friesen, *Christian Peacemaking*, p. 210.
[349]Friesen, *Artists, Citzens, Philosophers*, pp. 224-26.

Menno, Dirk, Hoffman, some early Swiss, Hubmaier and possibly Schlaffer and Denck. I disagree with Hubmaier, however, over Christian participation in coercive government and government's right over citizens' lives (in the military). I find Marpeck's general outlook most helpful: participate in government and society's service functions when possible but avoid coercive ones. But do not expect to find the former wholly free of the "world."

4. Postscript: universality and particularity. To articulate the significance of the new creation's missional dimension in today's globalizing world, theology must make several universal affirmations. Mission announces and actualizes Jesus' universal kenotic lordship consistently with biblical narrative's universal horizons. Since God desires that all be saved and intends this lordship for all creation, the world (process) as created is also, despite its extraordinary variety, an integrated whole with common characteristics. Further, since opposition to God's goal is not simply ad hoc and occasional but comprehensive and systemic, the "world," however disintegrating its effects, is also a single process with some general features.

Beyond these three, however, this chapter has ventured few universal affirmations. I have, indeed, added that (finite, limited) creativity and shalom (as a goal) always characterize the world, and an ontology of violence, the "world."[350] But central as such universals are in mission's overarching framework, most missionary knowledge comes from interaction with particular contexts. The latter emphasis is postmodern, but not only so. Anabaptist concerns about specific behaviors and particular needy peoples foster a very practical, observant mission orientation. Moreover, efforts to embody universally valid behaviors through visible alternatives, especially when they apparently conflict with all societies, require careful examination of every setting.

Anabaptist mission, that is, brings into sharp relief the scandal of particularity. God attains universal goals not by working everywhere in the same way—say, through conscience, natural law, human social construction or self-realization. Instead, God makes these goals known chiefly by embodying them vividly through particular persons and groups. God initially chose the tiny nation Israel for this (Ex 19:4-6; Deut 4:6-8). But as the nation as a whole turned away, Yahweh focused this through an increasingly dwindling remnant and finally a single individual, Jesus. God's particular vehicles are now churches, aptly called eschatological sacraments.

While the scandal of particularity characterizes Christian faith generally, the

---

[350]Several other universal characteristics could be mentioned. I have not derived the ontology of violence biblically for lack of space. I would begin by showing how murder was one of sin's first consequences (Gen 4:8-12), how quickly it spread (Gen 4:23-25; 6:11-13) and how it was attributed at bottom to the serpent (Gen 3:15) or devil (Jn 8:44).

Anabaptist perspective, I submit, heightens it more than most. This is why Anabaptism can draw a very sharp contrast between the church and the "world," yet insist that Jesus' lordship, including his way in many specifics, is for everyone. This is why mission must be deeply concerned with particular contexts (as postmodernists and marginalized churches stress) and concentrate mainly on visible alternatives, yet give significant attention to broader and ultimately global processes and issues (as ecumenical churches stress).

PART III

THE CONVICTIONAL
FRAMEWORK

Part two of this book sought to articulate what lay at historic Anabaptism's heart to provide a center for a contemporary theology in Anabaptist perspective. While I declined to identify this with Anabaptism's essence, I proposed that it could be usefully described as the coming of the new creation, an all-embracing apprehension that life in every dimension was being significantly transformed and would soon be wholly transformed by divine energies. Although I specified three dimensions of this coming—personal, communal and missional (chaps. 5-7) for historic Anabaptists these were inseparable.

Contemporary Christian groups, however, often emphasize one or another of these. Many evangelicals, for instance, prioritize the personal dimension, while many ecumenical communions highlight the communal. Some churches consider mission their reason for being. Others seldom look beyond themselves. But since Anabaptists did not really make these distinctions, I proposed that this allegedly "sectarian" perspective might suggest ways of integrating them today. These could be quite practical, for Anabaptists have long been respected for practicality. Yet since they have done relatively little formal theology, it seemed unlikely that they could contribute there.

Historic Anabaptists, indeed, were mostly concerned with the new reality's vivid inbreaking and immediate, concrete responses. The great majority were peasants or artisans. Most educated leaders had been eliminated early on. Few had training or time to address issues commonly considered more theological.

Nonetheless, their practices clashed sharply enough with those of their era to endanger and often cost them their lives. Anabaptists would scarcely have lasted a few decades, let alone centuries, had they not been nourished and motivated by what Robert Friedmann calls an implicit theology, and James McClendon, indispensable convictions.[1] Part two showed that historic Anabaptists indeed explicated these somewhat.

Above all Jesus played a crucial role. Anabaptists experienced personal salvation as participation in his life, death and resurrection. They structured church life around his commands. Their mission message focused on him; and their interaction with others, like their personal and communal lives, was patterned after his way. Clearly, convictions about who Jesus is and what he did and does—which often led Anabaptists to their own crosses—were essential to this movement.

Accordingly, though Anabaptists reflected less often on such convictions than on the new creation's actuality, the former were indispensable to the movement. They formed a constitutive framework without which it would never have taken the shape it did. Accordingly, I consider this framework, which chapters eight through ten will explicate in part, as basic to theology in Anabaptist perspective as the vision expressed in chapters five through seven.

Part three first addresses Christology. Congruent with the importance Anabaptists give Jesus' historic and risen activity, I commence with what he did, does and will do: his work. This leads intrinsically to who he was and is, or his person, including his human and divine aspects, and then further, to what divine reality must be. I also include Polish Anabaptism's distinctive contributions. This progression clarifies a "framework" issue that began emerging in part two: the nature of spiritual reality and its relation to matter, or matter-energy as it is better named today.

Since Jesus' work through his Spirit deeply transforms people, conforming them to his own human character, convictions as to what humans are like were also indispensable to Anabaptist practice. These occupy chapter nine. Our capacity for relationship with God and our spiritual and material features come to the fore, along with sin's nature and extent.

Anabaptist response to the new creation was shaped by convictions that it was arriving within a cosmic horizon. Chapter ten explicates this eschatological vantage point, from which this volume's main themes are reviewed. Though Anabaptism's convictional framework includes other loci, such as creation and revelation, space concerns forbid their inclusion.

Although contemporary Anabaptist theologians seldom discuss personal salvation (chap. 5) or church practices (chap. 6), they ponder Christology often, as they do church mission (chap. 7). Accordingly, in chapter eight I interact with J. Denny

---

[1]Robert Friedmann, *The Theology of Anabaptism* (Scottdale, Penn.: Herald, 1973), pp. 21-22; James McClendon, *Systematic Theology*, vol. 2, *Doctrine* (Nashville: Abingdon, 1994), p. 29.

Weaver in considering Jesus' work, Norman Kraus and James McClendon regarding his person, and again Kraus on God's nature. I add the valuable contributions of Walter Wink on Jesus' work and Elizabeth A. Johnson on the Trinity. Chapters nine and ten incorporate movements not yet directly considered. Reformed theology, particularly its twentieth-century giants Karl Barth and Reinhold Niebuhr, helps me develop my anthropology. My eschatology takes shape in dialogue with some current evangelical theologies and another Reformed theologian, Jürgen Moltmann.

8

JESUS AND DIVINE REALITY

A̲nabaptists sought to foreground Jesus, and especially his concrete, earthly way, much more than they thought other movements did. This deeply affected not only their personal lives but also their reshaping of church practices and their missional relationship to society. As we turn from these concrete concerns toward the framework of convictions that shaped them, convictions about Jesus will be central.

Although historic Anabaptists affirmed Jesus' universal lordship, Western imperialism co-opted this claim. To avoid this I defined this lordship as kenotic. Christology asks, in much more detail, how churches can portray such a Jesus and a God who is truly liberating for all people in our globalizing era. To do so Christology further probes how Jesus can be both particular and universal, both physical and spiritual, both divine and human. This will provide the appropriate center from which to consider the mission issues more generally.

Formal Christology often distinguishes Jesus' person from his work. It usually commences with the former, focusing first on Jesus' divine side and then its connection with his humanity. Next, under his work, this Christology examines what Jesus did (and sometimes what he does and will do) to bring salvation. This orientation corresponds generally with that of traditional systematic theology. It usually begins by considering God and then moves toward what God means for human life. Consequently, Jesus' person, along with the Trinity, often appear near the beginning of traditional theologies. Discussion of these exalted topics usually requires technical vocabulary, much of it adapted from philosophy. The understandings developed in this way significantly influence subsequent considerations of Jesus' work and its saving significance for people.[1]

---

[1]Thomas Finger, *Christian Theology: An Eschatological Approach* (Scottdale, Penn.: Herald, 1985), I:103-5, 257-59.

Christologies that commence with Christ's person and deity are often labeled "from above." However, another orientation, beginning from Jesus' historic work, or "from below," appeared in Anabaptism and has become more common over the last 150 years. Anabaptism's stress on Jesus' earthly career, along with its practical orientation, suggest that Christology might start from Jesus' work and move toward his person.[2] This need not imply that Anabaptists were chiefly concerned about the human Jesus, and only secondarily about how he might be divine. Beginning with his concrete work, however, will help clarify the concrete meaning of subsequent statements about his person, which sometimes are unavoidably complex.

In considering the mystery of God, Anabaptist theology might well continue along the same path, approaching the divine nature from the standpoint of the divine work. Biblical narrative generally operates this way, reciting numerous divine acts and portraying God's character in light of these. Said otherwise, Anabaptist theology might begin, broadly, from soteriology, as historically enacted and experienced, and then proceed toward its divine source. I adopted this orientation by surveying "The New Creation's Coming" (part two) before probing its "Convictional Framework" (part three). I will extend this in the present chapter, progressing from Christ's work to Christ's person and on to divine reality, particularly the Trinity.

We have discovered that today's Anabaptist theologians discuss certain areas quite thoroughly, like mission and society (chap. 7), but others very little, such as church practices (chap. 6) and personal salvation (chap. 5). Since current Anabaptists do write about Christology, they will provide several dialogue partners here. I will consider Denny Weaver's Christus Victor reading of Christ's work which, he claims, conflicts with the classical creeds. I will interact with Norman Kraus's somewhat neo-orthodox approach to Christ's person, along with James McClendon's attempt at a two-narrative rather than two-nature model. Turning finally to Godself, I will again reference Kraus, but chiefly Elizabeth A. Johnson's feminist Catholic reading. Under Christ's work I will include Walter Wink.

To adequately consider how classical Anabaptist Christology might be, the sec-

---

[2]Modern impetus arose from early nineteenth-century "lives of Jesus." In 1874 Albrecht Ritschl first worked "from below" systematically (*The Christian Doctrine of Justification and Reconciliation*, vol. 3 [Clifton, N.J.: Reference Book Publishers, 1966]). Ritschl and his liberal descendants, up to the 1930s, focused very largely on Jesus' life and death, considering his birth and resurrection accounts unreliable. When I examine historic Anabaptists "from below," I will accent how they both understood his historical career and experienced his present salvific activity. However, my own construction "from below" will mean (1) deriving the significance of Jesus' work and person from what specific biblical passages about his life, death and resurrection meant in their time, (2) interpreting broader biblical statements on his work and person in light of these, and (3) conveying this significance in contemporary concepts.

ond and third sections will expand beyond the usual three historic sources to examine Polish anti-Trinitarian inclinations. As this chapter unfolds, the character and relationships of spirit and matter-energy will increasingly be probed.

THE WORK OF JESUS CHRIST

Jesus' work is often called "atonement." This can include all aspects and phases of at-one-ment among God and creatures—past, present and future. Yet theologians focus mostly on atonement's meaning for humans. Further, they usually concentrate on the past—Jesus' birth, life, death and resurrection—and finally, among these, on his death. Consequently, atonement, despite its cosmic implications, often connotes theories about the cross.

Approaches are often grouped into three main models. To unearth historic Anabaptism's specific contributions, I cannot, of course, equate them with any one. Nonetheless, if I approach the tangle of expressions by looking for elements of each model, they together can provide a helpful exploratory framework for several reasons. First, all three views existed in Reformation times. The theology of any Christian communion is shaped by others' theology, and historic Anabaptists were influenced by these models, sometimes consciously, sometimes not.[3]

Second, some Anabaptist theologians debate these models today. The three can provide entrée into this discussion. Third, these models still lurk in current Christology's hinterground and should be reckoned with in efforts to contribute to it. Traditional atonement models then will function as exploratory frameworks or lenses, helping us discern how closely historic Anabaptism's apprehensions fit them, and to search for other understandings when they do not.[4]

The *substitutionary* theory was formalized by Anselm of Canterbury (1033-1109). The Reformers often thought along these lines, as have the Protestant orthodox and many current evangelicals. In this model humans were created to honor God or obey God's law and by doing so continuously to merit the reward of eternal life.[5] However, every person has broken this law, forfeited eternal life and deserved instead the penalty of eternal death. Jesus' work substituted for our failures. His obedient life merited eternal life as a reward. His cross paid the penalty of eternal death. When we accept his work for us, this payment and his merits are transferred, or imputed, to us or to our account. We are exempted from

---

[3]Cf. pt. 18 on p. 101 above.

[4]For fuller accounts of these inevitably oversimplified summaries, see Finger, *Christian Theology*, 1:303-24. McClendon also introduces Jesus' work by discussing these three models (*Systematic Theology* 2: 199-213).

[5]Cf. pp. 110-13 above.

eternal death and receive the reward of eternal life. Substitutionary theorists tend to stress God's wrath or judgment or the demands of God's righteousness, conceived in legal terms. They enlist biblical language about sacrifice and price especially in support of their view.

The *moral influence* theory was popular among Protestant liberals, though it was pioneered by Peter Abelard (1079-1142). Many ecumenical Protestants find its general outlook congenial today. Here humans were created to join in moral endeavor leading to God's kingdom, conceived largely in earthly and social terms. Such endeavor is better motivated by awareness of God's love than fear of God's wrath. From this perspective Jesus' work consisted mainly in his moral teaching and example and his manifestation of divine love. His death was a supreme expression of this love, which motivates people to live for God's kingdom, rather than satisfaction of divine wrath.

Christus Victor was prominent in the patristic era and still is in Eastern Orthodoxy. It is not a precise theory but a broad motif whose details can vary. Nearly all variations, however, include the following features. Humans were created to attain divinization by walking with God, but they followed the devil instead. This subjected them to the dominion of evil powers, corruption and death. God punishes sinners not so much directly as indirectly, by handing them over, individually and corporately, to the forces they have obeyed. At times this punishment is also construed somewhat as in substitution: by obeying Satan humans break God's law, which entitles Satan to hold them prisoner, unless paid a ransom.

Jesus walked in God's way and resisted the evil powers. Yet they apparently conquered him on the cross. But through Jesus' resurrection God vindicated him and judged the powers, divesting them of their dominion over humanity. In some versions Jesus also conquered the powers on the cross by offering them his life as a ransom. These features of Christus Victor might be called its conflictive dimension.

A transformative dimension is also involved. Through Jesus' obedient life he increasingly experienced divinization. Resurrection drew his humanity fully into the fellowship, initiated during his life, with his Father and Spirit. Through Jesus' life, death and resurrection people joined to Jesus are released from the powers' dominion and participate in his entrance into trinitarian divinization. While most theology after the fourth century interpreted the powers as entirely spiritual (as sin, the devil, etc.), some earlier theologians (esp. Justin Martyr [100?-164?]) perceived them acting through sociopolitical forces.

Historic Anabaptist Perspectives

Switzerland. Except for Balthasar Hubmaier, Swiss Anabaptists seldom reflected explicitly on Christ's work. Michael Sattler affirmed that Christ reconciles people with and gives them access to the Father.[6] Sattler, who contrasted church and "world" dualistically in the Schleitheim Confession, similarly distanced Christ from the devil, the "prince over the whole world."[7]

Hubmaier often used substitutionary terms. Since the Father was angry toward sinners, Christ's blood was "payment and satisfaction" for sins.[8] Forgiveness came only through Christ's suffering, and favor only from his merits.[9] Yet Jesus' payment of this price, his "anxiety and distress, torment and bitter dying," also revealed the "greatest and highest love," as moral influence theory stresses.[10] The Lord's Supper vividly pictured this, arousing "heartfelt fervent" response.[11] Jesus' sufferings indeed were necessary for us to "acquire" a merciful Father. Yet this Father did not merely remit penalties but also received us into "the favour, grace, and good will" he has for his Son.[12]

Faith, accordingly, was "knowledge of God's mercy" shown in "offering his only begotten Son."[13] It was this "grace and kindness," not legalism or perfectionism, that engendered commitment to the strenuous new life.[14] Precisely speaking, Jesus' death bestowed forgiveness. His resurrection brought righteousness, or justification.[15] The risen Christ, though distant from the Lord's Supper, was very active through the preached Word, as the physician who gently healed.[16]

Hubmaier connected substitutionary suffering not only with moral influence language but also Christus Victor. For him, to say "sin produces an unpayable debt" was much like saying "we are in bondage to sin and consequently death and the devil." Similarly, to conceive atonement as payment of a debt was much like conceiving it as liberation from debt and those powers. For this, however, Jesus' res-

---

[6]Michael Sattler, *The Legacy of Michael Sattler*, ed. John Howard Yoder (Scottdale, Penn.: Herald, 1973), p. 22.

[7]Ibid., cf. p. 38. To Christ's blood Schleitheim attributed forgiveness (p. 43); and also *Vereinigung*, or unification, which Yoder translates "atonement," in concert with the "gifts of the Spirit—who is sent by the Father" (p. 34, cf. p. 42). I am not attributing "On the Satisfaction of Christ" to Sattler (pp. 108-18).

[8]Balthasar Hubmaier, *Balthasar Hubmaier: Theologian of Anabaptism*, ed. Wayne Pipkin and John H. Yoder (Scottdale, Penn.: Herald, 1989), p. 332.

[9]Ibid., pp. 116, 424, 443-44.

[10]Ibid., p. 236.

[11]Ibid., p. 395, cf. p. 355.

[12]Ibid., p. 116, cf. p. 146.

[13]Ibid., p. 32, cf. pp. 355, 395, 399-400; cf. note 219. Faith was trust in a "gracious, good, gentle, benevolent and merciful Father in heaven, who carries, protects, and shields us as . . . his child, or like a hen her chicks under her wings" (p. 116).

[14]Ibid., p. 117.

[15]This theme appeared more often in Hubmaier's Swiss writings (ibid., pp. 86, 100, 115, 117) than in his later writings (e.g., p. 348).

[16]Ibid., pp. 84-85, 144.

urrection was also necessary. When he descended to hell, Jesus, through the Spirit, proclaimed this "satisfaction" to the Old Testament saints who were captive there, yet had believed God's promise of future salvation (cf. I Pet 3:19-21). Then Jesus reunited his "spirit, soul, and body in the grave," and by rising led forth those captives "as a strong and mighty Victor over death, hell and the devil."[17]

Hubmaier understood sin as bondage in another sense, via his tripartite anthropology.[18] Sin arose when the soul obeyed the body (by taking the apple), allowing the body's desires to overwhelm it. This virtually extinguished the soul's awareness of and ability to choose between good and evil.[19] The body simultaneously took the spirit captive. Though the spirit maintained its orientation toward God, now it could only cry out as a prisoner. Release from this bondage, Hubmaier insisted, "must, must, must take place through a new birth."[20] Only through renewal by the Word and Spirit could the soul be made whole again and the spirit be freed from the body's harm (though the body would remain bound by sin until the resurrection).

This living Word who healed the soul was, or directly conveyed, the risen Jesus. This Word, with the Spirit, bestowed salvation in the sense most important for Hubmaier: ontological transformation (by, but not into, divine being). Since this increasingly released one from captivity, Hubmaier could express it in Christus Victor language.

Hubmaier described personal salvation as justification, or righteousness, in both Protestant (imputed) and Catholics (imparted) senses—but above and beyond these, as ontological transformation (chap. 5). He also described Jesus' death both as substitution and something like moral influence (though chiefly the former). Yet crucial as this historical event was in Jesus' work, his risen, present bestowal of ontological transformation was its apex, fittingly portrayed by Christus Victor terms. Although ontological transformation involved ethics, Hubmaier seldom connected it or Christ's work in any other sense directly with Jesus' life.[21]

When Hubmaier considered the powers as barriers to transformation, he con-

---

[17]Ibid., p. 236, cf. pp. 347-48.

[18]See chap. 9, cf. pp. 259-60 above.

[19]Hubmaier, *Balthasar Hubmaier,* pp. 361-62.

[20]Ibid., p. 445, cf. pp. 361, 431.

[21]Hubmaier once recommended preparing for the Supper by recalling how Christ "was a man, a prophet, mighty in works and teaching before God and all people, and how the highest bishops among the priests and princes gave him over to condemnation and death" (ibid., p. 394). Hubmaier included Jesus' intercession in his risen work as the kind physician, but viewed this as largely substitutionary pleading, in view of the favor he had won, that the Father "abstain from his anger" (p. 145). Though Jesus had delegated the keys to the church at his resurrection, these would be returned at the end so he could execute final judgment (pp. 413-16, 546).

nected them with the body, "our greatest enemy";[22] and as barriers to forgiveness, with the "harsh and frightful" law (102). In his turbulent times, he found the powers active in additional ways. As Schleitheim declared, the devil was the prince of this "world." This meant that even Christians were so enmeshed in it that some of them needed, and others should wield, the sword.[23] The devil turned most governments against the gospel, instigating all-to-frequent persecutions.[24] Eventually, however, God would punish evil authorities in Christus Victor fashion, handing them over to other fallen powers.[25]

South Germany-Austria. I. Jesus' work was apprehended far less through atonement theories than understandings of his person, which will receive most attention. Divinization involved mystical and ethical participation in Jesus' birth, life, death and resurrection. Yet this process was knowable outwardly in "all creatures" or inwardly through the Word or the Lamb suffering from the world's foundation.[26] Did these terms indicate some divine principle or salvific potential immanent in everyone?[27] If so, Jesus' work would not be strictly necessary for salvation, though it might aid some in moral influence fashion. However, if Jesus was the Lamb or Word in a unique sense, his birth, life, death and resurrection would also originate or constitute atonement.

• *Hans Hut.* Terms obviously associated with atonement models were not used

---

[22]Ibid., p. 243; for a close parallel between the flesh and the devil see p. 442. Hubmaier occasionally attributed the body/flesh's incorrigibility to the serpent's poison (e.g., pp. 438, 446).

[23]Cf. pp. 291-93 above. If we are stuck in "the kingdom of this world, which is a kingdom of sin, death, and hell right up to our ears" (Hubmaier, *Balthasar Hubmaier,* pp. 496-97) it is unclear how fully we were liberated from the powers. Hubmaier could advise Christians to confess themselves "captive . . . in the kingdom of sin, of the devil, hell, and eternal death" (p. 242).

[24]Ibid., pp. 311, 495.

[25]Ibid., pp. 309, 488, 498.

[26]Hans Denck, *The Spiritual Legacy of Hans Denck,* ed. Clarence Bauman (Leiden: E. J. Brill, 1991), pp. 89-91, 225; Hans Hut, "On the Mystery of Baptism," in *Early Anabaptist Spirituality,* ed. Daniel Liechty (New York: Paulist Press, 1994), pp. 73, 75; Leonhard Schiemer, "The Apostles' Creed: An Interpretation," in *Spiritual Life in Anabaptism,* ed. Cornelius Dyck (Scottdale, Penn.: Herald, 1995), p. 38; Leonhard Schiemer, "Ein epistl an die gemain zu Rottenburg darin huebsche erklearungen der 12 hauptsteuck unseres christlichen glaubens begriffen sein, " in *Glaubenzeugnisse oberdeutscher Taufgesinnter* (= Quellen und Forschungen zur Reformationsgeschichte), ed. Lydia Mueller (Leipzig: M. Heinsius Nachfolger, 1938), 20:55, 74; Hans Schlaffer, "Instructions on Beginning a True Christian Life," in *Early Anabaptist Spirituality,* ed. Daniel Liechty (New York: Paulist, 1994), p. 103; Hans Schlaffer, *Selections,* in *Spiritual Life in Anabaptism,* ed. Cornelius Dyck (Scottdale, Penn.: Herald, 1995), p. 203; Hans Schlaffer, "Ein kurzer Unterrich zum Anfang eines recht chrislichen Lebens," in *Glaubenzeugnisse oberdeutscher Taufgesinnter* (= Quellen und Forschungen zur Reformationsgeschichte), ed. Lydia Mueller (Leipzig: M. Heinsius Nachfolger, 1938), 20:96, cf. p. 109.

[27]This question was asked on pp. 260-63 above, under the heading "Evangelism."

by Hans Hut. For him humans were created as lords of other creatures, yet they became overly attached to them and served them instead.[28] Salvation consisted in painful crucifixion of such attachments and eventual filling by the resurrection Spirit.

Jesus experienced all this. Yet Hut critiqued those who said that Christ did everything for salvation so that we need do nothing.[29] For we must experience whatever Jesus did. But then did he accomplish anything necessary for us, or did he simply exemplify the salvation process? Hut often mentioned sharing Christ's sufferings. Yet this may only have meant participating in those of the community, or "Christ's body."[30]

Hut also declared that baptism's "essence" as a mystical process began with Adam. Jesus' baptism was but an "example" of it. Nonetheless, this event involved something unique: it instituted the baptismal ceremony, which we must follow.[31] Further, Jesus then took upon himself "our prideful nature, which is departed from God" and "brought it again under God."[32] Moreover, Jesus' "own person" was not really touched by sin, even though he suffered under sin for our sake.[33] Did Hut mean that starting with baptism Jesus bore a burden we could not bear and initiated a sinless way of relating to God into which we must enter—but could not unless he had borne this burden? Possibly. But his extant remarks are too sketchy for us to know.

• *Leonhard Schiemer.* Hut was often echoed by Leonhard Schiemer. Christ's work happened mostly "through his conception, birth, death and resurrection in us." His cross mostly meant detachment from creatures. Schiemer critiqued Lutherans for knowing Christ only according to the flesh: as next to but not within us.[34] Yet

---

[28]Hans Hut, "Ein christlich Unterrich, wie goettliche Geschrift vergleicht und geurteilen solle werden," in *Glaubenzeugnisse oberdeutscher Taufgesinnter,* (= Quellen und Forschungen zur Reformationsgeschichte), ed. Lydia Mueller (Leipzig: M. Heinsius Nachfolger, 1938), 20:33.

[29]Hut, "On the Mystery of Baptism," p. 68.

[30]E.g., Hut asserted that Christians suffer "Christ's suffering and not our own." Yet the reason was that "we are one body in Christ" (ibid., p. 75). Hut declared that "not only Christ the Head was crucified, but *rather* Christ in all his members" (p. 67, italics mine). Somewhat like Denck, Hut mentioned that God's Word must born in us as it was in Jesus. We must receive it with trembling like Mary and become Christ's mother, brother and sister ("Ein christlich Unterrich," p. 34). It is through our experience of death and resurrection that we know Christ is come in the flesh (ibid., p. 35).

[31]Hut, "On the Mystery of Baptism," pp. 73, 66-67.

[32]Ibid., p. 78.

[33]Ibid., p. 80.

[34]Leonhard Schiemer, "Three Kinds of Grace," in *Early Anabaptist Spirituality,* ed. Daniel Liechty (New York: Paulist Press, 1994), pp. 84-85.

Jesus emerged more clearly as the agent of a distinctive work, not simply an exemplar. He not only initiated the baptism of obedience but also suffered historically for us.[35] Jesus was the only mediator, who united us with God, and our master in heaven, to whom we pray.[36]

Schiemer found the devil very active in the opposition he experienced, but his extant works did not connect this with Christ's work.

• *Hans Denck.* God's Word works in everyone to take them through the *Gelassenheit* process, according to Hans Denck. This wrought humility, which included serving creatures.[37] Jesus often seemed to simply be a human who opened himself fully to this Word. Jesus, Denck said, became one with the Word through suffering, for the Word wrought grace in him according to his measure of faith.[38] Moreover, "God created all people like *[gleich]* himself," but Jesus alone never lost this perfection[39] and remained "entirely like *[ganz gleich]* the Father."[40]

Critics objected that if Jesus accomplished what everyone could, he was unnecessary for salvation. Denck replied that anyone who attained salvation had "merely taken from him, that is, righteousness out of grace." They enjoyed it only because the Word "became human in Jesus" to make this process visible, for people could not know God's love unless God manifested it through particular persons. This occurred supremely through Jesus, whose unity with God had been so perfect that his suffering was reckoned "the very suffering of God." True love, in fact, could not "be known otherwise than through him."[41]

Such affirmations seemed to identify Jesus uniquely with God during his

---

[35]Ibid., p. 95; Schiemer, "Apostles' Creed," p. 35.

[36]Ibid., p. 216, 221, cf. Schiemer, "Three Kinds of Love," p. 97.

[37]Denck, *Spiritual Legacy*, pp. 97, 157. This service was voluntary, in sharp contrast to the servitude which arose from inordinate attachment to creature, from which *Gelassenheit* freed us.

[38]Ibid., p. 223.

[39]Ibid., p. 97.

[40]Ibid., p. 101. *Gleich* can be understood loosely as "like" or precisely as "equal to." I follow Bauman's loose translation, rather than Williams and Mergal: "created all persons equal to *[gleich]* himself" (George Williams and Angel Mergal, eds. *Spiritual and Anabaptist Writers* [Philadelphia: Westminster Press, 1957], p. 102). Though Bauman translates *ganz gleich* as "entirely like," he adds "completely equal to" in a footnote (Denck, *Spiritual Legacy*, p. 101); Williams and Mergal use the latter in their main text (*Spiritual and Anabaptist Writers*, p. 102). Denck clearly meant to indicate not only Jesus' similarity with all persons but also a difference. It is unclear whether the difference and his being *ganz gleich* the Father was due to his work, his obedience to his Father in everything, or his person, being "the Son" who shared God's love "from eternity."

[41]Denck, *Spiritual Legacy*, pp. 97, 101, 185, 187. God's perfect love involves becoming as nothing for the needy (p. 187, cf. p. 89). Love denies itself, and would will to die or cease to be for the beloved's sake (p. 183).

life—and even, through the Spirit, from the beginning.[42] But do they clash with others about the inner Word's sufficiency to lead everyone, Jews and pagans included, to salvation?[43] I can resolve this only in "The Person of Jesus Christ" (see pp. 370-73).

In any case, when treating Jesus' work, Denck stressed that he made visible not only the human path to salvation but also God's self-giving love, as does moral influence theory. Unlike Hubmaier, who connected this almost entirely with Jesus' death, Denck included Jesus' life. But Denck put little emphasis on his resurrection, again unlike Hubmaier.

Denck sometimes used substitutionary language—but to lend it another meaning. For instance, Jesus "made satisfaction," but this was by pioneering the way no one else could find.[44] Jesus fulfilled the law for us, but "to give us an example for following him."[45] Denck meant that Jesus fulfilled the law's inner intent, which is love, and can motivate us to do so. Among traditional atonement categories, Denck clearly approximated moral influence most closely.

• *Hans Schlaffer.* Christ's work was verbalized by Hans Schlaffer with greater variety than other early South German-Austrians. He also understood salvation as incorporation into Jesus' life, death and resurrection.[46] As for Hut, this consisted largely in sharing life with others in Christ's body. The flesh and blood that people gave in dying was not theirs but Christ's.[47] Like Hut and Schiemer, Schlaffer rejected the notion that since Jesus had done everything, we need only believe.[48]

Yet Schlaffer also affirmed that the body's suffering "goes primarily by the head."[49] Jesus' blood, sacrifice and resurrection also referred to redemptive historical

---

[42]"Nach dem geyst von anbeginn eyns mitt Gott gewesen" (ibid., p. 186). Denck's wording seems more classically trinitarian than Liechty's: "He was one with God's Spirit from the beginning" (Daniel Liechty, ed., *Early Anabaptist Spirituality* [New York: Paulist Press, 1994], p. 114; further references in note 251 of this chapter).

[43]Cf. p. 261 above.

[44]Denck, *Spiritual Legacy*, p. 133; see p. 120 note 60 above. For this translation and related passages. Jesus also fulfilled "all righteousness," including the law's commands "from the smallest to the greatest," but "as an example for us" that we should not despise them (p. 195).

[45]Ibid., p. 133.

[46]Schlaffer, "Ein kurzer Unterrich," p. 95; *Selections*, pp. 204-7, 196.

[47]Schlaffer, *Selections*, p. 205; "Ein kurzer Unterrich," p. 109. Like Schiemer, Schlaffer insisted that for Jesus' work to benefit us, we must experience it. Jesus, for instance, remitted sins by sprinkling our consciences and showing brotherly love, so we would shed our blood for others (*Selections*, p. 206). We must also participate in Jesus' descent to hell ("Ein kurzer Unterrich," p. 96) and resurrection (ibid., p. 95; *Selections*, p. 196).

[48]Schlaffer, "Ein kurzer Unterrich," p. 95.

[49]Ibid., p. 96, cf. pp. 106, 114.

acts. Schlaffer conceptualized the first two as substitution.[50] Gethsemane did not simply exemplify suffering but somehow included all suffering from the beginning.[51]

Far more clearly than Hut, Schiemer or Denck, Schlaffer considered Jesus God's eternal Son, through whom God created the worlds.[52] To pray through Christ was to participate in his "depth" and to appeal to the Father "for what he has done on our behalf."[53] Christ's eternity entailed that his words, including his baptismal commands, would never pass away.[54]

For Schlaffer Jesus conveyed God's love, as in moral influence. Yet important as his historic ministry was, Jesus accomplished this mainly in the present by illumining our hearts and sealing them with the Spirit.[55] Through this we know that the Father loves and accepts us, as Hubmaier underscored, though he had focused on the cross.[56]

Alone among early South German-Austrians, Schlaffer employed Christus Victor imagery often. Jesus, he said, triumphed over the devil in the wilderness, suffered under the "Prince of this world" and was delivered over to the Serpent's cunning.[57] Like Hubmaier, Schlaffer envisioned Satan behind this "world's" darkness and raising up sects.[58] The "world" was so entrapped by sin that it was God's enemy from which Christians must turn.[59]

2. Substitutionary language was occasionally used by Peter Riedemann. The Father laid our transgression on his Son, who stilled his wrath.[60] Yet much as Hubmaier declared, this resulted in "knowing that I have a gracious God who has discounted, remitted and forgiven me" and "offered himself to me in Christ as Father."[61] Such phrases often appeared in conjunction with Christ's present renewing work, which renders us "partakers of his nature, character, and being."[62]

---

[50]Ibid., pp. 91, 110, 111; Schlaffer, "Instructions on Beginning," pp. 105, 106. Jesus died for sin and rose for righteousness, as Hubmaier often said (p. 115, cf. p. 114).

[51]Ibid., p. 95; Schlaffer, *Selections*, pp. 202-3.

[52]Schlaffer, *Selections*, pp. 195-96; "Ein kurzer Unterrich," pp. 98-99.

[53]Schlaffer, *Selections*, p. 208.

[54]Schlaffer, "Instructions on Beginning," p. 107.

[55]Schlaffer, *Selections*, pp. 196, 202; Schlaffer, "Instructions on Beginning," p. 99.

[56]Schlaffer, *Selections*, p. 202.

[57]Schlaffer, "Ein kurzer Unterrich," pp. 107, 98, 124.

[58]Schlaffer, *Selections*, p. 199; "Ein kurzer Unterrich," p. 99.

[59]Schlaffer, "Ein kurzer Unterrich," pp. 113, 112.

[60]Peter Riedemann, *Peter Riedemann's Hutterite Confession of Faith*, ed. John Friesen (Scottdale, Penn.: Herald, 1999), pp. 70, 73.

[61]Ibid., p. 196.

[62]Ibid., p. 75, cf. p. 66.

Riedemann portrayed Jesus' historic atonement chiefly in Christus Victor imagery. God had created humans in the divine image to dwell in them. Yet they were deceived by Satan, lost all grace, took on the devil's image—lying, sin and injustice—and became idols' temples.[63] The inclination toward sin energized all human behavior, bringing everyone under God's wrath.[64]

Christ came to lead the human race back to God, to gather those who belonged to God and lead them into the liberty of heirs.[65] He became a lowly servant to guide and instruct us, especially in face of wealth and power.[66] Jesus withstood all temptation and illumined the darkness that imprisoned us.[67] He overcame the unclean spirits, bound them and delivered us, whom they held captive unto death. Riedemann connected this conquest of death, devil and hell, mainly with Jesus' cross.[68] Jesus' Father then raised him to be firstborn and Lord of the saved.[69] Riedemann connected this entire past work directly with Christ's ongoing conquest of evil. Since sin binds us to the devil, Christ delivers us by divinizing us, which destroys sin's actual power.[70]

Riedemann insisted that only divine power could accomplish all this. For this reason Jesus had to be the Word himself who "took upon himself human nature," although "the divine nature remained completely in him." However, since death had come through a human, it had to be conquered by the resurrection of one who was human.[71] This view of Christ's person, different from Hut's and Denck's, was closely intertwined with this different Christus Victor reading of Christ's work.

Like Hubmaier and Schlaffer, Riedemann and his Hutterites found the devil working everywhere in the "world." Established churches had originated from sacrifices to devils.[72] Things like concern about adornment, "standing drinks" and marriage for money or beauty were from the evil one.[73] God governed the "world"

---

[63]Ibid., pp. 91, 90, 171.

[64]Ibid., pp. 91-93.

[65]Ibid., pp. 176, 181.

[66]Ibid., pp. 71, 66, 120, 134.

[67]Ibid., pp. 65, 69, 72

[68]Ibid., pp. 65, 67, 71, 181, 185.

[69]Ibid., pp. 65, 71, 175. Jesus also descended to hell, or "the place of captivity," to proclaim salvation not, as for Hubmaier, to those who had believed God's promise but those who had disbelieved (p. 70). Riedemann briefly mentioned Jesus' present intercession, foregrounding the comfort it gives. Jesus knows our weaknesses, having being tempted in every way (p. 72). Jesus would return as Judge to pronounce sentences previously passed (p. 73).

[70]Ibid., pp. 67, 74, 176.

[71]Ibid., p. 65.

[72]Ibid., p. 124.

[73]Ibid., pp. 154, 156, 150, 128.

mainly by delivering evil forces over to each other, as Hubmaier also said. Government was the rod of God's anger that brought people's evil on their own heads. God gave disobedient populations and governments over to each other for mutual destruction.[74] Through rebellions God handed rulers over to and punished them with the consequences of their own sins.[75]

3. Like Riedemann's, Pilgram Marpeck's chief imagery was Christus Victor. He utilized substitutionary terms more than Riedemann, though not as prominently as Hubmaier.[76] Marpeck often mentioned sin's forgiveness through Christ's blood.[77] Sin's seriousness was indicated by how much God demanded from his Son.[78] These phrases, however, appeared within a broader drama that, as we might expect from Marpeck's sacramental vision, restored relationships between Spirit and matter. Not unlike Hut and Denck, Marpeck taught that humans were created to serve God and to rule other creatures through their spirits but serve them through their bodies.[79]

- *Christus Victor (transformative).* Humans, however, obeyed the serpent's urging to rise even above God. But through this disruption of the created order, they lost their rule over creatures and became subject to, or lower than, them through idolatrous attachments.[80] Humans and all other creatures became ashamed and fearful; sin, death and hell became our lords.[81] Evil seed and the serpent's poison spread through the race. The serpent became head of the body of humankind and prince of this "world."[82]

Sin, otherwise described, involved the human spirit's effort through reason to rise above the flesh. But through this, paradoxically, it fell under the flesh and was

---

[74]Ibid. pp. 130-31.

[75]Ibid., p. 215.

[76]E.g., Jesus bore our sins, weaknesses and guilt, and fastened them to the cross (Pilgram Marpeck, *The Writings of Pilgram Marpeck*, ed. and trans. William Klassen and Walter Klaassen [Scottdale, Penn.: Herald, 1978], p. 124). He became a sacrifice to the Father for us (ibid., p. 125); J. Loserth, *Pilgram Marbecks Antwort auf Kaspar Schwenckfeld's Beurteilung des Buches der Bundesbezeugung von 1542* [Vienna: Carl Fromme, 1929], p. 77). Through sacrifice Jesus expiated sin and paid our debt (Marpeck, *Writings of Pilgram Marpeck*, p. 236). His righteousness and innocence were valid before God's face (p. 154).

[77]E.g., Marpeck, *Writings of Pilgram Marpeck*, pp. 115, 337, 354, 470, 550. Christ's sacrifice assuaged the Father's wrath and repaid unrighteousness with his blood (p. 175).

[78]Loserth, *Pilgram Marbecks Antwort*, p. 265.

[79]Marpeck, *Writings of Pilgram Marpeck*, pp. 113, 83; for a fuller account see Thomas Finger, "Pilgram Marpeck and the Christus Victor Motif," *MQR* 78, no. 1 (2004):53-77.

[80]Loserth, *Pilgram Marbecks Antwort*, pp. 193, 194; Marpeck, *Writings of Pilgram Marpeck*, pp. 83, 414, 477.

[81]Marpeck, *Writings of Pilgram Marpeck*, pp. 113-14.

[82]Loserth, *Pilgram Marbecks Antwort*, pp. 192, 452, 208; Marpeck, *Writings of Pilgram Marpeck*, p. 114.

imprisoned by its obscurity.[83] Humans could be freed only if their spirits were again opened to God's Spirit to work through and renew their flesh, and only if the original order were restored, where human spirits served God and ruled creatures, and human bodies served their own spirits and creatures too.

Jesus conveyed God's Spirit to us through his pure flesh and blood.[84] Historically and contemporaneously, this was partly epistemological.[85] Just as we apprehend others' inner thoughts through their outer actions, we come to know God's mind through Jesus' earthly deeds. His flesh provided a clear, sinless channel for this.[86] In this way, Jesus' teaching and example comprised a major portion of his work.[87]

Marpeck also indicated that Jesus, as the first to incorporate an entire human life into the Spirit's transforming dynamic, forged a new human reality that others could participate in. This humanity attained full maturity only with Jesus' resurrection. Accordingly, the Word (or Lamb) could not have been savingly present in everyone since history's beginning, at least not as early South German-Austrians implied.[88] On the contrary, the Word took on flesh and bone to become the root of a new humanity that our flesh and bone would no longer be tainted through Adam's flesh but renewed through his.[89] Only as Jesus became the first human to walk in holiness was Adamic flesh cleansed and rejuvenated.[90] This alone enabled us to participate in that process by which Jesus overcame flesh's weakness and was taken up into the Godhead.[91]

This transformative side of Jesus' work clearly resembled Christus Victor. Yet how literally did he convey bodily renewal? Recall that although bread and wine could be of the Lord's Supper's essence, Marpeck still called Christ's presence there

---

[83]Marpeck, *Writings of Pilgram Marpeck*, pp. 76, 79, 322. For Marpeck flesh in the negative sense meant not the body but largely the "self-enclosed, self-rationalizing mode of existence in which all of humanity was trapped. One seeks a self-sufficient existence, without reference to any reality beyond the self" (Stephen Boyd, *Pilgram Marpeck* [Durham, N.C.: Duke University Press, 1992], p. 70).

[84]Marpeck, *Writings of Pilgram Marpeck*, p. 83.

[85]Primarily so, according to Neal Blough, *Christologie Anabaptiste* (Geneva: Labor et Fides, 1984), p. 56.

[86]Marpeck, *Writings of Pilgram Marpeck*, pp. 63, 76, 78, 81-82, 99, 435.

[87]Ibid., pp. 466-67.

[88]Before Jesus humans possessed only natural piety that at best could produce awareness of sin and hope for grace, such as through the Old Testament law (cf. chap. 7). The "Spirit of God would have remained an eternal secret without the humanity and the physical voice of Christ" (ibid., p. 76). Marpeck critiqued those who believed otherwise for attributing too much power to the human will or to God's image in humans (p. 79, cf. p. 60).

[89]Loserth, *Pilgram Marbecks Antwort*, pp. 287-88; cf. pp. 552-53.

[90]Ibid., p. 288.

[91]Marpeck, *Writings of Pilgram Marpeck*, pp. 322, 508-9.

spiritual.[92] Accordingly, Neal Blough maintains that when Marpeck mentioned Christ purifying our flesh, he meant this spiritually.[93] Yet Marpeck often stressed that matter truly participated in spiritual transformation. I agree more with Stephen Boyd:

> Because Christ shared the nature of the human being, that nature was opened or received the capacity to share in the divine life. Therefore, created reality, including the material, became, in the person of Jesus Christ, the mediator of that capacity and participation.[94]

- *Christus Victor (conflictive)*. How did Jesus accomplish this side of his work: releasing creatures from imprisonment under death, sin, hell and the curse?[95] Since the serpent instigates sin through reason's pride, sin can be defeated only when reason is humbled, when reason has to confess the weak, reviled, human Jesus as God's true revelation.[96] Jesus, that is, overcame Satan through his patient, humble way, which opposed all pride. This involved loving enemies and overcoming evil with good, which led to the cross. This is the only truly human path to overcoming opponents and eventually attaining glorification.[97] Marpeck, then, conceived Jesus' earthly work not only in moral influence but also in Christus Victor terms.

In this context, though, something like moral influence appeared. Jesus' cross was the culmination of his love.[98] It revealed that God sent his Son out of tender love. God loved us in this way that we might love God and gave his Son that we might give ourselves to God.[99] In Jesus' death the Father's mercy triumphed over judgment. It took away the fear that keeps us in bondage.[100] Marpeck, like other South German-Austrians, also regarded Jesus' cross as a participatory event in which our flesh and blood with their lusts are buried.[101] This goes beyond moral influence.

Marpeck underscored Jesus' descent to hell, the nadir of his humility, mentioned at length only by Hubmaier so far. Jesus remained captive there until he had

---

[92]Cf. pp. 184-208 above.

[93]Blough, *Christologie Anabaptiste*, pp. 71, 181-82.

[94]Boyd, *Pilgram Marpeck*, p. 74; cf. Marpeck, *Writings of Pilgram Marpeck*, pp. 197, 379, 389.

[95]Marpeck, *Writings of Pilgram Marpeck*, pp. 121-24.

[96]Ibid., pp. 79-80, 316-18, 337-38.

[97]Loserth, *Pilgram Marbecks Antwort*, p. 141; Marpeck, *Writings of Pilgram Marpeck*, pp. 434, 461, 548. Patience was also indispensable for church discipline (pp. 214-16 above).

[98]Marpeck, *Writings of Pilgram Marpeck*, pp. 148, 274.

[99]Loserth, *Pilgram Marbecks Antwort*, pp. 442, 446, 484; Marpeck, *Writings of Pilgram Marpeck*, pp. 189-90, 534-35.

[100]Marpeck, *Writings of Pilgram Marpeck*, p. 360.

[101]Ibid., p. 322.

paid fully for sin.[102] Then the life in him broke forth, annihilating the dominion of death and the devil. Jesus ascended in glory, taking along death's prisoners and "the prison itself."[103] By these acts the "world" and its prince were judged.[104]

The risen Jesus then presented to his Father, through his humanity, the right-eousness the Father required.[105] Substitutionary notions like this appeared amidst Marpeck's Christus Victor imagery, though much less often than in Hubmaier's. Those who participate in Jesus' resurrection are ruled only by God, no longer by sin, death, the devil, hell or creatures.[106] The created relationships among God, humans and nonhumans were restored.[107]

During Jesus' life, his human spirit and flesh were increasingly transformed by God's Spirit,[108] although the Spirit continued to minister largely through him. On the cross, however, his body was pried open and the Spirit released.[109] Jesus' resurrection also initiated the Spirit's outpouring. With his resurrection Jesus' human nature was more fully divinized, and through him the Spirit be-came available to others.[110] His resurrection, like his cross, became a participa-tory reality through which he lives in Christians, and they dwell in his risen body along with his Father and Spirit.[111] For Marpeck, as for Hubmaier, Schlaf-fer and Riedemann, Jesus' atoning work continued in the present. (He did not,

---

[102]Ibid., pp. 432-33.

[103]Ibid., p. 433.

[104]Loserth, *Pilgram Marbecks Antwort*, p. 200, cf. pp. 217, 317.

[105]Ibid., p. 110.

[106]Marpeck, *Writings of Pilgram Marpeck*, pp. 83, 414.

[107]In redemption "the life and deeds of all true believers serve all creatures. Their spirit is lord of all things through Christ, and they are again restored to the first glory of Adam so that nothing may rule over them, neither sin, death, nor hell" (ibid., p. 83; cf. pp. 430, 476). Though inordinate attachments to creatures must still be overcome, true conversion involves regarding "God together with his creatures . . . true and good" (p. 493). Marpeck briefly indicated that this involved recon-ciliation of the cosmos (Loserth, *Pilgram Marbecks Antwort*, pp. 198, 206). All this occurred because the Lord "became a natural man for natural man in order that that he [the natural man] might be translated, by the natural [Jesus], from his destroyed nature into a supernatural and heavenly being" (my translation. Marpeck wrote, in order that "er auch durch das natuerlich ubersetzt wuerde auss der zerstoerung der natur in das uebernatuerlich und himmlisch wesen" [Pilgram Marpeck, *Ain klarer vast nützlicher Unterricht* (Strasbourg: Jakob Commerlander, 1531), Bvi v = photocopy p. 26]). Klassen and Klaassen translate: in order that "by the natural, the destruction of his nature might be translated again into the supernatural and heavenly nature" (*Writings of Pilgram Marpeck*, p. 85). This might seem to mean that Jesus destroyed our nature.

[108]This point is somewhat disputed and will be addressed in "The Person of Jesus Christ" on pp. 377-79 below.

[109]Marpeck, *Writings of Pilgram Marpeck*, p. 431; cf. Boyd, *Pilgram Marpeck*, p. 151.

[110]Loserth, *Pilgram Marbecks Antwort*, pp. 302, 502, 535.

[111]Marpeck, *Writings of Pilgram Marpeck*, pp. 90, 91, 94, 436.

however, single out intercession as a distinct function.)

Nonetheless, Christ is not yet fully glorified. Marpeck called the church Christ's unglorified body and its ceremonies and actions the continuing humanity of Christ.[112] This body would not be glorified until the final resurrection, corresponding with Jesus' bodily return.[113]

Finally, like Schleitheim, Hubmaier, Schlaffer and Riedemann, Marpeck found demonic powers active in the political realm. He regarded governments more positively than most Anabaptists, as "intermediate gods" between good and evil.[114] Yet since they often failed to protect good and restrain evil, these "fallen angels and men are delivered over to each other as the greatest enemies with never ending enmity, envy, and hate," as Riedemann affirmed.[115] This corresponded with God's way of exercising judgment in Christus Victor: turning from people who turn from God, thereby delivering them over to and allowing them to become slaves of sin, death, hell, pain and the devil.[116] Satan, Marpeck claimed, had raised up the Peasants' War, Zwingli and Münster. The powers of "this world" ruled in the churches.[117] The devil was leading many astray through false teachings, attacking God's people and constant disputes.[118]

The Netherlands. I. Like many Anabaptists, Melchior Hoffman conceived certain foundational aspects of Christ's work substitutionarily, such as that he paid for the world's sins.[119] Hoffman taught that a first justification covered original sin, sins prior to conversion and continuing weaknesses (chap. 5). This came through Christ's merits.[120] Hoffman could also underline in moral influence fashion how Jesus' sacrifice revealed God's mercy.[121]

But since the first justification freed peoples' wills to accomplish a second, how else did Christ bring salvation? By walking before his flock as a model. Jesus betrothed or offered himself to his Father at baptism, as we should. Jesus followed the Spirit into a wilderness struggle with Satan, as we should too. He became de-

---

[112]Blough, *Christologie Anabaptiste,* pp. 57-59.

[113]Marpeck, *Writings of Pilgram Marpeck,* pp. 314, 415.

[114]Ibid, p. 537; cf. pp. 296-97 above.

[115]Ibid.

[116]Ibid., pp. 215, 430; cf. p. 344.

[117]Pilgram Marpeck, "Exposé of the Babylonian Whore," trans. Walter Klaassen, in *Later Writings by Pilgram Marpeck and his Circle,* ed. Walter Klaassen, Werner Packull, and John Rempel (Kitchener, Ont.: Pandora, 1999); Marpeck, *Writings of Pilgram Marpeck,* p. 299.

[118]Marpeck, *Writings of Pilgram Marpeck,* pp. 75, 164, 486, 546.

[119]Melchior Hoffmann, "The Ordinance of God," in *Spiritual and Anabaptist Writers,* ed. George Williams and Angel Mergal (Philadelphia: Westminster Press, 1957), p. 186.

[120]Klaus Deppermann, *Melchior Hoffman* (Edinburgh: T & T Clark, 1987), pp. 61, 229, 234.

[121]Ibid., p. 83.

tached from his own will and absorbed into his Father's.[122] Those who follow this way will finally conquer sin and join Christ in his eternal kingdom.[123]

All this occurred against the backdrop of struggle with Satan, who ruled this "world." Jesus' sacrifice also delivered us from Satan, though converts, as we might expect, had to lead themselves out of his kingdom.[124] Hoffman's emissaries were busy gathering prisoners out of Satan's realm.[125]

Satan and sin, in fact, had so corrupted human flesh that Christ's had to be heavenly to be pure enough to pay for sin.[126] This flesh also nourished people in the Lord's Supper, bringing divinization.[127] Hoffman presented Jesus as the crucified, roasted and baked paschal lamb as this true nourishment, yet he also was very much the heavenly Lord.[128] Hoffman's imagery overran yet included traditional atonement categories. Perhaps it approximated Christus Victor more often than others.

2. While most Anabaptists employed some substitutionary language, Menno Simons and Dirk Phillips used it quite often. They frequently described God's righteousness as a legal standard and Jesus' work as fulfilling the law.[129] Menno habitually unrolled lists of what Jesus provided in our stead: for example, "His merits, righteousness, intercession, word, cross, suffering, flesh, blood, death, resurrection, kingdom . . . without recourse to merit, graciously given."[130] Such substitutionary notions were most often associated with Jesus' death. In this context Menno and Dirk insisted, like Hoffman, that Jesus' flesh could be pure enough to pay for sin only if it came directly from God, not from Adam through Mary.

Occasionally these Dutch leaders presented Jesus' sacrifice as cosmic, reconcil-

---

[122]Hoffmann, "The Ordinance of God," pp. 189-90.

[123]Ibid., pp. 191-92.

[124]Deppermann, *Melchior Hoffman*, p. 225; Hoffman, "Ordinance of God," p. 186.

[125]Hoffman, "Ordinance of God," p. 185. Like Hubmaier, Riedemann and Marpeck, Hoffman envisioned God exercising wrath primarily by delivering some sinners over to others—by punishing sin with sin (Deppermann, *Melchior Hoffman*, p. 62). For other Christus Victor imagery, see ibid., p. 191.

[126]Deppermann, *Melchior Hoffman*, pp. 215, 225.

[127]Cf. pp. 194-95 above.

[128]Hoffman, "Ordinance of God," pp. 184, 186.

[129]E.g., Menno Simons, *The Complete Works of Menno Simons*, ed. J. C. Wenger (Scottdale, Penn.: Herald, 1956), pp. 70, 147, 157, 336, 391, 439. For Dirk, Jesus' first reason for coming was to take away sin (Dirk Philips, *The Writings of Dirk Philips*, ed. Cornelius Dyck, William Keeney, and Alvin Beachy [Scottdale, Penn.: Herald, 1992], p. 161). God's righteousness was revealed in how severely he beat his Son, before he would be reconciled to us (ibid., p. 163, cf. pp. 256, 362; Simons, *Complete Works*, p. 336; cf. Loserth, *Pilgram Marbecks Antwort*, p. 265).

[130]Simons, *Complete Works*, p. 95, cf. pp. 98, 504.

ing all things in heaven and earth.[131] Jesus' blood, too, was not always understood as a payment but sometimes as cleansing or sanctifying.[132] Yet terms like *sacrifice, payment, merit* and *reconciliation,* which appeared often, usually implied substitution.

Dirk and Menno also underlined the importance of Jesus' teaching and of his life course as an example.[133] It provided divinization's christomorphic pattern (chap. 5). Yet Dirk could specify that Jesus was first of all deliverer, mainly in a substitutionary way, and secondarily teacher.[134]

Christ's work also manifested divine love. His incarnation proceeded from love, which was displayed most movingly in his death.[135] Such love, and not command, provided the true motive for ethical obedience.[136]

For Menno, however, the incarnation also occurred because everyone belonged to the devil.[137] Satanic opposition seemed even stronger to the Dutch than to other Anabaptists. Governments, established churches in league with them, and numerous sects appeared to be energized by demonic forces. It seemed natural to construe Christ's work as liberation from such opposition, which paralleled Israel's deliverance from Egypt.[138]

For the Dutch these conflicts also had ontological roots. Adam and Eve had suffered "the bite of the serpent," which became "the poisoned root of the sinful flesh."[139] Like Hubmaier and Marpeck, though more graphically, Menno envisioned sin spreading from them like a contagion.[140] Since Adam was of the earth and cursed, curse and death alone could be expected from the earth and his flesh.[141] Small wonder that struggles with the "world" seemed so intractable. They raged between two antithetical groups born from incompatible seeds: the serpent's and the Word's.[142]

---

[131]Ibid., pp. 108, 219; Philips, *Writings of Dirk Philips*, pp. 193-94.

[132]Simons, *Complete Works*, pp. 152, 326-27, 492, 707; Philips, *Writings of Dirk Philips*, pp. 124, 130.

[133]Simons, *Complete Works*, pp. 389, 586; Philips, *Writings of Dirk Philips*, pp. 299-301.

[134]Philips, *Writings of Dirk Philips*, p. 416.

[135]Simons, *Complete Works*, pp. 144, 147, 283, 430, 832. For Dirk, Jesus' second reason for coming was to manifest God's love (*Writings of Dirk Philips*, pp. 164-65, 257-58; cf. pp. 102, 148). This love was especially astounding because we were God's enemies (p. 164). Like Hoffman, Dirk called Jesus the paschal Lamb, roasted through the fire of love for us, alluding to Anabaptist martyrdom by fire (pp. 124, 130, 272, 324, 329, 416).

[136]Simons, *Complete Works*, pp. 307, 885; Philips, *Writings of Dirk Philips*, pp. 70, 164-65.

[137]Simons, *Complete Works*, pp. 147, 817.

[138]Philips, *Writings of Dirk Philips*, pp. 96-97, 126, 161, 249-50.

[139]Ibid., p. 160.

[140]Simons, *Complete Works*, pp. 816, 818.

[141]Ibid., p. 438.

[142]Philips, *Writings of Dirk Philips*, p. 141; Simons, *Complete Works*, pp. 55, 504, 804.

How then did Jesus conquer the devil, sin and death? Menno stressed Christus Victor's conflictive side but usually as little more than substitution (as Hubmaier sometimes did and Marpeck occasionally did). That is, since humans came under the devil's power by disobeying God's commands, Jesus' compensatory obedience released them. On one level this apparently occurred on the cross, since Menno, unlike Hubmaier, Riedemann and Marpeck, seldom emphasized Jesus' resurrection. Yet Jesus also overcame the devil transfomatively in the present. His heavenly flesh, derived from the seed of the Word, enlivened Christians and overwhelmed the devil's seed.[143]

Dirk developed Christus Victor more fully and transformatively. To elevate us to participation in the divine nature, Christ took on human nature in its weakness, temptation and mortality.[144] He became our brother, had compassion on our weakness and was tempted in every way.[145] In fact Jesus reversed Adam's path toward sin and led us to God.[146] Dirk named Jesus the pathfinder, forerunner and pioneer, apostle and beginner.[147] Jesus repented on our behalf.[148] In the wilderness he struggled with and overcame Satan, as Hoffman stressed.[149]

Dirk, like Menno, gave Jesus' death a central role in defeating Satan, often conceived in substitutionary terms.[150] Yet other expressions appeared: for example, Jesus' eternal life slew death; he swallowed up death; his sacrifice through the Spirit brought others to spiritual birth.[151]

Dirk gave greater weight than Menno to Jesus' resurrection. It exalted him over all evil powers.[152] Jesus had taught and lived as he did that we might be conformed to his image, and indeed, through his resurrection we are "created anew" according

---

[143]Simons, *Complete Works*, pp. 805, 821, 870.

[144]Philips, *Writings of Dirk Philips*, p. 146.

[145]Ibid., p. 258.

[146]Ibid., pp. 295, 311, 353, 361, 455-57. Menno developed this once (*Complete Works*, pp. 816-17) but more often contrasted Jesus drastically with Adam (e.g., pp. 438, 795).

[147]Philips, *Writings of Dirk Philips*, pp. 97, 107, 300, 465, 64, 387.

[148]Ibid., p. 124.

[149]Ibid., pp. 280, 334.

[150]Christus Victor expressions often followed substitutionary ones immediately, apparently as alternative expressions for or consequences of the latter: e.g., Jesus "has fulfilled all the righteousness of God for us, taken away all our sins, stilled the wrath of God, made peace between ourselves and God, and more than conquered Satan, the world, hell, and death for us" (ibid., p. 68; cf. pp. 126, 161-62).

[151]Ibid., pp. 326, 416, 320, 122.

[152]Ibid., p. 327. Like Riedemann, Dirk stressed that Jesus could accomplish this victory only if he possessed divine power (pp. 136, 362, 416). Yet he had to be human to be our high priest and offer himself to the Father (pp. 136, 416).

to this image.[153] Jesus' resurrection transplanted us from fleshly, Adamic nature into the heavenly, divine nature.[154] We already rise to union with the Father and eternal glory.[155] Dirk, of course, was extolling the same divinizing participation in the heavenly Christ, which expunged the serpent's seed and was experienced in the Supper, as Menno. For both Dutch leaders, as for most Anabaptists, much of Christ's work occurred in the present.[156] Yet Dirk connected entrance to it more closely than Menno with Jesus' resurrection and with Christus Victor overall.

Summary. Historic Anabaptist views cannot be simplistically identified with traditional models. Some Anabaptist expressions, however, were clearly substitutionary. Most Anabaptists thought that Jesus' death at least cancelled the judgment that sins deserve. Yet substitution was really dominant only for Menno, somewhat less for Dirk and for Hubmaier when considering Jesus' historical work, in contrast to his present work.

Dutch Anabaptists, along with Hubmaier, Riedemann and Marpeck, also regarded Christ's substitutionary sufferings as manifestations of divine love, which moral influence theory emphasizes. They found these manifestations in other aspects of Christ's work, including his incarnation. Something like moral influence predominated among early South German-Austrians. For all but Hubmaier, Jesus' life and teachings contributed much to salvific influence of this kind.

Schlaffer, Riedemann, Marpeck and to some degree Dirk also perceived Jesus' acts as phases in an ongoing struggle with evil. Marpeck explicitly and Riedemann more implicitly identified Jesus' way of peace, patience and servanthood as his main means of opposing demonic forces, who operate through pride and oppressive power. Marpeck, Dirk and Riedemann (more sketchily) portrayed Jesus as Christus Victor's second Adam, who traveled the human path ahead of us, overcoming demonic opposition and attaining our destiny: divinization. For nearly all Anabaptists, Jesus' death also overcame the powers, though it was not always clear how. Hubmaier and Menno attributed this to Jesus' substitutionary payment of legal claims by which the powers held us prisoner.

For Humbmaier, Riedemann, Marpeck and Dirk, Jesus' triumph climaxed through the resurrection. This was chiefly because the risen Jesus through the Spirit continued to energize ontological transformation (by, but not into, divine being). This alone counteracted the powers' main means of oppression: not legal claims but the corruption or poison or fear, aggression and pride that pervade people, individually and corporately.

---

[153]Ibid., pp. 161, 295.

[154]Ibid., p. 76.

[155]Ibid., p. 258.

[156]Dirk conceived of Christ's continuing intercession as substitutionary (ibid., p. 384), but more often he mentioned Christ comforting and enlivening through the Spirit (pp. 103, 121, 127, 619).

Use of traditional atonement models has also helped us spot where historic Anabaptists differed from them. They linked Jesus' work more concretely with the particularities of his ministry and crucifixion. Yet they also experienced Jesus' present, participatory work more vividly. That is, Jesus initiated a very specific way of life to shape a new creation and kept bringing people into its transforming reality to participate in it with him.

These emphases, however, fit within a Christus Victor framework, which furnished not only Riedemann and Marpeck's primary model but significant images for all but Hut, Schiemer and Denck. Other main Anabaptist notions are compatible with it. Among traditional models, then, Christus Victor can be called historic Anabaptism's primary expression of Jesus' work—providing we add that they experienced this as more present and participatory, and more specifically shaped by Jesus' life than most.

Contemporary Appropriations

Some Anabaptists today favor one of the three traditional models.[157] In the nineteenth and early twentieth centuries, many espoused substitution and regarded it as evangelical.[158] Since about the 1940s some socially oriented Anabaptists have found moral influence more congenial. Kraus develops some of its themes but does not adopt it entirely.[159] Christus Victor's emphasis on conflict with the powers has

---

[157]McClendon treats the three traditional models as valid readings of major biblical trajectories and combines them in his own view (*Systematic Theology* 2, esp. pp. 229-37). Friesen lists three traditional metaphors: satisfaction, expiatory sacrifice and ransom to Satan—all substitutionary. He critiques them for supporting "the myth of redemptive violence" (Duane Friesen, *Artists, Citizens, Philosophers* [Scottdale, Penn.: Herald, 2000], p. 116). Friesen often utilizes Christus Victor's images (e.g., release from bondage) but does not discuss it as a model. He roots Jesus' conquest of the powers in revealing an alternative way of life, and Jesus' work mainly in modeling it, but mentions no similarities with moral influence (cf. note 422 of chap. 8).

Yoder, in an early, extensive discussion mostly critiqued Christus Victor (*Preface to Theology*, pp. 289-90), moral influence (pp. 291-92), and substitution, though he discerned certain strengths in the latter, such as taking sin seriously (pp. 304-5). Yoder highlighted Jesus' obedience, including nonresistance, in restoring communion with God (pp. 307-13). Noting Yoder's later emphasis on the powers, socially understood, Murphy and Ellis identify Christus Victor as his primary atonement model and adopt it (*On the Moral Nature*, p. 184; cf. esp. Yoder, *Politics of Jesus*, pp. 135-62, and p. 354 note 188 below]). Kaufman, with Christus Victor, finds Jesus' resurrection reversing meaning of his cross—but negatively by replacing "absolute self-sacrifice" with triumphalism, which "laid the foundation for later Christian imperialism" (*In Face of Mystery*, pp. 378, 379).

[158]This is detailed in J. Denny Weaver, *Keeping Salvation Ethical* (Scottdale, Penn.: Herald, 1997).

[159]See esp. C. Norman Kraus, *Jesus Christ Our Lord* (Scottdale, Penn.: Herald, 1987); cf. Thomas Finger, "From Biblical Intentions to Theological Conceptions: Some Strengths and Some Tensions in Norman Kraus' Christology," *CGR* 8, no. 1 (1990): 72-75.

attracted attention since the early 1980s. Having determined this model's importance among historic Anabaptists, I will sharpen my focus through lenses provided by J. Denny Weaver and Walter Wink. I will then formulate my own view, asking how this component in Anabaptism's convictional framework might further illumine mission and several related issues: the nature of the demonic, the "world," and spiritual reality.[160]

Christus Victor today. I. Like Yoder, McClendon and Kraus, J. Denny Weaver grants primacy to the unique narrative centering on Jesus (chap. 3). Weaver foregrounds the cosmos' "horizontal," or historical, dimension, and while he affirms Jesus' resurrection, he ascribes little if any theological significance to a "vertical" or an "inner," personal realm. Weaver's preference for Christus Victor may derive at least as much from his sharp church-"world" contrast as his narrative orientation.[161] He insists that the church must be and act other than the "world" more strongly than I find in Kraus, Friesen or Kraybill, and more as I recommend.

Weaver highlights confrontation between Jesus "as the bearer and representation and embodiment of God's reign" through his "life, deeds and teaching," and the reign of forces that killed him.[162] This clash emerged vividly in Peter's objections to Jesus' suffering way and Jesus' rejoinder: "Get behind me, Satan!" (Mt 16:23).[163] The overall confrontation became most visible at the cross.[164]

Weaver also stresses Jesus' resurrection, which conquered the ultimate enemy, death.[165] But while Weaver steps beyond the horizontal realm here, the resurrection mainly signifies that God now reigns in history.[166] Weaver calls his treatment of Christus Victor "historicized." Demonic forces are neither personal nor spiritual but the inner side or ethos of earthly social structures, much as Kraus and Friesen

---

[160]Cf. pp. 310-22.

[161]J. Denny Weaver, "Atonement for the Nonconstantinian Church," *Modern Theology* 6, no. 4 (1990): 208, 318.

[162]J. Denny Weaver, "Christus Victor, Ecclesiology, and Christology," *MQR* 68, no. 3 (1994): 284.

[163]Ibid., p. 282.

[164]J. Denny Weaver, "Some Theological Implications of Christus Victor" *MQR* 68, no. 4 (1994): 488.

[165]Weaver, "Atonement for the Nonconstantinian Church," p. 309.

[166]Weaver "Christus Victor, Ecclesiology, and Christology," pp. 280, 288; "Atonement for the Nonconstantinian Church," p. 313. Jesus' resurrection also "embodies a future consummation" (J. Denny Weaver, "Mennonites: Theology, Peace and Identity," *CGR* 6, no. 2 [1988]: 127). Weaver leaves room for "a wide variety of understandings about the way in which the resurrection was real." He finds it "more real than the vivid memories of liberal Protestantism" but less literal than the fundamentalists' "reanimation of specific atoms" ("Atonement for the Nonconstantinian Church," p. 322). Citing Wink, Weaver affirms that Christ's victory "established a transformed reality which has both spiritual and earthly or material dimensions" (ibid., p. 313).

maintain.[167] Christus Victor's cosmic imagery refers not to entities but expresses the ultimate meaning of Jesus' work.[168]

In contrast to Christus Victor's narrative shape, Weaver finds substitutionary and moral influence models employing static ontological categories, such as deity and humanity (as in the Nicene Creed, 381 C.E., and Chalcedonian Definition, 451 C.E.), and minimizing Jesus' resurrection.[169] Weaver treats these two models as products of Constantinianism, when the church forgot its radical historical memory of Jesus and surrendered its task of confronting the "world." He finds them basically individualistic and Christus Victor intrinsically social.[170] For sanctioning government violence Weaver further critiques Anselm's substitutionary paradigm, where God must punish sin to preserve his honor.[171]

2. Walter Wink, the author of the most extensive and influential recent works on evil powers, declines to affirm any atonement theory.[172] Weaver attributes the notion of powers as inner dimensions of social institutions to Wink.[173] As in Weaver, Kraus and Friesen, powers are not distinct spiritual beings for Wink; New Testament writers who thought so were projecting their experiences into the sky.[174] Wink supposes that the powers are impersonal, but does not pronounce definitively on this.[175] He also maintains that the powers, though fallen, are redeemable—as do Friesen, Kraus, Murphy, Ellis and Yoder.[176]

Wink draws on a broader understanding of spirit and matter, an issue at Anabaptism's heart. He espouses a panentheism where God, by nature, is not distinct from but is essentially interrelated with the cosmos. Heaven, or the spiritual realm, is not distinct from earth. These two, rather, are inner and outer aspects of a single

---

[167]Weaver, "Some Theological Implications," pp. 489-90; cf. pp. 305-6, 308 above.

[168]Weaver "Christus Victor, Ecclesiology, and Christology," p. 281.

[169]Ibid., pp. 287-88.

[170]Weaver, "Atonement for the Nonconstantinian Church," pp. 315-16; "Christus Victor, Ecclesiology, and Christology," p. 288. Weaver discusses Anselm's substitutionary model and Abelard's moral influence view (ibid., pp. 10-11). For the last two centuries, however, moral influence has been expressed chiefly in liberal theology's highly social categories. Governance of society was central to Anselm's pivotal notion of God's honor.

[171]J. Denny Weaver, The Nonviolent Atonement (Grand Rapids: Eerdmans, 2001), pp. 179-204.

[172]Walter Wink, The Human Being (Minneapolis: Fortress, 2002), pp. 104-12.

[173]Weaver, "Atonement for the Nonconstantinian Church," p. 313.

[174]Walter Wink, The Powers That Be (New York: Doubleday, 1998), pp. 25-26.

[175]Ibid., p. 27.

[176]Wink, like these Anabaptists, concludes that church mission should recall the powers to their original divine vocation (ibid., pp. 29-36). His only strong text for this is the usual one, Col 1:20. But he may derive this mostly from his panentheism, which makes final separation of any creature from others or God hard to conceive (cf. ibid., p. 36).

reality.[177] "Heaven is the transcendent 'within' of material reality."[178] In process theology terminology, heaven is the home of possibilities for enrichment that God offers humans to affirm and actualize. Though these possibilities emerge "from the internal decisions and interactions of the present world," they are not inherently distinct from matter.[179]

Wink's way of conceiving spiritual reality attracts many like Weaver, for it requires no vertical realm distinct from the horizontal. How well can the Anabaptist intertwining of spirit and matter-energy, and of inner and outer, be conceptualized thus? This issue will keep resurfacing as we proceed to the sections on the person of Christ and God.

Whatever the powers may be, how do they function? For Wink they operate most devastatingly through the myth of redemptive violence: "that violence saves, that war brings peace, that might makes right."[180] In all societies violence is curbed by finding scapegoats—humans or animals—on whom the society's deepest rage is vented, after which it feels purged and cleansed. Most sacrificial rituals enact this symbolically. Since such sacrifices seem to bring purification and peace, religions teach that they are willed, often indeed demanded, by God.

Jesus overcame the powers by heralding, with maximum clarity, "God's domination-free order of nonviolent love."[181] He promoted social values like egalitarianism and economic equality.[182] A single humble man, Jesus took on the entire domination system of his day and remained nonviolent in face of its final sanction: death.[183] In this way he took on himself the violence of the entire system and absorbed its momentum in his body.[184] Jesus, in other words, became the last scapegoat. This broke the spiral of violence, reconciling all people to God.[185] By this same activity Jesus made manifest the evil nature of the powers who killed him.[186] Wink associates this mostly with the cross. Unlike Weaver, he seldom mentions Jesus' resurrection.

Though Wink does not promote Christus Victor, he finds his own outlook, which resembles it, the antithesis of substitution. Like Weaver he claims that in sub-

---

[177]Ibid., p. 20.

[178]Walter Wink, *Naming the Powers* (Philadelphia: Fortress, 1984), p. 118.

[179]Ibid., p. 120.

[180]Wink, *Powers That Be*, p. 42.

[181]Walter Wink, *Engaging the Powers* (Minneapolis: Fortress, 1992), p. 65.

[182]Ibid., pp. 65-66.

[183]Ibid., p. 141.

[184]Wink, *Powers That Be*, p. 69.

[185]Ibid., pp. 87, 92.

[186]Ibid., p. 83; *Engaging the Powers*, pp. 140-41.

stitution God demands violent sacrifice. This provides ultimate sanction for the domination system.[187] Wink acknowledges that substitutionary expressions appear in the New Testament, but he argues that these reverse the meaning of the cross, interpreting it as the final sacrifice demanded by God rather than the termination of this notion altogether.[188]

Like many moral influence advocates Wink protests that "God is a loving parent who forgives us even before we repent." "Jesus simply declared people forgiven, confident that he spoke the mind of God."[189] Wink often critiques notions of God's wrath or judgment. Still these can be understood, in Christus Victor fashion, as God " 'giving us up' to the consequences of our own violence (Rom 1:18-32; Acts 7:42)."[190]

People can respond to Jesus' work somewhat as early South German-Austrian Anabaptists taught: not only by opposing unjust social patterns outwardly but also by dying inwardly and painfully to the way these have shaped and now bind us.[191] Our egos can then be organized around a new center as we surrender to divine initiatives in the struggle against the powers.[192]

Citing Weaver, Wink maintains that Christus Victor began losing favor in Constantine's time and was replaced by individualistic atonement theories. The church forfeited its radical social message, projected God's kingdom into the afterlife or far future and made Jesus divine.[193] But Jesus, in Wink's kind of Christology from below, remained below. God did not become incarnate in him. He incarnated God in "the same way that we must."[194]

An Anabaptist response. The Anabaptist perspective recommends beginning from below with Jesus' life—and examining his death and resurrection in connection

---

[187]Wink, *Engaging the Powers*, pp. 149-50; *Powers That Be*, p. 87.

[188]Wink, *Engaging the Powers*, p. 148; *Powers That Be*, p. 88; cf. Friesen, *Artists, Citizens, Philosophers*, pp. 102-3. "God has renounced any accounting of sins; no repayment is required or even possible" (Wink, *Engaging the Powers*, p. 151). Wink draws largely on Rene Girard (esp. ibid., pp. 144-52). While Nancey Murphy and George Ellis adopt Christus Victor, they treat New Testament substitutionary expressions as an *anomaly* for which it cannot account. They employ Girard's notion of sacrifice as an *auxiliary hypothesis*: not a contradiction to Christus Victor but a way of explaining substitutionary expressions compatible with it (Nancey Murphy and George Ellis, *On the Moral Nature of the Universe* [Minneapolis: Fortress, 1996], pp. 187-90, 228). Yoder, however, critiqued the notion of atonement as absorption of evil (John Howard Yoder, *Preface to Theology* [Grand Rapids: Brazos, 2002], pp. 296-97).

[189]Wink, *Powers That Be*, pp. 80, 88.

[190]Ibid., p. 93.

[191]Ibid.

[192]Ibid., pp. 96-97; cf. Gal 2:19-20.

[193]Ibid., pp. 89-91.

[194]Wink, *Human Being*, p. 89.

with it. Historic Anabaptists linked these most often in Christus Victor fashion. They found Jesus' way of peace central to his life. They also posited a sharp conflict between church and "world." We will follow these Anabaptist pointers to Scripture, the chief source and sole norm of my theology. Can they, now refined by historical research and contemporary considerations, help us connect Jesus' life with the church-"world" conflict, with his way of peace and also his death and resurrection? Will any of this resemble Christus Victor?

1. The conflictive dimension. Struggle with demonic forces forms an overarching pattern in the Synoptic Gospels. Immediately after his baptism Jesus wrestled with Satan in the wilderness. Satan offered him all the world's kingdoms if he would adopt the widely expected warrior-Messiah pattern for his mission (Mt 4:8-10; Lk 4:5-7). But Jesus chose instead the suffering Servant pattern.[195] This decision for a peaceful over a violent way launched his historic work. Jesus' mission was highlighted by opposition from and exorcism of demons.[196] Later, in a major showdown with his religious opposition, Jesus cited his exorcisms as evidence that a battle between kingdoms was raging and that God's kingdom was plundering Satan's. His opponents were apparently on the latter side (Mt 12:22-32; Lk 11:14-22).

The Synoptics reach a high point at Peter's confession of Jesus as Messiah (Mk 8:27-30 and parallels). But Peter, who would have expected a warrior Messiah, opposed Jesus' Servant path. Jesus rejected this as from Satan. Luke detected demonic forces behind Jesus' betrayal (Lk 22:31, 53). Then at Golgotha, the tempter's plea to adopt the warrior pattern surely echoed again: "Let the Messiah, the King of Israel, come down from the cross now, so that we may see and believe" (Mk 15:32 & pars). Yet it was the Romans and Israel's religious leaders who crucified Jesus and jeered him. The Synoptics often link demonic opposition with their opposition, without reducing it to the latter.[197]

Conflict with the demonic is also prominent in John, where "the Ruler *(archōn)* of this world" instigated the crucifixion (Jn 14:30). He was judged and driven out

---

[195]Mt 4:1-11; Mk 1:12-13; Lk 4:1-13. For this and what follows, see N. T. Wright, *Jesus and the Victory of God* (Minneapolis: Fortress, 1996), pp. 457-58; Oscar Cullmann, *The Christology of the New Testament* (Philadelphia: Westminster Press, 1959), pp. 122-24, 276-77; John Howard Yoder, *The Politics of Jesus* (Grand Rapids: Eerdmans, 1972), pp. 30-34; Thomas Finger, *Self, Earth and Society* (Downers Grove, Ill.: InterVarsity Press, 1997), pp. 239-40, 253-55.

[196]James Robinson identifies many similarities between Jesus' exorcisms and teaching, especially as declarations of God's kingdom coming in power (*The Problem of History in Mark* [London: SCM Press, 1957], pp. 33-42). This suggests that Jesus' teachings could be better characterized by a Christus Victor than a moral influence model (cf. Wright, *Jesus and the Victory of God*, pp. 195-96). These teachings were not simply ethical instructions but also expressions of God's saving presence.

[197]Finger, *Christian Theology*, 1:291-98.

(Jn 12:31), at least in part by the resurrection (Jn 16:7-11). Jesus told the human ruler Pilate that Jesus' kingdom was not from "this world," not that it existed elsewhere but that it did not arrive through violence (Jn 18:36, cf. Jn 18:10-11). The overall conflict was even more evident in John's pervasive contrasts between darkness and light, Jesus' followers and the "world" (esp. Jn 17:6-19), and freedom and truth in Jesus versus slavery to sin and the devil's lies.[198]

Early Christian preaching heralded Jesus' resurrection victory over opposing powers—whether in Acts,[199] other kerygmatic formulae[200] or via the oft-quoted Psalm 110:1 ("The LORD said to my Lord, / 'Sit at my right hand / until I make your enemies your footstool' ").[201] Continuing struggle with demonic forces also pervaded Revelation, clearly connecting them with the Roman Empire and false religion, and attributing victory to Jesus' conquest of them.[202] Since I am tracing conflict with the demonic through Jesus' life up to his resurrection and for lack of space, I must omit the considerable remaining material in the epistles.[203] Hopefully I have shown (as well as a quick sketch can) that Christus Victor's conflictive dimension has significant biblical basis, rooted in the Jesus narrative, where his way of peace was central.

Weaver and Wink helpfully illumine Christus Victor's social dimensions, explaining how Jesus, through his Servant pattern, brought God's domination-free,

---

[198]On the latter see esp. Jn 8:34-52; Jesus was accused of having a demon (Jn 7:20; 10:20-21); Judas was motivated by the devil (Jn 6:70; 13:2). Such themes permeate the Johannine epistles: the "world" as a realm of evil (1 Jn 2:15-17; 3:1, 13; 4:3-5; 5:4-5, 19), darkness-light conflict (1 Jn 1:5-7; 2:8-11). The devil (diabolos) occurs only in 1 Jn 3:8-10 but a relatively new term, "the evil one," in 1 Jn 2:13, 14; 3:12; 5:18-19 (once in John's Gospel [17:5]). "Antichrist" emerges in 1 Jn 2:18, 22; 4:3; 2 Jn 7.

[199]Acts 2:22-24, 34-36; 3:13-15; 4:10-12; 5:30-31; 10:38-40; 13:27-30; cf. Acts 4:25-28. McClendon highlights the resurrection for understanding Jesus' work and person (Systematic Theology 2: 238-79).

[200]Rom 8:34; Gal 1:3-4. The kerygma included the Acts texts and others accenting Jesus' resurrection (Rom 1:4; 10:8-9; 14:9; 1 Cor 15:3-7; 1 Thess 1:10) (C. H. Dodd, The Apostolic Preaching and Its Developments [New York: Harper, 1964]). Jesus' lordship, inaugurated by his resurrection, was "the center of the faith of primitive Christianity;" most early New Testament confessions connected it "with characteristic regularity," with "the subjection of the invisible powers under him" (Oscar Cullmann, The Earliest Christian Confessions [London: Lutterworth, 1949], p. 59).

[201]Mk 12:36; Lk 20:43; Acts 2:35; Heb 1:13; 10:13. See also these allusions: 1 Cor 15:25; Eph 1:22; Col 3:1; Heb 12:2.

[202]Esp. Rev 1:5-6, 9; 2:9-10, 13, 24-28. Weaver rightly enlists Revelation as a key expression of Christus Victor ("Atonement for the Nonconstantinian Church," pp. 311-15; "Christus Victor, Ecclesiology, and Christology," pp. 279-81). In such contexts, pistis Iēsou is often best translated as "faithfulness of Jesus," not "faith in Jesus," as in many texts bearing on justification (cf. chap. 5).

[203]Some are briefly mentioned on pp. 310-11 above. In Naming the Powers Wink presents much of this material. For an overview, see James Dunn, The Theology of Paul the Apostle (Grand Rapids: Eerdmans, 1998), pp. 102-27.

nonviolent kingdom. In biblical narrative, however, victory and defeat or condemnation and justification are conveyed through events.[204] Wink and Weaver rightly indicate that Jesus' cross revealed the oppressiveness of forces opposing him. But by itself the cross would not have signified this but that God had cursed Jesus and vindicated his enemies (cf. Gal 3:13). Consequently, only Jesus' resurrection (emphasized by Weaver but not Wink), which reversed this verdict and energized early Christian proclamation, can climax the Christus Victor narrative.[205]

Viewed from this angle Jesus' victory consisted largely in revelation. For the powers make heavy use of illusion: they strive to appear as humankind's ultimate benefactors, guarantors of its security and prosperity (Lk 22:25). But Jesus' resurrection revealed how thoroughly and cruelly they had opposed God and operated quite otherwise. By making "a public example" of "the rulers and authorities," Jesus "disarmed" them of this weapon of illusion (Col 2:15).[206] Resurrection, further, revealed Jesus as Messiah and his kingdom as God's alternative way of life. "Contemporary Appropriations" (pp. 319-22) identified the promotion of visible alternatives to the "world's" ways as a major mission task. Now we see how this is rooted in and extends Jesus' work as Christus Victor. Phrased differently, this revelation of evil also formed a reverse side of the justifying revelation of God's righteousness through the faithfulness of Jesus Christ.

Current Anabaptist theology, then, can indeed incorporate Christus Victor's conflictive dimension and the mission implications consistent with it. My fuller treatment of Scripture here, however, confirms what I found in chapter seven: the powers were implacably hostile to Jesus' historic work. Colossians 1:20 alone hints that it altered this opposition at all. I remain skeptical, then, of rhetoric about Christian mission redeeming the powers.

Jesus' work can further illumine a related issue: whether the powers are human constructs, as Kraus and Friesen maintain. Weaver and Wink apparently concur, calling the powers the inner ethos of social institutions. But doesn't this reduce the transcendence of Spirit over human life and matter-energy? Wink's panentheism and Weaver's critique of the vertical dimension apparently point this way, though Weaver makes room for Jesus' resurrection. This issue can be approached by considering additional biblical data relevant to Christus Victor.

2. The transformative dimension. In Christus Victor as it is usually understood, Jesus opened humankind internally, and thereby all creation, to the divinizing dynamic. Wink discusses an inner dimension of Jesus' work; though so far as I can see

---

[204]Cf. pp. 137-42 above.
[205]Cf. Finger, *Christian Theology*, 1:349-59.
[206]Yoder, *Politics of Jesus*, pp. 147-50.

Weaver does not. Historic Anabaptists, however, underlined not only the specific features of Jesus' historical work but also its present, participatory character. Salvation, that is, was not only christomorphic but also divinization, bestowed by the risen Jesus (chap. 5). We can best explore the latter biblically by examining, in greater detail than in chapter seven, how Jesus' work was connected with the Holy Spirit's.

God's Spirit, who was credited with begetting Jesus, prepared the way for him and inaugurated his ministry at his baptism (Mk 1:10-11 and parallels).[207] The Spirit then impelled Jesus into the wilderness encounter with Satan and back to Galilee (Mt 4:1; Mk 1:12; Lk 4:1, 14, 18). The Spirit continually guided and empowered Jesus, particularly his exorcisms. Indeed, Jesus may have become convinced that the kingdom was coming through his "awareness of otherly power working through him. . . . In his action God acted. . . . [T]he sufferer was relieved, the prisoner freed, the evil departed. This could only be the power of God."[208] Jesus' exorcisms "by the Spirit" provided the main evidence that God's kingdom was plundering Satan's (Mt 12:28; cf. Mt 12:31-32; Lk 11:14-22). Then through the Spirit, Jesus offered himself to God on the cross (Heb 9:14). In turn the Father raised him through the Spirit (Rom 1:4, 8:11; 1 Tim 3:16; 1 Pet 3:18-19).

With this exaltation, as Marpeck stressed, Jesus entered a divine communion so full that he began bestowing the Spirit on others.[209] This meant not that Jesus remained distant but that through the Spirit he came to them (Jn 14:16-19, 26; 16:13-15; 1 Jn 3:24; 4:13). A few texts nearly identified the work of Jesus and the Spirit (1 Cor 15:45; 2 Cor 3:17). In other texts the Spirit led humans into the divine.[210] The same Spirit surged through the whole creation (esp. Rom 8:18-27).

Viewed from this angle, Jesus' victory consisted largely in ontological transformation (by, but not into, divine energy). For the powers operate through not only outward illusion but also what Anabaptists called inner corruption or poison, which pervades people individually and corporately.[211] Jesus' resurrection bestowed the Spirit who alone could clear out that channel, opening it toward God. The New

---

[207]On Jesus' conception: Mt 1:18, 20; Lk 1:35. In Luke the Spirit heralded Jesus' coming through John's conception (Lk 1:15), Elizabeth (Lk 1:41), Zechariah (Lk 1:67) and Simeon (Lk 2:26-27). By baptizing with the Spirit Jesus' ministry contrasted with John's (Mk 1:8 and parallels; Acts 19:2-6).

[208]James Dunn, *Christology in the Making* (Philadelphia: Westminster, 1980), p. 47.

[209]According to Acts, Jesus received the Spirit from the Father, whom he then poured out (Acts 2:33) and continued to send in many ways (e.g., Acts 9:17; 13:2), especially on those being baptized in his name (Acts 2:38; 10:44-45; 11:15-17; 19:5-6; cf. Jn 15:26; 16:7; Eph 1:13).

[210]1 Cor 2:9-13. "Human wisdom" (v. 13) is that hid from rulers of this "world" who crucified Jesus (1 Cor 2:6-8; also Eph 1:17; 2:18; 3:16-19; 5:18-20). Through God's Spirit humans also opposed demonic forces (Acts 7:54-55; Eph 6:17-18).

[211]The New Testament often designates this by "flesh" (*sarx*) and other terms that may seem to denote the body per se. Chapter 9 will untangle these.

Testament then represents Jesus' present work much like Christus Victor, in its transformative dimension. But does Scripture depict its historical prelude in the specific way that this motif does?

Before Jesus came, according to Christus Victor, the powers, by ruling humans through their own corruption, blocked the Spirit from transforming them. In the Old Testament, to be sure, the Spirit broke through that barrier occasionally in special ways (e.g., to Israel's judges). Despite such exceptions, though, the Bible portrays humans as communal beings to be transformed as they receive and channel the Spirit from one to another, to dwell ever more deeply within and among them. But before Jesus, in Christus Victor, everyone was bound by the powers' dominion and corruption. No one could transmit the Spirit in this fully human way. Atonement then required that some human remain free from the powers to receive and be transformed by the Spirit—which was, in fact, the destiny which God intended for all.

The New Testament portrays Jesus not only as wholly led by the Spirit but more specifically as the second Adam who reversed the path by which the first had brought humans under death's reign, so that they might reign eternally in life (Rom 5:12-21; cf. I Cor 15:45-49). Hebrews in very similar terms depicted Jesus as salvation's "pioneer" (*archēgon*, Heb 2:10; 12:2), who fully shared our humanity to conquer death and the devil (Heb 2:11-15; cf. Acts 3:15; 5:31). Jesus learned and struggled as he walked ahead of us on the human path (Heb 2:10, 18; 4:14-15; 5:7-9; 12:2-4, cf. Heb 10:24). The similarity of his human path to ours is also clearly implied in many New Testament passages about our present participation in his suffering and resurrection. Since they affirm Jesus' presence with us along our own earthly journeys, his "suffering" or "death" must include not only his cross but also what he experienced throughout his own journey.[212]

Viewed from the transformative angle, Jesus' teaching and example, including his peaceful way, again appear essential to his work. They were intrinsic to his own path and to revealing and preparing the path that all humans must take to salvation. Jesus provided the "structural model" for our lives.[213] Many themes associated with

---

[212] 2 Cor 4:7-11, 14 (in the context of 2 Cor 3:17-18; 4:16-18, which more directly express a divinizing dynamic); Rom 6:3-10; cf. Rom 8:10-11; Phil 3:10-14; 2 Tim 2:8-12; I Pet 2:19-23; 4:1-2; Rev 1:9. The New Testament, however, does not explicitly mention Jesus' increasing participation in the Spirit during his life, though the Gospels indicate some such increase at his baptism. But this can be inferred from passages about his developing in fully human ways, which included his relationship with God (Lk 2:52 and the texts in this paragraph from Heb and Acts). McClendon favors a notion of Jesus' gradual divinization as, e.g., in the Cappadocian fathers (*Systematic Theology* 2: 254, 271).

[213] Jon Sobrino, *The True Church and the Poor* (Maryknoll, N.Y.: Orbis, 1984), pp. 128-29; cf. p. 244 above.

the moral influence model emerge. Jesus' concern for people suffering poverty, discrimination, illness and demonic affliction was motivated not only by justice but also very much by love. By adhering to this way of love in the teeth of dominating, demonic opposition and by refusing to abandon its nonviolent character in face of death, Jesus certainly revealed God's passionate, compassionate love.

Yet moral influence cannot express the depth of that love, of the opposition to it and of the struggle between them. As Marpeck perceived, Jesus' nonviolent, servantlike humility did not simply set an example, even a highly inspiring one. It was a Spirit-imbued comportment through which Jesus resisted and countered the powers' domineering, violent energy. This spiritual energy alone, released at his resurrection, could dissolve the poison which that violent energy had spread through all other people; it alone could rip up the roots of the fear, aggression and pride which that energy aroused and by which it had taken them captive.

I propose then that theology in Anabaptist perspective affirms many moral influence themes—but not that model's usual reductive, historicist framework. Anabaptist theologians can better express these through Christus Victor's transformative conceptuality. Indeed, given the deep spiritual conflict it expresses, theologians will distort Christus Victor and the biblical themes it illumines if they adopt its conflictive dimension alone or wholly historicize it.

The Spirit's major role again suggests that both God's atoning work and its opposition, which transform human and material reality, also transcend them. This complex issue can be addressed by pursuing Christology from below further into Anabaptism's convictional framework: by considering those questions about Jesus' divine side and his relation to the Holy Spirit which arise from examining his work.

3. Substitution? Most historic Anabaptists employed the substitution model, though seldom as primary. Wink and Weaver, however, find it diametrically opposed to Christ's work. Substitution, they protest, represents God demanding violent punishment as atonement's actual vehicle; yet this concept undergirds that very domination system that Jesus the Victor dethroned. Does affirmation of Christus Victor entail total rejection of substitution? Or might historic Anabaptism's occasional use of the latter point toward some positive features?[214]

---

[214]Kraus, like Friesen, is quite critical of substitution, but rethinks the cross at length (*Jesus Christ Our Lord*, pp. 147-68, 205-26; cf. my comments ["Biblical Intentions," pp. 68-75]). Rachel Reesor stresses atonement language's metaphorical and affective features, and proposes that when viewed from this angle, critique of substitution "does not require a wholesale rejection of talk of satisfaction, debt, sacrifice or blood" (Rachel Reesor, "Atonement: Mystery and Metaphorical Language," *MQR* 68, no. 2 [1994]: 217). While recognizing, with feminist critics, that atonement theology can

• *Legal terminology.* Historic Anabaptists critiqued substitution as well. Perhaps early South German-Austrians were most outspoken in response to what they heard Protestants say: to be saved, simply believe that Jesus died historically, outside of us. But as Schiemer protested, unless Christ dies in someone, "Christ did not go to heaven for him."[215] Yet we have noticed how, in emphasizing such experiences, these Anabaptists could reduce Jesus from salvation's unique origin to its exemplar, or to a symbol of one's experience.

To be sure, substitution can connote something done wholly apart from us, without any real effect on us. But might one of its intentions be to emphasize that Jesus is distinct from us, that as salvation's origin, he did something for us that we could not do for ourselves? I will review my Christus Victor account to ascertain whether concepts of a substitutionary sort could help express this. (Regrettably, I can only relate these models very generally, leaving many good questions and criticisms unanswered.)

In both models Jesus' lifelong obedience brought eternal life, which we could not attain on our own. Substitution conceptualizes the benefits of this obedience as merits. Merits earn eternal life as a reward. This can be transferred to our account. In Christus Victor, Jesus' obedience brought his human life into full communion with God. This communion itself is eternal life. This "reward" affects us when the risen Jesus, through the Spirit, incorporates us into his journey and hence his communion with God. We indeed obtain what we could not attain on our own, but mainly by being drawn into it and participating in it.

Both models also affirm that Jesus' cross rescued people from eternal death. Substitution conceptualizes this death mainly as punishment for breaking a law, which incurred a debt that no one could pay on their own. Jesus' death is a payment that nullifies that debt when it is transferred to our account. Christus Victor conceives death as the inevitable consequence of transferring one's ultimate allegiance from God, the source of life, to lesser powers who are likewise turned toward death. Since these powers are stronger than anyone, no one can avoid death on their own. Though death, or final separation from God, at bottom results from turning from God, the powers, so to speak, actually administer it, or inflict this punishment.

Since Jesus walked the human path as God intended, he inevitably opposed the powers—but in the peaceful way consistent with it. The powers, however, ulti-

---

function abusively, Reesor draws several positive meanings from a feminist perspective (ibid., pp. 212-17). For a treatment of similar issues in light of Luke-Acts, see Mary Schertz, "God's Cross and Women's Questions: A Biblical Perspective on the Atonement," *MQR* 68, no. 2 (1994).

[215]Schiemer, "Apostle's Creed," p. 35.

mately operate by violence.[216] Jesus, a true human who remained within human limitations, was weaker than they. Consequently, they inflicted violent death upon him. Because their punishment finalizes separation from God, Jesus experienced death in this sense. Did this accomplish something we could not do for ourselves?

Jesus passed alone through the horror of final separation from God, but he was raised to life by his Father through the Spirit. Consequently, when people joined to the risen Jesus are dying, this one who was crucified accompanies them. They are not abandoned to death but are finally raised to life. People under death's dominion cannot do this for themselves.

Some versions of Christus Victor explain aspects of this in substitutionary terms (recall Hubmaier and Menno). They might say, for instance, that people who are deprived of life by turning from God incur a debt (maybe like "oxygen debt") that they cannot pay. Or that by committing themselves to lesser powers, people disrupt God's order, or break God's law. Or that by that very act people give, and therefore owe, their lives to such powers. In consequence, when people are wholly deprived of life or are destroyed by these powers, they receive the penalty, or punishment, they rightly deserved. Now Jesus was deprived of life and destroyed by such powers in a way that means that we need not be. Theology, accordingly, might appropriately say then that he paid our penalty or suffered our punishment as our substitute.

But how adequately can that be conceived as making a payment transferable to our account? In Christus Victor that "benefit" reaches us much as his obedience does: when the risen Jesus, through the Spirit, incorporates our dying into his dying and companions us through it. The chief overall "reward" of Jesus' work, then, is communion with God in life and death. This work by definition continues in the present and is participatory. Therefore, while theology can speak of penalty or punishment, these features, at least, are not best described as transfer of a payment.

• *Divine violence?* What of Weaver and Wink's stronger complaint: by attributing the demand for violent punishment to God, substitution contradicts the nonviolent core of Jesus' work? In Christus Victor God does punish sin, but indirectly in nearly all versions. Since people sin basically by choosing other lords, God hands them over to those lords. God does not act violently. But the powers that humans choose as rulers do. The powers then punish sin directly and violently. It was they who ex-

---

[216]Said otherwise, an ontology of violence is a primary, intrinsic feature of the "world." Cf. Irenaeus's classic statement of Christus Victor: Jesus redeemed us "not by violent means, as the [apostasy] has obtained dominion over us at the beginning, when it insatiably snatched away what was not its own" (*Against Heresies,* in The Ante-Nicene Fathers, ed. Cleveland Coxe [Grand Rapids: Eerdmans, 1979], 5:528).

ecuted Jesus. Such judgment is God's, but only in the sense that in ordering the cosmos God allows the powers to rebel, humans to follow them and the powers to inflict penalties that inevitably arise from human choices. Since God is sovereign, some versions of Christus Victor say that God demands and executes such penalties—but again indirectly. Even then God's direct will is revealed only by Jesus' way. This will opposes the powers so strongly that they and their judgments are judged and overthrown.

Viewed from this angle Jesus' victory involved not only revelation (of the powers' and the kingdom's true character) and ontological transformation but also judgment—of the powers. Jesus' resurrection, which vindicated or justified him, simultaneously condemned his enemies. This theme and others, then, sometimes acquire legal phrasing in Christus Victor. This judgment, for instance, can be called just by explaining that while the powers had the right to punish other humans, they overstepped these legal limits with Jesus. (This jars, however, with the notion that the powers could rightly demand Jesus as a ransom.) God's role in condemnation can be called just because God simply grants humans what they want.[217] I lack space to pursue these concepts or intriguing connections between Christus Victor and justification as the revelation of God's righteousness through the faithfulness of Jesus.

I am trying to show that Weaver and Wink's critique of substitution does not disqualify all legal concepts (perhaps they might agree). A theology highlighting atonement's present, participatory character might consider some of these. For participation can become so prominent that past events which accomplished something decisive fade to the periphery—the more so that theologians treat religions and religious experience as constructions of contemporary communities. When overstressed, present participation can also dissolve distinctions between the Initiator and respondents—so that transcendent reality is dissolved into human experience, or ethics means copying Jesus exactly.

These tendencies were already visible, though perhaps not taken far, among early South German-Austrians. For most Anabaptists, however, salvation's present, participatory character was intrinsically shaped by its origin in Jesus' particular history and its bestowal by the same person now risen. Since such distinctions are blurred more often today, legal concepts, including some substitutionary ones, as indicated above, can play some role in sharpening them.

4. *Summary.* In a contemporary theology in Anabaptist perspective, Christus

---

[217]Despite his reservations about judgment Wink speaks of it this way (*Powers That Be,* p. 93; esp. Rom 1:18-32). I am not implying that in their rejection of substitution Wink and Weaver dismiss all legal notions whatsoever.

Victor can provide the chief model for Jesus' saving work. Its Jesus is relevant
for marginalized people especially and indeed for everyone who often feels
overwhelmed by gigantic, uncontrollable forces. Through his earthly mission
this Jesus provides a challenge and pattern for engaging these forces, and as
risen, he provides great strength, assurance and comfort amidst the conflict,
through God's Spirit. Christus Victor's conflictive and transformative dimensions are mutually reinforcing. Each is weakened and distorted if separated
from the other. Jesus the Victor locates struggle against evil at the heart of the
Christian life—and the joyful assurance that evil will never prevail because it
has already been decisively defeated.

Christus Victor is not a precise theory but a broad motif or framework. Anabaptist theologians can incorporate a variety of images and concepts, including
some from moral influence and substitution. I find, however, that Christus Victor's
narrative structure clashes with the overarching historicist and legal conceptualities
that usually shape the former and latter respectively.

In appropriating Christus Victor, Anabaptist theology again finds itself surprisingly close to Eastern Orthodoxy. Many marginalized groups also appreciate
Christus Victor, or they will when they hear of it. In this instance Anabaptists find
themselves further from those who favor substitution (conservative Protestants and
Catholics, including many evangelicals) and from those favoring moral influence
(liberal Protestants and many ecumenicals).

Anabaptists might make closer contact, however, by incorporating themes from
these models into a new framework, which might illumine the same themes for others. Anabaptists might contribute most to current Christology by underlining the
centrality of Jesus' way of peace in combating evil, and also by showing how following this way is strengthened by and strengthens participation in the risen Christ.

Jesus' victory revealed both the evils of life under the powers and God's new creation alternative. This is why mission promotes visible alternatives to the "world."
Moreover, the Holy Spirit played a large role in defeating the powers. This makes
it more plausible that they are distinctly spiritual in some sense. In fact, Jesus' work
was so intertwined with the Spirit's that perhaps our topic's traditional title, the
work of Christ, is incomplete. Even further, if salvation is the work of both, the
question of the Trinity emerges from below—from biblical narrative, not later
Greek speculation.

Before we consider the Trinity, we will look at the person of Christ, for Jesus' saving acts alert us to paradoxes that deserve prior attention. Who was this strange person who, when challenged by his enemies to prove himself Son of God, answered—
affirmatively—by becoming a suffering Servant? What kind of a person could be
killed but also be the Author of life (Acts 3:15-16)? Approaching Jesus through his

work, or the biblical narrative of his acts, has led, as narrative readings often do, to questions about the actor's identity that can transcend narrative categories.

THE PERSON OF JESUS CHRIST

Since historic Anabaptists often apprehended Jesus' significance from below, we cannot determine how they understood his person simply by noting how frequently they affirmed or disaffirmed the classical creeds.[218] We must ask, primarily, what their convictions about his work implied about his person, not simply whether they thought Jesus was human or divine but what their statements about this, and others bearing on who he was, meant for them.

Nonetheless, the deity-humanity issue profoundly shaped Christology from the start, and historic Anabaptists were hardly immune to it. Moreover, the debates that led to the Chalcedonian Definition (451 C.E.) help clarify some issues involved in approaching Jesus from below and from above. In addition, the deity-humanity question, like the traditional atonement models, is often discussed by Anabaptist and other theologians today. For these reasons this question can provide an exploratory framework for asking how Anabaptists understood Christ's person. It will help us discover where they agreed or disagreed with an influential tradition, but need not force every statement onto this grid. For it will also help us spot where and how Anabaptists viewed this mystery in other terms.

Chalcedon was preceded by debates between two schools. (To provide useful lenses, I must accent their differences more than occasional similarities.) Theologians from Antioch wanted to stress Jesus' full humanity (somewhat from below). They did so by affirming or implying that in his personal center, or person, he was entirely human. Antiochenes also called Jesus divine. They expressed this mainly by saying that the divine Word indwelt him. This Word, however, was also a person. It could appear then that their Jesus had not only two natures (human and divine) but also two persons. Further, if God were present in Jesus by indwelling him, it could appear that the man Jesus had performed the real saving work by opening himself to this indwelling. Jesus might also seem to be one of many whom the Word had indwelt, making him salvation's exemplar, but not its origin.

Theologians from Alexandria wanted to stress God's initiative in salvation. So they insisted that the divine Word brought salvation not by indwelling a complete human person but by taking on human nature (from above). Jesus' personal center then was this divine person. Further, whereas Antioch foregrounded the distinction between Jesus' two natures, Alexandria underlined the unity of his person. But since this person was divine, their Jesus could not really possess a

---

[218]Cf. Friedmann, *Theology of Anabaptism*, pp. 55-56.

complete human personal center. Consequently, Alexandrians could underplay Jesus' humanity. He could appear to have not only one person but also one nature (both divine).

As Chalcedon drew near, Alexandrians spoke more often of Jesus' human nature. But since they kept insisting that was Jesus just one (divine) person, this human nature lacked a full human person. Such a nature therefore could seem to be an abstraction, not concretely real. Chalcedon combined the Antiochenes' two natures emphasis with the Alexandrians' one person. Still, the deity of Christ's person seemed to mandate that his human nature lacked a human person.

Officially, Chalcedon proclaimed Jesus "one and the same Son . . . complete in deity and complete in humanity . . . consubstantial [homoousion] with the Father as to his deity and consubstantial [homoousion] with us as to his humanity, like us in all respects, apart from sin." In Jesus, this "one person [prosōpon]" and "subsistence [hypostasis]," human and divine "natures [physesin]" existed "without confusion, transmutation, division or separation [asynchytōs, atreptōs, adiairetōs, achōristōs]."

Today, evangelically inclined Anabaptists observe that most Anabaptists/Mennonites historically affirmed the creeds. Arnold Snyder includes classical Christology in historic Anabaptism's theological core.[219] For these people, this history provides a reason to advocate such a Christology. Others, more favorable toward ecumenical social activism, often stress Anabaptism's distinctive concern with Jesus' humanity. They tend to consider past and present affirmations of his deity, if not incorrect, at least of small consequence. Denny Weaver complains that Snyder ignored Polish Anabaptists and that had he included them this second orientation might appear more genuinely Anabaptist.[220]

Since Snyder defines historic Anabaptists as all sixteenth-century groups who practiced believers' baptism, I, like Weaver, find it inconsistent to omit the Poles.[221] Since Polish sources contain significant Christological options, I will include them in this and the following sections. In constructing my own view I will continue along the path "from below," interacting with two Anabaptist advocates of "the unique biblical narrative": James McClendon and Norman Kraus. They not only view Jesus' person in light of his history but exhibit some similarities with two Polish tendencies. All along I will keep Weaver's larger claim in mind: creedal Christology conflicts with Christus Victor.

---

[219]C. Arnold Snyder, *Anabaptist History and Theology* (Kitchener, Ont.: Pandora, 1995), pp. 84-85, 366.
[220]Cf. p. 55 note 39.
[221]Snyder, *Anabaptist History*, p. 6.

Historic Anabaptist Perspectives

Switzerland. Swiss Anabaptists, save Hubmaier, left few clues as to how they viewed classical Christology. They were chiefly concerned that Christ be obeyed. Still, this Christ was not only the human teacher but also a risen, transforming presence.[222] Sattler once referred to Christ as the "of one essence *[eingewesen = homoousios]* true God and Savior."[223]

Hubmaier's eucharistic teaching clearly distinguished Christ's deity, which was omnipresent, from his humanity, which was solely in heaven and could not be in the elements;[224] neither could the human Jesus exercise the keys of discipline, which he had hung at the church's side.[225] Nonetheless, Hubmaier occasionally worshiped and prayed to this risen Jesus, even during the Supper.[226]

This Jesus, however, was directly present in the preached Word.[227] Sometimes Hubmaier referred to the Word as a verbal message sent by Christ (or pointing to him) and thus apparently distinct from him. At other times, however, Christ seemed to actually be this preached Word, to be "God himself . . . which has become human."[228] Hubmaier depicted Jesus, in the repentance struggle, speaking directly to the convert of his atoning work, healing as a physician does.[229] Even though Jesus was in heaven, the Word was not simply a message about him but a dynamism through which he was so active and present that it could be equated with

---

[222]Michael Sattler called Christ "Prince of the Spirit, in whom all who walk in the light might live" (*Legacy of Michael Sattler*, p. 22). Conrad Grebel hoped his mother would put on Christ and become "a new creature born again of the divine Spirit" (Leland Harder, ed., *The Sources of Swiss Anabaptism* [Scottdale, Penn.: Herald, 1985], p. 195). Felix Mantz mentioned dying and being buried, and rising to new life with Christ (ibid., p. 313).

[223]Sattler, *Legacy of Michael Sattler*, p. 63, cf. n. 41.

[224]Hubmaier, however, rejected the distinction between the two natures reflected in the ancient Nestorian claim that Mary could not be Mother of God *(theotokos)*, but only mother of the human Jesus *(Christotokos)* (*Balthasar Hubmaier*, p. 538).

[225]See p. 187 note 149. Before the incarnation the Father exercised all power, but he transferred much of it—the keys—to Jesus while he was on earth. Jesus would again assume the kingdom bodily at his return as "God and Savior," and the keys would revert to him (Hubmaier, *Balthasar Hubmaier*, pp. 237, 505). Then at the very end, he would return them to the Father (1 Cor 15:28; cf. ibid., pp. 415-16, 546). Presently, Christ was sole intercessor with the Father and of equal majesty with him (pp. 237; cf. pp. 33, 335). Jesus lived as high priest in eternity (p. 398).

[226]Hubmaier, *Balthasar Hubmaier*, pp. 236-40, 302-3, 355, 395.

[227]Cf. p. 259.

[228]Hubmaier, *Balthasar Hubmaier*, pp. 248, 473, citing Jn 1:1, 14.

[229]E.g., Christ "brings along medicine, namely, wine and oil, which he pours into the wounds of the sinner. He . . . softens his pain and drives it away and says, 'Believe the gospel that clearly shows that I am . . . the only giver of mercy, reconciler, intercessor, mediator, and peacemaker toward God, our father' " (ibid., p. 84, cf. pp. 105-6). This is a good example of something like moral influence in Hubmaier.

him.[230] Jesus actively performed the divine work of pardon and salvation, which involved ontological transformation (by, but not into, God).

Accordingly, Hubmaier occasionally elucidated Christ's saving work by connecting it with classical affirmations of his deity. Christ existed "from eternity," he is "God and Lord" and "true God."[231] Hubmaier urged Christians to not just affirm this but understand it well, for "Jews, heathen, and bad Christians unite . . . in this error that Christ is not God."[232] Further, Son, Father and Spirit were one true God.[233]

Hubmaier probed Jesus' divine side a bit further in distinguishing God's hidden and revealed will. Hubmaier critiqued predestination for being based on claims about things beyond our knowledge, like God's omnipotence and omniscience, for these belonged to God's hidden will. Hubmaier conceded that God, being omnipotent, could do anything—even damn people before they were born. However, we can learn what God actually does only from "the revealed and preached will of God, which is God himself, and which has become human." "We should listen to the incarnated God" and cease making claims about what is hidden.[234]

Since Hubmaier was discouraging speculation, he did not distinguish in detail God as hidden and as incarnate. He was concerned with revelation's dynamism, as when he discussed the preached Word. Yet God's revealed will or Word hardly seemed a secondary expression of or something less than God. If anything, God was most fully active and real as "the incarnated God." Still, there was a clear distinction. Humbmaier could even say that "God is captured, bound and overcome by his own Word."[235] Recall too Hubmaier's definition of faith: trust in "the favor, grace and good will which God the Father has for his most-beloved Son."[236] Genuine love flowed between them. Divine love was revealed by not only the Son (á la moral influence) but also the Father's love for the Son.

---

[230]Ibid., pp. 100, 294, 403, 439. Though Christ was not on earth in his body, he was present "in his Word and through his disciples" (p. 104). People should receive the Word much as Mary received him, and "be conceived a new man and be born again in thy living, indestructible Word" (p. 236). To receive this Word was to receive the tender lamb, Jesus, so that one no longer lived, but he lived in one (p. 85). Similarly, the name of Christ, in which baptism takes place, was the grace and power of Christ (pp. 86, 113).

[231]Ibid., pp. 105, 397, 538, 539.

[232]Ibid., p. 539. He often declared that the church was built on the confession that Jesus is the Christ, the Son of the living God (pp. 352, 539, cf. p. 235).

[233]Ibid., pp. 238, 539.

[234]Ibid., pp. 473, 467.

[235]Ibid., p. 474.

[236]Ibid., p. 116 (cf. p. 333 above). In this context Hubmaier ascribed to Christ Yahweh's claim to be "the one who blots out sin for my own sake" (p. 115; Is 43:24-25).

Hubmaier also affirmed, in somewhat classic terms, that this Son became human that humans might become God's children and that he was "true God and man."[237] Jesus, like all of us, was composed of three substances. Hubmaier asserted, without much explanation, that Jesus acquired something for us through each: his body earned final resurrection, his soul regained knowledge of good and evil, his spirit freed ours from harm by our bodies.[238] Jesus, however, was somewhat unlike us in body. The human body was chiefly responsible for the first sin and had to pay with death. Through it we are "conceived and born in sin" and immediately begin decaying into earth.[239] Jesus, however, "was conceived and born without sin." This was why he alone could say, "'My kingdom is not of this world,'" whereas Christians live in this "world" and need to be ruled by, and could rule by, the sword.[240]

In sum, when Hubmaier spoke of who Jesus was, he was mainly considering his revelatory, salvific activity. Yet classical Christology well expressed Hubmaier's understanding of Christ. Revelation and salvation emanated from the Word, or divine personal center, identified with Jesus and different from his Father. Jesus' human features retained their distinctness, somewhat as the ancient Antiochenes stressed, for his deity did not overwhelm these even after his resurrection. Yet Hubmaier did not really envision the Word indwelling Jesus, as they did, or his life contributing greatly to salvation. Given the drastic effects of being conceived in sin, one also wonders how fully someone exempted from this could really share a common humanity. Hubmaier's Christ often seemed closer to the Alexandrians' divine Word who came to die and rise for us. Yet his outlook closely resembled neither classical option.

South Germany and Austria. I. By underscoring the reality of Jesus' sufferings and the necessity of following him, the earliest Anabaptists affirmed his full humanity. They also regarded the Word, or Lamb slain from the beginning, which indwelt him as somehow divine. But did they identify Jesus with that Word in some unique sense that made him divine in a way no one else could be? Or was Jesus simply a man who manifested and obeyed the Word in a way better than, but not qualitatively distinct from, others?

- *Hans Hut.* Few clues are provided by Hans Hut. He declared that "no one

---

[237]Ibid., pp. 236, 539.

[238]Ibid., p. 446. His obvious anthropological reference makes it most likely that the last term meant Jesus' human spirit, not God's Holy Spirit. If Hubmaier intended the latter, he would be vulnerable to the (Apollinarian) charge sometimes raised against Marpeck, that his Jesus was not fully human. In any case, Jesus' death sundered the three substances, but he united them in the grave and rose (p. 236).

[239]Ibid., p. 434, cf. pp. 361, 518.

[240]Ibid., p. 497; cf. pp. 391-93 above.

comes to the Father without the Son" or without "Christ the crucified." Yet Son
or Christ may simply have designated that mystical principle or process, open to
all people, that he called crucifixion.[241] However, Hut may have meant Jesus was
unique in affirming that he took "our prideful nature" on himself and "brought
it again under God" and that our sin did not touch his "person."[242] Since Chalcedon distinguished Jesus' person from his human nature and regarded the
former as divine, might Hut have meant that Jesus' person was uniquely divine?
Perhaps. But Hut also affirmed that a justified individual "becomes one with the
person of Christ."[243]

• *Leonhard Schiemer.* Christ functioned two ways, according to Leonhard Schiemer.
First, Christ is the light that indwells everyone (Jn 1:4-5), especially through conscience, teaching them how to obey God in a general way.[244] This first grace then
pointed toward the second grace of the cross.[245] The latter, however, also worked
internally for the most part. Schiemer interpreted the events recited in the Apostles'
Creed almost entirely in this sense: for example, "Christ's suffering destroys sin,
even as he suffers in me," and "not unless he suffers in me."[246] In both functions
Christ could be a principle or process operating in everyone, not uniquely identified with Jesus.

Yet Schiemer was more inclined than Hut to speak of Jesus Christ as distinct
from us and apparently as divine. Jesus was "the ruler of heaven" to whom all power
was given, in whom God's fullness dwelled bodily, and our only mediator, who
united us with God, to whom alone we pray.[247]

Hut and Schiemer's extant writings raise our major issue, but too briefly to determine how they really saw it. The next author was not so brief.

• *Hans Denck.* On one hand, Hans Denck developed a sophisticated concept of the
Word that worked in everyone through creation, conscience and above all *Gelassenheit.* This Word, which called and drew people purposefully, was in some sense an

---

[241]Hans Hut, "On the Mystery of Baptism," in *Early Anabaptist Spirituality*, ed. Daniel Liechty (New
York: Paulist Press, 1994), p. 74. This possibility is strengthened by the fact that Hut often called
the Christian community, collectively, "Christ" (ibid., pp. 75, 79; "Ein christlich Unterrich," pp.
33-34).

[242]Hut, "On the Mystery of Baptism," pp. 78, 80; cf. p. 336 above.

[243]Hut, "On the Mystery of Baptism," p. 79.

[244]Schiemer, "Three Kinds of Grace," pp. 85-90; cf. pp. 261-62 above.

[245]Ibid., pp. 90-93. His terminology was sometimes inconsistent, as in calling the first grace the law
(something external) but Christ the second grace (internal; p. 90), but including Christ as the internal Light in the first grace, and as incarnated, crucified and resurrected in the second.

[246]Schiemer, *Selections*, p. 34.

[247]Ibid., pp. 32, 216, 221; cf. "Three Kinds of Grace," p. 97.

agent or person, and given its goal (divinization) it was divine. On the other hand, Jesus was a genuine human, "born according to the flesh, in time, and, except for sin, subject to all human infirmities."[248] To clarify how Denck connected these two, I will employ our provisional classical framework.

While Jesus obeyed and manifested the Word better than anyone else, Denck usually distinguished it from Jesus' personal center, or person, as Antiochene Christology did. Did Denck ever identify Jesus' person more directly with the Word, as in the Alexandrian option? That would seem possible if he ever identified the Word, or an equivalent divine reality, as the direct subject of the earthly Jesus' actions. In at least three places he perhaps did.

This seems most likely in the passage recently quoted. The one who was "born according to the flesh" also was "never divided from God but from the beginning was one with God through the Spirit."[249] Second, Denck identified God's "firstborn" as the one who gave up everything to be "transformed into our nature" and also "became our bread."[250] Third, Denck referred to "a gelassenheit which is the means of coming to God, that is Christ himself, not to be regarded physically, but rather spiritually." So far, this simply sounds like the eternal Word, perhaps apart from Jesus. But Denck added "as he himself also proclaimed before he came in the flesh."[251] How consistent were these three passages with Denck's overall Christology?

I can best answer by glancing ahead to the Trinity, to the threefold dynamics of that mysticism that nourished all South German-Austrian Anabaptism but which Denck alone described with specificity. God, in that medieval tradition, was the one true Being. As such, God neither changed nor suffered. Yet God was also good. God

---

[248] Denck, *Spiritual Legacy of Hans Denck*, p. 187. Jesus supremely manifested not only God's love for humans but also human love for God. Jesus acted according to *[nach]* his humanity, yet not from *[von]* it, but as God instructed him (pp. 184, 185). In general, humans can fulfill God's law, though "not as humans *[menschen]*, but as those who are one with God and all creatures" (p. 133). Denck could say that Jesus' will was "not his own . . . but that of the ONE from whom he received it" (p. 265). Yet he seems to have meant that Jesus unified his will with God's (p. 267, cf. note 254 of this chapter).

[249] Ibid., p. 187 (cf. note 43 above). Sounding more orthodox than usual, Denck indicated this as the reason why "All who are saved must be saved through this Jesus" (though he added "to behold perfection in the Spirit," perhaps implying that near perfection was possible otherwise). Denck's common, more Antiochene themes also appear in this context: e.g., Jesus as our "forerunner." "All who have sought and found God's way have become one with God" (p. 187). Jesus was God's "firstborn through the Spirit *[seinen erstgeboren nach dem geyst]*" [p. 188]), though this might refer to his resurrection, or his life, probably as climaxed by it (I disagree with Bauman's translation: "according to the Spirit of Jesus, his first-born" [p. 189]).

[250] Ibid., p. 195.

[251] Ibid., p. 93.

did not want that goodness to remain hidden but to be revealed and praised.[252] So God birthed a Word that flowed forth through God's Spirit and created a universe.[253] This Word, which gave rise to creatures, speaks within them and through the Spirit continually leads them back to their immutable Origin.[254]

But although the One generated this cosmic process, it sometimes seemed less real than the One itself. For if humans are to return praise to God, they must do so freely, being capable of resisting that return journey. Yet resisting would be turning away from the one true Being and apparently toward nothing. In this sense then human resistance seemed ultimately unreal. Turning from this one true good, of course, was also evil. Yet since this was that same turn toward nothing, evil could also appear unreal.[255] Even the material cosmos could seem less than fully real, for Denck's Word operated "as long as there is time or space."[256] But in contrast, insofar as someone was "one with God, he is free of all time and space and unbounded by their laws."[257] In the ultimate sense salvation was not "bound up with flesh and blood, time and place." Nonetheless, since these features characterize all created beings, salvation "is not possible without these."[258]

Perhaps this cosmic process seemed somewhat unreal because its purpose was not to change anything. It existed to reveal what was already and always true, not, that is, to bring anything genuinely new into being but to more fully manifest the one true Being, who was wholly spiritual and beyond it. This process of emanation and return seems repetitive and cyclic, not a directional sequence that any temporal

---

[252]God is "eternally immutable" and must love himself in accord with the goodness which he receives from himself (ibid., p. 185). To be "extolled with full reverence . . . was the first and only reason" why God created. Had God not "then he would not have been recognized other than by himself, which was not adequate to his glory" (p. 81). Packull traces this general view back to Eckhart and shows how it emerged in South German-Austrian Anabaptism (Werner Packull, *Mysticism and the Early South German-Austrian Anabaptists* [Scottdale, Penn.: Herald, 1977], esp. pp. 17-34). It appeared in the *German Theology*, which Denck republished (*The Theologia Germanica of Martin Luther*, trans. Bengt Hoffman [New York: Paulist, 1980], esp. pp. 101-3, 131, 138-40). Some "propositions" briefly outlining a mystical system were appended to it about that time. Bauman attributes these to Denck (Denck, *Spiritual Legacy of Hans Denck*, pp. 261-67). I find them close enough to cite as from him.

[253]Denck, *Spiritual Legacy of Hans Denck*, pp. 221-23, 265-67.

[254]Ibid., p. 221.

[255]"In truth the understanding, will, and power of all creatures are God's own and united with God" (ibid., p. 133; I added "with God" to Bauman's translation). It was illusory to suppose that one had an understanding or will that opposed God, or that God opposes anyone, for God "truly was never against anything" (p. 135, cf. p. 87). Though oneness would seem to have lost some freedom through creatures who oppose it, "it never actually lost" this (p. 265).

[256]Ibid., p. 223.

[257]Ibid., p. 155.

[258]Ibid., p. 187.

event could alter decisively. It seems especially unlikely that the Word itself would be altered by taking on human characteristics.[259]

I doubt then that Denck meant that the Word and Jesus' personal center, which later acquired human features, were exactly identical from eternity in the Alexandrian sense. Did this mean that Jesus was simply a human like any other, not the Word in some unique sense? Denck apparently intended to identify them uniquely, but in the more Antiochene way, where Jesus' human center was increasingly assimilated to the Word the more that the Word indwelled him.

Jesus "through his suffering became one with God and his Word."[260] Through this indwelling, God was "so perfectly united in love" with Jesus "that all that God would do is done in him." In this way the "suffering of this Man is reckoned the suffering of God," and Jesus was divine.[261]

Denck, I suspect, found this identity so close that he could occasionally sound Alexandrian. But did Denck's Antioch-like approach really overcome the common criticism that he made the difference between Jesus and us one of degree, not of kind?[262]

• *Hans Schlaffer.* Unlike his three contemporaries Hans Schlaffer intentionally affirmed a classical Christology. Writing to a "weak brother" apparently troubled by the view that Christ was simply a prophet, Schlaffer insisted that he was God, the Word or Son through whom the Father made the cosmos, who became a true human through Mary.[263] Subsequently, Christ became all that Adam was to become and led humankind to an even higher state.[264]

For Schlaffer, like all early South German-Austrians, we participate in and are transformed by Jesus' sufferings, for he is the pattern for us all.[265] Yet Jesus was not simply an instance or example of a general process. For in dying and rising for us,[266]

---

[259]In Alexandrian Christology the Word changed not in the sense of becoming something else but by fully incorporating something else (human nature) while still remaining himself. Dutch Anabaptists would insist, like Alexandrians, that the Word did not indwell a human but became flesh—yet in way that could imply that the Word changed into something else.

[260]Ibid., p. 223, cf. p. 155.

[261]Ibid., p. 185. Other important passages that seem best explained in this Antiochene sense are on pp. 101, 155, 229, 265-67.

[262]Packull, *Mysticism,* p. 49.

[263]Schlaffer, "Ein kurzer Unterrich," pp. 107, 110. Christ is the "eternal Word and only Son," the "eternally remaining Word of God . . . the only savior" (pp. 84, 98; cf. p. 99), who came not from humanity (*Selections,* p. 196). God created the world through the Son and gave him all power in heaven and earth (ibid., p. 195). Since he is this eternal Word, his earthly words will not pass away (p. 107).

[264]Schlaffer, *Selections,* p. 197.

[265]Schlaffer, "Ein kurzer Unterrich," p. 95.

[266]Ibid., pp. 110, 114-15; cf. the special character of his suffering in Gethsemane (pp. 95; *Selections,* p. 203). Schlaffer often demarcated Jesus' initiatory role further by distinguishing us as his body from

in cleansing us and returning to judge,[267] Jesus did things for us that we could not do for ourselves. Yet he did not do this simply as an external agent. He now illumines our hearts, seals us with his Spirit and directs us to the Father by dwelling in us as we dwell in him.[268]

2. The aim of Christ's work, according to Peter Riedemann, was leading the human race back to God.[269] For several reasons, this required that he be divine: (1) because only divine power could overcome death, which blocked us from that goal, (2) because return involved being born from God, which only God could effect.[270] But while Riedemann, like his predecessors, found divinization central to Christ's work, unlike Hut, Schiemer or Denck, he rooted this in a more traditional Christology.

God's Son was that Word uttered by the Father in the beginning, through whom the Father created all things, upholds them and will complete them. Yet that Word remains in the Father. They are one God, distinct from the creation.[271] "The Son is the brightness of the Father's glory and the image of his nature." Yet "Though there are two names, there is one power and one essence."[272]

This Word "took upon himself human nature," not only to divinize it but also because death came through a human, and therefore salvation and resurrection had to come through a human.[273] Christ's "human nature" arose from union of the Spirit with virgin Mary's faith in the Word. (Jesus did not, as the Dutch were saying, bring it from heaven.)[274] Yet as Hubmaier perhaps allowed, this unique birth made Jesus "a different human being" from Adam's descendents, for he lived through divine power with no inclination to sin.[275]

Jesus was put to death in the flesh, which came from Mary. In him the weakness of human nature died. His "divine nature," however, did not die but forsook the human at this point. Still, Jesus rose victorious over death and the devil, and the

---

him as head ("Ein kurzer Unterrich," pp. 106, 111, 114; *Selections*, p. 203).

[267]Schlaffer, "Instructions on Beginning," pp. 108, 105.

[268]Schlaffer, *Selections*, pp. 196, 202, 208; cf. "Ein kurzer Unterrich," p. 96.

[269]Riedemann, *Peter Riedemann's Hutterite Confession*, p. 176.

[270]Ibid., pp. 65, 176.

[271]Ibid., pp. 64-66.

[272]Ibid., p. 66.

[273]Ibid., p. 65.

[274]Ibid., p. 68, cf. p. 102.

[275]Ibid., pp. 69, 109. He evidently equated human weakness with sin. Riedemann denied Jesus any inclination to sin, yet called him "a genuine and real person, who was tempted and tested in all things" (p. 69, cf. p. 72). Riedemann apparently attributed Jesus' ability to withstand sin to his divine nature, for "the fullness of the Godhead dwells in him," yet he taught that "the Word had stripped himself of his radiant glory" (pp. 69, 72).

Father bestowed on him the power and glory he had before creation.[276] As the Swiss insisted, his "human form" remains in heaven, though his "divine nature" is everywhere.[277] Yet from heaven Christ makes us his dwelling and transforms us into the divine nature, somewhat as Schlaffer said.[278]

Though Christ accomplished much the same goal—christomorphic divinization—as for Hut, Schiemer and Denck, Riedemann envisioned this Word as not always immanent in humans but coming from a transcendent realm, as Hubmaier and Schlaffer did. To become immanent the Son had to first become a specific human. Only so could he overcome obstacles to God's wider presence among the race: death and the devil. Jesus was not one instance of the Word's general indwelling but its unique incarnation.

Jesus, that is, was not so much a man who opened himself to the Word, in Antiochene fashion, as the Word who, in Alexandrian fashion, "took upon himself human nature" or "put on a human body and a human nature"—a nature, perhaps, not quite fully human.[279] Christ's person was not so much the man of Nazareth as the divine Word. His divine nature was not so much an indwelling presence as his own eternal reality. Christ's human nature arose not through earthly processes alone but was assumed by the Word through a unique conception and birth.

3. Writing extensively about Christ's person, Pilgram Marpeck produced some unconventional formulations. For this reason, some scholars pronounce features of his Christology heterodox. George Williams, for instance, suggests similarities with the Polish Unitarian Faustus Socinus, whom we will shortly meet.[280] However, Marpeck was highly creative and unable to study theology formally.[281] To determine what he intended by his idiosyncratic expressions, we will approach them from the standpoint of Christ's work.

---

[276]Ibid., pp. 69-72

[277]Ibid., p. 115.

[278]Ibid., pp. 67, 74-75.

[279]Ibid., p. 65.

[280]Williams also finds resemblances to the Italian Unitarian Giacometto Stringaro (George Williams, *The Radical Reformation*, 3rd ed. [Kirksville, Mo.: 16th Century Journal Publishers, 1992], pp. 865-67). He maintains that Marpeck eventually found no significant difference between his own Christology and the Dutch heavenly flesh (p. 1217). For Williams's nuanced discussion of Marpeck's Christology, see pp. 682-87, 703-21 of his book.

[281]Blough believes that Marpeck did not interact with Nicea and Chalcedon until his *Verantwurtung* of 1542 (*Christologie Anabaptiste*, p. 168), and never really reconciled biblical with dogmatic language (pp. 189-90; cf. John Rempel, *The Lord's Supper in Anabaptism* [Scottdale, Penn.: Herald, 1993], pp. 143, 149, 160).

- *God's coming.* Marpeck critiqued speculation that began "from above," with "the height and divinity of Christ" by persons unprepared "to go down with Christ into death and be buried with Him."[282] He found it contradictory to "speak high spiritual words" about "the loftiness of the Godhead and Christ . . . but deny the lowliness and deep humility of Christ."[283] Marpeck was thinking especially of Spiritualists who communed with a glorified Christ but underplayed his earthly humanity and denied its continuation with the church's activities and structures.[284]

Nonetheless, for Marpeck Christ's work had profound spiritual dimensions. Christ was "the ever-coming love of God," "the full love of the Father," "the fulness of love, and God Himself."[285] This love brought rebirth when Christ, the eternal Word, went forth "from the mouth of the Father," who "kisses the hearts of all the faithful" with that Word, so that "the divine nature of the children of God is conceived and born from the love of the Word, the imperishable seed."[286]

As for Hubmaier, this often transpired through the preached Word, in which Christ was dynamically present. Yet Marpeck often waxed more mystical. Echoing the Song of Songs, he variously portrayed the church as the Father's or Son's bride, and the Spirit or Word as the impregnating agency, blurring distinctions as happens in mystical language.[287] Yet viewed from the standpoint of Christ's work, Marpeck clearly meant to foreground the centrality of the Word or Son or Bridegroom in God's dynamic, divinizing advent.

Marpeck verbalized Christ's coming in classical concepts as well. He stressed, for example, that Christ had not "just become love" but was "the breaking in of time out of eternity and into eternity."[288] Christ the Word was eternal, true God, Creator, the Father's glory from eternity who ordered all things.[289] More than any other Anabaptist, Marpeck sought to express Christology in classical terms.

This Word was not active among humans before Jesus in the way Denck, Schiemer or Hut's Word was. Marpeck's Word had to enter history in a unique manner, as did Riedemann's, Hubmaier's and Schlaffer's. This Word was aptly described as "God

---

[282]Marpeck, *Writings of Pilgram Marpeck*, pp. 434; Loserth, *Pilgram Marbecks Antwort*, p. 266.

[283]Marpeck, *Writings of Pilgram Marpeck*, p. 381.

[284]Marpeck thought spiritualists knew "a proud, lofty, arrogant Christ, for whom poor folks are far too unimportant." He and his followers, however, had "no other consolation but to put forward our poverty with all lowliness" (*Writings of Pilgram Marpeck*, p. 384).

[285]Ibid., pp. 530, 329, 533.

[286]Ibid., p. 393.

[287]Ibid., pp. 391, 392, 399, 518, 523, 524, 525.

[288]Ibid., p. 535.

[289]Ibid., pp. 422, 434, 67, 132, 113, 388, 400, 408, 535, 256, 341-42.

and Man, Man and God, two natures, one God, and also two natures, one Man."[290]

Accordingly, though Marpeck eschewed mere speculation from above, he found it necessary to stress the heights to rightly apprehend God's descent to the depths. For Christ's work involved an extraordinary humbling. Its beginning was well expressed in traditional terms: he "took upon himself the seed of Abraham," or the Word became flesh.[291] Marpeck insisted this flesh came through and from Mary.[292] Yet Marpeck's Anabaptist orientation drew him much further. He underscored Jesus' descent into the form of a slave and ultimately hell to battle and finally conquer the powers.

• *Jesus' humanity.* To conquer the powers Marpeck's Jesus walked with God as no human had, opening a relationship through the Holy Spirit in which others could participate. What must Jesus' humanity have been like for this to occur? Some debate exists, so we must untangle it in light of Jesus' work. Marpeck's Jesus received the Spirit's fulness only at his resurrection. This raises the possibility that until then Jesus lacked any strong relation to the same and only became divine when adopted, through the Spirit, at his resurrection.

However, Marpeck clearly, if seldom, mentioned the Spirit in Jesus' earthly life.[293] Marpeck also used *Spirit* broadly to denote the general character of deity or Jesus' spiritual dimension. He could apply *Spirit* along with terms like *Word* to Christ from eternity and insist that Christ continued to be Spirit when he became flesh.[294] Since salvation involved the uniting of Spirit and flesh, the Savior would need to possess both. Recall also that Marpeck also identified the Holy Spirit with Christ's deity. These multiple uses of *Spirit* are indeed confusing. Yet they clearly im-

---

[290]Ibid., p. 535; cf. p. 530; Loserth, *Pilgram Marbecks Antwort*, p. 501. The one Word of the Father emerged from him as a stream from its source, became incarnate and now flows on by means of the apostles through the gospel (Loserth, *Pilgram Marbecks Antwort*, p. 298). Marpeck once said that Christ became a creature "according to his nature and person" (ibid., p. 234).

[291]Marpeck, *Writings of Pilgram Marpeck*, p. 381.

[292]Ibid., pp. 212, 233, 274, 317, 467, 508. "Mary prepared this flesh and blood" (p. 447). Like Riedemann, Marpeck was rejecting Melchior Hoffman's claim that the "Word became flesh from itself" (Loserth, *Pilgram Marbecks Antwort*, p. 544).

[293]The last days began at Jesus' birth with the Spirit's richest outpouring until then (Marpeck, *Writings of Pilgram Marpeck*, p. 60). Jesus was conceived through the Spirit, through whom he took Abraham's seed upon himself (p. 318). During his life Jesus never spoke without the Spirit (p. 378). Through God's Spirit he overcame the flesh's weakness and put it to death (p. 322). By the Spirit the Father committed all things to Jesus, who responded through the Spirit (p. 378-79) and lived as the Father's Son "according to Spirit, Word, and Power" (p. 314). Marpeck also depicted Jesus' body as an ark containing the Spirit's virtues and gifts, which was opened only on cross (p. 431). This very likely meant that God's Spirit was very active in Jesus' life but only given to others at his resurrection (cf. Boyd, *Pilgram Marpeck*, p. 151). Blough, however, finds both the question of the Spirit in Jesus' life and his deity before his incarnation unresolved in Marpeck (*Christologie Anabaptiste*, pp. 184-93).

[294]Marpeck, *Writings of Pilgram Marpeck*, pp. 379, 314.

ply the presence of the Holy Spirit in Jesus' life and perhaps explain why Marpeck seldom mentioned it. If he simply assumed this, why bother saying it often?

A further indication of the Spirit in Jesus' ministry appeared in several late passages portraying God's Spirit as so dominant in Jesus that it took the place of a human spirit.[295] This, of course, raised the opposite problem. If Marpeck consistently thought this, he was not espousing adoptionism but Apollinarianism.[296] Marpeck may also have underplayed Jesus' full humanity another way: by regarding him, somewhat like Hubmaier and Riedemann, as separated from sin by his unique birth. This kept the general consequences of Adam's fall from touching him and rendered him unable to sin.[297] This concern might have been consistent with denying Jesus a human spirit since only the devil's activity in the human spirit could produce sin.[298]

To interpret all these remarks, we need to recall Marpeck's overall account of Jesus' work. The powers draw people into sin by enticing their spirits to rise above their earthly limitations. When the human spirit attempts this, it forsakes obedience to God's Spirit and becomes imprisoned under the flesh.[299] The powers then rule humans through the flesh.

In describing Jesus' work Marpeck repeatedly underlined the weakness of Jesus' flesh. Jesus kept his flesh obedient to God's Spirit so this Spirit could again reach us through his pure flesh. Jesus remained obedient as a weak, patient, true human, as we should. Precisely through his weakness and humility he conquered Satan.[300] Marpeck's dominant theme, then, was not simply that Jesus was human in the same basic ways we are but that he became the second Adam, or authentic human, precisely by accepting human weakness and dependence on God far more than we do.

This account clashes with Marpeck's few remarks about God's Spirit taking the human spirit's place in Jesus, or performing its functions—if interpreted *substantially,* as if one "thing" (God's Spirit) were located in a "place" in Jesus where a different thing (a human spirit) is located in us. For if Jesus' decisions to be humble and nonviolent were directly enacted by a superhuman, divine Spirit, how could he possibly have accomplished the human task?

Marpeck's account of Jesus' work fits well with his remarks about Jesus lacking a human spirit, however, if they are interpreted *functionally,* as meaning that God's Spirit directed and energized Jesus' actions very differently than our spirits energize and direct

---

[295]Loserth, *Pilgram Marbecks Antwort,* pp. 496, 541.

[296]Apollinarianism is an extreme Christology from Alexandria where Christ's deity took the place of what Chalcedon later called his human, rational soul.

[297]Loserth, *Pilgram Marbecks Antwort,* p. 542.

[298]Ibid., pp. 251, 255-56, 542.

[299]Marpeck, *Writings of Pilgram Marpeck,* pp. 76, 322.

[300]Ibid., pp. 79-80, 232, 317-18.

ours. This would mean that Jesus opened himself to allow God's Spirit to act through him in this way. So far as I can see, however, this makes sense only if Jesus did this through some human capacity—what Marpeck called a human spirit and Chalcedon called a rational soul—even though Marpeck did not explicitly mention this. But even if Marpeck's Jesus exercised such a human capacity, he may not have been quite fully human since, like Hubmaier's and Riedemann's Jesus, he was wholly unable to sin.

Earlier I noted that Marpeck occasionally equated Jesus' deity with the Holy Spirit. I argued that this too is best understood functionally. That is, Pilgram meant to affirm that Christ was present in the Lord's Supper not substantially, since his body remained in heaven, but dynamically, through the Spirit.[301] Indeed, Marpeck could express such unity in action by differentiating Word and Spirit, and then by calling them "one thing [*ein Ding*] in the divine power of its activity [*göttlichen Kraft seiner Wirkung*]," for it (they) "is and works [*ist und wirkt*] with and through each other."[302] I now propose that when Marpeck named the Spirit the agent of Jesus' acts, he also meant this functionally—that Jesus, by opening himself in a fully human way in fully human choices, acted through or was empowered by the Spirit.[303]

• *Death and glorification.* Having patiently traversed the humble, peaceful path that alone leads to glorification, Jesus truly died in his humanity and sank into the devil's prison.[304] This human descent completed that divine descent from the heights into those depths we also must enter to eventually be raised with him.[305] Marpeck, however, exempted Jesus' deity from death.[306] Through his resurrection Jesus acquired the new fulness of the Spirit and greater divinization that God intends for all who complete his earthly journey. Marpeck sometimes spoke as if Jesus also became more fully divine, but he may have meant that Jesus' body also began participating in deity at that point.[307] By themselves, however, such statements could sound adoptionistic.

---

[301]See pp. 190-91 above.

[302]Loserth, *Pilgram Marbecks Antwort*, p. 516.

[303]The fluidity of Marpeck's terminology is evident in calling Christ, according to the inner person, not only the Spirit but also "Word, Holy Spirit and Godself" (ibid., p. 541). Similarly, he could name the inner essence of a reborn human the reigning Christ, Lord and God (p. 169). Marpeck hardly could have meant that these replaced a human mind or spirit.

[304]Ibid., p. 141.

[305]Marpeck, *Writings of Pilgram Marpeck*, p. 434, cf. p. 381.

[306]According to his Spirit, or deity, Marpeck's Jesus could not die (Loserth, *Pilgram Marbecks Antwort*, p. 542). This is how he took life back through his own power in Hades (Marpeck, *Writings of Pilgram Marpeck*, p. 434). Through the "glory, dominion, and power of life" within him he finally conquered death (p. 433).

[307]Loserth, *Pilgram Marbecks Antwort*, pp. 496-97, 500, 502, 534.

Yet they also make sense in light of Marpeck's dynamic orientation and the enormous contrasts in the Son's transition from the heights into the depths and back again. Marpeck was emphasizing that the Son "emptied himself" (*heauton ekenōsen*, Phil 2:7). It is difficult to express this kenosis without implying that Christ's deity was diminished thereby. Further, Marpeck was mainly tracing this one person's work through these widely contrasting phases. In terms of its active function the Son's deity could have appeared to diminish from his incarnation through his death and to increase again through his resurrection.

Since Marpeck was foregrounding the divine work, he was not predisposed to construe classical categories such as divine nature as fixed and static—a common complaint against classical Christology. Given the dramatic transformations in Jesus' atoning work, it perhaps seemed quite appropriate to say that in Jesus, God in some sense changed. For before this God had neither actually been human nor passed through suffering and death. Statements that apparently affirmed some post-resurrection increase in Jesus' deity then likely meant to add that this one person, who was divine, was also greatly transformed by resurrection and functioned quite differently thereafter. Marpeck probably did not mean a substantial increase in deity because he described the same reality as the Father returning to the Son his primordial glory.[308] But in any case, Jesus awaited yet further completion on the human side when his entire unglorified, earthly body would be glorified and join him.

This expectation was consistent with Marpeck's insistence that Jesus' body, though greatly transformed by resurrection, ultimately remained finite. God's fulness now dwelled there.[309] All creatures actually subsisted in it,[310] ruled by Jesus as the highest, though divinized, creature.[311] Further, since Jesus was taken up into the divine, triune dynamism, people could begin experiencing renewal through this body while on earth.[312] Sounding much like a spiritualist, Marpeck pictured Christ's risen body as a temple where believers, through the Spirit, could dwell, be transformed and praise the Father through the Son. Yet this communion affected

---

[308]Marpeck, *Writings of Pilgram Marpeck*, p. 535.

[309]Loserth, *Pilgram Marbecks Antwort*, p. 500.

[310]Ibid., p. 500. This is apparently incongruous with saying that Christ's spiritual body filled everything (p. 493). But Marpeck also claimed that Christ worked through bodily parts like arms and mouths, which yet were the "Spirit [*geist*] of God the Father" (p. 542), and that while Christ's body was at God's right hand (p. 500), God was all in all both with and without location (p. 501). However opaque these affirmations are, Marpeck meant to indicate that Christ's saving work touched all creation and opened materiality to the Spirit.

[311]Ibid., p. 538.

[312]Marpeck, *Writings of Pilgram Marpeck*, pp. 175-76, 530; Loserth, *Pilgram Marbecks Antwort*, p. 137.

their bodies, somewhat as the Eucharist did.[313]

• *Conclusions.* Despite some conceptual imprecision Marpeck intended to affirm a classical Christology. Christ's two natures lay at the heart of his concern, as Neal Blough and John Rempel agree.[314] This was chiefly because salvation involved transformation of human reality by the divine, which was no impersonal, static quantum. It was a dynamism bestowed through the personal address, or "kiss," and indwelling of the "ever-coming love of God," which descended from beyond time and space, all the way to hell's abyss. At the heart of this coming, and not simply its secondary agent, was the Son or Word himself, as in Alexandrian Christology.

Jesus' way of servanthood and peace were the direct outflow of this descent and the means by which he overcame the pride through which the powers hold us captive. Since salvation also connects humans intimately with God, in this descent the Son also took on the full range of what we are. (Though Marpeck, like some other Anabaptists, exempted him from any possibility of sin.) Jesus Christ triumphed completely when his human reality was fully transformed and raised through divine power.

I find this christological uniting of deity and humanity consistent with that intertwining of spiritual and material, and of inner and outer, that Marpeck constantly stressed. Christ's two natures, despite possible limitations of that term, were hardly abstractions of Constantinian Christology but were central to his profound Anabaptist theological vision.

The Netherlands. All the above writers sought to affirm Jesus' full humanity. Hubmaier, Schlaffer, Riedemann and Marpeck expressed this traditionally—God's eternal Son took on full humanity from Mary—though they protected him from any possibility of sin. The Dutch, however, conceptualized this more questionably, despite protests that they upheld Jesus' full humanity.

1. Salvation was understood as an intense kind of divinization by Melchior Hoffman. Like Marpeck, he valued nuptial imagery. The gospel was "the kiss rich in joys from the mouth of the Bridegroom."[315] In the Lord's Supper the

---

[313]Marpeck, *Writings of Pilgram Marpeck*, pp. 441-63, cf. pp. 231-32; Loserth, *Pilgram Marbecks Antwort*, pp. 500-501. They would never lose their identity and be absorbed in God (*Writings of Pilgram Marpeck*, p. 531).

[314]Blough, *Christologie Anabaptiste*, p. 24. More precisely, Blough declines to select either this or essence as the intertwining of inner and outer, as Marpeck's most fundamental notion (p. 199). Rempel finds Christ's taking on our nature and our being transformed by his nature central to Marpeck's eucharistic theology and theology as a whole (*Lord's Supper*, pp. 93-163; cf. Marpeck, *Writings of Pilgram Marpeck*, pp. 81, 509).

[315]Hoffman, "Ordinance of God," p. 186. Calling Jesus "the mouth of the Most High God" (ibid.) was perhaps similar to naming him the Word. Like Hubmaier, Hoffman found Christ present in the word of forgiveness (Deppermann, *Melchior Hoffman*, pp. 131, 151).

Bridegroom's blood became one with the bride's, so that they were "one body, one flesh, one spirit and one passion."[316] Hoffman expected this transformation to occur rapidly and thoroughly. Some of his followers anticipated being invulnerable.

Since Christ bestowed such dramatic alteration, it is not surprising that Hoffman thought he had only one nature, the divine, and that whatever flesh he had he brought from heaven.[317] Christ, contrary to Chalcedon, only passed through Mary, receiving nothing from her. "He did not take flesh upon himself, but became himself flesh."[318]

Yet this Christ was perhaps not fully divine either. Melchior tended to regard the Son and Spirit as transitory modes of the one God.[319] Jesus may have acquired full divine honor and power only at his resurrection, in adoptionist fashion, as some Polish Anabaptists would say.[320]

The earthly Jesus provided a model. He betrothed himself to the Father at baptism, followed the Spirit into the wilderness and trod the path leading to God's kingdom. He was "detached from his own will, and . . . absorbed into the will of his exalted Father."[321] While we cannot read much into this statement, it resembles the ancient heresy of monotheletism, where Jesus had no human will but only a divine one. This would be somewhat like saying that he had no human spirit but only the divine Spirit, as Marpeck occasionally seemed to imply, or that Jesus lacked a rational soul contra Chalcedon.

Since Melchior placed this occurrence at Jesus' baptism, he presumably possessed a distinct will before then. Yet the extent to which Jesus' humanity could apparently assimilate with the divine seems to parallel Hoffman's demand that a convert's "will,

---

[316]Hoffman, "Ordinance of God," p. 194.

[317]According to Williams, Hoffman's Jesus need not have been identical with us, for salvation was a transaction between God and Satan (Williams, *Radical Reformation*, p. 495). Williams proposes that heavenly flesh was suggested by the medieval Eucharist. If Christ's body and blood were literally present in the elements, they must have first descended from heaven invisibly. As analogies, Hoffman mentioned the dew that became manna (Ex 16:13-15), which Jesus recalled in naming himself bread from heaven (Jn 6:48-51), and pearls, which medievals believed to be solidified dew. In these analogies one substance, originally invisible, took on visible qualities without altering essentially. Williams discusses such views in Hoffman, Clement Ziegler, Caspar Schwenckfeld (Marpeck's spiritualist nemesis) and Michael Servetus (*Radical Reformation*, pp. 488-504). For Hoffman, Christ had a body before birth, as the Spirit had the form of a dove (Deppermann, *Melchior Hoffman*, p. 177).

[318]Hoffman, "Ordinance of God," p. 198.

[319]Deppermann, *Melchior Hoffman*, p. 228.

[320]Hoffman, "Ordinance of God," pp. 184, 186, 190.

[321]Ibid., p. 190.

life, desire, spirit, and passion be wholly slain" and that the bride be "one spirit, will and mind" with the Bridegroom.[322] The authentically human seemed to slide into the divine. Perhaps this explains Melchior's avoidance of two natures vocabulary.

When Jesus died, it was crucial that his flesh be pure and heavenly. Corrupt flesh, derived from Adam via Mary, could never have paid sin's price. Jesus then rose in a visible body.[323] Yet the risen flesh and blood of which believers partake seems almost entirely etherialized into the spiritual, consistent with very lofty expectations of divinization.[324]

2. The later Dutch leaders, Menno Simons and Dirk Philips, continued to understand salvation as christomorphic divinization. And although they rejected the Melchiorites' prophetic and sociopolitical extravagances, they defended their unorthodox Christology—especially Menno, late in life, in two lengthy, repetitious and often vituperative treatises.[325] Since Menno's presentation was more detailed and its intent differed little from Dirk's, I will reference it more often.

• *Incarnation.* Viewed through classical christological lenses, these later Dutch appear somewhat like ancient Alexandrians. They sought to stress that God had brought salvation, which bestowed participation in the divine nature (2 Pet 1:4). Not surprisingly, they often affirmed Christ's deity in traditional terms. He was the Word through whom all things were created,[326] the Firstborn of creation (Col 1:15)—though not in the Arian sense of being a creature.[327] Christ was eternally born or begotten of the Father.[328] Menno, however, rejected an image for this sug-

---

[322]Ibid., pp. 187, 194.

[323]Ibid., p. 198.

[324]According to Deppermann, Jesus' glorified humanity was not creaturely for Hoffman (*Melchior Hoffman*, p. 216).

[325]"The Incarnation of Our Lord" (in Simons, *Complete Works*, pp. 785-834) and "Reply to Martin Micron" (ibid., pp. 838-913). This teaching, Menno reported, was unknown to him when he became Anabaptist, and he struggled greatly before accepting it (pp. 668-673). Dirk covered Christology most fully in "The Incarnation of Our Lord Jesus Christ" (*Writings of Dirk Philips*, pp. 134-51) and "Concerning the True Knowledge of Jesus Christ" (ibid., pp. 152-72).

[326]E.g., Simons, *Complete Works*, pp. 305, 336-38, 351, 428, 810, 990; Philips, *Writings of Dirk Philips*, pp. 63, 136, 158-59, 361. More often than Dirk, Menno added that the Word fills heaven and earth (*Complete Works*, pp. 817, 881, 909; *Writings of Dirk Philips*, p. 119) and provides for all creatures (Simons, *Complete Works*, pp. 209, 338). For many other divine titles applied to Christ, see Simons, *Complete Works*, pp. 339, 493-94; Philips, *Writings of Dirk Philips*, pp. 154-60.

[327]Simons, *Complete Works*, pp. 492, 802, 860. He found Arianism erroneous (pp. 175, 747, 758, 760-61) but critiqued the harsh treatment meted of Arius (p. 65). Menno regarded the Nicene Creed positively (pp. 667, 734, 758, 967), which he thought taught that the Son remains in the Father (p. 862).

[328]E.g., ibid., pp. 80, 368, 491, 810, 815, 838; Philips, *Writings of Dirk Philips*, pp. 63, 155, 157, 257, 633. Menno often said we are Christ's brother, not from any common humanity but because we are also born from the Father (e.g., *Complete Works*, p. 772).

gested by his opponents: the Son is forever seated next to the Father.[329] For this implied too great a separation—that the Son was not "of complete divine Substance or Being, in God and with God."[330] Menno envisioned the Son always remaining within the Father, as had Erasmus, Luther and Riedemann.[331] Yet the Son was also distinct, so that the Father did not send to earth "an angel, a patriarch, or a prophet, but His eternal Almighty Word, His Eternal Wisdom, the brightness of His glory."[332]

Menno challenged talk of this Son's two natures. He could not conceive of a human nature existing apart from a fully human personal center, or person.[333] When his opponents mentioned Jesus' human nature, however, they did mean a nature without a person—to ensure that Jesus would be only one divine person, as in classical Christology. But Menno thought they meant a complete human person: a man of Adam's flesh born of Mary. Accordingly, if Christ had two natures, he must have been not one person but two.[334] More significantly, the human person would have been salvation's agent and merely indwelt by the Word.[335]

Menno was critiquing his contemporaries much as Alexandrians critiqued Antiochenes. Menno and Dirk wanted to portray salvation, which came solely from God, as an outpouring of God's burning love.[336] To underscore this they stressed

---

[329]Simons, *Complete Works*, pp. 860, 865.

[330]Ibid., p. 862, cf. p. 873. Dirk emphasized that the Son was one being (*Writings of Dirk Philips*, pp. 64, 156, 160, 414), substance (pp. 136, 156) or nature (p. 147) with the Father. But neither he nor Menno employed such terms uniformly.

[331]Simons, *Complete Works*, p. 802, cf. pp. 845, 861-62.

[332]Ibid., p. 144.

[333]Ibid., pp. 825, 901-2. Consequently, he often wrote as if nature and person meant the same (e.g., p. 792). Menno supposed that *hypostasis*, which meant person in classical Christology, was equivalent to *ousia*, which meant essence, or nature (p. 803). Dirk once affirmed Christ's divine and human natures formally (Philips, *Writings of Dirk Philips*, pp. 63-64). He clearly regarded Christ's person as divine (p. 64), though he seldom used the term. Dirk once said that Christ "has a fully human person" (p. 119), but was not addressing classical issues. By *nature* Dirk and Menno frequently meant what classical Christology did by *ousia*, but often with the added sense of "character": e.g., "the friendly, amiable Spirit, nature, and disposition of Christ" (Simons, *Complete Works*, p. 779; cf. Philips, *Writings of Dirk Philips*, p. 303). Other Anabaptists included this dimension, like Riedemann, who very often mentioned Christ's "nature and character."

[334]Simons, *Complete Works*, pp. 334, 415, 428, 764, 792, 801.

[335]Ibid., pp. 829-30, cf. p. 763. He noticed that distinguishing a human person from a divine person in Christ could lead to adoptionism: to the first being adopted by the second (pp. 765, 883; cf. p. 199). Menno once said that the Son "became incarnate in a human being" (p. 808) but evidently was speaking imprecisely. Dirk averred that if Christ had sprung from "natural human seed," humanity would have played too great a role in its own salvation (*Writings of Dirk Philips*, p. 141). True salvation was possible only if Christ was "entirely heavenly, entirely from God" (p. 416).

[336]Simons, *Complete Works*, pp. 428-29, 431, 306-7, 873-74; Philips, *Writings of Dirk Philips*, p. 416.

that the Son diminished and emptied himself—laid aside his divine prerogatives and glory[337]—and died for us.[338] This entire divine Christ—not simply Mary's human son—suffered in flesh, soul and spirit.[339]

Alexandrians also underlined this. Yet they distinguished this one divine person from his human features by saying that he took on human nature. In this way he remained the divine Word. Nevertheless, since he took on human features as his own, his sufferings were God's very own. Menno and Dirk, in contrast, identified the one divine Word directly with the whole Jesus, including his humanity. The Word did not take on flesh but literally "became flesh" (Jn 1:14). That raised a possibility Chalcedon sought to exclude: the Word did not remain divine but transmuted into something else.

Why did Menno and Dirk reject the classical alternative? Because, they insisted, their view was the plain meaning of John 1:14. But they had another reason. Like Hoffman, they considered all flesh descended from Adam too corrupt to provide a pure atoning sacrifice or to nourish believers, as in the Lord's Supper. Jesus then could not have received or taken on his flesh from Mary. His flesh could be pure enough only if it were the Word's very own. Menno and Dirk, however, allowed that this Word became flesh and was nourished in Mary, avoiding Hoffman's cruder talk about him bringing it from heaven.[340]

• *Jesus' humanity.* Dutch Anabaptists buttressed this view with an understanding of reproduction where the father bestowed the form that structured the fetus. The mother merely provided a receptive matter. Mary then could hardly have contributed what was essential for being human to Jesus.[341] Menno complained that if Jesus really had taken on our nature, Joseph would have been Jesus' father, not the heavenly Father.[342] But what if mother and father contributed equally to the fetus,

---

[337]Simons, *Complete Works*, pp. 437, 796, 814-15; Philips, *Writings of Dirk Philips*, p. 139; cf. Phil 2:5-8. Menno said that Christ "surrendered" his divine "attributes" (*Complete Works*, p. 815).

[338]Simons, *Complete Works*, pp. 335, 771.

[339]Ibid., p. 438, cf. pp. 334, 765, 813, 848, 902. Dirk supported this by citing the rejection of Nestorius, an Antiochene, for restricting Christ's suffering to the man born of Mary (*Writings of Dirk Philips*, p. 147).

[340]Simons, *Complete Works*, pp. 336, 428, 794; Philips, *Writings of Dirk Philips*, pp. 137, 361. Heavenly flesh, then, is not really an accurate name for later Dutch Christology. Menno did say once that "Christ had but one body which was heavenly and from heaven" (*Complete Works*, p. 967). Yet he specifically rejected Hoffman's view (p. 905). Since the former statement was a passing remark, it is best regarded as carelessness.

[341]Simons, *Complete Works*, p. 768. Experience, he admitted, seemed to indicate that mothers, who invest about ten times the effort of fathers during pregnancy and infancy, were the primary source of children. Still, objective exegesis supported the fathers' primacy (pp. 768-769, 890)!

[342]Ibid., pp. 867, 898.

as some people in that era thought? Menno responded that Christ, once again, would have been two persons (with God providing the divine, and Mary the human, person).[343]

Despite this contrast between Jesus' humanity and ours, the later Dutch insisted that Jesus was fully human, like Adam before the fall. Despite reservations about *nature*, Menno conceded that since Christ was truly God and also a true human, "there were two natures in the only, undivided person and Son of God, Christ."[344] Yet Menno recognized no similarity between this claim and his opponents', with their alleged two persons. Menno and Dirk's assertions about Jesus himself then were broadly Chalcedonian, though seldom stated that way.[345] Their view of Mary's role, however, was not.

Different as it was from ours, Jesus' flesh was weak and liable to death.[346] Apparently unlike Riedemann and Hubmaier, Menno, who felt constantly assailed from within and without, allowed that Jesus experienced "the same temptation, battle, misery, anxiety, and fear of death" that we do. Consequently, Jesus could rescue those "tempted by the world, hell, sin, devil, and death."[347] Jesus' flesh was still stronger than ours, for he fulfilled the law, which our flesh was too weak to accomplish.[348]

Since Jesus' humanity was like Adam's before the Fall, he accomplished the task allotted to him. Yet because Adamic humanity was hopelessly corrupt, Jesus did not really redeem it but created a new humanity. He did not so much partake of our humanity, as in classical Christology, as enable us to partake of his, mainly

---

[343]Ibid., p. 792.

[344]Ibid., p. 902, cf. pp. 430, 808, 871-72. Dirk affirmed this vocabulary at a key point (*Writings of Dirk Philips*, pp. 63-64). Still, they resemble the Oriental Orthodox (Armenian, Syrian and Coptic) who rejected Chalcedon because they felt it divided Christ's natures too sharply and attributed too much to the human. Other Christians often regarded Orientals as monophysite (affirming one nature, the divine). Today, however, Orientals insist that they always acknowledged two natures but disagreed with Chalcedon's conceptualization (see Paul Fries and Tiran Nersoyan, eds., *Christ in East and West* [Atlanta: Mercer, 1987]).

[345]Williams, though, finds Dirk "anti-Nicene" since he once wrote that Christ said to the Father: "'You have prepared a body for me,' so the body of Christ may actually not be held for [to be] God, but in the body dwells the entire fulness of deity bodily" (Philips, *Writings of Dirk Philips*, pp. 633). Williams thinks Dirk meant that the Son received a celestial body "before creation" and that since this body was not fully divine, the Son was not so before his incarnation (ibid., pp. 740-41). Dirk, however, did not assert that this occurred before creation. He likely meant only that Jesus' earthly body, considered in and of itself, was not God. Williams apparently assumes that Dirk, like Hoffman, believed in a celestial flesh predating the incarnation.

[346]Simons, *Complete Works*, p. 492.

[347]Ibid., p. 828; cf. Philips, *Writings of Dirk Philips*, p. 258.

[348]Simons, *Complete Works*, pp. 336, 439.

through communion with his risen flesh. Dirk identified this flesh, even more closely than Jesus' earthly flesh, with "the Spirit and the Word of God," minimizing, perhaps even erasing, human features.[349] Dirk could even say that "he who died as man rose from the dead as God," though he elsewhere propounded the common Anabaptist view of Jesus' body at the Father's right hand.[350] The church was also "made of His most holy and life-giving flesh," raising behavioral expectations very high.[351]

Interim summary. So far our provisional, classical christological framework has helped us spot significant differences among historic Anabaptists. Denck resembled the Antiochenes in important respects. Perhaps he, and possibly Hut and Schiemer, treated Jesus' deity as something not only indwelling him but also attained through his human acts. At the other extreme Menno and Dirk clearly expressed Alexandria's concerns along with its tendency to dilute Jesus' humanity. In between, Hubmaier, Schlaffer, Riedemann and Marpeck affirmed Jesus' deity and humanity in classical terms but also in ways intrinsic to their theologies. Riedemann and Marpeck leaned toward Alexandria. All but Schlaffer, however, perhaps slighted Jesus' humanity.

So far we find historic Anabaptism, on balance, not prioritizing Jesus' humanity but more nearly overprioritizing his deity. Yet perhaps, as Denny Weaver suggests, this picture will change if the Poles are included.[352]

Poland (and Italy, Lithuania and Romania). George Williams treats Polish Anabaptism and its Christology as legitimate expressions of historic Anabaptism. Yet he traces this Christology's development from different, mostly Italian, origins. Many Italian intellectuals viewed classical creeds as instruments of that oppressive church-state linkage, which humanists and then Anabaptists sharply critiqued. Moreover, they found the Christ of the creeds impersonal and distant; quite unlike the compassionate, concrete Jesus whom both humanists and Anabaptists admired.[353]

1. Italian Anabaptism. The Jesus of Italian Anabaptism could be viewed as Mary and Joseph's natural son whom God eventually adopted by resurrection to deity. Some Italian Anabaptists were influenced by this notion and also by Evangelical Rationalists who scrutinized church beliefs in light of original bib-

---

[349]Philips, *Writings of Dirk Philips*, p. 147, cf. p. 138. According to his humanity, Christ offered himself a sacrifice (p. 136) and is now high priest (p. 416). In rising, Christ reconciled us to his Father and accomplished his will according to his divinity (p. 136) and now intercedes in his heavenly being (p. 102).

[350]Ibid., p. 139.

[351]Simons, *Complete Works*, p. 772.

[352]Weaver, "Atonement for the Nonconstantinian Church," p. 43.

[353]Williams, *Radical Reformation*, pp. 945-47.

lical texts and promoted ethical religiosity.[354] By including this group with Anabaptists and Spiritualists in the Radical Reformation, Williams links their Christology more closely to Anabaptism than most previous historians. He notes, however, that the mystical strain prominent in Germanic and Dutch Anabaptism was largely absent from this orientation.[355]

In the first extant Italian Anabaptist writing, Giacometto Stringaro described Jesus as Joseph's son, "born" through the Spirit as God's Son at his baptism. The Spirit raised Jesus, transforming his flesh, and Jesus then acquired power to save. He was God's true Son, but not God.[356] For another early leader, Il Tiziano, Jesus was also Joseph's son, adopted by God at his baptism.[357] Though north Italian Anabaptists, influenced by Germanic Anabaptism's greater orthodoxy, disputed such teachings, the Venice Synod (1550) affirmed Joseph's paternity and limited Jesus' work to his teaching and self-sacrificing witness to God's love.[358]

2. Michael Servetus. Polish Anabaptism was also more directly shaped by Evangelical Rationalists, though these Rationalists were not as obviously adoptionist. Many of them, who fled Italy to Swiss and German intellectual centers, garnered much from Michael Servetus. Though Servetus was condemned for denying the Trinity and endorsing believers' baptism, he never received the latter. Since he does not fit the common definition of Anabaptist (one who practiced believers' baptism), I am not considering his theology Anabaptist. Nevertheless, he is crucial for understanding the Poles.

Servetus sought to derive his view of Christ solely from the Greek and Hebrew biblical texts, an ideal that humanists and Reformers shared. Most classical christological concepts, he argued, were abstract inventions of Greek philosophy. But the Bible, he claimed, began with the man Jesus, and Servetus sought to do the same (from below).

Servetus argued that *Son*, in Scripture, always meant the human Jesus, never an

---

[354]Williams characterizes Evangelical Rationalism as "a fusion of Italian humanism or critical rationalism with selected ingredients of two kinds of Italian Anabaptism and a visionary Spiritualism" (ibid., p. 836). It involved "sober philological observation, subtle and almost perverse doubting, persistent uncertainty, and diffidence in the face of all allegedly final solutions" (pp. 877-78). Explicit opposition to the Trinity was limited largely to Evangelical Rationalists (p. xxxi).

[355]Ibid., pp. 16, 804, 1301.

[356]Ibid., pp. 866-67. As mentioned, Williams finds Marpeck's Christology somewhat like Stringaro's (p. 375 note 280), although my reading doesn't. Perhaps Stringaro thought of the risen Christ and the Spirit working in the church as one.

[357]Ibid., p. 869.

[358]Ibid., pp. 871-72. The Synod denied the existence of Satan, hell and the wicked after death, but affirmed resurrection of the righteous. Some delegates refused to accept all these decisions. They were excluded from the Anabaptist communion.

eternal being. God's *Son*, then, could only have been "begotten" through and "born" from Mary (though not via Joseph but through God, as the Bible said), and did not exist before his human conception.[359] However, Servetus acknowledged that God's Word, in Scripture, existed before Jesus. He added that much as Christians are conceived from the seed of that Word (a favorite Anabaptists theme), Jesus was too.[360]

This Word, though, was no eternal being. It was God's speech, with its inherent logic or pattern. The Word emerged when the one God, the Father, said "Let there be" and created the cosmos. Servetus called this Word a person—but in, he claimed, the biblical sense: someone's outward appearance or expression.[361] In this way Servetus called Jesus this Word, or this person, made flesh (Jn 1:14). Jesus, that is, was a concrete expression of God's creative speech. But this creative speech, or Word, was a pattern or form. It was a person not in the sense of some preexisting entity but of an outward expression of another agent. Servetus initially described the Word fading away when Jesus gave it bodily existence. Later, however, he envisioned it remaining, as embodied in Jesus.[362]

Though Servetus's exegesis was extremely complex and sometimes confused, it often followed this pattern. He started and stayed with the man Jesus, regarded in no way as a supernatural being. Servetus then interpreted terms thought to denote supernatural entities, such as *Word*, in what he said was their biblical sense. These turned out to be expressions or dispositions of the one God. Since the Bible applied these terms to Jesus, he turned out to be not an ordinary man but a very special expression or embodiment of God.

For instance, Servetus claimed that nature and substance in Scripture do not

[359]Michael Servetus, *The Two Treatises of Servetus on the Trinity*, trans. Earl Wilbur (Cambridge, Mass.: Harvard University Press, 1932), pp. 85-86, 171.

[360]Ibid., p. 13.

[361]Ibid., pp. 57, 145. He also called this Word and the Spirit, a disposition, or way God disposes or conducts Godself (p. 126). When God said, "Let there be light," God brought God's own self forth from darkness and presented it in a distinct way (p. 191). The invisible God became the Creator. Yahweh became Elohim (which involved plurality for Servetus). The Word, that is, emerged when God acted in a new way and took on a new role. But God did not create or beget another Being (p. 187)—even though Servetus could say that God, in his sense, directly became Jesus the Son, or brought forth the Son from himself (p. 207).

[362]In his first book on the Trinity (*On the Errors of the Trinity*, in *Two Treatises*, pp. 3-184), Servetus could say that "when the being [Christ] itself comes, its personal representation [the Word] ceases" so that now "there is no such Word" (p. 143). Later, however, Servetus sought language less discrepant from orthodoxy. This enabled him to protest: "I have never admitted that the Word has ceased to be. On the contrary . . . the same Substance of the Word is in the flesh to-day" (*Dialogues on the Trinity* in *Two Treatises*, p. 190). In this second treatise, Servetus sometimes appeared to treat the Word as a substantial being, despite disclaimers.

mean something metaphysical but a characteristic way of acting. This enabled him to affirm, sounding quite classical, that the one divine nature and substance of the Father actually became flesh, became human, became Jesus. Jesus was no mere man but shared God's nature and substance. Yet this meant that Jesus characteristically acted as God did. They were, figuratively speaking, of one mind.[363]

Servetus sounded like Menno in denying that the Word was simply joined to another entity, a human nature, which Servetus also supposed meant an entire human person.[364] For "every quality in the Nature of the Word has passed over to the man, who is now God in the same way in which the Word was formerly with God."[365] Recall, though, that the Word was a pattern or way in which God expressed Godself; Servetus then was calling Jesus God in the sense of expressing God in every way that the Word had. Overall, Servetus divested Jesus of deity in the sense of our classical framework. Yet he affirmed Jesus' full humanity and granted him a crucial role in revealing God and bringing salvation.

It is appropriate then to ask Servetus what I asked many Anabaptists: Was Jesus only an exemplar of this revelation or also its unique origin? Servetus meant the former, for God could share "the fulness of his deity" with any human.[366] Servetus exhorted people to follow Jesus daily because he was God in a sense to which they

---

[363]Servetus, *Two Treatises*, pp. 36, 148-49, cf. p. 57. Servetus critiqued adoptionism, which appeared among Italian Anabaptists, for regarding Jesus as a mere man—and then concluding that he could only be divine by adoption. Servetus agreed that Jesus' flesh was conceived in Mary and was fully human. But, he countered, Jesus' flesh was also born from God's substance, and "by its own Nature it has a divine Substance" (p. 208, cf. pp. 175, 187, 197). This sounded like Dutch Anabaptism's heavenly flesh. But it meant, again, that Jesus in his bodily life acted as God did. Still, Jesus' earthly flesh was etherialized after his resurrection and functioned as "bread from heaven," spiritually consumed in the Lord's Supper and otherwise (pp. 26-27, 77-78, 187, 200, 206). Servetus went further than Dirk. When Jesus arose, he laid aside his creaturely existence. He was in no way animal (p. 212), but God—"in reality, just as he was formerly with him in Person" (p. 166).

[364]Ibid., pp. 130, 203; cf. pp. 18, 92. Any conjunction with a distinct being, including the flesh, would render the Word less divine (pp. 78, 90, 143, 174, 198). Servetus opposed a Nestorian two persons in Christ (p. 60). He claimed, like Menno, that his opponents taught "two beings in place of the one man Christ, the Son of God" (p. 187), not "one Son, but two half ones" (p. 202).

[365]Ibid., p. 175.

[366]Ibid., pp. 19, 45, 158. To deny this was to degrade human nature (p. 23). Though Servetus once mentioned Christ being God "not by nature but by grace" (p. 21, cf. pp. 29-31), he usually identified him and us more directly with God (cf. Roland Bainton, *Hunted Heretic* [Boston: Beacon, 1953], p. 64). Servetus understood salvation as divinization, that is, becoming divine in essence, not, with the Anabaptists, as christomorphic transformation by divine energies (see chap. 5). Calvin was apparently most upset by Servetus's view of the divine-human relationship (Bainton, *Hunted Heretic*, p. 195).

could aspire.[367] Servetus found biblical support for this in the Old Testament Elohim, which was applied not only to God but also occasionally to angels and people.[368] And despite his critique of "Greek philosophy," Servetus buttressed this by his own philosophical cosmology, in which "manifold rays of divinity proceed" from the highest being, "which all are Essences of God, and he is in them." For "God himself is the Essences of things."[369]

Servetus, then, could call Jesus fully divine—though hardly in an exclusive sense. But Servetus most influenced Polish Anabaptism by (1) claiming that the Word (and the Spirit) were not eternal beings but expressions of the one God, the Father,[370] and (2) predicating all christological terms of the man Jesus.

3. Polish tritheism and ditheism. Peter Gonesius picked up Anabaptist ideas at Padua, read Servetus and returned to Poland, where unusual theological views could be openly debated. There (in 1556) he declared the Trinity an unscriptural Roman invention. Gonesius proposed what became a hallmark of early Polish Anabaptism: the Father as the one true God.[371] The Son was born from the seed of the Father's Word in Mary and was not consubstantial with him.[372]

Gonesius's initial proposals were sharply rejected and the classical Polish Reformed Christology largely affirmed until about 1562. At the same time they were insisting that the Bible was the only source of doctrine. From this they later concluded, like Servetus, that classical Christology was unscriptural.[373]

Most Polish Reformed also accepted a tenet put forth by Francis Stancaro: that a mediator must be inferior to the one to whom he intercedes. Against people like Gonesius, Stancaro strove to affirm Christ's equality with the Father. Yet from his definition of mediation Stancaro concluded that Christ could be Mediator or Savior only in his human nature.[374] Most Poles, however, believed that Christ's divine nature also mediated salvation. But once they accepted Stancaro's tenet—that a

---

[367]Servetus, *Two Treatises*, pp. 45, 209.

[368]Ibid., pp. 23, 149, 173.

[369]Ibid., pp. 157-58. In Servetus's *Restitution of Christianity* (written c. 1546-1547, published c. 1552) God not only infused divine essences into everything but also was the form that structures all matter (Bainton, *Hunted Heretic*, pp. 130-37). Yet Servetus could also say that God existed only in Christ and could be known only through him (*Two Treatises*, p. 165).

[370]Servetus, *Two Treatises*, pp. 45, 53.

[371]Dariusz Jarmola, "The Origins and Development of Believers' Baptism Among the Polish Brethren in the 16th Century" (Ph.D. diss., Louisville: Southern Baptist Seminary, 1990), p. 67; Williams, *Radical Reformation*, p. 1043.

[372]Williams, *Radical Reformation*, pp. 1009-10; Jarmola, *Origins and Development*, pp. 306-7.

[373]Jarmola, *Origins and Development*, pp. 58-63; Williams, *Radical Reformation*, pp. 1018, 1025, 1041-42, 1111.

[374]Williams, *Radical Reformation*, pp. 1026-29.

mediator must be inferior—they began concluding that Christ's deity must be somewhat less than the Father's.[375]

Despite its general acceptance of the Father's superiority, the first phase of radical Polish Christology is often called tritheism (c. 1562-1565). Proponents did not downgrade the Son and Spirit so much as locate their divinity not in a common substance but in mutual interaction. Some eventually affirmed, with Servetus, that the Word originated only with creation, and was not really God's Son before his human conception.[376]

But Laelius Socinus, another Italian rationalist, had taken this further. He exegeted *word (logos)* in John I as the *sermo* heard in Jesus' earthly preaching. Laelius also interpreted John's "beginning" *(archē)* as the start not of the universe but of Jesus' ministry; and "world" *(kosmos)* as not the cosmos but the fallen human "world." Laelius's Jesus, like Servetus's, was virgin born, but without premundane status.[377] Laelius, however, was opposed by Poles who feared that Jesus was being understood as a mere man, empowered by God in adoptionist fashion.

As a result ditheism prevailed from about 1566-1568. Ditheists dropped the Holy Spirit's full deity. But they insisted that salvation had to come from one sent by God from heaven, not a human adopted as Son.[378] Gonesius joined them, deciding that the Son had been divine in form even before creation. If not born of the same substance as the Father *(homoousios)*, his Christ was born of like substance *(homoiousios)*.[379] Ditheists, like those tritheists who insisted that Christ was Mediator in his deity, wanted to emphasize salvation's divine origin.

4. Unitarianism. Gaining strength in Lithuania and Transylvania as well as Poland during the 1560s, unitarianism pervaded Polish Anabaptism by decade's end. It was expressed most definitively by Laelius Socinus's nephew, Faustus (who actually arrived in Poland in 1580, just after historic Anabaptism, in my usage, ended).

Tritheism and ditheism, though they subordinated the Son to the Father, thought of the Son coming from above, from God, as did ancient Alexandrian Christology; and likewise Hubmaier, Schlaffer, Riedemann, Marpeck and the Dutch. Unitarianism, in contrast, thought of Jesus being raised to deity, as did ancient adoptionists, some Italian Anabaptists, perhaps some Antiochenes and

---

[375]Ibid., pp. 1027, 1030-131, 1045.
[376]Ibid., pp. 1037-38.
[377]Ibid., pp. 970-71.
[378]Jarmola, *Origins and Development,* pp. 69-70.
[379]Ibid., p. 69.

Denck, and possibly Hut, Schiemer, and Hoffman.

Fasutus Socinus approached Christ from below and sought to define him by his earthly office, not his nature, and by his will, not his essence.[380] Like Servetus, Faustus meant to adhere strictly to Scripture. As an Evangelical Rationalist, he expected it to accord with reason. Correct understanding of its doctrines and fulfillment of its precepts were requisite for salvation.[381]

Faustus denied the soul's natural immortality. Jesus' saving task was to walk, and thereby show, the way to resurrection, which Faustus could call divinization.[382] Faustus claimed that Scripture conceived God chiefly in terms of will, not essence. For him, like tritheists, any unity among divine persons had to be of their wills. Like Servetus and many rationalists, Faustus denied that God's Son existed before Jesus' conception in the virgin.[383] Jesus was chiefly a prophet whose office was to reveal God's will.[384] In this sense, God's Word and will appeared in the flesh in him, though he had but one nature—the human.[385]

Much of Christ's saving work consisted in this prophetic task of teaching God's way to resurrection. Jesus' death was largely a marker on his journey to this event,[386] which glorified and transfigured him.[387] Those who followed would be resurrected at his second advent.[388] Further, through his resurrection and ascension, God conferred divine, ruling power on Christ, making him fully divine in this adoptive manner.[389] This adoptionist view had already been expressed in the Transylvanian Unitarian Confession (1579), which called Jesus "God" because he was conceived by God's Spirit, who anointed him above all others, and because he received majesty at the resurrection from his Father, who would restore all things by him. It was appropriate to invoke Jesus for good things because he had conferred these while on earth and because the Father had brought all things together in him, including eter-

---

[380]Williams, *Radical Reformation*, pp. 979, 981.

[381]Ibid., p. 1162.

[382]Ibid., p. 1163.

[383]Ibid., p. 981.

[384]Ibid., p. 982.

[385]Ibid., p. 985. Precisely speaking, Jesus' human nature was more susceptible to exaltation to divine dignity than others' (ibid.).

[386]Socinus endorsed neither moral influence nor Christus Victor models of the cross, and he sharply critiqued substitution. He did, however, view Jesus' resurrection as God's vindication of him, as does Christus Victor (ibid., p. 985). Jesus' prophetic office occupied his life. His kingly office commenced at his resurrection, with his priestly office, when he began presenting his sufferings to the Father and cleansing us from sins (pp. 983, 1168).

[387]Ibid., p. 985.

[388]Ibid., p. 1162, cf. p. 1303.

[389]Ibid., p. 985.

nal life, to channel them through him to us.[390]

5. Summary. While various Christologies appeared along the Polish trajectory, at its climax conclusions consistent with some underlying themes were drawn. A hallmark belief, the Father as the one and only God, became unitarianism. Jesus was granted a kind of deity via adoptionism, a popular option in the rationalistic humanism predating the trajectory's origin. Adopted deity, however, nearly always seems inferior to the Father's. Some Poles drew this consequence by declining to worship Christ (chap. 2).

Overall summary. How does our fourth source in the historic Anabaptist stream alter the broad portrait drawn from the other three? In particular, does the portrait now validate as an Anabaptist option a Christology foregrounding Jesus' ethical and socially relevant human features, and backgrounding his deity, or treating it as emerging from these?

The Polish trajectory surely indicates that Anabaptism's distinctive concern with Jesus' life (and following it) can take that direction. It also indicates, however, that this endeavor involved rationalistic, humanistic assumptions different from those that other Anabaptists generally shared. While this humanism's concern with original texts was congruent with the biblicism of mostly illiterate Anabaptists elsewhere, its temper and method were quite different. Its challenge to traditional doctrine involved an intellectual skepticism, an "almost perverse doubting, persistent uncertainty" that had found adoptionism congenial from early on.[391]

Polish Anabaptism also lacked the spiritually transformative notion of salvation found in the other three branches and the mystical orientation in all but the Swiss. This gave Jesus' life and teachings a quite different role, climactically expressed by Faustus Socinus. Much as Jesus' own acts brought him adoptive deity, his followers' corresponding acts gained a future salvation. But for other Anabaptists, Jesus' life formed the outward pattern of a present salvation that was also vibrantly inward and spiritual—and directed, of course, toward future culmination.

Very broadly, I propose that within the Polish trajectory Anabaptist themes, as they were shaped by humanism, began pointing "forward" toward modernity. Within the other three branches, however, those themes more often referred back toward features of medieval mysticism and communalism, and ultimately the New Testament.

If some Anabaptists today favor Christologies like the Poles', I do not think they will gain much if they simply cite Polish Anabaptists as legitimation. For historic Anabaptists espoused many unpalatable views (e.g., violent revolution). To

---

[390]Ibid., pp. 1131-33.
[391]Ibid., p. 877.

simply claim Anabaptism for one's position is to obscure one's real reasons for accepting some views but not others.

In our broad, historic Anabaptist portrait, viewed provisionally through classical lenses, Polish Unitarians, Denck and perhaps Hut, Schiemer, and Hoffman, display an Antiochene inclination unlike Chalcedon. The others appear broadly Chalcedonian. Not that they often argued in classical concepts—Menno, like Polish tritheists and ditheists, critiqued these, while Marpeck could become confused when he tried. Neither did the Dutch affirm Chalcedon's role for Mary. Yet for all these, Jesus' work brought the kind of salvation—transformative communion with the divine—that only God could bestow. It was salvific precisely because it flowed from a fully personal, eternally existing reality. The saving Word was not simply God's speech (Servetus) but God's self-bestowing reality.

Since this communion renewed all of human life into its bearer's likeness, his humanity had to be enough like ours to follow. To be sure, Dutch Christology probably fell short of this soteriological criterion. Most others hedged a bit. Broadly Chalcedonian Anabaptists, however, envisioned Jesus fulfilling Adam's human task.[392] If they differed from Chalcedon's affirmations, it was in not quite affirming that Jesus was fully human. All Anabaptists, however, diverged from Chalcedon's focus by keeping the kind of human he was, as servant and peacemaker, at the center of his work.

Did this broadly Chalcedonian orientation clash with Christus Victor, as Weaver maintains? Hardly. All those who utilized the latter affirmed the former (Hubmaier, Schlaffer, Riedemann, Marpeck, Menno, Dirk), with one exception (Hoffman). Their basic reasons, again, were intrinsic to their soteriologies: only a divine power could overcome death and bestow a life strong enough to purge its effects. So oppressively did the powers rule history that God alone could break in and make a new beginning. Christus Victor imagery was absent only from Denck (whose historical process seemed cyclic and perhaps, along with evil, less real than cosmic oneness) and from Hut and Schiemer (perhaps for the same reasons). Yet these three alone, with Hoffman, tilted away from Chalcedon. Riedemann and Marpeck, who developed Christus Victor most fully, were most Alexandrian.

This means that for most Anabaptists what Marpeck called Jesus' uniting of two natures was not only consistent with but really the source of that sacramental interweaving of Spirit and matter, inner and outer, religious life and daily existence,

---

[392]Due to limitations in Dutch and Polish, I am not sure what Hoffman and Polish tritheists and ditheists held on this. For this reason, I omit the Poles also from the next issue, coherence with Christus Victor. However, Polish tritheist and ditheists may have been broadly Chalcedonian or close to it.

at the movement's heart. This union, however, was no abstract conjunction of substances. It occurred within Jesus' history, whose specific character Anabaptists stressed more than most.

Contemporary Appropriations

The Polish Anabaptist trajectory culminated in adoptionism. As an overall Christology, this may be limited. Yet when theology puts to Scripture those questions about Jesus' person that arise from his work, something like adoption soon appears. At his baptism Jesus heard the declaration, "You are my beloved Son" (Mk 1:9-11 and parallels); this echoed Psalm 2:7, which adds: "today I have begotten you." Within the kerygma of his resurrection we hear that "God has made him both Lord and Messiah" (Acts 2:36) and that Jesus "was declared to be Son of God with power according to the Spirit of holiness by resurrection from the dead" (Rom 1:4).

From a Christus Victor perspective Jesus' resurrection, as his triumph, surely enhanced his human reality. Marpeck not only stressed this but occasionally spoke as if even his deity might have increased. Moreover, Jesus, as Christus Victor's second Adam who shared our human path, in some sense progressed toward that climax. "Jesus increased in wisdom and in years, and in divine and human favor" (Lk 2:52). He "learned obedience through what he suffered" (Heb 5:8; cf. Heb 2:10, 18; 4:14-15; 12:2-4), not least through struggle with death and the devil (Heb 2:14-18).

On the current scene an adoptionistic, or at least broadly Antiochene, orientation has been congenial for two centuries. In societies where a spiritual, eternal realm seems unreal, many people can still picture Jesus as an ordinary man who walked in close enough communion with whatever was divine to eventually become one with it. This approach can portray Jesus as a pioneer in ethical, social or psychological transformation. By elucidating his fully human processes and struggles, it can bring Jesus closer to the increasing multitudes who feel marginalized and dehumanized in our globalizing world.

For these reasons and because historic Anabaptists foregrounded the particular character of Jesus' humanity, I will keep notions of his development, including adoptionism, in mind as I pursue my contemporary Christology, again from below. Since Polish Anabaptists focused on such issues, I will dialogue with two current Anabaptists, James McClendon and Norman Kraus, who raise them in similar ways. However, our classical christological lenses showed that many historic Anabaptists were broadly Chalcedonian. Consequently, I will next ask whether biblical presentations of Jesus' development might be compatible with that framework.

Today's Anabaptist theologians differ over classical Christology, particularly "the creeds." Quite early, Yoder critiqued the Nicene Creed's political context and ontological terms. Yet he found it "the best answer" to the crucial question, How are Jesus' normativity and God's uniqueness related?[393] Yoder was far more negative toward Chalcedon and Alexandrian Christology, construing them as nearly Apollinarian.[394] Before long, however, he was recommending his own position as "more radically Nicene and Chalcedonian than other views."[395] For though the creeds scarcely mentioned Jesus' life and teachings, Yoder began insisting that Chalcedon's affirmation of Jesus' full humanity entailed their normative character. He enlisted the creeds to persuade ecumenicals and evangelicals to take Jesus' "politics" seriously.

For Weaver, in contrast, the creeds' political context, ontological terms and silence on Jesus' life conceal rather than help people recognize Jesus' ethical normativity. Regarding Jesus' deity, so far as I know Weaver simply says that he is "of God," while the only meaning Yoder mentions is that it sanctions his normative humanity. Both may find classical expressions too culturally relative to convey anything today, except Jesus' full humanity.[396]

Current Anabaptist Christologies. I. Even though James McClendon consults biblical narrative often, he begins inquiring about Jesus' person, not with his history (from below) but his risen presence.[397] McClendon insists that the risen One who encounters us is divine.[398] Accordingly, he credits Nicea and Chalcedon insofar as they "attributed full deity to the living, risen Christ. Hence, the very substance of God could be encountered in Christian practice and worship."[399] However, like Weaver, McClendon critiques these creeds' neglect of Jesus' earthly story and Christian discipleship, and the political factors in their formation and use.[400]

McClendon also criticizes the Alexandrian notion that because God's eternal Son formed Jesus' person, he took on human nature but was "not a human be-

---

[393]Yoder, *Preface to Theology*, p. 204.

[394]Ibid., pp. 213-16.

[395]Yoder, *Politics of Jesus*, p. 105.

[396]For these issues in Yoder, see Thomas Finger, Review of *The Politics of the Cross*, by Craig Carter; *Preface to Theology*, by John H. Yoder; and *Mennonites and Classical Theology*, by A. James Reimer, in *Perspectives in Religious Studies* 28, no. 2 (2002); and "Did Yoder Reduce Theology to Ethics?" in *A Mind Patient and Untamed*, ed. Gayle Gerber Koontz and Ben Ollengburger (Telford, Penn.: Cascadia, 2004). For Kaufman, by identifying "Christ" who was fully divine with Jesus, Chalcedon reified "mythopoetic expressions" about him "into metaphysical fact" (Gordon Kaufman, *In Face of Mystery* [Cambridge, Mass.: Harvard University Press, 1993], pp. 384-85). But if "Christ" includes the broader community involved in the Christ event, something of Chalcedon's intent can be retrieved—to show who are "the true God" and "true humanity—humanity responding in faith and love to God" (ibid., p. 405, cf. pp. 375, 456).

[397]McClendon, *Systematic Theology* 2: 239-40.

[398]Ibid., pp. 240-42.

[399]Ibid., p. 253, cf. p. 256.

[400]Ibid., pp. 253-57.

ing."[401] Much like Weaver, Yoder and Kaufman, McClendon finds models from different eras so incompatible that one "cannot be successfully grafted into another." Without explaining specifically why, he infers that we cannot take "Nicea or Chalcedon at face value without archaizing ourselves."[402]

Consequently, McClendon argues not that two natures meet in Christ but in contemporary language that two narratives do. One is humanity's lengthy, convoluted search for fulfillment and God. The other is God's self-expending approach to humanity. These stories are and remain distinct, implying a permanent Creator-creature differentiation. Yet in Jesus they became one. Here "the action of Jesus is God's action; what Jesus suffers, God suffers."[403]

During Jesus' human journey his communion with God gradually increased.[404] This combined narrative climaxed with his resurrection. This event, as a Christus Victor reading asserts, reversed "history's judgment as represented by the authorities," which found Jesus guilty and his opponents just, for Jesus' resurrection incriminated his opponents and justified him. According to McClendon, this event reversed things further by "identifying the life of Jesus of Nazareth afresh with God's own life, so that from this time . . . the history of this man . . . was to be counted identical with God's inner history." Through resurrection, Jesus was "re-identified." He became "the unique sharer of God's own identity" so that "the whole story of Jesus is God's own story. His entire story is now . . . eternally God's own."[405]

This construal of Jesus' deity resembles Polish unitarianism. Is it adoptionistic? Adoptionism, McClendon answers, teaches that God did not act until a human appeared who merited adoption as a reward. McClendon insists, however, that God always intended, even "before all worlds," "to redeem the world by identifying Jesus' life with God's own life," to exalt "this One who was God's self-giving presence."[406]

For McClendon, then, as for Socinus and Servetus, Jesus' essential self need not have existed before his conception. Nor need one ask how it could have taken on humanity. The nativity stories portrayed God's Spirit involved in Jesus' coming, but need

---

[401]Ibid., p. 255.

[402]Ibid., p. 265, cf. p. 276. Though he respects these creeds as historic efforts, McClendon asserts without discussion that "the puzzles of substance and *hypostasis*, of *ousia* and *persona* . . . were alien puzzles when read into the gospels" (p. 278, italics in original) and that Chalcedon's "severe paradoxes finally choked out the two-natures model" (pp. 256, 257).

[403]Ibid., p. 276.

[404]Ibid., pp. 254, 271.

[405]Ibid., pp. 247-48.

[406]Ibid., pp. 248, 272.

not rule out two human parents.[407] However, because God identified with Jesus in death, God tasted "human death at its godless worst."[408] And because our bodies "constitute the possibility of our engagement with one another," it is most fitting to assume that Jesus' resurrection transformed his body, but not to insist on it.[409]

To oppose a deifying role for Jesus' resurrection, the Alexandrian orientation has often enlisted Philippians 2:5-11. Theology has usually understood the "form of God" in which Christ initially existed as his divine nature (v. 6), and the "human likeness" in which he was born as his human nature (v. 7). This text, which praises Jesus' humility and servanthood, has long been extolled by Anabaptists. In the way it expresses Jesus' Lordship I find the evangel's "central universal affirmation" (chap. 7).

As McClendon interprets this passage, however, the "form of God" was nothing divine. It was that human image of God that Eve and Adam initially possessed. "Being born in human likeness" (v. 7) and humbling himself (v. 8) meant undertaking the human task or path that they were assigned but did not complete.[410] So read, Christ's preexistence was absent from this passage, but he was exalted to deity at the end (Phil 2:9-11). Murphy and Ellis and perhaps Yoder share this interpretation.[411]

Christology in Anabaptist perspective must take the specific character of Jesus' life and the narrative of its development seriously. But is it really convincing to affirm his deity if it was bestowed only at his resurrection and if his personal center existed nowhere before his conception? Some notions developed by the next author may help this seem plausible.

2. Displaying affinities with neo-orthodoxy, C. Norman Kraus differentiates God's revelation sharply from other sources of knowledge. These include Greek ontology, which he claims conceived reality in terms of static substances and was foundational for classical Christology. Like Anabaptists, including the Poles, and Evangelical Rationalists, Kraus seeks to derive Christology from the Bible, whose language he finds quite different: a historical mode where acts of personal agents are central.[412]

Kraus often affirms Christ's deity. Yet he rejects the notion of God's Son as a preexistent, subsistent being (*hypostasis*, the classical Greek term for "person"). Jesus, rather, was one with God as God's self-revelation or self-expres-

---

[407]Ibid., pp. 269-70.

[408]Ibid., p. 272.

[409]Ibid., pp. 249-50, cf. pp. 271-72.

[410]Ibid., pp. 266-69.

[411]Murphy and Ellis, *On the Moral Nature*, pp. 176-78; Yoder, *Preface to Theology*, pp. 80-88.

[412]C. Norman Kraus, *Jesus Christ Our Lord* (Scottdale, Penn.: Herald, 1987), pp. 46-57.

sion;[413] he is "God in his self-revealing action."[414] Kraus finds this occurring throughout Jesus' ministry but climaxing with his resurrection.[415] Kraus draws on Wolfhart Pannenberg, who finds the risen Jesus so integral to the resurrection's revelatory content that he and God, in Kraus' words, share an "identity of selfhood" or an "essential self-identity."[416] This identity, however, is a unity in work, not substance.[417]

In several ways Kraus reminds one of Servetus. Kraus begins with the man Jesus and also identifies Jesus with God's preexistent Word. This Word, further, was no distinct being but the self-expression of the one God, of this God's love and power.[418] Again as for Servetus this Word apparently emerged at creation. Interpreting "In the beginning was the Word" (Jn I:I), Kraus takes "the beginning" to mean "God's expression of himself in creative, salvific action." To ask what occurred before this beginning is to ask "what God is 'in himself.' " But knowledge of God "in himself" lies beyond what Scripture tells us.[419]

Incarnation then means, as for Servetus, that God's creative self-expression, or Word, was fully embodied in Jesus.[420] This is the way Kraus conceives what Mc-

---

[413]C. Norman Kraus, *God Our Savior* (Scottdale, Penn.: Herald, 1991), p. 23.

[414]Kraus, *Jesus Christ Our Lord*, p. 110. Jesus was the "self-disclosing presence of God . . . in a fully human life" (p. 42), the fullness of God's self-disclosure (*God Our Savior*, p. 29). As "Immanuel," he was God's expression or act, God-reconciling-us (*Jesus Christ Our Lord*, p. 59). Jesus was functionally equated with God's salvation (ibid., p. 82) and, much as Denck said, participated in the divine reality he represents (ibid., p. 96).

[415]Kraus, *Jesus Christ Our Lord*, pp. 88, 90; Kraus, *God Our Savior*, pp. 26-27.

[416]Kraus, *Jesus Christ Our Lord*, pp. 113-14, cf. p. 117; *God Our Savior*, p. 39. "In the resurrection, as Pannenberg observes, God decisively identified with and vindicated the faith, life and teaching of Jesus. God is one with Jesus in his revelation to us" (Kraus, *God Our Savior*, p. 46; cf. Wolfhart Pannenberg, *Jesus: God and Man* [Philadelphia: Westminster, 1968], pp. 66-73, 126-41).

[417]Kraus, *Jesus Christ Our Lord*, p. 112.

[418]Ibid., pp. 106, 104.

[419]Ibid., p. 100. This apparently is a major theme (e.g., Kraus, *God Our Savior*, pp. 69, 93, 132). Yet Kraus rarely seems to indicate otherwise. For instance, the Word "always existed in God" and is "the eternal self-expression of God" (ibid., p. 25). Paraphrasing Jn I, Kraus avers that Jesus "did not become the 'Son of God' . . . at creation . . . but he shared God's eternal glory," and in more intimately personal terms "he was sent from the bosom of the Father" (*Jesus Christ Our Lord*, p. 104, cf. p. 112).

[420]E.g., Kraus, *Jesus Christ Our Lord*, pp. 97, 100; *God Our Savior*, pp. 27, 29. Somewhat like McClendon, Kraus says that "Christ" was "before all things" in the sense of being in God's intention and plan "before creation" and being "the principle and goal of creation" (*Jesus Christ Our Lord*, p. 104).

Friesen briefly approves Nicea and Chalcedon for declaring "that in Jesus we find God and our humanity most vividly illuminated" (Friesen, *Artists, Citizens, Philosophers*, pp. 108-9). However, the significance of Jesus' person, in Friesen's christological section, consists entirely in his earthly embodiment and revelation of human fulfillment, God's kingdom and God (ibid., pp. 108-20; cf. note

Clendon also maintains: that Jesus of Nazareth's personal center did not exist before his conception. Jesus, indeed, was not of the same substance *(homoousios)* as the Father—for then he would have existed as the Son from eternity.[421] The virgin birth, moreover, should be understood not literally but as poetry or allegory, indicating that "Jesus' true origin and identity was not 'according to the flesh' but from the Spirit."[422] For Kraus this reading rules out adoptionism. In paraphrasing John 1, he opposes the notion that Jesus became God's Son "through a historical sequence of events."[423]

Jesus, then, apparently had no divine nature in the substantial sense. Like McClendon, Kraus also critiques the notion of human nature that seems most consistent with Chalcedon: the Alexandrian. For Alexandrians, Jesus' personal center was the eternal Son, so that his human nature lacked a human personal center. Like Menno, Kraus finds this notion of a nature without a person abstract and at odds with Jesus' full humanity.[424]

Kraus' fully human Jesus—contra some historic Anabaptists—acquired no special protection from a unique birth but shared our "handicap of a 'sinful nature.'"[425] By this Kraus means "not a corruption of individual substance" but being affected by humankind's sinful solidarity. Jesus, however, never consciously opposed God.[426]

Although Kraus finds Jesus embodying the Word throughout his life and critiques adoptionism, remember that his Jesus was most fully identified with God by resurrection, as for adoptionists. Not unlike Socinus, Kraus claims that only then was Jesus "associated in the most immediate and intimate terms with the divine presence, power, and purpose," only then was he endowed with "a divine identity and status . . . proper to his divine role."[427] Can the adoptionistic implications of this be avoided?

Perhaps they could in Pannenberg's way—though Kraus does not explicitly take

---

158 of this chap.). I find no reference to Christ's agency in relation to a preexistent Word or as resurrected. Friesen treats "the resurrection of Christ as the manifestation of the Spirit in a new humanity" (p. 96). He may conflate these events, for the Spirit is the only agent under this heading (pp. 117-20).

[421]Kraus, *Jesus Christ Our Lord*, p. 105, esp. n. 2; cf. Kraus, *God Our Savior*, p. 93. If we inquire about Jesus in terms of identity with God's revelation rather than of ontological essence, "we are brought directly to the historical word spoken in Jesus and not to some prior word" (*Jesus Christ Our Lord*, p. 101).

[422]Kraus, *Jesus Christ Our Lord*, p. 78.

[423]Ibid., p. 104.

[424]Ibid., pp. 47-48, 70.

[425]Ibid., p. 71.

[426]Ibid., p. 72.

[427]Kraus, *God Our Savior*, p. 39.

it—through an eschatological notion of truth: whatever something turns out to be at the climax of God's saving work is what it was all along. Pannenberg concludes that since Jesus, at the proleptic climax of this work—resurrection—was identified with God, he always was divine.[428] Here is another way of affirming Christ's preexistence without maintaining that Jesus' personal center existed before his conception.

3. Our two Anabaptist theologians connect Jesus' deity closely with his human character and development, as should any Christology in Anabaptist perspective, especially if shaped by Christus Victor. Both are generally Antiochene: Jesus was divine through the Word's indwelling. Though both reject the adoptionist label, their Jesus was most fully identified with God through resurrection. By denying preexistence to Jesus' personal center, they apparently avoid the problem involved in affirming it: depriving Jesus of a human center since this preexisting person would be divine.

Nonetheless, *God,* in biblical narrative, means the eternal One, the cosmos's Creator. Can any human who began existing at conception—no matter how fully indwelt by, united with or foreordained by God—really be God in this monotheistic sense? We recall that most historic Anabaptists were broadly Chalcedonian, more often in an Alexandrian than an Antiochene way. It is time to ask whether Jesus' genuine humanity can be expressed biblically and constructively in this manner.

An Anabaptist Christology. Turning toward Scripture, Philippians 2:5-11 stands out. Perhaps no text encapsulates Jesus' significance for Anabaptists as well. It vividly portrays his particular human character and course. By summarizing these as obedience (v. 8), it connects with other major passages on Jesus' humanity (Rom 5:19; Heb 5:8). Few texts have been enlisted so often to support an Alexandrian orientation. Much then will hinge on its exegesis. If the traditional reading is sound, a broadly Chalcedonian Christology will seem more credible. If McClendon's reading is more plausible, so will be a Christology like his and Kraus's. I will accordingly examine this crucial text in detail, then briefly connect my results with others bearing on Christ's person.

1. Biblical considerations.

• *Philippians 2:5-11.* Most scholars agree that this passage rests on an Aramaic hymn from early, pre-Pauline communities. Nonetheless, scholars often posit that Christ's preexistence emerged in late New Testament writings, influenced by Greek thought. James Dunn's impressive study of preexistence tends to reinforce this. Dunn provides exegetical grounding for McClendon's reading and for much that appears in Servetus, Socinus and Kraus.

---

[428]Pannenberg, *Jesus: God and Man,* pp. 135-36, 150-58; cf. Kraus, *God Our Savior,* p. 46.

Dunn claims that the earliest Christology did not mention preexistence but began from Jesus' resurrection to Lordship (expressed in the kerygma: Acts 2:31-36; Rom 1:3-4).[429] Before long, Jesus was being perceived as the last Adam, who shared our solidarity in the first one's sin. Yet he followed the path that Adam should have, through to resurrection.[430] From this an early Christological pattern emerged, with two stages: Jesus' earthly path and exaltation—but not a preceding stage, his preexistence. This Adam Christology seems compatible with Christus Victor, and the two-stage pattern seems compatible with adoptionism. Philippians 2, Dunn insists, must be understood within this framework.[431]

Like McClendon, Dunn interprets the "form of God" (*morphē theou*), which Jesus originally possessed (Phil 2:6), as the image and glory of God that Adam initially had. Jesus' refusal to grasp "equality with God" was the opposite and reversal of Adam's sin (cf. Gen 3:4-7, 22). The crucial notion of self-emptying (*heauton ekenōsen*, Phil 2:7) then meant that Jesus emptied himself not of divine glory but of Adam's initial glory, and embraced fallen Adam's lot. This involved making himself powerless.[432] Jesus, that is, began not as divine but as a human in one kind of condition, and he took on another human condition.

Christ also took on "the form of a slave" (*morphēn doulou*), which Paul contrasted directly with his original "form [*morphē*] of God." For Dunn the latter form meant slavery, along with Adam's descendants, to either corruption or the elemental spirits (cf. Gal 4:3, 9). Dunn translates the next phrase (*en homoiōmati anthrōpōn genomenos*, Phil 2:7) not as "being born in human likeness," which is more usual, but as "becoming" in this likeness, or as sharing generally in fallen humanity's fate.

Dunn takes the next phrase, "being found in human form" (*schēmati heuretheis hōs anthrōpos*, Phil 2:7) to summarize what the hymn has proclaimed so far. He understands all three terms in verse 7 ("form of a slave," "human likeness" and "human form") to indicate the same thing: fallen humanity. Further, Jesus' self-emptying and assumption of this condition indicated not a specific act, supramundane or mundane, but the general character of his life.[433] Following this, Dunn proposes, the first stage

---

[429]Dunn, *Christology in the Making*, pp. 33-46.

[430]Ibid., pp. 98-128.

[431]Ibid., pp. 114-15. Dunn rightly identifies Jesus' resurrection as the epistemological starting point for much early Christology. He shows how a Christology stressing resurrection can underline many emphases consistent with Anabaptism, but which can be lost when preexistence and incarnation are stressed (pp. 267-68, cf. pp. 128, 195). Yet this does not show that resurrection and preexistence-incarnation are necessarily incompatible. Recently Dunn revisited Phil 2 and added some interesting nuances, but has not substantially altered his interpretation (*Theology of Paul*, pp. 281-88, cf. pp. 245-52).

[432]Dunn, *Christology in the Making*, p. 117.

[433]Ibid., p. 120.

of this Adam Christology climaxed with Jesus' "death on a cross" (Phil 2:8).

The second stage, Jesus' exaltation (Phil 2:9-11), brought him to that point of rule over creation that Adam was meant to attain (cf. Ps 8:6). The language of these verses, Dunn says, describes "generally God's purpose for man."[434] Dunn hardly mentions that Christ was given God's own name (v. 9) and was worshiped by all creatures in terms clearly echoing allegiance to Yahweh alone (Phil 2:10-11; recalling Is 45:23). What should we make of this reading, which omits Christ's preexistence?

I find that Dunn's two-stage reading jars with this text's hymnic form. The passage makes far better hymnic, dramatic sense if it begins with a first supramundane stage and decision, ending with "born in human likeness" (Phil 2:6-7a); then a second stage descending to the nadir of "death on a cross" (Phil 2:7b-8); and then a third, ascending back to the zenith (Phil 2:9-12).[435]

Further, such a three-stage or "V-shaped" pattern existed in pre-Christian Judaism, especially in its Wisdom literature.[436] One can hardly insist, like Dunn, that early Palestinian Christians knew only two stages. Further, language about a supreme supramundane agent through whom Yahweh created and guided the universe was widespread in Judaism. The earliest Christians, in seeking to praise and understand the Jesus exalted to universal Lordship, likely drew on this cosmic language and its V-shaped expressions as well as Adam traditions.[437]

Although the Adam theme appears in our text, the three-stage pattern makes better sense of it. Christ's refusal to grasp equality with God (Phil 2:6) indeed contrasted with Adam's sin, as Dunn says. But if the "form of God" was simply the image humans bear, why did Christ have to radically empty or strip himself of it to take on the "form of a slave," "human likeness" and "human form" (Phil 2:7)?

---

[434]Ibid., p. 119.

[435]Such a reading reaches the nadir at exactly the halfway point. For a hymnic reconstruction, see Reginald Fuller, *The Foundations of New Testament Christology* (New York: Scribner's, 1965), who regards this as the three-stage Christology's earliest expression (though he derives this, as I do not, from Hellenism).

[436]Ben Witherington III, *Paul's Narrative Thought World* (Louisville: Westminster/John Knox, 1994), pp. 94-97; and his *John's Wisdom* (Louisville: Westminster/John Knox, 1995), pp. 49-52.

[437]While figures such as God's Wisdom and Word were known in Judaism, they were personifications of Yahweh's activities, not distinct beings—much as Servetus said. They were never worshiped, for worship belonged to God alone. In contrast, the risen Christ was worshiped and experienced directly as divine. This is mainly what made the Christ of Phil 2 unique. Larry Hurtado finds this also in other early hymns, prayers, references to Christ's name, the Lord's Supper, confession of Jesus and prophecies from him (Larry Hurtado, *One God, One Lord* [Philadelphia: Fortress, 1988], pp. 100-114). These convictions about Christ's divine significance seem "to have appeared without any . . . traceable process of long ideational development" (ibid., p. 122). Hurtado agrees with Dunn, however, that all reflection on Jesus' person and work flowed from the earliest community's belief in his resurrection (p. 94).

Even if these terms denoted humans under sin, wouldn't a human existing in God's "image" naturally empathize with them? Why would one radically relinquish that image to do so? The hymn's radical contrast, however, makes sense if Christ surrendered some features of his preexistent deity.

Further, "form of a slave" can hardly mean slave to corruption, as Dunn proposes. For the text's ethical intent is to commend Jesus' slavelike or servantlike behavior. Paul hardly advises becoming corruption's slaves! To be sure Jesus identified with sinful humanity in the sense of sharing its afflictions and serving it. "Form of a slave" aptly depicts this. But neither "form of a slave" nor "human likeness" nor "human form" expresses well humanity's fallen condition.[438]

Moreover, being "in the form of God" (v. 6) contrasts more strongly with being "being born in human likeness" and "being found in human form" (v. 7) than the contrast Dunn proposes: between being in God's human image and identifying with sinful humanity. Since the contrast involved a radical self-emptying, the phrases "being born," and "being found" (v. 7) more naturally denote becoming human in the first place, while "form of God" (v. 6) better indicates a preexistent divine state—which was personal, for it involved a self to be emptied and the ability to do so.

Overall, if Christ's preexistence is eliminated from this hymn, its major phrases must be interpreted quite awkwardly. To be sure, it movingly portrays Jesus' life and a resurrection through which he received God's name ("Lord," vv. 9-11). But even though this text and several others invest Christ at his resurrection with deity in some sense (e.g., Acts 2:31-36; Rom 1:3-4), they hardly support adoptionism. As Dunn recognizes, such passages did not deny that he was divine beforehand. This issue was not in view at that time, and they did not even address it.[439]

In Dunn's and McClendon's readings, God's initiative virtually vanishes. Without it this passage can read much as Socinus saw it: styling Jesus as an extraordinary human who attained resurrection and then exhorting us to repeat this performance.

However, if this Jesus was God's own self-emptying, self-giving approach to us, God's initiative was at the core of this text. More precisely, this hymn would identify God's coming as Christ's own kenotic coming—a Christ who preexisted not simply as a pattern of the Father's expressiveness (Servetus) but as one who, out of his own unfathomable love, voluntarily descended from the heights into the lowest depths. This reading does not minimize his human walk but identifies it with God's continuing descent as well as the task assigned to Adam (v. 8); nor does it minimize

---

[438]McClendon reads *morphēn doulos* as "a servant role" but then proceeds to interpret *homoiōmati anthrōpōn* as "likeness of Adam's race," presumably meaning sinful humanity (*Systematic Theology* 2: 268).

[439]Dunn, *Christology in the Making*, pp. 62-63.

the astounding resurrection reversal and exaltation over all creatures (vv. 9-11).

• *Some other texts.* Most scholars agree that the foremost passages on Christ's per-son—especially Colossians 1:15-20, Hebrews 1:1-4, John 1:1-14—also reflect earlier hymns. If the first such hymn, Philippians 2, stressed Christ's preexistence, and if Wisdom speculation, with its V-shaped pattern, was widely known in earliest Christianity, it is very plausible that preexistence would be found in the others. High Christology then would not be a late, Greek-oriented product.

Dunn acknowledges the influence of Wisdom concepts. Yet he finds New Tes-tament writers speaking so fully from the angle of Jesus' resurrected lordship that when they called him Wisdom they did not mean that he preexisted (with the ex-ception of Jn 1). Instead, they asserted that Wisdom, which was always a feature or pattern of God's activity in Judaism, became fully embodied in Jesus. The man Jesus expressed God's Wisdom so fully that he could be identified—only in light of his resurrection—with it and with God.[440]

Dunn arrives at this reading, which resembles Servetus's and Kraus's, by starting from a resurrection standpoint and playing this off against God's incarnation at Jesus' advent. Yet if resurrection and prior incarnation can appear in the same texts, and do very early in Philippians 2, a major objection against finding Christ's pre-existence in others falls. It becomes quite plausible that the extraordinary V-shaped transition from the heights into the depths and back, which Marpeck also por-trayed, appeared early and late in the New Testament.

• *John 1:1-14.* What then of the Word and Servetus's and Kraus's claim that it de-noted not a person but a pattern of God's expressiveness? Dunn finds everything in the hymn underlying John 1 up to verse 14 consistent with Hellenistic Judaism, where the Word was a personified attribute of the one God.[441] But then, when the preexistent "Word became flesh . . . full of grace and truth," "the transition from impersonal personification to actual person" at last occurred. Finally at this late point in the New Testament God's utterance was no longer merely embodied through a person but became that person.[442] Dunn does not base this on one verse

---

[440]Dunn approaches virtually all the important texts this way: Col 1:15-20 (ibid., pp. 187-96); 1 Cor 8:6 (pp. 181-83); 2 Cor 8:9 (pp. 121-23); Gal 4:4 (pp. 38-44); Rom 8:3 (pp. 44-46); and Heb 1:1-4 (pp. 206-9). However, he insists that authors who connected Jesus with Wisdom did not think he was a man adopted by God but that God's Wisdom became Jesus. They regarded Christ as divine in the sense that he "fully embodies the creative and saving activity of God, that God in all his fulness was in him, that he represents and manifests all that God is in his outreach to men" (p. 212).

[441]Ibid., p. 241.

[442]Ibid., p. 243.

but also many Johannine texts where God sending his Son meant sending this heavenly person.[443]

In my view the Word of John's prologue surpassed the personified attribute of Judaism and Servetus in additional respects. In revealing his glory by dwelling, or making his tent *(eskenōsen)* among us (Jn 1:14), the Word resembled the Shekinah, the presence of Yahweh's living holiness in the Israelite tabernacle. This glorious Word was also "full of grace and truth" (Jn 1:14), a fullness that bestowed "grace upon grace" (Jn 1:16) so that those who received him were "born of God" (Jn 1:12-13). The Word's eternal relationship with the Father was also deeply personal. He was the Father's only Son (Jn 1:14), dwelling in his Father's heart or bosom (Jn 1:18).[444]

The Word also appears in I John, as the "word of life" (I Jn 1:1). Dunn equates this simply with the preached message.[445] Yet this "eternal life . . . was with the Father" *(ēn pros ton pater,* I Jn 1:2), as the Word of John 1:1 "was with God" *(ēn pros ton theon).* I John also proclaims that "we have looked at" *(etheasametha)* what concerned this Word of life (v. 1), while John reports that "we have seen *[etheasametha]* his glory" (Jn 1:14) This beholding bestowed divine life, or "fellowship . . . with the Father and with his Son Jesus Christ" (I Jn 1:3). In the prologues to both John and I John, then, the Word was too much a participant in and direct agent of divine reality to be a mere pattern. He did not emerge with creation, as Servetus said. Neither did his presence "in the beginning" (Jn 1:1) mean at creation but not before, as Kraus maintains.[446]

---

[443]Jn 3:17; 10:36; 17:18; I Jn 4:9 (Dunn, *Christology in the Making,* pp. 42-43, 56). For Dunn, other references to God's sending his Son meant an earthly figure (pp. 12-64). Dunn finds New Testament authors tracing this divine sonship from the resurrection back through Jesus' ministry, then to his conception and finally eternity (pp. 60-62). Preexistence, then, emerged quite late (p. 256). Again, Dunn reaches a major conclusion by playing off a resurrection against an incarnational starting point.

[444]Jn 1:18 most likely called the Word the "only-begotten *[monogenēs]* God," not "only-begotten Son" (Raymond Brown, *The Gospel According to John* [Garden City, N.Y.: Doubleday, 1966], p. 4). *Monogenēs* essentially meant unique or special (pp. 13, 17). Like Dunn, I find this theme elsewhere in John. The Father sent his "only-begotten" Son into the world (John 3:16, 18) as love's deepest expression (I Jn 4:9). This Son shared the Father's glory before the world's foundation (Jn 17:5; cf. Jn 17:24). He descended from heaven and ascended again with his resurrection (Jn 3:3, 7, 13, 16, 19; 6:33, 38, 62; 8: 38, 42, 58; 10:36; 16:28). Jn 10:33-36 distinguished those whom the Old Testament called "gods" because they received God's "word" from the Son whom God sent and can be uniquely called God. That rare Old Testament tendency to call humans or angels *elohim,* which Servetus cited to show that all humans can be God, actually stresses Jesus' unique way of being the Son, the Word himself, and not simply one who received or embodied it.

[445]Dunn, *Christology in the Making,* p. 245.

[446]Kraus, *Jesus Christ Our Lord,* p. 100. The beginning of creation first appeared in Jn 1:3 (Brown, *Gospel*

- *Summary.* My historical and contemporary investigations demanded that Jesus' person be closely connected with his particular human character and development. (Biblical texts that confirm this appear on pp. 396, 359.) I have been asking whether Scripture perceives Jesus' divine side in a general Antiochene manner: as the indwelling of God's Word, which Jesus embodied and manifested so vividly that he was identified with God. Admittedly, relatively few historic Anabaptists took this approach (Denck, Polish Unitarians and perhaps Hut, Schiemer, and Hoffman). Yet I consider it important because McClendon and Kraus now take it, and it is fairly intelligible in our modern-postmodern context.

I asked in particular whether Jesus' personal preexistence might be eliminated, and his deity attributed largely to his resurrection (McClendon, cf. Socinus). I pressed further, asking whether the preexisting Word or Son, in Scripture, might be not a person but a pattern (Kraus, cf. Servetus). But I concluded that the crucial passage, Philippians 2:5-11, cannot be read as McClendon proposes (with Murphy, Ellis, Dunn and perhaps Yoder). Drawing on this I briefly indicated why other "preexistence" texts probably cannot be either (esp. Rom 8:3; 1 Cor 8:6; 2 Cor 8:9; Gal 4:4; Col 1:15-20; Heb 1:1-4; cf. note 442). I also found the Word's preexistence in John and 1 John quite personal.

2. Theological construction. If important New Testament passages affirm Jesus' personal preexistence, as did most historic Anabaptists, the classical conundrum resurfaces: Can this be conceived without downplaying Jesus' humanity, especially by depriving him of a human person? This prompts me first to ask, How adequate are classical, Greek categories? I will then develop my own view under the headings "Person," "Nature" and "Jesus' Humanity," and summarize my perspective on the person of Jesus Christ and "the creeds'" significance. All this will provide material for further reflection on a recurring issue—the nature of spiritual reality.

- *Greek categories.* Many contemporary theologians, including Kraus, McClendon, Weaver, Yoder and Friesen, fault classical Christology's concepts for being static, ontological and impersonal rather than dynamic, narrative and personal. Menno, Evangelical Rationalists and Polish Anabaptists thought similarly. Today theologians often characterize Greek concepts as rigid, fixed grids into which dynamic, diverse biblical materials were jammed. But this appraisal is binary and stereotyped, not really historical. Many patristic debates arose precisely because meanings of key

---

According to John, p. 4). Existence before creation was explicit in Jn 17:5 and entailed in Jesus' self-references as "I am" *(ego eimi)*, Yahweh's eternal self-declaration (Jn 6:20; 8:23-24, 28, 58; 13:19; 18:5). Many uses of "I am" with phrases like "the resurrection and the life" (Jn 11:25) also implied this (Brown, *Gospel According to John*, pp. 533-38).

terms, even in Greek philosophy, were varied, fluid and often unclear.

For example, *ousia* ("substance," Lat. *substantia*), the term central to the creeds' claim that Son and Father are *homoousios* ("of the same substance"), carried at least two quite different meanings. In Aristotelian tradition *ousia* meant a subsisting individual. In Platonism it meant a characteristic shared by many individuals. The Council of Nicea (325 C.E.) intended the second meaning. This meant that Son and Father were distinct. Yet many others understood *ousia* in the Aristotelian sense. They thought the council was proclaiming that Son and Father were one individual (or modalism, which most of them rejected). Between the Councils of Nicea and Constantinople (381 C.E.) much energy was expended in deciding what *ousia* should mean, partly by searching for other terms to express the distinctness of Father and Son (such as *hypostasis* and *prosōpon* [person]).

Careful research shows that patristic theologians did not often cram biblical notions into prefabricated alien categories; instead they usually loosened Greek concepts from their original frameworks and sought to transform them in light of biblical meanings. Most Greek concepts fit within a worldview that sharply separated spirit and matter, time and eternity. But classical Christology, whatever its shortcomings, sought to redeploy these concepts to affirm the contrary: the uniting of these realms in an historical person.

In approaching classical Christology (and any past theology) I will first ask what it most basically intended to say; not lock it into standard definitions of its categories. I must indeed examine the original meanings of these categories. But as Kraus urges, theological concepts, which often originate in other fields, must be allowed to operate flexibly and analogically—though he often denies this to Greek and other philosophical terms.[447]

• *Person.* As patristic theologians sought to express the Father-Son distinction intended in the Nicene Creed, no good candidates appeared among Greek concepts. Of the two eventually chosen to denote a distinct agent, *hypostasis* often overlapped with *ousia*, even in the New Testament.[448] *Prosōpon* (Lat. *persona*) often indicated a superficial appearance or mask.[449] Nonetheless, these two became virtual syn-

---

[447]Kraus, *Jesus Christ Our Lord,* pp. 40-57.

[448]Heb 1:3, 3:14; 11:1 (*hypostasis* appears only twice elsewhere: 2 Cor 9:4; 11:17); see Helmut Koester, "ὑπόστασις," in *Theological Dictionary of the New Testament,* ed. Gerhard Friedrich, vol. 8 (Grand Rapids: Eerdmans, 1972). Recall Servetus's claim that *hypostasis* and *ousia* meant much the same in the New Testament (Servetus, *Two Treatises,* pp. 148-49, cf. p. 57).

[449]*Prosōpon* was given content "only in the course of theological debate. The fathers adopted a word which had a wide range of meanings and could thus be given the more precise sense which it received in theological discussion" (Eduard Lohse, "πρόσωπον κτλ.," in *Theological Dictionary of the New Testament,* ed. Gerhard Friedrich [Grand Rapids: Eerdmans, 1968], 6:778).

onyms. To understand what classical Christology meant by them, we must ask why and how they were used.

One major purpose was to express the genuinely mutual interaction between Father and Son (and Spirit) found in the New Testament. *Prosōpon* could accent the particular activity, or appearance, of each; *hypostasis* could accent each one's continuing identity. By designating both agents as *homoousios* ("of the same substance") as well, their equality, and hence their authentic reciprocity, could also be underlined, despite their very different functions. To call this common *ousia* divine meant that this interactivity, though it was apprehended from below, had always characterized divine reality. It did not originate when Jesus appeared. Sharing a divine *ousia* provided a way to indicate that the Son's love was of the same quality as his Father's and, as Marpeck would, that divine love perpetually flowed "from the heavenly Father into Christ and from Christ into the Father."[450]

Patristic theologians did not select and transform such concepts to speculate about God "in himself," but to elucidate the kind of salvation Jesus brought. The *homoousia* helped them portray his coming as the overflow of this eternal, mutual love—not simply an expression of the Father's love channeled through a human. By distinguishing the Son's *hypostasis* from the Father's they could stress that this love was also the Son's own, ceaselessly directed to the Father and ceaselessly reciprocated, and that by directing it to us through his teachings, sufferings, and rising, this Son was salvation's direct agent. Such a love drew people into that interchange between Father and Son (and Spirit).

If *hypostasis-prosōpon* and *ousia* function this way, they can well express how most historic Anabaptists understood Jesus to bring salvation. Salvation, for most, involved breaking into and destroying death and the powers' reign, which God alone could accomplish; and also being brought into communion with God, which alone could transform people into their true destiny and purge death's corrupting effects. For most Anabaptists Jesus brought direct communion with God because he himself was God's self-bestowing, transforming coming, or Word.

Hypostasis-prosōpon can also help describe the Word as John did—as "the word of life" (I Jn 1:1), "full of grace and truth" (Jn 1:14), bestowing "grace upon grace" (Jn 1:18), God's own light, truth and glory, as Jesus in whom we abide (Jn 15:1-11; I Jn 2:5-6), as the Son who brings his Father and Spirit with him to abide

---

[450]Pilgram Marpeck, "Ein Epistel meldend von der christlichen Kirchen und das agareischen," in *Das Kunstbuch*, ed. Joerg Propst Rothenfelder, auch genant Maler (manuscript, 1561). Photocopy in Goshen College Historical Library: Nr 33, Bl 264CI (p. 305), translating "into Christ" and "into the Father" rather than "in Christ" and "in the Father" (as translated in Marpeck, *Writings of Pilgram Marpeck*, p. 381) due to the clear sense of the original.

in us,[451] whose coming and indwelling destroy the devil's works.[452]

This full coming of this divine person into human reality revealed not only God's love, which humans did not know, but also the love humans should have for each other (1 Jn 4:9-12). In giving his life for us Jesus not only actualized God's love but also showed that we should give our lives and goods to each other (1 Jn 3:16-17; cf. Jn 13:34-35). For John, as for historic Anabaptists, abiding in and being transformed by God's Son, or Word, was inseparable from following his commands. Jesus' life and teachings were a continuing expression of the Word's own personal coming.[453]

The divine *hypostasis-prosōpon* concept can also convey the significance of perhaps the premier Anabaptist text: Philippians 2:5-11. As Marpeck intimated, the wider the transition from cosmic heights to cosmic depths in this text appears, the more astounding does the love it expresses. The transition will seem wider the more clearly the radical self-emptying, obedience, suffering, crucifixion and resurrection involved can be apprehended as God's own. Yet this need hardly obscure Jesus' humanity. For this hymn narrates in outline those human changes and their specific character that a Christology from below must highlight. That human path was God's, but also the true Adam's and is now ours.

This way of conceptualizing salvation as God's very own act(s) and initiative, by foregrounding Jesus' *hypostasis-prosōpon* is broadly Alexandrian. Its problems will soon be addressed. Yet it seems to me that the Antiochene orientation has difficulty presenting salvation this way. For if Christ's active, personal center was the human Jesus, can it really be affirmed that God came, suffered and rose? Didn't God work mostly by empowering or indwelling the man Jesus, who actually performed the saving acts? Might even his deity have emerged, in part, from his acts?

Even if the Word filled Jesus and profoundly empathized with his suffering, was this really "the very suffering of Godself"?[454] Or did God's deepest center still remain somewhat aloof? This aloofness would be greater if that Word were simply God's expressiveness, and Jesus simply embodied that expressiveness (Servetus, cf. Kraus). Further, if Jesus became one with God only at his resurrection (Socinus, cf. McClen-

---

[451]Jn 14:17-26; 16:13-15; 17:21-23; 1 Jn 2:24-27; 3:24; 4:13-16; 2 Jn 9.

[452]1 Jn 2:14; 3:8-10; 4:4; 5:18-20; cf. Jn 16:7-11, 33.

[453]Jn 14:15, 21-24; 15:10-14; 1 Jn 2:3-6; 3:7-10, 22-24. While John described Jesus' life less concretely than the Synoptics, Jesus' humanity was central. John framed his Gospel by pointedly affirming Jesus' humanity (Jn 1:14; cf. Jn 1:10-11; 20:27-28; 21:12-14). The Johannine Epistles identified its denial with antichrist's message (1 Jn 4:2-3; 2 Jn 7; cf. 1 Jn 2:18-22).

[454]Hans Denck, "On True Love," in *Early Anabaptist Spirituality*, ed. Daniel Liechty (New York: Paulist, 1994), p. 113.

don), even less can theology conceive his life and death as God's true coming.[455]

In any case, to underline that "our Lord Jesus Christ" was "one and the same" divine agent from eternity and through all phases of his work, Chalcedon called him *hypostasis* and *prosōpon*. Over three centuries, Christology had greatly altered these Greek concepts. They had not simply rendered biblical notions static and impersonal but gained a capacity to express a novel understanding of being as personal.[456] Nonetheless, under modernity's influence *person* has become too individualistic, I believe, to express Jesus' character and agency—unless it is interconnected with the *hypostaseis* of his Father and Spirit (as I will show below under "The Trinity").

• *Nature.* Despite the varied meanings of *physis* (nature) and *ousia* (substance) in Greek thought, Chalcedon used them similarly. Jesus' existence in *duo physesin* (two natures) meant much the same as being *homoousion* (of the same substance) with the Father in his deity and with us in his humanity. With critics of Chalcedon I agree that *physis* and *ousia* become problematic if they connote some additional thing, perhaps static, which entities possess or in which they participate. Critics often claim that Chalcedon expressed this thinglike understanding when it declared that Jesus' natures retained their "properties" *(idiotētos)* and existed in him without "confusion, transmutation, division or separation" (*asynchyktōs, atreptōs, adiairetōs, achōristōs*).

When historic Anabaptists critiqued classical concepts, it was often for the same reason. Polish tritheists rejected not so much the deity of the three persons but a common divine substance that seemed to them a fourth thing or god. Tritheists could call the three one in the sense of sharing a common work *(unum)*, but not as sharing or being the same thing *(unus)*. Menno apparently thought of human nature as some thing, though of course a rational, volitional something. In this light his denial that this nature could exist by itself—without the thinking, willing human person—made sense. So did his inference that if Jesus had a human nature, he was a complete, human person, independent from the divine Word.

Even in Greek culture, however, *physis* and *ousia* could indicate processes or ac-

---

[455]I find McClendon, Kraus and Pannenberg's retroactive interpretation of Jesus' resurrection unconvincing (that what Jesus then became he always was: God). Theology must indeed allow Scripture to define God, perhaps in surprising ways. However, the biblical God originally created the cosmos and maintained it for eons before Jesus' birth. To exist in this way is very different from being eternally foreseen in God's intention (esp. McClendon, *Systematic Theology* 2:247-48, 272) or becoming directly identified, eons later, with God's purpose.

[456]John Zizioulas, *Being as Communion* (Crestwood, N.Y.: St Vladimir's Seminary, 1985), pp. 15-65.

tivities.[457] So far I have described Christological use of *ousia* and *homoousia* as ways of saying that Christ exercises and participates in divine activities, such as sharing love with his Father and bringing salvation as an equal. From this angle those who reject divine substance *(ousia)* as an additional thing but consider the three persons and their acts fully divine are basically trinitarian.

Chalcedon, I believe, employed *ousia* and *physis* not in specific, static, Greek senses but to refer, more loosely, to what any reality most basically was. This need not clash with today's more dynamic apprehension of existence, where *substance* can mean something like a characteristic way of acting. This notion seems broadly biblical, though not if substances are sheer processes operating by themselves. In biblical narrative, acts proceed from agents who are more than their sum—though agents are also shaped significantly by their actions and interactions. An agent, further, can only act in a way characteristic of many others if it possesses those capacities necessary for such action: to act in a human way, for instance, one must have a human body.

If we consider *nature* and *substance* as characteristic ways of acting in this sense, they can still, despite their limitations, play some role in Christology. Jesus' human and divine natures *(physeis)* can function as ways of saying that whatever is most basically involved in being human and divine, Jesus was, is and will be fully that. Christology can let Scripture fill in the content of each, not pressing for more than it can provide. And though these natures and their borders will remain a bit fuzzy, affirming them can still have import.

To affirm a real distinction between them, even if not precisely defined, means that human fulfillment involves remaining fully human. Fulfillment is not gradually sliding into deity, as intimated at times by Hoffman and often by spiritualities that appeal to searching people today.[458] True divinization is not becoming essentially God. What humans are and what God is can never be confused *(asynchytos)*, or transmuted into each other *(atreptos)*. But Christology adds that these distinct natures have actually been united in one person. This can mean something else significant for spiritually hungry people: we and God need not remain divided *(adiairetos)* or separated *(achoristos)*. That is, becoming fully human also involves

---

[457] *Physis* came from a verb for "to become" or "to grow," mainly referring to plants. Initially it meant something like budding, growth or development (Helmut Koester, "φύσις," in *Theological Dictionary of the New Testament*, ed. Gerhard Friedrich [Grand Rapids: Eerdmans, 1974], 9:252; for subsequent varied uses see pp. 253-77).

[458] Chalcedon meant that Jesus' full, distinct humanity came from Mary. Not surprisingly, Dutch Anabaptist denials of this, despite assurances that Jesus' full humanity was still affirmed, slid precisely in this direction. Chalcedon's term for Mary, *theotokos* (God-bearer, Mother of God) can overvalue her. But *theotokos* was meant in an Alexandrian sense: since Mary was Jesus' mother, and since Jesus was one divine *prosopon* and therefore God, Mary was God's mother—only "in respect of his humanity."

deep transformation by God's nature, or God's own energies.

I find it crucial to add, however, that this divine *physis* is not immanent in or always accessible to humans as Denck's Word apparently was. For it to become available, this unique person had to not only unite the natures but also overcome powerful forces blocking humans from God. Since only God could accomplish this, the *prosōpon* who united these *physeis* had to be divine. They will not, then, interact as closely in us as in him. In this way also Christology cautions that being fully human involves transformation by, but not becoming, God.

I am portraying Chalcedon, like classical Christology in general, as an effort not to jam Jesus into rigid, antiquated molds but to illumine his saving activity. In this sense even this Christology "from above" was shaped "from below." Still, its framers weren't mainly seeking to describe their experience but what its source was like. If we allow their concepts to stretch and not insist that these mean exactly what Greeks meant (assuming we could determine that!), it becomes evident that Chalcedon provided only a very broad framework for the mystery of Jesus. To ascribe natures to him that were without "confusion, transmutation, division or separation" set outer limits for what could be said. Within these, a wide variety of formulations and experiences are possible.

• *Jesus' humanity.* So far, my Christology is broadly Alexandrian. Finally, then, I must confront the major objection: Alexandrianism diminishes Jesus' humanity. First, by stressing the deity and unity of his person, it denies Jesus a fully human personal center. Second, even if I admit that our knowledge of divine and human natures is limited, don't the divine nature's attributes—say, power and knowledge—so utterly transcend their human counterparts that any being with the former could not possibly possess the latter?

The Anabaptists' beloved kenosis hymn provides a plausible response, which again shows how distinguishing *person* from *nature* can be useful. When Christ, who was "in the form of God . . . emptied himself" (Phil 2:6-7), he hardly surrendered his divine agency. For his emptying, obedience and dying were its supreme expressions. Christology can say, then, that he remained the same divine person.

Self-emptying, however, meant ceasing to act in some divine ways. Now if *nature* denotes characteristic ways of acting (along with capacities needed for it), theology can say that Christ no longer acted according to his divine nature in many respects—though not that he surrendered his deity (as do Kaufman and Abe).[459] For he continued to exercise love, righteousness, peace and other attributes of his divine nature. However, since Christ, by emptying himself, took on fully human ways of

---

[459]Cf. pp. 287-88 above.

operating, theology can say that he took on a fully human nature, which involved acting through fully human capacities.

But still, since his deepest personal center was not human, was Jesus really fully human? Christology cannot explain how all this happened. The incarnation's full mystery remains beyond our grasp. However, Christology can seek to show that in light of what we know, its models are plausible. I find kenosis, as just described, plausible—though not fully comprehensible—in light of the following considerations.

A human person or self is not a uniform, individual unit, as modernity assumed. A self develops by introjecting attitudes and behaviors impressed on it by many others. A child learns to play different roles in relating to parents and teachers and friends. Roles involve diverse activities, but form consistent, coherent behavior patterns. At various developmental stages these patterns coalesce to form provisional selves that remain largely intact through later stages. Throughout life, persons introject, reject, weave and reweave a variety of patterns.[460]

I do not mean that a human person is a sheer, postmodern plurality of behaviors. Coherence, agency, responsibility and love will emerge, I believe, only if, beginning from an incipient ego, a personal center (person, *hypostasis-prosōpon*) develops.[461] This person unfolds in response to God's call.[462] Its full reality, then, is eschatological (or future). Still, a person may sometimes apprehend this full or authentic self, though only partially, as an unformed horizon toward which one journeys.[463]

A human's personal core, then, can be distinguished from (1) a variety of roles and provisional selves, (2) its full, future self, and (3) human capacities; for someone can lose arms or legs, or hearing or vision, or much memory or mobility and still be the same person. (Nevertheless, these distinctions are intellectual. No human person exists apart from capacities, roles and subselves. None of these exist apart from persons. None of the foregoing are distinct, subsisting things. More

---

[460]Introjection of other selves or aspects of selves is stressed in object relations theory (Jay Greenberg and Stephen Mitchell, *Object Relations in Psychoanalytic Theory* [Cambridge, Mass.: Harvard, 1983]). For internal selves, see Richard Schwartz, *Internal Family Systems Therapy* (New York: Guilford, 1995), pp. 8-60. Similar notions appear in many psychologies: e.g., Freud's id, ego and superego; Jung's archetypes; Transactional Analysis's child, parent and adult (cf. p. 463 note 735 below).

[461]This is initially shaped (though not entirely determined) by a bundle of preferences, inclinations and aptitudes closely connected with a person's physical organism. Though each ego can develop in a variety of directions, this will occur within the framework of the foregoing, which form essential features of a person's individuality (Finger, *Self, Earth & Society*, pp. 285-86).

[462]Ibid., pp. 263-66; cf. pp. 500-501 below.

[463]On the true human self as future, or eschatological, see Jürgen Moltmann, *Theology of Hope* (New York: Harper & Row, 1967), pp. 91-92, 196-97, 285-88, 333-38. On awareness of this self as an unformed horizon, see Karl Rahner, *Theological Investigations*, vol. 5 (Baltimore: Helicon, 1966), pp. 199-211.

broadly, I maintain, as did the Cappadocian fathers in forming classical Christology, substances and natures [*ousiai* and *physeis*] only characterize—exist nowhere but in—actual beings.)[464]

The human person's identity then is continuous but continually developing and changing. Self-consciousness involves consciousness of roles and provisional selves. Some persons take on vastly different roles. A missionary, for instance, can become fluent in the language and adopt the lifestyle and many thought patterns of a very different culture. Some people can adapt to another culture fully enough to keep their former identity secret.

Since humans take on and relinquish roles requiring different—sometimes vastly different—actions and capacities, I find it plausible, though not fully comprehensible, that God's eternal Son remained who he was at the deepest level, yet operated in entirely human ways through human capacities. Further, human persons are not simple individual units, and self-awareness includes various roles and provisional selves. I also find it plausible then, though not fully comprehensible, that Jesus' self-consciousness was "that of a human male, a Jew, a self-educated 'rabbi' and prophet from Galilee" without wholly excluding another level.[465]

Jesus, indeed, might have apprehended his deepest personal center somewhat as we apprehend our full, future selves. As his self-consciousness developed in an entirely human way, perhaps he dimly apprehended but only gradually realized that he was God's beloved Son. Some such process, indeed, makes sense of episodes that resembled adoption, for in these Jesus recognized his sonship (esp. in his baptism, transfiguration and resurrection). The human growth and change that a Christology from below traces would include something like this.

All this makes it possible that Jesus' resurrection, the perfecting of his humanity, especially in Christus Victor, coincided with full self-awareness of his deity. If it did, being declared "Son of God with power" (Rom 1:4), receiving God's own name (Phil 2:9-11) and being made Lord and Christ (Acts 2:36) would reverse Jesus' horrified sense of forsakenness on the cross (Mk 15:33-37; cf. Mk 14:34-42). These declarations would announce his resumption of divine functions suspended at his self-emptying—not his becoming divine for the first time. Still, the divine-human manner in which Jesus began operating was new.[466] It is comprehensible how Marpeck could say, as he perhaps thought the New Testament some-

---

[464]Catherine Mowry Lacugna, *God for Us* (San Francisco: Harper, 1991), pp. 69-70. Consequently, neither does any divine substance exist in addition to the trinitarian persons, as Polish tritheists rightly maintained. Nor does any human nature exist without a person, as Menno rightly surmised.
[465]Kraus, *Jesus Christ Our Lord*, p. 70.
[466]This makes sense out of Jesus' appointment to certain functions, such as final judgment (Jn 17:21-23, 25-26; Acts 17:31; cf. Mt 25:34-46).

times did, that Jesus' deity (which for him was no static substance) increased at that point.

• *Summary.* I am considering questions about Jesus' person raised, from below, by his work, chiefly understood as Christus Victor. His saving work entails that as conqueror of death and the powers and bestower of divinization, Jesus is divine. He is divine mainly because he performs saving acts, which God alone can perform (esp. Is 43:11-13; 45:21-23; fulfilled in Phil 2:9-11). Jesus' work also entails that as bestower of christomorphic divinization or as the Adam who completed the path intended for all humans and who draws us, inwardly and outwardly, into his journey, Jesus is entirely and normatively human.

Given the importance of Jesus' path, Christology in Anabaptist perspective should not simply show that he was fully human but also what kind of human he was and what kind of path he trod. Jesus fulfilled his messianic calling not as a warrior but as the peaceful suffering Servant. Philippians 2:5-11 links this suffering with his obedience, self-giving and the contours of his path. Focusing on it I asked whether Christ's deity might flow not from his personal preexistence but, in broadly Antiochene fashion, from his earthly acts, climaxing with his resurrection—as some historic Polish and current Anabaptists maintain.

This text, I concluded, affirmed Christ's preexistence and thereby his self-giving servanthood as profoundly divine, not only human. It vividly expressed God's advent as Christ's radical involvement in human limitations, suffering and death—it portrayed Jesus as God's ever-coming, outpoured love amidst our deepest struggles, as Anabaptist and other marginalized Christians have known.[467] The Antiochene approach could not express this divine initiative well. Yet the Alexandrian alternative, which highlights it, has often underplayed its fully human terminus.

Nonetheless, by employing more complex, dynamic notions of *person, nature* and *essence,* I sketched a broadly Alexandrian Christology. Philippians 2 can help us perceive the divine initiative, or Christ's own divine person and nature, precisely in his self-emptying, or suspending all divine ways of acting that conflicted with fully human, servantlike behavior. As a result, though, the divine power impelling his ministry was not his but the Spirit's, through Jesus' fully human channel. This recalls the Spirit's major role in Jesus' work. Christ's deity also means that he draws us into the love he shares with his Father and Spirit. These themes, perceived from below, direct us further into Anabaptism's convictional framework, the Trinity.

3. The creeds. Classical Christology has provided lenses for viewing not only historic Anabaptism but current issues as well. Obviously, my perspective

---

[467]Esp. Simons, *Complete Works of Menno Simons,* pp. 306-7; Marpeck, *Writings of Pilgram Marpeck,* p. 434.

on the creeds had something to do with selecting it. Since I aim to make my method transparent, I will sketch this rather briefly.

Like their critics I examine the creeds' meaning in their historical context, though I find this meaning more flexible than most do. But whereas Weaver, Kraus, McClendon, Kaufman and Friesen relegate the creeds largely to that era, I view them primarily as confessions continuing to function in the present. Anabaptists and others who scarcely use creeds seldom appreciate how widely they are employed or the Nicene Creed's liturgical and aesthetic qualities, so often set to music. If churches are not simply contemporary but historic communities, and if numerous communities claiming to be churches confess creeds, can a church-oriented theology today ignore the creeds or freeze them in antiquity?

To be sure, creeds can function to equate faith with verbal profession or to sanction the status quo, and even imperialism, since they omit Jesus' ethics. Yet this was hardly inevitable, even in the fourth to fifth centuries. For while the Nicene Creed (325 C.E.) was formulated in Constantine's reign, it emerged not from Constantinianism (Weaver) but over two prior centuries of reflection in countercultural churches.[468] This creed, further, was not fully received by churches until 381. Between 325 and 381 its supporters often opposed Constantine and his successors, who generally favored Arianism.[469] Moreover, the value of what creeds *do say* is not undone by what they *do not say* or how they can be *used*.[470]

With Yoder, I recommend that Anabaptists utilize the creeds as points of contact with many evangelicals and ecumenicals. This can challenge such bodies to take their radical implications seriously. For creedal confession of Jesus' full humanity entails that his life and teachings are normative. Further, I find the creeds compatible, at the least, with the Anabaptist theme of Christ's kenotic Lordship. God's radical self-emptying can be heard in Nicea's declaration that the "Light from Light, true God from true God; . . . For us and our salvation came down from heaven, was incarnate by the Holy Spirit and the Virgin Mary and became human. For our sake he was crucified under Pontius Pilate; he suffered death and was buried" (ecumenical version).

Into Nicea's broad outline, drawn from biblical narrative, Anabaptism's most distinctive contributions can appropriately be inserted: Jesus' peaceful, servantlike way, through which he conquered the powers and their opposing ways, and his followers' participation, already, in the kingdom which "shall have no end" and in

---

[468]Thomas Finger, "Christus Victor and the Creeds," *MQR* 72, no. 1 (1998); cf. p. 64 note 83 above; A. James Reimer, *Mennonites and Classical Theology* (Kitchener, Ont.: Pandora, 2001), pp. 269-70.

[469]George Williams, "Christology and Church-State Relations in the Fourth Century," *Church History* 20 (November 1951) and (December 1951).

[470]Thomas Finger, "The Way to Nicea: Some Reflections from a Mennonite Perspective," *Journal of Ecumenical Studies* 24, no. 2 (1987).

"the resurrection of the dead and the life of the world to come." From this perspective confession of Jesus' lordship and deity hardly supports imperialisms. Rather, amid today's pervasive injustice, war and poverty, often intensified by mammoth globalizing forces, it announces the opposite: that kenotic love and peace form not only the optimum human lifestyle but also, despite all contrary appearances, the most real and powerful divine forces in the cosmos. These not only sustain us in struggle and sorrow, they also raise the dead and usher in a whole new creation.

Such a christological confession means that the radical contrast between Jesus' way and that of the powers' is rooted in a yet wider contrast between Christ's divine person and his kenotic love, and the creaturely world distorted by the rebellious "world," which his kenosis wholeheartedly embraces. In this embrace, by taking our concrete humanity into his very self, healing divine energies began transforming all creation. This interweaving of Spirit and matter-energy, of inner and outer, flows from what we can still confess as the union of two natures in one person, properly understood.

Spiritual reality. As a contemporary theology delves into Anabaptism's convictional framework, such assertions about deity and Spirit raise further questions. Modern and postmodern thought, with their historicist bent, typically conceive spiritual reality as one aspect of a single, monistic continuum—the "transcendent 'within' of material reality."[471] Has what theology calls Spirit then always been intertwined with the material universe? Was God never independent of or ontologically distinct from matter-energy or bio-history (Kaufman)?

This issue first surfaced in Weaver's, Friesen's and Kraus's treatment of the powers as human constructions or the inner ethos or negative momentum thereof.[472] By inquiring from below into the salvation process originating in Jesus' work, I found it most plausible that these powers possess some sort of spiritual reality distinct from and transcending human structures. For though they often operate through these structures, Jesus confronted them on their level, and the church can continue this work only through the Holy Spirit.[473]

What has reflection on Christ's person added? It has highlighted that extraordinary transition from cosmic heights into the depths vividly expressed in Philippians 2:5-11. Construed somewhat literally, this height and depth could signify an extreme contrast within a monistic continuum. However, if divine, or Spiritual (upper case), reality has always been interconnected with or a dimension of the physical universe, the agent of this kenosis could not really be distinct from it. Nor could he have decisively chosen to embrace it as something truly different. This

---

[471]Wink, *Naming the Powers*, p. 118.
[472]See pp. 305-10, 351-53 above.
[473]See pp. 311-12, 317-18, 357-60 above.

agent, rather, would always have been interconnected with the cosmos and its human inhabitants, and would have been unavoidably affected by their actions. But the sense of this passage is quite otherwise. "Height" and "depth" strain, figuratively, to express a quite different contrast.

They point toward a self-giving and self-emptying unlike anything we know, because it was wholly voluntary—neither necessarily conditioned nor determined by anything else. It was entirely self-initiated. This kenosis entered a situation (and its sorrow and misery) by which its agent was not intrinsically or unavoidably conditioned.

To be sure, this agent was not wholly unrelated to, or distant from, this situation. The creatures involved had originated from him—but from his free spontaneity, out of overflowing love. Through the same love this agent became deeply involved in and affected by that situation, yet not from necessity but wholly from grace.

Everything in our cosmos, however, is interconnected by its very nature. Each thing is unavoidably conditioned, affected, shaped by other things. A wholly self-initiated, kenotic love, then, must arise from beyond this mutually conditioned realm altogether. This further reality is what I mean by *Spiritual* in the foremost sense. This Spiritual reality, however (like divine or human natures and essences), exists nowhere but in volitional, personal agents. *Spiritual* designates no thinglike quality, attachable to other things and persons. Spiritual agents, intrinsically, are unconnected with and unconditioned by material reality and evil, though they can and do interconnect themselves with it. Christ in his divine nature and person was and remains Spiritual.

Since all created beings are interrelated in some way, none are Spiritual in this foremost sense. Only the Creator is. All creaturely acts are mediated through created connections. In biblical narrative, however, some acts of some creatures are not wholly reducible to these connections. Though formed and conveyed through creaturely channels, these acts also connect in some more immediate way with a divine spiritual agent. These agents include humans and powers (like angels) who obey God. I find it helpful then to call them spiritual (lower case) in a secondary sense.

Note that spiritual indicates not an agent's creaturely capacities (e.g., whether bodily or not) but solely its potential for direct contact with God. In this way—but only this way—spiritual agents transcend created connections. I include disobedient powers here because they oppose the Holy Spirit and interfere with divine-human interaction fairly directly. These powers, to be sure, often operate through human and material structures, psychological and social. Yet they transcend matter's "within" and the "inner ethos" of human constructions.

As science keeps revising basic physical concepts, talk of spirit and matter, or matter-energy, waxes increasingly complex. I cannot explicate or support my usage further now. Perhaps better terms can be found. Yet current theology, I believe, needs some term like *Spirit* to underscore that God's saving acts arise from sheer grace, as typified in Anabaptist perspective by kenosis, and also *spirit*, to stress that discipleship involves divinization or direct interaction with (but not transformation into) Spiritual agency, and with other agents operating in that dimension.

THE TRINITY

This chapter has shown how Jesus' saving work was and is closely aligned with the Holy Spirit's, whose actions, like the Father's, express personal agency. This brings our exploration, from below, of convictions framing Anabaptism's apprehension of the new creation to the Trinity.

At this point, some readers may wonder whether this path is heading away from Anabaptist sensibility and mission concern. Perhaps they would agree that Jesus, portrayed as compassionate and servantlike, and opposing depersonalizing, power-hungry global forces, might have wide appeal today. Perhaps his lordship or deity would also be appealing if presented kenotically: as unmasking and critiquing all oppressive claims to ultimacy. But for many Anabaptist and other Christians, the Trinity is an abstract conundrum. If Anabaptists promote something so abstruse as this, won't they lose today's needy, experientially oriented multitudes? Won't Anabaptists appear to be endorsing a rather static, institutional Christianity and some of its oppressive features?

These questions remind us that theology is undertaken by the church to enhance its worship, fellowship and mission. Since this always occurs in a sociocultural context, theology will not achieve these aims unless it is intelligible and relevant in that context. Theology, then, should not merely follow the unfolding logic of a theme, however biblical.

To connect the Trinity with my context, I will interact with a movement that emphasizes lived experience and critiques static, oppressive traditions: feminist theology, represented by Elizabeth A. Johnson. (I will first glance briefly at Norman Kraus, to link this section with the previous one.) Johnson does not aim simply to be contemporary but critiques and retrieves features of her own Catholic tradition. To connect my retrieval with hers, I will approach historic Anabaptism in light of classical trinitarianism. While this exploratory framework may at first seem distant from Anabaptism, it will help us discover whether Anabaptists expressed anything similar, and how often and why they developed different views, like Polish tritheism and unitarianism.

Early Christians, who referred to Jesus and the Holy Spirit in terms appropriate to God, were accused of being tritheists. In response theologians insisted on divine unity and explained it by means of three main models. Modalism emerged first. It perceived the three biblical agents as ways, or modes, in which the one God appeared to and worked among humans (usually as Father in the Old Testament, Son in Jesus' career and Spirit since his resurrection). But while modalism took historical revelation seriously, it experienced difficulties in accounting for biblical distinctions between and interactions among the agents. From early on theology usually rejected modalism.

Modalism also aroused objections that if the three were simply manifestations of God, the true God had not actually been revealed. To consider this sort of issue, theologians eventually distinguished the economic Trinity, or Trinity as it operated in history, from the immanent Trinity, or Trinity in itself, with its eternal interrelations. Modalism could be critiqued by saying that its Trinity was merely economic (historical), not immanent, or characteristic of God's true being.

Further trinitarian reflection was closely linked to Christology. Formulae such as three persons (*hypostaseis, prosōpa*) but one essence (*ousia,* Lat. *substantia*), resembled Christology's one person (*hypostasis, prosōpon*) in two natures (*physeis,* sometimes *ousiai* or Lat. *substantiae*).

By the fourth century Eastern Christianity commonly attributed divine unity to God the Father, mainly by conceiving him as the source of the Son's and the Spirit's deity.[474] This solution risks subordinating the latter two, making them less than fully divine. But in any case, these two themselves are equal, for both derive directly from the Father: the Son by being begotten and the Spirit by proceeding from the Father, as in the Nicene Creed (381 C.E.).

Against modalism, the Eastern solution stresses distinctions among the persons (*hypostaseis*), though still by means of actions: only the Father begets and spirates, only the Son is begotten, only the Spirit proceeds. In the East, divine unity was conceived as operating within and among the persons as the continual flowing back and forth of love, energy and delight, or *perichorēsis*. Each *hypostasis* draws the others so close that they dwell in and through each other, yet without losing their distinctions. Moreover, the divine essence (*ousia*) exists only in each of the persons.[475] *Ousia* does not designate some ontological category or thing subsisting apart from each.[476] Further, whatever this *ousia,* or essence, is, humans will neither know it nor participate in it, now or in eternity. This is why divinization can only be participation in divine energies, not the divine essence (*ousia*),

[474]LaCugna, *God for Us,* pp. 53-79.
[475]As I affirm. See pp. 411-13, 416, 419-20 above.
[476]LaCugna, *God for Us,* pp. 69-70.

and can only be transformation by God, not into God.

Western theologians, in contrast, tended to locate divine unity in a divine essence, or substance, common to the persons. Heaven will involve direct contemplation, or a beatific vision, of this essence. This enables Westerners to stress the equality of the persons, for each shares fully in this substance. Moreover, each divine person participates in every divine action. This tends, however, to underplay the distinctness of each.[477]

Nevertheless, subordinationism crept into the West another way. Whereas the Spirit, according to Nicea (381 C.E.), "proceeds from the Father," Western churches added, in the sixth century: "and the Son *[filioque]*." Yet if the Spirit issues not directly from the Father but from both Father and Son, the Spirit would seem subordinate to both. Further, many Western theologies conceive the Father perpetually begetting the Son out of overflowing love and the Son—as expression, image and reflection of that love—returning it and receiving and returning it again eternally. I find this vision, which Marpeck appropriated, biblical.[478] By itself, however, it tends to place Son and Father on the same level, but only includes the Spirit simply as this love, or its flow, not really a distinctive agent.

As Westerners and Easterners refined their concepts, they focused increasingly on the immanent and less on the economic Trinity, or God's historical activity. They all assumed, however, that it was the immanent Trinity who acted economically. These were not two Trinities, but one, viewed from different angles.

Historic Anabaptist Perspectives

Switzerland. The Schleitheim Confession, written to forge unity (*vereinigung*) among Anabaptists, found this unity being created by the divine persons. It wished readers the Father's peace through the "unification" (*vereinigung*) of Jesus' blood and the gifts of the Spirit sent by the Father.[479] *Vereinigung* appeared at the top of the cover letter, and *vereinigt*, meaning "we have been united," introduced six of the seven articles. Its authors sensed "the unity of the Father and of our common Christ" present in "their Spirit."[480] Schleitheim's main author, Michael Sattler, elsewhere referred to the Father, Son and "their Spirit," perhaps reflecting the Western filioque. Christ was also *eingewesen*, meaning *homoousios*, Nicea's term for "of the same substance."[481] Sattler called

---

[477]Ibid., pp. 81-109.
[478]See esp. Marpeck, *Writings of Pilgram Marpeck*, p. 391.
[479]See p. 333 note 7.
[480]Sattler, *Legacy of Michael Sattler*, pp. 34-35.
[481]Ibid., pp. 56, 63, cf. n. 41.

Christ "the Prince," or source of the Spirit but also the Father the one who teaches through the Spirit.[482]

Sattler frequently mentioned the divine persons' combined work in past and present salvation: Christ freed us and fitted us to serve God and the Spirit, whom he has given us; God gives the Spirit that we might walk in Christ's way; the Father has kindled "knowledge of him and the light of the Spirit."[483] Denny Weaver shows that other Swiss Anabaptists also referred to Father, Son and Spirit in terms of their actions and found these harmonious. However, they mentioned the Spirit least often. Grebel, Blaurock and the Zollikon believers perhaps foregrounded the Father; Mantz, possibly the Son.[484]

The favorite Anabaptist Scripture overall was perhaps Matthew 28:19-20, for it apparently placed preaching and repentance before baptism. Many Anabaptists found it hardly incidental that this baptism was in the triune name. Some, like Balthasar Hubmaier, also pointed out that the one explicit mention of threefold baptism—of Spirit, water, blood (I Jn 5:8)—followed specific reference to the Trinity (I Jn 5:7).[485]

For Hubmaier the three "powerful and unfathomable" names underlined the weighty importance of believers' baptism. Nowhere else in the Bible were "such high words put together in such an explicit and clear way."[486] Hubmaier also acknowledged baptism in Jesus' name alone, for this too was in Scripture (esp. Acts). Yet the latter was valid, theologically, because "the name of the Father and Son and Holy Spirit . . . is one power."[487] Both the three names and the one name invoked the same power.[488] This invocation was no mere formality. Hubmaier insisted that baptizands could promise to live as Christians only in the Father, Son and Spirit's power.[489] Baptism also included confession of faith in the Father, Son and Spirit, shaped by the Apostle's Creed's three articles.[490]

---

[482]Ibid., pp. 22-23.

[483]Ibid., pp. 38, 23, 56.

[484]J. Denny Weaver, "The Doctrines of God, Spirit and Word in Early Anabaptist Theology 1522-1530" (Ph.D. diss., Duke University, 1974), pp. 28-82.

[485]Hubmaier, *Balthasar Hubmaier*, pp. 226-27. Erasmus, however, had shown that the original text lacked verse 7.

[486]Ibid., p. 122, cf. pp. 263-64.

[487]Ibid., p. 201.

[488]Ibid., pp. 86, 113, 384.

[489]Ibid., pp. 86, 101, 121, 142, 146, 197, 201, 226-27, 349, 556-57. He did not insist, however, that baptism would be invalid without the three names (p. 142). He likely recognized that some Anabaptist baptisms were performed by untrained people.

[490]Ibid., pp. 117-18, 260, 349, 388, cf. p. 439. He cited the Nicene Creed as an authority for baptismal practice (p. 351). Hubmaier's baptisms required acquaintance with the Apostles' Creed (p. 387), by which he organized his own confession (pp. 235-40).

For all Anabaptists God's work in baptizands commenced before the water ceremony, as the Spirit cooperated closely with the Word.[491] For Hubmaier the risen Christ acted so directly through this Word that he often equated it with him. This initial baptism of the Spirit (Hubmaier sometimes added "and fire") made one alive and whole through "the fire of the divine Word through the Spirit of God."[492] Baptism of the Spirit was "inner illumination of our hearts . . . by the Holy Spirit through the living Word of God."[493]

More precisely, the Word began by drawing a person outwardly, while the Spirit convicted that person internally, making the Word "live, turn green, blossom, and bear fruit."[494] The "life-giving Word" granted forgiveness, while "the Spirit of God makes and effects this enlivening internally."[495] Word and Spirit interacted dynamically in bringing salvation—something only God could bring.

These dynamics continued beyond conversion. Hubmaier could say that the soul was awakened by the Father, made whole by the Son and enlightened by the Spirit.[496] While he sometimes ascribed overall agency to the Father, Hubmaier more often attributed personal renewal to the Word and many of its dynamisms to the Spirit.[497] In church life, however, the Spirit occupied the foreground, leaving the Son and Father more distant, in heaven, especially from the Lord's Supper and discipline.[498]

Hubmaier also differentiated the Son's and Father's work in ways implying not only economic but also immanent trinitarian distinctions. By sending the Son, the Father demonstrated his own love and mercy.[499] Yet the Son reconciled with the Father through his suffering, which won back for us the Spirit, who was withdrawn by the Father due to our sin.[500] Through the Spirit Christ preached to souls in hades.[501] The risen Christ now intercedes with the Father, who bestows on us the same favor that he has for his Son, for genuine love flows between them.[502] Hubmaier also expressed this Father-Son distinction as a contrast be-

---

[491]Cf. pp. 160-68 above.
[492]Hubmaier, *Balthasar Hubmaier,* p. 100.
[493]Ibid., p. 349.
[494]Ibid., pp. 362, 431, 145.
[495]Ibid., p. 100.
[496]Ibid., p. 439.
[497]Ibid., for Father see pp. 236, 337, 457; for Word see pp. 399-400, 403, 553; for Spirit see pp. 87, 147, 242, 400.
[498]Ibid., pp. 351, 414.
[499]Ibid., pp. 87, 147, 245.
[500]Ibid., pp. 84, 236.
[501]Ibid., pp. 236, 247.
[502]Ibid., p. 145; cf. pp. 116, 237, 348.

tween God's hidden will and revealed will, which was also the Word, or "God himself . . . which has become human."[503]

Nevertheless, Hubmaier cautioned that there were not "two wills in God" but "one single will." He spoke of two because "one must speak humanly about God."[504] Did this imply that this distinction was simply between modes? I have not found modalistic language elsewhere in this or any writing of Hubmaier's.[505] I know no other reason to assume that his trinitarian terms indicated anything but real distinctions. He formally affirmed the Trinity, including the filioque, and addressed the Father and Son personally.[506] Yet Hubmaier, a strong nominalist, evidenced no interest in elaborating the immanent Trinity further. He was chiefly interested in God's economic work, past and present, whose dynamics, for him as for Sattler, were triune.

South Germany-Austria. I. Earliest years.

• *Hans Hut.* Like many Anabaptist evangelists, Hans Hut often organized messages around the Apostles' Creed's three articles, which his mostly illiterate audiences knew by heart. Hut insisted that Scripture and God's work could be understood rightly only on a trinitarian pattern.[507] Salvation had to be experienced in three phases: (1) the Father's omnipotence (known through creatures), (2) the Son's justification (known through our detachment from creatures), and (3) the Holy Spirit's goodness (known through God's filling as we become detached). Hut called each a "part *[tail]* of the divine essence *[wesen]*."[508] Those who completed this *Gelassenheit* journey participated in the Trinity.[509]

These triadic references, then, were not merely pedagogical. Hut was referring to intrinsic, distinguishable phases of an apparently cosmic process, though the divine names he gave each sometimes varied. This process may have been largely immanent, for people who traversed it could know "the entire divine essence *[wesen]*

---

[503]Ibid., p. 473, cf. pp. 248, 469, 472-76. He also declared, though somewhat figuratively, that "God is captured, bound and overcome by his own Word" (p. 474).

[504]Ibid., p. 475, cf. p. 473.

[505]Although Hubmaier's remark on God's single will appeared in a scholarly work ("Freedom of the Will I," *Balthasar Hubmaier*, pp. 427-48; cf. "Freedom of the Will II," pp. 450-91), this was but one of many issues connected with his theme, and he probably was not treating it with exactitude. While his comment on the baptismal formula might sound modalistic ("the name of the Father and Son and Holy Spirit . . . is one power," p. 201), he was not considering this issue in any detail.

[506]Especially in his "Twelve Articles in Prayer Form" (*Balthasar Hubmaier*, pp. 235-37). To "my God, my Lord," Hubmaier once added "my Comforter" (p. 238, cf. p. 539). He concluded by beseeching the Father, through the Son, to send the Spirit (p. 240, cf. p. 244).

[507]Hut, "Ein christlich Unterrich," pp. 28-31.

[508]Ibid., p. 28.

[509]Ibid., p. 34.

in humans."[510] It is unclear whether each phase was activated by an agent, or hypostasis, in any classical sense. Since Hut's Jesus perhaps was an exemplar of the second phase,[511] Father and Spirit possibly were general names for the first and third.

In the broad sense of regarding God and God's work as triadic, Hut was strongly trinitarian. His two extant writings dealt mostly with the Son—his crucifixion and justification. But in Hut's apocalyptic preaching, the Spirit leaped into the foreground with multiple revelations. Early, grassroots South German-Austrian Anabaptism was highly pneumatic.

• *Hans Denck.* The genuinely metaphysical Anabaptist, Hans Denck, outlined the sort of cosmic trinitarianism that Hut presupposed. God was Being: wholly one, wholly good, but also impassible.[512] But since this God wanted to be known and praised, God birthed a Word that flowed forth through God's Spirit and created a cosmos.[513] The Word now ceaselessly departs from and returns to the One through the Spirit. This Word is goodness diffusing itself to multiply good, or love which "desires only to be beneficial and good to others."

Jesus, according to Denck, became "so completely united in love with" the Word that all God's work became his work and his suffering was reckoned as God's. As the Word returned to the One through the Spirit, this Spirit worked through every event in Jesus' life.[514] The Spirit now operates through us by returning to the Father what we had stolen, like thieves, by turning away from him.[515] Complete return, or "perfection in the Spirit," is the goal of Christian life.[516] Along this return path the Father draws, the Son leads and the Spirit strengthens people in the Father's will.[517]

But while Denck sometimes spoke triadically, he ascribed nearly all divine, saving functions to the inner Word, even some allotted to the Father in the New Testament. Nearly everything Denck said about the Spirit he could say of the Word. Denck did not contrast these two like Hut, with one (most often called Son) descending with us into crucifixion, the other (most often called Spirit) answering our cries for resurrection, then multiplying apocalyptic revelations. Denck usually attributed both crucifixion and resurrection to the Word.

---

[510]Ibid., p. 28.

[511]Cf. p. 335-36 above.

[512]Denck, *Spiritual Legacy of Hans Denck,* p. 223; for much of what follows, see also pp. 370-73 above.

[513]Ibid., pp. 221-23, 265-67.

[514]Ibid., p. 185.

[515]Ibid., p. 221.

[516]Ibid., p. 187.

[517]Ibid., p. 197.

Denck's Word operated agentially, much like an *hypostasis-prosōpon*. Yet it apparently was not Jesus' personal center. Neither did Denck really envision this Word, like Hubmaier's, as the risen, personal Lord approaching us from without, while a corresponding agency confirmed and applied what it spoke within. Denck's Word, of course, vividly manifested God's love by being embodied in Jesus. But Hubmaier's Word did so more relationally: as the beloved Son sent by a merciful, gracious Parent, who restored the Spirit to us and drew us back to that caring Parent, and into the love flowing between them.

For Denck, then, as for Hut, divine reality operated through a triadic process. Its phases, though, were neither as sharply contrasted as Hut's nor as personal as Hubmaier's. Denck's second phase, or Word, occupied the foreground. The third, or Spirit, which perhaps was Hut's dominant phase, seemed functionally subordinate. Further, since Denck's space-time cosmos was perhaps less real than the One, might both Word and Spirit, which arose with this cosmos, have been less fully divine? Denck's Son and Spirit, as in Eastern theology, evidently derived their deity from the Father. But here, perhaps, they were more clearly subordinate. And if the Spirit was further subordinate to the Son, Denck's Trinity was hierarchical.

• *Leonhard Schiemer.* Like Denck, Leonhard Schiemer regarded God as the supreme good. Those who truly apprehended this good would love God so dearly that "a pure joy would surge through" them, rendering even their bodies "wholly without pain or suffering, immortal and glorified."[518]

Like Hubmaier and Hut, Schiemer sometimes articulated his beliefs in creedal form.[519] He also expounded a three-phase mystical process like Hut's, though his three persons interacted somewhat in each phase (or grace). The first grace involved awareness of God the Father Almighty through creation but also through the light in everyone (Jn 1:1-5), which was the Word.[520]

The second grace was the Son's cross and was connected with the baptism of blood (though it corresponded roughly to baptism of the Spirit).[521] One could surrender to Christ and confess his name only when the Father sent the Spirit in that name.[522] The Father also bestowed the Spirit when someone took up the cross.[523] This process originated when Jesus, at his baptism, presented himself as obedient

---

[518]Schiemer, "Three Kinds of Grace," p. 92.

[519]Schiemer, "Apostle's Creed," pp. 30-40.

[520]Schiemer, "Three Kinds of Grace," pp. 85-86; "Apostle's Creed," p. 32.

[521]Schiemer, "Three Kinds of Grace," pp. 90-93, 95-96.

[522]Schiemer, "Apostle's Creed," pp. 219-21.

[523]Schiemer, "Three Kinds of Grace," pp. 88-91; "Apostle's Creed," p. 38.

to the Father unto death.[524] Jesus, though, was not only a historical exemplar but also God's eternal Son. Finally Schiemer, like Hut, aligned the Spirit—the secret, subtle, "effective power of the Almighty God"—more directly with the joyous, restorative third grace.[525]

Schiemer's brief, popular writings explicated no formal Trinity. He portrayed personal salvation, from below, more as an interactive process among three indispensable agents, like Hubmaier's, than among three phases, like Hut's or Denck's. These agents' functions overlapped a bit more than in other Anabaptists so far.

- *Hans Schlaffer.* While neither Hut nor Denck clearly affirmed Christ's deity in a Chalcedonian sense, Schiemer did and Hans Schlaffer expounded it in some detail. Similar contrasts appeared regarding the Trinity. Writing to the "weak brother" concerned about Christ's deity, Schlaffer argued (citing many biblical texts) that since the Father was God, and the Word and Spirit were one with him, they too were God. The three were inseparable, one God eternally.[526] Schlaffer offered an illustration: my speech is a unified phenomenon, although I am one thing, my word another and my breath a third.

For Schlaffer, like Hubmaier, the baptismal formula was no mere formality. Facing martyrdom, he cried for help in the name in which he was baptized: Father, Son and Holy Ghost, "one powerful, mighty God from eternity to eternity."[527] Also like Hubmaier, Schlaffer noticed that I John mentioned the baptisms of water, Spirit and especially blood (I Jn 5:8), along with the Trinity (I Jn 5:7, though the original text, Erasmus had shown, lacked v. 7).[528]

Schlaffer found the three agents interacting in salvation's impartation. This was often experienced in prayer. To pray through Christ, for instance, was to enter into that "depth" where the Son was in the Father and the Father in the Son, much as partaking of the Supper was incorporation into the Son in his oneness with the Father.[529] Christians also prayed to the Father to illumine them through Christ, the light, and to send the Spirit, through whom they could offer back prayer, as Christ taught, and call the Father "Abba!"[530] These three agents were distinct from those who prayed, not simply phases of an immanent process in which they participated.

Accenting the Son's agency slightly more, Schlaffer prayed that the Father's

---

[524]Schiemer, "Three Kinds of Grace," p. 95.
[525]Schiemer, "Ein epistl an die gemain," p. 56; "Three Kinds of Grace," pp. 93-95.
[526]Schlaffer, "Ein kurzer Unterrich," p. 108.
[527]Ibid., p. 125.
[528]Schlaffer, "Instructions on Beginning," p. 108; *Selections*, p. 208.
[529]Schlaffer, *Selections*, pp. 208, 204.
[530]Schlaffer, "Instructions on Beginning," pp. 99, 106.

light in Christ would illumine hearts and mark people with the Spirit, so that
through Christ they might know him as their true God and Father. Jesus had
baptized in the Spirit, bestowing power to become God's children. Since Christians, thereby, have Christ's Spirit, Christ "lives, suffers and dies" in them that
they might participate in his resurrection.[531] Schlaffer called this discipleship:
following Christ according to the Father's will in the name of the Spirit who did
all things through the disciple.[532] For if the triune dynamism were truly active
in prayer, Supper and baptism, it surely would energize people in following
Jesus' way.

Such passages (and there were many) mentioned the Father and/or Son as divinizing salvation's source and the Son and/or Spirit as its dynamism, though
which, in some texts, praise returned to the Father and/or Son. Sattler and Hubmaier often depicted divine activities overlapping, but usually ascribed each activity
to a distinct agent. As we move from Hut to Schiemer to Schlaffer, we increasingly
find some activities overlapping enough to be assigned to more than one agent.
These varying references, however, were not simply sloppy. They indicated how
closely these persons worked with each other and with humans in the same activities. On the whole, Schlaffer did distinguish these agents as salvation's ultimate
source (Father), most concrete dynamism (Spirit), and personal energy (Son) flowing from the first and impelling the second, yet also receiving from the second and
returning toward the first.

2. Following the Apostles' Creed in part of his major work, Peter Riedemann
expounded divine reality more fully than Schlaffer or Hubmaier.[533] God's foremost attribute was omnipotence—fittingly, since salvation was chiefly a conquest
of evil powers. God was distinct from the universe, having created it from nothing by so mighty an act that all powers should tremble.[534] Christ was divine because only divine power could conquer death and bring divinization. But more
precisely, the Spirit was "the power of God, doing, working and perfecting everything."[535]

Like Denck's and Schiemer's God, Riedemann's was "overflowing Goodness."[536] The Father had given "the fullness of all good things" to the Son and
poured them through him into us.[537] The Father, further, was truth, who spoke

---

[531]Schlaffer, *Selections,* p. 196.

[532]Schlaffer, "Ein kurzer Unterrich," p. 99.

[533]Riedemann, *Peter Riedemann's Hutterite Confession,* pp. 57-83.

[534]Ibid., pp. 59, 62.

[535]Ibid., p. 76.

[536]Ibid., p. 63.

[537]Ibid., pp. 80, 98, cf. pp. 74-75.

the divine Word that was rendered active and powerful through the Spirit, as is a human word through breath.[538]

The Father, moreover, had nothing for himself. He shared everything with the Son, as the Son shared all with the Father.[539] Christians, accordingly, were to own nothing but be one with each other and the Son as the Son was with the Father.[540] This was possible because the Holy Spirit, who had established the original community of goods, gathered the church and made it of one mind like Christ.[541] Community, in other words, was rooted in the Trinity. Further, since Father and Son were one, they could not rule over separate spheres—state and church—and sanction contrary behaviors in each.[542]

For Riedemann, the divine attributes of power, goodness, truth and unity were not abstract qualities. They were dynamisms that initiated and effected creation and salvation, and also flowed through each other.[543] Moreover, much as fire could not be separated from its light or heat—and if any were missing, so was fire itself— so there was no God without Father, Son and Spirit. Although there were three divine names, just as fire is one power, "one substance, one nature, one essence," the three names were "only one being."[544]

Riedemann drew the same conclusion from baptism. It was performed in the triune name because the Father required the Spirit to carry out what the Word showed. The three cooperated so closely in this activity that whoever lacked one lacked all, while whoever truly had one had them all, much as Hubmaier taught.[545] Although the Three were perpetually active, they always existed in and with each other.[546] Unlike our weak words that leave us, the Word spoken by the Father never

---

[538]Ibid., pp. 66, 75-76, cf. Schlaffer, "Ein kurzer Unterrich, p. 108.

[539]Riedemann, *Peter Riedemann's Hutterite Confession*, p. 80.

[540]Ibid., pp. 119, 80.

[541]Ibid., pp. 121, 77, 122-23.

[542]Ibid., pp. 204, 220. This seems inconsistent with his claims that government originated in the Father's wrath and had no place in Christ (pp. 221, 225, cf. pp. 294-95, esp. note 214, above.

[543]Other divine attributes included holiness, which underlay Hutterite efforts to separate from evil (ibid., p. 163). It set God off from the universe as its Creator *ex nihilo* (pp. 59, 62). Yet God was also omnipresent, filling creation with glory (pp. 59, 66, 115).

[544]Ibid., pp. 75-76, cf. p. 67. Though Riedemann employed technical terms more than most Anabaptists, he usually used them loosely, as in this passage, where he called fire "eine Substanz, Materie und Wesen . . . nur ein Wesen" (Peter Riedemann, *Rechenschaft unserer Religion, Lehr und Glaubens, von den Bruedern, so man Die Hutterischen nennt* [Wiltshire, England: Verlag der Hutterischen Brueder, 1938], p. 29). He affirmed the Western filioque (Riedemann, *Peter Riedemann's Hutterite Confession*, p. 75).

[545]Riedemann, *Peter Riedemann's Hutterite Confession*, pp. 197-98. Hutterite baptisms, like Hubmaier's, involved confession of faith in the Trinity, presumably recalling the creed's three articles in some way (p. 111).

[546]Ibid., pp. 75-76.

left him. The Word remained in him, while the breath emanating from the Speaker and Word remained in both.[547]

The Father then was no impersonal source. He offered himself in Christ that we might know him as a beloved parent, who, as Hubmaier also said, will always give us what is good. The Father wants to care for us as children, giving us everything through Christ and giving the Spirit as internal witness of this.[548] People come to Christ only when the Father draws them.[549] Riedemann could describe the Father as he often did the Son or Spirit: working in all our members, accomplishing everything in us.[550]

The Spirit, as for Hubmaier, was that breath or energy that enlivened the preached Word, bringing people to cling to, love and follow it.[551] The Spirit, Riedemann often affirmed, sealed the Word's work or God's work or our faith within us.[552] The Word, of course, operated in a similar, functionally divine manner. Precisely speaking, however, the Spirit was the agency by which truth was "expressed, confirmed, and put into action."[553] The Spirit was God's power, in the most active sense, who brought "comfort, delight, fruitfulness" and "confirms, strengthens and accomplishes all things."[554]

Historically, the Spirit had energized Jesus' work, anointing, raising and declaring him Son of God by resurrection.[555] Thereafter, people became Christ's children and called him Lord only through the Spirit.[556] While divinization involved becoming one plant and organism with Christ, the Spirit grafted and planted people into him.[557] Christ was the root; the Spirit, the sap rising from it, making the branches fruitful and of the same divine nature.[558] Riedemann was not thinking of the Spirit's work in individuals as often as Schlaffer and Hubmaier, but mainly as gathering and energizing the church corporately.[559]

Riedemann, as just noticed, occasionally ascribed the same divine act to different agents. The Father, for instance, sent the Word from heaven, "grafted us

---

[547]Ibid., pp. 66, 75, briefly affirming the filioque.

[548]Ibid., p. 196. This thus fulfills the original purpose of God, who is all good and who created us to dwell in us (p. 171).

[549]Ibid., pp. 174-75.

[550]Ibid., p. 62.

[551]Ibid., pp. 79, 100-101, 167, 76.

[552]Ibid., pp. 61, 97, 166, 183, 197.

[553]Ibid., p. 78.

[554]Ibid., p. 76.

[555]Ibid., pp. 61, 65, 69.

[556]Ibid., pp. 66-68.

[557]Ibid., p. 116.

[558]Ibid., p. 197.

[559]Ibid., pp. 76-77.

into his divine nature" and "sealed us with his Spirit."[560] However, the Spirit usually imparted divinization most directly. Shifts among divine agents indicated interweavings among their activities, as they did for Riedemann's South German-Austrian predecessors. Riedemann perceived divine unity in the historical (economic) saving work of the three but also in their remaining and working in and through each other eternally (immanently). Yet while he glimpsed a bit further than Hubmaier into this immanent Trinity, he did not assign unity, in a classical way, to either the Father (as in the East) or a common substance (as in the West). This dynamic interweaving of agents and their activities, however, sounds something like perichoresis.

3. Like his christological language, Pilgram Marpeck's trinitarian vocabulary was rich, variegated and sometimes confusing. Marpeck assumed that he wrote within classical trinitarian and christological frameworks.[561] But according to John Rempel, he was not developing strict ontological categories but painting various pictures of divine interaction with the world.[562] Marpeck treated the persons of the Trinity more interchangeably than even Riedemann or Schlaffer. This variety, along with his profundity, defy brief summarization.

• *Sacraments.* As in his Christology, Marpeck's trinitarian concerns were chiefly soteriological and often elicited by church ceremonies.[563] With all Anabaptists Marpeck considered water baptism an outer, public expression of an earlier, internal baptism, wrought by the Spirit along with the preached Word, which he more or less identified with the risen Lord, like many others.[564]

More clearly than others, however, Marpeck perceived the outer ceremony not mainly as a human response to the earlier, inner experience, but as a continuation of the interplay between outer and inner divine activities in those earlier events. God, who is Spirit, had reached human spirits through Jesus' physical humanity, which continued in the church.[565] God now worked simultaneously or cowitnessed both internally and through this materiality. Specifically, baptism (1) commemorated a history where the Father, out of tender love, committed himself to us by sending his Son, who was crucified as "a clear sign of this grace," and (2) assured us of this grace through the Spirit, poured

---

[560]Ibid., p. 61.

[561]Rempel, *Lord's Supper,* pp. 143, 149.

[562]Ibid., p. 160.

[563]Ibid., p. 94.

[564]For Marpeck's virtual equation of preached and divine Word, see *Writings of Pilgram Marpeck,* pp. 302, 460; Loserth, *Pilgram Marbecks Antwort,* pp. 297-98, 518, 522. Like other Anabaptists, he also distinguished the two (e.g., *Pilgram Marbecks Antwort,* pp. 295-96).

[565]See, e.g., Marpeck, *Writings of Pilgram Marpeck,* pp. 95, 103, 378, 455.

out through the Son, that we might give ourselves back to the Father through the Son.[566]

Baptism, that is, not only recalled that history, but reenacted its dynamics. The "Father, as Spirit" worked internally while Son worked externally through the ceremony, as an extension of his humanity. The underlying dynamic continued as baptizands, who were "born of the Spirit and nature of Christ" or being divinized, performed externally whatever "the Father, through the Spirit, performs in the inner man."[567]

These three agents interacted so harmoniously that one could not be without the other.[568] This, as for Hubmaier and Riedemann, provided the reason for performing baptism in the triune name.[569] In Marpeck's baptismal ceremonies, like theirs, baptizands confessed a triune faith, presumably on a creedal pattern.[570]

Marpeck, then, found baptism's inner-outer intertwining continuous with that of preached Word and inner conversion, and with that history which preaching and the sacraments re-presented. At salvation's heart, that is, God worked not as a single entity but as an interactivity among several agents. Divine reality, approached from below, intrinsically involved cowitness among personal forces, whose integration of matter and Spirit mirrored their interaction among themselves.

• *Divine initiative.* Marpeck traced all such salvific activity to a divine source, where he also found a reciprocity operating. He could equate Godself with love, eternally flowing back and forth between Father and Son.[571] Divine love was movingly manifested, as for Hubmaier and Riedemann, when the Father gave us his Son.[572] Marpeck even envisioned the Father subjecting himself to or becoming captive to love in this act.[573] Marpeck repeatedly defined eternal life as knowing the Father and Son, that is, experiencing their mutual indwelling in and among us (Jn 17:3).[574]

---

[566]Ibid., pp. 189-90.

[567]Ibid., p. 195.

[568]Ibid., p. 127.

[569]Ibid., pp. 171, 175-76, 184.

[570]Ibid., pp. 199, 226-27.

[571]Ibid., pp. 391, 530, cf. p. 517.

[572]Ibid., p. 274.

[573]Ibid., pp. 328, 319. Cf. God's "hidden will" in Hubmaier, checked by his "revealed" will, so that "God is captured, bound and overcome by his own Word" (*Balthasar Hubmaier*, p. 474). Divine omnipotence, moreover, was limited when God "sealed his might in the order of the Word" (Marpeck, *Writings of Pilgram Marpeck*, pp. 255-56). In such statements Marpeck sought, like Hubmaier, Schiemer and Denck, to counter claims that God predestines people to damnation (*Writings of Pilgram Marpeck*, pp. 341-42).

[574]Marpeck, *Writings of Pilgram Marpeck*, pp. 419-21, cf. pp. 126, 168, 312, 363, 466.

For Marpeck as for Riedemann, triunity provided the model and source of unity in the church.[575]

Marpeck also depicted the Spirit bringing this eternally flowing love down from the "highest height" to creatures, then drawing them up into the triunity.[576] Divine love drew people by awakening a longing for virtues of the Spirit,[577] who renewed them inwardly and united them corporately with the Father and Son.[578] But while this love flowing among the three persons divinized humans, it always remained in God.[579] Correspondingly, humans would never lose their creaturehood, never be wholly absorbed in God.[580]

Marpeck's moving devotional language, however, sometimes interchanged and apparently confused the persons' roles.[581] This, with his other conceptual irregularities, raises questions about his trinitarian terminology.

• *Trinitarian terminology.* Most of Marpeck's terminological puzzles can be resolved, I propose, by recognizing that he often expressed himself dynamically. One major way was by assigning multiple agents to divine acts, even more often than other South German-Austrians. To cite a few among countless examples: Jesus was "Son of God according to Spirit, Word and power;" he rose again "through the nature of God, Spirit, and Word." Christ was "Word, Spirit and life from eternity."[582]

In some such expressions, *Spirit* or *Word* may have denoted trinitarian persons. Yet Marpeck also used *Spirit* to mean divine reality in general and *Word* to mean the preached or written message. Read as distinctions among divine agents, such usages simply sound muddled. As ways of underscoring that the acts involved were divine, they seem more coherent.

I previously proposed that Marpeck, in two problematic usages bearing on the Trinity, was speaking in this flexible, agential way. First, he occasionally mentioned Jesus' deity increasing after his resurrection. This, I proposed, meant not that Jesus then became God or more fully God but that, functionally, he resumed the exercise of divine powers suspended during his earthly life. Marpeck, second, sometimes equated the Holy Spirit with Christ's deity. I interpreted this as a way of highlight-

---

[575]Ibid., pp. 74, 435, 420, 526.

[576]Ibid., pp. 391-92, 422-23, 530.

[577]Ibid., pp. 391-92, 410, 444, 523, 533-35. Marpeck, like most Anabaptists, also mentioned the Father drawing people to the Son and his fulness (pp. 76, 432, 454).

[578]Ibid., p. 522.

[579]Ibid., pp. 460, 518.

[580]Ibid., p. 531.

[581]As when he painted an "inner church" and its treasures (ibid., pp. 418-63, cf. note 312 above) or echoed the Song of Songs (esp. pp. 390-401, 516-48).

[582]Ibid., pp. 314, 379.

ing Christ's presence in the Lord's Supper, functionally, through the Spirit.[583] Marpeck likely perceived the Spirit flowing from and back to Christ, cowitnessing with him through the Supper's actions, elements and experiences.

• *Modalism?* Read functionally, Marpeck's shifting and overlapping ascriptions of divine agency nearly always appear purposeful, not simply confused. But could they be modalistic? Was Marpeck referring not to distinguishable agents but to how God was experienced by humans? For instance, when "the Father, as Spirit" worked internally and the Son externally in baptism,[584] were "Spirit" and "Son" simply names for different acts and experiences of one agent, the Father? Moreover, since Marpeck used other words for divine activity, such as love, might God have included additional modes?

A modalistic interpretation seems unsuitable mainly because salvation, for Marpeck, meant being addressed and indwelt by genuinely personal agents and thereby being drawn, individually and corporately, into a very real communion among them. This communion reflected the one Marpeck found operating in salvation's historical origin, between Jesus and the Spirit. Such kinds of communion were possible only among distinct agents, not modes. For Marpeck, this interaction was not only economic (historical) but also immanent (eternal).

Further, while Marpeck portrayed divine agency in multiple ways, no other names appeared nearly so often as the traditional three. Nor did any other function as a distinct salvific source. Love, for instance, was the very interaction among the Three: that giving and receiving, flowing back and forth among truly different, cowitnessing Sources. Marpeck meant that humans experience divine love through this triune interaction—hardly as a fourth mode. Neither did love, or any other name, designate a divine substance or essence uniting the Three. Marpeck rarely mentioned God's "essence" *(wesen)*. His fluid agential language precluded consistent expression of divine unity in usual Western or Eastern ways.[585]

---

[583]Marpeck also distinguished the risen Christ from the Spirit (cf. Rempel, *Lord's Supper*, pp. 156-57). Christ promised to send the Spirit, who would differ from the sender (Loserth, *Pilgram Marbecks Antwort*, p. 502, cf. p. 500). Moreover, Jesus' divine and human natures were united in heaven (ibid., p. 485), and both the risen Son and the Spirit existed, distinctly, in the Trinity (p. 534). At least once, Marpeck interpreted "the Lord is the Spirit" to mean that Christ was present in the Supper in his divine nature, for his human nature was not omnipresent (p. 486; 2 Cor 3:17). He concluded that this one Jesus, with his two natures, was present "through his divine power as Holy Spirit, and nevertheless with his body, flesh and blood, he remains wholly undivided in heaven" (p. 515). Recall also that Marpeck often used *Spirit* as a general term for God, and could call Christ "Spirit" adjectivally, to indicate his deity (e.g., Marpeck, *Writings of Pilgram Marpeck*, pp. 314, 332, 379).

[584]Marpeck, *Writings of Pilgram Marpeck*, p. 95.

[585]On *wesen*, see, e.g., Loserth, *Pilgram Marbecks Antwort*, pp. 515, 551. Marpeck once mentioned Word

The variety of Marpeck's interactive patterns points to a dynamic apprehension of the divine. It intimates that each agent executed fully divine functions.[586] Marpeck's persons apparently were united—God was One—chiefly through the love and energy that circulated among them and then flowed forth, incorporating creatures into communion with them and each other.[587] Marpeck's apprehension sounds something like perichoresis, where the persons dwell and work in and through each other, circulating and interchanging divine energies among them.

Perichoresis and divine energies are central notions in Eastern Orthodox trinitarianism. Interestingly, Westerners often critique divine energies for multiplying divine agencies.[588] It may not be coincidental then that Marpeck often appeared to posit multiple divine agents. The Orthodox, however, never thought of more or less than three divine persons. I doubt that Marpeck did either.

Marpeck used multiple agency language even more frequently than other South German-Austrians. His intuition of something like perichoresis seems similar to Riedemann's apprehension of God and perhaps Schlaffer's. Like all Anabaptists so far, Marpeck scarcely mentioned terms like *substance* or *essence* in any technical way. Still, in most of Marpeck's many hundred references, and most remarks by all others save Denck and Hut, three agents operated within a broad but traditional framework. The Father emerged as salvation's ultimate source, the Spirit as its most

---

and Spirit coming from the Father's "nature and essence," as in Eastern Orthodoxy (ibid., p. 542). He also depicted Word and Spirit proceeding from the risen Christ as they did from the Father before the incarnation—possibly locating the filioque in the economic Trinity, beginning with Jesus' resurrection (p. 515). Yet Marpeck occasionally used phrases like "the Spirit of God and Christ" (Marpeck, *Writings of Pilgram Marpeck*, p. 224) perhaps echoing the filioque (e.g., ibid., pp. 212; *Pilgram Marbecks Antwort*, pp. 135, 137, 554.)

Other remarks fit neither pattern: e.g., Christ is "the Spirit of the Father, one God and one essence" (Marpeck, *Writings of Pilgram Marpeck*, p. 467), and "Word, Spirit and Life from eternity," the "same as the Father in essence" (p. 379). More dynamically, Marpeck said that the Father and Son "certify" each other "in" each other as "one God, manner, nature and divine essence," and that the Father further "certified God" in Jesus "through the power of His divine essence" by miracles and other means (p. 314).

[586]One of Marpeck's clearest Spirit-Son differentiations highlighted the Spirit's kenosis. God's Spirit "does not strive to rule, but . . . divests Himself and divests everything at the feet of Christ. He does not consider all things as things to be grasped" but "humbles himself for servanthood" (*Writings of Pilgram Marpeck*, p. 146, cf. Phil 2:5-11). Since the Spirit's role was so similar to the Son's, it is hard to regard the Spirit as really subordinate here or in Marpeck's frequent trinitarian formulations that assigned agency to the Spirit. Marpeck, in fact, occasionally called the Son the Godhead's "third person" (e.g., Loserth, *Pilgram Marbecks Antwort*, pp. 76, 131, 137). Williams concludes that his triadology (like his Christology) was somewhat heterodox (*Radical Reformation*, pp. 684-85, cf. note 282 of this chapter). This places too much weight on one formulation.

[587]Cf. Rempel, *Lord's Supper*, p. 134.

[588]LaCugna, *God for Us*, pp. 186-92.

concrete dynamism, with the Son sharing features of both.

The Netherlands. 1. Evidently Melchior Hoffman regarded the triune agents as modes. His Jesus, though God's "Mouth" and quasi-divine from conception, perhaps became fully divine only through resurrection. Considered economically, however, the three agents interacted constantly in the salvation process. Jesus became fully absorbed in the Father's will, as we should be in Jesus' will. He was empowered and guided by the Spirit, as we should be.[589] Baptism in the three names (Father, Son and Holy Spirit) meant submitting to transformation through their interworking.[590] As for other Anabaptists, Word and Spirit interacted dynamically in this, although Melchior's apocalyptic intensity, like Hut's, lent greater weight to the latter and its revelations. But beyond the three actors, apparently, lurked the one God, who was supremely good, who granted freedom, yet was a fearful Judge.[591] This shows that modalism is a possible outcome of approaching God economically, or from below.

2. The only Anabaptist treatise outside Poland on the Trinity was authored by Menno Simons.[592] This doctrine threatened to divide Dutch Anabaptists in 1546-1547, when Adam Pastor denied the Trinity along with Christ's preexistence.[593] While Menno resisted extensive speculation on the Trinity, he considered it crucial for sound faith.[594] With Dirk, he excommunicated Adam.

As in Christology, Menno shied away from traditional terminology. He preferred three "names, activities and powers" over persons, and oneness in "deity, will, power and works" over substance.[595] The three powers could no more be separated than could the sun from its brightness and warmth, as Riedemann also said. To adduce the Son's and Spirit's deity, Menno began from their works. At least ten of the Son's activities and titles, he argued, could only characterize someone divine.[596] Similarly, Menno cited numerous works performed by the Spirit in

---

[589]Hoffman, "Ordinance of God," p. 190.

[590]Thereafter baptizands lived "solely in the Spirit, and the mind, and the will and from the wisdom of God, and the eternal Word of life" (ibid., p. 187). The Savior will be in the bride "with his Word, Spirit, mind, will, and well being," and they will be "one temple . . . and true city of the entire divine, almighty sovereignty of God and of his eternal Word and high Holy Spirit and mind" (p. 197). Though this process was clearly interactive, divine agency sometimes bore more than three names, as with other Anabaptists.

[591]See ibid., p. 198; Deppermann, *Melchior Hoffman*, p. 222.

[592]Simons, *Complete Works*, pp. 497-98.

[593]Williams, *Radical Reformation*, pp. 739-42.

[594]Simons, *Complete Works*, pp. 497-98.

[595]Ibid., p. 496. On rare occasions he said that the Son and the Father were of the same "substance" (pp. 862, 873, 907).

[596]Ibid., pp. 491-95. E.g., "Can anyone forgive sins and grant everlasting life except the only and eter-

biblical history and present experience that could only be God's.[597] However, he characterized the Father by more traditional attributes: source of all good, beyond change and suffering, and yet "mighty, holy, terrible, majestic, wonderful, and a consuming fire."[598]

Although Menno explicitly affirmed the deity of each power, he strained to avoid tritheism.[599] Perhaps partly for this reason he may have derived their unity, like Eastern Orthodoxy, from "the incomprehensible Father" from whom everything derives.[600] As in Orthodoxy, the Spirit proceeded from the Father, though through the Son.[601] Nevertheless, the Spirit "ever remains with God and in God, and is never separated from the being of the Father and the Son."[602] Further, while Menno acknowledged that Scripture never described the Son's eternal origin, he critiqued any intimation that the Son emerged after his Father or was overdifferentiated from him (e.g., by being eternally seated "next to" him).[603]

Like Riedemann, Menno stressed divine unity, often by envisioning Son and Spirit, despite their outgoings, remaining with and in the Father and each other. Yet they were not, as Hoffman perhaps thought, modes of something prior. For if Son and Spirit were not inherently, or ontologically, divine, God would be "without wisdom, power, life, light, truth."[604]

While Menno discussed the Trinity more explicitly than any Anabaptist save perhaps Riedemann, trinitarian phraseology appeared most often in depictions of salvation, clearly understood as christomorphic divinization. Baptism in the triune name meant that all three agents worked in regeneration.[605] Yet as with most Anabaptists, Menno's names for agents were sometimes multiple and interchangeable. Christ, for instance, very often appeared with his Word and "Spirit," not always equivalent to "Holy Spirit." It has been argued that while Menno formally affirmed the classical, immanent Trinity, his practical Trinity consisted in economic interaction among Christ's nature, Word and Spirit.[606]

---

[596]Ibid., pp. 491-95. E.g., "Can anyone forgive sins and grant everlasting life except the only and eternal God?" (p. 494). Menno critiqued Jan van Leyden, who called himself King David, by enumerating the true David's functions in ways that often presented him as divine (33-42).

[597]E.g., justifying, cleansing, sanctifying, reconciling, adorning with divine gifts (ibid., pp. 495-97).

[598]Ibid., pp. 811, 814, 821; 437, 771; 491.

[599]Ibid., pp. 802, 860.

[600]Ibid., p. 496, cf. p. 860.

[601]Ibid., pp. 496, 810.

[602]Ibid., p. 496, cf. p. 760.

[603]See ibid., pp. 862, 860, 865.

[604]Ibid., p. 497.

[605]Ibid., pp. 120-23, 265, 270-72, cf. p. 496.

[606]John Loeschen notes that Menno often used multiple terms, not unlike Marpeck, to indicate Jesus'

3. In contrast, Dirk Philips mentioned just the three persons, without interchanging them very often. He found the Trinity taught clearly in Matthew 28's baptismal command.[607] Dirk frequently described how the three agencies cooperated in baptism.[608] He reported, as did Hubmaier, Riedemann and Marpeck, that baptizands made explicit trinitarian confessions.[609]

Dirk also described the new birth, or divinization, as a trinitarian operation. Like other Anabaptists he often equated Jesus the Son with the Word or "imperishable seed of God the Father" received through the Spirit by faith. This created life in people's hearts that "thoroughly penetrates, purifies, and renews, and finally drives, leads, and transposes to the origin from which it has sprung, namely, eternal divine life itself."[610] In this process, that is, a person "is born anew out of God through faith in Jesus Christ in the Holy Spirit. The heavenly Father generates or bears the new creature, but the Word of the heavenly Father is the seed out of which the new creature is born and the Holy Spirit renews, sanctifies, and keeps the new creature in a divine nature. . . . Such a new birth . . . comes from the almighty and most high God through Jesus Christ in the Holy Spirit."[611]

This birth rendered people "participants in the divine nature" (2 Pet 1:4). Dirk portrayed this in triune terms too often to have meant acquisition of some "static" substance rather than involvement in an interpersonal dynamic.[612] This dynamic not only transformed individuals but also established and sustained the church.[613] Divine unity, as for Marpeck, was the source of church unity, including, as for

---

divine agency. In such contexts *Word* most often meant Scripture, not Jesus' deity. Loeschen calls such an economic Trinity as Menno's a real one, because he only knew "a 'one-level' universe," not two levels, including "a 'really real' above or under 'mere appearance' " (John Loeschen, *The Divine Community* [Kirksville, Mo.: 16th Century Journal Publishers, 1981], p. 60). I strongly disagree with the last assertion and attribute Menno's relative silence to his stated reluctance to speculate. I disagree with some of Loeschen's other main assertions: e.g., Menno had no " 'strong' doctrine of original sin as a corrupted ontological state" (p. 81); faith, for him, was simply "intellectual assent to the truth of the scripture" (p. 83).

[607]Philips, *Writings of Dirk Philips*, p. 62.

[608]Ibid., pp. 76, 78, 79, 303, 420.

[609]Ibid., pp. 87, 99, 110, 177-78.

[610]Ibid., p. 149.

[611]Ibid., p. 296.

[612]E.g., ibid., pp. 191, 221, 281-82, 285, 299, 310, 312, 345, 360, 384, 413, 417, 620. Like Schlaffer, Dirk described prayer's triune dynamics (pp. 131, 259, 641). The greatest joy was knowledge of the Father and Son imaged through the Spirit in our hearts (p. 66, cf. pp. 358, 361, 366). Eternal life would involve vision of the Trinity (pp. 626-27). Yet we would always remain creatures; we will never become God (pp. 145-46).

[613]Ibid., pp. 236, 337, 340-41, 380-81.

Riedemann, its economic sharing.[614] Dirk referred to this unity's source, or immanent Trinity, more than any Anabaptist so far.

Father and Son were "one undivided, incomprehensible, inexpressible, and living God and divinity in eternal unity, power and activity of the one and eternal
true Holy Spirit."[615] Perhaps recalling the dispute with Adam Pastor, Dirk underlined the necessity of confessing the Son's and Spirit's deity.[616] Like Eastern Orthodoxy and perhaps Menno, Dirk may have regarded the Father, the "fountain
of all good," as the source of the Son's and Spirit's being and thus of divine
unity.[617] Like Menno he spoke of the Spirit proceeding not from the Father and
Son (filioque), but from the Father through the Son.[618] Seldom, though more often than Menno and most other Anabaptists, Dirk employed technical terms like
nature, substance and person.[619] Father and Son, he once said, share not only "the
same divine nature" but, perhaps recalling Hoffman, even one will.[620] Nature,
however, indicated not only ontological status but also character, or ways of acting, as for most Anabaptists.

Like Menno, Riedemann and Marpeck, Dirk sought to keep trinitarian affirmations from undercutting divine unity. He insisted, for instance, that although the
Son went forth from the Father, he was still one with him.[621] Though the Son was
born or begotten from the Father (before creation), this occurred "naturally," "as
beams from the sun and the reflection from fire."[622] The Son, therefore, was the unblemished mirror and image of divine goodness. Dirk's point though was not simply metaphysical but that, since Jesus was this mirror, to participate in God's goodness one must examine and follow his practice.[623]

Nonetheless, Dirk probably viewed the Trinity more often from above than other
Anabaptists. Among "the principle articles of our salvation" he placed "true knowledge

---

[614]Ibid., pp. 157, 408-9, 481, 518.

[615]Ibid., p. 160, cf. p. 363.

[616]Ibid., pp. 177, 256-60.

[617]Ibid., pp. 62-63, cf. pp. 361, 413, 500.

[618]Ibid., pp. 259, 362, 381, 496. Dirk once spoke of the Son proceeding from the Spirit (p. 63). Once
he called the Holy Spirit the "Spirit of both the Father and Son" (p. 65).

[619]Ibid., pp. 135, 136, 156, 140.

[620]Ibid., p. 157. But Dirk was not speaking technically. He also called the Son the Father's "essential,"
not spoken, Word (p. 135). He referred to the persons in terms of being (pp. 156, 258, 328, 362),
perhaps because he called new creation in Christ the beginning of true being, in contrast to Old
Testament shadows (pp. 251, 303-4, 351, 356, 378). Dirk, like Menno, also denoted the three
agents by terms like *name, power* and *office* (pp. 362, 453).

[621]Ibid., p. 156.

[622]Ibid., p. 157.

[623]Ibid., pp. 299, 353.

of God" before faith, love and hope.[624] The first thing to be confessed about Christ and the Spirit was their deity.[625] To considerable extent, however, Dirk, like Menno, regarded the Spirit and Christ as divine because they performed divine functions.[626]

Poland. All Anabaptists just investigated affirmed the Trinity, at least in the sense that Father, Son and Spirit were each direct agents of saving activities. However, Michael Servetus was executed for denying the Trinity. Evangelical Rationalists who strongly influenced Polish Anabaptism rightly deplored this political and ecclesiastical use of the doctrine. This colored their perception of it.

I. Michael Servetus. Word and Spirit, in Scripture, were tendencies or dispositions *(oikonomiai)* in God, according to Michael Servetus.[627] Servetus also called them hypostases, classical theology's word for subsistent divine persons, but in what he claimed was its biblical sense: character or appearance.[628]

Much as the Word emerged when God decided to create, the Spirit arose as the breath, or power, of what was uttered.[629] God created the cosmos through his Word and adorned or vivified it through his Spirit.[630] The Word was God's presence; the Spirit, God's power.[631] Servetus called both wholly divine persons—but again, in his sense: as outward appearances or expressions of God, as divine activities, not distinct beings.[632]

Further, just as the Word acquired a substantial presence through embodiment in the thoroughly human Jesus, so by becoming the Spirit of this Word made flesh—by proceeding from the (human) Son—God's Spirit acquired "a certain substantial semblance of the human spirit."[633] In this sense Servetus affirmed distinctions among divine persons.[634] He also called both fully divine since the Spirit was God's self acting within us, just as was Christ living in us.[635] Yet in classical terms their deity consisted in being *modes* of the Father's activity.

This Spirit, however, became Holy Spirit only when it dwelled in humans through Jesus.[636] In its operations elsewhere Servetus called it the Spirit of God.[637]

---

[624]Ibid., p. 256.
[625]Ibid., pp. 257-59.
[626]Ibid., pp. 65-66, 154-55, 159, 163.
[627]Servetus, *Two Treatises*, pp. 124, 131-34, 174-78.
[628]Ibid., pp. 98, 163-64.
[629]Ibid., pp. 98, 193.
[630]Ibid., pp. 102-3.
[631]Ibid., p. 221.
[632]Ibid., p. 102.
[633]Ibid., pp. 97, 219.
[634]Ibid., p. 105.
[635]Ibid., pp. 104, 220.
[636]Ibid., pp. 132, 169.
[637]Ibid., p. 96.

Yet in both cases Spirit was the energy that brought matter to life and kept it in motion—it was God's active presence in everything.[638] Though Servetus insisted that there was only one God, he could easily affirm Jesus' and the Spirit's deity since the inner essences of all things were divine.[639]

Though Servetus was not adoptionistic, as Polish Unitarians would be, he opened a major pathway in that direction: the notion that Word and Spirit were only expressions, activities or embodiments of the one God. Servetus further claimed that the traditional Trinity was unthinkable: we cannot conceive of three existing persons (*hypostaseis* in the classical sense) without really regarding them as three separate beings (*ousiai*), sharing a fourth being or substance in common.[640] Servetus argued that in Scripture oneness meant harmony among different beings, not their substantial union, and that *ousia* meant "power," not essence.[641] Father, Son and Spirit then should be thought of as sharing the same power.[642] However we evaluate these claims, we recall that all Anabaptists stressed divine interactivity and shied away from classical concepts, especially a common divine substance.

2. From tritheism to unitarianism. Polish Anabaptists explicitly rejected the Western location of divine unity in a common substance. They considered it a philosophical abstraction, posing as a fourth, superior divine being.[643] In their tritheist phase (1562-1565) most Poles sought to conceive the three agents as "one" God and even as having the same nature, but adverbially, as sharing a common work (*unum*) rather than nominally, as being the same entity (*unus*).[644] Tritheists affirmed that the Godhead exists in each of the three persons, but not in itself, or separately, as a substance.[645] They were concerned that distinc-

---

[638]Ibid., p. 94.

[639]Bainton, *Hunted Heretic,* pp. 131-33. Consequently, "Our spirit dwelling in us is God his very self. . . . There is in our spirit a certain powerful and hidden energy, a certain heavenly feeling, and a hidden divine something."

[640]Servetus, *Two Treatises,* pp. 50-57.

[641]Ibid., pp. 3, 36, 100.

[642]Ibid., p. 36.

[643]They often mentioned Joachim of Fiore (c. 1132-1203 C.E.), who complained that this essence did not beget like the Father, was not begotten like the Son and did not proceed like the Spirit— so was really a fourth God with superior status. Servetus made the same criticism (ibid., p. 161). The Fourth Lateran Council (1215 C.E.) condemned Joachim, whose eschatology influenced many Anabaptists (see chap. 10).

[644]Williams, *Radical Reformation,* pp. 1045-46.

[645]Much tritheist language sounded somewhat traditional. E.g., even if the three "are divided by number and form, they are one personality on earth and in heaven. But they are so strangely united in the one divinity, that neither one nor the other is belittled, but all are in one nature, and of one will

tions among the persons and their activities should not be blurred.

At the same time they tended to regard the Father as the sole true God. While these two inclinations seem inconsistent, they resembled Eastern Orthodoxy in several respects: divine reality existed nowhere but in the three persons, and the Father was the source of divine unity. Other Anabaptists, similarly, scarcely mentioned a divine substance but emphasized the agents' activities and considered their ontological status in light of these. Only some, however, hinted at the Father's priority.

Unlike the East, however, in Poland the Father's priority gradually diluted the other two persons' deity. The Holy Spirit came to be regarded as a power, not a person, in the ditheist phase (1566-1568). Still, in order to maintain that salvation originated from God alone, ditheists continued to regard the Son as consubstantial *(homoousios)* with the Father and eternally existent.

The Poles, however, sought to be rigorously biblical. During the ditheist phase they were increasingly persuaded that in Scripture the "Word" *(logos)* meant a disposition in God, not a person (Servetus), or perhaps only the verbal message of the human Jesus (Laelius Socinus). By 1570 unitarianism began to dominate, and God's Son became identified strictly with the man Jesus, who did not preexist his birth, though he was raised to deity (Faustus Socinus). If Poles still thought of divine threeness, this was markedly subordinationist. The Father was the sole eternal deity; the Son, a man on whom the Father bestowed a portion of his reality; and the Spirit, the influence that emanated from both.

Summary. Utilized as an investigative framework, classical trinitarianism, unlike historic Anabaptist expressions as they initially appeared, has helped us discover much about the latter. Hoffman and Servetus, and Poles influenced by him, show that theologies that approach the divine mystery from below can remain there. They can treat distinctions in experiences of God as modes, or finite expressions or embodiments, that could hardly characterize God's own self. All other historic Anabaptists surveyed, however, found God's self directly present in the diverse but nonetheless unified activities of those whom they called Father, Son and Holy Spirit. Many found this unity paradigmatically expressed in the all-important baptismal command (Mt 28:19-20).

All Anabaptists, except perhaps Hut and Denck, regarded these agents as personal. None really treated any agent as subordinate, with the exception of Polish ditheists and Unitarians and perhaps Denck. While echoes of the filioque can be

---

and form, and so strangely are these three united in one, that correctly are they called by one form" (Gregory Paul, quoted in Jarmola, *Origins and Development,* p. 66). For some Italian roots of tritheism, see Williams, *Radical Reformation,* pp. 950-53, 958-59, 975-77.

detected among Anabaptists, these were rare and very faint. This Western affirmation, which apparently subordinates the Spirit, evidently lingered on as unassimilated, not consciously appropriated, tradition.

Nearly all Anabaptists considered the persons known in their economic activities as equal. They assumed further that these acts flowed from some eternal (immanent) unity. Yet Anabaptists almost never discussed the immanent Trinity in classical or any other terms. Menno and Dirk hinted that divine unity might derive from the Father, as in Eastern Orthodoxy. Like Easterners, they also avoided the filioque clause (and emphasized an Alexandrian Christology and divinization). Dirk and several others mentioned substance or some equivalents sparingly. But we discerned no inclination to base divine unity on this, as in the West.

Seen in this light the so-called Polish tritheists expressed some major Anabaptist inclinations: to understand the persons' deity and unity in terms of their actions and to avoid positing any other source. But as I read it, the Polish trajectory arrived at unitarianism not mainly through biblical exegesis but by drawing out the implications of something largely, even if vaguely, assumed from the start: the Father as the only God. I also suggested that adoptionism was on the scene from the beginning (pp. 394-96 above). From this perspective the Spirit's decline (ditheism) and subsequently the Son's (unitarianism) were idiosyncratic departures from the divine mutuality underscored by tritheists and other Anabaptists, impelled at least partly by Italian rationalism's monistic inclinations and discomfort with paradox.

Classical trinitarianism, however, offers one more model, predominantly Eastern, for conceiving divine unity: perichoresis. Here divine substance (essence or nature) exists nowhere but in the persons themselves. They are united through their ceaseless giving and receiving of love, glory, energy, joy and praise among themselves.[646] Riedemann, Marpeck, Menno and Dirk glimpsed something like this when they insisted that despite the Son's and Spirit's outgoings and diverse activities all three persons remained and worked in and through the others. Something like this is consistent with the overlappings among divine activities and agents found in these four Anabaptists and others, and the multiplication of names for these, especially in Marpeck and Menno.

No plausible channels for receiving these notions from Orthodoxy are known. Perhaps Anabaptists knew some of them from Catholicism.[647] Primarily, it seems

---

[646]While the Orthodox derive this interaction ultimately from the Father, they point out that this origin makes perichoresis and divine reality personal, as substance notions cannot (Zizioulas, *Being as Communion*, pp. 40-44; LaCugna, *God for Us*, pp. 63-68, 243-50, 302-4).

[647]For similarities between medieval Catholic and Orthodox notions of Trinity and divinization, esp. Palamas and Aquinas, see A. N. Williams, *The Ground of Union* (New York: Oxford University Press,

they intuited them by staying close to Scripture, with its many depictions of and names for God and God's activities. Anabaptists likely intuited them, further, from their experience of God's action in and among themselves in multiple ways. To account for such diverse yet direct touches of God, Orthodoxy refers to divine energies. *Energies* is a fairly adequate general term for Anabaptism's more concrete biblical expressions. This notion, however, is critiqued for introducing too great plurality into God. Yet as we will soon see, it opens new avenues for speaking of God today.

Earlier, I suggested that God's kenotic embrace of humanity and materiality, traditionally called the union of Christ's two natures, was central to the convictional framework shaping historic Anabaptism's efforts to connect Spirit with matter-energy and inner with outer reality (see pp. 418-19 above). The framework's trinitarian features place that union within a yet broader horizon. They connect Christ's deity more explicitly with the Father's governance of the cosmos and his humanity with the Spirit's groaning in all creatures. We can now recognize the original creation's diversity and the new creation's reconciling impetus as expressions of the triune interaction. We can now perceive Christ's extraordinary, kenotic self-giving originating from the Trinity's mutual self-giving, and new creation communities formed and sustained by this divine community. Historic Anabaptists, of course, did not express all these notions directly. I propose, however, that these explicate many implicit convictions that energized their communal and missional emphases.

Contemporary Appropriations

With their strong desire to live concretely in the new creation and scant opportunities for theological study, historic Anabaptists usually focused on particular features of its coming (see chaps. 5-7). It is now clear, however, that Father, Son and Spirit played indispensable roles in that coming and that nearly all Anabaptists assumed that each was fully divine. Yet while they occasionally affirmed the Trinity and often cast evangelism, teaching, and baptismal profession in triune form, historic Anabaptists showed little interest in discussing it.

What might this imply today, when many people hardly know what Trinity means and many who do know find it abstruse and linked with formal, oppressive institutions? Should Anabaptist theologians avoid it and focus on urgent social and global issues and the fragmentation and personal isolation cresting in their wake?

My reading of historic Anabaptism suggests perhaps not. To be sure, Anabap-

---

1999). I point out Anabaptist-Orthodox similarities to suggest possibilities (virtually unexplored) for interaction today, not to assert that Orthodoxy directly influenced historic Anabaptists, though I find this plausible and intriguing.

tists nearly always avoided complex theological terminology. Nevertheless, they frequently referred to three divine agents' actions and interactions in biblical narrative and present experience. While they seldom classified the divine mystery directly under three headings, Anabaptists often expressed awareness of interweaving and overlapping activity among these agents and names. Could a trinitarianism developed from this perspective connect more closely with current experiences and concerns than traditional formulations would lead one to expect?

I will focus on two issues. First, the Anabaptist approach to God from below can remain below, as Hoffman, Servetus and Polish ditheists and unitarians testify. Later, as transcendence seemed to dissolve under modernity's critical gaze, it appeared increasingly unlikely that God-affirmations could reach beyond history. Today, of course, interest in spirituality is resurging. Yet its spokespersons often contrast *knowing* God sharply with *knowing about* God and therefore intellectual affirmations. Postmodern influences tend to reduce God talk to cultural or personal perceptions.

In this atmosphere, nonetheless, adoptionistic treatments of Jesus, which foreground his human traits and leave his God rather vague, can attract attention. So can modalistic accounts of God, which draw on various religious experiences and expressions but remain imprecise about their source. Today, a trinitarian theology from below could lead toward modalism, as it did with the aforementioned historic Anabaptists. Should contemporary Anabaptist theology then be modalistic? And if not, why not? To clarify this issue I will first turn to Norman Kraus.

In recent decades a second issue has received wide attention. Trinitarian language is largely masculine. Often, this has not only devalued women, but the Eastern priority of the Father and Western priority of Father-Son have often fostered hierarchy—not merely in doctrine but also church and society, as Servetus's execution gruesomely testified.

Yet Anabaptists very seldom espoused the Father's priority. The relations they depicted among the persons were congruent with the mutuality they desired in church and society, whether explicitly intended or not. Might an Anabaptist trinitarian theology then display commonalities with feminist criticisms of divine and social hierarchy? I will consult Elizabeth A. Johnson on these issues. Then I will develop my trinitarian theology, first asking where and whether the Trinity might be found in Scripture.

Current Anabaptist trinitarian reflection. Reflection on the Trinity is fairly prolific among contemporary Anabaptists. It generally faults classical efforts for conceiving God as thing-like substance(s). Kaufman, however, lauds perichoresis for treating the persons as "so involved with one another, so relationally interconnected in their being" that none can be "substances who have their being or can act" independently of the others.[648] Partly to avoid substantial under-tones, Kaufman calls them three intentions or motifs. In his Trinity the motifs are inseparably interconnected, not only with each other but also, especially through the third (the Spirit), with the "creative trajectory . . . of biohistorical forces."[649]

Friesen finds trinitarian patterns implicit in Scripture, but also critiques sub-stance and favors process concepts.[650] His treatment often echoes Kaufman's.[651] For Friesen trinitarian notions are creative constructions that draw heavily on hu-man experience, but cannot describe "the way things really are."[652] Much like Kauf-man, he deals almost entirely with the economic Trinity and perhaps depicts the persons as modes. Yet unlike Kaufman, Friesen's God transcends the universe and brought it "into being."[653] Nevertheless, God never intervenes in natural processes, as Murphy and Ellis also maintain.[654]

Weaver, so far as I know, does not discuss the Trinity apart from his critiques of the creeds. Yoder, in contrast, affirms this ecumenical symbol, but does not develop its transcendent meanings, just as he does not develop classical Christol-ogy's. Yoder rejects an inference often drawn from the Trinity: that its distinc-tions among the three persons legitimate different ethics. An ethic of the Father, for instance, has often been contrasted with the Son's pacifism and used to sanc-tion government violence. But, for Yoder, the Trinity really means that the one God "is most adequately and bindingly known in Jesus," whose ethics are nor-mative everywhere.[655]

For McClendon, *person*, classically modeled on substance, connotes something so individualistic that it "should be abandoned."[656] Nonetheless, Scripture's narra-tive accounts of divine agency lead to the economic Trinity. If this is indeed the true God, it must be the immanent Trinity as well.[657] This God must transcend the world process not only as Creator but also as Redeemer in order "to ensure that finally all shall be well."[658]

In protesting the reduction of theology to historicism and social ethics, Reimer

---

[648]Kaufman, *In Face of Mystery*, p. 412.

[649]Ibid., p. 420.

[650]Friesen, *Artists, Citizens, Philosophers*, pp. 90, 92.

[651]See ibid., pp. 90-94; Kaufman, *In Face of Mystery*, pp. 412-25.

[652]Friesen, *Artists, Citizens, Philosophers*, p. 94.

[653]Ibid., p. 100, cf. p. 107.

[654]Ibid., pp. 100-102.

[655]Yoder, *Politics of Jesus*, p. 101.

[656]McClendon, *Systematic Theology* 2: 320.

[657]Ibid., pp. 321-22.

[658]Ibid., p. 314.

often champions the classical Trinity.[659] The "inner trinitarian life of love (immanent Trinity) is the foundation of the economic Trinity."[660] Yet, without significant discussion Reimer designates the three agents by a term classical trinitarians found quite problematic: *modes*. He also underscores distinctions among the modes, most significantly describing the first as "beyond good and evil, not captive to moral and ethical systems."[661] This mode, unlike the second (Son) is "not a pacifist."[662] Contra Yoder, the first mode legitimates some uses of violence. Still, the second mode reveals that the "nonviolent way of the cross" will ultimately triumph in history and calls us to immerse ourselves in this "undercurrent."[663]

For many Anabaptist theologians today, trinitarian "structure" is no abstract issue but, as for Johnson, closely connected to social and political debates. Modalism and the related question, whether an immanent Trinity exists or can be known, are also important. I will first ask whether an approach from below must lead to modalism and a wholly economic Trinity, and second, whether and how any trinitarian structure arrived at might be relevant to contemporary concerns.

Modalism? Norman Kraus, like me, finds Scripture presenting the Son and Spirit's work as divine and the Spirit, like the Son, as "a fully personal divine center of activity."[664] Like Friesen, however, Kraus insists that language about Father, Son and Spirit expresses "our perception or experience of God's presence" and does not analyze "the ontological nature of God."[665] Does this mean that Son and Spirit are modes through which we experience God? Kraus critiques modalism for failing "to depict the richness of God's manifold personal character."[666] He defines *person* as "a being-in-relation with other persons."[667]

---

[659]See esp., Reimer, *Mennonites and Classical Theology*, pp. 247-71.

[660]Ibid., p. 487.

[661]Ibid., p. 495, cf. pp. 379, 487, 493.

[662]Ibid., pp. 486-92.

[663]Ibid., p. 492. The third mode (Spirit) calls the church to make "genuinely new judgments" that go beyond biblical texts "while remaining fundamentally true to them" (p. 371). Yoder, in contrast, critiqued appeals to the Spirit's distinctness to sanction "the whole body of decisions and precedents, arrangements and adaptations which have been made between Christ and culture throughout the history of Christendom" for they "have by and large led away from an ethic of the Son" (*Politics of Jesus*, p. 103). Reimer notes that historic Anabaptist trinitarianism had "something in common with the Eastern theological tradition," especially its notion of divinization (*Mennonites and Classical Theology*, p. 264, cf. 369, 398).

[664]Kraus, *God Our Savior*, pp. 136, 133.

[665]Ibid., p. 132.

[666]Ibid., p. 90; cf. *Jesus Christ Our Lord*, p. 97.

[667]Kraus, *God Our Savior*, p. 93.

Kraus is attempting a biblical approach that neither ascends to an immanent Trinity in one direction nor descends to modalism in the other. How then does he conceptualize the Son and Spirit's "fully personal" character as found in Scripture?

For Kraus, somewhat as for Servetus, God's Word is God's self-expression, apparently existing since creation, but not a subsistent person. Jesus embodied this Word, or self-revelation, and was united with God—not in a "substantial union" but "a union or unity of purpose, character, and will."[668] Continuing from below, Kraus adds that during Jesus' ministry, the Spirit was God's "immediate, abiding, identifying presence" in him.[669] Jesus' authority and work were identified with the Spirit's so that Jesus was also "the embodiment of the Spirit of God."[670] Then after Jesus' resurrection, his presence was expressed through and became "identified directly with" the Spirit's.[671]

So far as I can tell, Son and Spirit for Kraus are personal in Servetus's general sense. Word and Spirit initially were and remain particular aspects or specific functions of the one God.[672] Apparently, they were differentiated and personalized when Jesus embodied the Word, and the Spirit operated through him, similar to what people call a "human spirit" operates through them. Since the resurrection, however, "the Spirit's character and work coincide precisely" with the earthly Jesus'.[673] Despite Kraus's critique of modalism, he calls the activity and presence of each a "mode." For although the "identity" of the Son's and Spirit's presence is the same, "the mode of presence is different."[674] Kraus also calls their current relationship "dynamic equivalence" and "functional identity"[675] in character, work and power.[676]

By limiting descriptions of trinitarian relationships and persons to their economic functions, Kraus avoids talk of immanent relationships and persons. How

---

[668]Kraus, *Jesus Christ Our Lord*, p. 112; see pp. 399-402 above.

[669]Kraus, *God Our Savior*, p. 140.

[670]Ibid., p. 36.

[671]Ibid., p. 137.

[672]Ibid., pp. 132, 134.

[673]Ibid., p. 36.

[674]Ibid., p. 148.

[675]Ibid., pp. 137, 143.

[676]Ibid., pp. 137, 143, 147. This volume (less polemical than *Jesus Christ Our Lord*) affirms traditional language about the " 'substantial' or 'essential' unity of the Son and the Spirit" (p. 36). Yet I cannot see how Kraus can appropriate these, except perhaps in the sense Nicea rejected—one essence (*ousia*) equals one distinct being (*hypostasis*)—or as pointers toward the unity he espouses: not of substance but of work (pp. 91, 93, 136), or simply of character and power (p. 84) or will and purpose (p. 85). Since the Spirit now "proceeds from" Jesus as well as the Father, Kraus finds the filioque clause somewhat plausible (p. 36, cf. p. 132).

adequately has he described the Son and the Spirit biblically each as "a fully personal divine center of activity"?[677]

Feminist contributions. I. Gender language. Elizabeth A. Johnson also reflects on trinitarian relationships from below. She is less concerned about modalistic construals than classical trinitarianism's hierarchical cast. Although tradition affirmed the persons' equality, it portrayed divine reality flowing from the Father to the Son, with the Spirit receiving from one or both.[678]

Johnson notes, however, that the Bible presents various patterns of interrelationship. For instance, the Spirit not only proceeds from Father or Father and Son, but is also "the glorifying God from whom Father and Son receive their glory; the unifying God who gives them their union; the active subject from whom Father and Son receive the world as their home."[679] In Scripture, Johnson observes, "the three interweave each other in various patterns . . . such as giving over and receiving back, being obedient and being glorified, witnessing, filling, and actively glorifying."[680] This "fluidity of usage" belies the notion that certain names (such as Spirit) must always denote only one person.[681] I have shown that fluidity in names and patterns abounded among historic Anabaptists.

Johnson is a Catholic feminist, retrieving from tradition whatever she can. She finds the notion that unity must emerge from a single source rather than mutual reciprocity, pre-Christian and philosophical. She credits Nicea's *homoousios* for countering this.[682] Johnson finds it incongruous that the Spirit, especially in the West, is commonly portrayed as the love flowing between Father and Son, and yet the Spirit is said to receive that love passively from them. But love is originative and creative.[683] Love does not flow down from hierarchy but subverts it through its mutuality.[684]

Partly to counter all patriarchal God concepts, Johnson considers the Spirit first.[685] Commencing from below with the divine historical manifestations, she travels to their primordial source, retracing the path from Spirit to Son to Father by which faith arises.[686] It is as Spirit that Johnson finds God "freely pervading the world, quickening creation, and working toward the renewal of all creatures."[687]

---

[677]Ibid., p. 133.
[678]Elizabeth A. Johnson, *She Who Is* (New York: Crossroad, 1992), p. 197.
[679]Ibid., p. 195.
[680]Ibid.
[681]Ibid., pp. 211-12.
[682]Ibid., p. 194.
[683]Ibid., pp. 145, 196.
[684]Ibid., p. 143.
[685]Ibid., p. 149.
[686]Ibid., pp. 122-23.
[687]Ibid., p. 123.

Through the Spirit we experience "the world and ourselves as held by, open to, gifted by, mourning the absence of, or yearning for something ineffably more than immediately appears." This often arises "in contrast to the powers that crush."[688] Historic Anabaptists, who celebrated and eagerly anticipated the new creation's coming, felt much the same.

Johnson calls God "Sophia," the Greek word for Wisdom. Wisdom, portrayed as feminine in the Old Testament and Apocrypha, participated in Yahweh's creating work. Perhaps this image appears marginal, selected to fit a feminist agenda. Yet Wisdom was the chief biblical root of John's *Logos* (Word), which dominated patristic discussion.[689]

Johnson continues on the path from below from Spirit-Sophia to Jesus-Sophia. Sophia, she concludes, "was sent one way that she might be with human beings . . . another way that she herself might be a human being."[690] From Jesus-Sophia, Johnson moves lastly to Mother-Sophia, the unoriginate origin, whose "creative, maternal love is the generating matrix of the universe, matter, spirit, and embodied spirit alike."[691]

Johnson, however, does not associate divine unity or essence preeminently with Mother-Sophia, as Eastern theology does with the Father, nor with a substance common to all three agents, as in the West. Instead, "being in communion constitutes God's very essence. Divine nature exists as an incomprehensible mystery of relation."[692] This implies that ecclesiastical and social institutions should not be structured hierarchically but through mutual interaction among all participants, as feminists recommend.

Many people today, however, not only advocate such an interrelatedness in human affairs but believe that it characterizes all reality. They assume that whatever spirit might be, it is not really distinct from matter. Nor is whatever God might be ontologically distinct from the universe but is intertwined with it. The divine "being" that Johnson calls "by nature relational" clearly includes three agents.[693] Does it also include the cosmos, as Kaufman and Walter Wink maintain?

---

[688]Ibid., p. 125.

[689]Ibid., pp. 86-100; cf. Dunn, *Christology in the Making*, pp. 163-76, 196-206; Finger, *Christian Theology*, 2:402-5. Wisdom's cosmic and saving role, esp. in Proverbs, Wisdom and Ecclesiasticus, shaped New Testament thought. Friesen affirms *Sophia* as a divine name, citing Johnson (*She Who Is*, pp. 106-107). McClendon (*Systematic Theology* 2: 321) and Reimer (*Mennonites and Classical Theology*, p. 369) also appraise feminine God-language positively.

[690]Johnson, *She Who Is*, pp. 156-57.

[691]Ibid.,. p. 179.

[692]Ibid., p. 227.

[693]Ibid., p. 227.

Johnson wants to affirm, with Catholic tradition, that "God creates creatures not necessarily, but in an exuberance of divine freedom," so that God's "relationship to a world is not a must."[694] She adds that God, who is "utterly transcendent, not limited by any finite category, is capable of the most radical immanence."[695] I find this beautifully expressed as the Son's (or Jesus-Sophia's) kenosis, and it is intrinsic to truly divine love and salvation by grace (cf. Phil 2:5-11).[696]

On the other hand, Johnson identifies her view with panentheism: "The belief that the Being of God includes and penetrates the whole universe" even though this "Being is more than, and is not exhausted by, the universe."[697] Perhaps above all Johnson seeks to envision both "freedom and relation" as "essential to one another," not only in healthy human life but also in God's interaction with the cosmos.[698] It seems to me, though, that if God's relationship to the cosmos is essential, God's being must include the cosmos and is intrinsically intertwined with and limited by matter-energy.[699]

2. Modalism? In her approach from below, Johnson, like other feminist theologians, stresses the role of experience. The "experience of Spirit" with which her trinitarian reflection begins often coheres "with women's experience."[700] Johnson considers not only biblical materials but also women's experience at length.[701] Some qualities ascribed to God's Spirit, important though they are, arise less from the former than the latter. For instance, the Spirit moves through "Finding one's own voice" and "taking responsibility for our own life and its impact on others." The Spirit is also mediated whenever "structural changes serve the liberation of oppressed peoples; when law subverts sexism, racism, poverty, and militarism."[702]

Does this mean that Johnson's trinitarian terms denote modes of human aware-

---

[694]Ibid., p. 226.

[695]Ibid., p. 229.

[696]See pp. 418-21 above.

[697]Johnson, *She Who Is*, p. 231.

[698]Ibid., p. 148.

[699]Johnson does call this relationship "asymmetrical. Insofar as the world is dependent on God in a way that God is not on the world" (ibid., p. 228). Yet she often presents this relatedness as constitutive of God's being: e.g., God imaged as Mother-Sophia "points to an intrinsic relatedness between God and the world . . . that belongs to the very essence of being a mother. A mother . . . is connected with another in a way that is constitutive of the self" (p. 185). We cannot mention any aspect of Sophia-Spirit "without factoring in the idea of relation in an essential way. Relationality is intrinsic to her very being as love, gift, and friend both to the world and within God" (p. 148).

[700]Ibid., p. 122

[701]Ibid., pp. 76-103, 61-75.

[702]Ibid., p. 126.

ness and activity, but not God's actual self? Does her approach from below remain below? Johnson certainly intends her concepts to refer to divine reality. Her Trinity is a "threefold movement, in eternal and hypostatic distinction;" a "threefold reality hidden in the fullness of [Sophia's] power, eternally uttering the distinct word of herself, and pouring forth her personal love."[703]

What is Johnson's rationale for this transexperiential reference? Basically, that what theology says about God is rooted in actual history, and her confidence that God "does not self-reveal in any guise other than the one which actually coheres with the essence of divine being."[704] Christians, that is, know God only through experience. Yet they believe that the way they meet God in Jesus and the Spirit corresponds to the way that God truly is, much as McClendon says.[705] In this way Johnson transcends modalism and passes through the economic to the immanent Trinity.

Theology then can speak of Godself truly. But Johnson hardly restricts this to a few traditional formulae. The deity's triune richness and dynamism can be conceptualized in many valid—though always partial—ways: for example, "the vitality of Wisdom's abyss, her personal word and her energy" or "Sophia's eternal communion in personal mystery, hidden, uttered, and bestowed." *Hypostases* and *persons* are also valid terms, for distinctions within God are genuine. Yet, much as Marpeck, Riedemann, Menno and Dirk insisted: "Each are in each, and all in each, and each in all, and all in all, and all are one."[706] Much as for historic Anabaptists, divine unity emerges not from hierarchy but from mutuality, relationship, interactivity, perichoresis.[707]

An Anabaptist response. For almost all historic Anabaptists, the Spirit, Son and Father were salvation's direct agents, and most regarded them as fully divine. Having examined historic Anabaptists through classical trinitarian lenses and my findings through current Anabaptist and feminist lenses, I am attempting to answer two questions: (1) Are personal distinctions immanent within Godself, or simply modes of our experience of God's economic activity? (2) Is trinitarian "structure" hierarchical or mutual? How might a theology in Anabaptist perspective address these?

Since the Trinity is little understood, theology could begin by showing how trinitarian notions make sense of some current issues. Johnson finds parallels in women's experience and liberationist concerns. Some such connections are crucial

---

[703]Ibid., p. 215.
[704]Ibid., p. 199, cf. p. 211.
[705]McClendon, *Systematic Theology* 2: 321-22.
[706]Johnson, *She Who Is,* p. 215.
[707]Ibid., pp. 220-21.

because theology seeks to express the kerygma in terms of concepts and issues familiar in its cultural context.[708] At times though some experiences and movements selected by Johnson seem to provide norms for discerning God's activity. Yet cultural experience is never neutral but is shaped by certain values and understandings. Theology must also test these. For this it needs ultimate norms from elsewhere. For me these come from Scripture.

I will first ask what biblical narrative contributes to questions about the immanent Trinity and trinitarian structure—or whether such refined issues are beyond its scope. In light of my findings I will then address these issues as thoroughly as I can.

1. The Trinity in Scripture? The Bible tells what God is like mainly by narrating God's acts. To determine whether Christ or the Holy Spirit are really presented as divine and how any such divinity might be connected with the Father's, one should first ask, Are they direct agents of divine acts (not merely instruments, such as the prophets)? Do they do what only God can do?

One preeminent divine act is salvation. For example, Yahweh proclaimed through Isaiah:

> There is no other god besides me,
> a righteous God and a Savior. . . .
> Turn to me and be saved,
> all the ends of the earth!
> For I am God, and there is no other. . . .
> To me every knee shall bow,
> and every tongue shall swear. (Is 45:21-23, cf. 43:11-13)

Consequently, if Scripture presents Christ and the Spirit as salvation's direct agents, it is presenting them as the one true God, however much this jars with commonsense God concepts, including the unitarian. I will explore this from two angles: (1) Jesus' history and (2) after his resurrection.

• *Jesus' history.* Many New Testament writers who portrayed Jesus as the Victor, conquering death and the devil and bringing eternal life, were attributing divine, saving acts to him.[709] His contest with the demonic centered on his identity as Son of God (Mt 4:1-11 // Lk 4:1-13; Mt 8:29 and parallels; Mk 3:11; Lk 4:41; Mt 27:40). Matthew, Mark and John structured their Gospels around the affirmation of Jesus as God's Son, meaning his deity.[710] Yet Jesus did not act alone.

---

[708]See pts. 3, 17 on pp. 96, 100-101.

[709]See Other features of Jesus' ministry seem appropriate to God alone: forgiving sin (Mk 2:5-12 and parallels), claiming authority superseding Moses (Mt 5:21-48), identifying the arrival of God's kingdom with his own arrival (cf. Finger, *Christian Theology*, 2:391-94).

[710]Mt 1:23 with 28:18-20; Mk 1:1 with 15:39; Jn 1:1-5 with 20:28.

Jesus' Father commissioned and affirmed him at his baptism, while the Spirit filled him and then impelled him into the wilderness and back. The Spirit's dynamic also pointed back to Jesus' unique birth (Mt 1:20; Lk 1:35). Through the Spirit Jesus healed, taught and exorcised, and claimed these as conclusive evidence that God's kingdom had arrived (Mt 12:22-32 and parallels, cf. Mt 11:2-6 and parallel). In the Synoptics, in fact, the Spirit more often appears as the divine agent, with Jesus as instrument, than vice versa. Jesus, a real human, may have become convinced that the kingdom was coming through "awareness of otherly power working through him. . . . In his action God acted. . . . The sufferer was relieved, the prisoner freed, the evil departed. This could only be the power of God."[711]

Jesus was also guided and strengthened through unique closeness with his Father,[712] with whom he often conversed and addressed by the unusually intimate "Abba!"[713] Jesus clearly understood his mission as carrying out his Father's will. Nevertheless, when Jesus reached Gethsemane, his Father's presence seemed to fade, and perhaps on the cross, even to vanish (Mk 15:34 // Mt 27:46).

Yet Paul (Rom 8:31-32; cf. Rom 5:8) and I John (I Jn 4:9-10) portrayed the cross as a momentous expression of the Father's love (as did Hubmaier, Riedemann and Marpeck). There is no reason to suppose that Father-Son unity weakened here, but there is much reason to suppose that they deeply shared death's grief: the Son's grief in actually dying, the Father's grief in losing a beloved.[714] Though the Spirit appears in the Gospels only briefly at this point (Mk 14:38 // Mt 26:41), Hebrews, which realistically portrays Jesus' struggle (Heb 2:17-18; 4:15; 5:7-9), tells us that Jesus offered himself through the Spirit to his Father (Heb 9:14). When Son and Father felt most separated in their agony, the Spirit still linked them.

According to Jürgen Moltmann, the cross above all must be understood in trinitarian terms. The simple word *God* cannot make important distinctions, such as

---

[711]Dunn, *Christology in the Making,* p. 47.

[712]This closeness is affirmed in a Synoptic saying with strong credentials for authenticity (Mt 11:27 // Lk 10:22) but dismissed by critics who presuppose that Jesus could have said no such thing (see Finger, *Self, Earth & Society,* pp. 241, 253; for the same general reason they reject Mt 12:29 // Mk 3:28-29; Lk 12:10 [see ibid., pp. 240, 253]). Jesus' constant dependence on and unity of purpose with his Father was portrayed broadly in the Synoptics and in greater detail in John (esp. Jn 5:19-47).

[713]*Abba* is Aramaic for something informal but trusting, like "Daddy!" Jesus' usage contrasted strongly with the Old Testament. Yahweh was not often addressed even as "Father," which could seem too familiar. An Aramaic term would hardly have appeared in Greek documents unless it were widely known and used. Many early Christians, prompted by the Spirit, also exclaimed "Abba!" (Gal 4:6). Jesus' Father also affirmed him explicitly at his transfiguration (Mt 17:1-8 and parallels).

[714]Jürgen Moltmann, *The Crucified God* (New York: Harper & Row, 1974), pp. 241-47. Precisely when "Father and Son are most deeply separated in forsakenness," they "at the same time are most inwardly one in their surrender" (p. 244).

between how God did and did not suffer. Precisely because it was a cosuffering where the Son's human suffering was joined by the Spirit with the Father's:

> All human history . . . is taken up into this "history of God." . . . There is no suffering which in this history of God is not God's suffering; no death which has not been God's death in the history upon Golgotha. There is no life, no fortune and no joy which have not been integrated by his history into the eternal joy of God.[715]

Finally, since God the Son truly died (as Alexandrian Christology meant to stress), he did not raise himself. The kerygma uniformly affirmed that he was raised.[716] This was precipitated by his Father,[717] or more precisely, the Father through the Spirit (Rom 1:4; 8:11; 1 Tim 3:16; 1 Pet 3:18-19).

When we review Jesus' history (far too briefly sketched), his saving activities appear intricately intertwined with those of his Father and Spirit, different though each one's was. At one point or another each exercised what we might call the dominant role. None was subordinate, an indirect agent of the process. They cooperated in a way that made salvation's advent a single work. These observations are relevant to issues of trinitarian "structure" and modes. They also entail that the three direct agents of this divine work, however different they are, must be divine.

• *Jesus after the resurrection.* After the resurrection Jesus was Lord in a way most Polish Unitarians even called divine. The early Aramaic hymn, where every tongue proclaimed him Lord, fulfilled God's promise: "To me every knee shall bow, / every tongue shall swear!" (Is 45:23; Phil 2:10-11). Another early Aramaic acclamation, Maranatha! ("our Lord, come!"), addressed him in worship (1 Cor 16:22; cf. Rev 22:20-21).[718] Since only God is worshiped, early Christian worship provides indications that Jesus was regarded as divine.[719]

He was also Savior and the anticipated transformer of the cosmos (Phil 3:20-21), and God in connection with this (Tit 2:13; cf. Tit 1:3-4) and in making humans "partakers of the divine nature" (2 Pet 1:1-4). Jesus was also Savior and the energizer of the gospel (2 Tim 1:10) and God our Savior through baptizing and justifying (Tit 3:4-7). The Johannine writings stress not only his preexistence and historic saving work but also his divinizing presence, in whom Christians dwell. Through the Son we dwell in the Father and Spirit and participate in their mutual

---

[715]Ibid., p. 246.

[716]See Acts 2:32; 3:15; 10:40; 13:33; Rom 8:34; 10:9; 1 Cor 15:4; 1 Thess 1:10.

[717]A very early New Testament title for God was "[the one] who raised Jesus from the dead" (Rom 4:24; 8:11; Gal 1:1; see Moltmann, *Crucified God*, pp. 187-96.

[718]See Cullmann, *Christology of the New Testament*, pp. 208-13.

[719]Hurtado, *One God, One Lord.*

communion.[720] It seems unnecessary to further indicate how Jesus was divine for early Christians, for (among other reasons) he not only brought salvation but also was bringing and would bring it.

After raising Jesus, being given by the Father to Jesus and then being poured out by him (Acts 2:33; cf. Jn 14:16; 15:26), the Spirit was often recognized as initiator of the saving process. The Holy Spirit was salvation's "guarantee" (*arraboñ*, 2 Cor 1:22; 5:5) and "firstfruits" (*aparchē*, Rom 8:23)—not as an extrinsic sign but an intrinsic energy. The Spirit was central in salvation's early stages (Rom 7:6; 1 Cor 12:13; Gal 3:2-5) and guided salvation toward its goal (Gal 5:5, 16-25; 2 Thess 2:13).

The Holy Spirit also bestowed "life" (*zōē*) directly: not biological longevity but the divine energy that raised Jesus from death's dominion (Rom 1:4; 8:10-11; 1 Tim 3:16; 1 Pet 3:18). One who directly imparts this personal vitality cannot be distinct from it.[721] This direct impartation was also expressed through the feminine metaphor of birth. For John, to be born of the Spirit (Jn 3:3-8) was to be born of God (Jn 1:13; 1 Jn 2:29; 3:9; 4:7; 5:1-4, 18; cf. 1 Jn 4:13). The Spirit's deity was also evident in the claim that the individual body (1 Cor 3:16-17; 6:17-20) was God's temple because the Holy Spirit indwelt it, as was the church body, at least by implication (Eph 2:21-22; cf. 1 Pet 2:5). For Hebrews, salvation made people partakers of Son and Spirit (Heb 2:14; 3:14; 6:4) while John clearly depicted it as participation in the triune dynamic.

The Spirit's salvific work in the church is especially evident in texts with a triune flavor: "There are varieties of gifts, but the same Spirit; . . . varieties of services, but the same Lord; . . . varieties of activities, but it is the same God who activates all of them in everyone" (1 Cor 12:4-5). "There is one body and one Spirit, . . . one Lord, one faith, one baptism, one God and Father of all, who is above all and through all and in all" (Eph 4:4-6). Such passages, most of which are liturgical, indicate that God's saving activity often exhibited a threefold dynamic (also 1 Pet 1:2 and of course the baptismal command, Mt 28:19).

In the early church then Spirit, Son and Father were experienced as salvation's direct agents, sometimes operating in a threefold, interwoven dynamic. This reveals much about relationships among them. It also entails that each one, and all together, are divine.

---

[720]See p. 411 notes 451-53 above.

[721]For identification of life with the Spirit, see Rom 8:6, 10-11; 2 Cor 3:6; 5:4-5; Gal 5:25; 6:8; 1 Pet 3:18; 4:6; Rev 22:17. First Cor 15:45 and 2 Cor 3:17 blur Spirit-Son distinctions, but this is because they ascribe divine reality to the Spirit (cf. Marpeck's problems with these at pp. 190-91, 378-79, 435-36 [esp. note 583]).

2. Intratrinitarian dynamics. Do New Testament texts describing the three agents' interactivity provide any clues about intradivine "structure" or divine unity? Biblical investigation reveals so many patterns, as Johnson notes, that apparently none can be called basic.[722]

If we ask how God operated before Jesus' coming, we obtain a broad impression of the Father working first through the Son (or Word *[dābār]* or Wisdom *[hokmâ]*) and then sending the Spirit. If we ask about Jesus' history, the Father apparently sent the Spirit first, and then they both sent the Son. Yet after the resurrection the Son sent the Spirit (Mk 1:8 and parallels; Jn 16:7; Acts 2:33), though the latter may have issued more originally from the Father (Jn 14:16, 26; 15:26; Acts 2:33; Gal 4:6). When we add that the Spirit was also called "God's Spirit" and "the Spirit of Christ" and "Christ's Spirit," the filioque dispute apparently escapes resolution on a strictly biblical basis.

The three patterns just mentioned are intersected by another pair. Moltmann points out that most trinitarian reflection has been protological: theologians usually locate divine activity in an originating source or cause (generally conceived as single) and then trace it forward through its effects. However, another direction of inquiry is at least as biblical: the eschatological. Theologians can ask how divine activity flows toward its final goal.[723]

When we think protologically, the Father appears as prior, the Son comes second and the Spirit third (even if theoretically proceeding from the first). That which plans, organizes or initiates can seem superior to whatever executes those plans in the cosmos. However, if we think eschatologically, we begin from the Spirit's present, dynamic activity, as Johnson does; this draws us toward the Son, who in turn draws us toward the Father. Here that which acts and serves can seem prior, and whatever channels its activity or provides its goal secondary.

Given the urgency with which Anabaptists experienced the new creation's realized and anticipated coming, we should not be surprised that they exhibited great interest in the Son's and Spirit's present activities and goals, and much less in how it all began. A contemporary theology in Anabaptist perspective, then, might highlight the eschatological direction more than most.[724] Yet since Scripture contains both patterns, theology needs to incorporate both.

These shifting interrelational patterns and equivalent protological and eschato-

---

[722]Johnson, *She Who Is*, pp. 194-97. Data for the following generalizations is in Finger, *Christian Theology*, 2:434-38, cf. 387-89. Johnson and I are indebted to Moltmann's sketch of such patterns (Jürgen Moltmann, *The Trinity and the Kingdom* [San Francisco: Harper & Row, 1981], pp. 61-96).

[723]Jürgen Moltmann, *The Future of Creation* (Philadelphia: Fortress, 1979), pp. 80-96.

[724]Cf. Finger, *Christian Theology*, 2:379-89.

logical orientations, so far as I can see, prevent theology, on biblical grounds, from definitively identifying any one pattern as *the* trinitarian structure, or one person or pattern as *the* source of divine unity.[725] Moreover, if substance *(ousia)* is used to indicate whatever the three have in common, it cannot be some "thing" which provides unity. For, as Eastern theology insists, deity exists nowhere but in the persons.

Divine unity, as Johnson claims, can only be understood in connection with the persons' mutual reciprocity—as something like perichoresis, an acting and dwelling in and through each other.[726] While this involves a circulation or interchange of distinctly divine energies, such as love (Marpeck) and praise, their sources also exist solely in the persons. Other names (e.g., love) can and should express divine energies and actions. They should not, however, be treated as persons, unless they clearly refer to the three biblical agents, as does Johnson's Sophia terminology.[727]

Esoteric as these reflections may seem, their significance for today's sociocultural context is great. Divine reciprocity, as Johnson stresses, implies that permanent hierarchical arrangements contravene God's intention. As Polish Anabaptists warned, trinitarian dogmas that imply hierarchy can function oppressively. Trinitarian mutuality, however, is mutuality-in-diversity. It does not suggest that everyone should function on exactly the same plane or be pushed into the same molds. Rather, it implies that political, social and ecclesiastical institutions should aim to incorporate wide diversities of individuals, social classes and ethnicities, opening full participation to all.

Since salvation is offered equally to both sexes, and since biblical Father-Son language symbolizes not gender but common purpose and intimacy, God is not more inherently masculine than feminine (or vice versa). Neither should gender be the sole basis for particular religious or social roles.[728]

Differences among the persons do not legitimate sharply contrasting functions

---

[725]Divine energy must often flow from Father through Son to Spirit. But this does not mean that it seldom flows in reverse. I am not denying that the Trinity has an immanent structure. It likely has multiple interacting structures. Neither am I denying that one structure could be basic or one person primary. On these matters, however, I maintain that precise knowledge surpasses theology's scope. (Thus theology cannot affirm the filioque as basic to trinitarian structure.)

[726]Though Scripture focuses on unity in divine work, I do not think trinitarian unity consists solely in this, as Polish tritheists and Kraus perhaps imply. True personal unity is not sheer activity but involves centers of activity. Existing, not simply acting, in and through each other is structure-like, though theology can say very little about it.

[727]Since the traditional names (Father, Son, Spirit) can acquire non- and antibiblical meanings today (e.g., patriarchal), alternate designations can express biblical meanings in theology and church practice. I prefer to show what Father-Son actually meant in biblical narrative (common purpose and intimacy, not gender) and retain them wherever feasible to keep theology and church practice close to Scripture (cf. Finger, *Christian Theology*, 2:485-90).

[728]See the fuller discussion in Finger, *Christian Theology*, 2:485-490.

among social institutions, as do Reimer's modes. Government's coercive role, for example, cannot be extrapolated from the Father's activities, and especially not from the cross. For while the Father handed the Son over to death, judgment and wrath were exercised directly by the powers. The Father's love remained constant and, joined with the Son's through the Spirit, passed with them through death. By raising Jesus, the Father, with the Spirit, judged the powers and installed the Son as eschatological Judge (Mt 25:31-33; Jn 5:27-29; Acts 17:31). Indeed, if Jesus is cosmic Lord, coercive government can only be ascribed indirectly to the temporary permission of the threefold God, whose direct work subdues the powers, and must be ascribed to the powers at least as directly as before.

I concur then with Johnson's vision of trinitarian unity or structure, and that it provides the source and model for human mutuality. I cannot agree, however, that the Trinity itself is ontologically interrelated with the cosmos. Johnson recognizes that to be truly creative and salvific, divine activity must be radically free and "transcendent, not limited by any finite category."[729] I argued earlier that Christ's self-giving could be the extraordinary act of love and grace that Scripture portrays only if it originated from a source unconditioned by the cosmos and its evil. I have now shown how his Father and Spirit participated intrinsically in that same salvific movement, and therefore initially, with the Son, in that source.

To be sure, through their creating and saving acts the divine agents have become deeply involved in the cosmos. But because this participation flows from a love conditioned only by itself, I do not see how theology can consistently affirm both its gratuity and that God's being includes the universe or that this relation is "essential" to God.[730] I find it better to insist that God's being or essence forever remains ontologically distinct from all creatures, and to speak of that which deeply transforms them as God's energies (though, of course, they also remain ontologically distinct). Admittedly, this Orthodox conceptuality raises problems by apparently adding divine agents. So does Anabaptism's multiple, shifting agential language. But as long as God remains ontologically distinct from the realms where God acts, I find this less problematic than locating God's being or essence partially in or expanding into the latter.

I find historic Anabaptism's Spirit/matter-energy dialectic extremely profound precisely because it flows from the kenotic meeting and embrace of truly distinct ontological realities: divine, spiritual and material human existence. The new creation did not evolve directly out of the old or the original creations. It arose from and involved something so new that only a radical lifestyle could em-

---

[729]Johnson, *She Who Is*, p. 229.
[730]Ibid., pp. 231, 148.

body it, even though this would be harmonious with some prior processes and structures.

3. Modalism and the immanent Trinity. I am arguing that the Trinity's economic activity flows from a reality immanent to the divine and ontologically distinct from the economic (spatiotemporal) realm. I have not fully decided, however, whether that immanent reality in itself need be triune. If a theology from below could show this, it would ascend far enough above to say something minimal about God's inner being. To decide whether it can, let me consider Kraus's claim that it need not, because biblical accounts of the Son's and Spirit's divine agency can be conceptualized as expressions, embodiments or modes of a single person.

Since I previously considered Kraus's account of the Father-Son relationship, I will focus on the Son-Spirit relation, where Kraus actually uses the term *mode.* Modalism, generally speaking, might seem plausible in light of postresurrection experiences. In these, divine agents often do not seem clearly distinct, but they interweave and overlap. However, I find it far less plausible in light of Jesus' history.

If Jesus operated in a fully human way, he had to act entirely through human capacities (suspending or greatly curbing any divine ones). His acts, at least those clearly manifesting divine power, must be ascribed most directly to God's Spirit. Jesus did not exorcise, heal and find courage to die directly from his deity—which would have made him extremely unlike us—but as a human wholly open to God's Spirit. The Spirit who performed these acts, who guided, even drove Jesus (Mk 1:12), who enabled him to offer himself on the cross (Heb 9:14) was no mere impersonal force or energy. All these were God's own intentional, purposeful saving acts. Jesus responded, opened, even surrendered himself not only to his Father but also to another will, another agent, whom he allowed to work through and with him. Kraus, however, largely dismisses this theme. The New Testament, he claims, makes "little direct reference" to the Spirit's work in Jesus' ministry.[731]

More generally, Kraus defines *person* as "a being-in-relation with other persons."[732] I find this accurate and congruent with Jesus' history, where he opened toward, served, pointed toward, received from and cooperated with two genuine, agential others. All three were full beings-in-relation with other persons. This kind of being-in-relation, however, is not possible with a person's own embodiments or expressions or modes, or between modes or expressions of the same being.

---

[731]Kraus, *God Our Savior,* p. 139.
[732]Ibid., p. 93.

In postresurrection experience, indeed, divine distinctions are often less clear. Yet many biblical texts on the Spirit indicate that similar intradivine relationships continue. For the Spirit takes on the role of openness, serving and pointing toward the two genuine others (Jn 15:26; 16:13-15; Acts 1:11; 2:33; Rom 8:26-27; 1 Cor 2:10-12; Gal 4:6). Jesus, of course, now comes to the world through the Spirit. But to call the Spirit "functionally identical" with him, or the two of them modes of the same being, misses that mutual sending and being sent, witnessing and being witnessed to, loving and being loved that many New Testament writers and historic Anabaptists found at God's heart. Such an interchange or perichoresis or community is not possible among modes, embodiments or expressions.[733] This divine being-in-relation with genuine persons is the deepest reason why the new creation's salvific reality must be communal. If God were less fully communal, so, it seems, would be the new creation's corporate dimension.

Salvation, as the triumph of eternal life over death and its powers, and renewal by the direct touch of divine energies, involves God's own coming, and thereby self-revelation. Theology therefore can conclude, with Johnson, that God "does not self-reveal in any guise other than the one which actually coheres with the essence of divine being."[734] In economic self-revelation and postresurrection experience, the three agents exercise equal, interactive roles. Accordingly, while theology can say very little about God's immanent being, it can affirm that it involves these persons and this kind of interactivity.[735]

All this, of course, does not prove that God is ontologically triune. But theology can show that if salvation is what Scripture says it is, divine triunity is a condition of its possibility. Theology can render this more plausible by showing how the

---

[733]Kraus may sometimes imply this. He argues that God's personhood cannot depend on any relationship to created persons and concludes that his relational notion of person "implies a necessary plurality in God," indeed, "in the eternal deity of his Godhead" (ibid.). This is where Kraus defines person "as a being-in-relation with other persons." Yet I find this incongruent with his dominant conceptuality, which is more consistent with what seems to be Kraus's primary God concept: God really has only one face, "always that of Parent-Creator" (p. 89).

[734]Johnson, *She Who Is*, p. 199, cf. p. 211.

[735]My concern with divine threeness has overshadowed concern for oneness. To redress this I could add to Kraus's concept of person (a being-in-relation with other persons) that a person, or self, is also intrinsically related to its own provisional selves and subselves (proposed to suggest how Jesus' divine consciousness might function harmoniously with a human self-consciousness [p. 415 note 460 above]). This concept of complex self-systems within an organizing, directing self might enhance the plausibility of God being truly three and one. Such a divine, interpersonal person would not need creaturely persons to be fully personal, but from its perichoretic fullness might well want to create others to share it.

Trinity deepens, enhances and exhibits profound connections among other Christian beliefs and activities. Theology also can, and must, show how trinitarian notions are plausible and make sense of some current issues. As a church task, however, theology does not base its affirmations on anything derived from its current context or any other.[736]

The transition from part two (The New Creation's Coming) to part three (The Convictional Framework) began a movement from below: from more direct soteriological experiences to general considerations implicit in them. This chapter has reflected on salvation in light of its divine source, also progressing from below: from Jesus' work and experience of it to his person to the Trinity. In today's modern-postmodern, historicist outlook, it seems plausible that God might not only be experienced and known but also emerge ontologically from below. My orientation, then, might seem to favor moral influence, adoptionism and modalism, with a panentheistic God-world relationship.

I have tried to show how a theology in Anabaptist perspective can emerge somewhat "above" these in a way significantly related to classical teachings important to ecumenical churches, namely, (1) Christus Victor, (2) a broadly Chalcedonian, somewhat Alexandrian Christology, and (3) a Trinity of three equal persons united perichoretically, transcending the cosmos ontologically. These constructions connect in various ways with many traditions, and considered together they perhaps resemble Eastern Orthodoxy most often.

At the same time these constructions can retain and enhance distinctively Anabaptist contributions important to many marginalized churches: (1) Jesus' sharp opposition to and triumph over the "world" and its powers, (2) his servantlike kenosis, and (3) mutually interactive community. Genuine trust in such a God and confession of such a Jesus as Lord engenders a life of discipleship in community guided by nonviolent shalom in every respect.

---

[736]See pts. 2 and 17 on pp. 96, 100-101 above.

9

HUMAN NATURE

Chapter eight recommended that contemporary Anabaptists draw on classical theology. This advice, however, seems incongruent with a common construal of historic Anabaptism as a forerunner of modernity.[1] In Anabaptism's voluntarism many scholars spot an early expression of the autonomous will. In its practical orientation they perceive an increasing concern with this earth and a decreasing interest in the divine. Anabaptism's spiritual understanding of church rituals, they allege, signaled sacramentalism's dissolution. Small, participatory Anabaptist congregations heralded democracy, while their critique of state-church monoliths signaled the dissolution of authoritarian civilization.[2]

To be sure, rationalist and humanist critiques of classical theology strongly influenced Polish Anabaptists. As they headed toward unitarianism, adoptionism and antitrinitarianism, the Poles indeed foreshadowed the Enlightenment. Yet their orientation differed significantly from Anabaptism's otherwise more mystical, medieval temper.[3]

Some recent Anabaptist theologians, such as James Reimer, incline toward the usual reading.[4] Critical of modernity's weaknesses and appreciative of strengths in historic Christianity, Reimer recommends that current Anabaptist theology incorporate many classical themes, including the creeds. Yet as Denny Weaver rightly asks: Why should a distinctively Anabaptist theology do so? What link(s) between historic Anabaptists and their foes' beliefs warrant inclusion of the latter today? It seems to me that Reimer, who finds Anabaptism and classical Christianity often at odds, provides few such links; he largely assumes the truth of much classical theol-

---

[1]See pp. 47-48.
[2]Esp. Ernst Troeltsch, *Protestantism and Progress* (Philadelphia: Fortress, 1986).
[3]See pp. 387-95, 442-45.
[4]A. James Reimer, *Mennonites and Classical Theology* (Kitchener, Ont.: Pandora, 2001), pp. 164, 167, 242.

ogy despite the apparent clash.[5]

In contrast, I have been proposing that historic Anabaptism, outside Poland, looked not so much forward toward secular freedom and democracy as back toward not only Scripture but also various medieval sources. Its social vision owed much to peasant communal ideals. Medieval mysticism profoundly shaped its soteriology. Some classical teachings need neither to be added to Anabaptist theology (Reimer) nor severed from it (Weaver). Links to them existed within historic Anabaptism itself.

Nonetheless, even though most sixteenth-century Anabaptists advocated nothing like modern freedom or secularity, their ideals eventually fed into currents flowing in that direction. As taken up, reinterpreted by and assimilated into other movements, Anabaptist emphases helped shape modernity. Consequently, I must ask how closely Anabaptism resembled not only earlier viewpoints but also later ones.

If historic Anabaptists approximated modernity at any point, it is often thought to be anthropology, particularly their view of freedom. Some presentations of Anabaptism assert straightforwardly that it affirmed free will. Free will was central to the Enlightenment. If anything, free will gained importance during the twentieth century—whether in modernity's vanguard, in existentialist resistance to impersonal, technocratic societies, or liberation struggles against systemic domination. Since Anabaptists knew oppression by similar structures, their notions of freedom can indeed contribute to such current concerns. Without qualification, however, free will today often means complete autonomy, as in the Enlightenment. It can be asked whether this ideal of freedom operating without restraints is attaining its ultimate expression, paradoxically, through today's massive forms of domination, which spread through globalization.

Theological anthropology includes humankind's corporate and personal dimensions. In the new creation's coming, Anabaptists found these inseparably linked. However, chapters six and seven covered many features of the corporate aspect. Further, Reformation era discussions of issues like freedom focused much on individuals. Consequently, this chapter will often work within that horizon, but it will acknowledge that this was an abstraction even then and will keep the corporate dimension in view.

This task will revisit in greater depth some issues from chapter five, particularly the relationship of divine and human roles in salvation. Since classical understandings of this shaped sixteenth-century discussions, I will utilize them as provisional lenses to discover where historic Anabaptists agreed, disagreed or saw things quite differently. Some Anabaptists reflected explicitly on this issue. Yet it was less a direct soteriological concern than an implication or feature of their convictional framework.

---

[5]Cf. pp. 70-72 above.

Around 400 C.E., Pelagius, a British monk, came to deplore the lax Christianity that imperial Roman sponsorship had made possible. He found this laxity condoned by claims that the will was too bound by sin for true holiness to be possible. Pelagius countered that all human wills were as free as Adam's originally was. To God's grace he ascribed little more than our creation as volitional creatures or the basic capacity to choose good or evil. Actual willing, or doing good or evil, were up to us. Pelagius insisted that if people could not really obey God's commands, God would be unjust and cruel in decreeing them. Pelagius anticipated the Enlightenment view in important respects.

In response, Augustine (354-430) claimed that the will was too bound by sin to obey God. It could be freed only by grace. Grace, for Augustine, meant a divine power. It so energized Christian acts that they could be ascribed more directly to God than their human agents. Augustine added that God had decided from eternity who would be freed (the elect) and who would not (the reprobate). This again aroused objections that God was unjust to command what reprobates (and even the elect, by themselves) could not do. Augustine's general orientation was adopted by most Reformers.

As debate intensified, semi-Pelagianism arose. It considered grace a divine power, as did Augustine, but human wills were free to interact with it. For this interaction to commence humans had to take the initial step. This position, like its two predecessors, eventually lost favor. What we might call semi-Augustinianism triumphed in 529 at the Second Council of Orange. For semi-Augustinians, as for semi-Pelagians, Christian life involved a dialectic between the divine and human wills. Both outlooks also granted humans some free choice, or ability to decide among options, in earthly affairs. Yet for semi-Augustinians the will initially was too enslaved by sin to choose God. Consequently, God had to awaken this capacity—taking the first step in the salvation process. This was substantially reaffirmed at the Council of Trent (1546-1547).

As we train these four lenses on historic Anabaptists, we should recognize that their chief interest was freedom's actual functions. When they mentioned views of divine will and knowledge, like predestination, which helped shape these lenses, they were much less concerned with theoretical aspects than their practical implications. Hubmaier, for instance, even in discussing freedom most academically of all Anabaptists, insisted that theology limit itself to God's revealed will in Christ, for he regarded predestination as illegitimate speculation about God's hidden will.[6]

As I survey historic Anabaptist anthropology, I will focus on freedom. We will often find this linked with questions about humankind's material-spiritual compo-

---

[6]Balthasar Hubmaier, *Balthasar Hubmaier*, ed. and trans. Wayne Pipkin and John Yoder (Scottdale, Penn.: Herald, 1989), pp. 472-78.

sition. In constructing a contemporary view I will dialogue with the major Reformation tradition not yet directly considered: the Reformed. While Lutherans also
taught bondage of the will, this became more foundational for the Reformed. The
twentieth-century valorization of freedom aroused Reformed theologians to wrestle with this issue anew. I will interact chiefly with two major shapers of recent Reformed theology: Karl Barth and Reinhold Niebuhr.

In today's rapidly globalizing era, what could an Anabaptist perspective contribute to the (perhaps postmodern) longings of particular, marginalized groups for
freedom? How would it assess globalization's massive homogenizing forces? Are the
latter opponents or perhaps the ultimate products of modern quests for freedom?
Can theology in Anabaptist perspective help the broader church and society better
understand diverse, even clashing, desires for freedom?

HISTORIC ANABAPTIST PERSPECTIVES

Switzerland

The Schleitheim Confession, in positing a sharp church-world dualism, styled people who had not united themselves to God as abominations from whom only
abominable things could come.[7] Schleitheim's author, Michael Sattler, underscored
the flesh's struggles against the Spirit and the Spirit's against flesh.[8]

Despite this negative evaluation of flesh, an early tract on divorce taught that
whoever cleaved to Christ was not only one spirit with him but also flesh of his
flesh and bone of his bone.[9] Fleshly relationships were significant enough that
those joining with a harlot became one flesh with her. This severed people from not
only their spouses, permitting the latter to divorce and remarry, but also Christ's
body.[10] One's relation with Christ, however, was most often called spiritual. It overrode a fleshly tie with an unbelieving spouse, allowing a believer to separate in case
of incompatibility, though to divorce only if one's partner became one flesh with
another sexually.

These few clues indicate a positive attitude toward *spirit*, though it is often unclear whether the human or divine spirit, or both together, were meant. *Flesh* usually

---

[7]Michael Sattler, *The Legacy of Michael Sattler*, ed. John Howard Yoder (Scottdale, Penn.: Herald, 1973), p. 38.
[8]Ibid., p. 22. Since he was probably referring to Gal 5:17, *gaist* very likely meant God's Spirit, not the
human spirit (cf. p. 23; Mandfred Krebs and Hans Georg Rott, eds., *Elsass, I Teil, Stadt Strassburg 1522-
1532*, Quellen zur Geschichte der Täufer, Band 7 ([Gütersloh, Germany: Gerd Mohn, 1959], p. 69).
Moreover, the flesh and its glory will pass away; only the Word of the Lord remains eternally (Krebs
and Rott, *Elsass, I Teil, Stadt Strassburg 1522-1532*, p. 59). For Grebel and Mantz on divine grace and
human works, see chap. 5.
[9]Sattler, *Legacy of Michael Sattler*, p. 103.
[10]Ibid., pp. 103-4.

indicated a negative quantum but could denote the vehicle of union among humans, and between humans and Christ.

Balthasar Hubmaier, a doctor of theology, investigated human freedom most meticulously among Anabaptists. In his early writings people often appeared wholly corrupt. Repentance was only possible by recognizing that "there is no health in us, but rather poison, wounds, and all impurity which cling to us from the beginning since we are conceived and born in sin."[11] Against Zwingli's view of children, which Hubmaier found too positive, he insisted that they all died in Adam and are "by nature children of wrath."[12] Even in his last writing, Hubmaier rejected Zwingli's reputed claim that original sin was "only a weakness," and asserted that it was "the matrix and root of all sins."[13]

The early Hubmaier often appeared to consider the will wholly depraved. Each person was "by nature an evil, worm-eaten, and poisoned tree, and neither can nor wants to bring forth good fruit." For this reason people could take the baptismal pledge and follow Christ only through the invoked Trinity's power.[14]

After arriving in Moravia, Hubmaier devoted two treatises to the will.[15] They deserve detailed examination. Soul, spirit and flesh were three distinct "essential substances." Each had its own will. Together they reflected the Trinity.[16] The spirit was directed Godward, the flesh earthward and the soul had to choose between them. Hubmaier pictured the soul as Adam in paradise: it was free to decide either way. But Adam chose to follow his flesh, which Hubmaier aligned with Eve—not without patriarchal bias—and forfeited freedom for all his descendants.

Hubmaier now attributed that hopeless depravity, which earlier seemed to pervade the person, especially to the flesh. The flesh could only sin, and not even wish to do good.[17] It "must daily be killed, since it wants only to live and reign according to its own lusts."[18] Hubmaier, that is, now lodged evil largely within one component of the person, which became one's "greatest enemy" (apparently outdoing sin or the devil).[19] The body, which Hubmaier usually equated with the flesh, had al-

---

[11]Hubmaier, *Balthasar Hubmaier,* p. 84.

[12]Ibid., p. 284; cf. pp. 139, 218, 361, 374, 456. This was due to the "old Adam," or "poisoned nature in which we are conceived in our mother's womb and born" (p. 86, cf. pp. 84, 146, 152, 218, 431, 433).

[13]Ibid., p. 540.

[14]Ibid., pp. 86, 100, 144. "There is nothing good in you and . . . you bring forth no good fruit" (p. 102). "We cannot do anything, but [God] must do it through and in us" (p. 105). "Believing is a work of God and not of a human being" (p. 204).

[15]Ibid., pp. 427-48, 459-91.

[16]Ibid., pp. 430, 432.

[17]Ibid., pp. 433-34; cf. pp. 442, 456.

[18]Ibid., pp. 87, 147.

[19]Ibid., p. 243.

ready been sentenced to decay back into earth.[20] It would, however, be raised as an immortal, spiritual body, a fit instrument for the soul.[21]

Hubmaier often painted the soul in similar somber colors. It had lost all knowledge of good and evil, and thus any ability to choose between them and do good.[22] Yet Hubmaier mitigated this slightly. The soul (Adam) knew that the fruit was evil and "preferred" not to eat, but he did so to avoid vexing his flesh (Eve). Thus the soul was "partly reparable" in this life.[23]

In contrast to flesh and soul, the human spirit never fell but continued to yearn for God. Yet because it was imprisoned "in the sinful and poisoned body" it could only groan like a captive.[24] The spirit was utterly helpless without God's Spirit, which had withdrawn from humankind at Adam's fall.[25] Hubmaier loosely identified the spirit with God's image or likeness, which still resided in people, though "dimmed, captured and bound." It was like a spark covered with cold ashes that "will steam if heavenly water is poured on it."[26] In his later writings Hubmaier found the claim that "nothing good" dwells in us exaggerated and true only of the flesh.[27] He even called the impotent desire to do good "a good work."[28] And God's image, like the law, taught people the good.[29] Hubmaier expressed the human dilemma more precisely: being captive in spirit, wounded in soul and completely corrupted in flesh.[30]

---

[20]Ibid., pp. 432, 441.

[21]Ibid., pp. 239-40.

[22]Ibid., p. 135.

[23]Balthasar Hubmaier, *Schriften,* Quellen zur Geschichte der Täufer, Band 9, ed. Gunnar Westin and Torsten Bergsten (Gütersloh, Germany: Gerd Mohn, 1962), p. 387. Hubmaier's editors and translators Pipkin and Yoder (*Balthasar Hubmaier,* p. 435) did not use "partly," although the original reads *"halb widerbrunglich";* cf. *Balthasar Hubmaier,* p. 441. At times, Hubmaier appeared to attribute much of the soul's evil to flesh, for the soul could not act except through the flesh (ibid., p. 435).

[24]Hubmaier, *Balthasar Hubmaier,* p. 360.

[25]Ibid., p. 437; cf. pp. 443, 236.

[26]Ibid., p. 360. It is the desire in all people to do right (p. 436), mentioned under "Evangelism" on pp. 259-60. Hubmaier also equated God's image with being "A corporeal reasonable creature, in body, soul and spirit" (p. 345).

[27]Ibid., pp. 360-61.

[28]Ibid., p. 462.

[29]Ibid., p. 361.

[30]Ibid., cf. p. 486. Or the soul's goodness was wounded, the spirit's was impeded and obscured by the body's darkness, while the flesh was completely ruined (p. 445); "the old serpent" almost "blacked out" the spirit "through sin" (p. 438). In contrast, Christ made people free in spirit, healthy in soul and rendered the Fall "completely harmless in the flesh" (p. 361). Jesus through his spirit rendered the body harmless to our spirits; through his soul he recovered the capacity to perceive good and evil through the Word; through his flesh he earned resurrection for our flesh, though it must first die (p. 446; on spirit, see p. 369 note 238 above).

Hubmaier identified the will with the power of the soul.[31] Was it in some sense free? Hubmaier found the Reformers' stress on inability to do good a dangerous "half truth."[32] If not balanced by biblical admonitions to choose, which presupposed freedom of some sort, it entailed that God was unjust in judging sinners and gave alleged Christians excuses for sinning. Hubmaier, like other Anabaptists, critiqued Protestant teachings on predestination, total depravity and the bound will less for theoretical reasons than their potential for undercutting discipleship and misrepresenting God.

Hubmaier championed freedom enough to sometimes sound Pelagian: "the person hangs freely in the balance and hovers between heaven and earth. One may freely choose—for the choice is given to one . . . good or evil, life or death."[33] Yet Hubmaier emphasized, in both earlier and later writings, that the soul could choose only when the Word awakened it: when "a new grace and drawing" granted one a "power of knowledge, willing, and working."[34] Only then, to the person so awakened, would God say, "Help yourself; then I also will help you." Only then would Hubmaier declare that "God has created you without your help, but without your help he will not save you."[35]

Rather than Pelagianism, Hubmaier was maintaining that God genuinely renewed the will and interacted with it, as did both semi-Pelagians and semi-Augustinians. He was not challenging the Protestant claim that God initiated salvation but their (Augustinian) perception that the will continued to be so bound that God virtually performed its positive actions. He insisted that salvation is not a monergistic but a dialogical process. Humans become genuine partners—even though God takes the lead and is every deed's "preeminent agent."[36]

In terms of our provisional categories, was Hubmaier basically semi-Augustinian or semi-Pelagian? The unfallen spirit directed toward God, the remnant of God's image, or the "spark" within, the desire for good which was a "good work"—did these indicate a human capacity to take the first step in salvation?

Hubmaier's repeated accounts of how the Word alone, usually through preaching, could bring us alive seemed to say no.[37] Only the Word could restore our lost

---

[31]Ibid., p. 443.
[32]Ibid., pp. 451, 482, 491.
[33]Ibid., p. 451.
[34]Ibid., p. 444.
[35]Ibid., p. 440.
[36]Ibid., p. 489.
[37]However, this was available to the patriarchs through the promised Christ (ibid., p. 454), as implied by Old Testament passages favoring free will (pp. 457-60, 532-34) and further back, since the Fall (pp. 459, 532-33).

knowledge of good and evil so that we could even begin to choose.[38] The Word
alone bestowed power to believe it and, by birthing us anew, to do what it commanded.[39]

Nonetheless, though free will itself was God's gift, Hubmaier, according to
Kenneth Davis's minutely detailed study, intimated that some human capacity preceded it. Hubmaier could say that the new "power of knowing, willing and working" is given to all "in so far as they themselves desire it."[40] Davis proposes that
Hubmaier distinguished full bestowal of free will from a prior, limited ability to
choose, even though Hubmaier "omits any direct mention of this step."[41] As support, Davis cites only the Hubmaier text just quoted.[42] Was this desire a semi-Pelagian first step? Davis evidently thinks it was not, but "a kind of first or prevenient
grace . . . latent until awakened by the gospel, or 'new grace.'" This meant that even
the "initial favourable response is an almost inevitably cooperative matter."[43]

Recall, however, that Hubmaier portrayed the human spirit desiring God, yet
wholly captive and unable to do God's will. This makes it plausible that "desire"
might not have implied any positive capacity. Moreover, mention of desire in the
relevant text was preceded by Hubmaier's familiar claim that one could not choose
unless knowledge of good and evil were restored through "a new grace and calling
by his life-giving Word."[44] Hubmaier, to be sure, insisted that Godward willing and
desiring were far from wholly destroyed by sin. Still, apart from one reference to
this desire as a "good work," I cannot find him affirming that these could move
toward God salvifically, even slightly, without God's prior movement, even if that
consisted mainly in imparting knowledge (though more was likely involved).[45] I
find little evidence that Hubmaier regarded salvation's first step as "cooperative" or

---

[38]Hubmaier put it this way in his treatises on free will (ibid., pp. 435, 439, 444, 446, 454, 466, 485).
   This seems implied in earlier writings where the law alone brought awareness of sin, and the gospel
   an awareness of salvation (pp. 102, 144, cf. pp. 340, 362).

[39]Ibid., pp. 204, 362, 466, 100-101, 105, 144, 403, 444, 457, 465, 477, 481-82, 553. Without this
   "our will is fully and completely in contradiction to [the] divine will" (p. 242). Hubmaier could
   even paraphrase a prayer of Augustine that Pelagius deplored: "Give us what thou commandest and
   command what thou wilt." For Hubmaier, doing God's commands "would be impossible for us in
   ourselves, without God's drawing. . . . Therefore we must first beg him and say, 'O Lord, give us what
   you command of us'" (p. 362).

[40]Balthasar Hubmaier, "On Free Will," in Spiritual and Anabaptist Writers, ed. George Williams and Angel
   Mergal (Philadelphia: Westminster Press, 1957), pp. 114-135, esp. p. 129; cf. Hubmaier, Balthasar
   Hubmaier, p. 444, cf. pp. 463, 553.

[41]Kenneth Davis, Anabaptism and Asceticism (Scottdale, Penn.: Herald, 1974), pp. 147-48.

[42]Ibid., p. 151.

[43]Ibid.

[44]Hubmaier, "On Free Will," pp. 128-29; cf. Hubmaier, Balthasar Hubmaier, pp. 443-44.

[45]Hubmaier, Balthasar Hubmaier, p. 462.

nearly semi-Pelagian,[46] and much more evidence that he considered it God's, like semi-Augustinians.

Whatever his views about freedom prior to conversion, Hubmaier's perspective on freedom afterward took two contrasting directions in his later theology. These corresponded with allocating evil almost entirely to one substance, the flesh, while pronouncing another, the spirit, entirely free from evil.

Earlier, Hubmaier had considered freedom damaged and limited even after awakening by the Word.[47] Later, however, he declared that the Word set our souls as free as Adam's in paradise to will good and evil.[48] At times Hubmaier affirmed that Christians had "complete freedom" and that following God's commands was "easy."[49]

Nevertheless, while Christians were Christ's members according their spirits and souls, according to their flesh they were not.[50] Their incorrigible bodies immersed Christians so deeply in "this world" that they needed discipline from not only the church but even the state (legitimating Christian use of the sword).[51]

This anthropology, it seems, could stretch a Christian to a breaking point—by expecting nearly flawless behavior from one part of oneself, even while one "strangles, crucifies and torments" incorrigible evil in another.[52] Hubmaier declared that when the soul united with the spirit, the flesh had to obey it, even if it had to go "into the fire."[53] However, his own recantations in Zurich and his concessions during his final imprisonment testified to the severity of this struggle—which he finally won.

South Germany-Austria

Earliest years. Jesus functioned as the model for both inner crucifixion of creaturely attachments and divinization's outward, public expression—and consequently as human behavior's ultimate norm. Although this *Gelassenheit* process involved much suffering, Packull claims that "God was immanent in the soul," and humans consequently "possessed . . . the potential to participate in . . . the divine."[54] Packull

---

[46]Davis, *Anabaptism and Asceticism*, p. 151.

[47]The convert surrendered only "As much as it is possible for a wounded person," and whatever "the wounded is not able to do out of his own capacity, the Physician counsels, helps, and promotes" (Hubmaier, *Balthasar Hubmaier*, p. 85, cf. pp. 98, 152).

[48]Hubmaier, *Balthasar Hubmaier*, p. 361, cf. pp. 439, 464.

[49]Ibid., p. 400.

[50]Ibid., p. 519.

[51]See pp. 289-323 above.

[52]Hubmaier, *Balthasar Hubmaier*, p. 401.

[53]Ibid., p. 441.

[54]Werner Packull, *Mysticism and the Early South German-Austrian Anabaptists* (Scottdale, Penn.: Herald, 1977), p. 25.

considers this anthropology Pelagian or semi-Pelagian.

I. Total personal renewal, where "all creaturely desires are rooted out and smashed," and the soul washed from all traces of carnality, was central to Hans Hut's preaching.[55] He styled this battle against lust for the creaturely as one between "spirit" and "flesh."[56] Hut also expected the Holy Spirit to transform all things eschatologically, and quite soon. Did all this entail that human desires and bodies were wholly incorrigible, as Hubmaier said?

When mystics and evangelists inveigh against creaturely attachments, they can appear to condemn all created reality and portray divinization as total transcendence of it. Yet for Hut creatures were not evil. Humans, though, had departed from God's intentions and put creatures to evil uses.[57] Humans accordingly needed purification inwardly, but also outwardly and physically, from "injustice in our way of living and our misuse of the creatures."[58] Christ's return would purify this material, social world, not replace it with a spiritual realm.

Hut portrayed the painful inner justification process as something passively undergone. Did it obliterate the will? Probably not. True passive justification, for Hut, was not simply letting oneself be declared righteous. It involved voluntary yielding, even though God performed the real work. Hut's extant writings, however, do not depict the human will recovering some original unity with God. The will, like the body, was transformed, but it apparently remained intact.

2. Much like Hubmaier, Leonhard Schiemer taught a trichotomous anthropology. Flesh and blood strove toward evil and darkness, opposing God's light. The soul was poised between the flesh and the light. Everyone, however, had turned toward flesh and was dead in soul.[59] But while Hubmaier distinguished the human spirit from God's Spirit, the uppermost role in Schiemer's anthropology belonged to the internal presence of God's Word, or Light (cf. Jn 1:1-5). While this included conscience, Schiemer also called it the first grace.[60] Apparently it was not a strictly

---

[55]Hans Hut, "On the Mystery of Baptism," in *Early Anabaptist Spirituality*, ed. Daniel Liechty (New York: Paulist Press, 1994), pp. 76, 78.

[56]Ibid., p. 77. Hut apparently meant the human, not the divine Spirit. He described it within humans (*"der in dem menshen ist"* ["Ein christlich Unterrich, wie goettliche Geschrift vergleicht und geurteilen solle werden," in *Glaubenzeugnisse oberdeutscher Taufgesinnter* (= Quellen und Forschungen zur Reformationsgeschichte), ed. Lydia Mueller (Leipzig: M. Heinsius Nachfolger, 1938), 20:24]) and in "conscience" (*"gewissen,"* p. 25). Further, he did not refer to God's Spirit in this context, though he did to Christ and God.

[57]Hut, "Ein christlich Unterrich," p. 33.

[58]Hut, "On the Mystery of Baptism," p. 70.

[59]Leonhard Schiemer, "Three Kinds of Grace," in *Early Anabaptist Spirituality*, ed. Daniel Liechty (New York: Paulist Press, 1994), p. 87.

[60]Ibid., pp. 88, 85.

human capacity but, as in the mysticism Packull mentions, a region where the human and divine intermixed.[61]

This light enabled people to know God through creation, mainly via the "Gospel of all Creatures."[62] When the light shines in people, they apparently possess sufficient free will to obey it and attain salvation by loving God and neighbor, or else to snuff it out.[63] The awareness obtained through this first grace, however, was chiefly of sin, much like that which Marpeck found possible through the law.[64] To those who greeted the light by opposing sin, God normally sent a second transforming, spiritual grace.[65]

This grace divinized people so fully that they passed beyond "the creaturely."[66] Yet Schiemer meant the creaturely realm not in itself but as the object of possessive grasping and also that very grasping.[67] He also affirmed the body's resurrection, and that divinizing energies could overflow from spirit and soul into the body, rendering it "unfeeling, impassible, immortal and glorified."[68] Schiemer was indicating something partially possible in this life. The body could be transformed through the soul and spirit, and was more directly related to them than for Hubmaier.

We notice that Schiemer, also unlike Hubmaier, delineated in detail a step to be taken before God sent the transforming Word. Yet might the light which made that step possible be attributed to God's initiative—since it was also the cosmic Word and a grace? If Schiemer had clearly distinguished this Word from a human spirit

---

[61]Beachy thinks that Schiemer derived this anthropology from Hubmaier, and Marpeck got it from Schiemer (Alvin Beachy, *The Concept of Grace in the Radical Reformation* [Nieuwkoop, Netherlands: B. De Graf, 1977], pp. 23-24, 37, 67-68, 173). While these three shared some conceptuality, I do not find the similarities among them substantive enough to support this derivation. Beachy also proposes that Anabaptists "saw human nature as retaining some region or faculty . . . not vitiated by original sin" (p. 227), much as in the preceding mystical tradition. Yet, he adds, they based free will chiefly on Christ's atonement (pp. 208-9, 211), or soteriology, though still, to a lesser extent, on anthropology (p. 229).

[62]See pp. 262-63 above.

[63]Schiemer, "Three Kinds of Grace," pp. 85-87.

[64]Ibid., p. 90.

[65]Ibid., p. 89. "Die creatur," in Leonhard Schiemer, "Leinharten Schiemers epistl an die gmain Gottes zu Rottenburg, geschriben 1527, von dreierlie gnadt," in *Glaubenzeugnisse oberdeutscher Taufgesinnter* (= Quellen und Forschungen zur Reformationsgeschichte), ed. Lydia Mueller (Leipzig: M. Heinsius Nachfolger, 1938), 20:67; yet even this divinization was "true human rest" (Leonhard Schiemer, "The Apostles' Creed: An Interpretation," in *Spiritual Life in Anabaptism*, ed. Cornelius Dyck [Scottdale, Penn.: Herald, 1995], p. 32). For discussion of this issue and translation of *"die creatur,"* see p. 121 note 69 above. Schiemer, somewhat like Hut, also affirmed that God hates sin, but not the creatures God made (Hut, "Ein christlich Unterrich," p. 32).

[66]*"Die creatur,"* in Schiemer, "Leinharten Schiemers epistl an die gmain," p. 67.

[67]See pp. 71-72 above.

[68]Schiemer, "Three Kinds of Grace," p. 92.

or capacity, we might conclude this. Yet human awareness and choice seem so intermixed with this light that their acts were apparently its acts too, at least in part. Human choice, then, did not simply respond to grace. It was so intermingled with it that humans could participate in salvation's first step. The process, however, involved continual divine-human interaction, and Schiemer was more nearly semi-Pelagian than Pelagian.

3. Human freedom was discussed by Hans Denck from two quite different perspectives. From the first, God originally gave and kept giving humans free will to respond to the Word.[69] This freedom to turn toward God also allowed people to turn away. Humankind had indeed done this and become inwardly entangled in creaturely lusts and values. Accordingly, when people sensed the Word's drawing, they experienced an opposing, deep-rooted, inborn willfulness or sickness.[70] Denck, like Hubmaier, usually called this the "flesh" and found it incorrigible.[71] But since created goodness was still manifest in all creatures, including humans, he did not link flesh as closely to the body as Hubmaier. Still, people who responded to the Word had to mortify this poisoned flesh as long they lived in the body.[72]

The flesh, however, could not negate freedom to respond to the Word. From this first perspective Denck often sounded optimistic about freedom. People could "very well" follow the Word, for it always spoke "clearly to everyone."[73] Like Hubmaier, Denck could call following God's laws "easy."[74] And while people would never be free from temptation, they could be from actual sin.[75]

From this first perspective Denck championed freedom against two of the Reformers' Augustinian doctrines: the bound will and predestination. These together, Denck protested, taught that God actually prevented people from choosing good, thereby making God responsible for ordaining evil.[76] This in turn excused people from acknowledging their own sin and responding to the Word's call toward good. But to Denck's Reformation opponents, his claim that people are free and drawn toward good sounded Pelagian.

In response Denck treated freedom from the second perspective. He countered

---

[69]Hans Denck, *The Spiritual Legacy of Hans Denck,* ed. Clarence Bauman (Leiden: E. J. Brill, 1991), p. 93.

[70]Ibid., p. 55.

[71]Ibid., p. 123.

[72]Ibid., p. 110, cf. p. 89.

[73]Ibid., p. 99.

[74]Ibid., pp. 135, 143, 151.

[75]Ibid., pp. 137, 253.

[76]Ibid., pp. 85, 213, 217-19.

that although the Word is *in* us, it is not *of* us. This meant that if I "run in the truth ... not I but God's Word runs in me."[77] Denck's freedom, like Hut's, was a response or surrender to the Word's work, letting it crucify inordinate attachments blocking us from good. And even this "activity is before God a passivity, our making before God a breaking, our something before God nothing."[78] At least when pressed by his opponents Denck affirmed that "whoever submits his will to God's will, is truly free and truly captive. Thus, it does not matter whether one calls it the free or captive will."[79]

This second response could raise the opposite objection: if God does all the acting, is freedom truly real? This objection also emerged from another angle.[80] While Denck's freedom allowed people to turn from God, God was the one true Being. To turn from this God and toward evil then was apparently to turn toward nothing. And despite sin's apparent actuality, it was already overcome in God's eternity.[81] Further, even though the Word had produced a world of creatures, all creatures in some deeper sense were one with God.[82] Perhaps then evil and even creatures were not ultimately real. But if so, could freedom to turn toward them be real?

Denck's two perspectives were highly paradoxical. From the first, freedom apparently involved taking initiative, changing things and challenging claims that the world order, and especially its evil, were unalterable. From there Denck appeared Pelagian or semi-Pelagian. But from the second perspective, freedom was largely passive response to the Word and its work: more nearly semi-Augustinian. This freedom opened one to a mystical union. There evil and distinctions between God and creatures, and consequently all change, perhaps became unreal. To the extent that they did, Denck was possibly even Augustinian. For all activities would have been God's, even apparently free human responses.

These considerations are intersected by another question: Was the Word really distinct from humans or immanent in their depths, as for some mystics in the preceding tradition?[83] When Denck described how freedom was experienced, he most often sounded semi-Augustinian. He ascribed initiative to the Word, which aroused a capac-

---

[77]Ibid., p. 87.

[78]Ibid., p. 89.

[79]Ibid., p. 253. After abandoning believers' baptism, Denck sought to settle in Basel. The Reformer Oecolampadius required a public statement of faith, which contained the quotation cited (ibid., pp. 247-59). It expressed Denck's beliefs, but packaged for a hostile audience.

[80]See pp. 371-73 above.

[81]Denck, *Spiritual Legacy of Hans Denck*, p. 81.

[82]Ibid., pp. 133, 155.

[83]Packull, *Mysticism and the Early South German-Austrian Anabaptists*, p. 25.

ity to respond in a receptive, perhaps passive, manner.[84] Yet even though Denck denied that this Word was "of us," I do not find him differentiating a human person, will or soul from it any more clearly than Schiemer. Only one aspect of the person seemed distinct from the Word: flesh (not body). Consequently, human freedom in its depths could well have intermingled enough with the Word to participate in salvation's first step. Yet since the process, like Schiemer's, involved continual divine-human interaction, Denck, from the first perspective, was also more semi-Pelagian than Pelagian.

4. Hans Schlaffer lamented that before his conversion God had long sought him, though he had strongly resisted.[85] But finally Schlaffer was convinced, as all who would be reborn must be, that he could not live by his own power.[86] Conversion involved becoming still and suffering Christ's work, as it was for his South German-Austrian colleagues.[87] Even faith was God's work in people.[88] They could continue as Christians only through the Spirit's power.[89] Unlike his colleagues, Schlaffer clearly differentiated the Christ who called from the people who responded, as Riedemann and Marpeck would. His concerns sounded semi-Augustinian (maybe even Augustinian, apart from the mystical outlook he shared with his colleagues).

For Schlaffer a human was a "bad tree" that could not make itself good. Though he said that this characterized humans "by nature," that meant "as soon as we come to know the difference between good and evil."[90] At the same time, he attributed this damage to Adam's fall. It involved fierce struggle between flesh and Spirit, as other Anabaptists underscored.[91]

---

[84]"No one comes of himself to Christ except the Father draw him. . . . [W]hoever . . . wants to come on his own initiative presumes to give God something which he has not received from him"; "without God, one can neither seek nor find him" (Denck, *Spiritual Legacy of Hans Denck*, pp. 111, 91). "As soon as a person becomes aware of the Word, he is again partly *[zum teil]* free . . . to sacrifice himself in suffering" (p. 218, author's translation). Yet "we indeed cannot do this, but must suffer God to do it" (p. 224, author's translation). "Where this has begun in a person and he ascribes it to himself, he robs God of his honor . . . [by] seeking to be something over against God" (p. 111).

[85]Hans Schlaffer, *Selections*, in *Spiritual Life in Anabaptism*, ed. Cornelius Dyck (Scottdale, Penn.: Herald, 1995), pp. 195-204.

[86]Hans Schlaffer, "Instructions on Beginning a True Christian Life," in *Early Anabaptist Spirituality*, ed. Daniel Liechty (New York: Paulist, 1994), p. 100.

[87]Hans Schlaffer, "Ein kurzer Unterrich zum Anfang eines recht chrislichen Lebens," in *Glaubenzeugnisse oberdeutscher Taufgesinnter* (= Quellen und Forschungen zur Reformationsgeschichte), ed. Lydia Mueller (Leipzig: M. Heinsius Nachfolger, 1938), 20:86.

[88]Schlaffer, "Instructions on Beginning," p. 105.

[89]Schlaffer, "Ein kurzer Unterrich," pp. 98, 99, 106, 112.

[90]Schlaffer, "Instructions on Beginning," p. 101.

[91]Schlaffer, *Selections*, p. 203. He probably meant God's Spirit, not the human spirit, since Gal 5 is written in the margin of the original (Hans Schlaffer, "Ein einfaeltig Gebet," in *Joerg Propst Rothenfelder, auch genant Maler*, ed. Das Kunstbuch [manuscript, 1561], line 121; cf. *Selections*, p. 102).

Schlaffer, however, located sin's source in not the flesh but the "the heart and mind."[92] The human body had been created good and was apparently being transformed along with the rest of the person.[93] For salvation was bringing people to a higher state than Adam's original one. Schlaffer, like Schiemer, taught that resurrection of the flesh occurred partially in this life, as people experienced Christ's sufferings in their bodies, and also climactically at the end.[94]

Peter Riedemann. Peter Riedemann represented those Anabaptists, the Hutterites, who worked out the new creation most radically in the material world: through sharing labor and possessions. Surprisingly, though, he considered material reality "alien to our true nature."[95] For humans were created as "heavenly beings" with a "heavenly body." Riedemann called this body God's "own breath and spirit" but also the human spirit.[96] This heavenly body, or spirit, was evidently still part of everyone and designed to lead their earthly bodies to God.[97]

Riedemann also described humans as created in God's likeness, which was spirit, whereas flesh and blood were earthly.[98] (However, he did not clearly differentiate God's likeness from God's image nor the human spirit from the soul.) But when Adam sinned he "cast aside God's image"—in the sense of "God's righteousness, purity, and holiness"—and received the devil's image or likeness: lying, sin and injustice.[99] Humankind's spiritual dimension probably remained in some sense. Still, Eve and Adam were "stripped and emptied" of God's grace, and with their descendants they came under God's wrath.[100]

Riedemann described sin several ways. Like Hubmaier, he attributed it mainly to Eve—yet not to her flesh but to her reason, as the desire "to be more clever than she had been made."[101] Along with many Anabaptists, Riedemann called sin "disobedience," which located it more in the will.[102] Like earlier South German-Austrians, Riedemann also highlighted the sin of idolizing the creaturely. Sin

---

[92]Lit. "kidneys"; Schlaffer, *Selections*, p. 198.

[93]Schlaffer, *Selections*, p. 199.

[94]Schlaffer, "Ein kurzer Unterrich," p. 95; *Selections*, p. 196.

[95]Peter Riedemann, *Peter Riedemann's Hutterite Confession of Faith*, ed. John Friesen (Scottdale, Penn.: Herald, 1999), p. 120.

[96]Ibid., pp. 88-89, 128.

[97]Ibid., p. 89.

[98]Ibid.

[99]Ibid., pp. 90-91, cf. p. 159.

[100]Ibid., p. 91.

[101]Ibid. Eve's sin was not desire for the fruit by itself but that inner desire plus the outward act of taking the fruit.

[102]Ibid., p. 92.

originated in "wrong taking" or grasping for possessions, which led to private property and conflicts over it.[103]

Humans also inherited a sinful nature from Adam.[104] Riedemann sometimes spoke as if this were a substance, such as "corrupting poison," a common term among Anabaptists.[105] But it was chiefly an inclination toward sin.[106] This "sinful nature" or "original sin" stirs up all other sins and leads to physical death. It once brought spiritual death too, but Jesus' atonement cancelled that penalty for everyone.[107]

Like most Anabaptists, Riedemann was rather rough on the flesh. Adam's sinful nature was transmitted through physical conception. The "weakness of the flesh" was a feature of this nature, not simply a finite limitation.[108] For Jesus to be free of it, he had to be "conceived in a completely different way", through God's power, which made him "a different human being."[109] Nonetheless, Jesus was truly born of Mary and "of David according to the flesh," which could not have been intrinsically sinful, though flesh seemed so in Riedemann's other uses.[110]

Riedemann seldom mentioned the will. Like Hubmaier and the Dutch, he insisted that repentance was active. People had to flee sin and conquer and subdue their flesh.[111] This sounds semi-Pelagian. However, it was the law, preached before the gospel, that induced awareness of sin and moved people to seek something better.[112] One's response was no work of "flesh and blood" or "personal choice."[113]

---

[103]Peter Rideman, *Confession of Faith* (Rifton, N.Y.: Plough, 1970), p. 58. See p. 33 note 32; Riedemann, *Peter Riedemann's Hutterite Confession*, p. 94, cf. pp. 87-88, 119-20 and pp 237-38 above.

[104]Riedemann, *Peter Riedemann's Hutterite Confession*, pp. 92, 109.

[105]Ibid., pp. 98, 159.

[106]Ibid., p. 92.

[107]Ibid., p. 93.

[108]Ibid., p. 68. He did not equate the serpent with "the curiosity and desire of the flesh" but insisted that this arose in response to the serpent's counsel (p. 91). It is not entirely clear that Riedemann's Adam was created with an earthly body. God's image, which Adam bore, was spirit and could not be "flesh and blood" (p. 89). Riedemann distinguished the serpent from Adam's flesh not because he originally possessed pure flesh but because he had no "mortality" (p. 91). Was Riedemann assuming that bodies were irreversibly mortal, and that Adam was not yet mortal and had no body? In this context, Riedemann mentioned the heavenly body that "shall lead the earthly body to God" (p. 89). In any case, he affirmed our resurrection in an "incorruptible body" (p. 82).

[109]Ibid., pp. 109, 68, 69.

[110]Ibid., pp. 68, 90, 96, 122, 174. Marriage, on one level, was a union of spirit and body where body could apparently be open to spirit in some positive way, and spirit need not simply oppose and subdue it. Yet attraction by youth or beauty was apparently following the flesh in the negative sense (pp. 127-29).

[111]Ibid., pp. 96-97.

[112]Ibid., p. 100.

[113]Ibid., p. 174.

The Word's efficacy "does not depend on human will or effort, but on God's initiative."[114] In conversion, then, divine initiation intersected with human response in semi-Augustinian fashion.

After conversion the "surrendered will interweaves itself with the divine will," and they "become one. From now on, God desires, chooses, and works everything in that person."[115] Christ and the Spirit transform people so thoroughly that the human will almost seems to vanish.[116] When he moved beyond conversion, Riedemann could sound more Augustinian than semi-Augustinian, as could Denck on occasion.

This lofty portrait of divinization spawned high behavioral expectations. Hutterites attributed lapses to the flesh's continuing clash with God's Spirit, and handled them mostly through discipline and banning. The stern discipline exercised in most Anabaptist communities owed something to an anthropology that justified both high expectations and harsh treatment for what opposed them.

Pilgram Marpeck. I. Reason, flesh and spirit. Marpeck foregrounded another human capacity: reason. Most Anabaptists who correlated sin with flesh noted that Eve found the apple "good for food" and "a delight to the eyes." Marpeck added, somewhat like Riedemann, that she also coveted its ability "to make one wise" (Gen 3:6). Sin consisted chiefly in the desire to possess knowledge of good and evil, for which she and Adam were banished from the garden (Gen 3:5, 22-23).[117]

Marpeck found reason's grasping most evident in the spiritualist effort to transcend earthly limitations and penetrate the divine secrets—though these remained eternally beyond its range.[118] Reason "presumed to be a god" who "can be saved or condemned by her own power."[119] Sin, that is, basically consisted in not capitulation to the body but desire to transcend it entirely. This arrogance was most pronounced among educated classes, who despised "simple, uneducated, coarse, faithful people."[120] Yet salvation required that reason be humbled at Jesus' physical feet

---

[114]Ibid., p. 178.

[115]Ibid., p. 179.

[116]Ibid., pp. 61, 67, 76, 97. Sin might stir in the redeemed, but it could not control them (p. 67).

[117]Like many Anabaptists, Marpeck also called sin unbelief and disobedience (Pilgram Marpeck, *The Writings of Pilgram Marpeck*, ed. and trans. William Klassen and Walter Klaassen [Scottdale, Penn.: Herald, 1978], pp. 337-38, 343), suspicion and mistrust of God (J. Loserth, *Pilgram Marbecks Antwort auf Kaspar Schwenckfeld's Beurteilung des Buches der Bundesbezeugung von 1542* [Vienna: Carl Fromme, 1929], p. 217), and idolatrous love of creatures and oneself, in the early South German-Austrian sense (*Writings of Pilgram Marpeck*, pp. 414, 479; *Pilgram Marbecks Antwort*, pp. 215, 259).

[118]Marpeck, *Writings of Pilgram Marpeck*, p. 83.

[119]Ibid., p. 317.

[120]Ibid., p. 370.

and that people admit they shared those weaknesses which his sufferings made evident. For Riedemann weakness arose from sin. Jesus overcame sin by being a different kind of human, imbued with power. Marpeck's Jesus, however, took on our
weakness and made it a source of salvation.[121]

Marpeck was not critiquing reason as God created it but its drive to penetrate
the divine realm and attain its own salvation. Reason was a function of the human
spirit, which Marpeck valued as "a sensitive, sublime creature" and an "image of
humanity's godlikeness."[122] Indeed, "rational man" was intended to be the highest
creature, and when it has been crucified "reason is again included in faith."[123]
Marpeck repeatedly defined eternal life as "knowledge" or "understanding."
While this mainly meant knowing God in a personal way, it included cognitive elements, as his complex theology evidenced.

Marpeck also insisted that flesh as created was not sinful.[124] Instead, sin dwelled
in the flesh; flesh had become sin's vehicle. This occurred when the human "spirit
once mingled with the flesh and fell into disobedience" and was imprisoned under
the flesh.[125] This may sound like Hubmaier's soul turning toward the flesh rather
than the spirit.

Yet for Marpeck the spirit transgressed, not the soul, by following reason, not
flesh. No capacity remained wholly directed toward God and unstained by sin.
Consequently, flesh in the negative sense was roughly synonymous with "fleshly
reason."[126] Sinful desires coursed through the mind as well as the body. Marpeck

---

[121]Ibid., pp. 317-18, cf. p. 232; cf. p. 378 above. Though Marpeck called "flesh and blood . . . the
very heel and lowest part of the inner man," Jesus crushed Satan "through weakness . . . in all patience" with such a heel, and his Spirit can also work through our "heels" (Writings of Pilgram Marpeck,
pp. 545-46). Marpeck seemed more realistic than Hubmaier about bodily fear of pain: the Spirit
could overcome this somewhat, but not entirely in this life (p. 329).

[122]Marpeck, Writings of Pilgram Marpeck, p. 79.

[123]Ibid., pp. 250, 129; cf. pp. 337, 366.

[124]"Flesh itself is not sin" (ibid., p. 108). Like Hubmaier and Denck, Pilgram wanted to clear God
from charges of ordaining evil (cf. pp. 471, 476). If flesh was created evil, he argued, God could
not be just in judging sin (Loserth, Pilgram Marbecks Antwort, p. 191). Neither could we anticipate
resurrection of our present bodies (ibid., p. 192). Marpeck found sin dwelling in the flesh, which
is not evil, in Rom 7, the text most cited by Reformers to support their view of sin (esp. Rom 7:17-
18, 20, 23). Still, Marpeck could occasionally portray flesh and blood wholly opposed to spirit,
even while alluding to this text (Writings of Pilgram Marpeck, pp. 321-22).

[125]Marpeck, Writings of Pilgram Marpeck, pp. 76, 79.

[126]Ibid., p. 79, cf. p. 206. The spiritualist tendency to soar above earthly life arises because "the flesh
seeks a quick release" (p. 91). Discord arises when our fallen flesh, blood and "understanding" mix
"into the knowledge of God" (p. 361). By ascribing humankind's chief sinful tendency to its highest capacity, the spirit, not the soul, Marpeck avoided Hubmaier's claim that this capacity was still
sinless. Marpeck generally affirmed trichotomy earlier, though he sometimes used spirit, soul and

did not often mention reason countering the flesh, for sin dwelt in both. Flesh, moreover, in many respects was not chiefly physical. It included, for instance, enthusiasm for "all ethical and human statutes."[127]

For Marpeck the will, like reason, was a function of the spirit and admirable as created. Yet he critiqued those who, much like Pelagius, attributed "all power and ability to man's free will."[128] Such persons were really lauding that energy by which reason strove to achieve salvation. What Spiritualists and some others called liberty Marpeck considered "freedoms of the flesh" and "most dire slavery before God."[129]

2. Human destiny. Since sin involved the desire to know, define and pursue good and evil apart from God, only those mature enough to attempt these could sin. In earlier writings Marpeck often inferred that children were free of sin and thus judgment because they possessed "the purity of creation" or were "innocent without guile."[130] Occasionally, he also attributed their safety to Jesus' reconciling work.[131] But later on Caspar Schwenckfeld called this ascription of sinlessness to children Pelagian.[132] Marpeck responded within an overarching conception of human destiny.

When Eve and Adam were created, they possessed only natural awareness of God.[133] They were merely the "image *[bild]*, not yet the essence *[wesen]*" of mature, supernatural humanity as God intended it.[134] Before they sinned, they were in a condition of "created simplicity."[135] Along with Western tradition, most other Anabaptists assumed that Adam and Eve, when created, were immortal adults. But when theology regards them thus, it usually construes sin as a drastic fall and salvation as restoration to their initial state.

Marpeck, however, sounded more like the early church father Irenaeus (c. 135-202 C.E.). Irenaeus portrayed our first parents as children, designed to receive the Spirit and attain immortality gradually through continuing obedience to God. Humankind was destined for a journey of spiritual, ethical and physical transformation. But Adam and Eve turned aside by obeying the serpent and came under its

---

body imprecisely. He formally affirmed it in his last work, mainly to stress that the whole person participates in sin and purification (e.g., Loserth, *Pilgram Marbecks Antwort*, pp. 113, 283, 286, 289, 446; cf. Marpeck, *Writings of Pilgram Marpeck*, pp. 192, 212).

[127]Marpeck, *Writings of Pilgram Marpeck*, p. 252, cf. p. 364.
[128]Ibid., p. 79.
[129]Ibid., p. 319, cf. pp. 323, 404, 406, 441.
[130]Ibid., p. 246.
[131]Ibid., p. 337.
[132]Loserth, *Pilgram Marbecks Antwort*, p. 189.
[133]Loserth, *Pilgram Marbecks Antwort*, pp. 220, 234, 235.
[134]Ibid., p. 203.
[135]Ibid., pp. 192, 195, 203.

rule of sin and death. Jesus, however, attained humankind's destiny by recapitulating the process intended for Adam and Eve, as in the Christus Victor motif. By following him in bodily obedience, energized by the Spirit, we too can gradually attain our supernatural destiny.

When our first parents left this path, the Spirit that led them withdrew. Humans, however, retained something of God's image or likeness. Marpeck correlated this more or less with a natural law, natural piety or, like Schiemer, Christ the light who enlightens everyone.[136] In responding to Schwenckfeld, however, Marpeck added that humans, including infants, are contaminated by original sin and thus are sinners by nature.[137] But how were they contaminated?

While Eve and Adam's transgression began as an inward desire, Marpeck insisted that it was not really sin until their bodies actualized it by taking the fruit. Just as their physical journey would have required spiritual receptivity, sin had to be expression of inward desires through outward acts.[138] Inwardly, this original sin also involved cooperation with the devil's spirit.[139] Marpeck, like many Anabaptists, conceived this as infection by Satan's poison.[140]

Whether this poison was quasi-physical or simply a spiritual attitude of greed and rebellion, it disordered the body-spirit relation. And since it affected the body, Marpeck believed that it could be passed on physically and affect infants. Eventually it brought physical death. Marpeck insisted, however, that this original sin produced only bodily, not spiritual, death. Further, the corruption in each person, not Adam's sin by itself, caused this physical demise.[141] In response to Schwenckfeld's charge of Pelagianism, Marpeck now affirmed that infants inherited an inclination to sin.[142] He acknowledged that sin shaped even children—yet reaffirmed that sin proper involved knowing volition.

However, Marpeck added that children also inherited the "breath or spirit" originally infused into Adam (Gen 2:7), along with Adam's "created simplic-

---

[136]Like Schiemer, Marpeck acknowledged some ability to let this light shine or not (ibid., p. 234, cf. *Writings of Pilgram Marpeck*, p. 58; cf. Beachy, *Concept of Grace*, p. 102; and p. 475 note 61 above). Yet natural piety or law could both arouse love for "honesty and natural virtue" and invent "all manner of idolatry" (Marpeck, *Writings of Pilgram Marpeck*, p. 479).

[137]Marpeck, *Writings of Pilgram Marpeck*, p. 245.

[138]Loserth, *Pilgram Marbecks Antwort*, pp. 251-52, 255.

[139]Ibid., pp. 251, 452.

[140]Ibid., p. 256.

[141]Ibid. Sin brought physical death by spreading organically from our first parents to everyone. Adam's transgression also carried a judicial penalty: earthly affliction (Gen 3:14-19), not eternal death. By tracing death, which was only physical, to Satan and Adam, Marpeck exonerated God from creating death, sin or evil (ibid., pp. 251-52, 256).

[142]"*Erbbresten*," lit. remnant of original sin, Loserth, *Pilgram Marbecks Antwort*, p. 198.

ity."[143] He then aligned this "breath" with that natural law or piety that granted everyone natural God-awareness and could produce natural and social virtues (but only incomplete supernatural salvation through hope in God's promise). This awareness was very like Schiemer's first grace, a term that Marpeck sometimes used for it. Yet it was intrinsic to the anthropological structure. I would not, then, attribute it entirely to God's initiative but rather to a region where divine and human activity intermingled, as found in Schiemer and Denck.

This awareness, then, implied some sort of semi-Pelagian ability—but only on the natural level. Unlike Hut, Schiemer and Denck, Marpeck distinguished two levels. On the supernatural level, his accounts of conversion, like Hubmaier's, Schlaffer's and Riedemann's, clearly prioritized grace.[144] There Marpeck sounded semi-Augustinian.

The Netherlands

Melchior Hoffman. Beginning his ministry as a Lutheran, Melchior Hoffman initially considered the will totally bound by original sin and humans wholly captive to Satan. He preached that when people accepted Christ's sacrifice, they were ransomed from Satan, justified and their wills set free.[145] Later he came to affirm, much like Hubmaier, that their spirits always remained righteous and yearned for God. Yet they were imprisoned in the body, while the soul's freedom was limited by lustful desires.[146] Still later, influenced somewhat by Denck, Hoffman taught free response to the Word, though he still granted the Word priority. Along with free will, ability to discern good and evil would be wholly restored.[147]

Thereafter, Hoffman expected perhaps more from converts than any other Anabaptist. They could pursue a second justification—by works—where, as we have seen, they would be awed by fear of God and learn that they could not live by their own strength.[148] Yet Melchior was confident that they could "lead themselves out of the realm of Satan," make a "complete, voluntary, loving surrender" to Christ and allow "their own will, life, desire, spirit and passion" to be "wholly slain."[149]

---

[143]Ibid., p. 207. Marpeck also ascribed childrens' status to God's promise of salvation in Christ (Gen 3:15), which preceded the promise to Abraham (ibid., pp. 198, 200-203). This provided all people another route to universal awareness of God. However, Marpeck's later writing also attributed forgiveness of children often to Christ (pp. 197-99).

[144]Marpeck, *Writings of Pilgram Marpeck*, pp. 120-26, 486-96.

[145]Klaus Deppermann, *Melchior Hofmann* (Edinburgh: T & T Clark, 1987), p. 191.

[146]Ibid., p. 224.

[147]Ibid., p. 229, cf. p. 373.

[148]Ibid., pp. 232-33.

[149]Melchior Hoffman, "The Ordinance of God," in *Spiritual and Anabaptist Writers*, ed. George Williams and Angel Mergal (Philadelphia: Westminster Press, 1957), pp. 186-87.

Unlike nearly all other Anabaptists, Hoffman often declared that conflict with the flesh would then cease. For though all people were activated by a sinful seed, its lusts and desires would die in the redeemed, so that they could no longer sin.[150] Yet Melchior interspersed such pronouncements with warnings about falling away and encouragement to persist to the end.[151]

Paradoxically, their free wills would lead such persons to relinquish them. They would live solely in God's will and become "one spirit, mind and will" with Christ, who had been "detached from his own will, and . . . absorbed into the will of the exalted Father."[152] Having surrendered their wills they would be wholly guided by the Spirit and live above the law.[153] In this heightened notion of divinization some basic human features may have dissolved into God. A sense of living above the law justified many questionable actions before, during and even after Münster.

Menno Simons and Dirk Philips. More than anyone considered in this study, Menno Simons and Dirk Philips sharply contrasted flesh and Spirit. Menno portrayed the seed of the serpent and the seed of the Word generating two natures that clashed in all respects. Someone born "of the earthly and devilish seed" was "altogether deaf, blind, and ignorant of divine things." Such a person "has nothing in common with God, but is . . . of a contrary nature . . . unmerciful, unjust, unclean, quarrelsome, contrary, disobedient, without understanding, and irreverent."[154] In contrast, those born of "the incorruptible seed" had the "divine nature. . . . Their thoughts are heavenly, . . . their works are holy and good, . . . they are holy vessels of honor, useful and ready to every good work."[155]

The corrupt nature emanated from Adam and Eve. They were created not as children, as Marpeck intimated, but wholly righteous and immortal after God's image.[156] They sinned chiefly through disobedience to God's command,[157] and lost

---

[150]Ibid., pp. 188, 201.

[151]Cf. p. 216 above.

[152]Hoffman, "Ordinance of God," pp. 187, 194, 190.

[153]"The law has no sovereignty over them any more, because they live unto righteousness and no longer unto sin. Therefore, the law cannot . . . show up blemishes and sports, because they are pure and live no more according to the flesh but according to the Spirit, and have been found unpunishable before the judgment seat of God" (ibid., p. 188; cf. Deppermann, *Melchior Hoffman,* p. 236).

[154]Menno Simons, *The Complete Works of Menno Simons,* ed. J. C. Wenger (Scottdale, Penn.: Herald, 1956), pp. 54, 55.

[155]Ibid., p. 58.

[156]Ibid., p. 503; Dirk Philips, *The Writings of Dirk Philips,* ed. Cornelius Dyck, William Keeney, and Alvin Beachy (Scottdale, Penn.: Herald, 1992), pp. 294, 352-53.

[157]Simons, *Complete Works,* p. 393; Philips, *Writings of Dirk Philips,* pp. 77, 294. Menno also called sin preferring the perishable to the imperishable (*Complete Works,* p. 68) and turning from the Creator to the creature (p. 155) as did South German-Austrian Anabaptists.

the reflection of God's image.[158] This image was no general human characteristic. Ultimately it was God's "invisible spiritual being" or that "eternal wisdom, power, and righteousness" that is "an unblemished mirror of [the Father's] divine glory," that is, God's eternal Son.[159] So dynamic a reflection could only be expressed actively through visible behavior. Consequently, when our first parents began sinning they lost this capacity. It could only be restored through Jesus' visible behavior, and subsequently through our following and thereby mirroring him.[160]

By losing immortality, Eve and Adam became subject to physical corruption. Menno and Dirk, like many other Anabaptists, sometimes called this satanic poison. They also substantialized it as an intrinsically evil nature (or flesh) passed on through literal human seed.[161] This corrupt nature, not our first parent's act, made all humans objects of a holy God's wrath.[162] Like Marpeck, Dirk and Menno maintained that it inclined infants toward sin.[163] Yet they also called children inherently pure or humble and pleasing to God—but only through Christ's atonement.[164]

This substantialized notion of sin makes it obvious why Jesus could not have come from human seed. That would have made him evil and placed him under wrath. How then could he have had a mother? Only if mothers did not contribute true seed to conception but merely a receptive matter. But then the sinful seed transmitted through the generations had to be correlated with the male sperm.

The Dutch sharpened the tension between their irredeemable fleshly nature and

---

[158]Philips, *Writings of Dirk Philips*, pp. 319, 320, 353.

[159]Ibid., p. 319, cf. pp. 289, 294, 386; Simons, *Complete Works*, pp. 56, 430, 441.

[160]Though this was Dirk's overriding emphasis, he also said that the image was restored to Adam and Eve through the promise of a savior (Philips, *Writings of Dirk Philips*, p. 353). Menno and Dirk, like Marpeck, affirmed Eve and Adam's salvation through the promise of Gen 3:15.

[161]While they seemed to consider flesh and body wholly evil, Dirk and Menno (rarely) spoke otherwise. Menno exhorted care for neighbors' bodies as well as souls and care for the poor because they were "brethren according to the flesh" (Simons, *Complete Works*, pp. 93, 366; cf. pp. 117, 526). Parents' "natural love" for children manifested love's true character (p. 338). Menno encouraged being "pious externally and internally, glorifying God both in body and spirit" (p. 184, cf. p. 327) and asked God to restore weak flesh to health (p. 616). Since the body was the Spirit's temple, both leaders encouraged cleansing of spirit and flesh (ibid., p. 561; Philips, *Writings of Dirk Philips*, pp. 367, 403-4).

Dirk insisted, against the spiritualist Sebastian Franck, that physical ceremonies were essential for the church because some goodness remained in material creation (*Writings of Dirk Philips*, pp. 455ff. he regarded Franck's spirituality, as Marpeck viewed the spiritualists,' as "fleshly": pridefully considering itself above physical ceremonies people really need [pp. 459-61]). Dirk critiqued followers who observed state church ceremonies for failing to praise God with body as well as spirit (p. 394).

[162]Despite Menno's strong disagreements with Reformed leader John à Lasco on many topics, they generally agreed on original sin (Simons, *Complete Works*, p. 420, cf. p. 563).

[163]Ibid., pp. 240, 272; Philips, *Writings of Dirk Philips*, pp. 92-93.

[164]Simons, *Complete Works*, pp. 135, 712; Philips, *Writings of Dirk Philips*, pp. 92, 299.

flawless new divine nature at least as acutely as other Anabaptists. Efforts to control the flesh fueled those banning controversies that marred Menno and Dirk's later years. Yet these two repeatedly countered charges that Anabaptists expected perfection, often with poignant realism: "They daily sigh and lament over their poor, unsatisfactory evil flesh, over the manifest errors and faults of their weak lives. Their inward and outward war is without ceasing. . . . Their fight and struggle is against the devil, world, and flesh all their days."[165]

Like many Anabaptists, these later Dutch mentioned spirit and soul more or less interchangeably.[166] They estimated reason more highly than most.[167] Consistent, with this, they believed that sinners knowingly reject truth and should be pressed to acknowledge it.[168] In fact, they urged repentance so earnestly that one wonders whether they, not unlike Hoffman, presupposed some degree of free will despite the flesh's corruption. Menno, for instance, exhorted people "to crucify the flesh with the affections and lusts, not to conform to this world, to put off the works of darkness and put on the armor of light."[169] This can sound semi-Pelagian.

Yet they conceived these actions as responses to the preached law, that aspect of the proclaimed Word that preceded grace.[170] I cannot find Menno or Dirk teaching that such acts could or should be performed prior to the Word's initiative. In fact, they often mentioned being given "such a heart, will, and desire that I willingly seek after that which is good."[171] This, they claimed, led to obeying God's commands freely "through the constraining power of love."[172] Moreover, like Marpeck, Dirk cri-

---

[165]Simons, *Complete Works*, p. 95.

[166]Menno mentioned Jesus' body, soul and spirit to emphasize that he was a complete human (ibid., pp. 428, 438). Dirk once listed these three to stress that the whole person would be resurrected (Philips, *Writings of Dirk Philips*, p. 626). Both affirmed bodily resurrection, apparently in some continuity with the present corrupted body (Simons, *Complete Works*, pp. 53, 61, 810; Philips, *Writings of Dirk Philips*, pp. 386, 408, 626). Yet Dirk's "new heavens" were "believers in whom God dwells," while the "new earth" was "hearts of Christians" (ibid., p. 318). He also said that at Jesus' return believers would be "conformed to the nature of angels" (p. 320)—perhaps not surprisingly if Jesus "died as man" but rose "as God" (p. 139).

[167]For Dirk reason was part of God's image (Philips, *Writings of Dirk Philips*, pp. 352-53), loss of knowledge was part of the Fall (pp. 97, 353) and knowledge of God basic to salvation (pp. 256-60, 282, 392, 465). Menno repeatedly appealed to the rationality of readers and government officials (with little success; see pp. 289-323 above).

[168]Simons, *Complete Works*, pp. 315, 678, 904, 982; Philips, *Writings of Dirk Philips*, pp. 117, 322. Menno testified that God made his sins known to him long before he truly repented of them (*Complete Works*, pp. 76-78).

[169]Simons, *Complete Works*, p. 113.

[170]Ibid., pp. 92, 336-43, 393; Philips, *Writings of Dirk Philips*, pp. 296, 358-60, 532.

[171]Simons, *Complete Works*, p. 310, cf. pp. 328, 610; Philips, *Writings of Dirk Philips*, pp. 69, 407, 532.

[172]Simons, *Complete Works*, p. 329, cf. p. 780; Philips, *Writings of Dirk Philips*, p. 70.

tiqued all freedom exercised apart from Christian truth and obedience as fleshly.[173]

Menno and Dirk, then, expected Christians to be active during and after conversion, but they meant to affirm that grace elicited this, in a general semi-Augustinian manner. Nonetheless, their stress on active response could be heard as an injunction to make oneself worthy of salvation and improve one's behavior through strenuous effort and fear of the ban.

Summary

Historic Anabaptists are often credited or critiqued for pioneering the modern notion of freedom, which resembles Pelagianism. How closely did they approximate Pelagianism or other traditional options?

While Denck and Schiemer intermingled human and divine willing too closely to be called Pelagian, they probably lent the former some initiating, semi-Pelagian role. For the most part, though, they pictured humans as dependent on and responsive to divine leading throughout the *Gelassenheit* process. Marpeck interconnected human volition with God's breath or light much like Denck and Schiemer, but only on the natural level. This could merely lead to a preliminary salvation through hope, far short of full, divinizing transformation. Hoffman perhaps viewed initial conversion in semi-Augustinian fashion. But afterward human wills responded to God's will in ways that often sounded Pelagian, until they virtually merged into it.

Otherwise, all Anabaptists surveyed, including Marpeck on the supernatural level, highlighted God's initiative more like semi-Augustinians. (Denck could even have been Augustinian, if freedom, evil and creatures were ultimately unreal for him.) Hubmaier, of course, highlighted human freedom's role in salvation. Yet I found extremely little evidence that he granted it rather than God an initiating (semi-Pelagian) role.

The mystical notion of God's immanence in the soul influenced Denck and Schiemer, possibly Marpeck (on the natural level alone), and perhaps Hoffman. Overall, though, Anabaptism's high behavioral expectations were rooted in soteriology—the new creations' initiating, transforming energy—not anthropology.[174] Freedom, for most, was possible only in response to a God who first made their response possible. This contradicts the modern notion of freedom as an autonomous human capacity.

Anabaptism's soteriological optimism was qualified (except for Hoffman) by our second anthropological theme, the ongoing struggle between human flesh and God's Spirit. Although they foregrounded concrete, bodily discipleship modeled

---

[173]Philips, *Writings of Dirk Philips*, pp. 392-93, 412, 556.
[174]Cf. p. 475 note 61 above.

on a very physical Jesus, Anabaptists seldom clearly differentiated flesh from the body. They often portrayed both as incorrigible. This in effect erected an *ontological barrier* between material, bodily existence and the spiritual energy through which they strove to transform it.[175] It fostered acute tensions between spiritual ideals and contradictory impulses, requiring continuous discipline and often the ban.

Only Marpeck, Schlaffer, Schiemer and perhaps Hut visibly loosened the virtual body-flesh equation. Marpeck unhooked sin far enough to conceive it as a drive—expressed more through reason than the body—to master reality and attain salvation apart from God. Body/flesh was not sinful. It could, however, become sin's vehicle when the human spirit yielded to the evil spirit. This distorted relations among not only human reason, will and body but also humans and other creatures, and Spirit and matter everywhere. Contrawise, when the spirit yielded to God's Spirit, the body became their vehicle for healing those distortions.

CONTEMPORARY APPROPRIATIONS

While theological anthropology includes humankind's personal and corporate sides, this chapter is focusing more on the former, at a point where Anabaptists differed from the Reformers and allegedly foreshadowed modernity. What can our study contribute to current theology? Compared with the Reformers, the Anabaptists' stress on active and, in some sense, free response to God was distinctive. Combined later with adulation of human initiative and equality deriving from other sources, it influenced authoritarian society's breakdown, democracy's rise, and eventually modernity.

By that time, freedom had become virtually Pelagian. Modernity's Enlightened progenitors and then their successors directed this freedom toward reshaping nature and society. Paradoxically, however, released from transcendent direction and restraints, freedom spawned new oppressions. The resulting technological progress, of course, benefited many people. But it also disrupted human ties with nature and numerous familial, communal and regional solidarities. This progress also despoiled much of the non-Western world, reduced many Westerners to faceless cogs in mammoth institutions and wrought armaments that wreaked unimagined destruction. Today the modern ideal of freedom without limits may be nearing its maximum expression through globalization.

During the twentieth century, numerous protests against such consequences arose. Yet nearly all lauded freedom in some manner. Existentialists championed the individual's ability to construct meaning amidst the Western world's suffocating impersonality. Liberation movements around the globe still exhort the op-

---

[175]See p. 190 above.

pressed to take charge of their own destiny. While unrestrained human freedom has produced serious bondage, almost everyone today prizes freedom.

Among contemporary Anabaptists, James Reimer warns that reductions of theology to historicist, social-ethical dimensions may strengthen modern freedom's drive toward domination. He promotes instead a classic voluntarism where human willing is "derived from and subject to" divine willing.[176] Reimer often critiques historic Anabaptists as progenitors of modern freedom.[177] Yet he allows that we can learn from some, like Hubmaier, who taught that "Our ability to choose comes from God, not our choice itself."[178]

It is not surprising that Gordon Kaufman's theology, which rejects Reimer's transcendent realm, is guided by a normative concept of the human. Reflexive self-consciousness, choice and taking responsibility for ourselves are central.[179] Kaufman endeavors to derive these from bio-history at length and to show thereby that freedom is not individualistic but must be "well-ordered": limited by the welfare of humanity as a whole and the environment.[180] Kaufman acknowledges that his notion of freedom is originally Western, as are the modernization and development processes it helped initiate.[181] These, however, he considers irreversible. This freedom then must guide these movements toward the optimum human future. Kaufman sharply critiques cultures and religions that resist these values (e.g., in India).[182] Despite his criticism of individualism and acquisitiveness, I wonder whether his theology ultimately encourages the spread of modernity.[183]

James McClendon develops no anthropology.[184] He frequently mentions liberation, but as freedom for discipleship and life in community, not autonomous free-

---

[176]Reimer, *Mennonites and Classical Theology*, p. 526. This emerged when "Classical Christian Orthodoxy creatively combined Hebraic personalism and voluntarism with Hellenistic metaphysics." Such formulations leave Reimer open to critiques that his view is not biblical and perhaps is even Constantinian (cf. Ben Ollenberger, "Mennonite Theology: A Conversation Around the Creeds," *MQR* 66, no. 1 [1992]; also p. 72 note 137 above.

[177]Reimer, *Mennonites and Classical Theology*, pp. 164, 167, 242, cf. pp. 526-27.

[178]Ibid., p. 534.

[179]Gordon Kaufman, *In Face of Mystery* (Cambridge, Mass.: Harvard University Press, 1993), p. 127.

[180]Ibid., pp. 127-32; cf. pp. 97-124, 141-93. Duane Friesen, like Kaufman, considers freedom a product of evolution, opposed to divine intervention (*Artists, Citizens, Philosophers* [Scottdale, Penn.: Herald, 2000], pp. 101-3) and creativity essential to being human (p. 87), especially creating culture (pp. 56-57). Unlike Kaufman, Friesen does not analyze freedom or its evolutionary emergence in detail.

[181]Kaufman, *In Face of Mystery*, pp. 133-34, cf. pp. 129, 289-90.

[182]Ibid., pp. 135-36, 220-21.

[183]Cf. pp. 277-80 above.

[184]James McClendon, *Systematic Theology*, vol. 2, *Doctrine* (Nashville: Abingdon, 1994), pp. 156-57.

dom from all relationships, beliefs or norms.[185] While not affirming original sin, McClendon credits it with illumining the priority of grace, the pervasiveness and inwardness of sin, and the shallowness of most views of human nature.[186]

Freedom is important for Nancey Murphy and George Ellis because the physical and social sciences are incomplete without ethical values.[187] Yet ethics is meaningless unless freedom is real.[188] Ethics in turn requires theological grounding. Anabaptism functions mainly to provide this for their ethic of *self-renunciation* against an *ontology of violence*.[189] This ethic presupposes that God does not coerce human actions, which entails, for them, that people are free to act in various ways.[190]

Norman Kraus, in contrast, considers human nature in light of the normative human, Jesus, especially as the primary of image of God (as did Dirk Philips) and the second Adam. Kraus roots human freedom and responsibility chiefly in God's call, particularly into covenant relationship.[191] Sin, conversely, arises from rejecting the personal God.[192] Human self-identity forms through relationships with God, other humans and other creatures.[193] Virtues develop through these interactions, rooted in acknowledgment of the absolute dependence of all creatures, especially oneself, on God. While Kraus underscores both divine priority and human response in these relationships, he considers Calvinist (or Augustinian) issues concerning their exact interconnections beyond theology's scope.[194]

Keeping in mind these current Anabaptist contributions and drawing on historic Anabaptist sources, what might I add? Since traditional schemas of divine-human interaction helped illumine these sources, I will continue dialogue with the tradition that has kept these issues most alive: the Reformed. Reformed theologians have affirmed not only the will's bondage but also predestination. However, the Reformed notion of divine sovereignty can be interpreted various ways. It can sanction traditional behavior and authoritarian structures, as it did in

---

[185]Ibid., pp. 120-21, 292-93.

[186]Ibid., p. 127.

[187]Nancey Murphy and George Ellis, *On the Moral Nature of the Universe* (Minneapolis: Fortress, 1996), pp. 91-103.

[188]Ibid., pp. 206-7.

[189]Ibid., pp. 107-40.

[190]For Murphy and Ellis freedom is incompatible with divine intervention (*On the Moral Nature of the Universe*, p. 207), as for Kaufman and Friesen, except perhaps at the quantum level (pp. 32-35).

[191]C. Norman Kraus, *God Our Savior* (Scottdale, Penn.: Herald, 1991), p. 117.

[192]Ibid., p. 122.

[193]Ibid., pp. 106, 108, 113.

[194]Ibid., pp. 83-84; cf. C. Norman Kraus, *Jesus Christ Our Lord* (Scottdale, Penn.: Herald, 1987), pp. 68-74, 87-97.

nineteenth-century America in the Reformed orthodoxy of Charles Hodge and others.[195] For many twentieth-century admirers, this kind of orthodoxy defined true evangelical theology. Such claims have increased recently, not least among socially conservative Reformed people who are wary of endeavors like evangelical-Catholic dialogue.[196]

Alternatively, the Reformed view of divine sovereignty can accent its dynamism in shaping reality and call humans to transform their worlds. This construal played a large role in authoritarianism's demise, and democracy and capitalism's rise (e.g., in Cromwell's attacks on British monarchy). Yet this freedom remained within transcendent limits. Many Reformed theologians, accordingly, were disturbed when nineteenth-century liberal theology seemed to promote unchecked modern freedom—especially when this freedom produced oppressive consequences, including world war. Reformed leaders of early twentieth-century neo-orthodoxy countered this not by valorizing traditional behavior and social structures, but by the dynamism of God's will and appropriate human response.[197] Since many Reformed theologians seek, against modernity, to reconceptualize Gods' priority in salvation and also freedom's importance in light of modern issues, they provide fruitful discussion partners for Anabaptists with similar broad aims.

Evangelical Reformed theologians have appropriated many neo-orthodox themes. Since this book proposes that Anabaptists can contribute to evangelical theology, it might seem advisable to interact with them. This might be most fruitful for Anabaptists, however, if we first consider their predecessors from our own vantage point. For this reason I will dialogue with Karl Barth (1886-1968) and Reinhold Niebuhr (1892-1971); Reformed evangelicals will appear in footnotes.[198] I will develop my own position on freedom and then body-soul-spirit, in-

---

[195]E.g., Hodge's interpretation of the ten commandments (Charles Hodge, *Systematic Theology* [London: James Clark, 1960], 3:259-65.

[196]This dialogue was mentioned on p. 134 note 160 above. Evangelical theology's increasingly Reformed slant is evident in "The Gospel of Jesus Christ: An Evangelical Celebration," *Christianity Today* 43, no. 7 (1999).

[197]Early on, Karl Barth inclined strongly to Swiss religious socialism. But he soon distanced theology from politics. This, say many critics, supported the status quo. Reinhold Niebuhr first favored communism but later became a major advocate of a generally conservative politics.

[198]Ray Anderson, *On Being Human* (Grand Rapids: Eerdmans, 1982), cf. footnotes 199, 200, 215, 229 of this chap.; Anthony Hoekema, *Created in God's Image* (Grand Rapids: Eerdmans, 1986); C. G. Berkouwer, *Man: The Image of God* (Grand Rapids: Eerdmans, 1962); Stanley Grenz, *Theology for the Community of God* (Nashville: Broadman & Holman, 1994), cf. footnote 207 of this chap. I will also consider James Boice, a conservative Reformed evangelical (cf. footnotes 214, 215, 218, 228 of this chap.) and Hendrikus Berkhof, whose critiques of his own tradition sometimes draw him close to Anabaptism (cf. footnotes 199, 221, 250 of this chap.).

vestigating biblical materials under each heading, and finally transcendence and sin, followed by some contemporary implications.

Twentieth-century Reformed Anthropology

Karl Barth. Critiquing human presumption, Karl Barth sought to reaffirm divine transcendence and Scripture. He did so by focusing on the dynamic divine will that breaks unpredictably into our world, which modern humans seek to control by sealing it off from God. So "Wholly Other" is God that we can know nothing of God unless God chooses to reveal it. Yet this revelation does not communicate propositions or principles. It is the personal, vivid, divine address that shatters self-enclosed pride.

Such an address does not strike its recipients as passive objects but actually constitutes them as active, responding subjects, much as Kraus also says.[199] Although in Reformed theology sinful humans cannot move toward God, Barth considered them beings who can become subjects when God encounters them. In this sense they bear the divine image.

Just as we know God solely through revelation, to understand human nature we must consult the same source. Barth accordingly developed his anthropology from neither fallen humans nor Adam, but from the one who revealed what it was to be fully human: Jesus. As for Kraus, Menno and Dirk, Barth's Jesus was God's true image, and Jesus showed that Christian life is discipleship.[200] Yet his call to discipleship is an offer of grace. We cannot follow on our own.

Since Jesus continually responded to God's address, he was continually constituted a free, responding subject. This meant, in apparent contrast to much Reformed theology, that the "decisive definition" of being a human subject was "free-

---

[199] Anderson, *Being Human,* pp. 56-58. Humans exist as response to what is said (Karl Barth, *Church Dogmatics* III/2 (Edinburgh: T & T Clark, 1960), p. 126) as answer (p. 175), as constituted in speech and hearing (p. 252) and in encounter, including with other humans (pp. 247-48). For many recent Reformed theologians some kind of response-ability is central to being human (cf. Hendrikus Berkhof, *Christian Faith* [Grand Rapids: Eerdmans, 1986], pp. 186-87). Emil Brunner called responsibility a formal divine image that remained despite loss of any material capacity to actualize it. Barth rejected this as an effort to attribute some redemptive capacity to humans apart from God. Any such structure, he insisted, arises only through God's address.

[200] On Jesus as the image, see Barth, *Church Dogmatics* III/1, pp. 201-2; III/2, pp. 206, 219, 222-23, 319, 323-24; cf. Anderson, *Being Human,* pp. 75-78. On discipleship, see Barth, *Church Dogmatics* IV/2, pp. 533-53. Barth sought to derive Christian ethics from Jesus in *Church Dogmatics* III/4. He wrestled with pacifism but finally allowed violence in some situations (pp. 397-469). Barth also called the "image" the male-female relationship, for this involves interaction between those who are both alike and different, distantly resembling divine-human and immanent trinitarian relations (*Church Dogmatics* III/1, pp. 181-91; cf. Kraus, *God Our Savior,* pp. 118-19).

dom." A "subject is something which freely posits itself in his own being."[201] Subjects are responsible. Their life "is one long responsibility."[202]

With contemporaneous existentialists, Barth also defined human existence as self-determination.[203] For when God acts, receptivity is not always the best reaction. An "active, spontaneous attitude" is sometimes better.[204] Self-determination, however, was not simply an individual matter, for people determine themselves largely through relations with others. Moreover, human subjectivity, shaped though God's Spirit, was not simply inward but, as Marpeck stressed, also outward and public.[205] To be human was to be intrinsically cohuman.[206]

Barth employed another existential term for self-determination: self-transcendence. Our being consists in seeking God.[207] We continually move toward the future. We are always possibility, never actuality.[208] This transcendence, however, never leaves the body behind. We always remain physical creatures.

Indeed, our bodies are linked inseparably with nonhuman creation. Through tilling the earth, humankind was initially commissioned to guide it toward a future fulfillment that Jesus would perfect.[209] Unlike most sixteenth-century Anabaptists and Reformed, Barth did not think that humankind's fall was from a perfect, immortal status. Humans were always designed to grow toward God's future, along with all creation.[210]

In this process human bodies and souls remain so entwined that Barth called people both embodied souls and ensouled bodies. This was a unity of "inner and outer," much as Marpeck said.[211] Yet a certain order is involved. Freedom belongs to the soul, and through the soul humans turn to God. The soul rules the body and the body serves the soul; people can be called souls of their bodies.[212]

Within this human structure Barth included a spirit. Yet it was so much the ac-

---

[201]Barth, *Church Dogmatics* III/2, p. 194.

[202]Ibid., II/2, p. 642, cf. III/2, pp. 174-79.

[203]Ibid., I/2, pp. 266, 364, 369, 373.

[204]Ibid., p. 267.

[205]Ibid., III/2, pp. 93-96, cf. Anderson, *Being Human*, pp. 62-63.

[206]Ibid., I/2, pp. 412-13; III/2, pp. 269-70, 285.

[207]Ibid., I/2, pp. 368, 391. This is similar to openness to the world, which Grenz, drawing on Pannenberg, makes central to his anthropology (*Theology for the Community of God*, esp. pp. 169-73; cf. Kraus, *God Our Savior*, pp. 117-18).

[208]Barth, *Church Dogmatics* III/2, pp. 110-13.

[209]Ibid., III/1, pp. 235-39. For Kraus also, Jesus as second Adam fulfilled this participation in the completion of creation (*God Our Savior*, pp. 111, 116, 123, 127).

[210]Barth, *Church Dogmatics* III/1, p. 200.

[211]Ibid., III/2, pp. 326-27.

[212]Ibid., pp. 332, 206, 351, 418-36.

tivity of God's Spirit that one should say, precisely, that a person "has spirit."[213] Since humans are not inherently immortal (even at creation) they can only live through this Spirit's continual renewal.[214]

For Barth, then, humans were extremely active. Apparently unlike much Reformed tradition, he found self-determination essential to being human, despite sin. Humans, moreover, continually transcend their given situations toward God and the future. Such notions were congenial to the twentieth century, with its activist orientation. Though Barth claimed to derive them strictly from the Word, he recognized their affinities with existential philosophy.

Examined further, however, Barth's notion of freedom appears increasingly Reformed. Champions of *freedom* often define it as the capacity to choose among options. The Reformed typically protest that this cannot truly be freedom, for it allows people to hurt themselves. True freedom, instead, must consist in attaining what is good. It must be not liberty for doing evil but liberation from whatever opposes good. Authentic freedom, then, can only confirm or actualize what God proposes.[215] For Barth this entailed that any such decision must be truly ours; God will not compel us. Barth often called such freedom what most Anabaptists did: obedience.[216]

Yet at times this obedience seemed to be not genuinely human activity, as most Anabaptists insisted, but really God's, as in Augustinianism. For since freedom is created by God's self-revelation, "In the last resort it can only be God's own freedom."[217] Like many Reformed, Barth also protested that if another agent were in-

---

[213]Ibid., pp. 334, 354, 356.

[214]Ibid., III/2, pp. 236-37, 259, 354-55; cf. Kraus, *God Our Savior*, p. 112. In contrast, for James Boice (a conservative, Reformed evangelical), as for most people at the Reformation, humans were created perfect and immortal (*God the Redeemer* [Downers Grove, Ill.: InterVarsity Press, 1978], pp. 23, 30). Whereas the spirit, for Barth, still animates all humans, for Boice it died when Adam sinned (p. 30).

[215]Barth, *Church Dogmatics* III/1, p. 264; cf. pp. 292-293; III/2, pp. 196-97; III/4, pp. 13-14; IV/1, p. 113; IV/4, p. 162; Anderson, *Being Human*, pp. 91-92; James Boice, *Awakening to God* (Downers Grove, Ill.: InterVarsity Press, 1979), pp. 144-45. Barth considered people free, apart from God's address, to realize all possibilities unique to humans, but not for communion with God. Boice agrees that humans are free in "nonessential things," but not in relation to God (*God the Redeemer*, pp. 44, 46; *Awakening to God*, p. 142). Like Barth, Boice views humans as subjects whose existence is based on decisions (*God the Redeemer*, p. 46).

[216]Barth, *Church Dogmatics* III/1, p. 263; III/2, pp. 179-86. However, God is not simply a commanding authority, for obedience involves "participation . . . in the being and life of God" (IV/1, p. 113). Barth said that we participate in God's "own divine essence" (III/1, p. 266).

[217]Ibid., I/2, p. 204. The "Bible nowhere speaks of anything that is real from man's side" (p. 205). "[T]he Word of God excludes every other freedom except its own" (p. 259, cf. p. 368). These emphases from Barth's earlier work were perhaps somewhat modified later, as when he mentioned "cooperation" with God positively (e.g., IV/1, p. 113). For an earlier account of divine initiative and human response, see I/2, pp. 274-275; for a later account see IV/2, pp. 553-84, 591-98.

volved, God's sovereign power would be denied.[218] Further, Barth appeared to evaporate the reality of human decisions when he maintained, somewhat like Denck, that any attempt to choose against God is to opt for "that which is in itself nothing."[219] Evil was a possibility that the all-sovereign God rejected at creation. Sin then was "an ontological impossibility," the "irrational and inexplicable affirmation of the nothingness which God as creator has negated."[220]

Despite his attempts to explain freedom in the twentieth century, Barth's efforts to underline divine sovereignty could resuscitate traditional Reformed problems. He lauded predestination as "first and last and in all circumstances the sum of the gospel."[221] There could be "no question of a child of God falling away."[222] Barth risked portraying decisions and realities that oppose God so chimerically that decisions for God appeared equally unreal. While traditional categories can hardly capture Barth's complexity, I suggest that he often sounded strongly Augustinian, but at times somewhat semi-Augustinian, when seeking to present freedom as real.

Reinhold Niebuhr. By adapting existential concepts somewhat differently from Barth, Reinhold Niebuhr stressed freedom in a way less likely to appear unreal. Niebuhr found his era valuing either the human body, seen as charged with positive potential (romanticism), or the mind, viewed as transcending the body, the source of error, toward truth (idealism). Like Marpeck, however, Niebuhr evaluated this confidence in mind/reason as pride, and the mind as the more serious source of error.[223]

Niebuhr attributed this striving to the spirit, modeled somewhat on existential self-transcendence, and called it "primarily a capacity for and affinity with the divine."[224] Though this spirit was finite, it stretched into eternity.[225] For Niebuhr, like Barth, the body was essential to being human. Unlike most Anabaptists, Niebuhr

---

[218]Ibid., I/2, p. 260. "Over against God the creature cannot produce or claim any inherent dignity, anything that is good within itself. It is obviously the creature's destiny to owe all that is good in its nature and existence as a creature to God alone.... [B]efore God even the good of its creatureliness as such is null and void" (II/2, p. 28). For Boice, God will not allow "the smallest human contribution" to salvation" (*God the Redeemer*, p. 51). Yet he discusses how we work with God in sanctification (*Awakening to God*, pp. 121-22).

[219]Barth, *Church Dogmatics* II/2, p. 316.

[220]Ibid., III/2, pp. 136, 146, 143.

[221]Ibid., II/2, p. 12. For a Reformed critique of predestination, see Berkhof, *Christian Faith*, pp. 203, 484.

[222]Barth, *Church Dogmatics* I/2, p. 268.

[223]Reinhold Niebuhr, *The Nature and Destiny of Man* (New York: Scribner's, 1941), p. 147.

[224]Ibid., p. 152. The spirit is a principle of the soul, distinguished though not separated from it (p. 151). The will is an activity of the spirit (pp. 258-60).

[225]Ibid., pp. 122, 124, 157.

recognized that by "flesh," Paul normally meant a principle of sin, different from the body.[226] Niebuhr, however, located the human dilemma elsewhere than Barth— in a tension between humanity's finitude, interconnected with matter, and its transcendent spiritual reach. Humans, limited by their bodies and minds stretch toward infinite possibilities. Yet they must choose specific courses of action.

To elucidate this dilemma, Niebuhr enlisted a favorite existentialist theme: anxiety *(Angst)*. Anxiety was the "internal precondition of sin."[227] It arises when we are confronted with choices. For we might reach too high, failing to accomplish our desires, or too low, forfeiting greater possibilities. Frightened by this dilemma, humans sin most often by striving toward the infinite on their own (pride), but at times by succumbing to material pleasures and fears (sensuality).[228]

For Niebuhr, however, anxiety did not need to produce sin. It was ideally possible "that faith in the ultimate security of God's love would overcome all the immediate insecurities of nature and history."[229] For humans were created to transcend many limitations and attain self-realization—though only in obedience to God.[230]

When they experience anxiety, people fear making wrong choices. When they choose wrongly, Niebuhr continued, they try to stifle this awareness by pretending, not always consciously, that their choices were better than they actually were. They act as if such choices and values conformed to a universal standard of righteousness. Niebuhr called this self-pretention. It was a chief expression of pride: that effort to surpass finite limitations and attain the infinite, including righteousness. Though people know their choices are basically selfish, they keep presenting them as unselfish and good.

For Niebuhr, pride and self-justifying excuses for it attained the greatest "heights of sinful pretension" in nation-states.[231] The sociopolitical realm, conse-

---

[226]Ibid., pp. 152, 245-46.

[227]Ibid., p. 182.

[228]Ibid., pp. 179, 185. Precisely speaking, pride and sensuality are the main forms taken by sin, which is lack of trust, or unbelief, in God. Unbelief, in turn, is influenced by a false interpretation of God "antecedent to any human action" (p. 180). Niebuhr identified this reality with Satan, whom he did not regard as a being (pp. 179-81, 252-54). Kraus finds distrust of God and exceeding creaturely limits central to Genesis 1–3 (Kraus, *God Our Savior*, pp. 127-30). For him "Selfish desire is the matrix of temptation and spawns sin (James 1:14)" (p. 126). Boice can call sin "unfaithfulness" (*God the Redeemer*, p. 20), but identifies apostasy, rebellion and pride as its three "root elements," with pride as its heart (p. 24). Sin is hatred and outright rebellion (pp. 21-22, cf. pp. 32, 50): "the unregenerate . . .do not even try" to meet God's standards (*Awakening to God*, p. 208).

[229]Niebuhr, *Nature and Destiny*, 1:183. I cannot agree with Anderson that "Niebuhr posits sin as the very presupposition of the self" and calls anxiety "the inevitable source of sin." But Anderson rightly points out that such a finite-infinite tension was not basic to created humanity for Barth, whom he largely follows (*Being Human*, pp. 93-103).

[230]Niebuhr, *Nature and Destiny*, 1:126, 251.

[231]Ibid., p. 218.

quently, was too pervaded by power politics for Christians to follow Jesus' teachings there. Yet it was still important to work for the best balance of power among evil forces. Niebuhr's self-transcendence directed individuals mainly upward, toward God's commands and ideals. In a world that fell far short, it also aimed forward, toward a somewhat better historical, material future—but more weakly.

Overall, sin for Niebuhr, as for Marpeck, involved succumbing to matter or the body far less than endeavoring to transcend them too far.[232] As such, sin could hardly be inherited by any physical process.[233] It was possible only because humans retained some freedom: to strive after the infinite and distort finite, corrupt values and motives into infinite goods.[234] Consequently, though our "essential nature," or God's image, often functioned badly, it had never been lost.[235]

Niebuhr, however, also highlighted original sin as the inexplicable paradox that all people sin (inevitably—but not necessarily) and thus are responsible. Original sin is a sickness of the will: the apparent absurdity that wills, while free, are somehow self-bound to evil.[236] People were free enough to recognize their own bondage and feel remorse. Yet only awareness of God's love could bring repentance.[237] Grace was chiefly mercy, or forgiveness, which releases people from the anxiety underlying their sinful strivings.[238]

Grace, for Niebuhr, was also power for new living. But emphasis on this, he warned, very often encouraged self-pretention (among, say, Catholics, liberals and Anabaptists). Accordingly, Niebuhr repeatedly cautioned that the will's sickness is never fully healed here below.[239] Among the major denials of this, Niebuhr mentioned the tendency to limit sin and all continuing imperfection to the body. This promotes legalism, for it fosters the illusion that the will can follow the law, yet it must obey it scrupulously to restrain the incorrigible body.[240]

In terms of traditional categories, Niebuhr's insistence on the will's bondage (which only grace can release) yet also on some real freedom, including some limited ability (when released by grace as mercy) to interact with grace as power—these seem most nearly semi-Augustinian.

---

[232]Ibid., p. 147.
[233]Ibid., p. 262.
[234]Ibid., pp. 270, 276.
[235]Ibid., pp. 269-76; *Nature and Destiny of Man* (New York: Scribner's, 1943), 2:117.
[236]Ibid., 1:241-44.
[237]Ibid., p. 257.
[238]Ibid., 2:100-104, 119-21.
[239]Ibid., pp. 110-19.
[240]Ibid., pp. 199-203.

An Anabaptist Response

Human freedom. Having considered (1) historic Anabaptist notions of freedom and (2) several recent ones, I will first treat freedom's role in human life and its relationship to divine freedom. Like historic Anabaptists, however, I will be concerned with how human and divine wills interact, and will consider most further questions about God's will and knowledge—for example, about predestination—beyond theology's scope.

I. Biblical considerations. For historic Anabaptists, and Barth, Kraus and myself, Jesus provides the norm for determining what it means to be human. Very early Christians expressed this by an Adam Christology. They contrasted Adam, who led humans away from God, with the second Adam, who brought them back into communion with God and attained the destiny intended for everyone (esp. Rom 5:12-21; I Cor 15:20-22, 45-49; Phil 2:7-9). The New Testament summarized Jesus' human activity as obedience (Rom 5:19; Phil 2:8; Heb 5:8-9) and also faithfulness—especially in Hebrews, where Jesus climaxed the history of those walking by faith (Heb 11:1–12:3; cf. Heb 3:1-6) and in Paul's focus on "the faithfulness of Jesus Christ."[241] Jesus was salvation's pioneer, breaking open the path to God, learning obedience through concrete human suffering.[242]

The Old Testament often represented such faithfulness as response to Yahweh's call. This call commenced when God breathed life into Adam (Gen 2:7). But when Adam and Eve sinned, they hid from God's call (Gen 3:8-10). Nonetheless, humans kept on being summoned by God's call or breath (often named "spirit" [*rûah*])—called to answer with their breath, or *rûah*, through confession and praise.[243] Especially in Wisdom writings, responsible hearing was "the root of true humanity."[244]

Israel's history began with a call to Abram and Sarai (Gen 12:1-3), whose response became the paradigm of faithfulness (Gen 15:6; Rom 4:17-25; Heb 11:8-19). Many of Yahweh's saving activities and the missions of Israel's leaders began with a challenging call.[245] Some Old Testament texts applied to Jesus stressed obe-

---

[241]*pisteōs Iēsou Christou:* esp. Rom 3:22, 26; Gal 2:16; 3:1, 5, 11, 23-26; Phil 3:9. Jesus' activity manifested God's faithfulness to humankind. But since he, as a human, accomplished it in faithfulness to his Father and the Spirit, faithfulness is also the human way to God; cf. pp. 140-43 above.

[242]See esp. Heb 2:10, which is amplified in Heb 3:1-2; 4:15; 5:7-9; 10:19-23; 12:1-3; cf. Acts 3:15; 5:31 (more fully discussed in Thomas Finger, *Christian Theology* [Scottdale, Penn.: Herald, 1989], pp. 93-96; and *Self, Earth and Society* [Downers Grove, Ill.: InterVarsity Press, 1997], pp. 262-66).

[243]Hans Walter Wolff, *Anthropology of the Old Testament* (Philadelphia: Fortress, 1974), pp. 59-60.

[244]Ibid., p. 74.

[245]E.g., Moses (Ex 3:1–4:17), which initiated the exodus of the nation, Samuel (I Sam 3:1-14), Isaiah (Is 6:1-13), Jeremiah (Jer 1:4-19) and Mary (Lk 1:26-38).

dient hearing (e.g., Is 50:4-5; Ps 40:6-8; cf. Heb 10:5-10). In the Old Testament, "Self-knowledge does not come about through self-reflection, but through the call which opens up a new vista."[246] I hardly need add that Jesus and the apostles continually called people to repentance and new faith journeys.

Though such calls were to obedience, this hardly meant rigid subordination to a domineering law. Biblical calls were personal addresses. Responses required risk, energy and creativity. To indicate this, I prefer to call such an orientation toward God "faithfulness," not obedience. Something like freedom is certainly central to biblical anthropology, though it arises from God's address, as Barth insisted.

Since Jesus actualized faithfulness most fully, and thereby the destiny intended for all people, Christian theology can infer that some general openness toward or dependence on God belongs to our created anthropological structure.[247] For human response to be possible, something like Barth's freedom, or self-determination, must be included. Since God's call is toward the future, self-determination must involve what Barth, Niebuhr and Kraus called self-transcendence.

But while freedom belongs to our created structure, dialogue with Reformed theology shows that this needs further definition, for quite different understandings of freedom are possible. Moreover, a definition of freedom's basic structure by itself will not tell us to what extent free acts are actual possibilities for humans now, given sin and the powers' effects. Let us first consider freedom's created structure, then its actuality.

2. What is freedom? For most opponents of Reformed tradition, freedom, at least in large part, is the capacity to choose among options. The biblical theme of faithfulness, however, shows that authentic responses to God lead to deepening relationships with God and others, and expand capacities for these. With the Reformed I agree that freedom in the foremost sense is fuller and deeper than the simple possibility of selecting among alternatives. Freedom must be continual choosing and enjoyment of God and of that to which God calls. But is this freedom opposed to the capacity to decide among options, as Reformed theologians often argue or imply?

If Jesus provides freedom's norm, the freest choices will involve self-giving and self-emptying (see esp. Phil 2:5-11). Freedom will be authentic dedication of oneself and true love to God and others. But how could we so commit ourselves unless we could, at least potentially, do otherwise, unless it were truly possible to act differently? Theology need not polarize freedom as complete dedication to God against a capacity to choose among options. The first is in-

---

[246]Wolff, *Anthropology of the Old Testament,* p. 73.
[247]Finger, *Christian Theology,* 2:93-96; *Self, Earth and Society,* pp. 262-66, 311.

deed freedom in the fullest sense. But it requires the second as one condition of its very possibility.

Barth often seemed not to attribute real freedom to humans but to God, in Augustinian fashion, to safeguard divine sovereignty.[248] In Anabaptist perspective, and much as Barth affirmed elsewhere, God's sovereignty operated most profoundly when God became vulnerable to human evil in Christ and suffered quite realistically under it—yet still brought and brings to pass the divine purposes.[249] For theology in Anabaptist perspective, consideration of God's nature must begin from below, with God as known in Jesus.[250] From this angle it must endeavor to express Scripture's representations of human freedom, even if it cannot determine their exact relationships with God's nature. The Bible grants humans enough freedom to oppose and really wound even God. Anabaptist-oriented theology, then, will not be Augustinian, if this means claiming ontologically that God virtually performs human acts. Biblical representations of human willing entail some genuine structural capacity for interaction with the divine will—even though the former's highest acts involve surrender to the latter, and Scripture does not tell us exactly how they interact.

3. Divine-human interaction. Historic Anabaptists insisted on the preceding point, and were often accused of asserting, like Pelagians, that humans could actually interact with God as they had been (structurally) created, unimpaired by sin or the powers. Given their strong apprehension of transforming grace, however, historic Anabaptists are better characterized as semi-Augustinian, though a few seemed semi-Pelagian. In other words, most Anabaptists believed that freedom's actual salvific interaction with God was initiated by God (semi-Augustinianism), not us (semi-Pelagianism). Even though the Bible leaves some questions about divine-human interaction unanswered, does it say enough to decide between these two alternatives?

I propose that Scripture substantiates something like semi-Augustinianism at least two ways. First, by showing that salvation originated, historically, from "God's righteousness through the faithfulness of Jesus Christ."[251] Salvation emerged from a trial that condemned the powers—along with all humankind they held captive (Rom 3:4-20). Humans were unable to escape the bondage of death (Rom 5:14, 18), sin (Rom 6:17, 19-20) or the flesh (Rom 8:6-8, 13),

---

[248]Barth, *Church Dogmatics* I/2, pp. 204-5, 260.

[249]Ibid., pp. 31-32.

[250]This was Barth's emphasis, but I do not find him consistent when he comes to this issue. For a Reformed treatment that comes close to Anabaptism, see Berkhof, *Christian Faith*, pp. 141-43.

[251]Cf. pp. 139-42 above.

all intensified by the law (Rom 7:5–8:2), and of many other powers (Rom 8:37-38).[252] God's saving righteousness intervened without assistance from anyone.

Second, when the New Testament considers actual human responses to these events, it often ascribes freedom's origin to God's Spirit. The Spirit releases us from sin and death's invincible bondage (Rom 8:2), reorients our conduct away from "the flesh" (Rom 8:6-17) and propels the whole creation toward our glorious liberty (Rom 8:21-27). For "where the Spirit of the Lord is, there is freedom" (2 Cor 3:17). Galatians, "the charter of Christian liberty," repeatedly attributes freedom from law and flesh to God's Spirit.[253]

These two biblical lines, I believe, can lead Anabaptist theology to affirm that salvation proceeds solely from God's initiative—yet that the consequent human acts are genuine responses by their agents. Theology can paraphrase this by saying that salvation includes genuine liberation of our structural capacities for response, which enable us, in some meaningful sense of the word, to choose among at least some options in relating to God. Still, as Reimer says, "Our ability to choose comes from God, not our choice itself."[254]

While God doubtless bestows this ability many ways, some not entirely conscious, biblical accounts, like historic Anabaptist accounts, normally attribute it to God's Word. This Word is or directly conveys the risen Christ and the good news of his atoning work. This atonement has at least three aspects, corresponding to the traditional models: forgiveness, awareness of God's love, and liberation from evil powers. Biblical freedom, then, is not generic volitional energy. It is response within and on the basis of a relationship where one feels forgiven, loved and free from domination by (though not always opposition from) hostile forces.

I could not, then, concur with Hubmaier if his desire for renewal by God's Word provided some actual basis for salvific response. However, desire and the spirit's ceaseless longing for God were likely ways of expressing that all humans, though unable to initiate salvation, are still God-related structurally. I agree with this intent. As Niebuhr indicated, our created structure enables us to choose many things, including some things related to God. Yet these choices, apart from grace, never actually break free enough of inner and outer bondage to connect salvifically with God.

In my theology the necessity of God's initiative and also distinct human response underscore divine-human differentiation. Semi-Pelagianism often does not express

---

[252]For more detail, see pp. 310-12 and esp. pp. 355-60 above.
[253]Gal 4:6-7, 22-31; 5:1, 13, 16; cf. Finger, *Christian Theology*, 2:133-34; *Self, Earth and Society*, pp. 272-73.
[254]Reimer, *Mennonites and Classical Theology*, p. 534.

this clearly enough.[255] This distinction, also formulated by Chalcedon, is consistent (though not identical) with my broader differentiation of Spirit from material creation.[256] Contemporary Anabaptist theology, in my view, should portray humans relating intimately with and even being divinized by God. Yet to conceptualize this as genuine interaction and avoid unrealistic expectations of transformation into, rather than by, God, it must insist on human nature's continuing integrity.

Historic Anabaptists, however, often attributed this interactive capacity to the spirit (or soul) and denied it to the body/flesh, even in the salvation process. This hardly sounds like continuing integrity. To affirm it, I must revisit these issues of anthropological structure.

Anthropological structure. Freedom as response to God's call is much like what Barth, Niebuhr and more recently Kraus named "self-transcendence." God repeatedly calls all people beyond their current, finite situations toward the divine infinity. This call, though, conflicts with features of the human condition. Niebuhr linked many of these with our finite bodies, but also our spirits or "capacity for and affinity with the divine," which stretch into eternity, though they too are finite.[257] With the help of this lens, I will consider the biblical words that correspond most closely with anthropology's main concepts.

Soul, in English Bibles, often translates the Hebrew *nepeš. Nepeš* can refer to the whole person as desiring, longing, or striving for life.[258] It can also indicate "the seat and action of other spiritual experiences and emotions."[259] Yet *nepeš* is not "an indestructible core of being, in contrast to the physical life." This word always refers to a "living being who has neither acquired, nor can preserve, life by himself, but who is eager for life, spurred on by vital desire."[260]

---

[255]I appreciate Denck's effort to insist that the divine Word existing *in* everyone was not *of* anyone. Still, insofar as the Word acted universally and was not uniquely identified with Jesus, it is hard to distinguish it from a general human capacity. Schiemer blurred the same lines by mentioning conscience, Christ the light and the first grace interchangeably. Perhaps Marpeck did so on the natural level by aligning a first grace with God awareness, though he contrasted this sharply with the Spirit-initiated supernatural level.

Paradoxically, Denck perhaps submerged divine-human differences another way: by suggesting that evil and creaturely distinctions were nothing, implying that God, or the One, alone was truly real. This sounds not wholly unlike Barth's insistence that evil was an ontological impossibility and that all freedom was God's. Such a strong (Augustinian?) move seeks to counteract divine-human mergings, such as in the South German-Austrian mystical heritage. Yet by evaporating humanity's distinctness from God it can merge them another way.

[256]See pp. 419-21 above.

[257]Niebuhr, *Nature and Destiny,* 1:152, 122, 124, 157.

[258]Wolff, *Anthropology in the Old Testament,* pp. 11-17 (e.g., 1 Sam 1:15; Ps 42:1-2; Prov 13:4, 19).

[259]Ibid., p. 17.

[260]Ibid., pp. 20, 24.

In the New Testament, *soul* often translates *psychē*. *Psychē* frequently denotes a person's life generally (Mt 2:20; Acts 20:24; Rom 11:3). It can also refer to inner deliberations and feelings (Lk 12:19; Jn 10:24; 2 Pet 2:8). If *psychē* carries a more particular meaning, this is probably "that specifically human state of being alive . . . as a striving, willing, purposing self."[261] As a person's true life, *psychē* can persist beyond death, but it can also be lost then (Mk 8:35-38). The *psychē*, then, is not inherently immortal. Words from this stem can mean "perishable," even carnal existence apart from God (1 Cor 2:14; 15:44-49; Jas 3:15; Jd 19). *Psychē* can become immortal only by continually receiving life from God (Lk 21:19; Jas 1:21). This corresponds with the way Marpeck, Barth, Kraus and most forms of Christus Victor viewed humans as created: not as immortal but designed to become so through living in response to God's Spirit.

The New Testament texts just cited, which underscore *psychē's* mortality, distinguish it from forms of *pneuma*, usually translated "spirit," for the latter connect humans directly with God.[262] *Pneuma* most often means God's Spirit, as does the Old Testament *rûaḥ*. When used of humans, *rûaḥ* indicates, above all, that dimension especially open to God's *rûaḥ*.[263] In the New Testament the human *pneuma* usually denotes the same.[264] Scripture provides some rationale then for calling humankind's orientation toward God "spirit," as did Barth, Niebuhr, Hubmaier and many other Anabaptists. However, this spirit can become unclean (1 Cor 7:34; 2 Cor 7:1; cf. Heb 12:23; Jas 4:12) and finally lost (1 Cor 5:5). It is not always pure, yearning wholly for God, as Hubmaier claimed, but can be directed away, as Marpeck and Niebuhr maintained.

Scripture, then, sometimes distinguishes *pneuma/rûaḥ* from *psychē/nepēš* —but not in a consistent way that denotes separable substances, as Hubmaier thought. For

---

[261]Rudolf Bultmann, *Theology of the New Testament* (New York: Scribner's, 1951), 1:205; stressing Phil 1:27.

[262]In Jude 19, *psychikoi* are those who lack God's Spirit (*pneuma*; cf. Jas 3:15). In 1 Cor 2:14, *psychikoi* neither receive nor understand the gifts of God's Spirit (*pneuma*), though *pneumatikoi* do (in 1 Cor 2:10-14). In 1 Cor 15:44-46, *psychikos* denotes merely the physical, corruptible body, but *pneumatikos*, the body which has put on "incorruptibility" from God.

[263]The new *rûaḥ* which will animate Israel will be Yahweh's own *rûaḥ* (Ezek 36:26-27; cf. Ps 51:10-12). This is the source of the life poured out where humans can only see death (Wolff, *Anthropology of the Old Testament*, pp. 33-34; as is the New Testament *pneuma* [Rom 8:6, 10-12; Jn 3:5-6; Rev 11:11]). *Rûaḥ* is the vital force without which no creatures could live (Job 34:14-15; Ps 104:29-30; Is 42:5). The human *rûaḥ* is something like what we call "will": it can be patient or proud (Eccles 7:8; Prov 16:18), endure or be broken (Prov 18:4). It is stirred up when Yahweh calls someone to a task (Judg 3:10; 6:34; Jer 51:11; Ezek 1:5), and energized to produce beauty (Ex 31:3; 35:31).

[264]E.g., Mk 14:38; Lk 23:46; Acts 7:59; 1 Cor 14:14-15. This is perhaps clearest in Rom 8:16: when we cry, "Abba! Father!" God's Spirit witnesses with our spirit that we are God's children. However, the functional intertwining in such passages sometimes leaves it unclear whether *pneuma* (like *rûaḥ*) indicates the human or divine.

instance, Paul sometimes closed letters with "the grace of God be with your spirit" (*pneuma*, Gal 6:18; Phil 4:23; Philem 25), but at others with "the grace of God be with all of you" (Rom 15:33; 1 Cor 16:23; 2 Cor 13:14). *Pneuma* in the first three benedictions clearly referred to the whole person(s), as it did in the last three benedictions. Similarly, every *psychē* in Acts 2:43 and Acts 3:23 means "everyone." Paul could write "my spirit had no rest" (2 Cor 2:13 [*pneumati*, though sometimes translated "mind"]), and a bit later "our bodies had no rest" (2 Cor 7:5). He was not referring to two distinct substances, but simply meant: "I (we) became tired." Soul and spirit are dimensions or particular orientations of one, unified human being—not parts of it.[265]

This view of the person is borne out by a term that incorporates its different dimensions, usually translated "heart." The Hebrew *lēḇ* (or *lēḇāḇ*) can, like *nepeš* (soul), mean desire and longing (Ps 21:2; Prov 12:12) but also emotions, especially courage and fear (2 Sam 17:10; Ps 40:12; Is 7:2) and what we call conscience and thought.[266] *Lēḇ* (or *lēḇāḇ*) also refers to a person's depths, which can contrast with outward appearance.[267] Its usage, finally, is not simply figurative, not entirely loosened from the physical organ, the heart. The New Testament *kardia* carries the same meanings and is the person's true center (Mt 12:34; Mk 7:18-23; 1 Pet 3:4).[268] *Lēḇāḇ/kardia* provides the main biblical source for the concept of person, or personal center, which I developed in Christology with help from current psychology.[269] Salvation occurs only when God transforms its depths.[270]

---

[265]Cf. Finger, *Christian Theology*, 2:121-23; *Self, Earth and Society*, pp. 272-73; Gustavo Gutiérrez, *We Drink from Our Own Wells* (Maryknoll, N.Y.: Orbis, 1984), pp. 61-64. Generally speaking, Scripture employs anthropological terms too loosely to denote distinct components, though at times consistently enough to differentiate broad functions. I do not deny that humans might have separable souls or spirits, but I consider this question beyond theology's range.

[266]Phrases like one's "heart smote" someone indicate something like conscience (1 Sam 24:5; 2 Sam 24:10; cf. 2 Chron 34:27). Whereas people today often contrast heart with head or feeling with thinking, *lēḇ* (or *lēḇāḇ*) "includes everything that we ascribe to the head and the brain—power of perception, reason, understanding, insight, consciousness, memory, knowledge, reflection, judgment, sense of direction, discernment" (Wolff, *Anthropology of the Old Testament*, p. 51). *Lēḇ* (or *lēḇāḇ*) appears most frequently of all Old Testament anthropological terms (ibid., p. 41; cf. Finger, *Christian Theology*, 2:122-126; *Self, Earth and Society*, pp. 273-74).

[267]Wolff, *Anthropology of the Old Testament*, pp. 43-44.

[268]*Kardia* can indicate what we call emotions (Jn 16:6; Rom 10:1; Jas 3:14), will or intentions (Jn 13:2; Acts 8:22; 1 Cor 7:37), thought (Mt 24:48; Lk 2:51; Acts 7:23), unconscious levels (Mk 11:23; 1 Cor 4:5; Heb 4:12) and physical drives (Mt 5:28; Acts 14:17; Rom 1:24). When people are truly united, this is "in heart" (Acts 4:32; Phil 1:7; Col 2:2).

[269]See pp. 415-17 above.

[270]Mt 13:14-15 and parallels, Jn 12:39-41 and Acts 28:26-27 all quote Is 6:9-10. Heb 8:8-12 and 10:16-17 quote Jer 31:31-34; cf. Mk 11:23; Lk 24:25; Acts 7:51; Rom 10:6-10. God alone knows and searches the *kardia*'s depths (Lk 15:17; Acts 1:24; 15:8; Rom 8:27; 1 Thess 2:4; Rev 2:23).

The unity of the person is further confirmed and amplified by the New Testament terms for body *(sōma)* and flesh *(sarx)*. Both can denote not only individual organisms but also channels that unite persons to realities beyond themselves, and thereby the corporate solidarity of such realities.[271] *Sarx* (flesh), however, also accents human frailty.[272] Paul often distinguished it further from *sōma* (body) to mean passions contrary to God (Rom 13:14; Gal 5:16, 24), expressed through idolatrous reliance on religious customs (Rom 2:28; 7:5-6; Gal 3:3; 6:13; Col 2:18-23) or human achievement and pedigree (2 Cor 11:18; Phil 3:3-7). Most often, *flesh* indicates the tendency to treat physical, measurable things as ultimate—"inordinate attachment to creatures" in South German-Austrian Anabaptist parlance. Fleshly conflicts destroy community (1 Cor 3:3; Gal 5:19-20). Ultimately, *sarx* is a superhuman power.[273]

In contrast, *sōma* (body) most often designates the human organism as created. This can be filled with either fleshly strivings or God's Spirit. When invaded by the former, under sin's dominion, the *sōma* can become the "body of sin" (Rom 6:6) or "body of death" (Rom 7:24; cf. Rom 8:13) and unify people in sin (1 Cor 6:16). However, God's Spirit can also indwell our bodies (Rom 8:11; 1 Cor 6:19) and join us to Christ (1 Cor 6:13, 17) and his church, appropriately called his body. Since *sōma* (body) is capable of these two orientations, it, like *pneuma* (spirit) and *psychē* (soul), signifies a dimension of the overall person rather than a part, or substance. When Paul called people to yield their bodies to sin or righteousness (Rom 6:12-14; 12:1), he meant: yield your entire selves. Yielding to righteousness incorporates whole persons into the Spirit's renewal of all creation.[274]

All this biblical material closely approximates Niebuhr's portrait of people rooted in finite concerns and values, largely through their bodies, but stretching far beyond, toward God, who calls them to transcend these. Given their bodies' weaknesses and incorporation into fleshly solidarities, plus the insecurities aroused by God's call, it is plausible how sin—working through their bodies—prompts people to grasp finite values or objects, giving these priority over God. Yet human bodies themselves do not become sinful. They only provide channels for the flesh's operations, as recognized by

---

[271]For *sarx*'s individual, physical meaning, see Rom 2:28; 1 Cor 15:39; for human solidarities, see Mk 10:7-8 and parallels, Rom 11:14; Eph 6:5; Philem 16; for the whole person, 2 Cor 7:5 (with 2 Cor 2:13). The Old Testament had only one word, *bāsār*, for what the New Testament distinguished as body and flesh. *Bāsār*, in fact, included all living creatures. For its meaning of human physicality, including genetic relatedness, see e.g., Gen 2:23; 37:27; 2 Sam 5:1; Neh 5:5.

[272]See e.g., 1 Cor 15:50; 2 Cor 1:17; Gal 4:13; as *bāsār* often did (e.g., Job 34:14-15; 2 Chron 32:8).

[273]Gal 5:17; Eph 2:2-3; Rom 8:3-8. The classic study on body-flesh is John A. T. Robinson, *The Body* (Philadelphia: Westminster, 1952); cf. Finger, *Christian Theology*, 2:116-21; *Self, Earth and Society*, pp. 270-72; Gutiérrez, *We Drink*, pp. 54-61, 64-71.

[274]Rom 8:11, 15-17. Recall that Barth expressed this unity by calling people embodied souls and ensouled bodies (*Church Dogmatics* III/2, pp. 326-27).

Barth, Niebuhr and Marpeck (almost alone among historic Anabaptists).

Nonetheless, even when bodies resist the flesh, some tension persists between them and the spirit and the Spirit's transcending movements. For bodily weaknesses and fleshly influences continue, as do God's calls toward apparent insecurity. However, if body and spirit are not separable substances but dimensions of the person, ongoing temptations cannot belong simply to the former, as most historic Anabaptists thought. Not bodily desires alone but tensions between them and spiritual aspirations provide temptations to or occasions for sin. Sin then belongs at least as much to the spirit (Niebuhr) or reason (Marpeck). In any case, whether being distorted by sin or transformed by divinization, the created human "structure," with all its interacting capacities, retains its integrity.

Depreciations of the body can be alleviated by appropriately affirming desire, a major theme of Melanie May and Scott Holland. While the most relevant New Testament words (*epithymia* and derivatives) usually present desires as vehicles of sin, they also indicate natural physical urges, desire for God (Mt 13:17; Phil 1:23) and the Spirit's striving against the flesh (Gal 5:17). People caught up in the new creation are passionate, in ways modeled and regulated by Jesus' passionate life and death.[275]

Niebuhr rightly warned that associating sin with the body, while exempting the spirit, can blind people to the depth of sin's continuing reality.[276] Not coincidentally does this attitude, shared by most historic Anabaptists, spawn legalism. The spirit, feeling able to obey the law, undertakes this somewhat arrogantly and suppresses the body with rigor. A biblical view, however, would locate sin and its persistence in the heart, exempting no dimension of the person.[277]

Transcendence and sin. If God's call and the spirit's transcendence are understood in accord with biblical narrative, preeminently through Jesus' faithfulness, they be will "upward" toward God (Niebuhr)—but only by also being "forward," through history, toward a spiritually transformed material world, as accented by Barth and Kraus. Sin will not as often be pride, or running ahead of God, and active commission of evil, as it was for Niebuhr, Barth and even Marpeck. Pride is most charac-

---

[275]Cf. Thomas Finger, "Overwhelmed by God," *Books & Culture* 5, no. 6 (1999). A review of *The Shape of Living*, by David Ford.

[276]Reinhold Niebuhr, *Nature and Destiny of Man* (New York: Scribner's, 1943), 2:199-203.

[277]E.g., Jer 17:9; Mk 7:21-23, Eph 4:18; Heb 3:7-12. I can affirm original sin in the sense that a strong inclination toward sin affects all people from birth (and perhaps prenatally), as most historic Anabaptists thought. I agree that all humans inevitably, though not necessarily, act in accord with it from their hearts, committing what Anabaptists called actual sin. This wounds the heart at a deep level. Niebuhr helps us understand how subsequent acts toward God can be paradoxically free, by operating according to freedom's created structure, but unfree because this self-inflicted wound prevents them from connecting actually and salvifically with God. A fuller treatment would take into account the inner and outer bondage occasioned by this wound and the demonic forces' role in this.

teristic of people who possess some power. But oppressed people, as liberation theologians point out, often succumb to another sin: turning aside or back from God's call. This was more common in biblical narrative.[278] For them sin is passivity, being less than one can be, and omission of doing good (which Niebuhr called, inadequately, sensuality).

If God calls people forward through history, their paths will pass through their natural and social environments. Faithful response will involve shaping those environments and also being shaped by them. Anabaptists, of course, will expect opposing forces to hinder these efforts, even more than the Reformed. Yet they will not, like Niebuhr, seek mainly to establish the best balance of power among them. They will rely on the new creation's potential to bring deeper, even if apparently limited, transformation patterned after Jesus, their anthropological norm.

This chapter has, somewhat artificially, mainly considered anthropology's personal side. But at this juncture the personal intrinsically points to the social, much as the new creation's personal dimension (chap. 5) repeatedly referred to its communal and missional dimensions (chaps. 6-7). A fuller anthropology would add, with Barth, that humans are not only *dependent on God,* and therefore called to *faithfulness,* but also are intrinsically *cohuman* and called to *mutual servanthood;*. they are natural creatures called to *stewardship of creation.*[279] Since one's body plays a major role in relations with other persons, institutions and creatures, elaboration of these last two features would more fully illumine the bodily, finite pole of transcendence.

Contemporary implications. Theology in Anabaptist perspective can affirm that people are created to be free and long for freedom, and yet that none are truly free apart from God's initiative. Many quests for freedom, both personal and social, may improve situations, relatively speaking. Anabaptist-oriented theologians can support some of these quests insofar as they promote the original creation's aims and do not contradict Jesus' way. Yet Anabaptists will be alert for pride and passivity within them. They will critique identifications of even laudable causes with God's.

Today's quests for freedom take at least two forms. One is for unlimited, autonomous modern freedom, largely motivated by pride. It operates most vigorously through globalizing forces that seek maximum control over raw materials, production, markets—and therefore people—without environmental, political or moral restraints.

---

[278]Sin reached its greatest heights in Jesus' crucifixion. Humankind was condemned as its agent (with the powers). Yet relatively few people, except the Romans and Jewish religious leaders, actively opposed Jesus. The great majority simply allowed it all to happen, turned aside and sought security by acquiescing to their leaders' unjust rule.

[279]Finger, *Christian Theology,* pp. 91-112; *Self, Earth and Society,* pp. 262-69.

In response, Anabaptist anthropology should insist, with the Reformed, that human freedom always operates within limitations. Yet not all limits are obstacles. For freedom is inherently relational.[280] It develops through interactions among individuals, groups, institutions and other creatures. Freedom is intrinsically cooperative, involving give-and-take. Paradoxically, it is fullest when it facilitates loving mutuality, which always curbs desires for autonomy. Human freedom is most limited—and energized—by God. But freedom's ultimate actuality and source is no autonomous modern individual but a loving, perichoretic interactivity of giving and receiving.[281] God bestows freedom by drawing creatures into this and other relationships.

Modern freedom is also highly future-oriented, thriving on "creative destruction" of the past.[282] Many theologies, often while promoting liberation of the oppressed, correlate authentic human existence with creating the new and sin with preferring the old. This orientation, however, can actually promote modern freedom. For it underplays the finite, bodily pole of transcendence, which connects people with the past and its traditions. Traditions and the past contribute some stability to the present, and are sources of wisdom and renewal. The new creation itself fulfills the original creation's aims and also ancient promises and prophecies preserved through venerable writings and institutions. Unhooked from the past, transcendence becomes an arrogant crusade to attain salvation and create a world autonomously, which has kept producing new bondages since the Enlightenment.

The quest for freedom's second form arises from oppression. People struggle for self-determination against controlling forces and often their own ingrained passivity. This requires a different approach. Anabaptists can, as Reformed theology sometimes has not, encourage such people to exercise freedom and creativity. Since God continually calls them, their responses are valuable in God's sight. While freedom develops within genuine relationships, which involve limitations, these are less possible the more people view themselves as passive objects defined by their environments. Growth in and expression of creativity, individuality and self-worth are essential for true relationships to emerge. Yet exercising freedom is risky and difficult. Oppressed people are deeply conditioned to suppress this. To counter sins of passivity, then, Anabaptists can encourage relatively autonomous expressions of freedom among them—remembering that freedom ultimately involves interdependence and utter dependence on God.

---

[280]McClendon, *Systematic Theology* 2: 120-21, 292-93.

[281]See pp. 459-62 above.

[282]Creative destruction is "the perpetual cycle of destroying the old and less efficient product or service and replacing it with new, more efficient ones" (Thomas Friedman, *The Lexus and the Olive Tree* [New York: Anchor, 2000], p. 11, see also pp. 7-16). The phrase is Joseph Schumpeter's.

Anabaptists' lower-class origins can help them minister in this way. Since their forbears critiqued oppressive structures and encouraged people to break with them, Anabaptists can support various social causes, sometimes radical ones. This will connect them often with marginalized churches and peoples. Yet to influence the global megastructures behind oppression, Anabaptists must also join with larger ecumenical communions.

When we consider the situations of people struggling against oppression, it may be clearer why Anabaptists, despite their reverence for God's initiative, still resist Augustinian ascriptions of all true freedom to God. These, with their predestinarian implications, often appear to sanction the status quo and imply that Christian activity must accord with it. Anabaptists, however, often find the new creation calling for radical departure from customary behaviors. It seems difficult to encourage this outlook, whose costs may be enormous, without a convictional framework that at some point grants some capacity for what people experience as genuine choice. Such a framework for action, however, need not resolve mysteries like predestination.

10

THE LAST THINGS

Human life, personal and corporate, involves a transcending movement toward a goal. Biblical narrative directs all divine and human acts toward a cosmic climax. In our day rapid renewal or destruction of all earthly life seems increasingly possible. Historic Anabaptists too anticipated the cosmic consummation of the new creation's coming. Chapters five through nine, in fact, have been written within this eschatological horizon.

Most historic Anabaptists, however, expected the future world to differ significantly from the present. They experienced this discontinuity already in sharp conflicts between the church and the "world," and between God's Spirit, who was bringing the new creation, and their bodies, which were rooted in the old creation. To be sure, some early Anabaptists envisioned a coming millennium in rather earthly terms. Their literalistic excesses, however, drove many others to more spiritual expectations.

Most historic Anabaptists, moreover, assumed that a conceptual ontological barrier blocked interaction between matter and spirit. Nonetheless, I have proposed that human transcendence—as they implicitly apprehended it and as we can explicitly conceive it today—intrinsically involves the shaping of earthly, physical reality. Anabaptist practices, including ecclesial ones like baptism and the Lord's Supper, denied this theoretical Spirit-matter disjunction. But does Anabaptist eschatology confirm, challenge or qualify my interpretation? To articulate contrasts such as Spirit-matter, body-spirit and church-society more precisely, I must directly examine that eschatological horizon within which the new creation's coming occurs.

This chapter will provide an overarching perspective for reviewing the preceding chapters. Like the kerygma itself, it will direct us toward the future. A theology in Anabaptist perspective, indeed, could begin with eschatology. James McClendon and I have done so.[1] Should I, then, have located eschatology within Anabaptism's soteriological core (the new creation's coming)?

In my view, eschatological expectations among historic Anabaptists were too diverse and functioned too differently to shape their core vision as consistently and explicitly as salvation's personal, communal and missional dimensions. Nevertheless, eschatology pervaded Anabaptist awareness thoroughly enough that without it, Anabaptism's salvific vision could not have been what it was. It belongs then among those belief complexes indispensable to Anabaptism's convictional framework.

As in previous chapters I will examine historic Anabaptist beliefs through the lenses of several traditional perspectives to discover where Anabaptists agreed and disagreed, and then bring these beliefs into dialogue with current eschatology, which these perspectives have also affected.

During the first few centuries of the Christian era most Christians associated Rome with satanic opposition to the church. They anticipated its overthrow, followed by Christ's return and reign on earth. Early Christians often identified this reign with the millennium (Rev 20:4-6). Jesus' advent, then, would be premillennial. After Constantine, the church increasingly spiritualized this demonic opposition and raised Christ's final reign to heaven. Following Augustine (354-430), the millennium was commonly disconnected from this final reign and identified with the dominion of the state-supported church on earth.

It was sometimes said that Christ would return and rule on earth after this reign had improved things. This position came to be called postmillennialism. Eschatological hopes and fears, however, were usually directed toward spiritual states entered immediately at death (heaven, hell and purgatory). Theologies that interpreted all eschatological themes as symbols of these states were sometimes called amillennial. Especially during the last half-century, however, theologies that construe eschatology within some kind of historical framework but reject a literal millennium have also been called amillennial. Pre-, post- and amillennialism will provide my three main lenses for viewing historic Anabaptism.

After Constantine and Augustine premillennial expectations subsided, only to flare up intermittently among groups who aligned the authorized church or state with final satanic opposition to Christ. Their leaders often identified figures and forces of their own time with "the abomination of desolation" (Dan 9:26-27), "the lawless one" (2 Thess 2:3-12), antichrist (1 Jn 2:18, 22; 4:3; 2 Jn 7), the two witnesses (Rev 11:3-12), the beasts along with their heads and horns (Rev 13; 17:7-14), the Babylonian whore (Rev 17–18), Gog and Ma-

---

[1]James McClendon, *Systematic Theology*, vol. 2, *Doctrine* (Nashville: Abingdon, 1994); Thomas Finger, *Christian Theology: An Eschatological Approach*, 2 vols. (Scottdale, Penn.: Herald, 1985, 1989).

gog (Rev 20:7-10) and other eschatological figures.

Joachim of Fiore (d. 1202) added a new dimension, dividing God's historical work into three (somewhat overlapping) eras: the age of the Father, ruled by the law; the age of the Son, governed by the Gospel; and the then-dawning age of the Spirit, where God would teach people directly, eventually transcending written Scripture. This age would be spearheaded by an elite spiritual community (monks for Joachim) and a returned Elijah. But the Spirit would also speak through simple people. Joachim expected the final conflicts to occur on earth, and he sought to identify antichrist, the beast and other figures. Christ's final reign seemed to be earthly, though it was so spiritually transformed that it was hard to tell.

As the Reformation approached, the Roman Church and more specifically the pope were increasingly identified with antichrist. The pope also became "the lawless one," for he exalted himself in God's temple with his "abomination of desolation," the Mass (2 Thess 2:4). As conflict between Rome and its opponents intensified and social unrest spread widely, most people expected the end shortly. Yet Anabaptists were affected more than most by eschatology, especially by the behavioral implications they drew from it.

Over the last thirty to forty years as humanity has become increasingly capable of self-destruction, theology has recovered a general eschatological orientation, especially through Jürgen Moltmann and Wolfhart Pannenberg.[2] Today as globalization multiplies the positive potentialities of technology and knowledge, great hopes for humankind's future are rising. But so is the frustration and anger of those who feel victimized by these processes. So too are forebodings of global destruction. Questions about future events and states, however, are being discussed mostly among evangelicals. (Popular end-time scenarios are usually elaborated by people who claim this label.)

While mainline theologians generally dismiss such concerns, other evangelicals are carefully though critically interacting with these visionaries. What, if anything, they ask, can be believed about future events and about the material and spiritual features of the consummation for which Christians hope? The Spirit-matter issue was central in historic Anabaptist eschatology and remains so for Anabaptist understanding. It will be helpful then to round off my sketch of a contemporary Anabaptist theology through dialogue with scholarly evangelicals, to learn what they might contribute to Anabaptists and vice versa. This interaction will lead me to include Moltmann's alternative and thereby connect with more ecumenical endeavors. I will often touch on creation, though I cannot allot it a separate chapter.

---

[2]Jürgen Moltmann, *Theology of Hope* (New York: Harper & Row, 1967); and *The Coming of God* (Minneapolis: Fortress. 1996); Wolfhart Pannenberg et al., *Revelation as History* (London, Macmillan, 1968); and *Theology and the Kingdom of God* (Philadelphia: Westminster, 1969).

HISTORIC ANABAPTIST PERSPECTIVES

Eschatological fervor ran high among peasants and artisans attracted to early Anabaptism. To recover their outlook we must rely, as with all movements from "the underside," on popular expressions of it, not simply more formal writings. Eschatology pervaded early Anabaptism in South Germany-Austria, preeminently through Hans Hut, and in the Netherlands through Melchior Hoffman. How did Switzerland compare?

Switzerland

For Ulrich Zwingli, early mentor of many Anabaptist leaders, God's kingdom and other eschatological realities had been present in the church from its beginnings, especially through the preached Word and the Spirit.[3] The Day of the Lord occurred when the Word was proclaimed. The Last Judgment took place in various historical catastrophes, such as Jerusalem's fall (70 C.E.). It could descend again on God's enemies through sociopolitical events.[4] This broadly postmillennial outlook included hope for the Word's further progress on earth, aided by the state.

At the same time, like most Reformation postmillennialists, Zwingli anticipated a final, future coming of Christ and identified some eschatological predictions with his own day.[5] He associated antichrist with not only the pope but also Conrad Grebel and Felix Mantz, and Anabaptists in general with the false prophets of the Last Days.[6] Yet Zwingli's attention and hope were focused not toward disruptive future events but on the Word's present progress in the church and state.[7]

Earliest years. Compared with Zwingli, Swiss Anabaptists sounded more premillennial and concerned with inbreaking events. This may have stemmed from a Zurich Bible study led by Nicholas Storch, who in 1521-1522 envisioned a new earth where justice would reign and the wicked would be destroyed.[8] In June 1525 a large Anabaptist group from Zollikon paraded into Zurich crying "Woe! Woe!" and giving the city forty days to repent. It called Zwingli the dragon of Revelation 12; his

---

[3] Claude Baecher, "Les Eschatologies Anabaptistes de la Haute Vallee Rehnane en Debat avec les Reformaeturs (1524-1535)" (Ph.D. diss., University of Strasbourg, 1996), pp. 139-43.

[4] Ibid., pp. 147-48, 150, 254.

[5] Ibid., p. 143.

[6] Ibid., pp. 140, 161.

[7] According to Baecher, Zwingli was motivated by a pragmatic spirituality, but Anabaptists by a mystical orientation flowing from medieval Rhineland sources (ibid., pp. 134, 157, 255).

[8] Ibid., p. 316. According to a less reliable report, Simon Stumpf prophesied that Christ would make war on the princes and the impious in two years, and the elect would reign on earth.

priests were the dragon's heads. These rural Anabaptists declared that everyone should share possessions, as they had upon being baptized.[9] Later on, some of them and others were ready to "testify with their blood" that Zwingli was a false prophet and the beast of Revelation 13.[10]

In Basel, Anabaptists proclaimed the imminent judgment of tyrants and the saints' millennial reign on earth. They named infant baptism the antichrist and abomination of desolation.[11] In the Hallau region Johannes Broetli warned people that antichrist governs by force and to guard themselves against false prophets.[12] As Anabaptists spread into St. Gall, various extravagances erupted. A certain Verena warned crowds that the Last Judgment was eight days off and that she herself would give birth to God's Son or antichrist.[13]

Conrad Grebel made some less spectacular identifications. Roman Catholic practices, especially the Mass and infant baptism, were antichrist's.[14] Zwingli was the beast of Revelation 13:10 who would soon go into captivity. His fellow clergy were the kings who gave the beast their power (Rev 17:12-13). Grebel also pictured these leaders as the abomination of desolation in the temple.[15] Yet he added, the Lamb "will defeat them in his own time" (cf. Rev 17:14), and he avoided precise predictions.[16] According to at least one witness, Grebel expounded the book of Revelation.[17] He warned Vadian, mayor of St. Gall, that unjust treatment of the innocent would be revealed on the Day of the Lord.[18]

Other Swiss Anabaptist leaders aligned eschatological events and figures with their own day in general ways. Felix Mantz regarded infant baptism as the invention of antichrist, the papacy.[19] George Blaurock stressed the coming judgment, but mainly as an incentive to repentance and holy living.[20] Zurich Anabaptists generally expected the Day of the Lord to fall on that city.[21] A tract often bound with

---

[9]Leland Harder, ed., *The Sources of Swiss Anabaptism* (Scottdale, Penn.: Herald, 1985), p. 410; cf. p. 235 above.

[10]Harder, *Sources of Swiss Anabaptism*, p. 435.

[11]Baecher, *Eschatologies Anabaptistes*, pp. 270-72.

[12]Ibid., p. 312.

[13]Ibid., p. 316.

[14]Conrad Grebel and Friends, "Letters to Thomas Müntzer," in *Spiritual and Anabaptist Writers*, ed. George Williams and Angel Mergal (Philadelphia: Westminster Press, 1957), pp. 75-82.

[15]Harder, *Sources of Swiss Anabaptism*, p. 283.

[16]Ibid., pp. 357-58.

[17]Baecher, *Eschatologies Anabaptistes*, p. 314.

[18]Harder, *Sources of Swiss Anabaptism*, p. 379.

[19]Ibid., p. 311.

[20]Thieleman van Braght, *The Bloody Theater or Martyrs Mirror* (Scottdale, Penn.: Herald, 1950), p. 432.

[21]Baecher, *Eschatologies Anabaptistes*, p. 327.

Michael Sattler's works identified current religious leaders with Babylon.[22] A second tract exhorted readers to flee this Babylon, with its "desolation and abomination," to avoid false prophets and await deliverance from antichrist and the powers of darkness "by the revealing of his Son."[23]

A third tract was more specific. The beast with seven heads and ten horns who recovered from a mortal wound (Rev 13:1-4) signified false Roman teaching, especially on baptism and the Eucharist. This Beast was seemingly defeated by the Reformers, but it revived when the Reformers taught much the same.[24] The Reformers were identified more precisely with the second beast, which caused people to worship the first (Rev 13:11-17). Together, Rome and the Protestants comprised the abomination of desolation, for they took over God's temple and drew worship to themselves. God's true people must flee this Babylon.[25]

Sattler's eschatological message was also somewhat specific. He warned his congregation at Horb that the abomination of desolation was already visible among them, and that the elect would soon be marked on their foreheads (cf. Rev 7:3; 14:1), just before the Day of the Lord.[26] Sattler drew on the apocryphal work now called 2 Ezra, especially the notion of the elect being rescued from this shadowy world and joining the Lamb's marriage supper (2 Ezra 2:34-37).[27] Second Ezra's eschatology was premillennial, stressing the asceticism, pacifism and mission activity of the elect. However, Sattler opposed "speculation," which apparently included more specific identification of persons, events and dates.[28]

Claude Baecher proposes that Sattler's stress on holiness, including pacifism, arose largely from this concern to become pure for Christ's coming. Further, Schleitheim's polarization of church and world anticipated this imminent separation of those destined for the Lamb's feast.[29] Baecher does not find this sharp distinction between an apparently spiritual new creation and the old material

---

[22]Michael Sattler, *The Legacy of Michael Sattler*, ed. John Howard Yoder (Scottdale, Penn.: Herald, 1973), p. 124.

[23]Ibid., pp. 127, 129-32, cf. Mt 24; I Thess 1:5-10.

[24]Ibid., p. 117.

[25]Ibid., p. 118, cf. Rev 18:4-8. Some scholars consider this tract South German-Austrian.

[26]Ibid., p. 61.

[27]Ibid., pp. 62-63.

[28]Ibid., p. 60.

[29]Baecher, *Eschatologies Anabaptistes*, pp. 414-18. Soon after declaring that nothing exists but good and evil, God's temple and idols, Schleitheim exhorted departure from "Babylon" to escape its coming torment (Sattler, *Legacy of Michael Sattler*, p. 38). It named infant baptism the pope's greatest "abomination" (p. 36).

world vastly different from premillennial hopes for earthly, revolutionary change, but an alteration of them.[30]

In sum, the early Swiss identified eschatological figures with those of their day. Yet they were less inclined to elaborate detailed scenarios than early Anabaptists elsewhere. The Swiss aimed not so much to make predictions as to assure the afflicted that God was in control. They underlined the coming judgment, but in calls to repentance and holy living, not mainly as one item on a future timetable. Though many Swiss may have expected Christ's reign to be earthly, little speculation about its features can be found.

Early Swiss Anabaptists contrasted Christ's future reign far more sharply with the present than Zwingli. Their present contained no hope for state-supported progress of the Word. Whatever these Anabaptists believed about a millennium, their sense of vastly worsening conditions before the parousia resembled premillennialism. Unlike Zwinglian postmillennialists, they could not consider any prior era an embodiment of God's rule.[31]

Soul sleep? These differences were linked with one of Zwingli's fervent allegations against Anabaptists: they taught that at death souls do not immediately enter heaven, purgatory or somewhere worse but "sleep" until the resurrection of whole persons (body and soul) at Christ's return.

Zwingli, in contrast, insisted that fully conscious eternal life, heavenly and hellish, began at death.[32] However, if each person's final destiny is realized at death, eschatology happens almost exclusively in the eternal realm. Jesus' return and a final resurrection, judgment and transformation of the temporal realm could add little to it. Even though Zwingli affirmed at least the first three of these events, his focus on eternity clashed with any possibility of history's future, drastic alteration. It allowed him, in practice, to ignore such eventualities and concentrate on improving present conditions by spreading the Word gradually, with state support. But if even the dead do not attain ultimate destiny until the final resurrection and judgment, eschatological hope must focus on Jesus' bodily return, which will affect history more radically.

---

[30]Baecher, *Eschatologies Anabaptistes*, p. 411; cf. C. Arnold Snyder, "The Schleitheim Articles in Light of the Revolution of the Common Man: Continuation or Departure?" *16th Century Journal* 16, no. 4 (1985).

[31]Baecher finds Grebel's notion of the Last Day close to Zwingli's (*Eschatologies Anabaptistes*, pp. 269, 315). Zurich Anabaptists, he maintains, refused to develop a future chronology or stress the Last Day's imminence, and were "true Zwinglians" in this sense (p. 331, cf. p. 327). The evidence, as I see it, is too scant to support this and mainly indicates differences from Zwingli.

[32]Catholics affirmed this but added purgatory, which most souls entered straightway. Rome was providing means to lessen purgatorial suffering for the dead and also the living in advance, including purchase of indulgences. But if souls were not conscious until resurrection, this penitential and financial scheme would collapse.

Zwingli insisted that Anabaptists taught soul sleep, and he critiqued it extensively, as did his colleague Heinrich Bullinger and later John Calvin.[33] Sebastian Franck, a more sympathetic and often accurate commentator, reported that many Anabaptists held this view, within a premillennial framework.[34] Schiemer indeed taught this, Dirk apparently did, and it perhaps influenced Sattler's perceived denigration of Mary and the saints.[35] Yet other evidence that specific Anabaptists promoted soul sleep is slim. Camillo Renato, Michael Servetus, Faustus Socinus and Simon Budny all affirmed it, but they drew it from Italian evangelical rationalism, not mainstream Anabaptism.[36] Still, the widespread association of Anabaptists with soul sleep makes it plausible that some believed it. This may have originated in Switzerland and later emerged in Germanic and French regions, though perhaps not the Netherlands. In any case, it would be consistent with views held by many Swiss.

Balthasar Hubmaier. Like many other Swiss, Balthasar Hubmaier viewed the Mass as the abomination of desolation, an idol erected by antichrist.[37] Infant baptism was the red dragon devouring children as they were born.[38] Hubmaier aligned the fall of sun, moon and stars with that of reputed church authorities.[39] The longer church and world lasted, the worse they became.[40] They were drawing upon themselves the predicted cosmic cataclysms, including conquest by Gog and Magog.[41]

---

[33]Baecher, *Eschatologies Anabaptistes*, pp. 146, 344-49, 361-64; George Williams, *The Radical Reformation*, 3rd ed. (Kirksville, Mo.: 16th Century Journal Publishers, 1992), pp. 63-72, 312, 507, 899-901, 922-32. Bullinger also accused Anabaptists of teaching universal restoration (see Williams, *Radical Reformation*, p. 312), which other critics associated with Hans Denck (see p. 525 note 72 above).

[34]Baecher, *Eschatologies Anabaptistes*, pp. 366-69.

[35]Leonhard Schiemer, "Three Kinds of Grace," in *Early Anabaptist Spirituality*, ed. Daniel Liechty (New York: Paulist Press, 1994), p. 92; Dirk Philips, *The Writings of Dirk Philips*, ed. Cornelius Dyck, William Keeney, and Alvin Beachy (Scottdale, Penn.: Herald, 1992), p. 66. When accused at his trial of despising Mary and the saints, Sattler insisted that though he revered Mary, she could not be our heavenly advocate, since "she like us must await judgment" (Sattler, *Legacy of Michael Sattler*, p. 72; cf. "The Trial and Martyrdom of Michael Sattler," in *Spiritual and Anabaptist Writers*, ed. George Williams and Angel Mergal (Philadelphia: Westminster Press, 1957), pp. 136-44; Williams, *Radical Reformation*, p. 295). Grebel was enthused by Gerhard Westerburg's *Sleep of Souls*. In 1524 he conversed with the author, who became Anabaptist in 1529 (Harder, *Sources of Swiss Anabaptism*, p. 295; Williams, *Radical Reformation*, pp. 196-98).

[36]Williams, *Radical Reformation*, pp. 840-42, 989, 1291.

[37]Balthasar Hubmaier, *Balthasar Hubmaier*, ed. and trans. Wayne Pipkin and John Yoder (Scottdale, Penn.: Herald, 1989), pp. 355, 302.

[38]Ibid., pp. 389-90, cf. Rev 12:1-4. Making plays on words, he aligned ministers and monstrances with the sea monster of Rev 13:1 (p. 335).

[39]Ibid., p. 176, cf. Mt 24:29.

[40]Ibid., pp. 176, 375, cf. Mt 24:12.

[41]Ibid., pp. 550-51, cf. Rev 20:7-9.

While Hubmaier declined to identify this foreign menace, his Austrian captors perhaps thought he meant the Turks, who were threatening Vienna.

Hubmaier declared that Christ's return was "closer than we know" and prayed for his swift advent.[42] Yet he loathed predictions. For while Humbmaier was building a large Anabaptist church in Moravia, Hans Hut, who was predicting an early parousia, visited and began drawing many away. Hubmaier complained that this lured many from responsible work and relationships. The two finally debated in public, but afterward Hubmaier banished Hut. He realized that Austrian authorities viewed Hut's forecasts as revolutionary.

Hut interpreted the roughly $3\frac{1}{2}$ year period of final tribulation in Revelation literally (Rev 11:2-3, 9; 12:6, 14). Dating it from 1525—the Anabaptist persecution in Switzerland—Hut arrived at Pentecost 1528 for the parousia. Hubmaier, however, countered that each year was a solar year (the time it takes the sun to complete its own orbit), so that $3\frac{1}{2}$ years equaled 1,277 ordinary years.[43] But rather than intending this number literally, Hubmaier was rejecting literal predictions altogether.[44]

In contrast, Hubmaier's substantive eschatology focused on the Last Judgment as a recompense for works and as vengeance, especially against authorities who persecuted the innocent.[45] Such an event would most likely influence conduct if its timing were unknown, requiring that people always be ready.[46] Further, even though undatable, the imminence of resurrection as well as judgment would encourage Christians, despite severe suffering, to persevere in following Jesus' way.

For Hubmaier, Jesus' body was in heaven, so that it could not be in the Lord's Supper, and so that Jesus' authority, including the ban, could be transferred to the church. Yet to complete salvation history Jesus would need to take back this authority. To do so, he had to return bodily. For Hubmaier, however, Jesus would return only to meet his saints in the air.[47] At this time their bodies, souls and spirits would be reunited. Yet their bodies would become so "impassible, transfigured, immortal" that they would never return to earth but remain forever in the air.[48]

For Hubmaier, in other words, the new creation would finally be spiritual. Eternal life would consist in the beatific vision of God's face, which is inconceiv-

---

[42]Ibid., pp. 542, 237.
[43]Ibid., pp. 542-43.
[44]Walter Klaassen, *Living at the End of the Ages* (New York: University Press of America, 1992), p. 27.
[45]Hubmaier, *Balthasar Hubmaier,* pp. 187, 237, 309, 364-65.
[46]Ibid., p. 406.
[47]Ibid., pp. 329, 364.
[48]Ibid., pp. 240, 415, cf. pp. 435, 446. Perhaps his low view of the body and even of material existence shows through here (cf. pp. 469-70).

able on earth.[49] Hubmaier was mainly concerned to assure the righteous of their reward and the unrighteous of the awful, equally eternal deprivation of God's countenance. In all this he resembled amillennialism more than most Swiss Anabaptists.[50]

Like other Swiss, Hubmaier then found eschatological forecasts being fulfilled, though he was less specific than most as to how. He resembled Zwingli not only in eucharistic teaching but also in establishing stable churches guarded by and promoting the sword.[51] Such churches, however, would be further than Zwingli's from the status quo. Hubmaier's main hopes were not directed toward extensive earthly transformations but the spiritual realm.

South Germany-Austria. I. Earliest years.

• *Hans Hut.* Hans Hut admired and sometimes accompanied Thomas Müntzer, leader of the Franconian Peasants' War, though Hut probably avoided fighting. Hut's Trinity involved a threefold revelatory process through the created order and mystical experience.[52] This somewhat resembled Joachim of Fiore's tripartite historical schema, where the Spirit, in the third age, began transcending Scripture and speaking directly to select leaders and then common people. Müntzer embraced similar views.

Following the peasants' drastic defeat (May 1525), Hut concluded, like Müntzer, that they had not sought God's will but their own. But now Hut moved among masses whose hopes for revolutionary change had been bitterly dashed. They had seen Reformers like Luther support their merciless noble conquerors. Was there any way out?

Hut retained his emphasis, generally shared with Müntzer, on *Gelassenheit:* inner detachment from creatures and Jesus-like suffering. But now he insisted that this should be expressed outwardly, in nonretaliatory behavior toward the godless rulers, until God intervened to destroy them. Only then—not before, as Müntzer had taught—could true Christians could join God against them, wielding the sword.[53]

---

[49]Ibid., pp. 240, 364.

[50]Ibid., p. 365. Hubmaier conceded to his Catholic captors, however, that impure Christians might experience hell as purgatory and find forgiveness in the next life. Yet he found no basis for a purgatory different than hell (p. 541).

[51]See pp. 291-93 above.

[52]See pp. 426-27 above.

[53]According to earlier interpretations by Harold Bender ("The Zwickau Prophets: Thomas Müntzer and the Anabaptists," *MQR* 27, no.I [1953]) and others (e.g., Herbert Klassen, "The Life and Teachings of Hans Hut," *MQR* 33, nos. 3 and 4 [1959]: esp. pp. 202-5), Hut relinquished all violence on becoming Anabaptist. This view was challenged (e.g., Roland Armour, *Anabaptist Baptism* [Scottdale, Penn.:

Until then, converts were to form small fellowships, share possessions, continue purificatory suffering and receive baptism as a sign of their election.

By about May 1526, Hut was evangelizing very widely and organizing many others to do so. Since he predicted Pentecost 1528 for Jesus' return, along with preceding events, converts' experiences of *Gelassenheit*, baptism and community would have to be intense and swiftly paced.[54] Moreover, while Swiss converts anticipated both Christ's return and judgment on their enemies, their salvation was seldom tied to a particular scenario. Hut's timetable was likely more central to his converts' notion of salvation. Understandably, when Hut expired before the predicted parousia, which then failed to arrive, his following dwindled rapidly. Only a few extremists like Augustine Bader recalibrated Hut's scheme and persisted. Others fled to Strasbourg where they influenced Melchior Hoffman.

Details of Hut's scheme are known largely from accounts of his and his followers' trials. Since torture and intimidation were employed, their accuracy is sometimes suspect. However, a reasonably reliable outline can be sketched. Hut's pronouncements fell under seven headings, or judgments, often identified with Revelation 7 and its book with seven seals. The first involved God's covenant, or the gospel of Christ, faith and baptism.[55] The second judgment concerned Christ's body, including the suffering church and the Lord's Supper. The third turned to "the End of the world." This may have meant God's purging of the earth before Christ's return, or perhaps been a heading for the last four judgments. These included (4) Christ's future coming and judgment,

---

Herald, 1966]), especially by Gottfried Seebass (*Müntzer's Erbe: Werk, leben und theologie des Hans Hut (gestorben 1527)*, [Erlangen-Nuernburg: Friedrich-Alexander University, Habilitationschrift, 1972]), whom Werner Packull (*Mysticism and the Early South German-Austrian Anabaptists* [Scottdale, Penn.: Herald, 1977]) and Stayer (*Anabaptism and the Sword*, 2nd ed. [Lawrence, Kans.: Coronado Press, 1976]) largely follow. They find Hut urging subjects to kill their rulers shortly after Frankenhausen (e.g., Stayer, *Anabaptism and the Sword*, p. 151) and underline Müntzer's continuing influence on him. It is now generally accepted that Hut never renounced violence wholly, but soon restricted it to the final stages of God's judgment. However, Packull and Stayer were challenging the standard pacifist reading and often interpreted contrary evidence maximally (cf. p. 293 note 205 above).

[54]The initial persecutions of Swiss Anabaptists, which for Hut initiated the final $3\frac{1}{2}$ years, coincided roughly with the peasant defeat at Frankenhausen. Hut apparently identified the two witnesses (Rev 11:3) with Müntzer and his lieutenant, Heinrich Pfeiffer. The final seven years probably began with the "Zwickau prophets" who claimed special revelations through the Spirit, challenged Luther's sole reliance on Scripture and influenced Müntzer.

[55]One of Hut's two extant writings, "On the Mystery of Baptism," the chief source for his soteriology, dealt with this judgment ("On the Mystery of Baptism," in *Early Anabaptist Spirituality*, ed. Daniel Liechty (New York: Paulist Press, 1994), pp. 64-81.

(5) the resurrection, (6) the kingdom of God, and (7) eternal judgment of the damned.[56]

Hut's eschatological predilection disturbed many Anabaptist leaders besides Hubmaier. At a gathering in Augsburg (August 1527), they asked him to henceforth preach only the first two judgments. Quite possibly, Hut did so when evangelizing but reserved the last five as secret teachings for the baptized.

As we can see, Hut separated a judgment at Christ's return (no. 4) from a final judgment of the condemned (no. 7). Apparently, he also distinguished a resurrection of the righteous (no. 5) from a final resurrection of the wicked. A first judgment and resurrection, then, might have introduced the millennium (Rev 20:4), with a second pair occurring afterward (Rev 20:11-15), as in standard premillennialism.[57] Hut expected the Turks to soon punish Christendom in concert with natural and supernatural disasters. Through direct revelation Hut identified several cities to be spared, where Anabaptists should flee.[58] Eventually the Turks would withdraw, leaving some of the godless alive. Then Christians could finally exterminate them.

Almost all trial accounts placed this slaughter at or shortly after Jesus' return. A few, however, hinted that it might occur beforehand.[59] The distinction is crucial. In this second scenario humans would prepare the earth for Christ through revolutionary violence. God's kingdom would be ushered in militarily, not wholly unlike in postmillennialism. Though Hut probably did not teach this, the Münsterites eventually would.

Hut shared the premillennial expectation that Christ would reign on this earth, with his true followers. Social distinctions would vanish, possessions would be shared, need would be eliminated—in short, that peasant-artisan vision dashed in

---

[56]Ambrosius Spitelmaier's testimony on judgments 4-7 appears in Walter Klaassen, ed., *Anabaptism in Outline* (Scottdale, Penn.: Herald, 1981), pp. 321-23. Other followers said that Hut had the seven-sealed book given to Daniel, and he thought he was Daniel. Hut may have regarded himself as John the Baptist/Elijah (Klaassen, *Living at the End*, p. 81).

[57]Packull, *Mysticism and the Early South German-Austrian Anabaptists*, pp. 82-83, 204n. 107. During interrogation, Hut insisted that he taught only a spiritual kingdom. Under torture, though, he confessed advocating violence. Hut also claimed that his seven judgments were not meant literally but to call sinners to repent (pp. 119-20).

[58]Some followers later mentioned Nicholsburg and St. Gall (Klaassen, *Living at the End*, p. 85); others mentioned the two Mühlhausens. One was not far from Strasbourg. The other, formerly controlled by Müntzer and Pfeiffer, was in Thuringia (Klaus Deppermann, *Melchior Hofmann* [Edinburgh: T & T Clark, 1987], p. 200). Hut also forecast that some Anabaptists would simply have to hide in forests. For a general account, see Klaassen, *Living at the End*, p. 26; Packull, *Mysticism and the Early South German-Austrian Anabaptists*, pp. 82-83; Stayer, *Anabaptism and the Sword*, p. 155.

[59]Armour, *Anabaptist Baptism*, p. 88.

the Peasants' War would soon be realized more wonderfully.[60] "Unlike the 'Swiss Brethren,' Hut did not want to establish a holy island in a sea of evil. He wanted to turn the whole earth into 'the Kingdom of God.'"[61] Like Joachim of Fiore, Hut was energized by a sense of God's Spirit unleashing a final age, speaking more directly to common people and making specific predictions through him.

2. Though Hans Schlaffer and Leonhard Schiemer were Hut's disciples, they developed his eschatological orientation differently. Schlaffer sounded somewhat like the Swiss. He spoke generally of these "last and most dangerous times" and expected the Day of the Lord soon.[62] But he also opposed speculation.[63] In contrast to Hut's literalism, but reminding one of Hubmaier, Schlaffer cautioned that a "day" from God's standpoint might be a thousand years.[64]

Schiemer, however, rejected figurative interpretations such as Hubmaier's.[65] Like Hut, Schiemer calculated how Christ's return would follow $3\frac{1}{2}$ years of tribulation and occur at Pentecost 1528. He detailed the events involved.[66] Despite his spiritualized understanding of Jesus' work, Schiemer stressed his bodily return, concluding an historical span during which the departed saints would sleep in the earth.[67] Consequently, Schiemer's claim that "the saints shall rule the world" might have meant "on earth."[68] Yet we find no mention of saints wreaking vengeance, as in Hut.

Also unlike Hut, Schiemer associated the two witnesses with Anabaptist martyrs (Rev 11:3-13) and a young man baptizing with Hut himself (Dan 10:5; 12:6). Further, Schiemer equated the abomination of desolation with the destruction of God's people and the "daily sacrifice" involved as Christians being martyred.[69] All this would climax a history somewhat like Joachim of Fiore's. The

---

[60]Klaassen, *Living at the End*, p. 89; Deppermann, *Melchior Hoffman*, pp. 200-201; Packull, *Mysticism and the Early South German-Austrian Anabaptists*, pp. 82-83. According to some followers, Hut himself would reign on earth as a channel for Christ's rule from heaven (Klaassen, *Living at the End*, p. 89; Deppermann, *Melchior Hoffman*, p. 200).

[61]Deppermann, *Melchior Hoffman*, p. 202.

[62]Hans Schlaffer, "Instructions on Beginning a True Christian Life," in *Early Anabaptist Spirituality*, ed. Daniel Liechty (New York: Paulist, 1994), pp. 106, 108, cf. p. 99.

[63]Hans Schlaffer, "Ein kurzer Unterrich zum Anfang eines recht chrislichen Lebens," in *Glaubenzeugnisse oberdeutscher Taufgesinnter* (= Quellen und Forschungen zur Reformationsgeschichte), ed. Lydia Mueller (Leipzig: M. Heinsius Nachfolger, 1938), 20:105-7, 110.

[64]Schlaffer, "Instructions on Beginning," p. 105.

[65]Leonhard Schiemer, "The Apostles' Creed: An Interpretation," in *Spiritual Life in Anabaptism*, ed. Cornelius Dyck (Scottdale, Penn.: Herald, 1995), p. 37.

[66]Ibid., pp. 37-38.

[67]Schiemer, "Three Kinds of Grace," p. 92.

[68]Schiemer, "Apostles' Creed," p. 36.

[69]Ibid., p. 37, cf. Dan 8:11-13; 11:31; 12:11.

number of the beast, 666, indicated six ages that Satan ruled (Rev 13:18). Yet in a seventh, a sabbath, creation would reach its true goal and humans would be fully divinized.[70]

3. Zwingli critiqued Hans Denck for premillennial tendencies.[71] Yet Denck's preoccupation with the inner Word, which eventually led him to minimize outward ceremonies, pointed away from concern about a spatiotemporal future. Further, time, matter and even evil could seem unreal in Denck's mysticism.

Other eschatological teachings, however, might have been congruent with Denck's orientation. Since the Word indwelt everyone, would it eventually purify them all? The less real evil or matter were, the more plausible would this seem. Denck was, in fact, charged with teaching that everyone would be saved (universalism), or perhaps that while the Last Judgment would condemn many, hell would function as purgatory and eventually redeem them all (universal restoration).[72] Neither view, however, appears in Denck's surviving works, which hardly mention eschatology. There he resembled other Anabaptists only in painting the world as more evil than ever and the final judgment as punishment for evil works and vindication for the oppressed.[73]

Peter Riedemann. For their beleaguered converts, Hutterites portrayed Christ's coming as blessed deliverance.[74] Yet in their evangelism it functioned as fearful judgment. Christ's vengeance "with flaming fire" on all wrongdoing "will be terri-

---

[70]Leonhard Schiemer, "Ein epistl an die gemain zu Rottenburg darin huebsche erklearungen der 12 hauptsteuck unseres christlichen glaubens begiiffen sein, " in *Glaubenszeugnisse oberdeutscher Taufgesinnter* (= Quellen und Forschungen zur Reformationsgeschichte), ed. Lydia Mueller (Leipzig: M. Heinsius Nachfolger, 1938), 20:49-50; cf. Schiemer, "Apostles' Creed," p. 38. A follower of Hut's testified that Hut also taught this scheme (Packull, *Mysticism and the Early South German-Austrian Anabaptists*, pp. 78-79).

[71]Zwingli referred to a Micah commentary, reputedly by Denck and Ludwig Haetzer (Baecher, *Eschatologies Anabaptistes*, pp. 163-65). Its author would neither reject all future earthly expectations nor comment on them (Packull, *Mysticism and the Early South German-Austrian Anabaptists*, pp. 64-65). Packull suggests that Denck may have agreed somewhat with Hut and did not oppose him at the Augsburg meeting (August 1527) as usually supposed (ibid., p. 119; cf. p. 46). But Denck developed the mysticism and pneumaticism he shared somewhat with Hut in directions with quite different eschatological implications.

[72]For contemporaneous reports, including Hubmaier's possible opposition, see Packull, *Mysticism and the Early South German-Austrian Anabaptists*, pp. 40-43 (cf. footnote 33 on p. 519). Denck was also occasionally charged with a plausible implication of these views: the devil's ultimate salvation. Packull concludes that Denck taught universalism (p. 44). For opposed interpretations, see William Klassen, "Was Hans Denck a Universalist?" *MQR* 39 (1965), and Alvin Beachy, *The Concept of Grace in the Radical Reformation* (Nieuwkoop, Netherlands: B. De Graf, 1977).

[73]Hans Denck, *The Spiritual Legacy of Hans Denck*, ed. Clarence Bauman (Leiden: E. J. Brill, 1991), pp. 67, 123-25, 233, cf. pp. 151, 233, 239.

[74]Klaassen, *Anabaptism in Outline*, pp. 325-26.

fying," especially for the saints' persecutors.[75] Indeed, Riedemann wrote his confession of faith, in part, to warn them and "as a testimony against the ungodly."[76] This harsh expectation no doubt reflected Hutterite experience of severe persecution and the implacable hostility they perceived between church and "world."

Like many other Anabaptists, Hutterites interpreted the Mass as antichrist occupying God's temple.[77] Somewhat uniquely, they identified themselves with the woman protected in the wilderness during the dragon's final raging.[78] Beyond this, Hutterites speculated about events, places and sequences less than the Swiss, likely in reaction to Hut's excesses. Though the judgment's timing was unknown, its certainty and the necessity of witnessing to the "world" until then kept them walking in Jesus' way.

Riedemann affirmed some continuity between the original creation and the future new creation. Eternal life, for instance, "begins here and now, and continues into the future, when it will be properly and fully revealed."[79] Given the care which Hutterites lavished on the earth, one might assume that it would remain in some form. Misuse of creatures was so serious that they would witness against humans at the judgment.[80]

Riedemann, however, did not address this issue. He only mentioned that Christ would "transfigure our insignificant body. It will become like his glorified body, and we shall see his resplendent brightness. We shall be where he is."[81] Might this be on earth? We recall that Riedemann called temporal reality "alien to our true nature"; the notion that God's likeness in us involved "flesh and blood" was foolish, for this could only be "spirit."[82] To be sure, these conceptual claims seem to contradict Hutterite practice. And if Riedemann envisioned a more material future, he might have kept silent to avoid identification with Hut. It is also quite possible, however, that he perceived eschatological existence as spiritual, like amillennialists.

Pilgram Marpeck. Like other Anabaptists, Pilgram Marpeck often mentioned "these last dangerous times" when errors proliferated, believers fell away and

---

[75]Peter Riedemann, *Peter Riedemann's Hutterite Confession of Faith*, ed. John Friesen (Scottdale, Penn.: Herald, 1999), pp. 72, 229.

[76]Ibid., p. 228.

[77]Klaassen, *Living at the End*, p. 70; cf. 2 Thess 2:4.

[78]Rev 12:4-6, 13-17; see Ulrich Stadler, "Cherished Instructions on Sin, Excommunication, and the Community of Goods," in *Spiritual and Anabaptist Writers*, ed. George Williams and Angel Mergal (Philadelphia: Westminster Press, 1957), pp. 281-82; Klaassen, *Living at the End*, p. 68. Hutterites saw themselves called through their communal labor to make this wilderness fruitful.

[79]Riedemann, *Peter Riedemann's Hutterite Confession*, p. 82.

[80]Ibid., p. 63.

[81]Ibid., p. 82.

[82]Ibid., pp. 120, 89, cf. chap. 9.

God's swiftly approaching judgment should instill fear in everyone. Marpeck often correlated antichrist with Rome and, like many Swiss, especially with infant baptism, the entrance to antichrist's realm.[83] Marpeck also called this antichrist the Babylonian whore (Rev 17–18), who masqueraded as Christ's bride. She arose when the pope, disguised as Christ, married Constantine's governmental power.[84]

From then on the dragon concealed himself under this pretended bride. But by the late medieval era his time was running short (cf. Rev 13:12). So he made the whore's error seem more godly by raising up false prophets, the Reformers.[85] Though their teachings were partly right, they reenacted antichrist's most basic apostasy: they married secular power anew and another antichrist was born.[86] They rejected the way of Jesus' cross and hid behind their rulers.

Marpeck predicted that these Protestants would perish with "more awful bloodshed than in the Peasant War."[87] True Christians, however, were to persist in following Jesus' patient, humble way until the imminent end—as had their predecessors since New Testament times. In general, however, Marpeck, like Riedemann and unlike Hut and Schiemer, hesitated to connect eschatological events specifically with his own time. He often preferred broad affirmations, such as that the gospel should be preached to "all nations," especially "in these last days."[88]

Did Marpeck expect a wholly spiritual end, as Riedemann well may have? Marpeck often insisted that Spirit was revealed and bestowed through matter and in turn transformed it through sacraments and divinization. Christ's work restored cosmic relations among God and all creatures, and enabled matter, though his per-

---

[83]Pilgram Marpeck, *The Writings of Pilgram Marpeck,* ed. and trans. William Klassen and Walter Klaassen (Scottdale, Penn.: Herald, 1978), pp. 259-60, 45-46, 145, 207. He also called the pope the abomination of desolation in the Holy Place (p. 558).

[84]Pilgram Marpeck, "Exposé of the Babylonian Whore," in *Later Writings by Pilgram Marpeck and His Circle,* ed. Walter Klaassen, Werner Packull, and John Rempel, trans. Walter Klaassen (Kitchener, Ont.: Pandora, 1999), pp. 38-39.

[85]Ibid., p. 26.

[86]Ibid., pp. 28-30, 39.

[87]Ibid., p. 28. He was critiquing Lutherans especially for encouraging princes to oppose the emperor (p. 26). But Christians must be subject to authority, as Christ was, which emperors will hold until the end (p. 27). Christians could appeal to emperors for change, but must simply be patient amid suffering if not heard (p. 29).

[88]Marpeck, *Writings of Pilgram Marpeck,* p. 48. Jesus was sending messengers ahead of himself to purify "spiritual Jerusalem"—believers' hearts (pp. 47, 421-22, cf. p. 352)—betrothing a new bride and expelling the whore ("Exposé of the Babylonian Whore," p. 25). He identified Elijah, whom many, like Hoffman, expected to return and spearhead such preaching and purification, with the earthly Jesus (*Writings of Pilgram Marpeck,* pp. 74-75).

son, to mediate divine life.[89] Then at the end, wouldn't the Spirit, again coming from the Father through the Son's bodily advent, bring physical reality to its highest actualization?

Surprisingly, Marpeck affirmed instead that all natural processes would then cease.[90] Neither time nor anything existing in time would remain, "such as animals, bird, fish, light, nor day." These were created solely for humanity's sake. People would no longer need them when eternity's inbreaking abolished time. Only beings that could live eternally would remain—including disobedient ones in everlasting torment.[91]

Marpeck, of course, insisted that natural realities alone can lead us into the supernatural. This however would only last until our physical life "is opened to its eternal unchangeable essence . . . after this fleeting, perishable time comes to an end."[92] Then—and not before, as Spiritualists supposed—our need for ceremonies, structures and all other externalities would cease.[93] This would coincide with Christ's bodily return and also our resurrection "according to the flesh," when "His glory shall glorify our bodies."[94] One wonders, though, how bodily we would be afterward. In any case, Marpeck rejected any ultimate loss of creaturehood and absorption into God.[95]

Further, the "first resurrection" (Rev 20:4-6), for Marpeck, would not be an historic event inaugurating a future millennium, as for premillennialists (probably including Hut). This resurrection, instead, had begun with Jesus' resurrection. Christians now ruled with him over evil and all other creatures. Marpeck, however, did not mention departed saints participating in this rule, as do amillennialism and postmillennialism.[96]

For Marpeck, like Riedemann, participation in the new creation included involvement in concrete structures and vocations. Yet they had seen predictions of an earthly millennium fail disastrously, heaping great notoriety on Anabaptists. They could perceive how such expectations had been shaped by vengeful desires and nar-

---

[89]Stephen Boyd, *Pilgram Marpeck* (Durham, N.C.: Duke University Press, 1992), p. 74.

[90]Marpeck, *Writings of Pilgram Marpeck*, p. 85.

[91]Ibid., pp. 536-37.

[92]Ibid., p. 86.

[93]Ibid., pp. 45, 47, 86.

[94]Ibid., pp. 314, 415.

[95]Ibid., pp. 530, 531. He said that we will remain flesh and blood "with Christ eternally" (p. 212), but also that we "remain human as long as we have not discarded the earthly . . . in physical death" (p. 379). While the latter by itself might imply that we will not be physical or even human thereafter, Marpeck attempted, somewhat awkwardly, to define even Jesus' risen body as creaturely and finite (see footnote 310 on p. 380).

[96]Ibid., p. 414; see "Contemporary Appropriations" in this chapter.

row vision.[97] Both then were understandably reticent to ascribe any spatiotemporal features to what Christ would bring. While Riedemann may have entertained several such expectations but kept silent due to prior events, Marpeck presented a systematic rationale for omitting them. He located hope for social transformation on that temporal plane where all creatures pass away, in contrast with eternity where alone abiding peace can exist.[98]

The Netherlands

Melchior Hoffman. Melchior Hoffman's preaching, like Hut's, was eschatologically charged, abounding in specific predictions that must have been near the center of many a convert's faith. Again like Hut, and recalling Joachim of Fiore, Melchior believed that history's final era had arrived: the Spirit was exceptionally active in converting, sanctifying and directly conveying Scripture's hidden meanings, especially among the theologically untrained. And, once more like Hut, Hoffman understood salvation mystically and expected it to proceed rapidly, but to even loftier spiritual heights.

Unlike South German-Austrians or Swiss, Hoffman, who believed that pious rulers might occasionally aid Christians, predicted that several would do so.[99] Yet he neither called converts to revolution nor promised that they would finally slay the godless. (Though he often appeared, curiously, in the vicinity of local disturbances.) Melchior granted the civil sword a greater role in aiding the saints than anyone so far, save perhaps Hubmaier.

For Hoffman the millennium had begun with Paul's binding of Satan, who was later let loose with the rise of the papacy, church-state union (especially under Constantine), infant baptism and the Mass.[100] Hoffman dated the seven final years from 1526 and therefore the end in 1533. (Hut's dates were 1521-1528.) Hoff-

---

[97]Ibid., pp. 541-42.

[98]Government belonged only to the temporal realm (ibid., p. 537). But Christians already ruled "outside of time." (This is why religions should never be bound to the state [p. 339].) After the last person was saved for the eternal realm, government would dissolve, followed by "war without any means of peace or rescue." Still, godly persons would be separated from this and gain eternal peace with Christ (p. 538). This sounds somewhat like the Great Tribulation and Rapture. By placing these in the future, Marpeck perhaps indicated that the Last Days were not quite there for him, though they were for most other Anabaptists.

[99]See pp. 297-98.

[100]The papacy became antichrist when the dragon (the emperor) gave his power to the beast from the sea (the pope, Rev 13:2; Deppermann, *Melchior Hofmann*, p. 248; Klaassen, *Living at the End*, p. 28). The pope usurped Christ's seat (Klaassen, *Living at the End*, p. 57; Deppermann, *Melchior Hofmann*, p. 72; cf. 2 Thess 2:4). The Mass was the continual burned offering (Dan 12:11) and abomination of desolation (Klaassen, *Living at the End*, p. 70). John Hus severely wounded the dragon (Rev 13:3), who gave the beast power to destroy him (Deppermann, *Melchior Hofmann*, p. 248).

man elaborated several not always consistent end-time scenarios. One emerged in 1526, before he was an Anabaptist. The most significant alterations occurred after 1530. We will consider the 1526 scheme first.

During the first $3\frac{1}{2}$ years, apostolic messengers would invite all people to the Lamb's feast, and many would respond.[101] The pope would be exposed, and this period would end with the "two witnesses" punishing the world for 1,260 days (Rev 11:3) or 1,290 days (Dan 12:11). Hoffman identified the witnesses as Elijah and Enoch, claiming that both were alive but as yet unknown.

Then the pope would call on the red dragon, Emperor Charles V (cf. Rev 12:3–13:2), who would kill the two witnesses (Rev 11:7-10) and many saints.[102] The seventh trumpet would be blowing (Rev 11:15), and Christians would flee into the wilderness, as Hutterites noted (Rev 12:6, 14). There God would teach them directly.[103] Other political forces would enter the fray. Two rulers, whom Hoffman identified, would lead the persecution, while two others would somewhat protect the true church. (These were unnamed in 1526, but in 1530 Melchior identified one.) Then pagan Gog and Magog would wreak greater destruction on all (Rev 20:8-9). Only Christ's return would overcome them.[104]

During 1529-1530 Hoffman visited Strasbourg. There he embraced Anabaptism and, influenced by Denck's followers, asserted the will's total freedom after conversion. His eschatology was affected by a circle of "Strasbourg prophets," including some of Hut's disciples who had fled there after his death. Many women belonged, such as Ursula Jost and Barbara Rebstock, another indication to Melchior that the Spirit was being poured out widely (cf. Acts 2:17-18). Through this circle's veneration, Hoffman began regarding himself as one of Revelation 11's two witnesses—Elijah—though the other's identity remained vague.[105]

After 1530, Hoffman incorporated some of the Strasbourg prophets' pre-

---

[101]Deppermann, *Melchior Hofmann*, p. 72.

[102]In 1530 Hoffman foretold the two witnesses' execution at an ecumenical council resembling the Council of Constance, which martyred Hus (1414 C.E.). Persecution would be launched by a hellish trinity of pope (beast), emperor (dragon) and monks (false prophets; see Deppermann, *Melchior Hoffman*, p. 254). Hoffman's first scheme appeared in chap. 12 of his Daniel commentary (1526 C.E.; Deppermann, *Melchior Hoffman*, pp. 72-78; excerpt in Klaassen, *Anabaptism in Outline*, pp. 326-28). The alterations came from his Revelation commentary (1530 C.E.; Deppermann, *Melchior Hoffman*, pp. 251-56).

[103]According to Hoffman in 1530, the apostolic messengers would lead people from literal to self-evident knowledge of God, a favorite theme of Joachim of Fiore. Hoffman included a conversion of Jews of this spiritualist nature (Deppermann, *Melchior Hoffman*, pp. 252-53).

[104]Ibid., pp. 73-74.

[105]Cf. George Williams and Angel Mergal, ed., *Spiritual and Anabaptist Writers* (Philadelphia: Westminster Press, 1957), pp. 211-12.

dictions.[106] He had previously affirmed, quite generally, that devout rulers would protect some saints during the final $3\frac{1}{2}$ years. This would now occur in specific cities, a notion found in Hut. The chief city would be Strasbourg, which would fend off the dragon (emperor). Anabaptists would not actually fight but dig trenches, stand guard and direct the whole operation. After this the apostolic messengers would evangelize the earth. Though unarmed, they would be invulnerable.

Before Christ could return, Babylon and its priests had to be destroyed. Though pious rulers would apparently perform this, Hoffman's new scenario depicted the saints not suffering to the end but joining the winning side after the Strasbourg siege. In 1533 he added that an earthly theocracy, ruled by Joseph and Solomon and inspired by Samson and Jonah, would reign between Babylon's destruction and Christ's return. The seventh trumpet, which in 1526 had introduced a final ($3\frac{1}{2}$ year) persecution of Christians, would now unleash God's wrath on the godless.

Up to 1530 Hoffman had depicted Christians as largely passive and devout rulers as only marginally successful during the final $3\frac{1}{2}$ years. After 1530 both appeared increasingly active in bringing about Christ's reign—consistent with Hoffman's new confidence in free will. Though he opposed the Münster endeavor and never called Christians to arms, this schema could certainly be enlisted in support of it.

Münster. Late in 1533, while Hoffman languished in a Strasbourg prison and Jesus remained in heaven, Jan Matthijs proclaimed himself Enoch and extended the parousia to Easter 1534. Through Matthijs, the Spirit identified the final city of refuge as Münster, not Strasbourg. Anabaptists were already taking power in Münster.

Bernard Rothmann, Münster's chief theologian, agreed that the Spirit was revealing such plans directly. Yet he sought to substantiate the course of events biblically. Rothmann did not simply identify certain Old Testament prophecies with current events, like Hoffman and Hut. The Prophets and Pentateuch became his canon within a canon. From this orientation he insisted that Scripture concerns "the time of this life upon earth." Consequently, everything prophesied about the Last Days had to be implemented here before Christ returned.[107] This included judgment of the wicked and erecting God's kingdom on an Old Testament model.

Unlike Hoffman, Hut and Schiemer, Rothmann interpreted the ubiquitous final $3\frac{1}{2}$ years neither literally nor wholly figuratively, like Hubmaier and Schlaffer.

---

[106]Deppermann, *Melchior Hoffman*, pp. 257-59; Klaassen, *Anabaptism in Outline*, pp. 328-29.
[107]Klaassen, *Anabaptism in Outline*, p. 334.

By complex calculations the church's subjugation to Babylon became 1,400 years.[108] The abomination of desolation, then, had taken over soon after the apostles, much earlier than Hoffman taught.[109] And while Hoffman expected some secular authorities to aid the saints, Rothmann traced all government to Nimrod and found it wholly opposed to the church (cf. Gen 10:8-11).[110] Nobody could help true Christians but themselves.

Further, since the church's $3\frac{1}{2}$ year tribulation (= 1,400 days) had just expired, the time of grace was past. Christians should now execute God's wrath, as Elijah had killed Baal's prophets after $3\frac{1}{2}$ years.[111] Moreover, the abomination of desolation was again patently visible in widespread, deliberate resistance to the gospel.[112]

For Rothmann, Scripture predicted that humans would actualize not only God's judgment but God's kingdom as well. Influenced by Hoffman's notion of a theocratic interregnum preceding the parousia, Rothmann and other Münsterites identified Christ not as the David who would establish the kingdom after his return, but Solomon who would reign after David introduced it on earth. David, of course, became Jan van Leyden. After Jan had subjugated God's enemies, 144,000 Münsterites would stream forth to convert whoever was left.

While Rothmann rooted his scenario in an allegedly biblical eschatology, his anthropology and soteriology played crucial roles. Like Hoffman, he taught the will's complete freedom, including ability to attain a second justification, after conversion. Rothmann expected similar rapid divinization—and loss of salvation for one deliberate sin.[113] This optimism fueled exhortations to judge God's enemies and build God's kingdom.

With Münster's tragic fall in June 1535, the Dutch Anabaptist situation recalled South Germany-Austria's in 1528 when Hut's predictions failed. Until then Dutch eschatology had been even more pronouncedly premillennial. (However, given its highly spiritualized soteriology and Rothmann's relegation of Scripture's significance to this world, even it may have ultimately expected a disembodied end.) We should not be surprised if Menno and Dirk's reactions were similar to Riedemann and Marpeck's.

Menno Simons. Echoing most Anabaptists, Menno Simons often called the pope and the Roman Church "antichrist." Antichrist worked particularly through infant bap-

---

[108]Klaassen, *Living at the End*, p. 30.

[109]Klaassen, *Anabaptism in Outline*, pp. 320-21.

[110]Deppermann, *Melchior Hoffman*, p. 347.

[111]Klaassen, *Living at the End*, p. 31.

[112]Klaassen, *Anabaptism in Outline*, pp. 332-33; Klaassen, *Living at the End*, p. 31.

[113]Deppermann, *Melchior Hoffman*, pp. 342-43.

tism, the Mass and the pride of theologians.[114] Shortly before he left Catholicism, Menno, jolted by Münster and his brother's death on the way there, first applied "antichrist" par excellence, along with "abomination of desolation," to Jan van Leyden.[115] For only Jesus could be the promised David. But Jan had dared assume that name—as David Joris later would and likewise be labeled antichrist and the man of sin.[116]

Resembling premillennialists at times, Menno spoke as if a particular scenario were unfolding. Menno insisted that God did not want the saints to punish Babylon (Rome). Instead, Babylon would attack and overcome them, allied with the beast (cf. Rev 13:7).[117] The present persecution would last until Christ returned with his saints for judgment. Then God would use the heathen to destroy Babylon, as in ancient times (cf. Rev 17:16).[118]

More generally, Menno declared that "the prophecy of Christ concerning the last days, as well as that of Daniel and of the apostles are being fulfilled in force."[119] The predicted signs were appearing in the heavens and in wars, famines, pestilences as well as "unheard-of wonders on the earth beneath."[120] The dragon, knowing his time was short, was savagely persecuting the saints. But at the same time, after centuries of darkness Christ was being manifested more clearly, as Hoffman had also announced.[121]

Nevertheless, while Menno mentioned such sequences, he often emphasized that no one could know when or how they would commence.[122] He was sharply critical of all who calculated the future by biblical timetables and models, as did Münsterites. Menno also denounced Münsterites for claiming, somewhat like Joachim of Fiore, that the Son's dispensation was past and a better one was beginning.[123] This had led them to rely on dreams and visions.[124] It also denied that

---

[114]Menno Simons, *The Complete Works of Menno Simons*, ed. J. C. Wenger (Scottdale, Penn.: Herald, 1956), pp. 128, 151-52, 303, 743, 775, 927, 943. He also identified the Roman Church with its priests and teachers with the beast of Rev 13 (p. 742). The priests were called "without exception" by the dragon and beast (p. 255). The pope was "the man of sin" (p. 232, cf. 2 Thess 2). Menno identified Protestant churches, with their baptism and Supper, as the Babylonian harlot (p. 517) and the Reformed Church of his opponent, Gellius Faber, with the man of sin and antichrist (pp. 756-57).
[115]Ibid., p. 37.
[116]Ibid., p. 1019.
[117]Ibid., p. 742.
[118]Ibid., pp. 47, 597.
[119]Ibid., p. 528.
[120]Ibid., p. 374.
[121]Ibid., pp. 581, 626, 962, cf. Rev 12:12.
[122]Ibid., p. 46, cf. p. 1035.
[123]Ibid., pp. 219-20.
[124]Ibid., pp. 218, 220.

Jesus, who had already brought "the dispensation of perfectness," was our behavioral example.[125] Only the resurrection would bring greater perfection.

Yet while the new creation involved this future dimension, Menno's major theme was that it had already come. His most comprehensive and theological treatise, *The Foundation Book* (1539), began by proclaiming that the day of grace is here—even though, in a sense, it also "approaches."[126] All Old Testament promises are fulfilled; all evil powers have been vanquished by Christ, even by "the children of God." The concrete implication: repent immediately and rise with Christ to new life![127] Don't wait for a time more convenient or conducive to this total transformation. Had the apostles done so, the gospel would never have gone forth.[128]

This last affirmation was at the heart of Menno's eschatology and his ethics. Though the new creation would sometime pervade everything, it was already here in the most important sense. Consequently, it was fully possible to live by Jesus' ethics and to undertake his mission. These need not wait until society became more hospitable to such idealism. This lifestyle must be adopted not simply because Jesus taught and exemplified it but also because through grace the eschaton was present in a way that made it attainable.

Eschatological existence, then, could commence immediately. Certain events need not transpire beforehand, nor need its final form arrive soon. Nevertheless, present experience was shaped by that future dimension. Converts would be sustained in suffering by anticipating God's final victory. Others would be called to accountability and changed by fear of final judgment. Everyone would be judged by their works.[129] Civil rulers, apostate church leaders and in some way even true Christians should tremble.[130] Yet if they endured, the latter would assist Christ in judging their persecutors.[131] These persecutors would recognize their fate in anguish, but too late.[132] Menno claimed that he did not desire vengeance but their salvation.[133]

The day of grace then was more fully actualized than the day of judgment. People could enter the former immediately, while the latter still delayed. Nonetheless, judgment could also fall in the present. Leaders of false churches, for in-

---

[125]Ibid., pp. 518, 216.
[126]Ibid., pp. 108-9, cf. pp. 206, 220, 375.
[127]Ibid., pp. 108, 220.
[128]Ibid., p. 110.
[129]Ibid., p. 833.
[130]Ibid., p. 966.
[131]Ibid., p. 81.
[132]Ibid., pp. 205, 225, 940, 1067.
[133]Ibid., p. 942.

stance, were "utterly past conversion" so that "the righteous judgment is come upon them."[134]

Given Menno's revulsion over Münster, we should hardly be surprised that he often described the eschaton's present reality as spiritual. It was "the fulfillment of all figurative transactions into a new, spiritual reality"; "the kingdom of Christ is not of this visible, tangible, transitory world, but . . . eternal, spiritual, and abiding."[135] The "first resurrection" occurred with conversion, much as Marpeck thought.[136] Those partaking of it "dwell in the heavenly reality" and "have come to the heavenly Jerusalem." This was the church, "the spiritual bride of Christ, His spiritual body."[137]

This heavenly existence, of course, already activated new creation communities in this material world. But it would pervade the new creation's consummation, when "there shall be no more time," which Menno expected to be spiritual.[138] Like Riedemann, Marpeck and Hubmaier, he perhaps retained a shred of materiality by affirming that "all human nature shall . . . arise . . . with a glorified body."[139] Yet Menno shared their broadly amillennial vision of our future as "heavenly" and even "of the angelic nature."[140] Like the early Swiss, Menno perhaps expected several events to precede Christ's return. Yet like them he preached these mainly not as a timetable but as a call to repentance and sanctification, and to assure the persecuted that God was in control.

Dirk Philips. Writing more systematically than Menno, Dirk Philips delineated more precisely the spiritual character of eschatological *restitution* (Rothmann's word for the Münsterite project). Dirk critiqued Münster and also Rome for believing that God's kingdom involved literal enactment of Old Testament promises and institutions. God's kingdom was "not of this world, but inwardly among all genuine Christians."[141] The new heavens were believers in whom Christ dwelled, and the new earth was their hearts.[142] The only "restitution" anyone could expect then was restoration of all things spiritually in Christ. The Old Testament simply provided

---

[134]Ibid., p. 91, cf. p. 318.

[135]Ibid., pp. 108, 217, cf. pp. 808, 819.

[136]Ibid., p. 58, cf. Rev 20:4-6.

[137]Ibid., p. 59, cf. pp. 74, 223, 993. Such passages sometimes referred to this as future also, showing how closely he intermingled the eschaton's present and future reality. God's kingdom is "here in hope, and after this in eternal life" (p. 94; for practical implications, see p. 613).

[138]Ibid., p. 109.

[139]Ibid., p. 810.

[140]Ibid., p. 708.

[141]Dirk Philips, *The Writings of Dirk Philips*, ed. Cornelius Dyck, William Keeney and Alvin Beachy (Scottdale, Penn.: Herald, 1992), p. 317.

[142]Ibid., pp. 318-19, cf. 2 Pet 3:13; Rev 21:1.

figures and shadows of this, which reached their end in Christ.[143]

Dirk expounded in detail how the New Jerusalem from heaven was, as Menno taught, the current congregation's spiritual reality.[144] Yet Jerusalem was also future because restitution existed in two phases: presently, in the Spirit's work; and finally in perfect, renewed, heavenly being.[145] Dirk repeatedly mentioned Jesus bringing "true being," which was spiritual, yet it was also "created," and people could begin walking in it immediately.[146]

By underscoring this present dimension Dirk differentiated himself from Hoffman's hyper-spiritualizing tendencies, especially concerning purely spiritual revelation unmediated by the "external word."[147] Perfect knowledge was unattainable in this life. Those who pretended to have it supposed that the Spirit had transported them beyond the gospel and apostles into that future that had not yet arrived. They likewise forgot that true spiritual birth had to be manifested now, as Menno also insisted, in concrete, Christlike behavior.[148]

Nonetheless, when Dirk turned to the future, the spiritual dimension again predominated. Like Hubmaier, he both affirmed that body, soul and spirit would be resurrected, and suggested that the first might then vanish.[149] The "earthly house" would be "broken," and our mortal flesh "laid off" as we are "clothed with an imperishable, immortal and glorious body."[150] Like Menno, Dirk expected us to "be conformed to the nature of angels."[151] Yet Dirk, like Marpeck, insisted that humans would always remain creatures and never actually become God.[152] Resurrection, moreover, would be a future historical event, not simply the soul's entrance into heaven or hell at death. Soul sleep would apparently precede the resurrection, for this would awaken all people, who had been "at rest from death."[153]

In other respects Dirk's eschatology resembled Menno's. The judgment would

[143]Ibid., pp. 347, 317.

[144]Ibid., pp. 376-82, cf. Rev 21:2–22:6.

[145]Ibid., pp. 404, 347-48, 377, cf. pp. 326-28, 347. "The creation of the heavens and the earth is spiritually restored in Christ until the time that the perfect transformation out of the perishable into the eternal imperishable and glorified takes place, and all believes shall inherit and possess the new heavens and the new earth" (p. 319).

[146]Ibid., pp. 317, 348, 351, 515. He tended to distance Christians as newly created from their original creation (pp. 320, 323, 353, 420) much as he did Jesus' heavenly flesh from their earthly flesh.

[147]Ibid., p. 290.

[148]Ibid., pp. 289-94.

[149]Ibid., p. 626.

[150]Ibid., p. 338.

[151]Ibid., p. 320, cf. chap. 9.

[152]Ibid., pp. 144-45.

[153]Ibid., p. 66.

shame those who persecuted the saints, as Hubmaier and Riedemann also maintained.[154] Dirk encouraged victims to be patient, for they would not be ashamed.[155] Rome was the Babylonian harlot, the abomination and antichrist that had set itself above God for many centuries.[156] Dirk discouraged attendance at Catholic worship by pointing to the final condemnation of the two beasts and their follower.[157]

Dirk perceived Satan being finally loosened in his own day, not after a future millennium (Rev 20:7-9). Dirk found his day more perilous than the apostles' because all governments persecuted his followers.[158] Yet it was also the day of salvation, as Menno insisted. People could step directly into God's spiritual kingdom and experience final purification.[159]

Summary

Most historic Anabaptist eschatologies, broadly considered, fell into two types. In the first, the new creation's final coming was preceded by sequences of specific events. Persons, groups, episodes and places involved, or soon to be involved, were correlated with biblical figures. Some literal predictions were attributed to the Spirit's climactic outpouring, which was bestowing unique insight into Scripture—and, for some, also transcending it. Specific scenarios were promoted by Hut, Schiemer, Hoffman, Münsterites and perhaps some early Swiss, especially in locales like Zollikon and St. Gall.

Such schemas located the future new creation on earth, following unprecedented tribulation. Hut, Schiemer and Hoffman (for most of his career) expected this future to commence with Christ's return, as in premillennialism. This focus on a future parousia was compatible with soul sleep until the resurrection (although, evidence that Anabaptists other than Schiemer and Dirk taught this is indirect).

For Hut, Münsterites and perhaps the later Hoffman, Jesus' way provided the behavioral norm until just before the kingdom's establishment, and again afterward. Violence, however, would be permitted to initiate God's reign. The Münsterites sought to establish God's kingdom fully before Jesus returned, investing great energy in this generally postmillennial sociopolitical task. Predictions were so intrinsic to these apocalyptic evangels that specific expectations must have contoured

---

[154]Ibid., pp. 177, 628.

[155]Ibid., pp. 238-40, 265, 303, 391-92.

[156]Ibid., pp. 188-89, 234, 239, 323.

[157]Ibid., pp. 187-88.

[158]Ibid., p. 404, cf. pp. 234, 198.

[159]Ibid., pp. 384-85, cf. 1 Cor 3:12-15; 2 Cor 6:2. Purification apparently could also occur after Jesus' return (p. 402).

many converts' faith. When these forecasts failed, such faith was likely shaken severely or destroyed.

Eschatologies of the second type also correlated biblical phenomena with a sense of final tribulation and the impending end. Like the first variety, they aligned anti-Christian figures with persecuting governments and Catholicism over many centuries, sometimes including Protestants as their extensions. This second type also found the Spirit uniquely active, though not transcending Scripture. However, timing and sequences were usually indefinite, particularly since most such eschatologies emerged after failures of the first type.

Though this second orientation included Christ's historical return, few material features were ascribed to what followed, except brief acknowledgments that human bodies would be transformed—and perhaps, therefore, not wholly spiritualized. Such perspectives were propounded by Hubmaier, probably most other Swiss, Schlaffer, Riedemann, Marpeck, Menno and Dirk. (Denck's was far more spiritualized.) Among traditional options they most resembled amillennialism.

This second type, which did not calendarize the Last Days, encouraged Jesus-like behavior in all of them, not only certain phases. Indeed, this perseverance formed the supreme test and medium for purification, avoiding judgment and entering God's final kingdom. Yet this was no interim ethic just for the Last Days. It was that normative Christian way that had largely vanished centuries ago.

Given their turbulent times and heavy persecution, most adherents of this second outlook probably expected the parousia quite soon. But since they set no date, they were ready to persevere when particular dating schemes failed. Jesus' early arrival was not intrinsic to their theological conviction that he would come. To be sure, most eschatologies of this type emerged later than the first. Their adherents were more concerned to establish things like stable churches that might last. Gradually, their anticipation of the end may have diminished *psychologically*. Still, I find no good evidence that their sense of living in the Last Days diminished *theologically*.

All these eschatologies, even the first type, were highly "realized." As Menno articulated most clearly, the day of grace had been present since the apostles—even though he, like others, sensed it operating and the day of judgment approaching with exceptional intensity. Anabaptist beliefs about the new creation's personal, communal and missional potentialities were inseparable from some such apprehension of its climactic, Spirit-imbued dynamism. Had this not shaped their convictional framework, Anabaptists would hardly have been so optimistic about embodying Jesus' life and teachings in discipleship.

CONTEMPORARY APPROPRIATIONS

Historic Anabaptists were energized by eschatology's "realized" dimension, or the presence of the new creation already in their midst. Many early converts expected this to climax in a wide-ranging transformation of society and the spatiotemporal universe. Some forecast the coming and character of this transformation in detail. But when events discredited them, Anabaptism's future hopes became almost wholly spiritual. Toward what, then, should a contemporary eschatology in Anabaptist perspective direct its focus? Future spiritual states, but not history and society's future course? Or this historical and social future, but not future spiritual states? Or perhaps features of both, but without reference to the world's future spatiotemporal structure?

Despite the "realized" dimension, historic Anabaptists also anticipated sharp discontinuities between present and future. The future states of individuals and of social and natural structures would greatly differ from present ones. Which of these discontinuities (personal, social or spatiotemporal) should current Anabaptist eschatology stress?

Among those contemporary Anabaptist theologians who consider eschatology, most devote significant attention to the social aspect, noticeably less to the personal, and very little to the spatiotemporal.

According to James McClendon, if we are to know "what lasts" in history and thus what we should promote, we must know "what comes last."[160] For McClendon, eschatology provides multiple pictures of the end. Yet their interconnections "need not be temporal, or spatial, or causal ones."[161] These pictures identify God's true history amidst all historical events.[162] But they yield no real clues as to when, how or even if this will prevail in human experience, or how any end might be related to other times or spatiotemporal structures.[163]

---

[160]McClendon, *Systematic Theology* 2: 75.

[161]Ibid., p. 77, cf. pp. 91, 93.

[162]E.g., Mt 25: 31-47 locates it among people beneath the threshold of ordinary awareness (ibid., pp. 78-80, 101).

[163]McClendon links his eschatology with his central baptist vision: "shared awareness of the present Christian community as the primitive community and the eschatological community" (James McClendon, *Systematic Theology*, vol. 1, *Ethics* [Nashville: Abingdon, 1986], p. 31; cf. *Systematic Theology*, 2: 82, 86, 92) This vision is "neither developmental nor successionist, but mystical and immediate" (*Systematic Theology* 1: 33). While McClendon's narrative emphasis checks the vision's tendency to reduce past events' meaning to some dimension of the present, it is less successful in avoiding reduction of the future to the present. Since McClendon is little concerned with specific future events, he can downplay Hut's misforecasts, as we might expect "of one who shared the baptist vision" (*Systematic Theology* 2: 95). He treats Hut as consistently pacifist. For detailed, mostly positive, interaction with McClendon's eschatology, see Thomas N. Finger, "Outlines of a Contemporary Believers' Church Eschatology: A Dialogue with James McClendon," in *Apocalypticism and Millennialism*, ed. Loren Johns (Kitchener, Ont.: Pandora, 2000), pp. 290-305.

Norman Kraus treats Jesus' resurrection as history's "normative center" and from it "projects the nature of the eschaton."[164] Eschatology assesses history's movement in light of Jesus' "revelation of human nature and destiny."[165] Yet Kraus sharply separates the meaning of God's historical acts from empirical historical knowledge.[166] Theology, consequently, cannot really say how Jesus' resurrection or eschatological events are related to spatiotemporal reality.[167] Kraus likes the notion of the "new" being both continuous and discontinuous with the "old." Yet eschatology, which seeks "to conceptualize the unimaginable," cannot prioritize this model. It must also affirm value in different, even contradictory, models.[168] Nonetheless, Kraus rejects "sudden intervention from heaven," and affirms a "qualitatively different existence" beyond temporality after death.[169] For the most part, Kraus' eschatology, like McClendon's, helps us to recognize God's reign in the present, but not to estimate where, when or how widely it might transform history or its spatiotemporal framework.[170]

Nancey Murphy and George Ellis reject divine intervention into this framework, except perhaps at the quantum level.[171] They treat higher levels in the universe, like divine action, as complex organizations of lower levels which incorporate the lower into their own functions without altering the lower's laws. Though Murphy and Ellis do not consider eschatology at length, their outlook raises the possibility that the consummation might introduce one or more higher levels into our world. Perhaps this would permit, say, bodies to rise and flourish eternally without altering the scientific laws we know. (Murphy and Ellis do not discuss this notion.)

Duane Friesen also highlights Jesus' way and its social significance, and rejects divine intervention.[172] Even human fallenness "will not be removed in his-

---

[164]C. Norman Kraus, *God Our Savior* (Scottdale, Penn.: Herald, 1991), p. 197.

[165]Ibid., p. 187.

[166]Ibid., pp. 194-98; cf. C. Norman Kraus, *Jesus Christ Our Lord* (Scottdale, Penn.: Herald, 1987), pp. 43-44, 52-58, 74-79, 88-91, 198-201.

[167]Kraus, *Jesus Christ Our Lord*, pp. 201-2, 221-22.

[168]Kraus, *God Our Savior*, p. 202. Those are translation "into an eternal spiritual kingdom," destruction of this earth and creation of a new one, and "successful completion of creation" (pp. 201-2). Kraus treats models of Jesus' resurrection (pp. 221-22) and the Last Judgment similarly (pp. 212-15, 221-22).

[169]Ibid., pp. 204, 218.

[170]Ibid., p. 205.

[171]Nancey Murphy and George Ellis, *On the Moral Nature of the Universe* (Minneapolis: Fortress, 1996), pp. 207, 214.

[172]Duane Friesen, *Artists, Citizens, Philosophers* (Scottdale, Penn.: Herald, 2000), pp. 101-3. Kaufman argues that if some eternal structure of reality transcends the cosmological-biological process, the latter, including human history, do "not have ultimate metaphysical significance" (Gordon Kaufman, *In Face of Mystery* [Cambridge, Mass.: Harvard University Press, 1993], p. 251).

tory."[173] Yet Friesen also underscores eschatology's importance as a vision for history: "we will not live by an alternative set of practices if we do not have an alternative hope for the future."[174] Here again eschatology helps to discern social discontinuity between the old and new creations. But when old creation forces oppose its vision as overwhelmingly as historic Anabaptists experienced, will theology's claims seem credible if it cannot affirm that this vision will indeed triumph—in some lasting, widespread, unhindered way in real human life? Can this be done without affirming something about our world's material future?

To pursue this question I will interact mainly with evangelicals who are discussing relations between the eschaton's social and material forms most thoroughly today. Issues for further Anabaptist-evangelical dialogue may surface. This interaction will lead me to include Jürgen Moltmann's eschatology.

Evangelical Eschatologies

Having employed pre-, post- and amillennialism as lenses for exploring historic Anabaptism, I will first consider their current shapes.

Dispensationalism. Pre-Constantinian eschatologies, as noted above, were mostly premillennial. They expected various cataclysms to destroy the Roman Empire, followed by Christ's return, transformation of this earth and Christ's reign on it. Premillennial eschatologies envision sharp discontinuity between present and future forms of social existence. Yet they anticipate some continuity as well as discontinuity between the current and coming physical cosmos. Premillennialism has appealed to many who oppose the status quo and long for peace and justice on earth.

Most popular eschatological scenarios today derive from a form of premillennialism called dispensationalism. It aims for consistent literal interpretation of Scripture.[175] It treats continuity-discontinuity issues by dividing history into dispensations. God's kingdom dispensation began with Israel as an earthly, sociopolitical entity. Jesus finally appeared as Israel's king and added his distinct teachings to its structure. But when Israel rejected Jesus, God's kingdom dispensation was interrupted. It will be reactivated fully, spiritually and socially—but only in the millennium—after Jesus returns.

Dispensationalism then envisions a social order like the Anabaptists' new cre-

---

[173]Stephen Mott, quoted in Friesen, *Artists, Citizens, Philosophers*, p. 237. Friesen does not want to divide "this life from the life to come" (p. 115), but I find him saying hardly anything about the latter.

[174]Friesen, *Artists, Citizens, Philosophers*, p. 124, cf. pp. 125, 172-73, 237.

[175]Charles Ryrie, *Dispensationalism Today* (Chicago: Moody Press, 1965), pp. 86-109; with recent exceptions, to be explained.

ation in that Jesus' teachings contribute to it, though along with many Old Testament features. Yet this order is not present or realized but postponed to the future. Its place is now taken by the church dispensation. Here spiritual matters alone are of real concern.[176] Sociopolitical affairs belong to the "world," which opposes the church, somewhat as historic Anabaptists thought. But Jesus' kingdom way cannot be followed until he returns and his enemies are destroyed in the way Revelation, read quite literally, describes.

Literal interpretation furnishes material for dispensational chronologies, especially of those final seven years that fascinated Hut, Schiemer, Hoffman and Rothmann. At their midpoint, dispensationalists usually insert a rapture, when the saints will join Jesus in the air.[177] The earth below will then undergo a final $3\frac{1}{2}$ year tribulation. The saints will remain with Jesus and return with him to establish the millennial kingdom.

Since dispensationalists read scenes of the earth's devastation fairly literally, it is often thought that they devalue the environment (e.g., Rev 8:7–9:20). However, despite discontinuities between present and millennial social structures, dispensationalists, with all premillennialists, envision important material continuities between the present and future earths. Nearly all dispensationalist theologians expect the millennium to bring human and nonhuman potentials to their highest actualization.[178] Indeed, they insist that they emphasize the material and social dimensions of God's kingdom—though by distancing these from the church's concerns.

Since about 1980 a *progressive dispensationalism* has acknowledged some figurative features of eschatological texts and somewhat less clarity about coming events. It softens the sharp distinction between kingdom and church dispensations by calling

---

[176]Dispensationalism originated with John Nelson Darby, who founded the Plymouth Brethren in late nineteenth-century England in hopes of restoring New Testament Christianity, or a believers' church. Darby conceived this true church as largely spiritual in contrast to the false (Anglican) church's temporal and material enmeshments (Donald Durnbaugh, *The Believers' Church* [Scottdale, Penn.: Herald, 1968], pp. 161-72). Craig Blaising associates Darby with *classical dispensationalism*, along with C. I. Scofield and Lewis Sperry Chafer. *Revised dispensationalism* flourished in the 1950s and 1960s under Alva McClain, J. D. Pentecost, John Walvoord, Herman Hoyt and Charles Ryrie (Craig Blaising and Darrell Bock, *Progressive Dispensationalism* [Wheaton, Ill.: BridgePoint, 1993], pp. 9-56). My brief description applies to both.

[177]The key text is I Thess 4:14-18. Yet while dispensationalists often call this rapture "secret," Jesus descends with a shout, an archangel's call and a trumpet (v. 16). This text likely means that the saints, after rising to meet Jesus, will accompany him back to earth in triumph rather than remaining above for a lengthy period. Some dispensationalists, however, place the rapture midway through or even after the tribulation. See Robert Gundry, *The Church and the Tribulation* (Grand Rapids: Zondervan, 1973), esp. pp. 9-28.

[178]Thomas Finger, *Evangelicals, Eschatology, and the Environment* (Wynnewood, Penn.: Evangelical Environmental Network, 1998), pp. 17-24.

the kingdom God's overall goal, actualized in diverse ways in different dispensations. Jesus' distinctive teachings become more applicable today. The church maintains its spiritual integrity not by separating from society but by witnessing to kingdom values in its midst.[179]

Postmillennialism. In ancient premillennialism the Roman Empire opposed Christ's millennial rule. In postmillennialism that Empire, by supporting the church, became a vehicle for Christ's rule. Postmillennialists affirm significant social continuity between today's world and the millennium. For the latter is already present, or realized, though quite differently than for Anabaptists. In Revelation 20:4-6 the martyrs come alive and reign with Christ. If this will not occur after Christ's return, as premillennialists believe, Christ and his martyrs must actually be ruling during a prior historical span. This must affect at least much of the earth, for Christ's enemies have been defeated (Rev 19:11-21) and demonic powers bound (Rev 20:1-3).

It is hard to conceive these saints reigning otherwise than through a church with widespread social dominance. Further, since the millennium affects every sphere of life, civil authorities must be aiding and participating in this church's rule. Jesus' way then cannot be normative for everyone. Postmillennialists minimize the distinctness of Jesus' way and the eschatological, countercultural suffering that might go with it.

Postmillennialism, in other words, regards certain institutions and leaders of its own day as fairly direct agents of Christ's end-time rule. It also tends to find that millennium being actualized progressively through ecclesiastical and social processes. Zwingli adopted this outlook. Münsterites also did, in the sense that God's kingdom would be initially governed by humans.

General expectations of social progress, like those in nineteenth-century liberal theology, also are broadly postmillennial. Here neither institutions nor individuals so much as widespread trends—democracy, socialism and so forth—become direct expressions of Christ's rule.[180] Today, however, these are often regarded as products of a particular, flawed, human outlook: modernism.[181]

In many postmillennial schemes, Christ's return climaxes such trends or is interpreted symbolically. The millennium, then, is also continuous with the cosmos' material structure. Evangelical postmillennialists, however, posit a brief flare-up of

---

[179]See Blaising and Bock, *Progressive Dispensationalism.*

[180]E.g., according to Social Gospel theologian Walter Rauschenbusch, "the development of a Christian social order would be the highest proof of God's saving power. The failure of the social movement would impugn his existence" (Walter Rauschenbusch, *A Theology for the Social Gospel* [Nashville: Abingdon, 1978], p. 178).

[181]Cf. pp. 313-14.

evil after the earthly millennium but before the parousia.[182] Afterward, the material earth will be transformed, both in continuity and discontinuity with what preceded, somewhat as premillennialists anticipate.[183]

In nineteenth-century America, many evangelicals were postmillennial in this sense. They were more socially oriented than premillennialists. This was because they envisioned the gospel advancing hand in hand with American democracy, industry, social welfare and global commerce.[184] This optimism, however, was diminished by the Civil War, financial crises in the 1870s and multiple social ills accompanying industrialization and urbanization. Dispensationalism, in fact, arose along with the consequent pessimism. Few twentieth-century evangelical theologians championed postmillennialism. Nevertheless, equations of any social institution or movement, such as America's war on terrorism, with God's purposes are basically postmillennial, whatever eschatology their adherents profess.

Amillennialism. I will use the term *amillennialism* to cover all views that believe Revelation 20:1-10 does not indicate a temporal span. It includes most eschatologies that invest ultimate hope in an entirely spiritual, heavenly realm; or an internal, existential sphere. Denck probably belongs here. Some amillennialists, however, turn much attention to historical and material reality.

1. Evangelical amillennialism. A final time of trouble, dominated by antichrist, the beasts and other biblical figures, is anticipated by evangelical amillennialists. These end-time characters, however, will be not so much individuals as climactic forms of forces that have opposed the church for centuries, as most Anabaptists saw them. After this, evangelical amillennialists expect Christ to return bodily and transform the material world in way both continuous and discontinuous with our present one, much as premillennialists envision.[185]

This broad chronology, however, does not include the millennium as a stage. For this would fragment eschatological hope. These amillennialists insist that Scripture links its central hope, Christ's return, intrinsically with the bodily resurrection, last judgment, defeat of evil and renewal of the cosmos. A spatiotemporal millennium, however, divides the resurrection and judgment in two (Rev 20:4 and Rev 20:11-13).[186] Evil's defeat becomes twofold (Rev 19:20–20:3 and Rev 20:14-15). So does cosmic renewal, arriving first with the millennium and later with the new heavens and earth (Rev 21:1–22:8).[187]

---

[182]Charles Hodge, *Systematic Theology* (London: James Clark, 1960), 3:792-800, 812-30; cf. Rev 20: 7-10.
[183]Ibid., pp. 851-57.
[184]Donald Dayton, *Theological Roots of Pentecostalism* (Grand Rapids: Zondervan, 1987), pp. 153-58.
[185]Anthony Hoekema, *The Bible and the Future* (Grand Rapids: Eerdmans, 1979), pp. 164-72.
[186]Dispensationalism nearly adds a third resurrection, the rapture.
[187]Cf. Finger, *Christian Theology*, 1:168-76.

But while denying a millennium, evangelical amillennialism refuses to spiritualize Revelation 19–22. God's kingdom, it insists, will finally be actualized on earth. For the Bible links humanity's creation with that of all other creatures. Humans were designed to rule them (Gen 1:28-30), though as stewards who care for and nurture them. This tie is so close that nonhuman creation is injured by humanity's sin (Gen 3:17-19), while humanity's liberation through Christ must include creation's liberation from this curse (Rom 8:19-22). In fact, Anthony Hoekema argues, if God would destroy or bypass the earth in saving humankind, "Satan would have won a great victory."[188]

Still, if Revelation 20:1-6 involves no particular timelike span, what does it signify? The usual answer is the one found in postmillennialism. The first resurrection was the martyrs' ascent to heaven to rule with Christ—though perhaps not as directly through or continuous with specific institutions, leaders and movements as in postmillennialism.[189] Nonetheless, evangelical amillennialists usually suppose that sociopolitical life is more positively affected by Christian forces and less by anti-Christian ones than do premillennialists.

In America this amillennialism has often characterized Reformed evangelicals, who enter the public arena more often than premillennialists, though probably less optimistically than postmillennialists. Amillennialists do not promote Jesus' way as the general behavioral norm, though they are more likely than postmillennialists to expect Christians to suffer.

2. Moltmann's amillennialism. Jürgen Moltmann is critical of postmillennialism for equating particular sociopolitical constellations with Christ's rule.[190] Moltmann, who is not evangelical in the American sense, insists that Jesus' rule is actualized not through those who claim to represent his cosmic authority but those who follow his cross.[191] When this crucified one arose, he opened up not "a possibility within the world and its history, but a new possibility altogether for the

---

[188]Hoekema, *Bible and the Future*, p. 281, cf. pp. 250, 274-87.

[189]Ibid., pp. 229-38. Hoekema indicates some uncertainty about the sociopolitical effects of the saints having "authority to judge" (Rev 20:4) by remarking: "Whether this means simply agreeing with and being thankful for the judgments made by Christ, or whether it means . . . opportunity to make their own judgments about earthly matters, we are not told" (p. 230).

[190]Moltmann, *Coming of God*, pp. 129-201.

[191]Regarding pacifism, Moltmann opposes nearly all wars, believing that "just causes" invoked for them will almost always be outweighed by actual injustices, especially in nuclear war. But so far as I know he is not a strict pacifist (Thomas N. Finger, "Moltmann's Theology of the Cross," in *Following Jesus Christ in the World Today*, ed. Willard Swartley [Elkhart, Ind.: Institute of Mennonite Studies, 1984]; see dialogue following this lecture in Willard Swartley, ed., *Dialogue Sequel to Jürgen Moltmann's Following Jesus Christ in the World Today* [Elkhart, Ind.: Institute of Mennonite Studies, 1984], esp. pp. 39-48, 60-62).

world . . . for history."[192] Like historic Anabaptists, Moltmann insists that the raising of this one so bitterly rejected by the "world" heralded a new creation.[193] Extraordinary potentials for personal and social transformation now flow perpetually from the risen Jesus.

Early on, Moltmann occasionally spoke as if the social discontinuity between old and new creations implied some material discontinuity: "It is not possible to speak of believing existence in hope and in radical openness, and at the same time consider the 'world' to be a mechanism or self-contained system of cause and effect. . . . [T]he openness of man is bereft of its ground, if the world itself is not open at all."[194] Nevertheless, the eschaton, for Moltmann, will not finally involve a different space or time but is "a change in the transcendental conditions of time."[195] It is not a time span but God's presence in temporal events, connecting them directly to divine eternity. It is a way or quality of life in historical time.[196]

This presence enables people to embrace life rather than defeat and fear of death. It arouses hope for a future toward which they can work together. The final resurrection, for instance, indicates not a future event but a quality of corporate life in God's presence, already experienced partially in places and worth attempting to realize more fully on earth. The first resurrection (Rev 20:4-6), in such a view, would not apply to departed saints ruling through a socially dominant church, as for postmillennialists and many evangelical amillennialists. It would likely characterize people living in Jesus' risen reality on earth, as Marpeck and Menno thought.

Moltmann's broadly amillennial outlook, then, underlines social discontinuity between the old and new creations much like historic and current Anabaptists. Moltmann also posits material continuity, like most of the latter. Historic Anabaptists, however, expected the consummation to be somewhat discontinuous with the old material creation or else sharply discontinuous—very largely or wholly spiritual.

Historic premillennialism. While it believes that much eschatological language refers to history, historic premillennialism rejects classical dispensationalism's literal hermeneutic and various features of its chronologies.[197] While historic premillen-

---

[192]Jürgen Moltmann, *Theology of Hope* (New York: Harper & Row, 1967), p. 179.
[193]Ibid., pp. 172-229.
[194]Ibid., p. 69, cf. pp. 76, 92, 179-82.
[195]Jürgen Moltmann, *The Coming of God* (Minneapolis: Fortress. 1996), p. 26.
[196]Cf. ibid., pp. 22, 70-71, 102-3, 192-96, 200, 291.
[197]George Ladd differentiated historic from dispensational premillennialism most influentially (esp. in *The Meaning of the Millennium: Four Views*, ed. Robert Clouse [Downers Grove, Ill.: InterVarsity Press, 1977], pp. 17-40). Unlike amillennialists, however, historic premillennialists identify distinguishable temporal periods in Revelation 19–22, namely, Rev 19:11–20:3; 20:4-6; 20:7-9 (or 10); 20:10 (or 11)-15; 21:1–22:6.

nialists seldom include a rapture, they do affirm a millennial period that divides the resurrection, judgment, defeat of evil and cosmic renewal each into two phases, against amillennial protests. In this scheme the first resurrection initiates the millennium (Rev 20:4-6). It is not ascent to heaven at death, with its usual consequence: Christ and the saints' somewhat direct rule in history. Instead, the saints might well "sleep" until the millennium, though most historic and dispensational premillennialists have not taught this.

Consequently, society, for historic premillennialists, is governed largely by anti-Christian forces. Christians will often suffer, as historic Anabaptists stressed, especially in the final tribulation. Yet God's kingdom is not in abeyance until the millennium, as for classical dispensationalists but, again as for Anabaptists, present in some realized way. The church then should not be purely spiritual and separate from society but witness to kingdom values in society, much as progressive dispensationalists urge. A premillennialist could argue that the more authentically the new creation is present, the more important is following Jesus' distinctive way.

With their sharp awareness of evil, however, many historic premillennialists promote "law and order" governments as bulwarks against it. This can promote social conservatism and separatism in practice. Overall, historic premillennialists anticipate significant social discontinuity between the present and the millennium but envision some material continuity along with discontinuity, as with nearly all evangelical theologians.

An Anabaptist Response

Anabaptism, with premillennialists and Moltmann, underlines sharp discontinuity between today's sociopolitical reality and the eschaton. Dialogue with evangelical eschatologies clarifies that Anabaptists cannot endorse post- or amillennial forms that align God's rule with past or present structures or movements, or treat the powers as largely redeemed (cf. chap. 7). In such post- and amillennialisms, history and society are insufficiently transformed.

For Anabaptists, God's new creation already affects all realms of life. Anabaptists, then, also cannot postpone living by its norms until a future millennium, as classical (but not progressive) dispensationalists and even some historic premillennialists attempt. As Moltmann maintains, the risen presence of the one crucified by this "world's" rulers calls and enables Christians to walk in his way.

But are the material relationships between the current cosmos and the consummation relevant to this realized, practical orientation? Does it make much difference whether (1) the latter is wholly spiritual and disconnected from the former, or (2) wholly spiritual but preceded by the former's demise, as most historic Anabaptists apparently envisioned, or (3) the latter's form is seldom or never mentioned, as by Moltmann and most current Anabaptists, or (4) whether the earth will be transformed, rendering the consummation's spatiotemporal character partly continuous and discontinuous with former, as for historic premillennialists, evangelical amillennialists and some early Anabaptists?

With these interrelated questions in mind, I now turn to Scripture, my theology's chief source and sole norm. I will first consider human and creaturely destiny broadly, then the final drama specifically.

Biblical considerations. I. Human and creaturely destiny.

• The Old Testament. As emphasized by evangelical amillennialists, the Old Testament links God's original purpose for humans closely with all other creatures', and similarly human sin with creatures' fate. Not only in Genesis 2–3 but throughout the Old Testament, humans were called to care for and nurture the earth. When they obeyed God's call, the earth flourished. When they disobeyed, the land languished, became polluted and cast them out.[198] The original, material creation was not some inferior, preliminary, dispensable stage in God's plan. Humans, of course, would be transformed by Yahweh's immaterial Spirit (Ezek 37:1-4; cf. Jer 31:31-34), but only through their bodies and surroundings.

Yahweh, of course, was not restricted by what we call natural laws. Prophetic portrayals of terrestrial and celestial upheavals were not always figurative. Cosmic alterations were sometimes in view (e.g., Is 24:21-23; 25:7; 26:19; 34:4; Dan 12:1-3; Amos 9:5-6). Yet even the creation of a new heavens and earth was depicted in highly physical terms (Is 66:17-24).[199] No warrant exists within the Old Testament for envisioning these or any future cosmos as mainly or wholly spiritual.

• The Synoptic Gospels. Existing societies are sharply contrasted with God's arriving kingdom in the Synoptic Gospels. Yet these Gospels and also Acts give little reason to think of it as nonmaterial. Through Jesus' mighty deeds God's power broke into the natural world. Jesus' resurrection, the first fruits of a future general resurrection (I Cor 15:20-26), clearly involved his body in the Synoptics, as in John (esp. Jn 20:19-28) and Acts (esp. Acts 1:9-11; 10:39-41).[200] At most, a few remarks may hint at a highly spiritualized future: for example, in the resurrection people do not marry "but are like angels in heaven" (Mt 22:30).[201]

• Jesus' resurrection. The strongest demonstration of God's capacity to not only

---

[198]Finger, *Christian Theology*, 2:108-10.

[199]Cf. Finger, *Evangelicals, Eschatology, and the Environment*, pp. 10-12.

[200]Cf. Grant Osborne, *The Resurrection Narratives* (Grand Rapids: Baker, 1984).

[201]This is perhaps a source of Menno and Dirk's notions of our future angelic nature.

"give life to the dead" but even "call into existence things that do not exist" is Jesus' resurrection.[202] Consequently, as Moltmann points out, it evoked new creation language. We too are being and will be raised by this power transcending matter-energy far enough to create it.

In his ascent, however, Jesus did not simply leave earth behind. He poured out the Spirit, who started transforming human and nonhuman creation.[203] Jesus began reigning over other creatures, which not only represented God's rule but also initiated humanity's cosmic destiny (Heb 2:5-9, cf. Rom 8:19-23). In a sense Jesus' enemies and the cosmos are already "under his feet" (Acts 2:34-35; Eph 1:20-23; Heb 10:12-13). Yet his enemies are not yet fully so, "for he must reign until he has put all his enemies under his feet" (1 Cor 15:25). Then by that same power he will transform our bodies into conformity with his glorified body (Phil 3:20-21).

For these reasons, as Hoekema and Kraus indicate, theology's main clues about the new creation's consummation must come from Jesus' bodily resurrection—especially if Jesus attained human destiny by walking its path of bodily obedience, and affirmations about the nature he shares with us are derived from his work.[204] Jesus' resurrection inaugurated humanity's "elevation" back over other creatures, under whom we had become subservient. Humankind's rule will be perfected when we join him.[205] This rule begins as the Spirit who raised him transforms our bodies christomorphically.

Authentic human existence, then, in its present and final forms, does not subordinate and eliminate other creatures. It cares for and nurtures them. It recognizes that we are interlinked with and even dependent on them in many ways. Does it seem likely, then, that our destiny could be attained and Jesus' reign be fulfilled unless that Spirit, who transformed Jesus' body and ours, would raise ours in some connection with those physical creatures who share our destiny?

• Heavenly destiny? Most churches, like many historic Anabaptists, have taught otherwise, by identifying ultimate human destiny with a wholly spiritual realm. Several texts are frequently cited in support. Didn't Jesus leave to prepare a place in his Father's mansions, so that he could take us to himself (Jn 14:2-3)? Didn't Paul

---

[202]Rom 4:17, 24-25; cf. 1 Cor 1:28-29. These texts, in my view, are most important for affirming *creatio ex nihilo:* creation of all things, including matter's most primeval forms, simply by God's power (Thomas Finger, *Self, Earth and Society* [Downers Grove, Ill.: InterVarsity Press, 1997], pp. 298-99, 303; *Christian Theology,* 2:408-12; *Evangelicals, Eschatology and the Environment,* pp. 162-65).

[203]Hoekema, *Bible and the Future,* pp. 245-50.

[204]Cf. pp. 330, 365, 396-97, 417.

[205]See esp. Marpeck, pp. 344-45 above.

long to depart and be with Christ rather than remain in the flesh (Phil 1:23-24), to put off his earthly tent and put on his "house not made with hands, eternal in the heavens" (2 Cor 5:1-4)? For "flesh and blood cannot inherit the kingdom of God," can they (1 Cor 15:50)? More generally, weren't New Testament hopes often directed toward heaven (Eph 1:18-23; Phil 3:20; Col 3:1-4)?

Certainly. But this need not mean that heaven itself was their final goal. Early Christians looked upward, toward heaven, because Jesus was there. But since he was returning, they looked more eagerly forward to his descent to earth. The texts just mentioned fit well within this framework, even if not all teach it explicitly.

Paul told the Philippians not only that he longed to "depart and be with Christ" (Phil 1:23) but even that "our citizenship is in heaven" (Phil 3:20). Yet Paul immediately added: it is "from there" that we expect Jesus, who will "transform the body of our humiliation that it may be conformed to the body of his glory, by the power that also enables him to make all things subject [hypotaxai] to himself" (Phil 3:21). As other texts indicate, this will climax Christ's present, heavenly reign (Acts 2:34-35; 1 Cor 15:25; Eph 1:20-23; Heb 10:12-13), bestowing the final form of being "with Christ" after we "depart."

Paul also longed for our "house not made with hands, eternal in the heavens" (2 Cor 5:1). He therefore wanted to put off his earthly "tent" (2 Cor 5:2). Yet Paul immediately clarified, not because he wished to be "naked" or "unclothed"—a bare soul without a body, it seems (2 Cor 5:3-4). Quite the contrary, Paul yearned to be "clothed with" (ependysasthai) by the heavenly dwelling. He did not desire that his body be eliminated but that whatever was "mortal" (to thnēton) be "swallowed up by life." This language, like Philippians 3:20-21, is quite compatible with the notion of divine life, which originates in heaven, reaching downward to take material reality up into itself and transform it, and it is also compatible with Jesus finally descending to raise earth into heavenly energies to bring it to its goal—not to abolish and replace it with a wholly different reality.

Further, Jesus' preparing a place for us in order to "come again and . . . take you to myself" (Jn 14:2-3) need not mean transporting us to a location. The main point is that he will take us to himself. That is compatible with Jesus returning here, bringing that "place" with him.

Finally, "flesh and blood cannot inherit the kingdom" because they, in themselves, are "perishable" (1 Cor 15:50). But this does not entail that the perishable body must be destroyed. Rather, it must be "raised" (1 Cor 15:52), must "put on [endysasthai] imperishability." Further, whatever is "mortal" (to thnēton) must "put on [endysasthai] immortality" (1 Cor 15:53). This language resembles 2 Corinthians 5:1-5 closely enough to be interpreted similarly.

I Corinthians 15, moreover, defends bodily resurrection: Jesus' resurrection, our resurrection and the link between them. The psychophysical body *(sōma psychikon)* is like a seed, and the coming spiritual body *(sōma pneumatikon)* is like the mature plant (I Cor 15:44). The difference may be very great. But the latter will clearly be a transformation of the former. Further, while this transition will occur dramatically at some future point, it has already been realized proleptically in history. For humanity (Adam) was originally created psychophysical, or "from the earth," while Jesus was ultimately spiritual, or "from heaven" (I Cor 15:46-47). The full transition from the first to the second occurred in Jesus. This was the "firstfruits" of what will happen to us at his parousia (I Cor 15:23). Then we who bear the image of the earthly human will bear the image of the heavenly human (but not necessarily "go to heaven," I Cor 15:48-49).

New Testament texts about Jesus' and our resurrection and reign, then, including those most cited to support a wholly spiritual afterlife, are at least compatible with a consummation in which the divine Spirit will greatly transform humans, probably with other creatures, and yet all will retain some materiality.

2. Eschatological texts. This conclusion, however, is further challenged by texts that apparently depict earth's final destruction, not its transformation.[206] While I cannot consider them all, they are most numerous in Revelation. I can best respond by indicating how the book as a whole can be read.[207] I will then compare this read-

---

[206]2 Pet 3:10 is often translated: "the heavens will pass away with a loud noise, and the elements will be dissolved with fire, and the earth and the works that are upon it will be burned up" (RSV). However, the word translated "burned up" is *heurethēsetai*, which means "to be found," or "disclosed." How could the elements' fiery dissolution lead to earth's being "disclosed"?

The word for "elements," *stoicheia*, could denote heavenly bodies or evil angelic powers who govern earth and cut it off from God by hovering in the air, as it were (see E. M. Sidebottom, *James, Jude and 2 Peter* [Greenwood, S.C.: Attic, 1967]; Richard Bauckham, *Jude, 2 Peter* [Waco, Tex.: Word, 1983]; cf. Gal 4:3, 9; Col 2: 8, 20, where *stoicheia* were objects of false worship; cf. Eph 2:2). If *stoicheia* are either of these, their destruction would not damage earth seriously. Instead, it would remove obstacles blocking God's vision of the earth, so to speak, laying it open for God to examine all human "deeds" *(erga)*, "everything that is done" (2 Pet 3:10) and judge the godless (2 Pet 3:7). This connects with Peter's main aim: stimulating behavior through which readers would be disclosed or "found" *(heurethēnai)* pure at this judgment (2 Pet 3:14).

This fire may seem destructive (2 Pet 3:7, 10, 12). In eschatological contexts, however, fire often tests or discloses the quality of things and also purifies them (esp. I Cor 3:11-14). Peter, then, likely spoke of a coming testing and purification, not total destruction. He had just declared that in Noah's flood, the world "perished" *(apōleto, 2* Pet 3:6). Yet Peter certainly believed that earth's geology survived, not to mention members of every major species. If so strong a word did not mean total destruction, we need not assume that his fiery forecasts did either (see my *Evangelicals, Eschatology, and the Environment*, pp. 2-6 for fuller exposition). Cf. note 219 on p. 558.

[207]Revelation can be read solely within its original historical context, but then any broader significance becomes quite indirect. It can be treated as wholly symbolic, but then it has no real meaning for future history. Revelation (chaps. 6-22 at least) can also be basically understood as a linear chro-

ing with a passage stressing continuity, Romans 8.[208]

• Revelation. The book of Revelation paints multiple scenes of destruction, many of them contents of seals (Rev 6:1-16), trumpets (Rev 8:6–9:21; 11:15-19) and bowls (Rev 16:1-21). Note that these are visions: distinct, highly imagistic snapshots. Consequently, may be somewhat discontinuous and need not harmonize entirely. For instance, although "every mountain and island was removed from its place" (Rev 6:14), the mountains remained stable enough for "everyone" to seek safety in them (Rev 6:15). Though turning all rivers and springs into blood (Rev 16:4) would likely kill everyone, great multitudes remained (Rev 16:10-16). John was describing one vivid image after another; he was not surveying one literal world whose features were always consistent.

Further, many such scenes are largely parallel with others. The first six seals (Rev 6:1-16), for instance, lead to a seventh, which begins a similar series (of bowls, Rev 8:1–9:21). The seventh bowl apparently initiates a series of trumpets (Rev 11:15-19; 16:1-21). Broadly speaking, destruction increases with each series. Their parallelism is not simply repetitive but progressive, pointing as a whole toward a climax.[209] Nevertheless, Revelation interconnects them dramatically, leaping forward and looping backward, not in linear, historical fashion. Despite their vividness, then, these scenes by no means imply the entire earth's destruction.

In contrast, joyous praise for God's creating and sustaining the world forms another major motif in Revelation. See how mightily the enthroned ones are praised for creation (Rev 4:11) by all creatures (5:11-13)! Christ is creation's "origin" (archē; Rev 3:14). God is glorified for creating heaven and earth, seas and springs (Rev 14:6-7; cf. Rev 10:6). Earth, at least once, is to be protected (Rev 7:1-3), while God will destroy "those who destroy the earth" (Rev 11:18). More broadly, when nonhuman creatures are destroyed, this is never because they are too lowly or evil to participate in the consummation. They suffer because they are so intertwined with humans that they cannot avoid sharing our fate.

Revelation climaxes with the "new heavens and a new earth" (Rev 21:1–22:6). Yet might they be wholly spiritual? For at the final judgment "the earth and the heaven

---

nology of specific events. Popular, mostly dispensational, expositions that insert many such events in the present usually follow this approach. Finally, the reading I adopt values the symbolic yet refers to real history from its original context up to some climax (similar to Hoekema's approach in *Bible and the Future* [pp. 223-27]).

[208]For 2 Pet 3:3-14, see note 206 above.

[209]E.g., one-fourth of humans are affected by at least one seal (Rev 6:8), one-third of the earth is devastated by some of the trumpets (Rev 8:7-12), while the whole earth is apparently damaged by some bowls (Rev 16:2-9). Chapters 17-18 may lead to the climax again. Still, this reading allows chapters 19-22, or portions thereof, to unfold further stages of the end.

fled, . . . and no place was found for them" (Rev 20:11)? Notice, however, that despite the apparent earlier slaughter of every king (Rev 19:17-21), numerous kings and peoples bring their nations' honor and glory—presumably, cultural and other achievements—into the New Jerusalem (Rev 21:24, 26). If a measure of sociocultural continuity survived scenes of annihilation, some material continuity almost certainly did.

Notice further that the new heavens and earth descend upon the old (Rev 21:2, 10)—like Paul's heavenly house and spiritual body, and Christ with his heavenly energies, drawing material creatures up transformingly into themselves. Indeed, the very Godhead descends to the New Earth (Rev 21:3-4, 22-25; 22:3-5). This broad, beautiful cosmoscape is not so much of people going to heaven as of heaven descending, dwelling among and renewing people and their earth.

• Romans 8. If such material continuity is less vivid than discontinuity in Revelation, it emerges clearly in Romans 8. This chapter climaxes the ascending triumph of life, righteousness and God's Spirit over death, sin, law and flesh (Rom 5–8). It finally exults that nothing in creation can separate us from God's love in Christ (Rom 8:38-39). Paul closely links the Spirit's raising of Jesus' body with the present spiritual transformation of ours (esp. Rom 8:11-14). This Spirit that groans within us also groans within and transforms the whole creation (Rom 8:15-27).

Indeed, creation's release from bondage and decay, inflicted due to humankind's fall under sin, now runs parallel with human renewal (8:20-23).[210] All creatures anticipate the redemption of "our body" (corporate humanity, not "bodies"; Rom 8:23) with great eagerness (Rom 8:19), for they will attain their liberation and fulfillment along with ours (Rom 8:21). Indeed, they "must be redeemed in order that redeemed man may have a fitting environment."[211] For God designed humans to attain their destiny in concert with nonhumans from the beginning.

Many more passages could be examined. One might argue that John, Hebrews or 1 Peter envisions the consummation as spiritual.[212] I can only indicate that within the overarching, canonical narrative of God's creating and saving activity,

---

[210]Commentators generally agree on this meaning for Rom 8:20 (e.g., James D. G. Dunn, *Romans 1– 8* [Waco, Tex.: Word, 1988], pp. 469, 472-73). Romans 8's teleology is hardly a smooth, optimistic progression, as sometimes found in postmillennialism. While it does not calendarize specific tribulations, eschatological "groanings" accompany the Spirit's renewal throughout (esp. vv. 18, 31-36; see Jürgen Moltmann, *The Way of Jesus Christ* [San Francisco: HarperCollins, 1990], pp. 151-59; Moltmann, *Coming of God*, pp. 225-35). Discontinuities of this sort abound amid the overarching continuity in Spirit and matter-energy's interaction.

[211]Dunn, *Romans 1—8*, p. 471.

[212]Johannine eschatology is largely realized. Future judgment and resurrection appear only briefly (Jn 5:28-29; 6:40, 54; 1 Jn 2:28–3:2; 4:17). But while Johannine writings say little about an eschatological future, let alone any material features, some major emphases are quite compatible with

where all biblical writings have their place, the spiritual is repeatedly expressed and fulfilled through the material, and most fully at the end.

Theological construction. The biblical materials above point to a consummation whose material form will be both continuous and discontinuous with our present spatiotemporal world, much as in evangelical amillennialism and historic premillennialism. To be sure, we can hardly imagine what its arrival will be like. This overall expectation, however, is coherent with those transformations of matter-energy by Spirit in chapters five through nine of this book. To many people today, nonetheless, it sounds like an odd intrusion into or sudden rupture of a universe adequately explicable by science. Since theology seeks to render the kerygma intelligible in the present, let me attempt this through three constructive tasks.

First, I will take up the question most pressing for Anabaptists: How is this future vision relevant for present practice? Anabaptist theology is not speculation but articulation of convictions that shape practice, even though these cannot be derived simply from it.[213] Second, I will enumerate several features of such a future world. Third, to resolve some remaining issues I will consider the millennium and final resurrection more closely.

Though I hope to make my view plausible in light of current thought forms and issues, these will not function as criteria for validating it. While it draws on many

---

this: e.g., Jesus' bodily resurrection (esp. Jn 20:19-28) and the Word truly becoming flesh (Jn 1:14; 20:19-28) so that denial thereof marks antichrist (1 Jn 4:3; 2 Jn 7; cf. 1 Jn 2:18, 22). Further, John's supposedly Platonic orientation appeared in contemporaneous Jewish writings that retained an earthly eschatology.

In Hebrews, Old Testament rites and objects were "sketches of the heavenly things" (Heb 9:23), "a mere copy of the true" (Heb 9:24), while Jesus passed "through the greater and perfect tent (not made with hands, that is, not of this creation)" to enter the true Holy Place (Heb 9:11-12). Many commentators find Platonic Form-exemplar conceptuality here. Further, salvation brings us to "the heavenly Jerusalem, and to innumerable angels, . . . to the spirits of the righteous made perfect" (Heb 12:22-23). (Menno and Dirk often depicted the church's spiritual nature with this imagery.) Moreover, God would shake earth and heaven (or perhaps already had) producing "the removal of what is shaken—that is, created things *[pepoiēmenōn]*—so that what cannot be shaken may remain" (Heb 12:27). Hebrews probably comes closest among biblical writings to actually teaching a spiritual new creation.

I find little to suggest that the consummation must include materiality in 1 Peter. The awaited inheritance was "imperishable, undefiled, . . . kept in heaven" (1 Pet 1:4). Peter often contrasted its imperishability with the perishability of readers' present lives (1 Pet 3:4; cf. 5:4), particularly their flesh, which withered like grass (1 Pet 1:23-24). The eschatological goal was salvation of their *psychai* (1 Pet 1:9; cf. 1 Pet 1:22; 2:11, 25; 4:19). This could mean their lives as wholes. However, since Peter also contrasted *psychai* with *sarx* (flesh), it could have meant something more like "soul" (1 Pet 2:11). Peter also used *pneuma* anthropologically, in contrast to *sarx* (1 Pet 3:18-19). However, none of this contradicts a future with some material dimension.

[213]See point 11 on pp. 98-99.

sources, my theology is a church discipline whose final norm is Scripture and one that seeks to explicate convictions rooted there.[214] Nevertheless, by clarifying such convictions and their interconnections in light of a cultural context, their plausibility can be enhanced.

I. Are cosmic questions relevant? If Christians underscore discontinuity between old and new creation's social forms, and work to actualize the latter in the present, does it matter what they believe about its final material form?

Billions of people have commenced that human journey which is intrinsically shaped by and shapes other persons, societies and creatures. Yet many have been halted quite prematurely through illness, accident, grave injustice or untimely death. Much of the injustice has been perpetrated by other persons, by some on thousands or millions of people. Not infrequently have the most righteous suffered most. Now if a just, loving God who fulfills creation's purposes exists, what of those billions unjustly deprived of fulfillment? Will they ever attain it? What of those who deprived them? Will they ever be called to account?

The final resurrection and judgment help answer these questions. They involve more than individual rewards and punishments. They are expressions, actualizations, of the climactic revelation of God's righteousness, manifested proleptically through the faithfulness of Jesus, of God's character and will for the cosmos. This righteousness does not simply pass verdicts on individuals, for it establishes righteous relationships—reverses things, sets wrong things right. Historic Anabaptists expected the eschaton to bring this kind of justice, to vindicate and bless those who had suffered horribly.

However, if final resurrection and judgment occur only in a realized way, wholly within current spatiotemporal structures, unrequited victims and perpetrators of the past will never experience this justice. Even if God's final purposes attain some expression in ongoing history, these persons themselves will have been extinguished and nearly all of them forgotten.

But when people are gravely injured by injustice and others agonize as they suffer or die, cries for justice include actual vindication and fulfillment for these persons—not simply greater earthly justice centuries later. An Anabaptist perspective, shaped by generations of much suffering, can sensitize theology to the cries of the marginalized. These cries are for victims created to walk the path to human fulfillment through bodily interaction with a material world. If God will really bring such people to fulfillment—not simply compensate a separated part of them in some different realm—resurrection of their bodies in something like their earthly surroundings must occur. This requires a spatiotemporal environment of some sort.

I find such a future quite relevant to Anabaptist practice. If churches truly follow

---

[214]See points 2, 9 and 15 under "The General Nature of Theology" on pp. 96, 98, 99-100.

Jesus, they will often find themselves among the billions most bitterly oppressed. Such churches will not simply be *for* the poor but also *of* the poor (Sobrino). Yet because the "world" opposes God strongly, some, perhaps many, such efforts to actualize the new creation will apparently fail. Some, perhaps many, unfortunate people whom churches seek to help will undergo tragic, apparently meaningless, suffering and death.

As Moltmann says, eschatological visions of justice and peace will guide these efforts, functioning as horizons or ideals that we will not fully attain. However, ministry to such people is best motivated, I think, if we also believe that what has begun for those who open themselves to the new creation will not cease when they die but be fulfilled—when they themselves rise. Efforts to better their social and natural environments are best inspired by confidence that such changes will somehow carry on into their actual, future life world.

I also doubt whether many deeply oppressed people can begin living in active hope against massive opposition if they believe that many of their friends, family members and projects will simply perish long before any lasting betterment is achieved. Can they really rejoice and trust in God's righteousness if they do not believe that some day, finally, it will prevail in a widespread, unhindered way—but believe instead that oppression and injustice will victimize untold billions century after century without real let-up?

It seems to me that eschatologies which deny or avoid mention of material discontinuity, as do most current Anabaptists and Moltmann, will have difficulty sustaining a praxis stressing social discontinuity—even more when opposition from the "world" and the powers intensifies. In brief: the distinctive Anabaptist emphasis on social discontinuity requires some ultimate material discontinuity along with continuity.

To affirm real fulfillment of personal and interpersonal hope without this, eschatology must relegate it to a spiritual realm. But then that very Spirit/matter-energy intertwining intended in the original creation and being actualized in the new creation will suddenly be abolished at the latter's consummation. Such an eschatology more consistently sustains practices prioritizing the spiritual realm far above the material, social and historical.

Historic Anabaptist precedent for this exists, however. Marpeck, who conceived spirit-matter interaction most profoundly, nonetheless expected physical life to cease when it was finally "opened to its eternal unchangeable essence."[215] Hubmaier, Denck, Riedemann, Hoffman, Menno and Dirk prioritized the human soul/spirit in ways compatible with this.[216] On this issue, then, my theology in

---

[215]Marpeck, *Writings of Pilgram Marpeck*, p. 86.
[216]Cf. chap. 9.

Anabaptist perspective diverges from most historic and contemporary Anabaptists! Methodologically, this is because I find my position more consistent with (1) the implicit vision or convictional framework (though sometimes not explicit conceptuality) that guided and guides Anabaptist practice, and (2) Scripture, interpreted in light of its historical narrative centering on Jesus' life, death and resurrection.

However, if Anabaptist practice is best guided by expectation of social and material transformation, we can hardly visualize what forms these will take. My eschatology's content is really rather modest.[217] Churches, accordingly, must undertake ministries humbly, never assuming that any directly mirror or lead into the consummation. Still, to guide hope and action at all, the new creation's consummation must have several specific features.

2. Specific features. From the new creation's present activity, as patterned after Jesus and initiated, ruled and indwelt by him and his Father and through the Holy Spirit, theology can infer the following about its consummation:

• Since salvation involves a deeply personal dimension and since the dawning days of grace and judgment call for individual decision, personal identity will persist. Moreover, since much richness in new creation communities flows from diversities among participants (esp. 1 Cor 12), we can expect these identities to preserve some individual differences. In fact, since everyone will attain their individual destiny, they will become most fully themselves and recognize and love others who attain this (cf. Rev 2:17).

• Since personal salvation occurs in corporate contexts, the consummation will include social groupings or solidarities. Since persons from every nation, tribe, people and tongue will be involved (Rev 7:9), theology can assume that various group as well as individual differences will remain. (Dispensationalism underlines this, citing Rev 21:24-26.) In becoming one (cf. Jn 17:11, 20-24) we will not all be the same but enjoy a harmony arising from and enriched by differences, though we cannot be sure exactly which.

• New creation communities and individuals now transform nonhuman creation, in a broadly sacramental way, mainly through daily activity and also church practices. When humans join Jesus in his rule over other creatures, we will continue to

---

[217]While biblical language about this future involves material and historical references, it stretches toward a newness transcending most literal references. Eschatology can only point to this in terms taken from the past or present. Yet if these cannot refer to something truly new, this very pointing will be undermined. This is the chief biblical reason for rejecting uniform literal interpretation and thereby many dispensational predictions. Historic Anabaptism provides vivid evidence that eschatological language defies consistent literal schematization.

interact with at least some, for the nonhuman realm will also attain its destiny (esp. Rom 8:20-21).

What forms will resurrected individuals, social groupings and other creatures take? Theology must observe Paul's caution (1 Cor 15:35-36) and simply affirm that these will be transformations of whole people and creatures in their environments, not replacements by something else (1 Cor 15:36-55). How great or small these transformations might be is unknown.

Might some higher level of organization produce these changes in the cosmos, without altering laws now governing lower levels (Murphy and Ellis)? Or would these laws themselves need to change? Such questions are significant but beyond the scope of this inquiry.

• Since Jesus, the first fruits of our resurrection (1 Cor 15:23), rose as a distinct, whole person, and since eschatological hope longs for greater closeness to him (Tit 2:13; 1 Pet 1:8; 1 Jn 3:2-3), Jesus will become present, or return, in some fuller, bodily way. The triune God will dwell in our midst, filling the earth "with the knowledge of the glory of the Lord, as the waters cover the sea."[218]

• Since the "world" opposes the new creation strongly, theology can assume that the latter's full arrival will include some destruction and judgment of the former. Since human participation in either solidarity involves personal choice, theology can infer that some people who opted for the former will be judged. The climactic revelation of God's righteousness, like its proleptic revelation through Jesus' faithfulness, will bring judgment as well as salvation.[219] Yet Jesus' followers can never presume to know who will be judged, nor desire any persons' judgment, even if they are bitter enemies. For we ourselves were God's enemies. Only Jesus' love for enemies saved us (Rom 5:10). We continue in his

---

[218]Hab 2:14; cf. Is 11:9; Rev 21:1-4, 22-23; 22:3-5. Murphy and Ellis's model suggests a way of conceiving how this movement might simultaneously draw earth up into heaven's transforming energies, or how mortal creatures might "put on [endysasthai] immortality" (1 Cor 15:53), or be "clothed with [ependysasthai] our heavenly dwelling" (2 Cor 5:2), without losing their basic features. A "descending" higher level of organization might reconfigure our earth without changing its physical laws. Or might the coming transformations be extensive enough also to require change in some laws? This question is too complex for the space available here.

[219]Final judgment could well be one result of the incursion of heavenly energies. Perhaps those who greet it will enter heaven as it pervades earth, while those who resist it will experience it as a burning hell. I find both positive and negative judgment strongly attested in Scripture—but no evidence of hell being ultimately redemptive, like a purgatory, or as in the universal restoration reportedly taught by Denck. It seems probable though that some who welcome Christ's coming will experience this fiery brightness as purgation (esp. 1 Cor 3:11-15). Eschatological fire tests and purifies as well as destroys. (See footnote 206 on p. 551 above; Finger, *Christian Theology*, 1:143-68).

love only by practicing the same, leaving judgment to God (Rom 12:17-21; I Pet 2:19-23).

3. Resurrection and millennium. Finally, since the new creation's consummation will involve some destruction and judgment of the old, can theology say whether everything will occur more or less together, as in evangelical amillennialism, or more sequentially, as in premillennialism? Will defeat of God's enemies occupy a temporal span (Rev 19:11—20:3), followed by resurrection of the righteous and another span—the millennium (Rev 20:4-6)—and only afterward resurrection and judgment of the unrighteous (Rev 20:11-15)? How theology answers (or whether it can answer) hinges significantly on its interpretation of the first resurrection (Rev 20:4-6).

Premillennialism's divisions of resurrection-judgment (Rev 20:4; 20:11-13), evil's defeat (Rev 19:20-20:3; 20:14-15) and cosmic renewal (Rev 20:4-6; 21:1—22:8) can appear awkward. Yet if the first resurrection is not a spatiotemporal event, distinct from the second, what might it be? It cannot be the ascent of souls at death to rule with Christ, for then they would have ruled history somewhat directly for centuries. This answer implies, further, that people attain their full destiny at death, in heaven or hell. But if they do, Jesus' return and a final resurrection, judgment and cosmic transformation can add little. We noticed how this outlook enabled Zwingli to marginalize expectations of radical historical, sociopolitical changes. More broadly, if people enter their full, final destiny at death, the Bible's eschatological framework undergoes four serious distortions:

- Hope for bodily resurrection becomes desire for purely spiritual survival.

- Christ's coming cosmic reign is replaced by individual bliss.

- The future eschatological horizon is scattered into countless punctiliar events.

- Hope's all-encompassing goal dissolves into multiple individual ends.

When amillennialists interpret the first resurrection spiritually, they subdivide the eschatological hope. But if the first resurrection will occur in history, only when Jesus returns, none of these distortions results.

This, however, raises a further question: If this resurrection is yet future, where now are the dead? Soul sleep, which various historic Anabaptists probably affirmed, provides an answer. If the dead are in some unconscious or dreamlike state, bodily resurrection will be their true, final awakening. (If, however, they already experience complete bliss, resurrection can only attach something insignificant to their souls.) Such an interval presents no real problem if theology simply affirms that deceased

Christians are "in Christ"—somehow in his care, safe from defeat and sorrow.[220] It is a secondary question whether they experience something like sleep, perhaps with pleasant dreaming, or are conscious of Christ, perhaps in heaven, but share his deep longing for the new creation's triumph at his return.[221] In any case, such an interval would seem far shorter to the departed than to the living.

If this future resurrection is the first (Rev 20:4-6), will it not introduce a time-like millennium and the entire premillennial sequence? Can theology affirm something so detailed, relying so heavily on a single text?

I do not know how theology, if it is sufficiently humble, can be certain that the premillennial sequence is erroneous. Yet I find that Revelation 20:4-6 can be interpreted much as Moltmann, Marpeck and Menno proposed. Since the eschaton has been significantly, though not fully, realized since Jesus, the first resurrection might well occur in this life. If so, his text would portray some present horizon of possibility. Reigning with Christ could signify times when Christians who have suffered actualize some measure of his peaceful reign in this world, unhindered for a time by evil forces. Revelation 20:7-8 then would not denote a subsequent historical period. Instead it would indicate that while evil forces sometimes subside in this life, they eventually resurface. Revelation 20:9-10, however, would foretell their final historical defeat.

So interpreted, this text refers to enjoying resurrection victory in limited times and places in this life, not sharing Christ's rule over institutions and movements from heaven or eventually on earth. Such sharing in his resurrection is consistent with sharing in his cross—indeed, it is central to the new creation's personal dimension. However, I distinguish this first resurrection from humankind's future, corporate resurrection. This I expect, unlike Moltmann, to bear specific spatiotemporal features. My overall outlook comes closest to evangelical amillennialism. It does not predict exactly how Christ's return, our bodily resurrection, judgment, evil's defeat and cosmic renewal—or events leading up to them—might be interrelated. It does emphasize, however, that all four are facets of one hope.[222]

---

[220] They will not be in purgatory, for if something like this exists, it will be at or after the parousia. My earlier treatment of the intermediate state perhaps suggested too strongly that deceased Christians were unconscious (Finger, *Christian Theology*, 1:136-41). My intent was to shake some readers out of traditional assumptions.

[221] The vision of martyred souls longing for final judgment but resting from their labor may hint at the latter possibility (Rev 6:9-11). Hoekema, who places departed saints in heaven, consistent with his amillennialism, still wants to affirm their future orientation (*Bible and the Future*, pp. 92-108).

[222] A premillennial reading of Rev 20, where these arrive in stages, might supply a cautionary note. It might remind us that even in the consummation, eternal life can never be a fixed, static possession. We live eternally only as we keep receiving life from God. Eternal life—transformation by the dynamic triune perichoresis—will keep transforming us forever. Perhaps for these reasons turning back or away from God's call are depicted as possibilities even after Jesus' return (Rev 20:7-10).

In brief I am recommending that Anabaptist eschatology stress

• that the eschaton's realized presence (not Jesus' commands and example by themselves) makes discipleship, with its social-ethical dimensions, possible

• more sharply than most theologies, the social discontinuity between old and new creations in order to highlight the new and derive from it creative alternatives to the old

• that amidst the old creation's opposition, the new will often seem unreal without the affirmation that it will actually triumph in a concrete, widespread, enduring way some day

This requires both material continuity and discontinuity with the present world, or the hope that God's original purpose—the transformation of matter-energy and history by Spirit, which divinizes peoples' full humanity—will be fulfilled.

Such a hope entails that everything done in the past and present to actualize the new creation will be retained in its consummation. This can encourage churches to become involved in situations that seem virtually hopeless to most people and to discern but also promote constructive potentials found in globalization and other trends. At the same time, awareness of the old creation's opposition can sensitize churches to the destructive potentials of such trends, the rage of those who feel oppressed and the possibilities of violent, apocalyptic conflagration.

SUMMARY

Although Anabaptism forms but a rivulet in the stream of Christian tradition, recognized, if at all, for its ethics, I have proposed that rich theological resources lie under its surface. The Anabaptist perspective can, for instance, suggest connections among realities commonly separated today: among Christian life's personal, communal and missional dimensions (chaps. 5-7); between soteriological concerns (part two) and theological convictions (part three); between evangelicals and ecumenicals, marginalized and mainline communions, and among Protestant, Catholic, and Orthodox theologies. Anabaptism offers such suggestions, however, not as mere compromises, but from a distinct and radical standpoint.

I consider my theology one among other valid contemporary Anabaptist approaches. To clarify its particular character and enable readers to evaluate it, I sought to identify my major assumptions early on (chap. 4) and my methodology throughout. To complete this process I will briefly outline its specific shape.

My theology is not the sum of two lists: a doctrinal one from some theology in general and an ethical Anabaptist one.[1] Instead, every locus is shaped by the Anabaptist perspective. The resulting affirmations, however, do not simply express Anabaptist distinctives, for whatever material the Anabaptist perspective shapes appears in at least some other traditions. Anabaptist configurations resemble and diverge from other theologies' in varying ways and degrees. The following themes contour mine most prominently.

THE COMING OF THE NEW CREATION

The primary accent falls on *new*. A way of life quite different from other options

---

[1]Agreeing with J. Denny Weaver (*Anabaptist Theology in Face of Postmodernity* [Telford, Penn.: Pandora, 2000], pp. 71-93).

is possible, for the energies that enable it already operate. This sense of newness, rather than any separatist notion, underlies Anabaptism's particularist orientation. Because a new lifestyle is really viable, the church cannot take its major bearings from or compromise with the old creation. This orientation, of course, harbors a risk of separatism, of disconnecting from past traditions, present societies and future responsibilities as far as possible.

This risk, however, is countered by *creation.* An all-encompassing transformation is at hand. Its thoroughness is a major reason why the lifestyle it elicits is so new and cannot be compromised with the old. Yet this vision is not sectarian, for it concerns all creation. Still, its contrast with the old creation can tempt people to spiritualize it or become sectarian.

These risks are further diminished by *coming,* understood as a dynamic process. Since this process already operates, we cannot simply await its future manifestation. Since it operates in our physical, social world, we must act in this theater, in visible ecclesial and public ways. Yet new creation dynamism transforms the whole world not in a general progressive manner but paradoxically amidst opposition that often suggests the contrary and raises doubts. These doubts are countered by the conviction that this coming is no endless process but will indeed reach consummation. Wrongly understood, this hope can weaken involvement in the present. Rightly apprehended it strengthens confidence that the new is truly here and efforts to embody it.

Spirit and Matter-Energy

Since the new creation arrives through God's Spirit, and since it reshapes the physical world, every theological locus is informed by the Spirit's transformation of matter-energy. Historic Anabaptists, however, often overplayed Spirit and downgraded matter. I attribute this largely to the (conceptual) ontological barrier that prevented the two from interacting. I find true Anabaptist convictions better expressed in their practices, which contradicted this assumption. Spirit-matter intertwining is particularly evident in the inseparability of the new creation's three dimensions: personal, communal and missional. Though I discussed them in this sequence (chaps. 5-7), I insisted that none held priority. To confirm this I now summarize Spirit/matter-energy interaction in reverse order.

The Missional Dimension

Because the Holy Spirit energizes and keeps bringing the new creation, persons and communities caught up in it cannot exit society. The Spirit keeps impelling them into it. Even if they legitimately avoid society's hostility at times, they must enter it often enough to call others to the new creation and align their own everyday physical activities with its coming. Such people call others to spiritual conversion that draws them into visible communion with themselves, expressed through daily interactions and celebrated through physical ceremonies. Their embodiment of convictions like peace and economic sharing suggest alternatives to common social practices. Their mission often focuses on local situations because spiritual conversions that energize radical, alternative, material practices usually make the greatest impact there. These alternatives, however, frequently suggest creative approaches to larger structures and trends, such as governments and globalization.

The Communal Dimension

The Spirit's mission through individuals and groups draws people into communities. These join very diverse persons in cooperative activities and structures. Through his Spirit, that is, the risen reality of Christ the Head attains physical expression in members of his earthly body. As chief expression and channel of the Spirit's shaping of matter-energy, the church is the primary sacrament, which derives from the primordial sacrament, Christ's incarnation through the Spirit. Its sacramentality is manifested mainly through members' daily lives, but it is also celebrated, symbolized and actualized in special ways through ceremonies called sacraments and sacramentals. The church that so embodies the new creation's coming is an eschatological sacrament.

Since it embodies what is coming to all creation and its mission and message are directed to everyone, the true church is universal and linked through channels of communication and organization. Yet its sacramentality is also expressed by communities distinct from the "world." Again in ecclesiology, visible newness and distinctness are most characteristically Anabaptist—because, paradoxically, such particular embodiments bear most effective universal witness to the new creation.

The Personal Dimension

Mission calls for personal conversion, and community life requires each member's participation. Personal salvation, initiated by mission and mediated through communal involvement, is thoroughgoing transformation by divine energies—divinization. This spiritual process revitalizes the body and often works gradually. Some historic Anabaptists, though, presupposing an ontological barrier, overlooked this, etherializing salvation and arousing unrealistic expectations. But divinization is christomorphic: patterned after Jesus' human comportment. It involves inward and outward participation in his life, death and resurrection. So understood, it can be called discipleship. Divinization is transformation by, but not into, God; an ontological transformation by, but not into, divine being. While highly spiritual, it takes distinct personal, physical forms.

God alone initiates divinization, which is received only by faith. Since inward faith receives the risen Christ, it intrinsically produces outward good works. Faith and works cannot be understood in generic terms, but only in light of the concrete, historical revelation of God's righteousness through the faithfulness of Jesus Christ. Since this revelation and righteousness affect all spheres of life and initiate universal mission, justification, while profoundly personal, spreads far beyond that dimension.

CHRISTOMORPHISM

While "the coming of the new creation" and "Spirit and matter-energy" refer to Jesus and his work, "christomorphism" must be even more central. For Jesus did—and does and will—bring the new creation and intertwine Spirit with matter-energy. These participate in the reality that his incarnation, life, death and resurrection inaugurated—briefly, they participate in him.

Jesus' way, including servanthood and overcoming evil nonviolently with good, should be followed because he taught and exemplified it. Yet Jesus was not simply or chiefly a teacher or example; he was more centrally the second Adam, salvation's pioneer. His way recapitulated the journey to which our first ancestors and all other people were and are called. Through this earthly walk, Jesus realigned psycho-physical humanity's relationship with God's Spirit, distorted in all others, culminating in his resurrection. He also overcame powers that keep humanity in spiritual and sociopolitical bondage—for these powers are spiritual agencies, acting through these psycho-material complexes. Jesus' resurrection broke their bondage and unleashed the Spirit for personal and corporate renewal. This opened Jesus' way to all who participate by faith in his risen reality. His Spirit spreads through them into nonhuman creation, which thereby participates in him.

While focus on Jesus beginning from his historical work (from below) can obscure the magnitude of divine reality, this can also make it obvious that he, his Father and the Spirit continually cooperated. While historic Anabaptists did not always explicate the following implications, I find them consistent with the convictional framework that sustained most of them.

Since Jesus and his Spirit, like his Father, were direct agents of salvation, which God alone can bring, they too were and are fully divine. Jesus' servantlike and self-giving comportment expressed not only his fully human character but also his wholly gracious and astounding divine character and self-emptying *(kenōsis)*. One who bestows salvation kenotically cannot be intrinsically enmeshed in our world but must approach us wholly by grace and thus be wholly Spiritual. God then is ontologically distinct from the cosmos, yet not prevented by some ontological barrier from interacting with it. God, in Christ, inaugurated the new creation's Spirit/

matter-energy interaction by crossing all barriers and, while remaining distinct from creation, making our materiality his very own (the primordial sacrament). Understood in light of the divine saving acts, God moreover is a dynamic, perichoretic triunity, the deepest source of the new creation's communality. Christomorphism provides the pattern for incorporation into divine, human and natural community, as well as ethics. Even divine reality, the most universal of all, has a personal, interactive, transforming character, which is most effectively revealed through particular communities in radical ways.

WORLD/"WORLD"

The preceding themes entail a positive valuation of the world (or original creation). Human bodies, social structures and other beings were created "very good" and designed for positive development. The world in this sense is being transformed by the new creation's coming, and it will be perfected at its consummation.

However, this positive, synthetic process is being radically opposed by divisive, destructive forces. Guided by spiritual powers, these oppose God's purposes and violate God's creatures systemically as the "world" (or old creation). Such an emphasis carries the risk of supposing that the world—the original creation's structures and processes themselves—has become ontologically evil. The "world," however, is a dynamism, not an entity. Though it sweeps creatures into its momentum, it can never wholly pervert their basic structures and functions. This is why all creatures, however warped, are always worth loving, and all collective activities and systems are worthy of our interest and our involvement unless it contradicts Jesus' way.

The paradoxical world/"world" clash makes it clear why the new creation's global transformation is no smooth, linear development. History is too entangled in networks of sin and evil. Transformation must often break into these from a distinctly different source. It helps explain why God's universal goal will be attained largely through particular activities and in specific times and places until the consummation. A theology shaped by this paradox can be deeply concerned about worldwide processes like mission and globalization but still prioritize radical transformation in local settings. It warrants great optimism about creaturely potential, and often pessimism or sober "realism" about current actuality.

BIBLIOGRAPHY

CGR = *The Conrad Grebel Review*
MQR = *The Mennonite Quarterly Review*

Abbott, Walter, ed. *The Documents of Vatican II.* New York: Guild, 1966.

Alliance of Confessing Evangelicals. "An Appeal to Fellow Evangelicals: The Alliance Response to the second ECT Document, 'The Gift of Salvation,'" August 1998, <www.alliancenet.org/CC/article/0,,PTID307086|CHID560462|CIID1415576,00.html>.

———. "The Cambridge Declaration," Thesis 4, April 20, 1996, <www.alliancenet.org/partner/Article_Display_Page/0,,PTID307086|CHID560462|CIID1411364,00.html>.

Althaus, Paul. *The Theology of Martin Luther.* Philadelphia: Fortress, 1966.

Anderson, I I. George, T. Austin Murphy and Joseph Burgess, eds. *Justification by Faith: Lutherans and Catholics in Dialogue VII.* Minneapolis: Augsburg, 1985.

Anderson, Ray. *On Being Human.* Grand Rapids: Eerdmans, 1982.

Aquinas, Thomas. *The Summa Theologica of Thomas Aquinas.* Great Books of the Western World 19, 20. Edited by Daniel Sullivan. Chicago: Encyclopedia Britannica, 1952.

Armour, Roland. *Anabaptist Baptism.* Scottdale, Penn.: Herald Press, 1966.

Austin, Gerard. *Anointing with the Spirit.* New York: Pueblo, 1985.

Austin, Gerard, et al. *Eucharist: Toward the Third Millennium.* E. Peoria, Ill.: Versa, 1997.

Baecher, Claude. "Les Eschatologies Anabaptistes de la Haute Vallee Rehnane en Debat avec les Reformaeturs (1524-1535)." Ph.D. diss., University of Strasbourg, 1996.

Bainton, Roland. *Hunted Heretic: The Life and Death of Michael Servetus.* Boston: Beacon, 1953.

Balthasar Hubmaier: Theologian of Anabaptism. Edited by Wayne Pipkin and John H. Yoder. Scottdale, Penn.: Herald Press, 1989.

Baptism, Eucharist and Ministry. Faith & Order Paper III. Geneva: World Council of Churches, 1982.

Barth, Karl. *Church Dogmatics.* 4 vols. Edinburgh: T & T Clark, 1956-1969.

Bauckham, Richard. *Jude, 2 Peter.* Waco, Tex.: Word, 1983.

Bauerschmidt, Frederick. "Baptism in the Diaspora." In *On Baptism: Mennonite—Catholic Theological Colloquium, 2001-2002.* Edited by Gerald Sehlabach. Kitchener, Ont.: Pandora, 2004. Bauman, Clarence, ed. *The Spiritual Legacy of Hans Denck.* Leiden: E. J. Brill, 1991.

Beachy, Alvin. *The Concept of Grace in the Radical Reformation.* Nieuwkoop, Netherlands: B. De Graf, 1977.

Beasley-Murray, George R. *Baptism in the New Testament.* London: Macmillan, 1962.

Bell, Daniel. *The Cultural Contradictions of Capitalism.* New York: Basic Books, 1976.

Bender, Harold. *The Anabaptist Vision.* Scottdale, Penn.: Herald Press, 1944.

———. *These Are My People.* Scottdale, Penn.: Herald Press, 1962.

———. "Who is the Lord?" In *The Lordship of Christ.* Edited by C. J. Dyck. Elkhart, Ind.: Mennonite World Conference, 1962.

———. "The Zwickau Prophets: Thomas Müntzer and the Anabaptists," *MQR* 27, no.1 (1953).

Bender, Rosalee. "Locating Ourselves in 'Godbecoming.' " *CGR* 10, no. 1 (1992).

Berkhof, Hendrikus. *Christian Faith.* Grand Rapids: Eerdmans, 1986.

Berkouwer, C. G. *Man: The Image of God.* Grand Rapids: Eerdmans, 1962.

Bernstein, Richard. *Beyond Objectivism and Relativism.* Philadelphia: University of Pennsylvania Press, 1988.

Biesecker-Mast, Gerald. "Spiritual Knowledge, Carnal Obedience, and Anabaptist Discipleship." *MQR* 71, no. 2 (1997).

Blaising, Craig, and Darrell Bock. *Progressive Dispensationalism.* Wheaton, Ill.: BridgePoint, 1993.

Bloesch, Donald. "An Evangelical Response." *Christianity Today.* October 7, 1996.

———. *A Theology of Word and Spirit: Authority and Method in Theology.* Downers Grove, Ill.: InterVarsity Press, 1992.

Blok, Marjan. "Discipleship in Menno Simons' Dat Fundament." In *Menno Simons: A Reappraisal.* Edited by Gerald Brunk. Harrisonburg, Va.: Eastern Mennonite College, 1992.

Blough, Neal. *Christologie Anabaptiste.* Geneva: Labor et Fides, 1984.

———. "Messianic Mission and Ethics." In *The Transfiguration of Mission.* Edited by Wilbert Shenk. Scottdale, Penn.: Herald Press, 1993.

Boff, Leonardo. *Trinity and Society.* Maryknoll, N.Y.: Orbis, 1988.

Boice, James. *Awakening to God.* Downers Grove, Ill.: InterVarsity Press, 1979.

—. *God the Redeemer.* Downers Grove, Ill.: InterVarsity Press, 1978.

Bowman, Carl, and Stephen Longenecker, eds. *Anabaptist Currents: History in Conversation with the Past.* Bridgewater, Va.: Penobscot, 1995.

Boyd, Stephen. "Community as Sacrament in the Theology of Hans Schlaffer." In *Anabaptism Revisited.* Edited by Walter Klaassen. Scottdale, Penn.: Herald Press, 1992.

—. *Pilgram Marpeck: His Life and Thought.* Durham, N.C.: Duke University Press, 1992.

Braaten, Carl, and Robert Jenson, eds. *Christian Dogmatics.* Vol. 2. Philadelphia: Fortress, 1984.

—. *Union with Christ: The New Finnish Interpretation of Luther.* Grand Rapids: Eerdmans, 1998.

Brauch, Manfred. "Perspectives on 'God's Righteousness' in Recent German Discussion." Appendix to E. P. Sanders, *Paul and Palestinian Judaism.* Philadelphia: Fortress, 1977.

Brown, Raymond. *The Gospel According to John.* Garden City, N.Y.: Doubleday, 1966.

Bryant, Darrol. "Response to J. Denny Weaver." *CGR* 3, no. 1 (1985).

Bultmann, Rudolf. *Theology of the New Testament.* Vol. 1. New York: Scribner's, 1951.

Calvin, John. *Institutes of the Christian Religion.* Philadelphia: Westminster Press, 1960.

Carter, Craig. *The Politics of the Cross.* Grand Rapids: Brazos, 2001.

Clarkson, John, et al., eds. *The Church Teaches: Documents of the Church in English Translation.* St. Louis: B. Herder, 1955.

Clouse, Robert, ed. *The Meaning of the Millennium: Four Views.* Downers Grove, Ill.: InterVarsity Press, 1977.

Cobb, John, and Christopher Ives, eds. *The Emptying God.* Maryknoll, N.Y.: Orbis, 1990.

The Complete Works of Menno Simons. Edited by John Christian Wenger. Scottdale, Penn.: Herald Press, 1956.

Cooke, Bernard. *The Future of Eucharist.* New York: Paulist Press, 1997.

—. *Sacraments and Sacramentality.* Mystic, Conn.: Twenty-Third Publications, 1983.

Crossan, John Dominic. *The Historical Jesus.* San Francisco: Harper, 1991.

Cullmann, Oscar. *Christ and Time.* Philadelphia: Westminster Press, 1964.

—. *The Christology of the New Testament.* Philadelphia: Westminster Press, 1959.

—. *The Earliest Christian Confessions.* London: Lutterworth, 1949.

—. *Early Christian Worship.* London: SCM Press, 1953.

D'Costa, Gavin, ed., *Christian Uniqueness Reconsidered.* Maryknoll, N.Y.: Orbis, 1990.

Dallen, James. *The Reconciling Community: The Rite of Penance.* New York: Pueblo, 1986.

Davis, Kenneth. *Anabaptism and Asceticism.* Scottdale, Penn.: Herald Press, 1974.

Dayton, Donald. *Theological Roots of Pentecostalism.* Grand Rapids: Zondervan, 1987.

Deppermann, Klaus. *Melchior Hofmann.* Edinburgh: T & T Clark, 1987.

Dintaman, Stephen. "The Pastoral Significance of the Anabaptist Vision." *MQR* 69, no. 3 (1995).

———. "Reading the Reactions to 'The Spiritual Poverty of the Anabaptist Vision.'" *CGR* 13, no. 1 (1995).

———. "The Spiritual Poverty of the Anabaptist Vision." *CGR* 10, no. 2 (1992).

Dodd, C. H. *The Apostolic Preaching and Its Developments.* New York: Harper, 1964.

Dunn, James. *Christology in the Making.* Philadelphia: Westminster Press, 1980.

———. *Romans 1–8.* Waco, Tex.: Word, 1988.

———. *The Theology of Paul the Apostle.* Grand Rapids: Eerdmans, 1998.

Durnbaugh, Donald. *The Believers' Church.* Scottdale, Penn.: Herald Press, 1968.

Dyck, Cornelius, ed. *Spiritual Life in Anabaptism.* Scottdale, Penn.: Herald Press, 1995.

Eller, Vernard. *In Place of Sacraments.* Grand Rapids: Eerdmans, 1972.

Empereur, James, and Christopher Kiesling, *The Liturgy That Does Justice.* Collegeville, Minn.: Liturgical Press, 1990.

Epp-Weaver, Alain. "John Howard Yoder and the Creeds." *MQR* 74, no. 3 (2000).

———. "Options in Postmodern Mennonite Theology." *CGR* 11, no. 1 (1993).

Epp-Weaver, Alain, ed., *Mennonite Theology in Face of Modernity: Essays in Honor of Gordon D. Kaufman.* North Newton, Kans.: Bethel College Press, 1996.

Erb, Peter. "Contemplation and Action in the Modern World." *CGR* 9, no. 1 (1991).

"Evangelicals, Catholics Pursue New Cooperation," *Christianity Today,* May 16, 1994.

Ewert, Merrill. "Humanization and Development." Monograph Series 2. Akron, Penn.: Mennonite Central Committee, 1975.

Finger, Lareta. "An Investigation of Communal Meals in Acts 2:42-47 and 6:1-6." Ph. D. diss., Northwestern University, 1997.

Finger, Reta Halteman. "Social Implications of the Lord's Supper in the Early Church." In *The Lord's Supper: Believers Church Perspectives.* Edited by Dale Stoffer. Scottdale, Penn.: Herald Press, 1997.

Finger, Thomas N. "Anabaptism and Eastern Orthodoxy: Some Surprising Similarities?" *Journal of Ecumenical Studies* 31-32 (1994).

———. "An Anabaptist/Mennonite Theology of Creation." In *Creation and the Environment.* Edited by Calvin Redekop. Baltimore: Johns Hopkins, 2000.

———. "An Anabaptist Perspective on Justification." In *Justification and Sanctification in the Traditions of the Reformation.* Edited by M. Opecensky and P. Reamond. Geneva: World Alliance of Reformed Churches, 1999.

———. "Appropriating Other Traditions While Remaining Anabaptist." *CGR*

17, no. 2 (1999).

———. "Are Anabaptists Evangelicals?" unpublished address in Harrisonburg, Va., October 1991.

———. *Christian Theology: An Eschatological Approach.* 2 vols. Scottdale, Penn.: Herald Press, 1985, 1989.

———. "Christus Victor and the Creeds: Some Historical Considerations." *MQR* 72, no. 1 (1998).

———. "Confessing Truth in a Pluralistic World." In *Practicing Truth: Confident Witness in Our Pluralistic World.* Edited by David Shenk and Linford Stutzman. Scottdale, Penn.: Herald Press, 1999.

———. "Did Yoder Reduce Theology to Ethics?" In *A Mind Patient and Untamed: Assessing John Howard Yoder's Contributions to Theology, Ethics and Peacemaking.* Edited by Gayle Gerber Koontz and Ben Ollenburger. Telford, Penn.: Cascadia, 2004.

———. *Evangelicals, Eschatology, and the Environment.* Wynnewood, Penn.: Evangelical Environmental Network, 1998.

———. "From Biblical Intentions to Theological Conceptions: Some Strengths and Some Tensions in Norman Kraus' Christology," *CGR* 8, no. 1 (1990).

———. "Is the Boundary Between Science and Theology Distinct?" *Perspectives in Science and Christian Faith* 54, no. 1 (2002).

———. "James McClendon's Theology Reaches Completion: A Review Essay." *MQR* 76, no. 1 (2002).

———. "Jesus Christ and Religious Pluralism," *Catalyst* 25, no. 3 (1999).

———. "Justification in Eschatological Perspective." Prague VI Conference. Strasbourg, France. February 13, 2000.

———. "Moltmann's Theology of the Cross." In *Following Jesus Christ in the World Today.* Edited by Willard Swartley. Elkhart, Ind.: Institute of Mennonite Studies, 1984.

———. "Outlines of a Contemporary Believers' Church Eschatology: A Dialogue with James McClendon." In *Apocalypticism and Millennialism.* Edited by Loren Johns. Kitchener, Ont.: Pandora, (2000).

———. "Overwhelmed by God." *Books & Culture* 5, no. 6 (1999).

———. "Pilgram Marpeck and the Christus Victor Motif." *MQR* 78, no. 1 (2004): 53-77.

———. "Response to Frederick Bauerschmidt's 'Baptism in the Diaspora.'" In *On Baptism: Mennonite-Catholic Theological Colloquium, 2001-2002.* Edited by Gerald Sehlabach. Kitchener, Ont.: Pandora, 2004.

———. Response to "The Final Reconciliation," by Miroslav Volf. Presentation to the Evangelical Theology Group, American Academy of Religion. Boston: November 20, 1999.

———. "Response to J. Denny Weaver." *CGR* 6, no. 2 (1988).

———. Review of *Anabaptist Theology in Face of Postmodernity*, by J. Denny Weaver. *Christian Scholars' Review* 30, no. 1 (2001).

———. Review of *The Politics of the Cross*, by Craig Carter; *Preface to Theology*, by John H. Yoder; and *Mennonites and Classical Theology*, by A. James Reimer. In *Perspectives in Religious Studies* 28, no. 2 (2002).

———. *Self, Earth and Society*. Downers Grove, Ill.: InterVarsity Press, 1997.

———. "Trinity, Ecology and Panentheism." *Christian Scholar's Review* 27, no. 1 (1997).

———. "Two Agendas for Baptist Theology." *Perspectives in Religious Studies* 27, no. 3 (2001).

———. "The Way to Nicea: Some Reflections from a Mennonite Perspective." *Journal of Ecumenical Studies* 24, no. 2 (1987).

———. " 'Universal Truths?': Should Anabaptist Theologians Seek to Articulate Them?" In *Anabaptists and Postmodernity*. Edited by Susan Biesecker-Mast and Gerald Biesecker-Mast. Telford, Penn.: Pandora, 2000.

Friedman, Thomas. *The Lexus and the Olive Tree*. New York: Anchor, 2000.

Friedmann, Robert. *Mennonite Piety Through the Centuries*. Goshen, Ind.: Mennonite Historical Society, 1949.

———. *The Theology of Anabaptism*. Scottdale, Penn.: Herald Press, 1973.

Fries, Paul, and Tiran Nersoyan, eds. *Christ in East and West*. Atlanta: Mercer, 1987.

Friesen, Abraham. *Erasmus, the Anabaptists, and the Great Commission*. Grand Rapids: Eerdmans, 1998.

———. "Present at the Inception: Menno Simons and the Beginnings of Dutch Anabaptism." *MQR* 72, no. 3 (1998).

Friesen, Duane. "An Anabaptist Theology of Culture for a New Century." *CGR* 13, no. 1 (1995).

———. *Artists, Citizens, Philosophers*. Scottdale, Penn.: Herald Press, 2000.

———. *Christian Peacemaking and International Conflict*. Scottdale, Penn.: Herald Press, 1986.

———. "Toward a Theology of Culture." *CGR* 16, no. 2 (1998).

Friesen, John, ed. *Peter Riedemann's Hutterite Confession of Faith*. Scottdale, Penn.: Herald Press, 1999.

Fuller, Reginald. *The Foundations of New Testament Christology*. New York: Scribner's, 1965.

Funk-Wiebe, Katie. "Reflections on the Conference 'In a Mennonite Voice: Women Doing Theology.' " *CGR* 10, no. 2 (1992).

Gaebler, Ulrich. *Huldrych Zwingli: His Life and Work*. Philadelphia: Fortress, 1986.

Gerber Koontz, Gayle. "As We Forgive Others: Forgiveness and Feminist Pain." *MQR* 68, no. 2 (1994).

————. "The Trajectory of Scripture and Feminist Conviction." *CGR* 5, no. 3 (1987).

"The Gift of Salvation." *Christianity Today*, December 8, 1997.

"The Gospel of Jesus Christ: An Evangelical Celebration," *Christianity Today* 43, no. 7 (1999).

Gray, Donald. "The Real Absence: A Note on the Eucharist." In *Living Bread, Saving Cup.* Edited by Kevin Seasoltz. Collegeville, Minn.: Liturgical Press, 1987.

Grebel, Conrad, and Friends. "Letters to Thomas Müntzer." In *Spiritual and Anabaptist Writers.* Edited by George Williams and Angel Mergal. Philadelphia: Westminster Press, 1957.

Greenberg, Jay, and Stephen Mitchell. *Object Relations in Psychoanalytic Theory.* Cambridge, Mass.: Harvard, 1983.

Grenz, Stanley. *Theology for the Community of God.* Nashville: Broadman & Holman, 1994.

Griffen, David, ed. *Spirituality and Society.* Albany: SUNY Press, 1988.

Grimsrud, Ted. "Constructing a Mennonite Theology in a Congregational Setting." *Mennonite Life* 52, no. 1 (1997).

————. *God's Healing Strategy: A Guide to the Main Themes of the Bible.* Telford, Penn.: Pandora, 2000.

————. "Mennonite Theology and Historical Consciousness: A Pastoral Perspective." In *Mennonite Theology in Face of Modernity.* Edited by Alain Epp-Weaver. North Newton, Kans.: Bethel College Press, 1996.

Gros, Jeffrey. "A Catholic Response." *Christianity Today*, October 7, 1996.

Gross, Leonard. Review of *Becoming Anabaptist*, by J. Denny Weaver. *MQR* 63, no. 4 (1989).

Guelich, Robert. *The Sermon on the Mount.* Waco, Tex.: Word, 1982.

Gundry, Robert. *The Church and the Tribulation.* Grand Rapids: Zondervan, 1973.

Gutiérrez, Gustavo. *The Power of the Poor in History.* Maryknoll, N.Y.: Orbis, 1983.

————. *A Theology of Liberation.* Maryknoll, N.Y.: Orbis, 1973.

————. *The Truth Shall Make You Free.* Maryknoll, N.Y.: Orbis, 1990.

————. *We Drink from Our Own Wells.* Maryknoll, N.Y.: Orbis, 1984.

Guzie, Tad. *The Book of Sacramental Basics.* New York: Paulist Press, 1981.

————. *Jesus and the Eucharist.* New York: Paulist Press, 1974.

Harder, Leland, ed. *The Sources of Swiss Anabaptism.* Scottdale, Penn.: Herald Press, 1985.

Harder, Lydia. "Biblical Interpretation: A Praxis of Discipleship?" *CGR* 10, no. 1 (1992).

————. *Obedience, Suspicion and the Gospel of Mark.* Waterloo, Ont.: Wilfred Laurier University Press, 1998.

————. "Postmodern Suspicion and Imagination: Therapy for Mennonite Hermeneutic Communities." *MQR* 71, no. 2 (1997).

Hays, Richard B. *The Faith of Jesus Christ*. 2nd ed. Grand Rapids: Eerdmans, 2002.

Hecht, Lydia Hubert, and C. Arnold Snyder, eds. *Profiles of Anabaptist Women*. Waterloo, Ont.: Wilfred Laurier University Press, 1996.

Hick, John. *An Interpretation of Religions*. London: Macmillan, 1989.

Hick, John, and Paul Knitter, eds. *The Myth of Christian Uniqueness*. Maryknoll, N.Y.: Orbis, 1987.

Hildebrand, Mary Anne. "Domestic Violence: A Challenge to Mennonite Faith and Peace Theology." *CGR* 10, no. 1 (1992).

Hodge, Charles. *Systematic Theology*. 3 vols. London: James Clark, 1960.

Hoekema, Anthony. *The Bible and the Future*. Grand Rapids: Eerdmans, 1979.

————. *Created in God's Image*. Grand Rapids: Eerdmans, 1986.

Hoffman, Melchior. "The Ordinance of God." In *Spiritual and Anabaptist Writers*. George Williams and Angel Mergal. Philadelphia: Westminster Press, 1957.

Holland, Scott. "Anabaptism as Public Theology." *CGR* 11, no. 3 (1993).

————. "Einbildungskraft: 1. Imagination, 2. The Power to Form into One." In *Mennonite Theology in Face of Modernity*. Edited by Alain Epp-Weaver. North Newton, Kans.: Bethel College Press, 1996.

————. "Even the Postmodern Story Has a Body: Narrative, Poetry and Ritual." In *The Presence of Transcendence: Thinking 'Sacrament' in a Postmodern Age*. Edited by Lieven Boeve and John Ries. Leuven, Belgium: Peeters, 2001.

————. "God in Public." *CGR* 4, no. 1 (1986).

————. "How Do Stories Save Us?" *CGR* 12, no 2 (1994).

————. "Mennonites on Hauerwas, Hauerwas on Mennonites." *CGR* 13, no. 2 (1995).

————. "The Problems and Prospects of a 'Sectarian Ethic.' " *CGR* 10, no. 2 (1992).

————. "The Resurrection of the Soul in the Anabaptist Body." In *The Believers Church: A Voluntary Church*. Edited by William Brackney. Kitchener, Ont.: Pandora, 1998.

————. Review of *The Lord's Supper in Anabaptism*, by John Rempel. *CGR* 12, no. 1 (1994).

————. "Theology Is a Kind of Writing: The Emergence of Poetics." *MQR* 71, no. 2 (1997).

————. "When Bloch Pointed to the Cages Outside the Cathedral." In *Anabaptists and Postmodernity*. Edited by Susan Biesecker-Mast and Gerald Biesecker-Mast. Telford, Penn.: Pandora, 2000.

Hubmaier, Balthasar. *Schriften*. In Quellen zur Geschichte der Täufer 9. Edited by

Gunnar Westin and Torsten Bergsten. Gütersloh, Germany: Gerd Mohn, 1962.

Huebner, Harry. "Within the Limits of Story Alone?" *CGR* 13, no. 2 (1995).

Hurtado, Larry. *One God, One Lord*. Philadelphia: Fortress, 1988.

Hut, Hans. "Ein christlich Unterrich, wie goettliche Geschrift vergleicht und geurteilen solle werden." In *Glaubenzeugnisse oberdeutscher Taufgesinnter*. Quellen und Forschungen zur Reformationsgeschichte 20. Edited by Lydia Mueller. Leipzig: M. Heinsius Nachfolger, 1938.

―――. "On the Mystery of Baptism." *Early Anabaptist Spirituality*. Edited by Daniel Liechty. New York: Paulist Press, 1994.

Irenaeus. *Against Heresies*. In The Ante-Nicene Fathers. Vol. 5. Edited by Cleveland Coxe. Grand Rapids: Eerdmans, 1979.

Jarmola, Dariusz. "The Origins and Development of Believers' Baptism Among the Polish Brethren in the 16th Century." Ph.D. diss., Southern Baptist Seminary, 1990.

"JDDJ: A Critical Evaluation." *Lutheran Commentator* 11, no. 5 (March-April 1998).

Jepsen, Alfred. "*amam, emunah, amen, emeth*." In *Theological Dictionary of the Old Testament*, edited by G. Johannes Botlerweck and Helmer Rinngren, 1:292-323. Grand Rapids: Eerdmans, 1974.

Jeschke, Marlin. *Discipling the Brother*. Scottdale, Penn.: Herald Press, 1973.

Jewett, Robert. "Are There Allusions to the Love Feast in Romans 13:8-10?" In *Common Life in the Early Church*. Edited by Julian Hills. Harrisburg, Penn.: Trinity Press, 1998.

―――. *Paul the Apostle to America*. Louisville: Westminster/John Knox, 1994.

―――. "Tenement Churches and Communal Meals in the Early Church." *Biblical Research* 38 (1993).

Johnson, Elizabeth A. *She Who Is*. New York: Crossroad, 1992.

Johnson, Maxwell, ed. *Living Water, Sealing Spirit*. Collegeville, Minn.: Liturgical Press, 1995.

"Joint Declaration on the Doctrine of Justification." In *Ecumenical Proposals*. Chicago: Evangelical Lutheran Church in America, 1996.

Käsemann, Ernst. *Commentary on Romans*. Grand Rapids: Eerdmans, 1980.

―――. " 'The Righteousness of God' in Paul." In *New Testament Questions of Today*. Philadelphia: Fortress, 1969.

Kauffman, Richard, ed. *A Disciple's Christology: Appraisals of Kraus's Jesus Christ Our Lord*. Elkhart, Ind.: Institute of Mennonite Studies, 1989.

Kaufman, Gordon. *An Essay in Theological Method*. Missoula, Mont.: Scholars Press, 1975.

―――. *In Face of Mystery*. Cambridge, Mass.: Harvard University Press, 1993.

―――. *God—Mystery—Diversity*. Minneapolis: Fortress, 1996.

———. "My Life and Theological Reflection: Two Central Dilemmas." *CGR* 20, no. I (2002).

———. "On Thinking of God as Serendipitous Creativity." *Journal of the American Academy of Religion* 69, no. 2 (2001).

———. "Religious Diversity and Religious Truth." In *God, Truth and Reality: Essays in Honour of John Hick.* Edited by Arvind Sharma. New York: St. Martin's Press, 1993.

———. *Systematic Theology: A Historicist Perspective.* New York: Scribner's, 1968.

Kavanagh, Aidan. *Confirmation.* New York: Pueblo, 1988.

———. *The Shape of Baptism.* Collegeville, Minn.: Liturgical Press, 1978.

Keener, Carl. "Aspects of a Postmodern Paradigm for an Ecological Age." In *Mennonite Theology in Face of Modernity.* Edited by Alain Epp-Weaver. North Newton, Kans.: Bethel College Press, 1996.

———. "The Darwinian Revolution and Its Implications for a Modern Anabaptist Theology." *CGR* I, no. I (1983).

———. "Some Reflections on Mennonites and Postmodern Thought." *CGR* II, no. I (1993).

Keim, Albert. *Harold S. Bender, 1897-1962.* Scottdale, Penn.: Herald Press, 1998.

Keller, Ludwig. *Ein Apostle der Wiedertaeufer.* Leipzig: S. Hirzell, 1882.

Klaassen, Walter. *Anabaptism: Neither Catholic nor Protestant.* Waterloo, Ont.: Conrad Grebel, 1973.

———. "'Gelassenheit' and Creation." In *CGR* 9, no. I (1991).

———. *Living at the End of the Ages.* New York: University Press of America, 1992.

———. "Sixteenth Century Anabaptism: A Vision Valid for the Twentieth Century?" *CGR* 7, no. 3 (1989).

Klaassen, Walter, ed. *Anabaptism in Outline.* Scottdale, Penn.: Herald Press, 1981.

———. *Anabaptism Revisited.* Scottdale, Penn.: Herald Press, 1992.

Klassen, Herbert. "The Life and Teachings of Hans Hut." *MQR* 33, nos. 3 and 4 (1959).

Klassen, William. *Covenant and Community: The Life, Writings and Hermeneutics of Pilgram Marpeck.* Grand Rapids: Eerdmans, 1968.

———. "Was Hans Denck a Universalist?" *MQR* 39 (1965).

Klassen-Wiebe, Sheila. "Response to Nadine Pence Frantz." *CGR* 14, no. 3 (1996).

Knitter, Paul. *No Other Name?* Maryknoll, N.Y.: Orbis, 1985.

———. *One Earth, Many Religions.* Maryknoll, N.Y.: Orbis, 1995.

Knitter, Paul, and Roger Corliss, eds. *Buddhist Emptiness and Christian Trinity.* New York: Paulist Press, 1990.

Kolb, Robert, and Timothy Wengert, eds., *The Book of Concord.* Minneapolis: Fortress, 2000.

Koontz, Gayle Gerber. "Evangelical Peace Theology and Religious Pluralism: Particularity in Perspective." *CGR* 14, no. 1 (1996).

Köster, Helmut. "φύσις κτλ." In *Theological Dictionary of the New Testament*, 9:251-77. Edited by Gerhard Kittel and Gerhard Friedrich. 10 vols. Grand Rapids: Eerdmans, 1964-1976.

————. "ὑπόστασις." In *Theological Dictionary of the New Testament*, 8:572-89. Edited by Gerhard Kittel and Gerhard Friedrich. 10 vols. Grand Rapids: Eerdmans, 1964-1976.

Krall, Ruth. "Anger and an Anabaptist Feminist Interpretation." *CGR* 14, no. 2 (1996).

Kraus, C. Norman. "An Anabaptist Spirituality for the Twenty-first Century." *CGR* 13, no. 1 (1995).

————. *The Community of the Spirit*. Scottdale, Penn.: Herald Press, 1993.

————. "Evangelicalism: a Mennonite Critique." In *The Variety of American Evangelicalism*. Edited by Donald Dayton and Robert Johnston. Downers Grove, Ill.: InterVarsity Press, 1991.

————. "The Faith to Doubt: A Theological Autobiography." *CGR* 20, no. 1 (2002).

————. *God Our Savior: Theology in a Christological Mode*. Scottdale, Penn.: Herald Press, 1991.

————. "The Great Evangelical Coalition: Pentecostal and Fundamentalist." In *Evangelicalism and Anabaptism*. Edited by Norman C. Kraus. Scottdale, Penn.: Herald Press, 1979.

————. *An Intrusive Gospel?* Downers Grove, Ill.: InterVarsity Press, 1998.

————. *Jesus Christ Our Lord*. Scottdale, Penn.: Herald Press, 1987.

Kraus, C. Norman, ed. *Evangelicalism and Anabaptism*. Scottdale, Penn.: Herald Press, 1979.

Kraybill, Ronald. "Peacebuilders in Zimbabwe: An Anabaptist Paradigm for Conflict Transformation." Ph. D. diss., University of Capetown, 1996.

Krebs, Mandfred, and Hans Georg Rott, eds. *Elsass. I Teil, Stadt Strassburg 1522-1532*. In Quellen zur Geschichte der Täufer 7. Gütersloh, Germany: Gerd Mohn, 1959.

LaCugna, Catherine Mowry. *God for Us*. San Francisco: HarperSanFrancisco, 1991.

Lakoff, George, and Mark Johnson. *Philosophy in the Flesh: The Embodied Mind and Its Challenge to Western Thought*. New York: Basic Books, 1999.

Lederach, John Paul. *The Journey Toward Reconciliation*. Scottdale, Penn.: Herald Press, 1999.

The Legacy of Michael Sattler. Edited by John Howard Yoder. Scottdale, Penn.: Herald Press, 1973.

Liechty, Daniel. "Communication Technology and the Development of Consciousness: Reframing the Discussion of Anabaptists and Postmodernity." *CGR* 18, no. 1 (2000).

———. "The Seamless Robe of Human Experience: An Essay on (Mennonite) Theological Method." In *Mennonite Theology in Face of Modernity.* Edited by Alain Epp-Weaver. North Newton, Kans.: Bethel College Press, 1996.

———. *Theology in Postliberal Perspective.* Philadelphia: Trinity Press International, 1990.

Liechty, Daniel, ed. *Early Anabaptist Spirituality.* New York: Paulist Press, 1994.

Lindbeck, George. *The Nature of Doctrine.* Philadelphia: Westminster Press, 1984.

Littell, Franklin. *The Origins of Sectarian Protestantism.* Rev. ed. New York: Macmillan, 1964.

Loeschen, John. *The Divine Community: Trinity, Church, and Ethics in Reformation Theologies.* Kirksville, Mo.: 16th Century Journal Publishers, 1981.

Lohse, Eduard. *"πρόσωπον κτλ."* In *Theological Dictionary of the New Testament,* 6:768-80. Edited by Gerhard Kittel and Gerhard Friedrich. 10 vols. Grand Rapids: Eerdmans, 1964-1976.

Loserth, J. *Pilgram Marbecks Antwort auf Kaspar Schwenckfeld's Beurteilung des Buches der Bundesbezeugung von 1542.* Vienna: Carl Fromme, 1929.

Luther, Martin. "The Address to the German Nobility." In *Luther's Works* 44. Philadelphia: Fortress, 1966.

———. "Admonition to Peace: A Reply to the 12 Articles of the Peasants in Swabia." In *Luther's Works* 46. Philadelphia, Fortress, 1967.

———. "Against the Murdering and Robbing Hordes of Peasants." In *Luther's Works* 46. Philadelphia: Fortress, 1967.

———. "The Babylonian Captivity of the Church." In *Luther's Works* 36. Philadelphia: Fortress, 1959.

Mantzaridis, Georgios. *The Deification of Man.* Crestwood, N.Y.: St. Vladimir's Seminary Press, 1984.

Marpeck, Pilgram. *Ain klarer vast nützlicher Unterricht.* Strasbourg: Jakob Commerlander, 1531. (British Museum Signature 3906.a.77. Photocopy in Goshen College Historical Library.)

———. "Ein Epistel meldend von der christlichen Kirchen und das agareishcen." In *Das Kunstbuch.* Edited by Joerg Propst Rothenfelder, auch genant Maler. (Manuscript, 1561. Photocopy in Goshen College Historical Library.)

———. "Exposé of the Babylonian Whore." In *Later Writings by Pilgram Marpeck and His Circle.* Edited by Walter Klaassen, Werner Packull and John Rempel. Translated by Walter Klaassen. Kitchener, Ont.: Pandora, 1999.

Martens, Jo-Anne. "Response to Lydia Harder." *CGR* 10, no. 2 (1992).

May, Melanie. *The Body Knows: A Theopoetics of Death and Resurrection.* New York: Continuum, 1995.

———. "The Pleasure of Our Lives as Text." *CGR* 10, no. 1 (1992).

McClendon, James. "The Radical Road One Baptist Took." *MQR* 74, no. 4 (2000).

———. "Response to Stanley Hauerwas." *CGR* 16, no. 1 (1998).

———. *Systematic Theology: Doctrine.* Nashville: Abingdon, 1994.

———. *Systematic Theology: Ethics.* Nashville: Abingdon, 1986.

———. *Systematic Theology: Witness.* Nashville: Abingdon, 2000.

McDonnell, Kilian. *The Baptism of Jesus in the Jordan.* Collegeville, Minn.: Liturgical Press, 1996.

McFague, Sallie. *Models of God.* Philadelphia: Fortress, 1987.

Meyendorff, John. *Byzantine Theology.* New York: Fordham, 1983.

———. *St. Gregory Palamas and Orthodox Spirituality.* Crestwood, N.Y.: St. Vladimir's Seminary Press, 1998.

Meyendorff, John, and Robert Tobias, eds. *Salvation in Christ: A Lutheran-Orthodox Dialogue.* Minneapolis: Augsburg, 1992.

Meyer, Christian, ed. *Zur Geschichte der Wiedertäufer in Oberschwaben, Teil I. Die Anfänge der Wiedertäufertum in Augsburg, in Zeitschrift des Historischen Vereins für Schwaben und Neuberg I* (= ZHVSN: Hut), 1874.

Millbank, John. "The End of Dialogue." In *Christian Uniqueness Reconsidered.* Edited by Gavin D'Costa. Maryknoll, N.Y.: Orbis, 1990.

Miller, Larry. "The Church as a Messianic Society." In *The Transfiguration of Mission.* Edited by Wilbert Shenk. Scottdale, Penn.: Herald Press, 1993.

Moltmann, Jürgen. *The Church in the Power of the Spirit.* New York: Harper & Row, 1977.

———. *The Coming of God.* Minneapolis: Fortress. 1996.

———. *The Crucified God.* New York: Harper & Row, 1974.

———. *Following Jesus Christ in the World Today.* Elkhart, Ind.: Institute of Mennonite Studies, 1984.

———. *The Future of Creation.* Philadelphia: Fortress, 1979.

———. *The Spirit of Life.* Minneapolis: Fortress, 1992.

———. *Theology of Hope.* New York: Harper & Row, 1967.

———. *The Trinity and the Kingdom.* San Francisco: Harper & Row, 1981.

———. *The Way of Jesus Christ.* San Francisco: HarperCollins, 1990.

Moody, Dale. *Baptism: Foundation for Christian Unity.* Philadelphia: Westminster Press, 1967.

Moore, Art. "Does 'The Gift of Salvation' Sell Out the Reformation?" *Christianity Today,* October 7, 1996.

Morris, Thomas. *The RCIA: Transforming the Church.* Rev. ed. New York: Paulist Press, 1997.

Mueller, Christian. *Gottes Gerechtigkeit und Gottes Volk.* Göttingen: Vandenhoeck & Rupprecht, 1964.

Mueller-Farenholz, Geiko, ed. *And Do Not Hinder Them: An Ecumenical Plea for the Admission of Children to the Eucharist.* Faith & Order Paper 109. Geneva: World Council of Churches, 1982.

Murphy, Nancey. *Beyond Liberalism and Fundamentalism.* Valley Forge, Penn.: Trinity Press International, 1996.

―――. "Non-reductive Physicalism: Philosophical Issues." In *Whatever Happened to the Soul?* Edited by Warren Brown Murphy and H. Newton Maloney. Minneapolis: Fortress, 1998.

―――. "Textual Relativism, Philosophy of Language and the Baptist Vision." In *Theology Without Foundations.* Edited by Nancey Murphy, Stanley Hauerwas, and Mark Nation. Nashville: Abingdon, 1998.

Murphy, Nancey, and George Ellis. *On the Moral Nature of the Universe.* Minneapolis: Fortress, 1996.

Murray, John. *The Epistle to the Romans.* 2 vols. Grand Rapids: Eerdmans, 1959.

Nellas, Panayiotis. *Deification in Christ.* Crestwood, N.Y.: St. Vladimir's Seminary Press, 1997.

Nickoloff, James, ed. *Gustavo Gutiérrez: Essential Writings.* Minneapolis: Fortress, 1996.

Niebuhr, H. Richard. *Christ and Culture.* New York: Harper & Row, 1951.

Niebuhr, Reinhold. *The Nature and Destiny of Man.* 2 vols. New York: Scribner's, 1941, 1943.

"Official Catholic Response to Joint Declaration." *Origins* 28, no. 8 (1998).

Ollenburger, Ben. "Mennonite Theology: A Conversation Around the Creeds." *MQR* 66, no. 1 (1992).

Osborne, Grant. *The Resurrection Narratives.* Grand Rapids: Baker, 1984.

Osborne, Kenan. *Sacramental Theology.* New York: Paulist Press, 1988.

Osmer, Richard. *Confirmation: Presbyterian Practices in Ecumenical Perspective.* Louisville: Geneva Press, 1996.

Packull, Werner. "Between Paradigms: Anabaptist Studies at the Crossroads." *CGR* 8, no. 1 (1990).

―――. "Gottfried Seebass on Hans Hut: A Discussion." *MQR* 49, no.1 (1973).

―――. *Hutterite Beginnings.* Baltimore: Johns Hopkins University Press, 1995.

―――. *Mysticism and the Early South German-Austrian Anabaptists.* Scottdale, Penn.: Herald Press, 1977.

―――. "A Reinterpretation of Melchior Hoffman's Exposition Against the Background of Spiritualist Franciscan Eschatology with Special Reference to

Peter John Olivi." In *The Dutch Dissenters: A Critical Companion to Their History of Ideas.* Edited by Irvin Buckwalter. Leiden: E. J. Brill, 1986.

———. "Research Note: Pilgram Marpeck's Uncovering of the Babylonian Whore and Other Anonymous Anabaptist Tracts." *MQR* 67, no. 3 (1993).

Palmer, Paul, ed. *Sacraments and Worship.* New York: Longmans, Green, 1957.

Pannenberg, Wolfhart. *Jesus: God and Man.* Philadelphia: Westminster Press, 1968.

———. *Theology and the Kingdom of God.* Philadelphia: Westminster Press, 1969.

Pannenberg, Wolfhart, et al. *Revelation as History.* London, Macmillan, 1968.

Paul VI. *Mysterium Fidei.* London: Catholic Truth Society, 1965.

Pelikan, Jaroslav. *The Spirit of Eastern Christendom (600-700).* Chicago: University of Chicago Press, 1974.

Pence Frantz, Nadine. "The (Inter)Textuality of Our Lives: An Anabaptist Feminist Hermeneutic." *CGR* 14, no. 2 (1996).

———. "Response to Melanie A. May." *CGR* 10, no. 2 (1992).

———. "Theological Hermeneutics: Christian Feminist Biblical Interpretation and the Believers' Church Tradition." Ph.D. diss., University of Chicago, 1992.

Pinnock, Clark. *A Wideness in God's Mercy.* Grand Rapids: Zondervan, 1992.

Pinnock, Clark, et al. *The Openness of God.* Downers Grove, Ill.: InterVarsity Press, 1992.

Placher, William. *Unapologetic Theology.* Louisville: Westminster/John Knox Press, 1989.

Power, David. *The Eucharistic Mystery.* New York: Crossroad, 1995.

———. "A Prophetic Eucharist in a Prophetic Church." In *Eucharist: Toward the Third Millennium.* Edited by Gerard Austin et al. E. Peoria, Ill.: Versa Press, 1997.

Powers, Joseph. *Eucharistic Theology.* New York: Herder & Herder, 1967.

Rahner, Karl. "The Comfort of Time." In *Theological Investigations III.* Baltimore: Helicon, 1967.

———. *Theological Investigations.* Vol. 5. Baltimore: Helicon, 1966.

Ramseyer, Robert. "The Anabaptist Mission and Our World Mission (I)." In *Anabaptism and Mission.* Edited by Wilbert Shenk. Scottdale, Penn.: Herald Press, 1984.

Rauschenbusch, Walter. *A Theology for the Social Gospel.* Nashville: Abingdon, 1978.

Redekop, Calvin. "The Community of Scholars and the Essence of Anabaptism." *MQR* 67, no. 4 (1993).

———. "Toward a Mennonite Theology and Ethic of Creation." *MQR* 60 (1986).

Redekop, Calvin, ed. *Creation and the Environment: An Anabaptist Perspective on a Sustainable World.* Baltimore: Johns Hopkins University Press, 2000.

Reesor, Rachel. "Atonement: Mystery and Metaphorical Language." *MQR* 68, no.

2 (1994).

Reimer, A. James. *Mennonites and Classical Theology.* Kitchener, Ont.: Pandora, 2001.

Rempel, John. *The Lord's Supper in Anabaptism.* Scottdale, Penn.: Herald Press, 1993.

Reumann, John. *Righteousness in the New Testament.* Philadelphia: Fortress, 1982.

Rideman, Peter. *Confession of Faith.* Rifton, N.Y.: Plough, 1970.

Riedemann, Peter. *Rechenschaft unserer Religion, Lehr und Glaubens, von den Brüdern, so man die Hutterischen nennt.* Wiltshire, England: Verlag der Hutterischen Brueder, 1938.

The Rite of Christian Initiation of Adults. Washington, D.C.: United States Catholic Conference, 1974.

The Rite of Penance. Washington, D.C.: National Conference of Catholic Bishops, 1975.

Ritschl, Albrecht. *The Christian Doctrine of Justification and Reconciliation.* Vol. 3. Clifton, N.J.: Reference Book Publishers, 1966.

———. *Geschichte des Pietismus, I.* Bonn: Adolph Marcus, 1880.

Robinson, James. *The Problem of History in Mark.* London: SCM Press, 1957.

Robinson, John A. T. *The Body.* Philadelphia: Westminster Press, 1952.

Roth, John. "Living Between the Times: The 'Anabaptist Vision' and Mennonite Reality." *MQR* 69, no. 3 (1995).

———. "Pietism and the Anabaptist Soul." In *The Dilemma of Anabaptist Piety.* Edited by Stephen Longenecker. Bridgewater, Va.: Penobscot, 1997.

Rothmann, Bernhard. *Bekentnisse van beyden Sacramenten.* In *Zwei Schriften den münsterischen Wiedertäufers Bernhard Rothmann.* Edited by Heinrich Detmer and Robert Krumbholz. Dortmund, 1904.

Rouillard, Philippe. "From Human Meal to Eucharist." In *Living Bread, Saving Cup.* Edited by Kevin Seasoltz. Collegeville, Minn.: Liturgical Press, 1987.

Rupp, Gordon. "Thomas Müntzer, Hans Hut and the 'Gospel of all Creatures.'" *Bulletin of the John Rylands Library* 43 (1960-1961).

Ryrie, Charles. *Dispensationalism Today.* Chicago: Moody, 1965.

Sanders, John. *No Other Name.* Grand Rapids: Eerdmans, 1992.

———. *What About Those Who Have Never Heard?* Edited by John Sanders. Downers Grove, Ill.: InterVarsity Press, 1995.

Sasse, Hermann. "κοσμέω κτλ." In *Theological Dictionary of the New Testament* 3:867-98. Edited by Gerhard Kittel and Gerhard Friedrich. 10 vols. Grand Rapids: Eerdmans, 1964-1976.

Schertz, Mary. "God's Cross and Women's Questions: A Biblical Perspective on the Atonement." *MQR* 68, no. 2 (1994).

Schiemer, Leonhard. "The Apostles' Creed: An Interpretation." In *Spiritual Life in Anabaptism.* Edited by Cornelius Dyck. Scottdale, Penn.: Herald Press, 1995.

———. "Three Kinds of Grace." In *Early Anabaptist Spirituality.* Edited by Daniel

Liechty. New York: Paulist Press, 1994.

Schlaffer, Hans. "Ein einfaeltig Gebet." In *Das Kunstbuch.* Edited by Joerg Propst Rothenfelder, auch genant Maler. (Manuscript, 1561. Photocopy in Goshen College Historical Library.)

————. "Ein kurzer Unterrich zum Anfang eines recht chrislichen Lebens." In *Glaubenzeugnisse oberdeutscher Taufgesinnter.* Quellen und Forschungen zur Reformationsgeschichte 20. Edited by Lydia Mueller. Leipzig: M. Heinsius Nachfolger, 1938.

————. "Instructions on Beginning a True Christian Life." In *Early Anabaptist Spirituality.* Edited by Daniel Liechty. New York: Paulist, 1994.

————. *Selections.* In *Spiritual Life in Anabaptism.* Edited by Cornelius Dyck. Scottdale, Penn.: Herald Press, 1995.

Schmemman, Alexander. *Of Water and the Spirit.* Crestwood, N.Y.: St. Vladmir's Seminary Press, 1995.

Schwager, Raymond. *Must There Be Scapegoats?* San Francisco: Harper, 1987.

Schwartz, Richard. *Internal Family Systems Therapy.* New York: Guilford, 1995.

Seasoltz, Kevin, ed. *Living Bread, Saving Cup.* Collegeville, Minn.: Liturgical Press, 1987.

Seebass, Gottfried. *Müntzer's Erbe: Werk, leben und theologie des Hans Hut (gestorben 1527).* Erlangen-Nuernburg: Friedrich-Alexander Universität, Habilitationschrift, 1972.

Senn, Frank. *Christian Liturgy.* Minneapolis: Fortress, 1997.

————. *Stewardship of the Mysteries.* New York: Paulist Press, 1999.

Servetus, Michael. *The Two Treatises of Servetus on the Trinity.* Translated by Earl Wilbur. Cambridge, Mass.: Harvard University Press, 1932.

Shenk, Calvin. *Who Do You Say that I Am?* Scottdale, Penn.: Herald Press, 1993.

Shenk, David, and Linford Stutzman, eds. *Practicing Truth: Confident Witness in Our Pluralistic World.* Scottdale, Penn.: Herald Press, 1999.

Shenk, Wilbert, ed. *Anabaptism and Mission.* Scottdale, Penn.: Herald Press, 1984.

————. *The Transfiguration of Mission.* Scottdale, Penn.: Herald Press, 1993.

Sidebottom, E. M. *James, Jude and 2 Peter.* Greenwood, S.C.: Attic, 1967.

Sider, Ronald. "Evangelicalism and the Mennonite Tradition." In *Evangelicalism and Anabaptism.* Edited by Norman C. Kraus. Scottdale, Penn.: Herald Press, 1979.

Snyder, C. Arnold. *Anabaptist History and Theology.* Kitchener, Ont.: Pandora, 1995.

————. "Anabaptist History and Theology: History or Heresy?" *CGR* 16, no. 1 (1998).

————. "Beyond Polygenesis: Recovering the Unity and Diversity of Anabaptist Theology." In *Essays in Anabaptist Theology.* Edited by Wayne Pipkin. Elkhart, Ind.: Institute of Mennonite Studies, 1994.

————. *From Anabaptist Seed: The Historical Core of Anabaptist-related Identity.* Kitchener, Ont.: Pandora, 1999.

————. "Orality, Literacy and the Study of Anabaptism." *MQR* 65 (1991).

————. Review of *Becoming Anabaptist,* by J. Denny Weaver. *CGR* 7, no. 1 (1989).

————. "The Schleitheim Articles in Light of the Revolution of the Common Man: Continuation or Departure?" *16th Century Journal* 16, no. 4 (1985).

Snyder, C. Arnold, and Lydia A. Huebert Hecht. *Profiles of Anabaptist Women.* Waterloo, Ont.: Wilfred Laurier University Press, 1996.

Snyder, Graydon. "The Text and Syntax of Ignatius Pros Ephesious 20:2c." *Vigilae Christianae* 22 (1968).

Sobrino, Jon. *Christology at the Crossroads.* Maryknoll, N.Y.: Orbis, 1978.

————. *Jesus in Latin America.* Maryknoll, N.Y.: Orbis, 1987.

————. *Jesus the Liberator.* Maryknoll, N.Y.: Orbis, 1993.

————. *Spirituality of Liberation.* Maryknoll, N.Y.: Orbis, 1988.

————. *The True Church and the Poor.* Maryknoll, N.Y.: Orbis, 1984.

Sobrino, Jon, and Ignacio Ellacuria. *Systematic Theology: Perspectives from Liberation Theology.* Maryknoll, N.Y.: Orbis, 1996.

Spiritual and Anabaptist Writers. Edited by George Williams and Angel Mergal. Philadelphia: Westminster Press, 1957.

Stadler, Ulrich. "Cherished Instructions on Sin, Excommunication, and the Community of Goods." In *Spiritual and Anabaptist Writers.* Edited by George Williams and Angel Mergal. Philadelphia: Westminster Press, 1957.

Stasiak, Kurt. *Return to Grace: A Theology for Infant Baptism.* Collegeville, Minn.: Liturgical Press, 1996.

Stayer, James. *Anabaptism and the Sword.* 2nd ed. Lawrence, Kan.: Coronado Press, 1976.

————. *The German Peasants' War and the Anabaptist Community of Goods.* Montreal: McGill-Queen's University Press, 1991.

Stayer, James, Werner Packull and Klaus Deppermann. "From Monogenesis to Polygenesis: The Historical Discussion of Anabaptist Origins." *MQR* 49, no. 2 (1975): 83-121.

Stoesz, Edgar. "Thoughts on Development." Monograph Series 1. Akron, Penn.: Mennonite Central Committee, 1977.

Stoffer, Dale. "Response to C. Norman Kraus." *CGR* 13, no. 2 (1995).

Stoffer, Dale, ed. *The Lord's Supper: Believers Church Perspectives.* Scottdale, Penn.: Herald Press, 1997.

Stoltzfus, Phil. "Performative Envisioning: An Aesthetic Critique of Mennonite Theology." *CGR* 16, no. 3 (1998).

Stuhlmacher, Peter. *Gottes Gerechtigkeit bei Paulus.* Göttingen: Vandenhoeck & Rupprecht, 1965.

Surin, Kenneth. "A Politics of Speech." In *Christian Uniqueness Reconsidered.* Edited by Gavin D'Costa. Maryknoll, N.Y.: Orbis, 1990.

Swartley, Willard, ed. *Dialogue Sequel to Jürgen Moltmann's "Following Jesus Christ in the World Today."* Elkhart, Ind.: Institute of Mennonite Studies, 1984.

———. *Explorations of Systematic Theology.* Elkhart, Ind.: Institute of Mennonite Studies, 1984.

Swartzentruber, Elaine. "Marking and Remarking the Body of Christ: Toward a Postmodern Mennonite Ecclesiology." *MQR* 71, no. 2 (1997).

———. " 'They Were All Together and Had Everything in Common': Subjectivity and Community in Modern and Postmodern Theologies." Ph.D. diss., Emory University, 1999.

The Theologia Germanica of Martin Luther. Translated by Bengt Hoffman. New York: Paulist, 1980.

Thompson, W. Scott, and Kenneth Jensen, eds. *Approaches to Peace.* Washington, D.C.: United States Institute of Peace, 1988.

Troeltsch, Ernst. *Protestantism and Progress.* Philadelphia: Fortress, 1986.

Van Braght, Thieleman. *The Bloody Theater or Martyrs Mirror.* Scottdale, Penn.: Herald Press, 1950.

Verduin, Leonard. *The Reformers and Their Stepchildren.* Grand Rapids: Eerdmans 1964.

Voolstra, Sjouke. "True Penitence: The Core of Menno Simons' Theology." *MQR* 62, no. 3 (1988).

Waite, Gary. *David Joris and Dutch Anabaptism, 1524-1543.* Waterloo, Ont.: Wilfred Laurier University Press, 1990.

Walpot, Peter. "True Yieldedness and the Christian Community of Goods." In *Early Anabaptist Spirituality.* Edited by Daniel Liechty. New York: Paulist Press, 1994.

Weaver, Dorothy Jean. "On Imitating God and Outwitting Satan." *MQR* 68, no. 2 (1994).

Weaver, J. Denny. *Anabaptist Theology in Face of Postmodernity.* Telford, Penn.: Pandora, 2000.

———. "The Anabaptist Vision: A Historical or a Theological Future?" *CGR* 13, no. 1 (1995).

———. "Atonement for the Nonconstantinian Church." *Modern Theology* 6, no. 4 (1990).

———. *Becoming Anabaptist.* Scottdale, Penn.: Herald Press, 1987.

———. "Christus Victor, Ecclesiology, and Christology." *MQR* 68, no. 3 (1994).

———. "Christus Victor, Nonviolence, and Other Religions." In *Mennonite Theology in Face of Modernity.* Edited by Alain Epp-Weaver. North Newton, Kans.: Bethel

College Press, 1996.

———. "The Doctrines of God, Spirit and Word in Early Anabaptist Theology 1522-1530: A Comparative Study in the Swiss and South German Lines of Anabaptism." Ph.D. diss., Duke University, 1974.

———. "The General Versus the Particular: Exploring Assumptions in 20th-century Mennonite Theologizing." *CGR* 17, no. 2 (1999).

———. *Keeping Salvation Ethical.* Scottdale, Penn.: Herald Press, 1997.

———. "Mennonites: Theology, Peace and Identity." *CGR* 6, no. 2 (1988).

———. "Narrative Theology in an Anabaptist-Mennonite Context." *CGR* 12, no. 2 (1994).

———. *The Nonviolent Atonement.* Grand Rapids: Eerdmans, 2001.

———. "Perspectives on a Mennonite Theology." CGR 2, no. 3 (1984).

———. "Reading 16th-Century Anabaptism Theologically: Implications for Modern Mennonites as a Peace Church." *CGR* 16, no. 1 (1998).

———. "Response to A. James Reimer and Thomas Finger." *CGR* 7, no. 1 (1989); 74-79.

———. Review of *Christian Peacemaking and International Conflict,* by Duane Friesen. *CGR* 5, no. 2 (1987).

———. Review of *The Nature of Doctrine,* by George Lindbeck. CGR 3, no. 2 (1985).

———. "Some Theological Implications of Christus Victor." *MQR* 68, no. 4 (1994).

———. "Understandings of Salvation: The Church, Pietistic Experience, and Nonresistance." In *Anabaptist Currents: History in Conversation with the Past.* Edited by Carl Bowman and Stephen Longenecker. Bridgewater, Va.: Penobscot, 1995.

Weiler, Barbara. "Response to Veronica Dyck." *CGR* 14, no. 3 (1996).

White, Stephen. *The Recent Work of Jürgen Habermas.* New York: Cambridge, 1988.

Wiebe, Dallas. "Can a Mennonite Be an Atheist?" *CGR* 16, no. 3 (1998).

Wiebe, Tim. Review of *Keeping Salvation Ethical,* by J. D. Weaver. *CGR* 16, no. 1 (1998).

Wilbur, Earl. *A History of Unitarianism: Socinianism and Its Antecedents.* Boston: Beacon, 1945.

Williams, A. N. *The Ground of Union.* New York: Oxford University Press, 1999.

Williams, George. "Christology and Church-State Relations in the Fourth Century." *Church History* 20 (September 1951 and December 1951).

———. *The Radical Reformation.* 3rd ed. Kirksville, Mo.: 16th Century Journal Publishers, 1992.

———. "The Two Social Strands in Italian Anabaptism, ca. 1526-1565." In *The Social History of the Reformation.* Edited by Lawrence Buck and Jonathan Zophy. Columbus: Ohio State University Press, 1972.

Wink, Walter. *Engaging the Powers*. Minneapolis: Fortress, 1992.

————. *The Human Being: Jesus and the Enigma of the Son of the Man*. Minneapolis: Fortress, 2002.

————. *Naming the Powers*. Philadelphia: Fortress, 1984.

————. *The Powers That Be*. New York: Doubleday, 1998.

Witherington, Ben, III. *John's Wisdom*. Louisville: Westminster/John Knox Press, 1995.

————. "Making a Meal of It: The Lord's Supper in Its First-century Social Setting." In *The Lord's Supper: Believers Church Perspectives*. Edited by Dale Stoffer. Scottdale, Penn.: Herald Press, 1997.

————. *Paul's Narrative Thought World*. Louisville: Westminster/John Knox Press, 1994.

Wolff, Hans Walter. *Anthropology of the Old Testament*. Philadelphia: Fortress, 1974.

Wright, N. T. *Jesus and the Victory of God*. Minneapolis: Fortress, 1996.

The Writings of Dirk Philips. Edited by Cornelius Dyck, William Keeney, and Alvin Beachy. Scottdale, Penn.: Herald Press, 1992.

Yamada, Takashi. "The Anabaptist Vision and Our World Mission (II)." In *Anabaptism and Mission*. Edited by Wilbert Shenk. Scottdale, Penn.: Herald Press, 1984.

Yoder, John Howard. *Body Politics*. Nashville: Discipleship Resources, 1992.

————. "How H. Richard Niebuhr Reasoned: A Critique of *Christ and Culture*." In Glen Stassen, D. M. Yeager and John Howard Yoder, *Authentic Transformation: A New Vision of Christ and Culture*. Nashville: Abingdon, 1996.

————. *The Politics of Jesus*. Grand Rapids: Eerdmans, 1972.

————. *Preface to Theology: Christology and Theological Method*. Grand Rapids: Brazos, 2002.

————. *The Priestly Kingdom*. Notre Dame, Ind.: University of Notre Dame, 1984.

Zartman, I. William, and J. Lewis Rasmussen, eds. *Peacemaking in International Conflict*. Washington, D.C.: United States Institute of Peace, 1997.

Zizioulas, John. *Being as Communion*. Crestwood, N.Y.: St. Vladimir's Seminary Press, 1985.

Zwingli, Ulrich. *Of Baptism*. Translated by Geoffrey Bromiley. Library of Christian Classics 24. Philadelphia: Westminster Press, 1953.